TIES THAT BIND,
TIES THAT DIVIDE

Ellis Island Series

VOICES FROM SOUTHEAST ASIA
The Refugee Experience in the United States
by John Tenhula

DISTANT MAGNETS
Expectations and Realities in the
Immigrant Experience, 1840–1930
edited by Dirk Hoerder and Horst Rössler

BRANCHING OUT
German-Jewish Immigration to the
United States, 1820–1914
by Avraham Barkai

FAITH AND FAMILY
Dutch Immigration and Settlement in the
United States, 1820–1920
by Robert P. Swierenga

Ira Glazier and Luigi de Rosa,
series editors

TIES THAT BIND, TIES THAT DIVIDE

100 Years of
Hungarian Experience
in the United States

JULIANNA PUSKÁS

Translated by Zora Ludwig

HM

Holmes & Meier
New York / London

TO MY BROTHER,

who for half a century did so much to help newcomers find their place on American soil, who provided support for most of my research, and who taught me to understand the immigrant fate.

Published in the United States of America 2000
by Holmes & Meier Publishers, Inc.
160 Broadway • New York, NY 10038

Typesetting by Coghill Book Typesetting, Chester, Virginia

This book has been printed on acid-free paper.

Manufactured in the United States of America

Library of Congress Cataloging-in-Publication Data

Puskás, Julianna.
  Ties that bind, ties that divide : 100 years of Hungarian experience in the United States / Julianna Puskás.
      p.   cm. — (Ellis Island series)
  Includes bibliographical references and index.
  ISBN 0-8419-1320-X (cloth : alk. paper)
    1. Hungarian Americans—History. 2. Hungarian Americans—Cultural assimilation. 3. Hungary—Emigration and immigration—History.
4. United States—Emigration and immigration—History. I. Title.
II. Series
E184.H95P89 1998
973'.0494511—dc20

                                                      96-18828
                                                         CIP

CONTENTS

Part Four
THE POSTWAR PERIOD

Figures

Tables

ACKNOWLEDGMENTS

There have been so many people who have contributed to the research of this book, that simply to list them all by name would fill several pages. I am particularly grateful to those Hungarian immigrants and their descendants, who understood the aim of my research and assisted it enthusiastically. The oral testimonies which they provided were of inestimable value in understanding the different patterns of migration and the changes in ethnic life. First among these Hungarian immigrants were those from my village of Szamosszeg. Without the support of my own relatives and other Szamosszegean immigrants, their children and grandchildren, I would never have gotten into close connection with their communities, their institutions, and the leaders of them. I also thank them for their hospitality for being able to get to so many places, among others to West Virginia, to Holden, to the mining settlement where for most of them, their American story began.

I would like to thank the directors of the Institute of History of the Hungarian Academy of Sciences and of the Central European Institute for backing my research and the boards of IREX, Fulbright, and OTKA for their financial support.

I was assisted considerably by the Immigration Research Center in Minnesota, and the Hungarian Foundation in New Jersey. I was able to do research at these institutions and could enjoy their financial assistance.

I also thank all my friends and colleagues for their helpful comments and suggestions: Zora Ludwig, for her tireless effort in translating my manuscript into English and Paula Benkart for her editorial direction in shaping the material into its present form.

Finally, many, very special thanks to my assistant, Mara.

INTRODUCTION

American connections were simply a fact of daily life in my native village of Szamosszeg in Hungary's Szatmár County during the 1930s. Almost every family in the village had members who had been in, were still in, or were thinking of going to the United States and specifically to New Brunswick, New Jersey. A number of villagers were even U.S. citizens, born while their parents were immigrants there. Tales of the transatlantic journey and life in the United States permeated the local folklore and were told and retold as villagers gathered on winter nights. My grandmother, who as a young girl spent a few years in the United States, used to tell me stories of her experiences, and—having seen a movie about the sinking of the *Titanic*—she always ended her story with a priest standing on the deck, holding a little girl exactly my own age in his arms as they were plunged under water. At that point she began to sing in Hungarian "Nearer My God to Thee," and I joined in.

Because America had also been an integral part of the village's economic life since the turn of the century, men such as my father, naturally thought of going there in times of crisis. Relatively prosperous peasants in the optimistic 1920s, the family had mortgaged its seventeen-acre farm in order to modernize the buildings and equipment, but in the midst of the Depression the payments became impossible and we had to subsist on a diet of potatoes and bread. My father's uncle in New Brunswick supplied the papers for him to immigrate, and my father sold some land that was in my mother's name (therefore not encumbered by the bank) to pay for the trip.

On a windy March day in 1938, I saw my father in modern clothes for the first time. After purchasing his ticket, he had enough money to buy a small traveling bag and a suit, but no overcoat. Friends took us by horse and wagon to the next village, where I saw a train for the first time. Despite all our expectations, however, my father managed to send us only twenty dollars before World War II cut off our communication with him. By the time the war ended, my father was a U.S. citizen and entitled to bring over his children. My older brother left in 1947 with what proved to be an unrealistic dream of attending medical school in the United States.

When my father, overcome by homesickness, returned to Szamosszeg the next year, he found the period of estrangement had been too long; separation had somehow become part of our family's way of life. He would soon go back

to his work in a Szamosszegean friend's butcher shop in New Brunswick. I
begged him to take me with him. A romantic eighteen-year-old, I dreamed of
being married in a long white gown like those the Szamosszegean girls wore
in the wedding pictures they sent back to the village from America. No, my
father said, in New Brunswick I would become either a housemaid or a worker
in the cigar factory. If I stayed in Hungary, he could finance my higher education
and I could become a schoolteacher. All that my no longer naive father said
was true and more. I was able to go away to school and board in the homes
of my teachers; my American father could obtain goods such as a typewriter
for one of my teachers, and even when I went on to the tuition-free People's
College in Budapest, I had a supply of American clothes to wear and share
with my fellow students.

I became an economic historian applying a statistical, or "macro," approach
to the modernization of Hungarian agriculture that began in the late nineteenth
century. In 1970, my institute assigned me to take on the developing field of
migration studies. When I began my research I was interested in the quantita-
tive aspects of the overseas migration process, and comparing its characteristics
with those of other countries. The paper of Frank Thistlethwaite which was
presented at the World Conference of Historians in Stockholm, 1960, was a
significant and direct stimulant to my research. Accepting his advice, I did not
plan to investigate solely in the country of origin, but wanted to follow the
Hungarian migrants in their new environment, to study the geography of their
settlements, the development of their communities, and ethnic institutions. I
tried to learn about factors which inspired or discouraged the Hungarian group
cohesion and conflict in the integration process.

In studying the international literature, and the American in particular, I
soon realized that the ethnic revival of the 1970s directed the attention of
social researchers to the history of Americans from Central and Eastern Europe,
and their changed social views and increased interest are reflected in the studies
published since the 1970s. Thanks to a veritable explosion of literature on the
subject over the past thirty years, our understanding of international migration
and ethnicity has dramatically increased. This literature has provided researchers with new data, new theoretical models, and new methodological approaches.
Generally these works have assumed the invalidity of the Melting Pot theory,
and by questioning the conventional concept of complete assimilation, have
emphasized the endurance of the ethnic legacy.

One of the most prominent and respected scholars in immigration history
during the early post–World War II period, Oscar Handlin, published in 1951
his famous book *The Uprooted*. He depicted the immigrants as a displaced
peasantry wrenched out of a communal past by the forces of modernization.
Thrust into the American industrial city, the newcomers were confronted and
often beaten down by the relentless power of the capitalist system. In the
ethnic ghettos of the new land, Handlin contended, the immigrants suffered
the destruction of their traditional cultures, social breakdown, personal disorganization as well as that of the family. At first, the newcomers found it difficult

to escape "the shock of alienation," but over time they became assimilated as schools, politics, popular culture, the mass media, and other American institutions silently melted the immigrants and their children into the American mainstream. His interpretation emphasized that "from the perspective of individual received, rather than the receiving society, the history of immigration is a history of alienation and its consequences." Since the early 1970s, a new generation of historians has seriously challenged this social breakdown and assimilationist interpretation. A stimulus to the new immigration history derived from R. J. Vecoli's study, *Contadini in Chicago: A Critique of "The Uprooted."* He found that Old World cultures survived the ocean crossing and significantly influenced adaptations in America.

With the development of the new social history, most of the subsequent studies have emphasized the carefully calculated nature of the decision to emigrate, the ubiquitous character of chain-migration, and the important role of family and kin in the process of migration and settlement; scholars have also shown that myriad immigrant and ethnic institutions were centrally involved in community and cultural maintenance. As a result, the young generation of immigration historians has also challenged virtually every aspect of the traditional assimilationist interpretation of American ethnic history—from the notion that assimilation occurred in "straight lines" (the Chicago School of sociologists) to the "melting pot" theory.

The model of chain-migration has replaced that of uprootedness. Chain-migration rather is based on networks of family ties, of friends and neighbors, on information, mutual help, and emotional and material resources which provided guidance and sustenance to the voyagers. It was important to distinguish the concept of chain-migration from the "push-pull" model based on economic rationality—in which migrants responded mechanically to labor markets. Researchers have begun to realize the need for more localized, village-oriented studies that examine the culture of migration and emigrant behavior on the micro level. The "history from-the-bottom-up" of the 1970s demanded that individual migrant's experiences be made visible.

However, as the momentum of the ethnic renaissance of the 1960s and 1970s slackened, the one-sidedness of the newly advanced theories became evident. The wholesale negation of existing paradigms that usually accompanies a novel approach, as Eva Morawska reminds us, is not the wisest strategy. Scholars of immigration began to realize that although Handlin may have overstated the misery of migration, his views deserve further serious investigation. Morawska, in particular, retained assimilation theory as one of a number of possible frameworks accounting for the immigrants' adaptation to the host American society. Lately, regardless of their position on assimilation, researchers have become more interested "in the processes of cultural and social change whereby immigrants ceased to be 'foreigners' and yet did not become 'One Hundred Percent Americans.'"

One of the obvious ways to study the organization of ethnic groups is to examine the leaders who facilitated the formation of the ethnic identity of their followers. Despite the popularity of social history in the United States, few American researchers have examined the role of ethnic leadership. Those inspired by the ethnic renaissance to study the history of immigrants and their descendants were generally biased against the elite. They chose instead to examine society from the bottom up, and leaders who had risen above the masses to function in a wider world appeared unimportant in the history of the rank and file. Relatively late in the development of American ethnic studies, John Higham first focused attention on ethnic leaders in a pivotal work he edited, where studies dealing with specific immigrant groups outline the principal roles and types of ethnic leadership.

As he emphasized, the increasing awareness of the new American ethnic identity was primarily the result of the migrant elite's mentality. They were the ones able to express themselves through the cultural and social activities of the groups, through the inventions of ethnicity. And yet only in 1987, did Victor R. Greene study the pioneer leaders of the large masses of Irish, Polish, German, Italian, and Jewish immigrants in order to gain insight into the formation of the communities they represented.

For decades, Emil Lengyel's monograph *Americans from Hungary*, published in 1948, was the only academic work on Hungarian Americans available. The field was dominated by amateur historians of Hungarian background for more than five decades. Fortunately the ethnic renaissance aroused interest in the history of Hungarian immigrants among researchers in social history. Beginning in the 1970s, a number of studies and three large-scale historical works were published in the United States. The application of the new sociological method is especially reflected in Paula Benkart's Ph.D. dissertation completed in 1975: "Religion, Family and Community Among Hungarians Migrating to American Cities, 1880–1930." The traditional method of historiography is followed by S. Papp in her monograph *Hungarian Americans and Their Communities of Cleveland*, which furnishes the most information to date on the Hungarians in Cleveland. With a more systematic method, in his book *The Hungarian-Americans*, Steven Béla Vardy surveys the various waves of the Hungarian immigrants to the United States and their socially differentiated groups, endeavoring to direct more attention to the Hungarians arriving after World War II while working in the frame of traditional historiography.

To understand the changes in the ethnic identity of their nations' emigrants, European researchers also need to direct much greater attention to the leaders of the communities that were formed overseas. From whom were they recruited? What special problems did they face? How did the relationships develop between leaders and followers? To determine what role various factors played in the common process of integration, researchers need to compare the various immigrant groups in the United States, as migrant communities and ethnic organizations were not built under identical conditions. Surely, arrival time, group size, the migrants' motivations, sociocultural characteristics, stimuli from donor and host societies, and the relationship between the two societies, as well as the quality and quantity of the ethnic elite, will all prove to be important. The larger the comparative framework in which the elite can be viewed, the fuller and more accurate will be our picture of how immigrant strangers were transformed into ethnic Americans. Modern society, it is asserted today by commentators on social change, is perfectly capable of accommodating ascriptive bonds and particularist orientation and of incorporating large sectors of traditional economic and social institutions.

Interest in the history of overseas migration grew among European scholars in the 1960s. In Hungary, a few historians began to concentrate on the migration process, but with special concern for its origins in and impact upon the sending society. I was the first who subsequently has tried to combine both of these new American and European approaches to cover the whole process with its complexity.

During the last two decades in Hungary a number of studies were published dealing with one or another aspect of the Hungarian diaspora. Linguists studied in particular the way they made changes in the Hungarian language, literary historians the literature of those Hungarians who wrote and published in the Western countries. In 1993, Zoltán Fejős wrote his dissertation with a new social-historical approach on the two generations of Hungarians who settled in Chicago.

Not only did the time arrive, but also the opportunity for synthesizing the literature with my basic research, after having published two books and a number of other studies. It is within this context that I intend to show how the process, the size, the mechanism, and the demographical and social characteristics of the Hungarian labor migration took shape and carried the greatest number of people to America. I will also try to integrate the competing macro- and micro-explanatory frameworks of international migration by introducing the mediating role of the local sociocultural environment from which the Hungarian migrants came to America. My approach relies on both micro- and macroanalysis, and on oral and written sources. For microanalysis of migration I chose my village, Szamosszeg, which is located in a migration region, and New Brunswick, New Jersey, as I knew since childhood that many people went there from my village. At that time I did not know that Szamosszegeans went not only to New Brunswick but to Holden, Dobra, and Granttown, West Virginia, and Detroit, Michigan.

Now at last it is time for me to synthesize the statistical "macro" data, the oral histories, or "micro" data, and my own personal knowledge of the Hungarian immigrant experience. I wish to interpret the complex material within the conceptual framework of international migration studies and to apply the model of global system/dependency (core and periphery) to explain mass migration from Hungary. Hungary's economic development was of a peripheral nature; the country was fundamentally dependent on the needs of its core, the Western Hemisphere. Between 1880 and 1914 Hungarian labor migrated in large numbers from the Central East European periphery to the Western Core. This movement was part of the circular exchange of capital and labor within the expanding Atlantic world economic system.

In the frame of one hundred years I analyze the waves of migration, their ebbs and flows, and the various types of migrants, the sojourners, the economic migrants, the forced migrants, the political émigrés, the refugees, throwing light upon the reasons for the departure of those different groups and the various social types among them. I am convinced that only a survey over a long period could present the social importance of migration in its complexity. I tried to discover the interaction between the subjective and objective aspects of the Hungarian migration experience. I placed more emphasis on local and personal developments, so that the individual migrants' experiences would be visible.

Therefore, the first of the volume's four parts outlines the main changes in the donor society in Hungary in the nineteenth century, the migration process, and the social and demographic characteristics of the migrants. Included here are the regional differences in emigration, personal and economic aspects of transoceanic chain-migration, and effects of overseas migration on the multinational donor society.

After exploring the migration process with its particularities, I follow the transformation of Hungarian Americans from the 1880s to the 1970s. I intend to give a detailed account of their expectations, how they perceived America and their position in it, how they organized their everyday life into meaningful patterns and strategies in pursuit of their jobs, and what they did and did not achieve: their specific acculturation experiences. My investigation of the internal dynamics of the Hungarian immigrant communities reveals that they were far from homogeneous enclaves. My empirical research is based on the theoretical concept of ethnic inventions. According to this concept, the development of ethnicity is a process that embraces, adapts to, and complements already existing community loyalties, cultural characteristics, and historical memories. The transformation from stranger to American is not linear but a dynamic process, driven by many kinds of relationships, especially competition, and causing many kinds of changes.

The Hungarian migrants settled in many parts of the United States, but their largest and most Magyar colony, the Buckeye neighborhood, developed on the East Side of Cleveland, Ohio. In Cleveland's Hungarian communities, in Buckeye and a smaller one on the West Side, can be found all that the Hungarian migrants brought with them as "cultural baggage," along with the ethnic inventions they created for adaptation in the United States, the intermixture of tradition and modernity, and the adaptation of peasant immigrants to American urban industrial society. I portray immigration as a process that entailed a fundamental social disorganization and personal demoralization affecting behavior, personality, and social life. As they created the new adaptive social organizations, specifically ethnic institutions, migrants could steer past many difficulties.

All the various types of community leaders and their ideologies are also visible in Cleveland, and their roles and effectiveness can be evaluated within a relatively wide social framework. This is why I focused my research on the Hungarian communities there, but I also tried to take account of the characteristics of Hungarian communities forming in other settlements, in mining and steel towns, for instance.

In Part II are outlined to the Hungarians' settlement patterns and the description of the work and life of Hungarians as sojourners. Also introduced in this section are the entrepreneur types, the individuals from the ranks of manual laborers who became independent businessmen and, at the same time, the leaders in building community organizations. I began with the hypothesis that two conditions were necessary for the organization of migrant communities: (1) leaders and opinion shapers, and (2) community institutions. Because these two conditions had a reciprocal effect on each other, outlining the characteristics, programs, and activities of secular organizations leads to research in the founding of Hungarian religious institutions and their activities and ethnic functions, as well as the roles and lives of the pioneer clergymen.

Most important, however, is the examination of the Hungarian-American press and the part it played in ethnic invention. I introduce the newspaper *Szabadság* from its foundation to the beginning of World War I, and I introduce Tihamér Kohányi, its publisher-editor, and several other well-known Hungarian writers in Cleveland, to describe the function of the press as community organizer. Finally, I describe the intermediary role of the Hungarian journalists and leaders in Cleveland in establishing political connections between the host and donor societies.

The last chapter of Part II reviews the particularly serious conflicts of dual loyalty and divisions within the Hungarian community and the conflicts with the "others" caused by World War I. Hungarians also imply that the Hungarian-American response to other ethnic and social groups was more complex than one based simply on competition. Often the association was greatly influenced both by historical European experience and by contemporary events in Europe.

Part III chronicles the last part of mass migration, its character (in particular, uniting families) and the changes that permanent settlement brought in the 1920s. Among them were the changes in the immigrants themselves, as well as in their environments, and as a result, the modification of their ethnic identity. This new phase of integration, which culminated during World War II, then, was affected by the Great Depression. Also discussed are the problems of the second generation looking for its own identity, and the growing gap between the generations.

The post–World War II period analyzed in Part IV, encompasses the immigration of the displaced persons and the Freedom Fighters of 1956. Both of these new waves considerably altered the Hungarian-Americans as a group. For the last fifty years they also have been characteristic segments of the Hungarian ethnic phenomenon, and played an important role shaping the Hungarian identity. I found it necessary to draw them into the overall picture to understand the colorful many-sidedness of the Hungarian ethnicity. They represent the problem of lack of interaction among Hungarians who arrived at different times and from different social milieus. U.S. census data of 1970 reveal the resulting social structure of Hungarian immigrants in the United States and show that nations such as Hungary were an important source of skilled and professional immigrants for the United States in the twentieth century.

It is not easy to reconstruct the history of immigrant groups in the United States, as documents are scattered and fragmentary. The various American ethnic groups did not form in the same manner as European ethnic minority groups, and historical study is further complicated by the fact that the immigrants' diverse old-country backgrounds must always be taken into account. However, the possibilities for collecting data are inexhaustible and never can be considered complete.

Besides the historical literature, I have studied a wide range of sources and made use of the most varied kinds of information. For the scope and characteristics of emigration and immigration, I examined Hungarian emigration statistics, U.S. immigration statistics, published census figures of both countries, and the reports of the Immigration Commission set up by the United States Congress to study the problems of immigration. Despite their biases, the commission's reports contain very interesting data on the economic circumstances, working conditions, wages, and lifestyles of the immigrants. For insight into the question of remigration, and the Hungarian government's emigration policies, I studied the published records of the Hungarian Parliament (minutes of the House of Representatives), the minutes of various conferences on emigration, and documents from special collections in Hungarian and American libraries. I have found the Széchenyi Library in Budapest to be the greatest depository of Hungarian-American newspapers; its collection is far from complete, but still is incomparably richer that any in the United States. The second-best collection of Hungarian-American publications and other historical documents in Hungary is in the Sárospatak Library. In the United States I studied the Hungarian collections at the Immigration History Research Center of the University of Minnesota, St. Paul, Minnesota, and the American Hungarian Foundation of New Brunswick, New Jersey, as well as the documents and publications stored in the Bethlen Otthon (Bethlen Home) of the Hungarian Reformed Federation of America in Ligonier, Pennsylvania, and in the private library of Lajos Szathmáry of Chicago, Illinois. Immigrants' letters to those at home in Hungary were useful, but hard to find.

Last but not least, in the course of my studies I increasingly stressed ethnographic fieldwork. Between 1972 and 1985, I spent more than two years of study trips among Hungarian-American families (immigrants and second and third generations). I visited homes, parishes, and different types of Hungarian ethnic organizations. I attended weddings, baptisms, funerals, religious and national celebrations; I was a guest at conventions of two fraternal associations with nationwide branches. I interviewed more than five hundred persons, mostly leaders of religious and secular organizations and members of the first and second generations, and occasionally members of the third generation. I was lucky, because with the help of my brother, I could make personal contact with many leaders of Hungarian-American organizations.

Comparing the richness of their stories in the oral testimonies with the limitation of the traditional sources, I became convinced that I should use the immigrants' own words to present their experiences.

PART ONE

MIGRATION

CHAPTER 1

Hungarian Society: Between Feudalism and Capitalism

FOR ELEVEN HUNDRED years the Magyar people have occupied the Danubian Basin of east-central Europe, the land other Europeans called Hungary after the federation of Magyar tribes. Árpád was the paramount chief of the tribal federation when the Hungarians invaded the Carpathian Basin. In 975 the Magyar chief Géza adopted Christianity and Hungary became affiliated to western Christianity. Géza's son, István, was the first Hungarian king crowned by the pope. István brought in foreign missionaries and artisans, established a church hierarchy, and gradually replaced the tribal system with a centralized structure based on counties.

Hungary served as western Christianity's outpost against the Turks from the middle of the fifteenth century until its defeat by the Ottoman army at Mohács in 1526. For the next century and a half Hungary was divided into three parts: the area ruled by the Turks; the northwestern region under the rule of the Habsburgs; and Transylvania, which was independent. One hundred fifty years later the Turks left behind a country depopulated and economically shattered. After the liberation from the Turkish yoke, the whole country was controlled by the Habsburgs, who built Hungary into the Habsburg realm.

At the beginning of the nineteenth century Hungary was by western European standards a backward country, underdeveloped, in many respects feudal, and with a national culture submerged by the use of the German language, as well as the traditional Latin in administration and education. In 1825 a new generation of Magyars began championing both cultural revival and political autonomy for Hungary. The country was the homeland of a variety of ethnic groups, of which the Magyars were only one but always a dominant group. The reformers fought for Magyar to be the official language of Hungary. The leader of the radical reformers was Lajos Kossuth (1802–1894), a lawyer and brilliant orator who denounced feudalism and its aristocratic defenders and

3

agitated for self-rule and parliamentary democracy, for the abolition of the constitutional distinction between noblemen and plebeians, and for economic modernization.

The revolutions of 1848 in Europe, first in France and afterwards in Vienna, helped to progress the movements of the Hungarian reformers, too. On March 3 the Hungarian Diet in an address to the king demanded constitutional rule for the peoples of the empire, independent government for Hungary, and some other bourgeois reforms. In Pest, on March 15, the resistance of the ruling circles was broken by the people's revolution, enabling the liberal nobility in the succeeding weeks to bring about the transition to a bourgeois state, to national independence, the reforms stipulated in their earlier plans, and a good deal more. On March 17, the king consented to the demands, and appointed Count Lajos Batthányi as Hungary's first independent prime minister. The implementation of these reforms had hardly begun when the Viennese court, having overcome its panic, resorted to the old "divide and rule" tactic. The national minorities were encouraged to challenge Hungarian predominance, and Serbs and Romanians mounted sporadic assaults on the Magyar population. In September 1848, an Austro-Croatian offensive led by the governor of Croatia, Count Jellasic, was repulsed. Thereupon the Austrians attacked in force and occupied Pest and Buda in early December; the peaceful revolution turned into a bitter war of independence. Kossuth, at the head of a National Defense Committee in the city of Debrecen, hurriedly assembled an army, and in April 1849 declared complete independence from the Habsburgs.

The 1848/1849 Revolution and War of Independence was suppressed, (with the help of Russian forces), but it paved the way for modernization in Hungary. The serfs were freed, the nobility lost its privileges, legal equality was introduced, and ownership of property was opened to all. The struggle for civil rights had been part of the battle for independence from the Habsburgs, and although the Austrians won the war with the help of the Russians, they left the civil program in force and directed its practical implementation.

Two decades after the defeat of the Revolution and the War of Independence, in 1867, an Austro-Hungarian Compromise was enacted.[1] The basic condition of the Compromise was the introduction of constitutionalism throughout the Monarchy by restoring the April 1848 Constitution, and granting Hungary self-government under a Habsburg king, though with joint administration of foreign affairs, defense, and finance. The multinational Hungary formed a single constitutional unit.

The Nationality Act of 1868 declared Hungary to be a "unitary national state", and its inhabitants members of the "unitary Hungarian political nation" taking note that most of "Hungarian citizens speak different languages." So the Act recognized only one political nationality and one official language: Magyar. At the same time it declared the civil equality of all nationalities and allowed the free use of their languages in the lower instances of administration and justice, and primary and secondary schools. It also guaranteed in principle the right of association and the autonomy of their churches. This politico-legal fiction disregarding the national identity of the non-Hungarian peoples, brought the protest of the nationalities at the time. Later on they would have accepted the Act as a basis of negotiation, but by that time the Hungarian government not only denied the spirit of the Act but did not even keep to its letter and made more and more attempts at assimilating the other ethnic groups.

The new political, economic and social conditions did not bring an immediate change in the structure that had developed during feudalism. The old feudal lords simply became the sole owners of the manorial estates, and their serfs became free peasants and sharecropper tenants. A very extreme division of property thus occurred, with a few thousand families controlling more than 50 percent of the country's territory. At the same time, approximately 70 percent of the millions of peasants occupied areas too small for them to scratch out even a subsistence living, while a portion of the landless emancipated serfs worked on the estates for wages or, more often, for payment in kind. Estates of ten thousand *holds* (one hold equals 1.42 acres) or larger were much more numerous in Hungary than in other European countries, as were the number of dwarf holdings and landless persons.

Population Growth and Economic Change

In the four decades between 1870 and 1910, the population of Hungary grew from 13.6 million to 18.3 million, or, including Croatia, from 15.5 million to 20.9 million. As the average annual rate of growth represented by the 5.4 million was .074 percent, the signs of the demographic revolution began to appear in Hungary in the second half of the nineteenth century. The middle period of a demographic revolution occurs when birth rates remain stable while death rates decrease, so that the consequent acceleration of the population increase creates a demographic explosion. This period was observable in Hungary in barely one decade, 1875–1885, and led to the sudden growth of a young population in need of employment by the turn of the twentieth century. The 15- to 19-year-old age group experienced a record growth of 26.4 percent in the years between 1890 and 1900. Within just a few years this group increased as much as it had in the previous twenty years. In the same decade the 20- to 24-year-old age group also had a notable growth rate of 11.9 percent compared to its earlier rate of 1.4 percent.[2]

As a result of this population increase, the peasant holdings were broken into increasingly smaller parcels and the large masses of the landless grew. By the turn of the century, more than one-fourth of the population were agrarian laborers, the majority of them (73.27 percent) leading a totally uncertain existence as freely wandering laborers. The other important part of the agrarian population (15.2 percent) consisted of the land parcel owners who were able to eke out only a partial, continually decreasing livelihood from their property.[3]

Between the Danube and Tisza Rivers the division of land continued until the physical limits of continued fragmentation were reached. Plots divided into six-foot units were not uncommon; in Kisvárda (Szabolcs County) the plots were divided not only lengthwise, but also widthwise, so that the owner of the middle plot found it difficult to cultivate, because there was no road for a horse-driven vehicle.[4]

In 1867, after two decades of absolute rule, the Habsburgs had arrived at a compromise with the Hungarian ruling class; the Hungarian Nationality Act of 1868 recognized only one political nationality and one official language, Magyar. This beginning of political consolidation also marked the beginning of industrialization in Hungary.

Hungary's role in the economic division of labor within the Dual Monarchy had always been that of supplier of raw agricultural products and foodstuffs to the more industrially developed areas. As manufacturing had never developed in Hungary, in the mid-nineteenth century the livelihood of approximately 80 to 85 percent of the Hungarian population was still based on agriculture. Because the capitalist class—largely through the intervention of the Austrian side of the Monarchy—was engaged in agricultural production, the development of the food industry continued to be Hungary's main role throughout the entire period of industrialization.[5]

The partial nature of Hungary's industrialization, combined with its late introduction and narrowly based foundation, resulted in a wide gap between the number and types of workers that industry needed and what was available from the agrarian population's large surplus of manpower. This disparity between supply and demand not only influenced the movements between the rural agricultural and the urban industrial sectors but also created continually strained relations between the two sectors.

The modernization of agricultural production brought with it the greater use of tools and agricultural machinery. These technical advances, in an area dominated by the use of manpower for cultivation and an undeveloped animal husbandry, made agricultural work even more seasonal and drastically shortened the employment period for the agricultural population. Whereas in 1860 the harvest had lasted an average of sixty days, by 1890 it had been cut in half to only thirty days. From the 1880s on, the demand for agricultural workers did not keep pace with population growth. In fact, by the first decade of the twentieth century the number of workers employed in agriculture had barely increased at all. Overpopulation and chronic unemployment had by then become endemic in the agrarian society of Hungary, particularly in some regions. The predicament of the agricultural workers was often exploited by employers: for example, only those workers who were willing to assume a certain number of unpaid labor days and side jobs were guaranteed contracts for harvesting and threshing.

In the thirty years between 1880 and 1910, the number of factory hands in Hungary increased two and one-half times and the number of those in the manufacturing sectors almost tripled. The pace of growth of the industrial workforce was most dynamic in the ten years between 1890 and 1900, the most active period of internal mobility in the country. This is reflected in the growth in the urban population and in the numbers who moved from their place of birth. The census found 74.5 percent of the total population still residing in their birthplace in 1880, 73.4 percent in 1890, 70 percent in 1900, and 68.6 percent in 1910. Although internal mobility slowed down somewhat after the turn of the century, the growth of the total industrial population remained dynamic. Out of the total number of those seeking work in the industrial sector and in mining, employment rose 32 percent between 1870 and 1890, 25 percent between 1890 and 1900, and 29 percent between 1900 and 1910. Because of the nature of industrialization, however, less and less of the enormous and ever-growing surplus of labor arising out of the agricultural population could be absorbed into industry.

A narrow industrial base, intense territorial concentration, and the particular structure of industry limited the possibilities for a massive flow of workers from the agricultural population into the industrial. The specific requirement for industrial workers in Hungary had been formulated by circumstances within the Monarchy favoring the development of Hungary's food industries on the one hand, and its iron and machine industries on the other.

The iron and machine industries always needed highly skilled workers but were unable to obtain them from the agricultural community or from the sparse group of domestic workmen and craftsmen, while the food production industries employed more seasonal than permanent workers. As a result of those circumstances, Hungary did not develop the natural movement of workers between agrarian and industrial sectors that occurred in western Europe. Instead, at the same time that there was conspicuous overpopulation in agriculture in Hungary, industry was struggling with a scarcity of manpower.

The agricultural population was able to supply industry only with unskilled helpers and seasonal laborers. The landless villagers first streamed to those branches of industry that were related to agriculture and had a seasonal nature: the mills, breweries, and brickyards. It was another step to find employment in the larger, more permanent branches of industry, where job stability did not coexist well with a second occupation. The path leading through the ranks of agricultural worker to urban day laborer, road or construction worker, and finally skilled laborer was narrow. In the majority of cases, the landless ended up stuck between agriculture and industry. When the first great impetus from the development of the infrastructure abated, the masses were forced back into agriculture.[6] This reversal occurred in several regions of the country, including the counties of Szatmár and Szabolcs, which became the centers of overseas emigration for the population whose native language was Magyar.

Not all the obstacles to movement between the agricultural and industrial sectors stemmed, however, from the character of Hungary's industrialization. The Hungarian agrarian structure's human connections, customs, values, and culture had evolved historically from the village way of life. Differing from those of the city, they served as a damper on development of a workforce for large industry.

Immigrant labor had become more important in the newly established spheres, which in some cases required higher qualifications and had higher levels of mechanization. The more industrially developed areas of the Monarchy became the sources of skilled workers for Hungary's needs. Migrant Czech, Moravian, and Austrian workers formed the vanguard of skilled industrial workers. In Budapest in 1870, for example, 25 percent of the factory workers and 35 percent of those employed in the iron and machine manufacturing industry, which demanded the most highly trained skilled workers, were foreigners. The main sources for this labor were Bohemia and Moravia, which provided 51.5 percent of foreign industrial labor migrants. With the advancement of industrialization the percentage of foreign skilled workers decreased, as did their absolute numbers after the turn of the century.[7] Nevertheless, the lack of skilled laborers remained a factor throughout the entire industrialization period, and after the turn of the century contemporaries attributed the slackening in the development of industrialization to the lack of skilled workers.

Migration and assimilation played an important part in the development of a working class in Hungary.[8] The first group of skilled laborers in Hungary came either from abroad or from an economically more developed territory within the Austro-Hungarian Monarchy. *Valcolás,* or "waltzing" abroad for the purpose of obtaining trade experience, was part of the education of the original Hungarian skilled workers, tradesmen, and industrial workers. They traveled throughout all the countries of Europe, but because they tried to go primarily to German-speaking areas, German became the trade language of the Hungarian industrial workforce. These "waltzing" workers and artisans also brought back the ideas of socialism from the more developed western countries. Under their influence the Hungarian workers' unions were established during a relatively early period of industrialization, and the workers' movement quickly reached the same level as in the developed European countries.

Those who were occupied in the traditional sectors—peasants, village artisans, and miners—witnessed a gradual deterioration of their lifestyles during the process of modernization. As has been noted, the upward demographic trend sped the fragmentation of small holdings, and the growth of the industrial sector was not enough to absorb the surplus workforce created by agrarian overpopulation. It was symptomatic of the period from the 1890s on that it always became more difficult for young people to find employment. Meanwhile, landowners increasingly had to take on mortgages in order to pay their local and national taxes; the rates were so steep that in some instances their total surpassed the small farmholder's real income.[9] Impoverished peasants had no choice but to sell what belongings they had in response to their creditors' demands. At the same time, the artisan's existence was jeopardized by competition from industry and the dismantling of the guild system. The network that developed with the building of railway lines, which themselves cut deeply into the earning possibilities of those who were transportation providers, spurred the growth of consumers' desires, slowly but surely changing lifestyles. As the village populations became accustomed to new consumer goods, their growing demands could have been fulfilled only by the increased production of those goods. There were, however, no possibilities for extensive expansion.

Because of high taxes and land prices and the entailment of a good number of the large estates, few were able to purchase land. The domestic management of the estates as well as the expansion of capitalistic land leasing increasingly forced out all forms of small tenancy. After the emancipation of the serfs, the peasants were squeezed onto less territory than they had occupied before emancipation.[10]

There were additional obstacles preventing conversion to an intensive agricultural system. Above all, the capital necessary for investment did not exist; loans were almost unobtainable. Under Hungary's notoriously bad credit conditions, the security that the large banking institutions demanded could be provided only with the greatest difficulties. For the most part, loans were obtained on usurious terms, which worsened conditions and more than once resulted in bankruptcy.[11] Educational and cultural factors also hindered the spread of more professional management. The complaint was constantly voiced that competence and technical training in agriculture were missing and that the peasants had "no business mentality." Essentially they had no economic experience.

The peasants sold their products individually and were forced to sell below market value because of the small volume, uneven quality, and often semifinished, non-transportable nature of their goods such as milk. At times there was no market at all for their products, and with inadequate storage facilities, they were not able to hold out. If they could not cover their urgent expenses by selling on the immediate market—sometimes at a loss—they had to resort to "advance contracts," as they lacked the reserve capital and credit resources to tide them over until their produce matured.

The peasants also were at a disadvantage on the consumption end as their purchases were not large enough to qualify them to deal directly with suppliers. Commodities reached the villages through a chain of middlemen, substantially raising the prices. The peasants purchased all their necessities from the village shopkeepers, who because of the isolation of villages, especially during autumn and winter, usually had monopolies. The peasants did not always have ready cash and so were forced to endure corrupt practices for fear of losing their credit with the village general dealer, who often was also the tavern keeper, usury banker, and buyer of their products. These dealers often exploited the ignorance of the peasants, who were doubly at their mercy and cheated when settling accounts, used false measurements, sold inferior or fake merchandise, and so on.[12] Extortion through the sale of goods occurred particularly during credit purchases and the measuring of drinks, infuriating the villagers. The proportions of this extortion sometimes were so great that official intervention became necessary.[13]

The peasant family's standard of living, particularly that of the agrarian proletariat, generally was low. They produced part of their necessities themselves at home and obtained much of the rest through trade. Thus it is easy to understand, and from the contemporary descriptions it is abundantly clear, that the poor of that era were inequitably and sparsely fed. In the mid-1880s according to reports from official circles in Liptó County—except in two villages—people used to eat bread only on Sundays and other festive occasions, like wedding celebrations. Their main source of nourishment was potatoes. "Meat is not eaten by them on weekdays, and only very scarcely on Sundays. Trencsén County also belonged to the 'poorly catered for' counties. They consume mostly potatoes here too, but meat is consumed very rarely and only the more well to do eat it." "Bereg County likewise, only on bigger holidays does meat get on the table of poor people. Here, because of the scarce and bad nourishment, well-developed bodies and strong physiques can be seen only very rarely, and people look very pitiful."[14] Contemporary official reports emphasized in all the counties of the northeastern region the excessive consumption of brandy. However, in the counties between the Duna and the Tisza and on the right banks of the Tisza the picture of nourishment is not as gloomy,[15] and that had an effect on keeping the population from emigration. Wages—especially real income—and the detailed analysis of changes in the cost of living are essentially an unexplored area in the economic history of this period in Hungary. During the 1880s, agrarian wages were so low, and the cost of living was so high, that in the less productive regions a poor harvest meant actual starvation for the populace.[16] During the first half of the 1890s nominal wages stagnated, while the mild tendency of real income to rise in both industry and agriculture was due to the fall in prices of food products and of manufactured articles. Nominal wages grew in industry from 1895 on, but in agriculture they grew only after the turn of the century. Significant rises in nominal wages, however, began in the first decade of the twentieth century when they grew approximately 40 percent in industry and approximately 80 percent in the agrarian sector.

For a family of five—reckoning with 15 crowns per metric centner and 2 metric centners per head—their bread grain requirement alone would cost 150 crowns. Their pay was scarcely enough for the raising of a pig, as 50 to 80 crowns were asked for a brood-sow, and 16 to 19 crowns even for a piglet less than a year old at the market of Munkács in 1900. Thus, nourishment was seldom enriched with a meat dish for most of the agrarian proletarians. Only a few of them had sufficient strength to buy and raise a cow, though milk and dairy products were important elements to supplement their nourishment. A milking cow would cost 200 to 320 crowns at the Debrecen market, and that would mean one year's wages, or even more, for a day laborer. To acquire a draft animal could hardly enter the mind of a farmhand or a day laborer, for it entailed serious effort on the part even of a small holder. In 1900, in the market of Gyula, a feeble ox found a purchaser for 340 to 480 crowns, and a pair of plowhorses, just ready to be used, cost 420 to 760 crowns. And even if the prize of products and animals did fluctuate according to regions, these data show national tendencies in the long run.[17]

Despite the rise in nominal wages for industrial workers, real income decreased as the cost of living grew faster than wages. It is much more difficult to estimate changes in the real income of the agrarian worker. The farm workers' wages showed an improvement in the first decade of the twentieth century, but we do not know to what degree the comparatively smaller opportunities for work and the lower value of wages paid in produce diminished the advantages. The latter method of payment played an important role in the life of the Hungarian agrarian worker, as did the various forms of payment determined in proportion to yield. On the estates, sharecroppers harvested the grain and cultivated the crops for a precontracted share of one-half, one-third, or some other proportion.

Those who contracted to do sharecropping generally worked in temporary associations that safeguarded their interests. Work associations or bands were organized by villages, and at times they were taken to work in distant areas of the country. Since the beginning of the nineteenth century, groups of men from the mountainous regions, separated from their families, generally had worked as sharecroppers from spring to fall. The migrant agricultural workers developed groups, such as the *summások,* which contracted for hourly or production wages or a combination of the two.[18] Contemporaries ascribed the growth of economic tensions in the 1890s to the reduction of the production share that employees received and to various new services required from them, for example, unpaid work for leased lands.[19]

Social and Cultural Life

At the beginning of the twentieth century, the entire life of the village population still was ruled by traditional social customs and mutual commitments. Most striking were the family division of labor, the moral commitment of assisting each other in any form necessary, and the rituals commemorating birth, marriage, burial, and certain holidays. Kinship, by long existing custom, regulated the private lives of individuals and guaranteed their cooperation. Obligations and prohibitions abounded within family life. The reciprocal giving and receiving of help in whatever form—work, money, or moral reinforcement—and whenever necessary was expected of all; to forget one's obligations to kin was considered shameful.[20]

For the agrarian family, where home and workplace were one and the same, there was minimal division between work and private life. This peasant way of life, which had been carried over from feudalism to capitalism, was particular to agriculture. The importance of continuing traditions from generation to generation was emphasized, placing the families of the youngest generation and the individuals within it in a subordinate position. Perpetuation of the race, economics, and education were stressed. Besides these main functions, historical data also show the defensive, emotional, cultural, and religious functions of the family.

In terms of composition there were three main types of family.[21]

1. The *nagycsalád,* the extended family, consisted of the circle of relatives and of other elements, encompassing three to five generations, which functioned through family cooperation. Capitalism partially dismantled the extended family and placed it under conditions that guaranteed its eventual complete dissolution.

2. The *törzs család* consisted of two families and two generations with close economic and marriage ties, generally parents and either their married son or married daughter.

3. The *kiscsalád,* the basic or nuclear family, consisting of a married couple and their children, gained ground as the transitional family form in this period, although the *törzs* family appeared most often.

In the first decade of the twentieth century, a functioning *törzs* family represented the coexistence of two generations. It was formed when a son or daughter married and had no choice but to live with the parents, who put one of the rooms or the pantry at their disposal. Because the two united small families of the *törzs* family often had no property beyond that of their house, the men went to work either as construction laborers or as sharecroppers in other parts of the country, and the women in their absence became used to sharing one household. This arrangement did not change even when the men returned home in the winter or when the young women gave birth; the two small families still lived together in one common household.

Until the turn of the century the division of labor within the family was rather rigid: men's work could only be done by men and women's work only by women. Cultivating, sowing, harrowing, plowing, reaping, sheaving, stacking of grain and corn, caring for the horses, manuring, and winter cutting of reeds and wood was men's work. Women's work was cooking, washing, cleaning, caring for the cattle, milking and preparing the milk, going to the market, and rearing the children.[22] A much harder role awaited the woman when the family was supported by income from two different sources, when the husband was far away as seasonal worker. After the turn of the century, the strengthening of the woman's role occurred with local variations. Women's participation in property ownership and in the workforce and their skillfulness in adapting to the realities of life to the market, and to people obtained for them an exceptional authority and independence in many places. In difficult situations they became the family's backbone, its protecting and uplifting strength. "If the family's situation improved, it showed the wife's strength; if it declined, her softness."[23]

Despite the changes in the personal relationship between husband and wife, the traditional interpretation prevailed throughout the entire period: women were not considered to have equal rights and rank. The husband was the family head; his status determined that of the entire family including his wife. The husband represented the family in public life, although from the beginning of the century onward wives, through their husbands, achieved continually greater influence in the public affairs of the village. The dominance of the husband in the family was emphasized in the vernacular by expressions such as "he is the master in the house" and "he wears the hat."[24] The husband was the family administrator. The wife usually handled the money, but the husband determined how much was to be spent. The wife dared not act on her own without her husband's permission; her independence could be achieved only through her husband.[25] During the transition from feudalism to capitalism, the social position of women did not undergo much change as they continued to remain workers not only in the management of the household but also in field labor, industry, and trade. Important changes did occur, however, in their property rights and in their guiding role within the family. The earlier custom, that mostly males inherited property while the females were given a lesser share which was paid in cash began to be replaced by equitable property assessments and the equal distribution of property inheritance.[26]

By contrast, a total subordination still prevailed between parents and children; the age and family situations created no exceptions. Even the fifty-year-old son and the married daughter owed obedience to their father if they lived on the father's property. His right to physical discipline was recognized until the children reached majority, or at least until they married. Age was not a restraint in joining the workforce, as in many places children were forced to work at the age of four, usually on their parents' property, although within a few years they could be sent to an unfamiliar environment, too.

In Hungary and in other European countries where the holdovers from feudalism were strong, every social stratum had its special lifestyle. An individual's class was clearly visible through his general deportment and in his every individual characteristic: his clothes, home, food, manners, and speech. Because it was possible to recognize at first glance a person's class and status, strangers were able to address each other according to their proper rank.

The function of clothing was to depict every nuance of status and to symbolize the individual's place within society. Clothing customs reflected the period, the family's position, and its prestige. The villagers evolved their own colorful national costumes in their Sunday clothing, and young and old took pains to be properly dressed for going to church. On workdays they wore linen trousers, cheap store-bought clothes, or patched garments, as was customary among the poor. The clothing of the most populous social class, the proletarians, had neither fashion nor style, for lacking both the money to spend on clothing and status within the society, they purchased their clothes secondhand.

When a girl at the age of sixteen laid aside her hair ribbons and clothed herself in many petticoats, it was a signal to the entire community that she had reached the age when she would accept the courtship of young men. From then on the community could not protest if she was seen walking together with a boy in out-of-the-way places. In the same manner, when a woman no longer wore colorful clothing but only black, she was openly declaring that she was aging. This indicated not only self-denial but also that she had assumed a new status, that of the "women dressed in black" who were the guardians of morals, customs, and behavior in the village. The dress code, which determined everyone's status, guaranteed the effective supervision by the community of all its members.

In addition to dress, social structure was reflected in housing and the seat occupied in church. Each class had its special form of housing, ranging from the luxurious homes of the middle class all the way down to the urban proletarians' overcrowded apartment buildings and the one-room houses of the poor peasants and the agrarian proletariat. The seating arrangement within the churches was hierarchical; the first rows in front of the altar or the pulpit belonged to the local lower middle class (the notary, teacher, and officials of the nearby large estate) who, ensconced in their prominent pews, proudly displayed their positions at the top of the local pyramid.[27]

Even in traditional society, peasants had not lived in total isolation from the world outside the closed circle of their village. There were, for instance, group meetings through which they could obtain information about events in distant places and could form opinions about the affairs of their own smaller circles. Yet from the beginning of the nineteenth century on, transportation and the market were the important agents in the transformation of the peasants' production techniques. With the development of commodity production, the peasants obtained more significant portions of their foodstuffs and household consumer goods from the marketplace. More and more industrially manufactured goods replaced those they used to make completely by themselves, not just plows and wagons but even wooden spoons and personal necessities.

The trade relationship between the city and the villages was loose; the smiths, tailors, furriers, tanners, and others who provided the peasants' necessities were scattered throughout the villages. Blacksmiths' shops, inns, and mills, places where a large turnabout of people had to wait, were both the providers of necessities and the stages for opinion formation through the gathering and dispersal of news. The importance of these market villages continued to grow for many long decades after the emancipation of the serfs.[28] The peasants took their surplus products exclusively there to be sold, and they purchased there their farm tools, clothes, and home furnishings. Going to market was not just an opportunity for buying and selling but a great event, an opportunity to see the world and come into contact with people from distant places. Sunday markets, particularity in the Alföld (the Plains) from the 1880s on, assumed the character of a "human market" in those towns where there was a large surplus of agricultural workers to be hired as weekly day laborers. Changes in the economic structure also brought changes in behavior. Inevitably the more mobile village population became better informed about the affairs of the larger environment, and their experiences influenced their daily life, particularly those of the younger generation.[29]

With the turn of the century the results of compulsory education became discernible. A law that in 1868 established four-year elementary schools made it possible, at least in theory, to acquire the basics of reading, writing, and arithmetic. Elementary education spread slowly, and illiteracy remained significant even after the turn of the century—although in varying degrees—dependent on the nationality of the multinational population. Reading and writing skills broadened horizons and brought new expectations. These, then, began to loosen the traditional ties of the society.

The impact of modern life, spreading in ever wider circles, influenced the still fairly isolated culture of the peasants in almost every respect, but its effect varied from region to region. Two elements were decisive in the development of education. One was the reading circle known by such names as the farmer's circle, reading association, or casino, which was also the place for educational lectures and amateur theater productions. Their influence included the development of previously unknown social ties for the peasants, who earlier had been limited to family and village community organizations. A decisive factor in raising social consciousness and organizing social and political endeavors, the associations played an immeasurable role in transforming peasant culture.[30]

The second agent that similarly influenced the formation of a modern cultural life was the press, which enabled the peasants to synthesize their acquired knowledge. Popular papers were already widespread by the 1880s, but even in the next decades newspaper reading was still not characteristic of the peasant. The mass influence of the press became evident only at the beginning of the twentieth century after reading and writing had become more common and education was no longer restricted to the associations. These two factors, the associations and the press, collectively had an all-encompassing influence on the social consciousness, world views, and education of the peasants. They also were instrumental in the emergence of individuals from the ranks of peasants, those with creative, organizational, and leadership abilities, to participate in reshaping and re-creating traditional culture.

Military service also played an important role in the development of national consciousness and served as a transmitter of revolutionary ideas. In the last third of the nineteenth century the idealized symbol of the Hungarian Revolution was Lajos Kossuth, leader of Hungary's fight for independence. Songs about him were popular among soldiers, who brought them to the villages. Cheap booklets or broadsides sold to the people also disseminated national symbols.[31]

The last decade of the nineteenth century in Hungary was marked by largely spontaneous mass actions of the agrarian workers and the poor peasants, who expressed themselves in various provinces through agrarian socialist movements and harvest strikes. These actions were local in most cases, and, in their choreography filled with rituals, symbolism, and mysticism, they were reminiscent of earlier primitive uprisings in western Europe.[32] It should be emphasized, however, that in the first decade of this century both the peasants and the agricultural proletarians throughout the country lived under the influence of the ideal of small ownership. The value system of the villages was strongly land oriented. As had been the case for generations, a person's worth was determined by his property and occupation, and the same factors also determined his willingness to participate in any political movement.

The echo of the Revolution of 1848 and the War of Liberation that followed in 1849 played an indirectly important role in the formation of national consciousness. During the Age of the Dual Monarchy (1867–1914), utensils ornamented with national symbols spread rapidly through the villages. In Protestant villages the walls of the houses were decorated with symbols of the lasting resistance against the Habsburgs: pictures of Kossuth or of the "martyrs of Arad," the thirteen Hungarian officers who had been executed in the town of Arad after the suppression of the Hungarian Revolution. In Catholic villages the worshiping of the four saints of the Árpad dynasty, the so-called Hungarian saints, spread rapidly.[33]

In the Age of the Dual Monarchy, following the liberation of the serfs, the identity of the Hungarian peasants was strengthened. Peasants developed a self-respect that was manifested in an improvement in their way of life: furniture, food, embroidered clothing. These changes, combined with the shortage of land, forced many into the cash economy through seasonal wage work, part-time carting services, and migration to construction sites or to the factories overseas. Former coexistence with other ethnic groups began to be replaced by conflicts when different interests clashed. Tensions increased because of the memories of the War of Independence, the years in the army in different cultural areas and the activities of intellectuals to raise the national consciousness. However, spontaneous acts of inter-ethnic solidarity have also been recorded. In this transitional period the peasants' values remained static among those with no surplus and led to new attitudes among others and to emigration for still others. Life as a rule was characterized by a greater emphasis on work. At the turn of the century, the Hungarian peasants still believed that their future rested in their land and in their efforts to enlarge their holdings, although they began to send their sons into trades or to schools. Slowly, folk customs began to change throughout the whole country. Peasant consciousness began to manifest itself in relation to urban workers, intellectuals, and the "gentlemen." While social distinctions came to the fore, there were greater aspirations to become similar to the higher social strata. Their forms of behavior were taken as models. This signaled a gradual movement of the peasants toward the mainstream of Hungarian national culture.[34]

It was because of these economic and social developments that the Hungarian masses joined the international capitalist labor market, and it now may be useful to summarize them briefly. Change took root in the social structure with the beginning of industrialization as the demographic explosion and agriculture's shortened production process accelerated the growth of the available workforce and made continuation of the traditional lifestyle increasingly difficult. At the same time, the expansion of modern transportation technology, especially construction of the railroads, the increase in the level of elementary education, and the appearance of two important agents of modernization, the reading associations and the newspapers, provided the peasants with information about the possibilities of a different way of life.

From the 1880s on, American industry also began a new period of development. The unique pace of its economic growth generated an enormous search for industrial workers, particularly at the cheap and unskilled level. Because such a workforce was unavailable in American society, the demand had to be filled from elsewhere. As a result, word of the work possibilities and higher wages in America spread into east-central Europe, attracting and mobilizing the population of the Danubian Basin that could not find a place in either the agriculture or the industry of its homeland. The following chapters contain an analysis of that mobilization and its consequences.

CHAPTER 2

The Pattern of
Migration: 1876–1910s

THE FIRST WAVE of emigration from Europe took place in the 1840s and
1850s and affected the peoples of the British Isles. Primarily Germans and
Scandinavians made up the second wave between the 1850s and 1870s. Although there were indications of emigration from central and east-central
Europe as early as the 1850s, large numbers of people began to leave the
region only in the early 1870s. From that time, immigrants to the United States
began to come from eastern Europe and Italy, rather than from northwestern
Europe, in part because governments abolished old controls on land in east-
central and southern Europe and, as a result, a new mobile, "propertyless"
class was created (as described in detail in the first chapter). Emigration
assumed such large proportions that in the first decade of the twentieth century
the records of United States immigration authorities show people from the
Austro-Hungarian Monarchy to be the largest single group among new arrivals,
accounting for 24 percent of the total.[1]

Figure 1 shows the evolution of migration from the 1860s to the 1910s
from Europe as a whole, from northwestern Europe, and from east-central
and southern Europe. The diagram reflects a fourfold growth from the 1860s
to 1910s.[2] This growth was not steady but took place in three waves, each
bigger than the last. In the first wave, the curve indicating emigration from
Europe as a whole is almost identical with that for overseas emigration from
northwestern Europe. Migration from east-central and southern Europe increased in the second wave, after the 1890s. In the third wave, around the turn
of the century, it accounted for the overwhelming majority of the immigrants to
the United States. The trends show the interdependence of the process of
mass migration from western and from east-central Europe.

Figure 2 shows the development of migration to the United States from
the Austro-Hungarian Monarchy, Italy, and Russia. The curves of migration

18

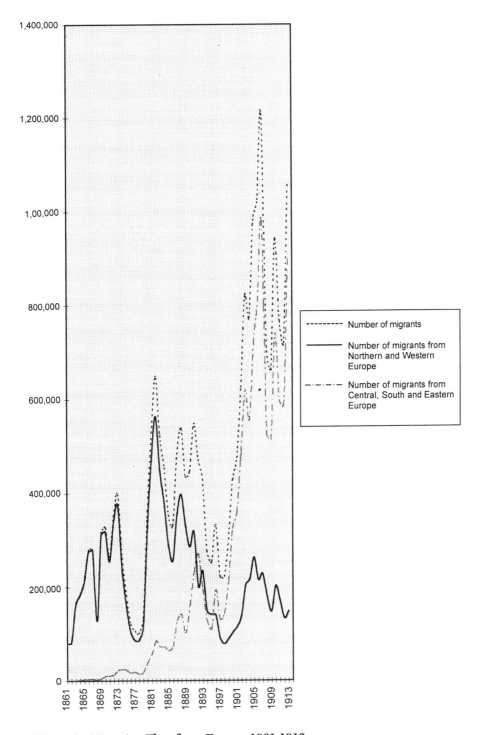

Figure 1. Migration Flow from Europe 1861–1913

Legend:
- - - - - - Number of migrants
———— Number of migrants from Northern and Western Europe
– · – · – Number of migrants from Central, South and Eastern Europe

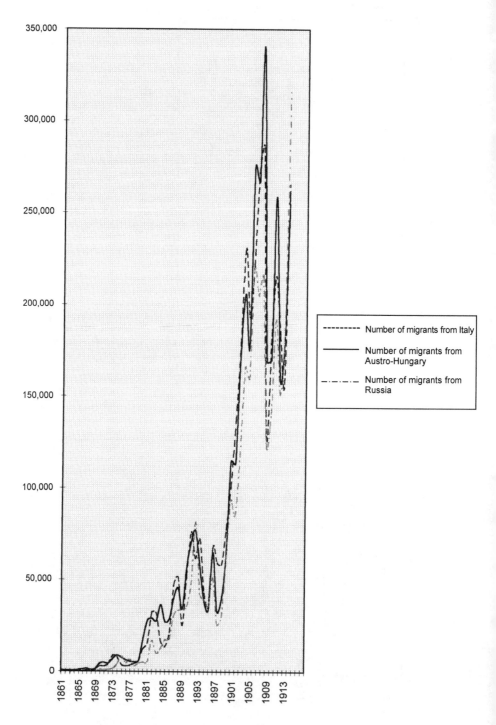

Figure 2. Migration Flow from Italy, Austro-Hungary, and Russia 1861–1913

are surprisingly similar. In east-central and southern Europe, the preliminary phase of mass emigration lasted until the mid-1880s. It was only then that the annual number of emigrants from each country rose to 10,000. The growth phase of mass emigration that followed lasted from the 1890s until 1905 to 1908. The few years before World War I can be regarded as the saturation phase of growth for the Austro-Hungarian Monarchy and Italy, where mass emigration reached a peak of more than 200,000 persons annually. The fourth phase, the slowing down of migration from the central European region, followed a different pattern from that affecting western and northern European countries.[3] In the Danubian Basin it was not local industrial development and absorption of the labor force that gradually reduced the impetus for overseas emigration; the restrictive immigration policy pursued by the United States put a sudden end to it. In the early 1920s, severe American immigration laws closed the gates of the country to "undesirable" immigrants.

Realistic estimates concerning the number of migrants in a given ethnic group are hard to obtain. From the Austro-Hungarian Monarchy, 3,765,381 immigrants were registered by the U.S. Office of Immigration between 1861 and 1913, with the majority (2,260,113) arriving after 1899. During the same period, 1,815,117 immigrants from Hungary entered the United States.[4] Although sporadic cases of emigration had already occurred in Hungary from the mid-nineteenth century on, the feverish overseas migration began with the 1880s.[5] The peak of its increase was the first fourteen years of this century.

Gross migration from the Austro-Hungarian Monarchy before World War I, therefore, can be put at three million people, an estimated one and one-half million of whom were migrants from Hungary. The number of external emigrants is two and one-half times greater than the number of migrants to internal industry. When Hungary's industrial workforce grew by 88,000 from 1880 to 1890, by 230,000 in the next decade, and by 260,000 in the decade after that, the numbers of Hungarian emigrants recorded at the seaports were 164,119; 261,414; and more than one million for the same decades, respectively.[6]

Three years stand out during the period of mass emigration from Hungary: 1905, with 7.9 emigrants per thousand inhabitants; 1906 with 8.1; and 1907 with 9.3. Thirty-eight percent of all emigrants from Hungary during 1889–1914 left in 1905–07. The emigration average of these three years is just twice the average of the next six years and three times that of former years.[7] Similarly, the two significant breaks in the otherwise constant increase in overseas emigration coincided with the American depressions of the mid-1880s and of the years 1907–08.

During the past fifty years the same emigration statistics have been used in the literature both by way of warning and as reassurance about the effects of the movement on Hungary.[8] In fact, a remarkable phenomenon, noticed also by contemporary economists and cited here from statistical records of Hungarian emigration, was that "the highest level of emigration from Hungary coincided almost completely with economic improvement."[9] For example, "in

1905 the harvest was fairly good, and in 1906 it was excellent and agrarian wages were steadily improving."[10]

The phases and extent of emigration from Hungary were by no means independent of the various phases of Hungarian economic development. The cycles, the short-term waves of emigration, and the fluctuations in the annual number of emigrants, however, show much closer correlation to the ups and downs of the American economy than to the Hungarian.[11]

Between 1899 and 1913, the overwhelming majority of the emigrants, 85 percent of the total, sailed to the United States.[12] Repeated passages overseas, and thus multiple registration of the same person, were by no means uncommon, however, so the above figures may be misleading. According to the Report of the Immigration Commission, 19 percent of all Slovaks and 11 percent of all Magyars who migrated to the United States from 1899 to 1910 had been there previously.[13] Their repeated round trips had earned them, as well as the Italians, notoriety as "birds of passage" among the United States authorities. Consequently, the actual number of immigrants could have been at least 20 percent less than the numbers going through the immigration process.

Before 1914, no large-scale immigration to the United States had taken place from any country to the east or south of Hungary, except for a massive exodus of Jews from western Russia to America. Furthermore, statistics of the number of overseas migrants compared with the total population in various countries show that emigration, not only from Ireland, but also from Norway, Sweden, and even Finland, was proportionately much greater than that from Hungary.

It becomes evident from the contemporary literature on emigration that the bonds and lifestyles of agrarian society impeded immigration to the United States less than they blocked migration to cities within Hungary. However, this is only a seeming contradiction: overseas migration lured the emigrants with the hope that their move would not be permanent. They expected to return to their original homeland and improve their life with the money earned abroad This hope was based on the differences in earnings which then existed between industry in the United States and both agriculture and industry in Hungary.[14]

By now it is generally accepted that migration overseas was not exclusively a unidirectional movement but had a back-and-forth transitional or circular character. Recent research has focused increasing attention on frequent return migration as one of the characteristic features of labor migration.[15] Still, return migration has not yet been given the attention its significance requires. The subjective reasons that motivate authors to exaggerate the dimensions of migration also exclude returns from their range of vision, or lead them to underestimate their importance.[16]

According to the research conducted by Gusztáv Thirring in the years 1895 to 1896, 23 percent of the emigrants were people who had been to the United States before.[17] The Lord-Lieutenant of Liptó County estimated the number of remigrants from America in his county at 50 percent in 1902.[18] The subprefect of Szepes County also reported to the Minister of the Interior in the autumn of 1914 that the first emigrants of the county "were almost entirely mineworkers, who owing to the closing down of the former flourishing mine-industry here, had remained without income to insure their livelihood, and so were virtually forced to emigrate."[19] T. N. Carver, professor at Harvard University, knew of such a Hungarian emigrant who crossed the ocean eight times.[20] A contemporary traveler who crossed the sea with Hungarian emigrants on the *Ultonia* met an emigrant from Hungary who made the journey to and from Europe and America nine times.[21] Such frequency would, of course, be rare. However, contemporary newspapers and official reports also emphasize that the same people repeatedly sailed to the New World en masse.

Remigration, this remarkable feature of the so-called new wave of immigration, reveals a characteristic pattern. First, data on a number of ethnic groups for the period between 1908 and 1924 indicate that remigration was closely correlated to the historical development of international migration. The longer the overseas migration of an ethnic group continued, the smaller the proportion of remigration; conversely, the more recent the migration was, the more people returned to their homeland.[22] Second, the fluctuation in the flow of migration was influenced by economic cycles and international difficulties; the general volume of returns varied significantly with both cyclical and seasonal fluctuations in the American economy. The economic crisis of 1905–1907 in the United States brought about a great wave of remigration to Hungary, for example.[23] In 1908 more returnees were registered than emigrants. Finally, when remigration did not occur, exceptional factors likely were at work in the country of origin. The data on age and occupation and the sex ratio for Jews thus shows that they sailed overseas with the intention of settling abroad for good after the pogroms in Russia and Romania.[24]

Official Hungarian statistics on remigration between 1899 and 1913 show that 32.9 percent of all emigrants eventually returned.[25] In reality, this figure must have been larger, because those who were in charge of compiling the data admitted that their files on remigration were incomplete. "It is more of symptomatic importance, it shows, so to say, the gross outlines, the tendency of the direction of the remigrant masses general movement."[26] When one also considers the data in American censuses on the segment of American population born in the Austro-Hungarian Monarchy or in Hungary itself, the proportion of those who returned can be cautiously estimated at 40–50 percent.[27] Remigration was mainly a "movement of the men"; women took part at a much smaller rate in remigration than in migration.

With regard to Hungary, the simultaneous study of emigration and returns is the sine qua non for understanding the nature of overseas migration. People who left this European region to improve their living condition planned their American stay to last for two to five years, expecting to halt the downward trend of mobility in their original surroundings. A temporary "voluntary degradation" to the ranks of the North American proletarians was endured to prevent their final degradation to the proletariat in their homeland.[28]

Some historians have suggested that returnees were likely to be the unsuccessful immigrants, others emphasized the conservative character of remigration.[29] However, available evidence clearly shows that most Hungarian
returnees improved their economic conditions and went back to Hungary to
their home districts because they had never thought of a permanent relocation
overseas. For most of them emigration to America was an emergency measure
to solve problems at home and to make money in order to buy land in Hungary.

Nevertheless, the first Hungarians who departed—although for a temporary emigration—faced the moral condemnation of a society that did not recognize the peasants' right to move about freely.

The Migrants

The most striking characteristic of immigrants from east-central Europe is
their ethnic and linguistic diversity, shown by census data from Hungary,
1899–1913,[30] and by statistics revealing the range of emigrant nationalities from
the Austro-Hungarian Monarchy.

TABLE 1.

Ethnic Composition of Overseas Emigrants from Austria-Hungary, 1899–1913[31] (in %)

Nationalities	From Austria-Hungary	From Hungary	Population of Hungary, 1900 Census
Polish	18.7	—	—
Slovak	15.4	26.8	11.9
Magyar	14.2	26.3	51.4
Croat-Slovenian	14.0	16.6	1.2
German	11.4	15.0	11.9
Hebrew	7.5	3.7	3.1
Ruthenian	7.3	2.1	2.5
Czech-Moravian	4.3	—	—
Romanian	3.1	6.9	16.6
Bosnian	2.7	2.4°	3.1°
Italian	0.8	—	—
Others	0.6	0.3	1.4
	100.00	100.00	100.00

°Serbian, Bulgarian

In actuality the picture is more diversified because these ethnic groups do
not encompass all the migratory peoples. In addition to the multitude of ethnic
groups, the table further indicates that during the years from 1899 to 1924,
Poles, Slovaks, and Hungarians represented the largest immigrant groups from
the Austro-Hungarian Monarchy: approximately 50 percent of the emigrants

were from their ethnic regions. The much smaller numbers of Czech-Moravians and Romanians each represented under 5 percent of the people who emigrated from the Austro-Hungarian Monarchy to the United States.

From the ten ethnic groups of Hungarian citizens, the most numerous were Slovaks and Magyars. More than 50 percent of all migrants from Hungary came from these two ethnic groups. Because the various nationalities did not emigrate simultaneously, their proportions were constantly changing. Overseas emigration from Hungary was started before the 1880s by Jews and Germans, intelligent and resourceful merchants and artisans, but by the turn of the century Slovaks were at the top of the list. In 1899 one out of four emigrants who went to the United States from the Monarchy was Slovak (25.2 percent), and virtually every second emigrant from Hungarian territory was Slovak (45 percent), while only one out of five was of Magyar nationality (20 percent).

Ethnically, the main characteristic of overseas emigration from Hungary was its multinationality. In 1900, when about half of the country's population was Magyar, the Magyars accounted for only slightly over one-fourth of Hungary's overseas emigrants.

The situation had changed by 1913, however. As the migration of Slovaks abated and their proportion went down to 22 percent of all emigrants from Hungary, that of Magyars increased to 25 percent.[32] Sixty-seven percent of the 1.2 million Hungarian citizens who left Hungary between 1899 and 1913 did not speak Hungarian as a mother tongue. Proportions are somewhat different in official Hungarian statistics, where the emigrants of the Magyar mother tongue include Jews and constitute about one-third of the total. These differences are not significant enough to cause a qualitative modification of the picture. Because the majority of emigrants were from the national minorities and not Magyars, overseas migration resulted in a special pattern of demographic, cultural, and political consequences for Hungary. The history of the national minorities and emigration in Hungary are inextricably intertwined.

This migration obviously was a movement of the young generation. The labor migration especially involved the most productive age groups of the population. In the 1905–07 period, 61.6 percent of the people who arrived in the United States from Hungary belonged to the 20- to 40-year-old age group. Teenagers (under 20 years) represented a relatively high proportion (23.2 percent) of the total and the number of children under age 14 was low all through this period in spite of a gradual increase.[33]

The pioneers from Hungary departed mostly in family units. Therefore, there were almost as many women among them as men: approximately 40 percent in 1878–1879.[34] In the years 1899–1913, in the first period of mass migration from Hungary, the proportion of women was approximately one-third: 33.9 percent. The role of the men became more dominant as the wave of migration unfolded. In 1902–03, the proportion of women did not even reach a quarter of all the migrants. In 1905–07 at the peak of the migration period this proportion was 30 percent.[35]

Thus, participation of Hungarian women in the process of overseas migration was strikingly low for some years prior to World War I. The same applies to the other ethnic groups in eastern and southeastern Europe. From 1907, however, the proportion of women rose continuously. In the six years prior to World War I almost 40 percent of the Hungarian migrants were women, and in 1913 it was already 53.8 percent.[36]

It is a widely held presumption that women have less enterprising spirit, therefore the view is held that migrant women were taken out of the original community by their husbands or their families. Without doubt, the reuniting of families played a role in the growth of the numbers of migrant women, but national statistics show that this was not the only reason.

Although from 1910 to 1913 there were many married men among the migrants, U.S. immigration officials registered only 37.2 percent of the Hungarian women as married. Indeed, the rate of single persons over 14 years of age was higher among the women than among the men (35.2 percent compared to 28.7 percent).[37] The marriages that took place among the immigrants once they were in the United States deserve much more attention than they have received as they offer an important insight into the formation of ethnic groups. In Hungary, contemporaries already realized that the inclination of women to migrate was stimulated by the growing demand for female labor in U.S. industry, especially from 1910 onward in the tobacco, cigar, and textile industries.[38] The women who migrated overseas from Hungary were strikingly young. From 1910 to 1913, 73.7 percent of them were between 14 and 21 years of age, and a mere 7 percent of them were over 30.[39]

The question of the occupational groups from which the migrant masses were being recruited concerned officials who prepared statistical documents in both Hungary and the United States. Hungarian accounts are of limited value because they cover only a few years and because their occupational categories do not fully express social stratification. Beginning in 1861, by contrast, authorities in the United States recorded the occupation of each immigrant although, as previously noted, for years emigrants from Hungary were listed jointly with those from Austria. Despite some problems, American records for the years beginning with 1899 are the most useful, being relatively detailed and registering the immigrants' occupations by ethnic groups. With the help of these later records, information from descriptive historical sources, and comparisons with data from other countries and ethnic groups, characteristics of the Hungarian emigrants' social structure can be outlined. Let us first consider the occupational distribution of the emigrants as reflected in the Hungarian records.

Thus, the overwhelming majority of the emigrants from Hungary were agricultural workers. The number of independent landowners among them was relatively small. Instead, most were agricultural day laborers, a category that included not only the landless agrarian proletarians but also the young members of small landowning families who did not yet have a plot of their own. The subprefect of Heves County did not stand alone in his opinion:

TABLE 2.

Occupational Distribution of Emigrants from Hungary[40]

Emigrants' Occupation	1905–06	1911–13	As % of Hungary's population in 1910
Agriculture	17.0	21.0	41.3
Agriculture and day laborers	51.6	47.4	20.4
Miners and mine laborers	1.2	0.9	0.8
Industrial workers	2.2	3.0	5.5
Tradespeople	0.3	0.4	1.5
Industrial and commercial help	11.3	8.4	13.7
Professional	0.5	0.7	4.5
Day laborers, not specified further	9.5	10.2	2.6
Domestic servants	5.2	5.3	4.4
Other occupations	1.2	2.7	5.3
Total	100.00	100.00	100.00

"Emigration with us is now a class movement. The movement is of the agricultural class. The movement in itself is not improvised, it is not of a transitory moment, but a manifestation arising as a consequence of the development of the peasantry's vital process."[41]

Within a relatively short time, by 1911–13, the number of independent landowners and independent craftsmen had increased considerably. Yet emigration had so impressed public consciousness with its agrarian character that it was generally considered to be a peasant movement.[42] And so it was, even though before the turn of the century, the nonagricultural element had played quite a significant role in initiating emigration, organizing it, and communicating to those still at home the attraction of the United States.

Among the works of contemporaries, an interesting report was submitted in early September 1888 by Consul Black in Budapest to his American superiors.[43] According to his experiences, Hungarian emigration may be divided into the following classes:

a. The rural population, which forms the bulk of the emigrants, are either farm laborers or are owners of small parcels of land. They have little or no familiarity with improved farming implements; they have a very primitive lifestyle, are frugal in their habits, except in the matter of alcoholic spirits in which they indulge immoderately. They are normally docile and peaceable unless under the influence of liquor, when they often give way to excesses, to belligerence.

The peasant often manages to get into debt, then has to mortgage his small property, and when he finds he is unable to repay the debt, resolves to go to the United States to earn enough to pay his debt and sometimes to buy additional land from a less fortunate neighbor. Because they go to the United States with no intention of becoming citizens, they leave their families here, to anxiously await the return of husband, father, or son with a well-filled purse. With rare exceptions they return successful, and their success motivates the entire neighborhood to likewise try their luck. We thus find entire villages in upper Hungary almost depleted of their able-bodied male population, who are temporarily residing in the United States earning money which they send to their families left behind. Millions upon millions of such money is received here annually. However, there are exceptions to this rule. There are some who find their condition so vastly improved in the United States that they decide to remain there permanently, and as soon as they have earned enough money, send for their families.

b. Small merchants, clerks, bookkeepers, and such who have no regular occupation. Members of this class emigrate to the United States to improve their living conditions and with the intention of becoming citizens of the United States. They are usually able-bodied, intelligent men and are from the most respectable group of the Hungarian emigrants.

c. Broken-down merchants, speculators, and such of the gentry who, by mismanagement or from other causes, have squandered their inheritance go to the United States without any fixed purpose, but with strong hopes of retrieving their lost fortunes. Being unused and unwilling to work they are doomed to bitter disappointment. As is usual in such cases they live on the proceeds of the honest earnings of others. Fortunately, this class forms but a small proportion of the emigration of this country.

d. Young men in their teens, who emigrate in order to evade military service. The greatest part, however, once there, remain in the United States and having come there when comparatively young in years, and belonging to the more intelligent class of people here, they generally prove useful citizens.

e. The usual sprinkling of defaulters, forgers, and other criminals who leave their native land for their country's good and to the detriment of the United States.

This gives only a rough and approximate picture of the emigrants' original occupations and social backgrounds. Other contemporary observers emphasized that the first to venture on the great trip were not peasants.[44] Rather, shopkeepers and artisans whose livelihood was threatened by emerging capitalism were most receptive to the idea of emigration and first gathered the remnants of their possessions and set out overseas. The characteristic emigrants of the 1870s were relatively prosperous bourgeois Germans from the western and southeastern parts of the Monarchy and miners from the north, the latter of whom first encountered the emigration agents scouring the coal, salt, and petroleum regions of Galicia for cheap European labor to staff the frenetically developing American industries. By the terms of their contracts, the first miner immigrants could leave the Pennsylvania coal mines only if they found someone else to replace them; this requirement naturally played a great role in their urging others to emigrate.[45]

From the 1880s on, bankrupt artisans (tanners, weavers, tailors, blacksmiths, cutlers) appeared alongside the miner emigrants in annually increasing numbers. Initially not many of those who emigrated were from among the totally destitute day laborers, who did not have the means to pay for their passage. But as competition among shipping companies led to reduction of fares and as the earlier immigrants, still few in number, began to send money and boat tickets home, more and more people were able to undertake the trip.

They were joined by young day laborers and jobless journeymen who could not find work in small industry or in the depleted mines. Later, and in ever increasing numbers, came the agricultural day laborers, cotters, and servants, and bankrupt small landowners. After the turn of the century, the occupational distribution of the emigrants tipped heavily toward day laborers. The emigration agents promoted the mass exodus of day laborers and agricultural workers by promises of job opportunities and work contracts and by lending them the money to pay their fares. Soon usurers, banks, and loan associations also recognized the possibilities inherent in loans to would-be emigrants and made this type of credit operation a booming business in northern Hungary. Day laborers made up a much greater proportion of the emigrants than of the Hungarian population, just as skilled industrial workers by this time comprised a smaller proportion of the emigrants than of the total population. It was when the migratory movement of artisans and craftsmen was joined by the agricultural population that it grew into a mass migration. Thus, although mass emigration from Hungary was without a doubt a rural movement, it would be a mistake to overemphasize the social homogeneity of the emigrants.

The varied occupational background of the nonagricultural population is illustrated in more detail by the records of the United States immigration authorities. According to those records, between 1900 and 1913 the Hungarian-speaking immigrants included 272 mechanical engineers, 257 musicians, 203 teachers, 175 clergymen, and 26,786 skilled workers. The largest groups in the latter were 3,526 carpenters, 3,511 tailors, 2,523 blacksmiths, 1,860 locksmiths, and 1,088 masons.[46]

The changes in occupational distribution found among Hungarian emigrants to the United States during the period of mass migration are similar to those for other European emigrant groups. Throughout Europe, the craftsmen and village artisans were the archetypical pioneers, and emigration became a mass movement only when the agrarian population joined in. Similarly, as the waves of emigration subsided, the proportion of the agricultural population

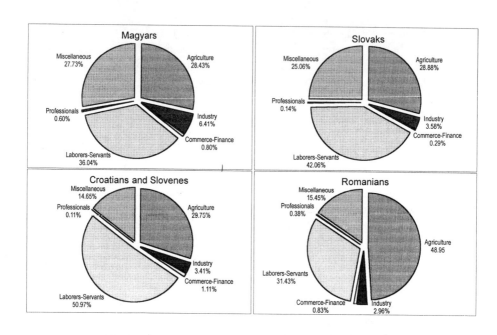

	Magyars	Slovaks	Croatians and Slovenes	Romanians
Agriculture	28.40%	28.89%	29.75%	48.95%
Industry	6.40%	3.58%	3.41%	2.96%
Commerce-Finance	0.80%	0.29%	1.11%	0.83%
Laborers-Servants	36.00%	42.08%	50.97%	31.43%
Professionals	.60%	.14%	.11%	.38%
Miscellaneous	27.70%	25.07%	14.65%	15.45%

Figure 3. Distribution of Immigrants by Occupation and Ethnic Groups, 1899–1924

among the emigrants likewise fell as already was the case in western Europe by the 1880s. The occupational structure of the American immigrants from southeastern Europe thus varied at any given time.

The diagram shows that the occupational distribution of the migrants differed considerably according to the ethnic group they belonged to. The proportion of agriculturalists (peasants and land laborers) was highest among the Romanians and lowest among the Magyars. The proportion of emigrants who worked in industry already in Hungary was highest among the Magyars, and lowest among the Romanians. Laborer and servant proportions were highest among the Croatians and Slovenes and lowest among the Romanians.

Intellectuals were few in numbers among all ethnic groups from Hungary—their proportion was under 1 percent. The Magyars were on the relatively highest level and the Croatians-Slovenians and the Slovaks on the lowest. Emigrants as a general rule tended to be more literate than their compatriots who remained at home although there were significant differences among the individual ethnic groups. In the years between 1899 and 1910 the American immigration authorities judged 88.6 percent of the Hungarians, 76.0 percent of the Slovaks, 65.3 percent of the Romanians, 63.9 percent of the Slovenes, 63.8 percent of the Croats, and 46.6 percent of the Ruthenes over the age of 14 to be familiar with the arts of reading and writing.[47] The differences in the occupational structure and in the level of literacy also reflect the different cultural and educational development of the various nationalities living in Hungary.

Up-to-date information on the occupational distribution of the Germans and the Ruthenians in Hungary can be gained from official Hungarian statistics. According to these the occupational distribution of the Germans of Hungary is similar to that of the Magyars; the proportion of industrial workers among them somewhat supersedes that of the Magyars. The occupational distribution of the Ruthenians was similar to that of the Slovaks, though the rate of peasants and agrarian laborers was higher than 80 percent among the Ruthenian emigrants from Hungary.

The Centers of Emigration

In all the European countries where migration unfolded, including the states where the population was ethnically more or less homogeneous, emigration spread primarily through certain regions, centers of emigration, which shared several common characteristics.[48] Foremost was a peripheral position, meaning that the regions were rather far from the industrial centers of the country and usually had less favorable economic and natural endowments than the rest of the nation. Often they were mountainous areas where households historically relied on handicrafts, artisanship, and commissioned work to supplement agriculture. The second and related characteristic of these emigration centers was a tradition of migrating. The strong susceptibility of Slovaks to the news of

possibilities provided in the New World was not independent of the centuries-
old Slovak tradition of seasonal migration, common among them since the early
nineteenth century. Their seasonal migrations were almost exclusively between
rural areas.[49] Likewise, it would be difficult to understand the relatively high
proportion of Germans among the migrants from Hungary without taking into
account their tradition of *valcolás,* itinerant learning of skilled work.

Third, in its topography, migration follows and clearly reflects the channels
of communication between regions and ethnic groups. Because in the nineteenth century communication moved from the north to the southeast, Jews,
Germans, and Slovaks living in the northern border zone formed the first
groups of Hungarian emigrants. The subprefect of Szepes County also reported
to the Minister of the Interior in the autumn of 1914 that the first emigrants
from the county "were almost solely mineworkers, who were virtually forced
to emigrate owing to the fact that they were obliged to ensure their living after
the once flourishing mining industry closed down completely, leaving them
without pay."

Several centers of emigration formed in Hungary relatively far apart from
one another. The largest, in the northeastern part of the country, encompassed
Szepes, Sáros, Zemplén, Abauj, Borsod, Ung, Szatmár, and Szabolcs Counties.[50]
Between 1899 and 1913, fully 31 percent of the emigrants from Hungary came
from this region, and its migration rates reached an average of fifteen per
thousand during 1899 to 1913.[51] There were smaller centers also in the Dunán-
túl (Trans-Danubia), mainly in Veszprém and Tolna Counties in the south of
Hungary, and in Temes and Torontó Counties, as well as in the southeastern
counties of Transylvania.

The main wave originated in the northeast of the country, in eastern
Slovakia, which was very mixed ethnically. Except in Sáros and Szepes Counties,
where Slovaks reached 58 to 60 percent, 90 percent of all Slovak migrants
came from the eastern counties. Masses of Magyar migrants (69.3 percent of
them in 1899) originated from this same area and from two neighboring
counties. Throughout the whole migration period communities in the above-
mentioned counties in the northeast were the main sources of all emigration
to America and were the places of origin of 60.4 percent of the migrants of
Magyar nationality; many Jews and Germans started from here, too.

In all regions the ethnic structure of migration was mixed, but in each case
the pioneers of migration overseas were the Jewish, German, and Slovak people.
The migration fever was spread by them both to their fellow nationals living
in other parts of the country and to the members of other ethnic communities
in their own neighborhoods. In the northeastern part of Hungary, it was
transmitted from the Slovaks to the Magyars; in Transylvania, from the Saxons
to the Romanians; and in Croatia-Slavonia, from the Slovenes to the Germans,
Croats, and Serbs.

The formation of emigration centers demonstrates that although general
economic and social conditions determine the possibilities and limits of human
life, the intentions and actions of individuals are influenced by the local environ-

ment and the information received in that environment. The shaping of actual emigration cannot be deduced directly from the macrostructure in any region; and in any given locality perception of pressure is not sufficient to induce people to leave their homes voluntarily and in masses. It is equally necessary to have a hint of favorable possibilities, the establishment of an information channel through which people can learn where and why it is worthwhile to emigrate. As these information channels were built up throughout Europe by reports of earlier emigrants, migration expanded everywhere along the personal communication chains of relatives, friends, and neighbors, which form the prime element of the expansion mechanism. This sort of self-generating characteristic was an inseparable part of the migration process that increased in some areas to such a height that it cannot be explained merely by correlation with economic or social factors.

The fact that the first and most important emigration regions in Hungary developed in the northeastern counties can be more or less related to the economic and demographic pressures that weighed on the region's population. The birth rate in these counties exceeded the national average of 39.2 percent; on the right bank of the Tisza, it was 42.7 percent. The population density was lower than that of the Alföld only in proportion to the total land area. Considering the available arable land, it was impressive, for much of the region was mountainous, the climate severe, and hardly suitable for agriculture. It serves as a good illustration of the fact that computing population density in terms of sheer square kilometers will hardly give a realistic picture of the region's economic problems.

The poor natural conditions of the northern regions and their lower level of productivity prevented them from being self-sufficient even before the demographic boom. The wages were only half of other counties. The migration of itinerant workers to do seasonal work on the plains at the center of the country was a traditional and organic part of the economic system there. This kind of division of labor between the mountainous and plain regions and the consequent early migration was characteristic of other European countries as well.

In the Danubian Basin, therefore, the centers of emigration were determined by the same rules and mechanisms for the spread of emigration that prevailed all over Europe. They clearly explain the multinational composition of Hungary's emigration and account for the higher proportions of national minorities, regardless of discrimination. The topography of emigration calls into question not only any political motivation ascribed to the mass movement, but also the hypothesis that automatically links emigration with the poorest, most backward areas.[52]

Both American and European researchers attribute the higher proportion of national minorities among Hungarian emigrants to the tension in the nationality situation. For instance, in recent Slovak and Croatian literature, political oppression ranks second only to economic factors as the general explanation of overseas migration.[53] It is difficult to detect and measure political motivations, however, especially in the case of individual decisions. To be sure, political motivations are clearly apparent in the case of some intellectuals and members of certain occupations, who left for America on account of national and political conflicts. Nevertheless, in the regions where mass emigrant movements actually took place, several factors contradict even the secondary role assigned to political motivations and raise questions about any relationship between the specific ethnic composition of the emigrants and the unresolved nationality issues. The lack of political motivations in the drive for overseas migration does not mean, of course, that the real seriousness of the nationality problems should be underestimated.

There is no explicit correlation between the various ethnic groups' intentions to emigrate and discrimination toward them; for instance, more Germans than Romanians left Hungary. Moreover, to use the example of the Slovaks, the centers of emigration were not in western Slovakia, where the nationality movement was the strongest. Finally, if even a secondary role is ascribed to the political motivations for mass migration, it still is impossible to explain why so many people returned to their original surroundings where in the meantime nothing had changed politically.[54] We are likely, therefore, to come closer to understanding the multinational aspects of migration by examining its own inner dynamics than by looking at its external political context.

The fact is that the economic factors determining the emigration process did not operate mechanically, as is shown by the great range in the number of the emigrants from villages that in other respects were more similar than different. Necessity often had the air of chance when it came to any given instance of emigration, which was much influenced by the success or failure of the neighbors who first sailed overseas. Good luck motivated others to follow their example, while bad luck weakened the desire to try.

The ethnic composition of the migration was relevant as well to a question that greatly interested its contemporaries, namely, how the returning migrants would use the cultural and political experience they had gained in America to influence their native environment. The answer, of course—as it can be read in later chapters—varied according to individual experiences and sometimes reflected contradictions between individual and group interests.

Overseas migration from Hungary also began only after decades of internal movement. Emigrants for the Americas slightly outnumbered the others when the mass movement started. The region of overseas migration in Hungary was one part of the region which developed in the northeastern part of the Monarchy.[55]

Workers moved from agricultural to industrialized areas, both within and across national borders. By the late nineteenth century, there was an industrial core stretching from the American Midwest to northwestern Europe. The large majority of migrants from Hungary went to the United States, but at this time many people took the way to less industrialized countries, such as Romania and Croatia, where labor scarcity made for high wages.

The changing position of an economy within the larger world economy can help explain one of the paradoxes of migration: why migrants leave less developed economies that are experiencing considerable growth.

We have to point out that Hungary sent large numbers of migrants to the United States when it was also undergoing industrialization itself in the early twentieth century. Workers were losing their traditional occupations through the very process of economic change. In many cases, these workers might prefer to take their chances on a better life in a more developed society than taking an unfamiliar and perhaps more difficult job in their own country.

CHAPTER 3

The Pattern
of Migration

The Village of Szamosszeg

To SPECIFY EXACTLY the characteristics of Hungarian migration requires a systematic microanalysis of individual migrants. In this study, however, sources and research conditions did not permit me to employ the methods of Swedish and Danish research, which extract a given amount of information about individuals from the available records and then use computers to create a typical profile.[1] Instead a more precise and detailed analysis of fewer cases appeared most promising. Just as the water of an entire ocean is embodied in a single drop, in the biographies of a small group (for example, the emigrants of a particular village and their children and grandchildren) international migration is likewise embodied in all of its complexity. For these family studies I selected a village from the northeastern part of Hungary, the important center of emigration from which transatlantic migration was most frequent.[2]

The choice of my native village of Szamosszeg in Szatmár County promised to be an especially advantageous one, for I already had a knowledge of the local community. My research trips to the United States took me to New Brunswick, New Jersey, where a good number of immigrants from Szamosszeg and their descendants now live. I was connected to several not only by personal contact and acquaintance but by family ties as well. These connections simplified the process of systematically collecting information in the settlement areas outside of the sending village.

Data were gathered from a wide range of historical sources. Besides conducting oral interviews, I consulted written documents and referred to photographs and other memorabilia.[3] I soon came to realize, however, that sources of written information such as personal correspondence, as well as passports and other documents, have survived only in rare instances. For the most part, it never occurred to the Szamosszegeans on either side of the ocean to keep such materials, nor did the political developments of the postwar period do much to encourage their preservation.

As a result, I began to place more and more emphasis upon the collection and analysis of oral sources. In gathering information on individual migrants from Szamosszeg, I interviewed those older villagers who were considered by the community to have the most knowledge about past events in the village. For each individual emigrant, I prepared a separate card on which I recorded all available information. This in turn gave me further leads to other village elders, to family members of the emigrants, and even to living emigrants themselves. I cross-checked the oral interviews against the available written documents—such as church registers in the village and in New Brunswick. Out of this mosaic of the various written and oral sources, then, I was able to reconstruct the more important episodes in the life histories of a number of individuals.

Collective memory proved useful as it widened and increased the number of sources of information and offered the opportunity to counterbalance various subjective evaluations. In the course of interviewing, I discovered that facts of importance in an earlier, older value system had become fixed in the memories of the elders with great exactness. Those interviewed on both sides of the ocean were able to relate accurately and without the least bit of doubt who had owned how much land in the village and how it had been obtained. With similar certainty, they were able to tie together the emigrants in terms of family lineages and extended relations. In the oral information they supplied on almost three hundred individual emigrants, their accounts differed only occasionally from what was written in the church records. In particular Ignác Kósa excelled with his very rich memory. Moreover, their information on property ownership was from time to time more accurate than the village records, for land had often been long divided among the children while the deed continued to list the parent as its owner.

Naturally, past experiences were viewed from the standpoint of the present and interpreted accordingly. When I asked a fellow migrant, "Why did such and such a person go to America?" or "Why did he come back to Szamosszeg?" I would invariably get more information than when I asked the migrants themselves, their own families, or the village elders. People tended to leave out those details of their past experiences and adventures, dealing with ideological or political developments to which they were no longer so partial. They had forgotten the radical behavior in the 1930s of their friends or family members. On this subject, it was rather the village "outsiders," who were not involved in the events, who were much more communicative.

In my original plan of research, I intended to interview at least one individual from each emigrating or remigrating family. But my original goal proved unrealistic. Although I made numerous personal contacts and held interviews outside of New Brunswick, I discovered that the emigrant generation, and particularly their children, have experienced such great geographic mobility that I was unable to visit all of their locations.[4] Fortunately, however, someone was always able to fill in the missing information on those families and offspring whom I was unable to visit personally. In this way, the gathering of information covered almost the entire emigrant group from Szamosszeg with only very few exceptions.

The emphasis of the questions was on uncovering, in as much detail as possible, the fate of the migrants themselves, the first generation.[5] I would ask the second generation primarily about their parents' lives instead of their lives or their children's. Regarding the second generation itself, I collected information about geographic and social mobility, language, and the connection to the ethnic community as it was reflected in choice of a marriage partner from within or outside the Hungarian community. In studying the second generation, then, I attempted to explore the path from one identity to another and so the changing manifestations of ethnicity and assimilation. In sum, I sought through microanalysis to discover more about the mechanism of migration and about the "transplanted community."[6]

I do not claim that the example of Szamosszegeans is valid for the peasant migration of every new immigrant group. Nor do I claim that no other patterns existed within Hungarian overseas migration. The history of the Szamosszegeans does, however, correspond to family histories already recorded in other Hungarian villages, and it confirms those trends already uncovered by macroanalysis.[7]

Back-and-Forth Migration: The Example of Ten Families

The migrations of the members of ten families from Szamosszeg give clear examples of multiple remigrations, of fragmentation of families, and of the different forms of family reunification, as well as of the return to the United States of children born in America but reared in the village. Through their existence as itinerant workers, these ten families typify the processes of chain-migration and of internal migration within the United States. Although emigration from the village also took simpler shapes and forms of movement (e.g., when the head of the family left the village and returned a few years later), the more complex types of migration represented by these ten families were more prevalent not only in the village of Szamosszeg but in other regions of Hungary as well.

The Family of Sándor and Zsuzsanna Kovács

This couple owned only a house and a small parcel of land, and the husband earned his living as a guard at the village cemetery. All three of the couple's sons migrated separately to the United States. Two of them were among the first from Szamosszeg to cross the ocean.

Their elder son, Sándor Kovács, Jr. (b.1877), trained to be a butcher. Married in the village in 1899, he left his wife and two children, Gusztáv (b.1899) and Irma (b.1901), and went to America in 1902. His father-in-law had already emigrated but soon returned to the village. Sándor worked at a mining site in

West Virginia. In 1904, his wife and children joined him in West Virginia where they went to the newly opened mines in Holden. A third child, Julianna, was born and died in Holden two years later. The couple's fourth, fifth, and sixth children, Sándor (b.1906), Ferenc (b.1908), and József (b.1910), were also born there.

In 1909 the parents sent the eldest son, Gusztáv, back to Szamosszeg with a relative to attend school, and the following year the rest of the family returned to the village. In the spring of 1912, however, the father again set off for Holden to be joined by the entire family in October. In 1913, another daughter christened Julianna was born. The father, Sándor, was twice widowed in the United States. In the early 1930s he returned alone to his native village where he soon died.

Gusztáv, the eldest child, was the first to leave Holden, working in the mines at Dobra and Granttown, West Virginia. In the early 1920s he went to Detroit, where he worked in a factory, but soon returned again to the mines of West Virginia. Finally he settled in Detroit and became a worker at the Ford plant.

The second child, Irma, married and moved to Bluefield, West Virginia. Her three younger brothers, like Gusztáv, went to Detroit to look for work, finding it first in a factory. Later the two youngest opened a grocery store.

Kálmán Kovács (b.1881) was the second son of Sándor and Zsuzsanna and the brother of the Sándor whose family has just been discussed. He trained to be a blacksmith before migrating to America in 1903. Kálmán worked in the mine at Cheswick, Pennsylvania, in 1904 and from there accompanied his older brother to Holden. In 1906 he went to New Brunswick to find a wife and there married Iza Sarkadi, an immigrant from Szamosszeg. Their marriage is the first entry from among the Szamosszegeans in the register of the Hungarian Reformed Church in New Brunswick, New Jersey. After their wedding the couple went to Holden, and their first child, Julianna, was born there in 1908. In 1909 the family returned to Szamosszeg where their second child, Marianna, was born later that same year. Probably in 1912 the husband went to America for the second time, and his wife and children joined him in 1913.

Because he had learned a trade, Kálmán made more money than his companions in the village did. He and his brother Sándor opened a butcher shop, but it did not succeed. In 1916 when Kálmán, Iza, and their daughters were living in Sharples, West Virginia, their third child, Kálmán, was born. Elizabeth, born in Cherrytree, West Virginia, in 1920 and George, born in Monaville, West Virginia, in 1922 followed. Their five children were thus born in five different places.

After living in West Virginia for thirty years, Kálmán and Iza moved to New Brunswick in 1945 and bought a house to settle there permanently. By that time, two of their daughters were still living with them, while the other children had scattered. Years later Marianna died in Charleston, West Virginia. Kálmán, Jr., lives in Texas; Elizabeth in Los Angeles; and George in Morgantown, West Virginia. Kálmán, Sr., and Iza died in New Brunswick. Julianna is still alive.

György Kovács (b.1887), third son of Sándor and Zsuzsanna, was an unskilled worker, who married in the village in 1910. In 1913 he left his wife there and went first to the mines in West Virginia and later to New Brunswick. In 1919, immediately after World War I, he returned to the village permanently, bought a house and approximately four hectares (9.88 acres) of land, and spent the rest of his life farming. After the death of his wife he remarried. Neither marriage producing any children, he reared an adopted son.[8]

The Family of Károly and Zsuzsanna Szabó

Károly and Zsuzsanna Szabó, who reared five children, were very poor and worked others' land as sharecroppers. One of their daughters, Erzsébet, learned to sew and went to find work in Budapest, where she also married. In the 1910s she became the *liferáns* (a German word with a Hungarian ending, meaning transporter or transportation agent) of the emigrants from Szamosszeg.

Eszti Szabó (b.1879), their other daughter, married István Puskás in the village and had two sons. A relative of István had gone first to America, and according to what could be recollected, István also had once been to America before returning there with Eszti. They left their two sons in the village, but later, accompanying an emigrating relative, the children joined their parents. István first worked in the mine at Holden and from there moved on to Granttown, the first of the Szamosszegeans to do so. Eszti kept a boarding house and in the interest of increasing business encouraged others from the village to emigrate.

In 1924 the couple remigrated to Szamosszeg, bought about 25 hectares of land, a house, and farm equipment. As a result, they rose to the level of rich peasants. When they called their son, István, Jr., who had been married in America, back home to farm, the son's wife was unwilling to remigrate and the marriage broke up. István, Jr., returned home and was killed in World War II. Because of both his wealth and his experiences, István, Sr., was elected community judge at the end of the 1930s, the first villager from a poor peasant family to attain this honor. In America he had become acquainted with socialist ideas, and as a village leader he supported the Social Democrats immediately after World War II.

Lajos Szabó (b.1885), son of Károly and Zsuzsanna, married in the village in 1909. His wife, Irma Paragh, came from a similarly poor family. At the urging of his sister, Eszti, and brother-in-law, Lajos and Irma also emigrated to America, joining them in Granttown in 1910. Lajos found work in the mines, while Irma followed her sister-in-law's example and ran a boarding house, washing, cooking, and cleaning for ten to twelve men.

Irma gave birth to thirteen children, eight of whom survived infancy. All were born in Granttown: László (b.1914), János (b.1915), Margit (b.1916),

Mária (b.1917), Árpád (b.1919), Lenke (b.1921), Lajos (b.1922), and Irma (b.1924). In order to support their large family and save a little money, the couple made *pálinka* (Hungarian brandy) and sold it to the boarders. The strain of her frequent pregnancies together with her strenuous physical labor ruined Irma's health, and she died in 1931 at the age of forty-four. The widowed Lajos returned to the village in 1933 with six of his children, bought a house, about twelve hectares of land, farm equipment, and settled down to farm.

His two eldest sons, László and János, who were nineteen and eighteen years old when their father moved back, stayed in Granttown and worked in the mine. Of the six children brought back to the village, three later returned to the United States: Margit, the eldest, in 1935 and Mária and Árpád in 1937. The two daughters settled in New Brunswick, the son in Granttown. So, from the family of Lajos and Irma Szabó, whose children were all born in the United States, two remained there permanently, three migrated to Szamosszeg temporarily, and three moved to the village permanently.[9]

The Family of Károly and Jusztina Bacskó

This couple reared four children in the village. The three sons, Bertalan, János, and Mózes, immigrated to the United States sometime between 1908 and 1910. At first they worked in the mines of West Virginia, then went from there to New Brunswick.

Bertalan Bacskó (b.1884), the eldest son of Károly and Jusztina, married in the United States an immigrant girl from a village near Szamosszeg. Their first child, Julianna, was born in New Brunswick. The couple and child returned to the wife's village just before World War I, and Bertalan died as a soldier during the war.

Julianna grew up in her mother's village and in the 1930s returned to the United States. She worked for a while in New Brunswick before marrying a Hungarian and settling in New York.

János Bacskó (b.1889) already had a fiancée when he left Szamosszeg, and the couple's daughter Irén was born in the village before their wedding. In 1911 at János's bidding, the child's mother joined him in the United States, leaving their little girl with her parents. In March of 1911 she and János were married at the Reformed Church in New Brunswick, and in 1914 their second child, Irma, was born there. In the same year the couple and their new baby remigrated to the village and bought two hectares of land which they then farmed.

Irma, who had been born in America, was sent back to the United States by her parents in 1930 at the age of sixteen. János's twin brother, Mózes, was asked to help Irma find work, and she worked for a few years as a housekeeper not far from New Brunswick. Later she became a factory worker, first in the cigar factory and later at the Johnson & Johnson plant, both in New Brunswick. Irma diligently sent home the money she saved: her family was able to buy an additional two hectares of land. In 1936 she married the American-born son of a Hungarian immigrant family. They had no children.

Mózes Bacskó (b.1889), the twin brother of János, was married in 1913 in New Brunswick to an immigrant girl from the northeastern region of Hungary. The couple worked as unskilled laborers in factories, the wife in the cigar factory. They also made and sold *pálinka* even during Prohibition. Their only child, Bertalan, was born in 1917. In 1920 they bought a house in New Brunswick, and in 1944 opened a saloon. They bought a few hectares of land in Szamosszeg as well, but the couple and their son stayed in New Brunswick for the rest of their lives.

Of the three sons of Károly and Jusztina Bacskó, two returned with wife and family to the village. Károly and Jusztina's two granddaughters, Irma and Julianna Bacskó, who had been taken back to Hungary, returned to the United States in the 1930s and settled there.[10]

The Family of Ádám and Jusztina Csóka

Among the first emigrants was Ádám Csóka (b.1857). Although he was no longer young by the time he decided to make the trip across the Atlantic, the fact that he and his family lived in a peasant house with his brothers and sisters and their children—thirty of them in all—probably played a part in his decision. Those who recalled those days frequently mentioned this as a conspicuous case of overcrowding.[11] After a few years, Ádám Csóka returned to the village, but his daughter, Juszti, followed his example by migrating in 1906.

Juszti Csóka (b.1890) was apparently married in the United States to Sándor Szabó, who had emigrated from Mátészalka, a small town next to Szamosszeg. Their names do not appear in the New Brunswick marriage records; however, their daughter Ida was born there in 1912. In December of the same year, Ida was sent back to Szamosszeg with a relative, to be cared for by her grandparents. Sándor and Juszti's second child, Margit (b.1913), was taken back to the village in 1914 by her mother, and was also put in care of her grandparents. Juszti returned to the United States that same year and went with her husband to Granttown, where he looked for work in the mine. There their third child, Sándor, Jr., was born in 1915. Later, the family moved to Detroit, where Sándor, Sr., and their son died. Juszti returned to New Brunswick and married József Biró, an emigrant from a village not far from Szamosszeg. The couple worked in factories in Staten Island, New York, and after retiring settled in Florida, where they lived until their death.

Margit, one of the little girls left in the village, died. The other, Ida, was brought up by her grandparents and rarely heard from her mother in America. When she was sixteen, she married Károly Filep, a Szamosszegean. Their marriage produced two daughters, Irén (b.1929) and Jolán (b.1931). The girls' father was killed by a falling tree while he was working in the forest in the winter of 1931. The widowed Ida married again in the village but was soon divorced. Ida was married for the third time in 1936, and had a third daughter, Magda.

In 1938 Ida and young Magda migrated to America, leaving behind in Szamosszeg Ida's new husband and, in the care of their paternal grandparents, Ida's two daughters from her first marriage. The strategy was for the family to reunite in the United States once Ida had managed to earn enough to pay for the trip. With the outbreak of the war, connection between the family members was severed for years. Ida's husband died during that time.

Only after World War II could the emigration of Ida's two daughters be considered. The elder of the two, Irén, was planning to marry and refused her mother's offer to help her emigrate, however, the younger, Jolán, joined her mother in 1947. In 1984 one of Jolán's sons, Juszti Csóka's great-grandson, who was born in America and Hungarian only on his mother's side, moved to Hungary, where he married. After a few years the young couple returned to the United States with their baby son.

Erzsébet Csóka (b.1892), Ádám and Jusztina's second daughter and Juszti's sister, migrated to the United States in 1911 and found a place in the cigar factory in New Brunswick. Soon her boyfriend Gedeon Kósa ran away from Szamosszeg, without informing his parents, to join her in New Brunswick, where they were married in 1913. Afterward they, like many other Szamosszegeans, went to West Virginia, in their case to Dobra. Gedeon worked in the mine while Erzsébet ran a boarding house. They had a son, Gedeon, Jr. (b.1922), and the couple returned with him to the village in 1924. There they bought a plot of land, a house, about eight hectares of farmland and opened a tavern. Gedeon, Jr., not only finished secondary school but graduated from law school as well. However, he could not build a livelihood worthy of his education.

Mária Csóka (b.1882), Ádám and Jusztina's eldest daughter, married Ádám Puskás in Szamosszeg in 1903. Their three children were born there: Ida (b.1905), Piroska (b.1907), and Borbála (b.1911). Ádám Puskás emigrated alone to America in the spring of 1914, but his wife and three daughters did not follow him until October 1923, when the family was finally united and settled in Granttown, West Virginia.[12] In 1924 two of the three girls, Piroska and Ida, went to New Brunswick with a Szamosszegean couple, József Paragh and Róza Varga. Soon after, the parents and Borbála joined them, and there a fourth child, Árpád, was born in 1925.

The parents and Árpád remigrated to Hungary in 1930. Ádám and Mária Puskás were the first Szamosszegeans who did not resettle in their home village but relatively far away, albeit in the same region of the country. There they bought a homestead and farmed. Their daughters remained in New Brunswick, worked at the cigar factory, and there married Hungarians, but not Szamosszegeans. In 1949 the elderly Ádám and Mária Puskás with their son, Árpád, again went to America and joined their daughters.[13]

The Family of Lajos and Amália Kósa

Lajos Kósa and Amália Puskás were from families that were better off than most. Their land was not only able to employ the labor of six children but large enough to allow sharecropping as well. In 1912 one of their children, seventeen-year-old Árpád, rebelled against his autocratic father, set off in secret on borrowed money, and only informed his parents of his intention to migrate to America once he had reached Budapest.

In the United States Árpád first looked up Szamosszegeans in New Brunswick. Later, according to what could be recollected, the young man turned up in the West Virginia mining sites, and in the course of his wanderings got as far as Texas. He returned to New Brunswick and tried different kinds of work, for a time working with a Szamosszegean friend as a streetcar conductor. Árpád Kósa married a non-Szamosszegean, Hungarian-speaking Slovak (tót-lány) in New Brunswick in 1917.

The young couple initially settled in Perth Amboy, New Jersey, and lived with relatives of the wife. Shortly thereafter they moved on first to McKeesport and then to Duquesne, Pennsylvania, where their daughter, Irén, was born in 1919. Árpád worked for about two years in Duquesne as an ironworker while planning with a friend to buy land which they could mine. Because his wife could not bear the sooty air of the steel town, however, they returned to New Brunswick and in the early 1920s bought a house and property there. In the meantime, Árpád had sent money back to his parents in the village to buy more land. In 1925 he sold his property in New Brunswick and together with his wife and daughter remigrated to Szamosszeg.

Árpád, his Slovak wife, and American-born child were not successful in fitting into the Kósa family or in adapting to the overwhelmingly Hungarian ways of the village. Within a year they were en route back to New Brunswick, where they finally settled. Once again they bought land there and built themselves a house.

The daughter, Irén, converted to Catholicism as a child. She finished high school and married a Hungarian who had been born in America. Their two daughters, both college graduates, do not speak Hungarian; their husbands are not of Hungarian ancestry and they have moved away from New Brunswick.[14]

The Family of Sándor and Zsuzsanna Bodó

Sándor and Zsuzsanna Bodó reared four children. József (b.1889) was unmarried when he left for America in 1914. His father, Sándor, had already been to the United States and upon returning had bought about five hectares of land.

In 1916 József married Zsuzsanna Kun, a Szamosszegean, in South River, New Jersey. They subsequently moved to Holden, West Virginia, where two children were born: Vilma in 1917 and Julianna in 1919. After József was disabled in a mining accident in the early 1920s, the couple along with their three daughters returned to the village. Because they had no savings and were unable to buy land, they remained poor. When they had three more daughters, Amália, Ilona, and Erzsébet, all born in Szamosszeg, their large family could survive only by sending the girls out to work on someone else's land.

The three daughters born in the United States each married a Szamosszeg-ean. In the 1930s the family decided that those three daughters, American citizens by birth, should go back to America. They went alone, one after the other, each leaving her husband behind in the village. It was the family's plan for the women to earn enough to buy boat tickets, then send for their husbands.

The sisters arrived in New Brunswick, where their mother's sister, Katalin Kun, helped them find work, first as housekeepers, later in the cigar factory. Vilma was able to bring her husband over immediately before World War II, but Zsuzsanna did not see her husband again until after the war in 1947, following an eight-year wait. Julianna did not send for her husband at all, but divorced him, remarried in the United States, and moved to Idaho. The children of Vilma and Zsuzsanna were born in New Brunswick. The remaining three sisters, who had been born in Szamosszeg, stayed there. The ties between the sisters in Szamosszeg and those in the United States became very loose.[15]

The Family of János and Lea Bodó

János Bodó (b.1873), also one of the "pioneers" and a relative of Sándor Bodó, married Lea Kósa (b.1880) in the village. They had three children: Vilma (b.1900), János (b.1902), and Julianna (b.1904). One hectare and a half of land did not appear to be sufficient to support the family, so János, following the example of the other Bodós, migrated to America in 1906 and began to work in the mine at Holden.

Recollections are unclear on whether or not János came home between 1906 and 1913, but in August 1913 Lea and the three children set off for Holden, where the couple's fourth child, Julius, was born in 1914. Lea's sister, Amali, was already in Holden, and soon they were joined by their other two sisters, Zsuzsanna and Julianna. Lea Kósa set up a peasant-style household at the mine site, growing vegetables and raising livestock in the yard of their company house. She also kept a boarding house.

In 1916 the Bodó family migrated to Detroit in the hope of making more money, but János and Lea realized that they had been better off in Holden, where Lea's contributions to the family income were more feasible. They returned there in 1917, and their fifth child was born in Holden.[16]

The subsequent changes in the lot of this miners' family with five children will be referred to several times in this book, as it is representative of the struggle generally experienced by Hungarian immigrants in the mining area.

The Family of Bertalan and Julianna Szögyény

This couple had ten children, of whom six survived. Lacking property, they were sharecroppers. In addition, Bertalan worked as a carrier with his two horses, and periodically he and the growing children did hired work, hoeing on a third-party basis. Of the six children, three went to the United States.

Sándor (b.1887) was the first of the Szögyény children to emigrate, running away in 1905 at the age of 18. The family found out about his intention to emigrate only when he wrote home from Budapest asking for money to buy a boat ticket, which his mother sent him. Typically, he went to Holden, West Virginia, and from there moved on. With his young friends he tried working at different mining sites, even working for a protracted length of time in Colorado. Also typically, Sándor Szögyény went to New Brunswick to get married. Sándor married a Szamosszegean, Vilma Varga, whose father, Károly Varga, had sent her to the United States. Károly Varga himself is remembered as one of those in the village who had crossed the ocean numerous times, although, unlike most migrants, Károly was illiterate and could only write his name. Károly's two marriages produced ten children. When he was in America, Károly is said to have supported the new arrivals from the village and directed them on their way. There were always boarders from the village living with him in the United States.

After their wedding, Sándor and Vilma went to West Virginia, where he worked in the mine at Dobra. Their son, Bertalan, was born there in 1915. Around 1920 the family remigrated to Szamosszeg and bought 10 hectares of land in Szamoskér, a neighboring village. Young Bertalan grew up and lived his life in Szamoskér.

Julianna Szögyény (b.1889), younger sister of Sándor, ran away from home with her friend, Lea Szász, in 1911. She recalled:

> I was twenty-two years old when I ran away from home and came to America with my girlfriend Lea in 1911. We got to Budapest but had no money at all. The sister of my mother lived there and she put us up in her home. Lea owned five dollars. "Don't be angry with me because I took five dollars from the bag," she wrote already from the railway waiting-room. They sent her money from home, and sent me some, too. They got it from uncle Balázs L., who used to be in America before, and had some money.
>
> I heard from everybody who came to America how good it is here. I also thought how good it will be, that one got rich quickly, can earn a lot easily. I thought that I would mind some children and will earn good money this way. Or I will go and manage their household for others. I did not think of factory work, but that is where I got to, in a cigar factory. My brother-in-law accompanied me to Vienna; he spoke German as his mother was German. We got a ticket for the boat in Vienna, her name was *New Amsterdam*.[17]

Julianna and Lea went to New Brunswick, found work in the cigar factory, and boarded in the home of Károly Varga, the future father-in-law of Sándor Szögyény, and a former neighbor of the Szögyény family in the village. Sándor, Julianna's brother, who had come earlier and worked in the West Virginia mines, had not wanted his younger sister to come to America, but she ignored him. In 1912 Julianna married József Sülő, who had emigrated from Nyirjármi, a village in the same region of Hungary as Szamosszeg.

The couple lived for a while in New Brunswick, but the job opportunities there were so bad that they went to the mining site in Dobra, where a number of Szamosszegeans were living. Their two children were born there before the family went back to New Brunswick in the 1920s. József found work in a factory making wire, Julianna a job in the cigar factory, and the family settled permanently in New Brunswick. Today their son lives there while their daughter lives in Ohio.

Zsuzsanna Szögyény, sister of Julianna, followed her sister's example and emigrated in the same year, 1911, to work in New Brunswick at the cigar factory. Later, Zsuzsanna migrated to Detroit, married a non-Szamosszegean Hungarian, and settled there permanently.

Of the six Szögyény children, three went to America and three remained in the village. Those who emigrated became relatively scattered. Sándor remigrated and settled in a village near Szamosszeg. The two children who remained in the United States were also separated from each other; Julianna lived her life in New Brunswick, Zsuzsanna in Detroit.

The Family of Lajos and Hermina Puskás

Lajos Puskás (b.1883), the youngest of seven children in a farming family, was still a bachelor when he sailed for North America in 1903. Some informants think Lajos may have been in America once before, but in any case, by 1903 he already had a sister living in the United States when he went to a mining area in West Virginia.

Among Lajos Puskás's associates from Szamosszeg during his time in West Virginia was Lea Lörinc. Although they did not marry, Julianna Lörinc was born to them, probably in 1905. Nevertheless, Lajos returned to the village in 1908 and soon married Hermina Ardai.The young couple lived with the parents of Lajos and worked the family plot. Two sons were born to them: József in 1911 and László in 1912. In 1913 Lajos returned to the United States, bringing Hermina Ardai with him, but leaving the two little boys in the village in the care of his parents. Initially Lajos Puskás again went to West Virginia, but he wanted to get away from the mines and took on a variety of odd jobs in a number of places. The three sons born to Lajos and Hermina in the United States were all born in different towns: Lajos, Jr. (1915), in Placement, New Jersey; Ferenc (1917) in Philadelphia; and István (1919) in New Brunswick.

After the end of World War I, the couple brought the three boys to Szamosszeg where they took the elder sons they had left with the grandparents back into their own care. Lajos and Hermina built a house with the money they had saved in the United States and bought twenty-two holds of land (a total of 31.24 acres), which they worked for themselves. One of their five sons, Lajos, Jr., finished secondary school, attended university, and became a Reformed minister. The other four boys completed elementary school and stayed on to farm their parents' land. In the 1920s and 1930s, the family property was nearly doubled to about forty holds by further land purchases.

At the end of the 1930s, two of the boys, who, as American-born citizens, did not fall under the immigration quota restrictions, returned to New Brunswick. Ferenc made the journey in 1938 and István in 1939, although István had been only two years old when his parents took him to Hungary and knew no English. With the outbreak of World War II, István was drafted into the U.S. Army, however, and learned the language.[18]

Both Ferenc and István married within the Hungarian-American ethnic group, forming the branch of the family that permanently settled in the United States.

At the beginning of the 1920s, Lea Lörinc also returned to Szamosszeg, bringing her American-born daughter Julianna with her. Lea Lörinc married a man from the village and had four more children. Daughter Julianna's first marriage was not a success, but soon afterward, in 1937 or 1938, she married again and took advantage of her American citizenship to move to the United States. Her second husband, Barna Bodó, was able to join her there before the war broke out.[19]

The Family of Gábor and Eszter Filep

Gábor Filep (b.1860) married Eszter Molnár, born 1877 in Szamosszeg. They had six children, including István, Anna, and Gábor. Twice Gábor, Sr., went to the United States alone, and the three children named above also emigrated. István (b.1896) emigrated in 1913 and, still single, wandered through West Virginia to Holden but finally settled in New Brunswick. There he married Julianna Kósa, who also came from Szamosszeg. The couple had six children. Two died in childhood; the other four were brought up in the United States.

At the beginning of the 1920s, István Filep, Sr., was followed to America by his sister Anna (b.1903). She also settled in New Brunswick where she married an immigrant, József Melcsák. Childless, both worked outside the home. They were able to purchase fourteen holds of land in Szamosszeg, which they later gave to her sister who stayed in Hungary.

Gábor Filep, Jr. (b.1908), married Emilia Dul from Ugornya in Szamosszeg. He managed to immigrate to the United States in 1938 and was followed in 1940 by Emilia, who came on the last boat available until after the war. They settled in New Brunswick. Childless like Anna and József, Gábor and Emilia Filep likewise were both wage earners. They also purchased land, five holds in Szamosszeg, and dreamed about their future life in the village.[20]

The Mechanism of Migration

Overseas migration from Szamosszeg, though it started slightly later, developed in the same way as Hungarian emigration at the national level. The beginning of the twentieth century witnessed a few sporadic departures from the village. Then, from year to year, the number increased at such a rate that by the

1910s—as the channels of information took shape—"migration fever" broke out.

The pioneers of migration to America, like those at the national level, were not the typical peasants of the village. They were craftsmen—half peasant, half tradesman—whose jobs had already given them a certain degree of mobility before their move to America. They thus were more receptive to the new opportunities presented by such work. News of their experience motivated their relatives, immediate neighbors, or closest friends to make the move as well, creating chain migration.

In almost every case, there was a blood relationship between those who left first and those who followed. The nearly three hundred individuals who left the village for the United States or Canada over the past seventy years can almost all be linked by family connections into a chain of migration that began with the first pioneers and continues to this day. The few exceptions had their own personal reasons for going.

Young men—married and single—were the first to migrate. Invariably, only one such family member left at a time. A few exceptions, heads of households, 35 to 40 years old, however, took a teenage son along. None of the migrant families set off together before the beginning of the 1920s as a complete nuclear family (i.e., both parents together with all the children). Rather, part of the family went and part remained in the village.

Before 1910 women seldom migrated to America from the village of Szamosszeg. A few wives later left with their husbands, while their children stayed in the village in the care of grandparents. Only one wife, taking two small children with her, in 1903 went in search of her husband, who had not given any sign of life for a year. And we know of a few single young women who were already in the United States before 1910.

The value system of the village was slow to accept and tolerate migration of young women. It was not so much their fathers' or brothers' examples that led those girls who did to leave the village but their own personal conflicts, chiefly disappointment in love, or family quarrels. The negative opinion of the community about some who migrated to America was even voiced in mocking poems.[21] The prejudice subsided by the 1910s. In the years 1912 and 1913, in fact, more women than men departed from Szamosszeg for America. A few left husband and children behind when starting off, but not necessarily to free themselves from a bad marriage. There also were those who were more confident than their husbands that they could hold their ground in the new surroundings. One of the latter, Irma Kun, spent three years in America and thus succeeded in paying off a heavy debt incurred for purchasing land in Szamosszeg.[22] The majority of female migrants, 76 out of 103, were single. That they were not going to a husband chosen for them in the village is shown by how many of them married men from outside the extended village community.[23]

The numerical data on Hungarian overseas migration suggest that women played a rather passive and inferior role in this formation of migration process. When I looked at my collection of documents, I was surprised that I also had submitted to this androcentric view of history. In my studies women got far less attention than they would have deserved, although I collected most of the "oral testimonies" from women.

Nevertheless, the oral testimonies testify that the women were the most active in building a social network which formed the mechanism of migration. They were also the ones who remained in touch with the family and with relatives, who wrote or had letters written. Those who were already overseas were the ones who gave detailed information to the people who remained at home. In the village, it was again the women who played a major role in spreading the news from the United States. In the spinneries and during other group activities they kept alive the stories of those who had returned. By their moral judgments, it was also the women who exercised the control of the sending community over the migrants' behavior.

Occasionally the women directly organized the migration from their village. Wives who kept boarders in America were led by their immediate material interests to send messages to the village, urging those who wished to migrate, with promises to find work for them and offering board. An immigrant woman from Szamosszeg had even had an assistant, her sister in Budapest, who gave instructions on a business basis to those who wished to leave without a passport and got them through the frontier. The villagers called her the *liferáns,* and she remained in the memory of the old people by this name.[24] Another, Iza Sarkadi, who had previously spent years in the United States, took a large group of girls to New Brunswick, in 1913. She became their "guardian mother," controlled their behavior during the journey, and placed them on arrival in the homes of villagers as boarders. She was following a tradition. In those villages from where the people regularly left for seasonal agricultural work, "guardian mothers" took over the mother's role for a certain time, particularly for unmarried women.

At the peak of the "emigration fever," the typical migrant was quite young, often sixteen or seventeen years old. Many who returned to visit the village took back to America a group of teenagers under their "guardianship." Naturally, when interviewed by immigration authorities, the youngsters would add a few years to their age.[25]

The patterns of group organization and daily life among the migrant workers assured a cohesive community away from home. One key function was to guard the women, particularly unmarried ones. Groups left the village each spring. Ties of kinship formations called *nagy bandák* (large work teams) were formed. Ties of kinship, of fictive kinship, and neighborhood played major roles in the organization of each team. As older villagers still recall: "Sure, we were far away from home, but the eyes of the village were always still upon us."[26]

Large families, those with six to eight children, were "thinned out" by the departure of three or four children, one after the other. The goal in every case was to work for the good of the family. Yet the family did not always decide which member would emigrate. Sometimes an example of a sibling or relative who emigrated or the stories told by those who had returned from America, building up and exaggerating its possibilities, carried away young people who never asked their families for permission to go. Overseas migration often meant for the individual liberation from family control and dependence.

Those who had no opportunity to work on their own land often had to make their living on the outskirts of the village, or even in a neighboring village, as seasonal workers or sharecroppers. "We sweated on somebody else's land," they recall. "Opportunities became fewer and fewer." "There were more and more people, and the bigger farms were always needing fewer and fewer workers."[27]

Most migrants came from those groups in Hungary—the overwhelming majority of the rural population—who had no land or owned a very small holding. In the village of Szamosszeg, the young women who migrated had previously worked as day laborers on the fields of rich local peasants or on the big estates surrounding the village.

Julianna Szögyény told her story this way:

We did not have any land, not a bit of it. We lived on what we earned. My father had two horses and a cart; he was carting goods. We were sharecroppers on the estate of the baron and the count. All of us, brothers and sisters, hoed and harvested along with our father. When the harvest began, my father mowed; I did the sheaf-binding; my sister Zsuzsi was the stripper; my brother Peter gathered the sheaves and raked up the trailings. I only finished four grades: I left school as I had to dig up potatoes and beets. At the age of nine to ten, I was already working: I worked as goose-girl, minded my sisters and brothers, and washed the smaller ones' clothes.[28]

Borbála Gergely recalled:

We had eight feet of grazing land, a tiny plot for potatoes and vegetables. My father was a sharecropper; we girls hoed corn on the basis of receiving two out of five shocks for the work done. I could not bear to live like this. I was looked down upon because we were poor and also because my sister had been seduced.[29]

Other informants provided similar accounts. The combination of demographic pressure and the modernization of farming methods on the large estates made it all the more difficult for the peasants to get by at the turn of the century. "The people lived in great poverty."[30] Under these conditions, temporary emigration of part of the familial workforce overseas became a more and more attractive alternative, particularly when families saw concrete proof of the opportunities for making money in America. In the village the most effective and alluring enticements for emigration came from those who had already emigrated.

Migration of individuals in most cases fit into a family strategy. Yet even if a member of the family left without consent, as happened quite often in Szamosszeg, the kinswomen took the initiative in helping him or her.

In any event, those who remained at home expected that the migrants would serve the interest of the whole family with the money they earned abroad. There are many examples in which a father who bought land from money sent home by son or daughter registered the property under his own name as a matter of course. An interview with Irma Bacskó was exceptional only for her earthy bitterness about the story she told.

> My parents screwed me out of every penny. I earned sixty dollars and always sent home fifty-five. I kept five dollars only to be able to pay my dues to the Rákoczi Fraternal Organization [an insurance association which provided workers disability and death benefits]. Do I know what they did with the money? The land wasn't registered in my name; my father registered it for himself. First he wrote that it would all be mine, and then he registered it for himself.[31]

It quickly became an integral part of the Szamosszegean peasants' view of the world that the reason to go to America was to make money in order to improve their lives in their native community. Their practical and concrete goals were to pay off taxes, redeem the inheritance (i.e., the house), and earn money for farm equipment and more land. There were young people who dreamed of even more than these things, especially getting out from under parental authority. Yet their dreams always revolved around the acquisition of land. After all, Szamosszeg was a Calvinist community where work and acquisition ranked first and foremost in the value system, and it also was part of the peasant world where land gave men and women honor and standing. "If I could just buy three holds of land, it would be just like I had six holds. In sharecropping I had to work six holds to get the produce of three."[32] This usually was the reasoning of the emigrants I asked about their original goals.

In the hierarchy of values, land occupied the first place, also because it was the basis for social status in the world of the peasants. The importance of property was emphasized by the Szamosszegean saying, "Even the sky over my land is mine." But as the peasant families grew, land became scarcer and harder to acquire. So hunger for land kept growing, and this manifested itself in the need for money. The day-to-day livelihood could be assured by the natural payment in kind they received for their labor, but land could only be bought with money (this is why the dollars that could be earned there made the United States so attractive to the villagers). According to the peasants' value system, acquiring land was worth any sacrifice. This is why wives let their husbands go to America,: sometimes they even were the ones who pushed them, and shouldered the burden of living separated from them for years. Opportunities in America were best if married couples went together; if they had children, they left them with the grandparents or close relatives, or if children were born in the United States, they were sent back to the village.

This family strategy occasionally led to tragedies. Mrs Sara Dienes, for example, took four children back to the old country to the grandparents. When returning to America, she could take back only two; the other children had died on the trip.[33] Ida Szabó sent her two little girls, one of whom was nine months old, back to her parents by relatives. The mother only saw one daughter again when she entered America after twenty-eight years of separation.[34]

Migration to America modified the cooperation and the division of labor within the family, but it did not stop the endeavor to safeguard the unity of the extended family household. The ones who stayed behind—the wife, husband, or children, the parents of migrating persons—"replaced" the one who departed by performing his or her tasks. The modification of the division of labor in the family owing to emigration put the main burden on those women, who remained at home with small children and had a small family farm.[35]

During their husband's long absences, women devised a number of ways to manage farm and family affairs. In times of particularly heavy or pressing work like plowing, sowing, harvesting, threshing, and mowing, village women assumed full responsibility and helped one another. Deputies in the Hungarian Parliament often drew attention to the village economies' "feminization," that "only women can be seen working in the fields."[36] The emigrant husbands, however, thought of themselves as continuing to manage the farm from overseas. They sent instructions about planting, purchasing livestock, renegotiating leases and the disposition of property when the wife was arranging to emigrate to follow her husband.

A return to the family and the sending community was always part of the plan, but in practice events did not turn out this way. Of those who left, only about half returned. The rest remained permanently in the United States. From the perspective of the emigrants' original plans, it is not those who returned who must be explained but rather those who settled in America. It was not necessarily the successful, more enterprising ones who stayed abroad, while the unsuccessful, more conservative ones returned to the village. Representatives of both types stayed and returned. Instead, their life stories suggest that more of the returnees believed that they had fulfilled their original purpose for going. The majority of those who returned bought parcels of land in the village, some as large as fifty to sixty holds, immediately raising their social standing to that of wealthy peasants. Among those who remained in America for ten to fifteen years, three families were able to free themselves from hired work and open their own saloon or butcher shop.

Whether they satisfied their original goals in Szamosszeg or in the United States, all the successful emigrant families managed to establish other sources of income besides wage work by using skills brought with them from the village. The larger savings that allowed the successful migrant to buy twenty or more holds of land in Hungary or to open a shop in America came in every case from a combination of three sources. The husband worked in the mine; the wife took in boarders; and the family made and sold *pálinka* to the boarders. This multifaceted activity required family cooperation and depended for the most part on the wife's energy. The main forces in the family "enterprises" were always the wives. Among those who remained in America, however, were some who admitted that they were ashamed to return home without money. Village opinion was fairly harsh on those who came back empty-handed. The decision on whether to remain in America or to return to the village was further influenced by developing family relations. A definite "yes" or "no" decision was formulated slowly, and the date of the return trip could be delayed. A number who finally decided not to settle in the village had already bought land there. In some cases, a firm decision was reached only after repeated trips back and forth. Usually, fathers who emigrated returned to their wives and children in the village, but in four cases, nuclear families were reunited in America, two of them after a number of transatlantic migrations.[37]

On the other hand, emigrants who married and began families in the United States tended to stay there permanently. There were quite a few of them: of 259 emigrants, 148 were single, and almost all of them married in the United States. In those cases, if one spouse was not from Szamosszeg, returning "home" was no longer a simple matter. Nevertheless, twelve of the couples who married in the United States actually returned to the village, bringing with them a total of thirty-four American-born children. But it also happened that parents who had left or sent their children back to the village with relatives never returned themselves This happened in the Oláh family. The couple remigrated in the twenties, but were disappointed when they realized that the husbands' parents had used the dollars sent home for their own benefit. Entrusting their small boy to the care of the wife's parents, they set off again. By this time they could only go to Canada, cross the border to the United States in secret, and remain there illegally. Their son grew up in Hungary, founded a family in Szamosszeg, and would have been very happy if his parents had taken him to the United States after World War II. His mother tried to explain in dramatic letters that they could not help him get out because of their illegal status. They tried to compensate him by sending many parcels and money.[38]

CHAPTER 4

"You Ask Me
Why I Came . . ."

THE EMIGRANTS' REFLECTIONS on the question "Why did I come to America?" not only portray a common fate but also provide a picture of individual lives within that fate. This chapter is a composite of information obtained from letters and interviews. The letters, dated 1909, were written to the most popular Hungarian-American newspaper of the time, *Szabadság*, in response to its contest entitled "Why did I come to America?" Although the published letters were obviously edited, their substance was not changed.

The interviews quoted in this chapter are from a collection of interviews that were prepared at the end of the 1960s with elderly people who had remigrated to their original village. These informants paint vivid and colorful pictures of their difficult living conditions and their yearning for a better life. Thus the contemporary letters and the much later interviews confirm each other's validity.

Letters to Szabadság

Here are some of the letters translated from Hungarian printed in *Szabadság*:[1]

> *Dániel Iváncza, Bishop, Pennsylvania:* I was an energetic man, but because I was propertyless I was forced to work as a day laborer; as a young single man I was unable to obtain a position as a hired hand or as a servant receiving payment in kind. Work being unavailable in my small village, every year I had to contract myself to the Kisbér Hungarian Royal Vasdinnye stud farm as a worker in the *Orbejckomendo* (*Arbeits-kommando*) designated draft, where monthly pay was a scant eight forints with room and board. From 160 to 190 persons, girls and men, old and young, were housed in a square stable, constructed of metal,

which even by standards of that time was unfit for pigs. Here, where we had to sleep together, we used straw for our beds. None of us could rest because we never had enough time to clean ourselves after the day's work, and consequently vermin fiercely attacked all of us. At best we could send one of us home once a week for clean clothing, our village being a good day's walk away. We were allowed few free days as we had to work almost every day, even on holidays and market days.

The work was hard; we worked from dawn to dusk. The food was extremely bad, as the slop that they cooked in one huge pot for all the workers was fit only for pigs. This was then sent after us to the fields in barrels. Someone who dared to demand better would be silenced by either the strong slap or cane of Ferenczi, the steward, or of his assistant, Orsonics, or of someone similar.

Once during the corn harvest I carried 300 sacks weighing 101 kilos of corn up and down the stairs on my shoulders. As a young boy I became ill and was unable to get up from the straw. Futó, the ranch boss, stood at my feet with a pizzle and after several strokes realized I was really unable to get up. There was no possibility of a doctor or medication; there wasn't even anyone to bring a little water. If someone managed to drag himself out for a drink and was spotted, he was immediately forced to go to work. According to them, anyone able to go out for water wasn't ill. Therefore it is no wonder that many people grew sick not only of working for the state, but got sick also from the state itself, and if they were able, emigrated to America.

Besides this, I also worked for a long time for Count M. Eszterházy's estates in Imréd and Vecsény, where the meager earnings were only enough for bread baked with raw potatoes. Therefore, I decided to go to the capital Budapest, where, thanks to God, the German culture had advanced so far that there I wasn't "you pig," but only "you stupid peasant." But I didn't give a damn—I was only interested in getting a job! And I quickly got one because they were preparing for the exhibition and needed workers. I was eager to work and save so that I would be able to improve on my poor old mother's miserable existence as soon as possible.

Unfortunately, when the exhibition closed, I was unable to find a job, and poverty set in. Since I was completely unwilling to go back to manorial work and particularly not to the state farms (I would rather die), I decided to go to America. Thank God! I have never regretted that decision. So it's not love of money that motivated me, nor was it the authorities chasing me that brought me here, but only the possibility of a livelihood. I believe many people will answer in the same vein.

John Szabó, Chicago, Illinois: I didn't leave because we were poor, as I was able to support my family quite well with my work. But being a thinking and sensitive person, I had always somehow felt that although I had everything I needed, still I wasn't the person that I had a right to be. So, slowly in my soul the desire to emigrate grew. I emigrated and got to know America, the land of the free. And although in the beginning I had to do without, and even now I am not bathing in milk and honey, I feel that now I am that man, who at home I only had a presentiment that I had a right to be, that is: an independent, free man. All this I learned in America.

What had I seen in public life, particularly in the official system? The same as in the army. What does an official of the city, county or the state do? Those who are supposed to be the servants of the people as their salaries are paid out of our bitter taxes. Instead of being courteous and obliging, they are arrogant and rude, of course only to those dependent on them; before their superiors they throw themselves on the ground, as the Mohammedan does before his Allah. In contrast what do we see in America? We see that Mr. Roosevelt, the head of the state, considers himself to be just as simple and useful a citizen as John Smith, who carries a baby in his arms or John Szabó, who is useful to the state only with his manual labor.

And in the offices? There is the greatest courtesy and simplicity: a person can drop in even if he doesn't understand a word of English. He won't be kicked out; he won't be spoken to rudely, nor will he be upbraided as in his beloved country back home. They will try in every possible way to understand him and willingly give him information; at the most they might smile a little at his simplicity.

These were the reasons I emigrated. All these things can be considered as sources of the rest of Hungary's problems.

János Jeszik, Tallapoosa, Georgia: It was twenty-three years ago that I took a walking stick in hand, when the Magyar language and gallantry were not yet so common on American soil. I came because in our poor Hungary, our Canaan where milk and honey flow, even with my willingness to do the most onerous work, I was unable to buy even the bare necessities. Although I left no stone unturned, I had no luck. This was the reason that in the prime of my life, at the age of thirty-seven, with heavy heart but with the greatest desire to work, I came to America so that I could help my family, whom I adored. I was not disappointed by my decision because a good worker could find a job. It's true that I only came out for three years, but when I saw life here and compared it to that in the old country, I realized that America was better. After three years I also brought my family out. Always living honorably, I supported my large family, faithful to my old principle, always keeping it before me the motto that we should not live to eat, but that we should eat to live. After being in America for eleven years, I left the factory, brought land in Georgia that the *Szabadság* had advertised, and have lived here for twelve years. We did not feel the recent economic crisis, and thus I am satisfied with my lot in life. However, it hurts when occasionally I read the bad news about my homeland in the *Szabadság*'s columns; I am only one of those whom my poor homeland lost, but when I reflect that in losing me it also lost my seven living children and numerous grandchildren, I am unable to be at peace with this.

Ferenc Tóth, New Philadelphia, Pennsylvania: What makes a man decide to sell his property and set out to change homelands? Let's look at a small town back home. The inhabitants of the small village appear very excited and why shouldn't they be? Lajos Szarvas, who left for America seven years ago, has just returned home. Just seven years ago the Szarvas family was so poor: now you only have to look to see what a difference there is. Even the chief magistrate doesn't have such clothes. I myself hardly dared speak to them; it was only from his wife, Örzsé, that I heard that in America every man is a gentleman: no one gives orders, everyone does what he wants. And that there aren't any peasants; there everyone dresses like the county's lord lieutenant back home. The women are well dressed; they wear hats on their heads, gloves on their hands. One woman is worth more than ten men. They don't go out to hoe and are not baked by the sun in corn fields from morning to night. And all that comfort, rocking chairs and who knows what all else. Therefore it is no wonder if we begin to think differently when we see such gentlemen come from America who tell us so many beautiful things about it.

Mrs. S. Farkas, New York: No one cheated us; only poverty chased us. We all came here only because of the need to make a living. There are towns and communities back home where only old people and children can be found. Houses and fields are ownerless and lie uncultivated because one can't bear the poverty and flees. You must escape—where? To America!

Here bringing up and educating children doesn't cost as much as back home because here a poor child can go to school even without money; he only needs an inclination and an aptitude for it. But in Hungary, if a poor man has five or six children, it often occurs that there isn't money to send them all to school.

The most important thing is the better life. Here if the family isn't too large, the father works and the mother is a good thrifty housewife, meat gets put on the table at least once a day. Back home it's served only on a special holiday, if at all. Why shouldn't one try for a better life when even the birds fly away after a better home.

Louis Teichner, New York: Why did I come here? Actually I'm not sure myself. Back home I didn't have to fear the bailiff, because I was fortunate—or unfortunate enough?—to be directly involved in the levying and collecting of taxes; so I didn't have to worry about my property being auctioned off—which by the way I didn't own any.

However, my curiosity gave me no peace. I wanted to see the skyscrapers and the great machinery about which I had learned so much, and I wanted to enjoy a little of the freedom and independence, which I had heard so much about.

Miklós Ladányi, New Kensington, Pennsylvania: Despite the fact that at that time I was a poorly paid clerk, the high praises of my friends for America didn't affect me at all. Even a few years later when my sibling went to America and with every letter held out promises of the most wonderful future, even that didn't have enough effect on me to make me want to emigrate to America. I was satisfied with my modest lifestyle and didn't desire after wealth; therefore it wasn't the desire for money that brought me here.

If I am to write down the real reason I came here, I will have to go back to when I met a poor but decent girl. In a short time our relationship developed into love. Then we vowed to each other that no matter what price or sacrifice, we would struggle until fate allowed us to be with each other. When I saw that we could not prosper at home, I decided that for the sake of our success we would have to find another home, and so I came to America. I came alone at first because we didn't have enough money for both of us to make the trip. True, in the beginning I had to work hard, but in a short time I was able to send for my beloved. And still loving each other, now we look happily back on those critical days, which made our situation so uncertain, and we bless America because it offered us work and the chance to be happy.

András Molitorisz, Allegheny, Pennsylvania: I was already a middle-aged, thirty-six-year-old man, when I came to the New World. In the old country, despite my diligence and outstanding conduct, I was unable to become successful even though I worked constantly. I earned just enough for my family to be able to lead a beggarly day-to-day existence. One day, after twenty-four years of diligent work, I thought it over well; if by then I still hadn't been able to accomplish anything, what will happen to my family and myself in the future when I would be getting old? I decided to set out for the promised land, and, for the time being leaving my beloved family behind, I arrived here alone. It's true that I found the beginning so difficult that I didn't even plan to stay a complete year, but in time, with great difficulty, I became so used to it that I have returned three times to the old country from here. Now that my eyes have been opened, after looking the working conditions over, I was unable to remain there under any circumstances and with my complete family I came back here again. If only I had done this twenty years ago!

Mrs. Lajos Jóos, Wilkes Barre, Pennsylvania (who won second prize, two and a half gold dollars): As a simple village woman I can tell you that village folk are not drawn by the home of the dollar. Oh, no. The simple child of the village will first move everything to save his tiny house, etc. He will go once again to the gentlemen at the tax office in the city and will ask and beg the prestigious gentlemen to have some patience. "But last year you came with the same reason," says the official. "I'm very sorry, but pay up!"

This cold ruthlessness completely squeezes his heart dry; his wife looks at him questioningly. He only replies, "The official has no soul, pack up my clothes, mother." "I knew," she bursts out weeping, "that it would end like this." The woman and the children cry. The husband doesn't weep; from the moment he left the office his heart has turned to stone. He no longer fears America; he yearns to be there with all his might. Within a week they have auctioned off his house, furniture, everything. The poor woman raged as one crazed.

Need I say more, gentlemen, about village life back home? Within six weeks the husband sent money, followed later by a picture of him marvellously attired.

Now the eyes of the villagers back home are also beginning to open. Here in America they not only open wide but sparkle in all their brilliance, when they compare the conditions here with those back home. Because, yes, here there is enough for plenty of meat and beer, and here we don't work from three in the morning until nine at night, and there is no overseer with a cane. Here the gentleman works just like the laborer, and here there is equality; no one makes the worker conscious that he is a common day laborer. I repeat, here the worker and the gentlemen are equal.

If the fact that we left hurts them back there, they shouldn't burden us to a breaking point with all kinds of taxes; they should support our industries and trades, instead of sending our money abroad. Let them quickly institute the independent tax district, etc. I think that the lack of these are the reasons for emigration.

Jenő Neumann, Passaic, New Jersey: I can state without any qualms that those who hold the reins of command in the government contribute to emigration. They only need to assure those in Hungary capable of working of their livelihood and to find some way that those who want to work do not succumb to starvation; to give fair and well-deserved earnings to those who are qualified for them. They should allow freedom of speech, not push us out of their offices if as a result of our lack of education (which is not due to our choice) we enter the room with our hats on. They should not attack us with policemen, gendarmes, or the military if we dare to raise our voices against injustice, and let them give back at least a small bit of those many undivided loaves, which we workers produced with the sweat of our brows.

Out with the answer then, my fellow countrymen, about why we changed our country. We have the freedom to write it down, even to express it because we are in America. In America where even if we don't have all, we still have lots more rights and the freedom to speak up than we did back home. Here for our honest work our reward is a fair living; this is what hurts, what even today is still missing, because were it not so I myself would be back home.

Miklós Krammer, Cleveland, Ohio: Not long ago someone came to study the situation of the Hungarians living here. He also came to Cleveland. How was the study conducted? It was very simple: instead of going to the schools to see what they know and what and how our children are taught; instead of going to the closest model factory, for example the old factory, where he would have seen how the Hungarian works as a laborer, how his shirt falls off from the heat and steam; or to plunge into a boarding house where eight or ten live, and to see with what joy they breathe each other's exhausted air, which contains enough alcohol that it would be possible to drive a car on it for a distance, and to see how many of them are working; or where the Magyar enjoys himself (the tavern), how they communicate with each other (with a knife), or to look into the smoky mine, from where so many Hungarians pay their respect and give their souls to the kingdom of heaven. However instead, after a few visits they threw a banquet, and with this the study was finished, with the difference being that back home the common coffers pay for the banquet and here everyone pays out of his own pocket.

And now it has become natural that in the old country the papers have numerous columns about what a great life the Hungarians have here, this itself greatly advances emigration.

This is my opinion, and this is why I came out.

Mrs. Nándor Bablanka, widow, Derby, Connecticut: It's been nine years since my husband died, leaving me a young penniless widow with five orphaned little boys between the ages of nine and a half, and four months old. My youngest son followed his father within ten months. I tried a new beginning for almost a year, but all for nothing, as it would not have been possible to make a living. As I didn't want my orphans to do without, I came to America.

I will never forget when I stood in the middle of the room, my heart filled with bitterness that I was among my beloved children for the last time. My six-year-old, Géza, knelt before me and placing his two hands together begged me, "My dear good little mother, please don't leave us, because we won't have anyone." This pain can't be expressed in words, it can only be felt.

And it has now been seven long years that here, where only the good Lord sees me, I struggle and cry. I only came to America so that I can provide a proper education, which soon I will be successful in, if God helps me.

Lajos Mészáros, New York City: I came to America because I was brought here. That is thirteen years ago, after my dear mother came to this country, within a few weeks I saw the light of day, and on this basis I have only half a right to enter this contest. With childish curiosity I ask my father and the Hungarians who come to our house, why was it necessary for them to come here from that good and beautiful country? As one, they answer that it isn't the country, but the government that is bad. At such times it involuntarily enters my mind that in my father's mother country even Providence is unkind because it doesn't send it a George Washington.

Kálmán Kassay, Cleveland, Ohio (the first prize winner of forty gold dollars): I come from a Reformed ministerial family; my parents tried to get me to also put on the robe of Christ, but my youthful spirit was completely captivated by the then developing engineering industry, and I was determined heart and soul, above all, to educate myself in this field. After I finished my education and received my diploma, I worked in prestigious factories as a group leader. I furnished my workshop and if then anyone would have indicated America as the stage for the realization of my knowledge, I would have laughed in his face. But it was all in vain; I was unable to come to terms with the corrupt system then in power; I myself joined the ranks of those developing an independent Hungary. But to be sure, I had to swallow many a bitter pill in the course of official pressure and troubles which appeared in all kinds of forms thanks to the chief magistrate. But I was unable to break the love of my soul towards my beloved country, not even when so-called gentlemen placed orders with me but even after receiving a fifth bill, still didn't pay. It ended up in court and even though I won I lost because the gentlemen in many cases can't be collected from. It was also the same with the prestigious and notable lords, but neverthless I put up with it.

After I saw that they were, in fact, driving the small-scale industry out, when I saw even those stronger than I break down, when I saw that every layer of society was contaminated with false slogans, I began to think about America and about emigrating at least while work was considered a shame in Hungary, while our capitalists are throwing away abroad that money which the Hungarian land gives them, while industry and business are allowed to stagnate, while the current government, paternally, only thinks of taxing the small landowners; while this goes on, the question of why the Hungarian comes to America is unjustly offensive back home.

Interviews with Remigrants (1969)[2]

O.F. (Megyaszó):
At the time of my emigration, my family owned three holds of land and a small plot of grapes. My father was the master of corn shocking for eighteen years for Squire Gyula Derék. He was an honest, fair person; the squire liked him as did the shockers.

There were three of us, I and my two sisters. As there were too many of us for the cultivation of our land, I also went into service at the squire's. We lived decently on our earnings.

Nowadays I can no longer figure out what our earnings were worth. At this time many Megyaszóans were already working in America. I had relatives there also. One was doing well; he had saved himself a little money; the other one had grown tired of the life there and had come home, but I also heard of those who would have liked to come home but did not have enough money to buy the boat ticket.

I did not like the life that was here; I tired of the collective work, I wanted to be my own master; therefore I decided to go to America, and I hoped to earn enough to at least be able to buy two or three holds of land. I wanted to be free of the *nagykepés* (an instrument). My mother did not want to let me go, saying that it's possible to earn a livelihood here too.

I don't remember whether anyone was organizing emigration to America. That didn't need organizing. What quickened one towards emigration was when someone came home with a lot of money.

F. O. (b.1887 in Megyaszó; in the United States 1904–1909):
I live in Nyiri. According to what I can remember, my parents had five holds of land: a part of this was pasture. The land was not enough to support the large family; the economy was very bad at that time, and we went into the forests around Mogyorós to work. There were eight of us children, four boys and four girls. Already, in my early youth, I went into the woods to work; we planted pine seedlings. I earned pennies.

I only heard good things about America, how everyone is happy there. This was true; I was very happy there. I even had relatives there; my cousin with her husband had long lived there. They also only wrote good things home.

At the age of eighteen, my two girlfriends and I often spoke about it not being good to live in indigence: we should somehow change the course of our lives and help ourselves and our families. In the end we decided to go to America.

Mrs. N.J., P.I. (b.1895 in Mogyorós; in the United States 1913–1921):
I live in Nyiri. My parents had twenty-four holds of land, maybe even more. All the members of my large family worked diligently on this estate; we never felt a need for anything. There were eight of us siblings, five girls and three boys. Before I emigrated, I worked around the house as I was still very young.

I already had heard about America before I went there. My father's sister, along with her husband, had emigrated five years earlier, and they wrote to us back home. As a child in the evenings, I often heard the adults talk about life abroad. They spoke about things such as everyone being given respect there, and whoever works and is thrifty can within a few years put together a nice sum of money. One summer when I visited my aunt's home, she also said that it's not bad out there.

Mrs. J.M., E.B. (b.1897 in Szaniszló, Szabolcs County; in the United States 1912–1922):
I live in Láca. My parents were servants on the Monyha ranch, which belonged to the estate of the Count Majláth. Naturally, they had no property. There were five of us siblings. As a child I became a day laborer and through this was able to add to the total sum of my family's income. I was not able to support myself. My wages as a day laborer were minimal, consisting of pennies.

I had numerous relatives and friends from Láca abroad, who wrote that a person who knows how to work can live better there. Therefore I decided to emigrate. Several persons wrote to us and invited us to go.

A.P. (b.1884 in Láca, Zemplén County; in the United States 1900–1910 and 1913–1920):
I live in Láca. I lived with my parents. There were six of us. At the end of the last century, my brother sneaked out to America. Twice he

came home, and the third time he again sneaked out. He was the one who took me out in May 1906, when I was sixteen years old.

Mrs. A.P., E.Sz. (b.1887 in Dóc; in the United States, 1906–1910 and 1913–1920):

I married my husband, I.S.M., in March 1891 in Láca. I live in Lácacsék, Zemplén County. At the time of my emigration, my family possessed twenty holds of land. The family at that time consisted of five members, myself as a widow and my four children. Two of these were married daughters, a seventeen-year-old son and a seven-year-old daughter. Before I emigrated, I worked in the household and in the fields. The income of the twenty holds was 60 to 40 hundredweights of wheat, rye, 100 hundredweights of corn, several wagons of hay, 300–400 hundredweights of potatoes, and a larger number of livestock. The family lived communally out of the pooled income.

I heard about America, that one can earn money there. And I had much need for money. My husband died in 1909; I became a widow with four children and many debts. My husband's illness had been very expensive; a doctor came to see him every day from Királyhely. One of the goals of my emigration was to pay the family debts. My other goal was to accompany my son, who was determined to go, and to stay with him for a while, so that I could guide him on his life and prevent him, as he was young, from falling into loose habits.

Mrs. I.S.M., widow, A.N. (b.1874 in Zemplénagárd; in the United States 1910–1920):

I live in Megyaszó. At the time of my emigration, my mother and my stepfather together had eight holds of land. I was the only child. Before my emigration, we worked the family land and lived pretty well off of it.

At this time there was a lot of talk about America. From Megyaszó and the region around it, many had gone abroad, and there were those who had already come back, but many were still there, and there were those about whom it was known that they would never come back. I also had relatives abroad; from Aszaló there was my uncle, who with his daughter had lived abroad for many years, and she had gotten married there. Those with whom I spoke had various things to say about America. There were those who praised it, but there were also those who told all the bad things about life there.

As I try to remember back so many years after my emigration about those years, it seems that my decision was not influenced by monetary difficulties because we lived well off the income from our lands and our work. Perhaps I was motivated a little by my occasional disagreements with my stepfather. But still the main element in my decision was that I wanted to get worldly experiences. I wanted to look around in America; I was curious about life there; I wanted to check things out myself. I wasn't out very long, a total of three years. This was enough for me to look around and to decide whether I should stay there or should come home.

I can't remember whether anyone ever organized emigration in the village or anyone agitating anyone to emigrate.

I found life there to be better than here at home; in general I liked the situation there, but it wasn't that much better than my life here at home to make me decide to stay there, even though there was a twenty-year-old girl who would have married me and whose parents were also there. They advised us young people to get married and to stay out, and they, the old couple, would come home to farm.

Sz. (b.1886 in Megyaszó; in the United States 1905–1908):

I live in Rics. My father, as the community's town crier, received payment in kind, but this alone was not enough to support the family. There were four of us children. I worked as a day laborer in the estates of the provost and the count, and in addition to this I accepted all odd jobs. My daily wages were twenty to twenty-five pennies.

At home we talked a lot about America. One of my uncles was there, with whom the family was in correspondence. He wrote such things as, the situation there isn't "Canaan" either but is a lot better than at home. It was pretty difficult for me to come to the decision of emigrating, but at home no matter where I turned, no matter what I tried, I couldn't get ahead. At last, when I saw that there was nothing else to do, I tried America. My uncle sent me encouraging letters and the notary took care of the official tasks.

K.P.V. (b.1884 in Rics; in the United States1908–1920):

I live in Rics. My family had no property. There were five of us children. Before my emigration, along with the other members of my family, we worked on the nearby estates as day laborers; in the summer we were shock harvesters, but we also accepted any available work. I remember the wages as being a few pennies a day. As the estate shockers, we received a third of the corn and a little potato land.

Now I can't remember what I heard about America before I emigrated since I was still quite young, but in the family it was decided that still it would be better to emigrate; the wages are better and the life is easier. Well, I became convinced later that while it was possible to earn more, it wasn't easy: you had to work very hard for the money. In the end I also wanted to emigrate, although I couldn't imagine what I was going to do there. In 1906, Sándor Persely, a Hungarian from Rics, came home to visit. He was already an American citizen. My parents entrusted him with power of attorney so that he could take me there and help me to get started in America. I was seventeen years old.

B.V.B. (b. 1889 in Rics; in the United States 1906–1913):

I live in Rics. At the time I emigrated, I already had established a family. I married one year before emigrating. Altogether we had one hold of land. Because we wouldn't have been able to live very well off this, I accepted any work that I could find. I also worked on the estate of the provost and on the manorial lands of the Majláths; in the summer I harvested shocks and hoed as a one-third sharecropper. The daily wages were around thirty pennies. We had enough for our daily needs. We were not in particularly straitened circumstances. I heard much about America. There were many from Rics there, or rather who had been there already. My father-in-law had been there for a long time, and we corresponded with him also. I decided on emigrating after my father-in-law first invited me to come in his letter. Then together with my wife, we decided that since we had a child on the way, we could not entrust the future of our family to two holds of land. Therefore, we have to go to America and earn enough money to be able to purchase the necessary land.

J.O., Sr. (b.1887 in Rics; in the United States 1912–1925):
My father died when I was half a year old and my brother was two and a half. My mother was in service with the wealthy, washing and cooking. Later she served in Pest.

At the age of thirteen, I went to Pest. I was alone. I learned the tailor's trade by observing someone, but it was hard to find a situation as I wasn't experienced enough. At the age of seventeen, I heard that abroad one had worth. In Hungary even when there was work, the pay was very small. In 1907, I went to Berlin, after that to London, after ten months to the provinces, then back to Pest. They called me into Szolnok for enlistment; I immediately got on a train and went to Vienna, from there to Paris, then Monte Carlo and from there to Menton. Again to London, then back to Paris.

I was still in Monte Carlo when a friend wrote from Cairo that we should go to America because "in Europe the bottom of the world will drop out." In 1912 it hung on a hair as to whether France and Germany would declare war. England was mixed up in it also. The Germans drew back. I said to my friend, "There is trouble coming." Daily before noon, we waited for the news at Le Matin. But by the time the war broke out, we were already in New York.

As mentioned before emigration got included in the villagers' scale of values as "men's activity," seasonal employment in a country very far away—at least till the 1910s. A part of the men living on the highlands performed their work in the spring, summer, and autumn generally far from their families, as laborers paid in proportion to yield, while the women, the wives, were laboring in the home economy the men left behind. This way a lifestyle tradition took shape bound to a divided family. Owing to the immense distance and the long time separation lasting much longer than any previous one, emigration to the United States put those affected to a bigger emotional test, than they were used to in the course of seasonal migration.

From the information individuals and the letters sent home by the emigrants, we can glean those emotional difficulties of the sentimental type, too, which was caused for young couples by the long separation for years. Extension of their stay in America by emigrants who were torn between a desire to save more money here and return to the family in the village often caused painful conflict on both sides of the ocean. The history of disappointment, unfaithfulness, and extramarital relationships remained an unwritten tradition and became very frequently the subject of the Hungarian-American newspapers and literature.[3]

More than one hundred "American letters" are stored in an Archive of Somogy County, which are valuable for researchers. Almost all of them were written by married people. Here is an example, written from the heart, translated in its original style:[4]

My beloved dear mate, my better half,

think of my happy life, i work day and night, if i have a night by chance, even then i don't know whether to rest or mend my clothes so my better half you must guess how happy i feel i pay so much for my board it would be enough for all of you if you were here, and for that one doesn't even have a satisfying meal, so my dear mate, what is our life worth, if you at home and i here am miserable, we do get married to at least enjoy each other as he is the unhappy one really, who cannot enjoy each other, and therefore you should get your passport as soon as possible and when we can see things to be good I have you brought out and if you could put the things somewhere then my dear mate i would like to relieve you from that abominable life as such people also get their family brought out who have land at home why should we then live miserably without each other believe me my sweet mate if you come out we shall live so happily as fish in the pond and if you have no money than write and i will send some as thanks to god i have a little money i can get you brought out any time with this i close my letter i remain your dear faithful husband till the grave i kiss you all you dears as a real father of the family god be with you and with me i send my greetings to the old people too. My address is Stefi Orbán chestnut st oil city p.a.

In these letters the longing for the family shines through; loneliness, the feeling of jealousy, and homesickness are reflected. The letters are bearers of such information, with the help of which we can see inside of the spheres unknown or hardly known of the "invisible history." Through them were put into words feelings, thoughts, emotions, and opinions that were usually left out from the official documents. In their lives—traditional life situations—it was not characteristic of peasants to reveal themselves emotionally. Getting into a situation never before experienced in their insular solitary position, languishing after affection and love, they were carried away by their feelings. They asked their wives more and more to follow them out, and to leave the children with the grandparents. The emigrants realized that the two of them would be able to acquire more income. There were husbands, too, who virtually blackmailed their wavering wives with threats that if they did not come to America, the husbands would never return home.[5]

The Integrated Macro- and Micro-Level Picture

Microanalysis—researching the stories of individuals—confirms such results of macro-level research as the role of itinerant labor in the process of migration from Hungary to the United States. At the same time microanalysis gives a better indication of immigrants who make choices because of culture and family ties as well as employment or economic opportunities. As Charles Tilly has put it, migrants to America formed networks: By and large the effective units of migration were (and are) neither individuals nor households but sets of people linked by acquintance, kinship, and work experience.[6]

From microanalysis we can answer the question "How did it happen?" with information about the very different motivations for migration in the same movements. How did members of individual families manage through the enormous geographical distances, often separated for years? Microanalysis reveals the necessary cooperation binding together members of a family laboring on two sides of the ocean, and the role played by the older generation, entrusted with the care of small children left behind or sent home later. An information chain also plays a role in the migration process. Whether verbal or not, it is always directly personal, of a face-to-face nature. These details cannot be conveyed through macro-level analysis. Such results also demonstrate how simplistic are those explanations which ascribe solely to economic factors the change from the originally "temporary migration" into "permanent migration." It becomes evident, too, that young people did not always start their journey within the framework of family strategy, but rather in the hope of self-realization.

Finally, what we have learned from the results of our microanalysis shows that it would be a mistake to emphasize only the fact that it took a man of some quality to make the decision to leave, in other words, to insist that it was always the most talented of the village or of a given social group who emigrated. What seems, rather, to have been the case is that the decision to emigrate was made by those who—for whatever reason—refused to accept their lot, who had a strong desire for change, and who consequently found it easier to make up their minds when the chance to emigrate presented itself.

CHAPTER 5

The Repercussions in Hungary of Overseas Migration: 1870–1914

WHAT WERE THE effects of migration on Hungary, when most of the pre-1914 migrants to America left intending only a temporary separation? What difference, if any, did it make that Hungary's peasant emigrants—and much of Hungarian society—still had one foot in the feudal past, and that this donor community was one in which peasant values, not middle-class values, predominated? And finally, how did the Hungarian population's multiethnic composition and the attendant ethnic tensions influence the impact of the migration process? These very important aspects of overseas migration must be analyzed, though the complexity of these questions permits only the sketchiest of answers here.

As the incidence of migration varied greatly from village to village and from region to region, so did the extent to which emigration became a formative influence on the donor communities. Differences of this kind are lost to macroanalysis, for they "average out" in the national statistics. It is only microanalysis, attentive to many kinds of local information, that reflects the true range of influence. Various bits and pieces of local information in themselves, however, will never add up to an authentic picture of the situation nationwide and are extraordinarily susceptible to subjective manipulation. The great differences from one area to the other in the frequency of migration also meant that the effects of migration varied greatly from one ethnic group to the next. This fact only compounds the methodological difficulty of keeping subjectivity to a minimum. It is not surprising therefore, that there has as yet been no systematic investigation of the repercussions of emigration in the donor societies.

The Demographic Effects of Emigration

It is well known that the internal migration caused by industrialization deeply changed the demographic balance among countries and, within countries, among certain regions. Geographically, it restructured the population even where mass external migration did not appear. In Hungary this restructuring affected each ethnic group in different ways and to different extents.[1] For a European country Hungary was not densely populated. Some parts of it had become completely depopulated during the century and a half of Turkish rule, and settlers still were being brought into those areas in the early nineteenth century. Thus Hungary experienced a demographic revolution which was more solid than that in western Europe.[2]

Nevertheless, the impact of emigration on Hungary does not appear to have been substantial. The census of 1880 recorded a population of 13.7 million; the 1910 census registered 18.2 million people, a population growth of 33 percent in three decades. During the same period, the country had an overseas migration traffic of 2 million, resulting in an actual population loss of 886,072 when people crossing the Atlantic repeatedly, the high percentage of remigrants, and immigration to Hungary from the surrounding countries are all taken into account. During these decades, when one-fifth of the natural population growth was lost through emigration, this net loss hardly slowed the rate of population growth on the national level. The net growth rates of the three decades from 1880 to 1910 were 10.3 percent, 10.3 percent, and 8.4 percent, respectively. Only in the first decade of the twentieth century, at the peak of the wave of migration, is there an actual drop in growth of 1.9 percent.

Although the emigrants were mostly young people of working age, the national average age composition of the population changed very little throughout this period. We find that the ratio of 20- to 39-year-olds in the population was 27.8 percent in 1900 and 27.7 percent in 1910; during this decade, the ratio of the 40- to 50-year-olds fell only .1 percent. What was lost through emigration, especially to America, thus appears to have been the population surplus resulting from the baby boom of the 1880s.[3]

Although both contemporary commentators and recent studies have spoken of the "feminization" of Hungarian society as one of the important consequences of the emigration of able-bodied men, census figures show that the surplus of women in the population antedated the migration wave. In fact, despite overseas emigration, on the national average the surplus of women tended to decline toward the turn of the century.[4] It was only in the 1900s that the surplus of women started to grow, but on the national average the male-female ratio in 1910 was the same as in 1890.

In contrast to what the national data indicate, however, population growth in the centers of migration fell substantially and was below the national average in 1890 and in 1910. In the center of overseas emigration in the northeastern part of Hungary, emigration as a percentage of the natural population growth for 1899 to 1913 was as follows: Szepes County, 159.2 percent; Abauj County, 157.7 percent; Ung County, 132.8 percent; and Zemplén County, 118.9 percent. In these counties the mass emigration of the young people brought the ratio of 20- to 39-year-olds in the population to well below the national average of 27.7 percent in 1910. In 1910 in Sáros County it comprised only 21.1 percent;

in Ung County, 22.4 percent; in Zemplén, 22.9 percent; and in Abaúj, 23.1 percent of the population.[5]

The male-female ratios in the emigration centers also show divergences from the national average. There the surplus of women grew until 1900, but declined during the first decade of the century, while the national surplus still grew from 1,009 women for every 1,000 men in 1900, to 1,015 women per 1,000 men. In Szepes County the ratio of women per 1,000 men fell from 1,113 to 1088; in Abauj from 1,123 to 1,106; and in Sáros from 1,161 to 1,137.[6] In these same counties the ratio of women emigrants grew the most conspicuously in this decade. The surplus of women due to emigration, then, was only a transitional phase. As emigration to America came to be regarded as a lifelong option, the sex ratio among the emigrants became more balanced.

In Hungary as a whole, the three prewar decades were a time of considerable population growth, but in the areas most affected by emigration, there was a population decline in both relative terms and absolute numbers. For instance, in 1910, Sáros County, which was affected first and most gravely by emigration, recorded a population smaller in two of its districts than in 1869. But villages with populations stagnating or declining in absolute numbers were registered only sporadically in other counties. The migrations generated by industrialization reshuffled the demographic and settlement structure of even those countries where there was no overseas emigration to speak of. In Hungary, this geographic redistribution of the population affected the various ethnic groups in different ways and led to a rate of population growth that differed from one ethnic group to the next.

At the time of the 1880 census, 6,404,079 people identified themselves as Magyar; in the 1910 census, the figure was 9,944,627, reflecting a growth of 3.5 million, or 59 percent in the country's Magyar population during thirty years. Within the same period, the non-Magyar population was growing at a much slower rate. Population growth among the Carpatho-Ukrainians (Ruthenians or Rusyns) was 31 percent, among the Romanians 22 percent, and among the South Slavs 17 percent. The Slovak population grew no more than 4.4 percent and the German, only .8 percent. By the turn of the century, the Slovaks and the Germans were nearing zero population growth, and in the decade from 1900 to 1910, there actually was a decline in their absolute numbers.[7]

The Magyars suffered some population loss through emigration, but on balance, they stood to profit from the internal migration. The towns functioned as melting pots; they had become the economic and cultural centers of Magyarization by the turn of the century. At the same time, all the non-Magyar nationalities suffered population losses during these thirty years as a result of both emigration and internal migration. By the end of the period Hungary's ethnic composition had changed to the point that the Magyars were an absolute majority. While the ratio of Magyars in the country's population was only 46.6 percent in 1880, by 1900 it was 51.4 percent, and by 1910, 54.5 percent.[8]

The gain in Magyar population by assimilation from other ethnic groups through internal migration was higher in numbers than the loss caused by Magyar emigration to America. Assimilation was such an important element of bourgeois transformation and social progress in Hungary, it is hardly possible by numerical estimates to determine its shape or to outline unambiguously its characteristics. Besides forced assimilation, to the Magyar population, assimilation occurred naturally through bourgeois development, urbanization, and moving out of traditional communities. It is difficult, therefore, to define the roles of the various factors in the process of assimilation and their relationship to the conflicts deriving from that process.[9]

The Economic Repercussions of Emigration

There is hardly a story, hardly a local legend of America that makes no reference to the dollars sent home. The dollars came through the mail or in the pockets of those returning for a visit or for good. There is absolutely no way of calculating just how much money was involved. Sources have estimated that the emigrants from Hungary sent home as much as 400 million crowns (i.e., 80 million dollars) in the years before the war.[10]

None of the contemporary commentators doubted that benefits were derived from the dollars sent home. What was debated was the exact amount and how far this amount compensated the country for the labor force lost through emigration. The consensus in the different opinions was that emigration meant a net loss to Hungary. The commentators arrived at this conclusion by putting in the debit column the travel costs and the amount of money the emigrants took with them. In addition, they argued that the emigrants, while growing up, had consumed some of Hungary's national wealth and upon reaching maturity, spent this capital invested in them overseas. Though the per capita estimate of "the full average value of the emigrants' labor" expressed in monetary terms was not overly high, the assumption was that every emigrant would have found employment at home.[11] The commentators were ignoring the rather well known fact that one of the causes of emigration from Hungary was the lack of job opportunities.

There can be no doubt that the dollars sent home from America boosted the Hungarian economy. They were one reason that the country had no deficit in its balance of payments and its imports could grow faster than its exports. Although the country's balance of trade showed growing deficits in the prewar years, it was evened out by the emigrants' dollars. The finest economist of the period, Frigyes Fellner, wrote, "As long as the national product does not decrease through emigration, far from being an ill, it is a downright blessing."[12] The benefit of emigration still outweighed the loss to Hungarian industry of a considerable portion of the country's labor force.

The dollars sent home had an even more evident salutary effect on the emigrants' local communities of origin, and the authorities had to concede as much in the preamble to the 1890 census:

> Emigration has proved to be a veritable boon. The impoverished popu-
> lace has been drawn off to where it has found lucrative employment;
> the position of those left behind, their work opportunities and standard
> of living, have undoubtedly improved thanks to the rise in wages, and
> thanks to the substantial financial aid coming into the country: sums of
> from 300,000 to 1,500,000 forints, depending on the county.[13]

Here is one opinion of a contemporary:

> By the 1910s, enthusiastic reports of how American dollars had trans-
> formed the emigration regions abounded. American wages have worked
> magic here in Hungary. America put money in the little guy's hand—this
> Hungarian capital would not have done. The villages are prospering;
> there's tiling in place of thatching on the roofs of the neat little houses,
> and there is agricultural machinery where not so long ago the most
> rudimentary implements were hardly to be had. The poor have been
> able to buy houses and land. Whence this miracle? True, America also
> profits. The emigrants invest their energies there; but it is a truism long
> recognized that one party's gain is not necessarily the other's loss. Here
> we have a case of both parties benefiting. For while America uses up
> some of the strength of the Hungarian manpower, the rest of it is
> multiplied in terms of value. America repays only a part of what she
> gets from Hungary, but that she pays in dollars. If, for instance, a
> Hungarian emigrant works for a year abroad he will indeed have en-
> riched America, but he will still be able to take home more than he
> would ever have been able to earn there. Here again, we see the magic
> dollar at work, the magic dollar with which they pay the emigrants'
> wages in America, and which in Hungary is exchanged at a rate of 22
> forints to the dollar. This is the reason that we, too, stand to gain
> from America.[14]

The "American houses" were so much larger and built so differently from the usual custom that in northeastern Hungary tin-roofed houses built in the new airy style were called American houses even if their owners had never been to America.[15]

A number of sources discuss the land purchases made with American money, although there are no statistics on the total of these purchases. From the recollections of contemporaries and from some case histories, it appears that many of those who had been to America bought plots in their own villages, most frequently of two to three holds, but many of five to six holds. There also were purchases of twenty-five holds or more, but these were infrequent. Some of the returnees cleared their debts and paid tax arrears with the dollars saved; others paid off co-heirs or redeemed "those parts of their plots which had been taken as collateral for unpaid taxes or personal loans."[16] There were those, too, who used the dollars sent or taken home to buy draft animals and farm implements in order to "rationalize their husbandry." Some thus managed "to secure a flourishing livelihood for themselves."[17]

The desire to acquire land in one's home village was so widespread among the emigrants that often land was bought before the emigrants finalized the decision not to return. It was mostly peasant lands that changed hands among the emigrants. But data mostly from Szepes and Sáros Counties indicate that *amerikások*[18] also bought up parts of the parceled-up estates of the gentry. As the chief constable of Homonna reported to the county authorities, "Whenever possible, the peasants buy up all the nobility estates, or at least some part of them."[19] If an emigrant did not have the full price on hand, his friends and fellow villagers would help him out with loans. On occasion, someone who had made up his mind to stay in America sold his newly acquired property to someone who had decided to return. The determination of the *amerikások* to acquire land created a rise in land prices. Only a part of the capital that they brought into the country, however, was used for direct productive investment. In fact, it was an exception when innovations aimed at increasing production were tried on the newly acquired land.

The most recent literature on emigration, therefore, calls return to the community of origin a conservative form of migration, a process contrary to the overall social trend.[20] There can be no doubt that returning to work the land conserved the peasant way of life with all its insecurities. Few of the *amerikások* managed to buy enough land and to modernize it to a degree sufficient to escape the hardships of the peasant life once and for all. Still, on the personal level, individual emigrants returning from America experienced as a great step forward everything that was an improvement on their earlier circumstances: moving into houses of their own, clearing their debts, and equipping their farms, however modestly. Emigration also had an indirect positive impact on the emigrant communities, where wages went up. Although other factors clearly played a part in the increases, the emigration of the surplus workforce improved local working conditions for those who stayed.

For individual emigrants, the years spent in America were not always positive in their long-term effects. Instead, a village constable in Trencsén County portrayed them to his superiors as overwhelmingly negative: "With a very few exceptions, those who have been to America for three or four years return as physical wrecks and broken in spirit. Men in the prime of life age before their time: their financial security disappears as they run out of the little they have put aside, and soon they are back where they started."[21]

For some local economies, too, mass emigration had adverse consequences when it led to labor shortages. "In many places, the land is carelessly cultivated, or lies completely neglected," reported the Hungarian census in 1891.[22] Similar statements are often to be found in reports by local and county authorities, and although they contain some exaggeration, they cannot be discounted.

The land purchases of the *amerikások* resulted in a conspicuous growth in the number of small homesteads and slowed down the proletarianization of the peasantry. However, even in the emigration regions there were places where no essential changes in the structure of the peasant holdings took place. Because the peasantry's tax burdens made it difficult for a great many of them to hold on to their lands, the *amerikások*'s land purchases usually meant that peasant land was changing hands. The total land area owned by peasants grew more slowly than the number of peasants during the period of mass migration.

An overview of the economic effects of emigration would be incomplete without at least passing reference to the social groups who tried to profit from overseas migration without actually migrating themselves. There were wealthy peasants or moneylenders who bought up estates to pass parcels of land on to the *amerikások* at a high profit. Others provided the emigrants with loans to buy their tickets, taking their land as collateral. Still others lent the emigrants' families money at an exorbitant rate of interest until the first dollars arrived. Providing loans of this sort grew into a veritable business concern in some regions of the country. At every step of the emigrants' way there were additional profiteers, from emigration agents to government agencies, that made them pay dearly for every document and every piece of information.

As we can see, the economic impact of emigration was threefold: on the national level, on the village level, and on the individual level. On the national level, the negative balance of trade was turned into a positive balance of payments by the migrants' remittances. This, however, did not mean that a conscious policy of investment and industrialization was pursued by the national government. Thus, the foreign currency did not have the effect it might have had. On the village level, the money spent led to some internal improvements and additional jobs. As regards individual migrants or their remaining families, they could improve their economic position (provided the migrant worker did not fall ill or became unemployed). For those who did remain in the new urban world, this might have become a permanent security. However, after return to the Old World, even under careful management, the accumulated savings were usually spent after a few months or years, and the cycle of impoverishment, migration, and proletarianization would begin anew.

The Cultural and Political Effects of Emigration

How did the experiences of the migrants enrich life in the Hungarian villages? Did contact with those who had been or still were in America foster receptiveness to the new? How did these contacts affect behavior and thinking in the communities of origin? Did the returnees exert an influence on village ways, or did the old culture prove stronger and reassimilate them? Journal articles, official reports, conferences organized on the subject, and the minutes of the parliamentary debates all indicate the importance that contemporaries attached to these questions. Many sources demonstrate that there definitely were changes in thinking and behavior. Where they disagree is in the evaluation of these changes. The following excerpts reflect the personal prejudices and interests of the commentators and show how one and the same phenomenon received diametrically opposite evaluations.

A correspondent of the *Schlesische Zeitung* made this comparison as he watched the crowds of emigrants heading for America rub shoulders with the crowds of returnees at the Prussian transit station of Odelberg: "There is little to be seen on those returning from America of the dirt and stupid indifference that clings to most of the emigrants. The returnees are more self-assured, move with greater confidence, and feel they are as good a man as their betters."[23] The positive effects of the American experience were what Ferenc Kossuth also emphasized in Parliament in 1902: "The emigrants return with a more modern outlook, having seen the world, and their experiences help broaden the vista of their environment as well."[24]

By contrast, the deputy lieutenant of Heves County had a more negative view of the consequences of emigration. "Getting to know the more developed form of government of the New World, the more perfect rule of law there, the more efficient administration and the lower taxes makes [the emigrants] discontent with conditions in the old country. And if they do return, it is to be feared that they will only kindle passion and discontent, and will become the enemies of public order and security. The soul of the emigrant has fallen prey to an insidious foreign spirit, and the family hearth is rent asunder."[25] Generally, Hungarian officialdom was critical of the changed behavior of the *amerikások*. Official reports often complained that the returnees "don't want to work," "are not patriotic," "don't go to church," and "spread Pan-Slavism."[26] The lieutenant of Turócz County was not the only one to make a statement in this vein: "The most characteristic feature of the returning emigrants was that during their stay in the United States they have adopted more free and democratic ideas and became more self-reliant and independent."[27]

The working-class press, however, attached great hopes to changes among those returning to Hungary:

> The remigrants are a particularly valuable group, for they have already seen an industrial culture. . . . They are a group tempered in their struggle with an industrial great power and know their own strength. Here, too, they will insist on the conditions they have become accustomed to in America.
>
> Those who have seen soapbox orators in America and have observed how the police take care lest some insult come to them, will not stand idly by when a popular demonstration is simply forbidden by the authorities. Those who in America had been part of the revolutionary movement of the world's industrial workers will be able to protect their own workers' associations from dissolution. Those who across the Atlantic have come to take for granted that freedom of expression, in speech and writing, is part of what cultural development is about will not let an overly zealous bureaucracy silence them. And those who have enjoyed

the blessings of industrialization—central heating, electricity, and the department stores—will not willingly give all this up just because their demands happen to impinge on the landowners' interests, i.e., the land-owners' due.[28]

With the wisdom of hindsight, it is perfectly obvious that both contemporary hopes and contemporary fears about the impact of American democracy on thinking and behavior were exaggerated. The hopes that certain of the working-class leaders attached to the returnees seem but romantic optimism in retro-spect. Few who saw their stay in America as temporary were willing to interrupt their work by striking for long-range goals. Few who had taken an active part in the American working-class movement returned. In terms of sheer numbers, they could hardly have formed the vanguard of the struggle for a democratic, and then a socialist Hungary. Still, in the emigration regions, many of the local activists who supported the Left in 1918–1919 turned out to have been *amerikások.*[29]

Contemporary commentators may have overstated the changes, but there was a great deal of truth in what they said. The image of a democratic America which those who stayed at home pieced together from overseas correspondence and from the stories of the returnees did influence the political climate of the donor communities. It undermined their tolerance for social and political subordination and made unquestioning, servile obedience a thing of the past. The incongruity of the two worlds was felt even more strongly by the returnees and was reflected in their failure to readjust. Their clashes with the local authorities left strong and lasting impressions on all the members of the commu-nity. It was often such conflicts that precipitated another trip overseas and confirmed the emigrant in his decision to stay in America for good.[30]

Nevertheless, it was more typical in the long run that on returning to his community of origin, the emigrant soon found himself thinking and acting in the old ways. The local ways quickly proved stronger than the influence of America. Those who had spent two or three years in the United States slaving down in the mines, on railroad construction, or in steel mills soon showed little sign of ever having been away. Their working and living conditions were backward, and so were those people among whom they lived and worked. Although it sometimes took them longer, even those who had worked in the cities in decently run factories, who had been away for many years, were also much more likely to readjust to the old environment than to transform it in any significant way on their return.[31] As one villager recalls:

> I too, saw many *amerikás* returnees when I was a child. What did they do? They bought land with the money they'd brought home, the land the others had lost because of the depression. They fell right back into the old conservative ways. They never wanted to go beyond the edge of the village. They differed at most in spending more time at the pub and in wearing their baggy *amerikás* trousers. But once their money ran out and their clothes wore out, there was no way of telling that

they'd spent twenty to twenty-five years in America. All their revolutionary spirit went up in smoke.[32]

The village community's power to reassimilate is emphasized in an ethnographic study that in 1901 analyzed the interaction of various ethnic cultures
in one of the centers of emigration in northeastern Hungary.[33] It likewise has
been borne out by the oral testimonies gathered in the course of much more
field work in the emigration regions. From these sources, then, a typology of
the returnees can be set up. As a group they did not stand apart from the
other villagers, but some enjoyed a great deal of respect because of their
breadth of vision and greater experience. "He knows a lot; he's been around,"
neighbors said of such a man. His opinion therefore carried much weight,
whether or not he had become rich in America.

Men who had grown wealthy in America fell into two distinct types. One
was receptive to everything new and, recognizing the advantages of education,
made more of an effort to give his children a higher education than did
wealthy peasants who had never left the village. The other type was decidedly
conservative in his views, and he bound his children to the land he had bought
with his dollars much more implacably than the better-off peasants who had
inherited their land. A stay in America had its effects on people's religious
beliefs as well. Some of the emigrants joined denominations or sects that were
unknown in their home villages and continued to practice their religion after
they returned. Migrants from America introduced Seventh Day Adventism to
Hungary, and the Baptists won many converts through the *amerikások*.[34]

The political repercussions of overseas emigration from Hungary were
complicated by the fact that the majority of the emigrants were not Magyars
but members of one of the national minorities, particularly Slovaks. The mass
of the emigrants, regardless of nationality, left Hungary for the same reason:
to make money in America and then return home. Only while in America did
this emigrant mass became politically differentiated, as was generally the case
in economic emigrations, which always contained an element of rebellion
against conditions prevailing at home.

The emigrants' nascent national consciousness was reflected back onto their
communities of origin in a number of forms. Some migrants served as personal
examples of commitment to the national cause; others provided the stay-at-
homes with information that encouraged them in their political activities. The
Pittsburgh consul had pointed out, as early as 1895, that the anti-Hungarian
campaign in the United States was making the returnees into eloquent apostles
of ideas dangerous to the state.[35] The ethnic newspapers published in America
gave glowing accounts of the immigrants' social and political activism in the
national cause and of the "aid" sent home in the form of money and anti-
Magyar propaganda. The Hungarian authorities classified these newspapers
as the most inflammatory of all and prohibited their postal delivery within the
country. Copies smuggled in were confiscated if discovered. In the ministers'

conferences between 1889 and 1913, the Minister of the Interior announced prohibitions on more than forty American-Slovak newspapers in Hungary.[36]

Finally, but not least important, were personal contacts—through letters or visits—gradually built up by the leaders of the national movements on both sides of the Atlantic. The self-important tone of many of these communications was not particularly conducive to strict factualism or to the realistic evaluation of any given situation. And distance, the vast expanse of the Atlantic, played into the hands of those bent on fostering illusions.

CHAPTER 6

Painting Pictures of
an El Dorado

THE FIRST REPORTS sent to the authorities on the rural population's emigration to America came from the districts immediately adjoining Galicia. Hungarian miners who formerly worked in the salt mines of Galicia brought back word of the opportunities in the United States. America was looking for workers, they said, and anyone who went to work in a mine or factory there would make wages he could not dream of making in any part of the Monarchy. It was money enough not only to support himself and his family, but also to buy a house and land on his return. Although those spreading these reports were authentic migrants, known to their neighbors, many of them were paid by the agents of the shipping companies, who practically overran Galicia in the 1890s as they tried to entice skeptical peasants to emigrate.[1]

Hungary's political and economic elite, primarily the landowners, reacted strongly to the first news of emigration to America, realizing that it would deplete their pool of cheap agricultural labor. From the 1880s on, they called for regulations to restrict emigration. However, after the Compromise of 1867, all the Hungarian governments professed liberal principles and could not question the freedom of individuals to emigrate. Instead, as a concession to the landowners, lobby laws were passed to control the process of emigration, and anti-emigration propaganda was encouraged.

"Heartless agents are luring the gullible people to America with false promises," read the reports of county authorities time and again. It was, therefore, the emigration agents who were brought under regulation. In 1891 the Minister of the Interior introduced a bill entitled "On Emigration Agents." Here are a few lines from its preamble: "Having studied the matter of emigration I have become convinced that the decision to emigrate is not one brought on by reflection by the individuals themselves, but was the result of the persuasion and heartless promises of various agents and profiteers."[2] The law permitted only officially licensed agents to operate, but while the authorities issued absolutely no permits, the wave of emigration continued to grow.

From the early 1880s on, the newspapers sensationalized the bitter experiences of the Hungarian emigrants working in America. The headlines themselves were designed to intimidate: "Emigrant Family Sick of Living,"[3] "Hapless Emigrants,"[4] "Flight Back Home,"[5] and so on. The *Népszava* (People's Voice), the paper of the Hungarian Social Democrats, refused to publish this type of anti-emigration propaganda. This same paper, however, also gave a less than optimistic picture of Hungarian immigrants in America "making their daily wages of $1.20 working 12.5 hours a day."[6]

In any case, the press campaign had little success. It was undermined, especially in migration centers, by county papers that carried letters and stories about the opportunities for success in America, as well as the hardships. The main reason for failure of the press campaign, however, was that the rural population most affected seldom saw a newspaper. Besides the Bible and little booklets of the lives of the saints, villagers read, at most, almanacs and penny dreadfuls recounting some historical event or legend. For this reason, one member suggested to Parliament that "the people be given popular booklets so they might get to know the lives and lifestyles of those who have emigrated to America. Let them find out that the amount of energy that here, in our dear homeland, is sufficient to make a living for a lifetime is soon exhausted in America; and even if the emigrant should return to the land of his fathers, he will do so a physical wreck with no energy left to earn his bread."[7]

As a result, a number of cheap, short booklets appeared in the first decade of the century, purportedly telling "true stories" of "experiences in America." One was entitled *The Happy Land As It Really Is.*[8] Its hero Michael, a young peasant lad, tells his distressing tale in a letter to a friend. On returning to his village after his stint of military service, he was met by poverty and the news that his sweetheart had been forced by her parents to wed "a well-off man." In his sorrow, he "longed for that distant land across the seas, where there is no misery and no poverty." He had heard emigration agents speaking of it. "They promised an El Dorado far across the ocean. You'll never be poor again, for the boat takes you to a country where poverty is unknown."

Michael's tribulations started in Hamburg. The agent, who had promised him wonderful wages in America, informed him that the ticket price they had agreed on would not get him that far. He made Michael sign a contract to work on the boat for the duration of the passage, and the crossing was dreadful. "We were in constant fear for our lives. There's nothing like a stormy ocean to teach a man to pray." Then when he finally reached shore, Michael discovered that the contract the agent had had him sign obliged him not only to work on the ship, but also to work six months on a farm in Dakota. "I've been deceived, frightfully deceived. Müller, who misled us all, is a heartless villain, who lives like a king on bamboozling unsuspecting simpletons to come to this strange land. He lures you to America, saying that here, everyone can get rich. It was only when I set foot on this land of liberty that I realized that I am a slave."

So wrote Michael from Dakota to his friend before heading posthaste toward home.

From New York, Michael wrote again. "There is no real air here; it sits heavy upon a Hungarian used to the open air of the plains. I set out for the coast toward America's largest city with the purpose of setting sail with the first available boat for the homeland I so faithlessly deserted. What a lot of stupid stories they tell folks at home of how here one can get rich without hardship or toil. I've never seen the least sign of it. If anything, I've seen that everyone works much harder for their daily bread."

In New York Michael also met some Slovak compatriots "who were seeking the Happy Land just like I was. What an air of misery, of poverty they had!" He invited the "hungry troupe" to eat at a saloon and was robbed while there. The stamp for the letter he earned helping the street sweeper for half an hour. The last station of Michael's calvary was a charity hospital. "It was charity that took me off the pavement where I had collapsed." After recovering at the hospital, he wrote to ask the Hungarian consul to arrange for his trip home.

The construction of the stories and the morals to be drawn from them were pretty much the same in all the popular pamphlets. The naive and gullible poor were lured to America "by perfidious agents making false promises and painting pictures of an El Dorado." After taking their last pennies, the agents left migrants to fend for themselves. Then comes the history of their miseries and exploitation as "slaves" in the New World. In the end they either perish, or the Hungarian consul appears and helps the disillusioned fortune seekers to return contritely to their homeland.

Preachers and teachers were called upon to help spread the negative image of America. For instance, there is the address to Parliament by Kálmán Török. "It is particularly priests and teachers who have the task—since the poor industrial and agricultural workers are lured by the siren's song of tinkling dollars—to call the attention of the [potential] emigrants also to that terrible, heartrending death rattle that breaks forth from the lead mines of America."[9] "Indeed, this is an issue that we must take up in the pulpits," responded one member who was a clergymen, Bishop János Hock, "for that is the priest's best opportunity to enlighten his flock as to the uncertain future and ceaseless toil that awaits them in America today, where there is an economic recession, and where, as here, they will be able to make only a subsistence living."[10]

Not all priests, teachers, and professionals in the villages were so inclined to propagate a negative image of America, however. On the contrary, some of them operated as emigration agents and thus had a financial reason to speak no evil of America. Others had firsthand knowledge of both the hardships the potential emigrants faced at home and the salutary effect that money sent from America was beginning to have in the villages.

Among the contemporary landowners as well, not everyone supported the campaign "to paint so dark a picture" of the fortunes of the emigrants. As Count József Majláth noted, "The fact that there are so many people who have improved their fortunes cannot be ignored, and under these circumstances, we hardly hope to impede emigration with such feeble methods."[11] The count was right; negative propaganda did not prevent some one and a half million men and women from Hungary from emigrating to America in the four decades preceding World War I.[12]

There were regions of Hungary, the centers of migration, from which conspicuously large numbers of emigrants sailed, and other regions from which hardly anyone left. Some village populations, then, cherished an image of America that differed from the views of the other social strata. The rural population received its information from relatives, personal acquaintances, and friends, and the emigrants' image of America was formed and confirmed by the chain-migrations that started in communities located along the country's northern borders. From these communities the news spread south, carried by Slovaks and Germans to the neighboring Magyars and other ethnic groups. An outline of this flow of information correlates with the spread of migration much better than does any map based on purely economic parameters.

The greatest attraction, as the rural population pictured America, was the money that could be earned, the dollars that could be sent or brought home. "With very few exceptions, the emigrants left determined to return home after having accumulated certain savings."[13] At the end of the nineteenth century, the village population of most regions of Hungary, especially the peasantry, could not readily accept the idea of ameliorating their lot by conclusively breaking with the community, let alone by settling permanently in another country. It was life in their community of origin that they wanted to improve with the money earned somewhere else.

Emigration to America was considered a temporary measure, much like going off to find work in other regions within or just outside Hungary. The sole difference was one of degree; because America was farther off, they would be absent longer. The temporary character of the emigration to America was repeatedly emphasized by all the officials of the counties affected by the exodus.[14] As late as 1913 the Minister of the Interior concurred: "The majority of our emigrants are motivated not by the desire to settle permanently in some foreign land, but the prospect of higher wages, and the greater possibility of striking it rich."[15] Furthermore, statistics supported these authorities.[16]

The salient feature of the image of America, therefore, was of its superior earning opportunities, an impression confirmed by the money the emigrants sent back. "There were known cases of substantial sums of money—and of purchases made using them—circulating among the people,"[17] recalled one emigrant. Another said, "The emigrants sent money to their relatives, and urged them to join them overseas in jobs they secured for them beforehand."[18] Land cleared of debts, "new houses with tiled roofs, the money regularly arriving from America and savings accounts are all mute, but eloquent emigration agents, ones that no earthly power can eradicate."[19] The entire face of the village was altered by the monies sent home. None could overlook the new "American houses" (those built by the *amerikások*), which were the largest and most modern in the community.[20] In the village of Mezokövesd, Americans investigating the roots of immigration reported in 1904, Pénzgödör (Money Pit) and Dollárhegy (Dollar Mountain) are the names of the areas where the remigrants from America have bought fields and built houses.[21] The dollars sent home, we are not surprised to read in the minutes of a meeting of the Szabolcs County Council, "created a blind faith in America being an El Dorado easily accessible to all, a place where everyone can achieve not only a comfortable livelihood but also riches without too much difficulty with the work of his own hands."[22]

In the 1980s those migrants who had ended up staying in America still recalled their original motivation in terms consistent with the contemporary Hungarian accounts. "We didn't come to America to stay here, but to make a few dollars; we'd buy a few holds of land and be able to live better at home," said one woman.[23] In contrast to their expectations, however, the first impression almost all of them had of America was one of disappointment; many of them wanted to turn back. "The women didn't like it here; no one did. But how could they have left; they had no means of leaving."[24]

Hungarian-American songs give a further glimpse of the disappointment and of the illusions:

> Of America I heard such fine things said
> That I set out to make my fortune and my bread.
> Nothing good, only bad luck came my way.
> Surely I'm the most unhappy stray.
> Here's America, better yet, misery-ca
> To think that I will never get home again!
> None here will encourage the poor wanderer.
> No pity for me, only sorrow, only pain.
> Hey America! with hills and valleys to the sea,
> If Hungarians' curses took, damned you'd be!
> Be damned forever, doomed for all eternity!
> To leave it all behind me, how happy I would be.[25]

Rather than go back home to dispute the favorable image of America, however, unlucky or unsuccessful emigrants were often ashamed to return to their communities of origin. Others made the trip home only to find they had retained memories of village life as idealized as their original notions about the United States had been. "It was a very difficult start for me here," wrote one of them. "It was so difficult that I didn't plan to stay even as much as a year. But in time I got used to it; and when I went back to the old country, three times in all, I couldn't help seeing the conditions of the workers with different eyes, and I couldn't have stayed there for anything. And so I took my family and came back here again. If only I'd done it twenty years earlier."[26]

A whole range of different reasons for staying away from Hungary can also be found in the hundreds of contest entries sent to the Hungarian-American paper *Szabadság* in January of 1909, quoted in the previous chapter.[27] Here are some more of them: "We came not to amass a fortune, but to make a decent living," was a sentiment echoed time and time again. To describe the initial motivation for leaving Hungary.[28] "If we had been able to make a living in Hungary with diligent work, as indeed we can here, I hardly think so many poor people would have taken the wayfarer's staff in hand and headed for America. No one lured us here; it was want that drove us."[29] Nevertheless, after the Hungarians arrived in the United States, acculturation drastically changed their plans. "Even at home the eyes of the village people are opening up; and here in America, one's eyes are not only open, but twinkle brightly on comparing conditions at home with the way things are here."[30] The democratic way of life had a profound impact on the immigrants. "Everyone here is simply Mister; there are no titles of the kind there are in Hungary," echoed one essay after another. "There's no looking down on one another; everyone's equal; people don't take their hats off either to one another, or to the authorities."[31] As one entrant summarized, attractive features of this sort confirmed them in their decision to stay for good. "Why it was that we changed homelands we can tell here on these pages, for we are in America, where though we cannot say everything, we have much more right and freedom to speak up than at home, the reward of diligent work is at least a decent living. What will always be a source of sorrow is that [in Hungary] this is still not to be had, for if it were, then I myself would still be there."[32]

The emigrants themselves were not inclined to paint a negative, or even a well-balanced, realistic picture of their American experiences to friends and relatives left behind. A number of complex factors led them instead toward a mixture of truth and wishful thinking. Because those who stayed at home were most interested in the wages that could be earned and in the job opportunities available, questions and answers centered on these two issues. Those contemplating emigration, especially in the early phases of the wave, had ears for little else. Moreover, those who were successful in their new life were more inclined to write home than those who encountered only failure.[33] It also should be kept in mind that, although most peasants were literate, they were not practiced in the art of letter-writing. Consequently, the letters they sent home were often composed for them by saloonkeepers, shipping line agents, parish priests, and others with a vested interest in the arrival of more immigrants.

As has been noted, the mass migration was not a movement of individuals; rather, the decision to emigrate was part of a family strategy. Before the emigrants left home, their work had been cut out for them, so to speak, and those waiting at home wanted to hear progress reports. Migrants thus were forced into a kind of role-playing that did not encourage them to say anything of the setbacks or often intolerable hardships of their day-to-day lives. In other words, they had to engage in a kind of deception by default. Some, however, misled their correspondents on purpose, lest they discourage their much-missed family members, particularly their wives, from joining them. One of the *Szabadság* contestants poignantly summed up this process of deception and disillusionment when he quoted this letter a fellow immigrant wrote: "'My dear wife: Come to America; here you'll be a lady; you needn't work here, there's everything here.'" The commentator continued his own letter with these remarks: "And then by the time the poor little greenhorn woman got there, all that had evaporated, and her husband had nothing but a great pile of debts. How gladly she would have worked, had she been able to get a job; but there's no place she can work, for she can't even speak the language."[34] At the same time, a satirical view of the emigrants' tendency to exaggerate was one of the mainstays of Hungarian-American humor.[35]

> If he writes home
> What does he tell his wife?
> Boastful and self-satisfied,
> He tell of his good life.
>
> If he picks turnips for a farmer
> He'll write he's bought a farm.
> Hundred and sixty acres' yield
> Will soon fill his barn.
>
> Or if he is a laborer
> He's sure to be in foreman's rank.
> He gives his orders in the bar
> But neither at work nor at the bank.[36]

There is absolutely no question that photographs sent from America appeared to validate the thousands of glowing words the emigrants wrote about the land of boundless opportunity. The pictures show elegant gentlemen, dressed in dark suits and leather shoes, many of them behatted and immodestly sporting what appear to be gold watch chains; women and girls are in their Sunday dresses, with handbags to match. People left behind in the village gazed at these photos with wonder and incredulity. "The wife stared and stared at the picture, and then ran to me, asking if that really were her husband. She even asked him in a letter, 'Is that really you, Istók? For you look like a veritable gentleman; even your cheeks are as round as if you ate meat every day and had a beer after.'"[37]

The pictures were indicative of far more than just prosperity to those looking at them in the village back home. In Hungary at the time, rural people still wore mostly homespun and home-sewn clothes. The closed social structure was reflected in the clothing typical of the various social classes. It was, therefore, startling if not shocking when the peasants saw their own relatives in clothes that in Hungary only "gentlefolk" wore. "Even the constable has no clothes like that!" a woman wrote to the *Szabadság*.[38] Immigrants sending the photos were very well aware of the impression they would make. "If only the priest at home could see me, or the schoolteacher, when I get all dressed up, he'd sooner doff his hat to me than I to him," was the way one of them put it.[39] Naturally, those with an interest in the growth of immigration also realized the potential impact of such pictures, and so urged the immigrants to have themselves photographed in all their American finery.

Nevertheless, a letter or even a picture from abroad could not compare in impact with a visit by someone from America.[40] The most conspicuous effect of emigration was the change in the returnee's personality.[41] Gone was the terseness of the written communications; now there was plenty of time to tell a long story in all its details. When the villagers assembled to listen to it, their attention never flagged. Face-to-face verbal communication was the most credited source of information in the closed world of the peasantry. The degree of credence given a story depended on whether it was firsthand experience that was being recounted or just hearsay. Personal experiences of mutual acquaintances were later passed on while the villagers were spinning together on a winter's night, cornhusking, or visiting with friends, neighbors, and family. Of course, being the center of attention inspired quite a few of the returnees to color and exaggerate their accounts. "If a man like that comes home dressed like a gentleman and speaking English, in his hard black hat, he is a more marvelous and more effective advocate of America than any agent. When he speaks, especially when he enjoys the attention he is getting and wants to make the best of it, he will exaggerate to those standing about him in awe. They will believe everything he says, and I have almost always found that following the return to the village by one or two emigrants who'd made good, the incidence of migration from that particular village always grows considerably."[42] The emigrants thus contributed to the development and conservation of an idealized image of America. When writing home, they always were at pains to show the positive side of the picture and reinforced it with the photos and monies sent. The difficulties they faced in adjusting to a radically different working-class life, their loneliness in an inhospitable environment, and their longing for home were given expression only in America, if at all. For those who stayed in the old country, nothing that contradicted the favorable view of emigration ever came through.

The determination of the donor community to cling to a positive image as its only hope out of a bad situation was a further filter on incoming information. It just could not tolerate the tarnishing of that image with either information on what it was really like to be an outcast "Hunky" (a nickname given by Americans to immigrants from Hungary) or with data on America's relatively large number of tragic industrial accidents. A Hungarian American who wrote to *Szabadság* could see what his compatriots at home simply could not. "The example of the unfortunates who'd perished abroad had no real impact. They spoke about them for a while, but then soon forgot them. Most people felt that they'd been misfits from the start. Those who came home empty-handed likewise went unnoticed, for they'd been no better off before; that was why they'd left."[43]

The image of an America where good luck, success, and happiness were the just rewards of hard, diligent work made no concession to individuals; if someone failed, was unhappy, or suffered an accident on the job, his own personal shortcomings were to blame. Hungarian peasants held on to this image of America, which—experience notwithstanding—permitted emigrants to set out optimistically for the great unknown.

With the passage of time, the image became more diversified but then gave rise to yet more powerful illusions. The few negative elements that could not be overlooked were all quickly forgotten. The myth of a land of boundless opportunity endured in the delivering communities, long after the chance of emigrating to it was closed to them for good.

CHAPTER 7

Emigration and Public Opinion in Hungary

GERMAN, ITALIAN, AND Swedish laws served as a model for the Hungarian government in 1902, when the first bill to control emigration was proposed.[1] In an economy that was more liberal in other respects and gave market forces more freedom, it would have been consistent to permit inhabitants to leave the kingdom. But from the very start, fear of losing their pool of cheap labor made the Hungarian landowning interests conservative opponents of emigration who tended to exaggerate the manpower lost. As early as the 1880s, they were calling on the government to take steps to restrict overseas migration, and some groups went so far as to demand its prohibition.[2]

Hungarian government circles, however, regarded it as a favorable phenomenon "from the aspect of the establishment of the Hungarian national state" that members of the national minorities constituted the majority of the emigrants. The resulting ambivalence of the government policy on emigration is reflected in the fact that while the official stand—adopted with an eye on the landowners' votes—was always opposed to emigration, all the governments throughout the entire period ignored the demands by various pressure groups for the prohibition of emigration.[3] The most that these groups could achieve was the passage in 1881 of the bill entitled "On Emigration Agents," which required emigration agents to be licensed by the authorities, who in turn dragged out the licensing process for years.[4] The preamble to the bill expressed the government's views very clearly: "Contemporary thinking does not allow the outright prohibition of emigration, for, as we all know, the right to emigrate is a constitutional right in a number of countries. Nor would a prohibition be enforceable, for since practically all the countries of the world can be visited without a passport, anyone wanting to emigrate could leave unnoticed."[5] Neither the 1881 law nor administrative restrictions imposed by the counties of northeastern Hungary stemmed the tide of overseas migration. The counties

89

turned again and again to the government, urging that effective legislation be brought to restrict emigration, but the first bill dealing with emigration as such was not passed until 1903. It contained the following definition: "Anyone going abroad for an indefinite period of time for purposes of full-time employment is considered an emigrant."[6] Although the bill included only some relatively mild restrictions on migration, its parliamentary debate provoked the most extreme reactions. The Hungarian Social Democrats charged that the purpose of the proposed legislation was "to add to the people's burden and at the same time to block the border, horsewhip in hand."[7] To adopt it was "nothing less than passing a law abolishing personal liberty."[8] Others, primarily landowners, claimed the law actually opened the way for a flow of people out of the country by allowing the government to contract with shipping companies. In the United States as well, the Hungarian government was accused of institutionalizing emigration.

The contradictory criticisms reflect the clash of various interests within Hungary over the country's unique population problems. In Hungary, where the effect of the demographic revolution was by no means as large as in regions of Western Europe, the first news of transatlantic migration produced a panic among the big landowners. With increasing urgency, they clamored for restrictions on the emigration of their cheap labor supply. The increasingly aggressive Hungarian nationalism and the illusion of a "Hungarian" empire thirty million people strong likewise demanded that the labor force be kept within the borders of the state.

The issue of nationalism in Hungary was very complex. Not only was the population multiethnic and brimming with national tensions, but the centers of migration tended to develop in the territories of the non-Hungarian nationalities. As a result, the mother tongue of approximately two-thirds of the emigrants was a language other than Hungarian. The secret exposé sent by Under Secretary of State Count Kuno Klebelsberg to Prime Minister Kálmán Széll in 1902 suggested that this emigration of the minorities could be a major advantage in building the Hungarian national state:

> For the institution of national statehood it is absolutely necessary that the ruling race—which has been called to uphold the national state and populate it—increase accordingly and thus after a while become the majority of the population. This increase can be brought about artificially, via assimilation. Nevertheless, as the smaller ethnic groups have recently been awakening to an ever increasing national consciousness, it is hardly possible to count any further on more extensive assimilation.
>
> Providence, however, at the same time that the natural increase of the Hungarian people has diminished, has granted another population factor which has significantly raised the proportion of the Hungarian element at the expense of the nationalities between 1890 and 1900 from 48.53 percent to 51.36 percent. This important new factor is the mass emigration of the non-Hungarian population.[9]

Official propaganda was directed against emigration in the interest of pacifying the large landowners. At the same time, the government resisted demands for an outright suspension of the freedom to migrate. The law tied departure to permission and passport. These could be obtained by anyone, although men liable for military service were allowed to leave only if they had received permission from the proper authorities.

On the strength of the emigration law, the government in 1904 signed a contract with the Cunard Steam Ship Company of Liverpool to transport Hungarian emigrants from the Hungarian port of Fiume and accept government control over them. In return, the Hungarian government would guarantee the company a traffic of 30,000 emigrants annually. The prime minister made no effort to deny the government's chief motive for making the contract: "I will not hesitate to declare that the idea behind this regulation of emigration was that the emigration traffic which presently goes through the German ports should be directed toward our own port, Fiume, so that those who till now enriched the German ports should not go there, but to Fiume."[10]

The other shipping companies did not welcome the contract between the Hungarian government and the Cunard Lines.[11] It was especially the German shipping companies, who earlier had enjoyed a practical monopoly of the overseas transportation of Hungarian emigrants, that attacked it in the press and applied economic pressure on Cunard, and diplomatic and political pressures on the Hungarian government. In the summer of 1904, the competing shipping companies began the great price war. Ticket prices plummeted from 240 to 90 crowns as the German shipping companies sold tickets under cost. The price war forced Cunard to reduce its fares to 120 crowns, and, by the time the fight stopped temporarily at the end of 1904, the German companies were estimated to have lost 8.5 million marks. Rumors spread, especially in the American press, that the Hungarian government was conspiring with Cunard to get rid of criminals, the insane, and the proletarians. In 1904, moreover, the German government refused to conduct trade negotiations with the Hungarian government until, "under conditions of reciprocity," it was agreed "that the governments concerned would not introduce regulations which would impede emigration through the German Empire by those individuals who want to emigrate, and had the right to do so under the existing laws on emigration."[12] In the United States, where by this time antagonism to the so-called new immigrants was increasing, the Cunard contract and the emigration policy of the Hungarian government provoked strong protest.[13] The Hungarian-American newspapers, such as *Szabadság* (Liberty) and *Bevándorló* (Immigrant), also attacked the contract and prepared to organize a boycott of the Cunard Lines.

Hungary's attempt to block the route leading through the German ports had failed, and its subsequent attempts to divert the emigrants toward Fiume were no more successful. They resulted only in considerable confusion and a great many delays for the would-be emigrants. In addition, the authorities were so arbitrary in providing or withholding passports and tickets that they were accused simultaneously both of preventing emigration and of encouraging or even organizing it.

The skyrocketing number of emigrants from 1904 on proves that the measures of the 1903 law availed nothing against mass emigration. Even men of military age had the chance to get emigration permits from the local authorities. The wave of emigration out of Hungary peaked at an annual rate of 100,000 in the years 1905–07. Forcing emigrants to take the Fiume route increased conflict to such a degree that finally the Hungarian government had to give up its ambitious plans. They had to permit a number of the emigrants, and a significant number at that, to buy their tickets from the companies of the Continental Pool, a consortium of transportation companies. On the ships of Norddeutscher Lloyd alone, more Hungarians left Europe (38 percent of all emigrants) than on the ships of the Cunard Line.[14]

In 1908 a new emigration law was presented in the Hungarian Parliament, which was ratified in 1909. Its purpose was to correct the deficiencies of Bill IV of 1903 and provide more effective supervision to control emigration.[15] The government also hoped by means of the new law to put pressure on the Continental Pool, with which it was negotiating. A provision of the bill stipulated that "only those companies will get permits to transport emigrants which recognize Hungarian law as binding, and permit the Hungarian authorities to exercise their right of inspection in the ports."[16] To make it more difficult for men liable for military service to emigrate, the law required prospective emigrants to deposit a hundred crowns as security and to obtain permits from the Minister of the Interior and the Minister of War. Finally, emigration agents operating without a license were subject to more stringent sanctions.

The pool companies still did not concede the Hungarian authorities permission to conduct inspection on their ships. Under the terms of the contract signed with the pool in 1910, the Hungarians had to do all their inspecting within the country, and the fact that the Hungarian government signed the contract at all was an admission that most of the overseas emigrants from Hungary would continue to sail on German ships. Once the passengers had boarded those foreign ships, Hungary had no right to ask them for their papers—not even those who were known to have left without a passport.[17]

The government's contract with the pool caused the expected stir in the Hungarian Parliament. The "agrarians," the deputies representing the landowners' interest, especially berated the government for its perfidy. A member of parliament, Barna Budai, in his lecture given to OMGE (Országos Magyar Gazdák Egyesülete [the National Association of Hungarian Landowners]) put his views in the following words: "I consider it a dangerous, nay, a criminal policy to demand money and men for the country's armament, while standing by as year after year ingenious smugglers of men rob the country of a contingent of Hungarian arms equal to twice what was lost in the Battle of Mohács."[18]

A government's policy is never what it says but what it does. Thus, the Hungarian government neither hindered nor encouraged overseas mass migration. It was imperial ambition, not support for emigration, that brought about the agreements made with the steamship lines and dragged the Hungarian government into a pitched international competition. The propaganda engendered by that competition, in turn, increased the antipathy of American public opinion toward Hungary and immigrants from Hungary.

During the relatively turbulent 1890s, when agrarian, social, and nationality problems increasingly threatened the stability of Hungarian society, the questions of land reform and abolition of the entailed estates were raised by the opposition in Parliament.[19] Nevertheless, the government was unable to face any practical question of land reform throughout the entire Dualist period. Consistent with a reluctance to alter the distribution of land was the longstanding belief that "land ennobles and industry belittles."[20] Those legislators who advocated the expansion of industrialization in Hungary knew that better working conditions and benefits in factories would contribute to employee satisfaction and might diminish the need for emigration. Bishop János Csernoch, a representative of the Catholic People's Party, meanwhile made concrete proposals for the maintenance of full employment, the modernization of agricultural methods, and the revision of the tax structure.[21] Generally, several speakers warned that in the absence of economic reforms, the effectiveness of the new emigration law would be limited.

The role of paid agents as a significant cause of emigration was emphasized from the beginning. The perceived importance of this role grew as the mass transportation of emigrants became an increasingly profitable business, and the shipping companies employed well-placed local individuals to act as their agents, to provide information, and to sell tickets, which they did with varying degrees of enthusiasm.[22] Laws were enacted in 1881 and 1903 to regulate the agents' activities, but they continued to be blamed for the rise in emigration. Prime Minister Kálmán Széll referred to them as "leeches," draining the nation's energy, and still further regulation was proposed.[23] A perception that the agents tended to be Jewish, although never fully documented, contributed to the debates, and the "pernicious activity" of Jewish newcomers as usurers, alcohol-sellers, price-gouging merchants, or emigration agents remained a topic of discussion.[24] Allegations made to incite anti-Semitism, however, were dismissed by government spokesmen.[25]

In its rate of emigration, Hungary ranked in the middle among the countries of Europe. About one-third of its emigrants were Magyars; the rest belonged to other nationalities. At first glance, therefore, the extremely strong and emotionally charged nationalist reaction against emigration from all segments of Hungarian society—political parties, literary men, and the public at large—seems quite inexplicable. However, the issue of emigration was well suited to exploitation, for it tied in with all the social and political tensions that had been built into Hungary's socioeconomic development. A catalogue of those tensions is almost overwhelming: the extreme inequalities in the division of land and consequent landlessness, the ethnic problems, the structural backwardness of society, the pressures of a semi-feudal system of land ownership, the difficulties of industrialization and of modernization in general, the legal ties with Austria, and so on. As a result, the debate over emigration became, after the turn of the century, a direct and effective political tool in the day-to-day power struggles of Hungary's parties and opposition groups.

It was always the negative effects of emigration that propaganda and politicians emphasized. Not even economic gains could offset the perceived enormous loss of manpower: data pertaining to the loss of population and the mass exodus of people could be used to demonstrate the imperiled state of the nation or of individual ethnic groups or to express all sorts of political sentiments. As a result, the emigration of one and a half million people from Hungary came to be interpreted as the emigration of one and a half million Hungarians. For Magyars, it was impossible to conceive of the various nationality groups as political communities. The so-called Nationality Act of 1868 declared Hungary to be a "unitary national state," and its inhabitants members of the "unitary Hungarian political nation," taking note at most only of "Hungarian citizens speaking different languages."

The sight of shiploads sailing off to America was a source of real anxiety to the elite of Hungarian society. The dramatic newspaper reports about the "poverty caravans," the shocking statistical data and personal experiences had made the question of emigration a central public concern; it was an everyday issue that gave rise to real and sincere anxiety in the minds of those honestly feeling responsible for the nation's fate. The struggle for national survival was an organic part of Hungarian history, dating back several centuries. The country and its people had been devastated by Tatars, Turks, and Germans, and these dramatic historical turning points had etched a profound sense of insecurity into the consciousness of the best of Hungary's public figures. The sense of impending national doom so deeply imprinted on the Magyar collective consciousness is reflected in the most effective poem of the great Hungarian poet of the period, Endre Ady:

> The whistle keeps calling him,
> Poverty is drumming it,
> That the Hungarians will come to an end
> As if they had never existed.[26]

Nevertheless, emigration also appeared in the political sentiment of the national minorities as an omen of the demise of their own ethnic groups. The Slovak *Narodne Noviny* (National Newspaper) articulated "the most widely held opinion, namely, that emigration weakened the Slovak nation in its struggle for survival and the survival of the Slovak language."[27] It was pointed out as early as 1903 in the Croat Parliament, "If the mass exodus continues, the very existence of the Croat people will be at stake."[28] Likewise, Croatian poet Antun C. Matol wrote desperately in 1911, "Our nation, the people of the village blindly rush out to America and the abandoned birthplaces are slowly but surely taken over by aliens. This is the terrible reality, the most timely and the most tragic problem which our sociologists, politicians and moralists face helplessly today."[29] In the case of the Slovaks, there was a real basis for envisioning popular destruction, but it was masked by the high proportion of return migration, which was highest among the other ethnics from Hungary. The flourishing of Slovak nationalist groups in America undoubtedly had a major role as well in easing the desperation Slovak leaders felt upon realizing the dimensions of emigration.

In multiethnic states, the unbalanced rate of economic development among various regions and the tensions that result always appear in the form of nationality questions. For Hungary's minorities, therefore, mass migration became the prime index of their unfavorable conditions and political oppression. In Hungary, however, all the various interest groups and parties overestimated the significance of the emigration issue. "Everybody tried to find a scapegoat: the government blamed the foreign shipping companies; the agrarians and the mercantilists blamed one another; the Social Democrats and the bourgeois radicals blamed the lords of semi-feudal Hungary, the big landowners and the big industrialists; and the leaders of the minority nationalities blamed the oppressive national policies of Vienna and Budapest."[30]

Those most vocal in calling for reform were the ones most likely to see mass emigration for what it was: the symptom of the backwardness of Hungary's economic and social structure. This group had a very clear idea of the country's social ills and took the opportunity that discussion of the emigration issue afforded to focus on the need for democratic reforms and to present their program for land reform. As the Committee on Land Policy of the Hungarian Sociological Society pointed out in 1908: "We are all agreed that a thoroughly thought out land reform organized by the government is necessary for stemming the tide of emigration, for transforming the millions of dollars sent home from abroad into effective investments, and for keeping those who came back from going abroad again."[31]

Mass migration came to an abrupt halt with the outbreak of World War I, but Hungarians today still see it in much the same distorted way that contemporaries did. Although historians might succeed in rectifying "the great and general misconception" that saw an ethnic Magyar lost in every Hungarian citizen who emigrated, the man in the street will not be easily disabused of his belief that "a million and a half Magyars" were lost through migration. This evaluation is so deeply rooted in Hungarian consciousness that it is difficult even for recent historical writing to avoid its influence and portray mass emigration not as national tragedy, but as it was, part of a general European movement.

CHAPTER 8

American Immigration Policy

The Era of Regulations, 1882–1914

BY THE TIME the gigantic Statue of Liberty, the symbol of freedom and of America's welcome to the immigrants, was raised on Bedloe's Island in 1885, the United States government had already begun to rescind its liberal immigration policy.

From the beginning of the nineteenth century to the 1870s, the states and various private organizations alike were busy enticing the people of Western Europe to immigrate with a variety of offers. The federal government spent a great deal of money to attract immigrants. Great quantities of advertising material were printed and distributed, and agents were sent to Europe, especially to the British Isles, Germany, and Scandinavia, to recruit immigrants.[1] Behind all this activity was the desire to promote economic development and to settle the unpopulated area as quickly as possible. The railroad companies were the most active and most successful in this. They offered free homesteads and handed out boat and railroad tickets at reduced prices. They organized entire settlements, especially in the Midwest, by guaranteeing long-term loans.

In 1882, Congress enacted the first comprehensive federal immigration law. Its major points were the following: each immigrant was to pay a fifty-cent tax on entry; and convicted criminals, the mentally ill, the mentally retarded, and all those who might not be able to support themselves were to be denied entry.[2] Three years later, in 1885, yielding to the pressure of organized labor, Congress passed a bill lobbied through the Congress by the Knights of Labor that prohibited the immigration of workers under contract.[3] It prohibited the recruitment of unskilled labor by prepaid passage and advance contracting, but it did not affect skilled workers, artisans, or teachers. For it was widely believed by the labor organizations that the industrialists' agents were recruiting masses of contract laborers, especially from southern and eastern Europe, to use as strikebreakers. What provided grounds for this accusation was the use of immigrants newly arrived from Italy and Hungary (the latter were mostly Slovaks) as strikebreakers in Pennsylvania in the 1880s. (Most of these men had immigrated on their own and were not on contract labor.) It is significant that the industrialists did not protest the prohibition. They knew full well that the contract laborers represented only a small part of the influx of immigrant manpower.

These laws did not yet reflect a concerted effort to limit immigration. Even those who urged their passing were only trying to resolve what they saw as special problems and to satisfy specific demands, never dreaming that these regulations were the beginning of a whole process of limitations. In 1885 an advocate of the Foran Act could remark that "this bill in no measure seeks to restrict free immigration; such a proposition would be odious, and justly so to the American people."[4]

The situation, and consequently the attitude toward immigration, began to change significantly in the second half of the 1880s. The economy became less stable: depression, industrial strikes, and social tension characterized a decade beginning in 1885. The growing social inequalities and sharper class divisions of a highly industrial society caused a new upsurge of xenophobia. Quite a few people responded to the explosive situation with outbursts of nationalism and the revival of the nativist movement. They sought a solution to the economic and social crisis in isolation from foreigners and in the overall restriction of immigration. More and more Americans saw immigration not as a precondition of progress but rather as a problem requiring speedy and drastic remedies.[5]

The workers' dissatisfaction, the economic struggles, and the strikes became increasingly connected with the influx of foreigners in the public mind. Although fear of an "imported revolution" had been expressed already in the 1870s in the mining regions of Pennsylvania and during the great railroad strikes, Americans came really to dread it only after 1886, when an anarchist's bomb exploded at the Haymarket in Chicago. From that time on, anxiety grew about the "wild-eyed foreign radicals" intent on undermining American society.

From the end of the 1880s, patriotic veterans' organizations and fraternal associations sprang up everywhere. Their members were recruited mostly from among such groups as the intellectuals, the clerical workers, the small shopkeepers, and the technicians, all groups that had been unfavorably affected by the status revolution and therefore reacted with special sensitivity to economic and social changes.

The labor organizations increasingly closed ranks with the above-mentioned groups in demanding that limitations be placed on immigration. Although the first mass labor organization in the United States, the Knights of Labor, had already fought in the 1880s for prohibition of the immigration of contract labor, at that time the Knights did not yet advocate a general restriction of immigration. At the end of the nineteenth century, trade unions were still unlikely to support demands for the restriction of immigration; their members were still too close to their immigrant past. Thus, the American Federation of

Labor, with its large immigrant membership and international outlook, refused to support the "literacy test"—designed to limit immigration—until 1897, and even then only after much bitter debate. All in all, however, as the last two decades of the nineteenth century wore on, even the employers, the main opponents of restricting immigration, began to give more weight to the supposed radicalism of the immigrants than to their contribution to the economy.

From the 1880s on, the American nationalists concentrated their antagonism and hatred on the new immigrants, who seemed to them a yet more worrisome group than the old immigrants. The Italian, Slovak, Polish, and Magyar peasants from beyond the Alps were still much closer to serfdom than the peoples of Northern and Western Europe. Jews from Galicia, Russia, and Romania were seeing the world outside the ghetto for the first time. By Western European standards, the new immigrant masses appeared bizarre in their attire and socially backward. Crowded into the slums of the cities of the eastern industrial states, increasing in numbers and thus becoming more conspicuous as a group, they became the target of the nativists' attacks.[6]

Altough by 1890 it was being claimed that the new immigrants represented a special danger, a line of demarcation between "old" and "new" immigrants, to the advantage of the former, was not drawn until after the turn of the century. The tendency of American immigration policy to differentiate among various groups of immigrants first occurred in the campaign to prohibit the entry of contract laborers. It was then, for example, that the Knights of Labor gathered evidence of the low standards of living among the immigrants who had come to America on contract from Italy and Hungary. Thinking in ethnic stereotypes, the nativists held the Southern and Eastern Europeans to be miserly and likely to commit violent crimes.

The monomania that the new immigrants were "the murderer breed of Southern Europe" and threatened the basis of American society was widespread. However, it was only a small group of racist New Orleans intellectuals who spread the doctrine of the racial inferiority of the new immigrants in comparison to the old. The economic value of immigration was made the object of "scientific" study, and "Ancestor Experience" was stressed as the criterion of the immigrants' value.[7] On this basis, the categories of "desirable" and "undesirable" immigrant were formulated. A great stir was created by the demographic study proving that the birth rate of the native population had declined because of the competition from immigrants. The new immigrants, thus, were not an addition to the old population but its replacement.

In 1894 the New England intellectuals formed the Restriction League to protect the future of the "Anglo-Saxon race" and of their class. It was a primary forum through which America's patrician elite expressed their fears. For the next twenty-five years, the League headed every movement for the restriction of immigration. The armory of their intellectual weapons built up gradually. In the 1890s they did not yet commit themselves to an expressly racist immigration policy. The campaign then was for the "literacy test" bill, which they hoped would, as a law, exclude the undesirable classes of Southern and Eastern

Europe. The literacy test bill was first submitted to Congress in 1896 by Senator Henry Cabot Lodge.[8] Its essence was to deny entrance to the United States to anyone who could not read at least forty words in some language.

Lodge demanded the supervision of immigration policy and urged restrictive legislation. Congress rejected the bill on the grounds that it would be an ineffective measure, and to pass it would be to deny America's historic role as an "asylum to the oppressed." Later attempts to get the bill passed in 1898, in 1902, and in 1906 met a similar fate at the hands of an adamant Congress. And when supporters of the bill finally succeeded in getting a Congressional majority to pass the measure, it was presidential vetos that frustrated their efforts (Taft's in 1911 and Wilson's in 1913).[9]

In 1896, those demanding the restriction of immigration were still convinced that they were in the majority and that the failure to get the bill passed was an insignificant and temporary setback. In fact, however, twenty more years had to pass until, in 1917, the League's campaign to limit immigration by introducing a literacy test finally met with success.

At first glance, this series of failures on the part of the nativists to restrict immigration is rather baffling. However, it becomes understandable when the factors influencing their activities are considered. The periodic ups and downs of the movement must be noted first of all, and the fact that the intensity of their activities was not caused by outside factors (the swelling of the wave of migrations), but by changes in American internal affairs. The intensity of anti–immigration activity lessened during times of economic prosperity and grew at times of economic depression. It would also be noted that various organized groups opposed the nativists. Big industrialists, interested in the free influx of cheap labor, hindered the efforts to curtail immigration, their organizations, especially the National Association of Manufacturers, continually lobbied in Washington against the restrictions. Effective opposition was organized among the immigrant ethnic groups themselves. Although the literacy test bill was clearly intended for use against immigrants from Southern and Eastern Europe, it aroused the opposition of every immigrant group. However, it was the newest groups of immigrants, especially the Russian Jews, who protested against it most vehemently and steadfastly. The National Liberal Immigration League, which functioned under Russian Jewish leadership, did much in 1906 and the years following to organize resistance to the demand for a literacy test.[10] Important organizations of old immigrant groups, such as the Ancient Order of Hibernians and the German-American Alliance, were also opposed to any kind of restriction of immigration (e.g., during the 1907 campaign).[11] Their protest carried a great deal of weight, since, as their members were moving into the middle class, their support had become important to the political parties. And naturally their vote went to the political party that promised to support their special interests. The Republican Party, which for over a decade had demanded the restriction of immigration, dropped it from its platform between 1904 and 1913. Accordingly, during these years, the Italian, Slavic, and Jewish voters were more inclined to vote Republican than Democrat.

During the twenty years preceding World War I, movements to restrict immigration had little effect upon the shaping of immigration laws and regulations. Although Congress kept enlarging the list of those not to be admitted to the United States, these restrictions did not affect the foundation and real framework of free immigration. For example, the law of 1891 prohibited the entrance of paupers, polygamists, and people with venereal and infectious diseases. Then, in 1903, exclusion was extended to epileptics, prostitutes, and professional beggars. And when the anarchist Leon Czolgosz assassinated President McKinley, the list was further extended to include anarchists and persons who might want to overthrow the government of the United States. Imbeciles, tuberculars, criminals, and the morally unfit were added to the list in 1917.[12]

With the growth of the list of exclusions, the entrance tax also grew from fifty cents to four dollars between 1882 and 1907. In addition, there were new measures for the stricter supervision of the immigrants. In 1891 immigration was placed under the authority of the federal government. The laws became more strictly enforced, although really effective supervision of the immigrants was practically impossible. The authorities were unable to examine thoroughly the ever-swelling crowds that arrived at the harbors. Immigrants who thought they could not pass inspection came to the United States through Canada.

The opponents of immigration, seeing that the series of mild regulations had hardly stemmed the tide, were not pacified. The greater success of their campaign against admitting Chinese immigrants was no adequate compensation. In fact, in 1902, the United States temporarily suspended Chinese immigration. Of course this did not stop the Chinese entirely, as many of them entered illegally through Mexico. However, the hatred they encountered and the various discriminatory measures taken against them compelled many of the Chinese to return home. On the West Coast, the protest against Japanese immigration also grew in intensity after the turn of the century. The labor organizations led the actions taken against both the Chinese and the Japanese immigrants, charging that cheap Chinese and Japanese labor endangered the living standard of American workers.

The anti-Japanese hysteria at the beginning of the twentieth century is an important chapter in the history not only of the West Coast. West Coast anxieties over the loss of white supremacy were the preliminary to a wholesale attack on the new immigrants. Racist feelings aroused by the "yellow peril" and belief in Anglo-Saxon racial superiority—strengthened by imperialism and justified by the new immigrants' difficulties in adapting—all favored the spread of the nativist point of view. Among the New England patricians and intellectuals, racial theories grew into uniform ideology, as the romantic cultural nationalism of the earlier period gave way to biological determinism. The development of European natural sciences provided additional ammunition for this theory, along with Darwin's theory of natural selection and the development of modern genetics—especially in its emphasis on inherited characteristics, traits that were beyond the environment's power to change. Belief in genetic determinism is expressed in the works of the social scientists writing at this time on the question of immigration. For example, in 1906, John R. Commons stated that even in America the immigrants could hardly overcome the handicaps of their heritage.[13] And Edward A. Ross spoke of the southeastern European immigrants as the "beaten members of beaten breeds."[14] Both relied in their theorizing on a work entitled *The Races of Europe* (1899), by the economist William Z. Ripley. He introduced Americans to the concept of physical anthropology, which divided the peoples of Europe into the Northern or Teutonic race and the Southern or Mediterranean race, each with its separate and unchangeable physiological characteristics. Nevertheless, in spite of the enormous quantity of effective nativist theory, the time for restricting immigration on racial grounds came only after World War I.

All the above notwithstanding, the racist content of early-twentieth-century nativist theory should not be overestimated. The new racial ideology was peculiar to a handful of intellectuals. Organized labor, which, by the first decade of the century, was steadfastly demanding the restriction of immigration, gave primarily social and economic reasons for its concern. The AFL's support of the literacy test after 1906 was the expression of opposition by trained, skilled workers to the widespread employment of untrained immigrants. The coal miners of Pennsylvania rejected Italian, Magyar, and Polish workers by arguing that they were members of an inferior, servile class, and that their presence neutralized efforts to win better wages and working conditions. It was these arguments that economists and a growing number of labor leaders transformed into a more general call to defend "the American way of life."[15] They demanded a selective immigration policy: in other words, that only those people be admitted who could rise to the living standards of the American workers. Otherwise, the native American living standards were in jeopardy.

Similar thinking prevailed among the members of the United States Immigration Commission, which sent delegates to the countries of Eastern Europe—to Hungary among others—to study conditions there and the causes and circumstances of mass emigration, including the governments' emigration policies.[16] The inspectors of the Bureau of Immigration were not unprincipled agents of some nativist preconception: they explained emigration from Hungary and the Monarchy by pointing to the poverty of the country and the backwardness of the economy. They did not present the immigrating masses as "races." It is sad—as Tibor Frank emphasized—that Senator Dillingham's congressional report of 1907–1911 did not consider their judgment.[17] Marcus Braun, inspector of the New York Immigration Authority, and members of the Dillingham Commision traveled to Hungary within the framework of this program.[18] Between 1907 and 1911, the Immigration Authority organized a comprehensive research project to collect statistics on the circumstances of the various immigrant groups. When submitted to Congress, their findings filled forty-two volumes, more than half of which contain information about the economic effects and results of immigration.[19] Comparing the various ethnic groups between 1899 and 1909, they tried to document the qualitative differences between the "old" imigrants and the "new." The western and northern Europeans made up the former group, southern and eastern Europeans the latter. Their report showed that the proportion of men, of skilled workers, and of the illiterate was higher among the new immigrants, and that the majority of them did not intend to stay permanently in the United States. They gave a detailed report of the role of the shipping companies and the emigration that had developed in the countries of southern and eastern Europe, especially in the Austro-Hungarian Monarchy and Russia.[20] They also listed the data giving statistical proof of the new immigrants' unfavorable classification. The commission was much concerned with the Magyars and with the immigrants from Hungary. The fact that after the turn of the century the Austro-Hungarian Monarchy had become one of the centers of emigration had drawn attention to the country, as had the press campaign waged by the competing shipping companies, to say nothing of the ensuing diplomatic complications.

The commission recommended further restriction of immigration in its "Brief Statement of the Conclusions and Recommendations of the Immigration Commission, 1910."[21] Its recommendation, however, was based not so much on racial prejudice, but rather on the consideration that the admission of foreigners must promote the economic and business interests that guaranteed American prosperity. According to the Dillingham Commission, the new immigrants were less skilled than the old, were motivated by economic considerations rather than political idealism, and were uncommitted to staying in America. The investigators also repeated the standard charges that the recent arrivals drove old-stock citizens out of some lines of work, undermined unions, resisted assimilation, and were inclined toward violent crime.

Whatever the considerations that convinced the members of the commission of the undesirable nature of the new immigrants, the fact is that they recommended the introduction of the literacy test as of utmost necessity for the immediate restriction of immigration. However, six more years had to pass before the commission's recommendation became law. The groups favoring restrictive immigration were able to get enough Congressional support to override the President's second veto only on the eve of World War I.

One of the founders of the science of modern anthropology, Franz Boas (1858–1942), received permission to do research with his team "regarding the physical traits of various races" at the immigration station of Ellis Island in New York.[22] In earlier research Boas had compared anthropometrical data on the Polish with that of the Czech, Hungarian and Slovak immigrants. In summary he stated: "The Czechs, the Slovaks and the Hungarians as well as the Poles, all of whom represent the Central-European type, show the same changes. The America-born descendants of this type show a growth in tallness, and both the length and the broadness of their head diminish."

Boas discussed the anthropometry of immigrants' children in detail for the first time in perhaps his best-known book, *Kultur und Rasse* (Culture and Race), issued in Leipzig in 1914. European readers could hear of the large-scale research in New York for the first time from this book, which later was published in many languages in many editions. As final explanation for the bodily changes, Boas pointed to the plasticity of the human types, and suggested that circumstances can influence the mental faculty even more than the bodily.[23]

Progressive scholars of the history of immigration, especially in the 1970s, have already pointed to the Immigration Commission's prejudicial handling of the data and the forced comparisons made in order to draw the desired conclusions. They have noted, too, the commission's failure to consider that the various phases of emigration from different countries took place at different times, and that there were changes in the immigrants' social composition and skills during the various phases of mass emigration. Indeed, the commission gave a synchronic comparison of all groups, disregarding the fact that these groups were then passing through different migratory phases. Sexual distribution, too, as we have seen, depended on when the given ethnic group had joined the stream of international migration; at the beginning of mass emigration, the proportion of men was always greater than in later phases. The situation is similar when we look at the immigrants' distribution by skills: at the peak of mass migration the number of unskilled peasants was always greater in every ethnic group than in the first phase, or after the peak of the migratory wave. As for the "temporary" nature of the new immigrants' stay, the revolution in transportation which had shortened to about ten days the two or three months' sailing of yore, to say nothing of the significant reduction of fares that the steamships had brought, created a basis for seasonal migration the like of which had been a technological impossibility in earlier periods.

The immigration policy of the United States before World War I, in spite of a growing number of limitations, was essentially an "open door" policy created by the demands for cheap labor for a rapidly expanding industry. The only source of this cheap labor was the mass of unskilled immigrants of peasant background, men willing to take on the most strenuous, the most physically demanding jobs, jobs that no American worker was willing to do. The immigrant peasant and worker masses of Central and Eastern Europe accelerated the social mobility of the native Americans. Their presence on the job market freed native manpower from the inferior jobs.[24] Thus, the children of the earlier immigrants could move more easily up on the social and occupational ladder, where, forgetting their parents' past, they looked down on the newcomers with considerable distaste. For the time being, economic and social interests pushed the growing hostility to the newcomers into the background, but the tensions that crystallized in the debates about immigration foreshadowed the future, the selective admission of immigrants. At this time, the native population expressed its anxieties by isolating the newcomers. Separate and secure behind its wall of prejudice, it could look down with the superiority of the insider. There can be no doubt that the social atmosphere around the new immigrants was frozen.

Fortunately—as we will learn—most of them were still so tied to the old country, lived their lives so much within their own ethnic groups, that little came through to them from the opinions formed about them, and if some of it did, the effect was mitigated by its having come from a foreign source.

PART TWO

THE FORMATION OF HUNGARIAN ETHNIC COMMUNITIES FROM 1880 TO THE 1920s

CHAPTER 9

Settlement Patterns

They come en masse,
a million,
their hope: treasures
their dream: wealth
barely able to keep body and soul together
they turn up
one in a mine, the other in a factory
silent
throughout the years.

Cities arise
in their footsteps, the flow of waters,
they beat into dams[1]

WHAT FORCES SHAPED the Hungarian immigrants' patterns of settlement, distribution, and grouping in the United States? Can we identify reciprocal influences between the migrant status of the workers and their settlements' locations and types? Were their communities characterized by continuity or constant reorganization? This chapter, by unfolding the development of the immigrants' wanderings and settlements, attempts to answer some of these questions.

Friends and acquaintances in the villages often began their long journey together. But even lone travelers found companions en route, on the train or at the seaports. Generally, the agents of the shipping companies organized the migrants into groups for segments of the trip and directed them to ports. The traditional route for emigrants to the United States was through Bremen and

Hamburg, in the ships of the Norddeutscher Lloyd or its subsidiary, the Missler Agency. The agents supplied the travelers with written directions and practical signs, and most migrants took a relative's or good friend's American address with them as well.

In transporting emigrants from Hungary, a leading role was played among the seaports by two cities of the German Empire, Hamburg and Bremen. (Nearly two-thirds, 62.7 percent, of the migrants embarked from those two ports.) Opened in 1904, the Cunard-Hungarian line (Fiume) also handled considerable passenger traffic until World War I. In 1910, Fiume was first among all the seaports as a point of departure for its emigrants from Hungary. The Cunard ships were not able to take on board everyone who wanted to go and the Adria, which worked in its stead, rerouted a large number of passengers to other lines.[2]

The steamships crossed the ocean with much greater safety and speed than the sailing ships that had transported the Western European emigrants.[3] Nevertheless, numerous personal accounts describe the hardships of the voyage, especially the overcrowded conditions, frequent illnesses, and other discomforts of the third-class or steerage accommodations. The more fortunate crossed the ocean in ten days, but those less so were stranded, sometimes for weeks, at a station or seaport. The Hungarian authorities added to the confusion from 1904 on, when they attempted to divert all the emigrants to the port of Fiume (at this time a Hungarian seaport) to ensure passengers for the Cunard Steam Ship Line.[4]

Local authorities required emigrants to buy their tickets only from licensed shipping companies. At the same time, Cunard did not send enough ships to transport the emigrants who had been driven to Fiume. To increase the attraction of Fiume, the MÁV (Hungarian National Railroads) gave a 50 percent reduction for groups of ten passengers. Tickets bought from other shipping companies or sent from the United States were confiscated.[5]

At the threshold of the New World, the immigrant masses, frightened and exhausted by the long journey, were placed under strict inspection by the American authorities at Ellis Island. Despite their confidence and hope, the question "Will I be allowed in?" filled them with fear. There always were some, if only a few, who were rejected on the basis of the immigration laws and mandatory health examinations.[6]

The majority passed through the sieve of the immigration authorities and continued their journeys for days by rail. Those in charge directed them to the correct routes based on the addresses and information pinned to their clothes by the agents who had recruited them to work in the United States or by their more experienced fellow countrymen. Some migrants had paid toll collectors just for providing these directions.

Since the first to make the long trip from Hungary were the Jews, Germans, and Slovaks, the first Hungarian neighborhoods in the United States were linked to them. Hungarians followed in their footsteps and joined forces with them on the East Coast, primarily in the states of Pennsylvania, New York, and New Jersey, as well as in Ohio. On Ellis Island, 80 percent of the Hungarians declared those four states as their journey's goal in the 1910s.[7]

The social background and the motivations of the later emigrants differed from those of the pioneers of labor migration, who from the 1870s on started to appear in New York, Cleveland, Bridgeport, Connecticut; and other places. Individuals came at first, but groups came from the turn of the century on. Craftsmen, merchants, and miners were the pioneers, the first links of the migration chain, which became a mass movement with the participation of the peasants and especially the agrarian proletariat.

The first groups of Magyars, along with Slovaks, settled in Pittsburgh and its environs, as well as in both smaller and larger mining settlements. The Slovaks clustered primarily in Pittsburgh and its vicinity, and their influx into the area became a mass movement in the 1880s. At that time the mines and the steel mills commissioned the German Missler Shipping Agents Company to recruit cheap manpower in Hungary. As a result, Hungarians were scattered throughout Pittsburgh, living near their workplaces. According to general belief, the majority lived in the nearby cities of Homestead, Duquesne, McKeesport, McKees Rocks, and Bellevue, and their main place of employment was the Carnegie iron- and steelworks in Homestead.[8] Outside the Pittsburgh area, Pennsylvania's Hungarians worked in relatively greater numbers in Bethlehem and Johnstown. In the latter town they were employed in the Cambriel Steel Company's mills and mines, as well as in the Camoria Steel Company's steel plants and brick factories. The largest concentration of ethnic Magyars in Pennsylvania, however, was found in Philadelphia; by 1920 it numbered 8,060 persons, of whom 4,767 were immigrants. For the most part, they were industrial and skilled workers.

By far the most populous and relatively most isolated Hungarian peasant workers' settlement in the United States developed in Cleveland, Ohio. In the early 1850s a few artisan and merchant families of Jews, Germans, and Slovaks from Hungary arrived in the city. In the 1880s ethnic Magyars joined them in increasing numbers until, by the 1920s, the Magyars represented the largest ethnic group among the immigrants from Hungary. There were then 97,962 immigrant Magyars, of whom 55,874 were living in Cleveland. Cleveland's Hungarian immigrant population rose from 9,558 to 43,134 by 1920. Hungarians constituted 8 percent of the city's foreign-born population in 1900, and 18 percent in 1920.[9]

Various forms of chain-migration had developed as the appeal of Cleveland became apparent to masses of Hungarians. In 1879 and 1880 most of them came from one county, Abauj, specifically from the villages of Buzita, Csécs, and Göncz.[10]

Although pioneers also came from other parts of the country, such as Sopron County, immigrants from Abauj County became the real founders of Cleveland's Hungarian neighborhoods. The fever that spread from this northern migration center, through kinship and friendly relations, to other parts of Hungary gave rise to other smaller and larger emigration centers. From 1874 to 1900, twelve thousand immigrants from Hungary were registered in Cleveland.[11] Undoubtedly, their actual numbers were even greater, as their geographical mobility made registration rather difficult. Those, for example, who had started working in the mines of West Virginia or Ohio and had arrived in the city on foot or by train were likely omitted from the count.

The Magyars worked for the National Malleable Castings Company, later calling it the "old" factory among themselves. The "new" factory, the Eberhardt Manufacturing Company, which made iron parts for agricultural implements, automobiles, heaters, kitchen ranges, and railway cars, recruited most of its workers from the Hungarian immigrants. In addition to those two factories, the immigrants worked in the rubber industry. Young women also worked by the hundreds in garment factories and in the city's business district, while skilled industrial workers were employed in many locations.

On the West Side of Cleveland, another Hungarian neighborhood developed. Much smaller than the one on the East Side, it also was much less isolated ethnically. Those who congregated on the West Side, for the most part, had worked as skilled craftsmen in Hungary, whereas settlers on the East Side were former agricultural workers, now laborers in the large factories. The West Siders "did not adhere as much to their national individualities. They had approached the immigrants from northwestern Europe with much greater ease, and lived in this section of Cleveland together with Germans and Czechs."[12]

One of the chief centers of Hungarian immigrants developed in New York City. Hungarian Jews lived here in large numbers. In New York, more than anywhere else, they were tradesmen, workers employed by tradesmen, and those providing personal services, such as maids, barbers, and waiters. Relatively few were factory workers, while even fewer were simple day laborers or former agricultural workers reluctantly compelled for a few years to become modern factory workers.[13] The Hungarian middle-class element also was most strongly represented in New York. Adapting to their surroundings with difficulty, they were most diligent in protecting their Hungarian characteristics.[14]

In 1890, there were 15,598, and in 1910, there were 96,813 individuals of various nationalities originating from Hungary in New York State. The 1920 census placed the number of immigrants in the state claiming Magyar as their mother tongue at 45,833, the overwhelming majority of them in New York City. The "Hungarian quarter" developed in the area bounded by Houston and Fourteenth Streets, Second Avenue, and the East River. It was named Gulyas Avenue after the favored dish of the Hungarian restaurants and taverns that were the meeting places of the New York Hungarians. Manhattan, with 29,977, was the central settlement of the Hungarian Jews.[15]

From Cleveland the Hungarians often migrated to the steel mills on the south side of Lorain, Ohio. Here, fairly early, they began to build "characteristically Hungarian, barrel roofed little houses," as the steel companies bought up some of the plots of land around their plants and resold them to the Hungarians to ensure a permanent workforce.[16] The 1920 census listed 4,210 inhabitants of Lorain with Magyar as their native language.

A significant Hungarian settlement also developed in Toledo, Ohio. According to a contemporary account, the closed settlement type with its "true Hungarian type houses, barrel-roofed with small gardens of rosemary are unique."[17] From 1891 on, after the National Malleable Castings Company built a large factory on the banks of the Maumee River, Hungarians slowly began to arrive in the city. The first immigrants, who arrived from the counties of Abauj, Heves, and Gömör, tried to settle together on Toledo's northeast side in the Birmingham district.[18] At first the Hungarian section consisted of approximately eighty houses and stood on a street without even a trace of a sidewalk. The overcrowded conditions of the boarding houses attested that "there were so many tenants in the houses, that it would have been impossible to squeeze more in even with a press."[19]

The first Hungarian in Youngstown, Ohio, arrived with Louis Kossuth, who was invited to visit this city on his American trip. From the 1880s on, more workers began to accept jobs in the steel mills. Their numbers had probably grown into the hundreds by the turn of the century. In 1900, a Hungarian banker and shipping agent moved into the city; with great vigor he negotiated the employment of Hungarians for the industries in Youngstown and Campbell (East Youngstown), Ohio, and Sharon, Pennsylvania, and organized their settlements. In 1907, an article in the *Szabadság Naptár* entitled "American Hungarian Settlements" estimated the number of Hungarian immigrants there at several thousand. The 1920 census counted 3,584 Magyars living near Youngstown in the settlements of Niles and Hubbard, Ohio, and New Castle, Pennsylvania, from which they commuted to work in the steel mills.

The Dayton Malleable Iron Works initiated the Hungarian settlement in Dayton, Ohio, in 1897, when it imported a foreman (János Liszák) from Toledo and entrusted a Hungarian merchant (J. D. Moskowitz) with the organization and leadership of a Hungarian settlement near its factory. The settlement, established with factory-owned houses on the east side of the city, was called Kossuth Colony. Only immigrants from Hungary were housed there, and the inhabitants had to shop exclusively at the company shops. Even their movement was limited, for their neighborhood, like those of slaves, was fenced in and guarded.[20] In Dayton the native-born Americans did not welcome the Hungarian "foreigners." However, the factory owners, seeing the possibilities of exploiting their workforce, preferred to hire them. Similarily in Columbus, Ohio, organized action established the small, more closed form of Hungarian settlement. There also a Hungarian immigrant merchant (Sándor Gál) recruited the immigrants, who were mostly from Transylvania and who settled primarily around Parsons Avenue.

On the East Coast, after the turn of the century, New Jersey became a center of the Hungarian immigrants. In 1890 those born in Hungary numbered 3,477; by 1910 there were 47,610; and by 1920, counting only those with Magyar as their mother tongue, there were 59,190 in the state. Numerically, their largest settlement was in Perth Amboy, where opportunities for work were available in the iron, wire, and copper industries, as well as in the cigar and chemical factories. In 1920 most Hungarian immigrants in Trenton worked in the Roebling wire factories. They were estimated at several thousand in number and were called "wire drawers" in the Hungarian-American vernacular.[21] The other large Hungarian colony in New Jersey developed in Passaic, where the rubber, wool, textile, silk, and oilcloth industries utilized female labor. Consequently, of those Hungarians who migrated there in the 1910s, 75 percent were young women. In New Brunswick the Hungarians were employed by the tanneries and by the cigar, tin, rubber, button, and paper industries and, later, by the ever-growing Johnson & Johnson chemical factories.[22] By 1920 there were 5,278 Hungarians living in New Brunswick and 4,399 in Perth Amboy.

One of the oldest and relatively most populated communities was formed in Bridgeport, Connecticut. Before World War I, it ranked third after New York and Cleveland for having the most Hungarians. They worked in the iron and machine factories, for the Automatic Machine Company, and for the Gramophone Company.[23] The Hungarians of this fairly populous settlement played an active role in the establishment of nationwide Hungarian-American organizations.

The western frontier of Chicago and its surrounding areas had already been sought out by adventurous Hungarian pioneers in the nineteenth century, as several families of refugees from the Revolution of 1848 had settled there. Along with New York, this was a city where the social strata and the background of the Hungarian immigrants were diversified from the very beginning. There was generally a larger number of merchants, small shop owners, skilled industrial workers, and intelligentsia among them.

The Hungarians settled mainly in South Chicago among various other nationalities, so the sources do not note isolated Hungarian quarters or streets. Those immigrants who came from a peasant background did not settle in the city; instead, they went to the outlying factory areas, with most working in the Illinois Steel Company's enormous steel mill.[24] In the West Pullman district, immigrants from Transylvania, Nagyida, and the county of Abauj worked in the machine factories and the iron foundry. Many of them settled in Burnside near the factories there. In Joliet the Hungarians were employed in the steel and cable factories and at the blast furnace. In Chicago in 1890, the census noted 1,818 immigrants from Hungary, and by 1910, it counted 28,938.

The only large settlement in Indiana developed in South Bend. By the 1910 census, 1,737 Hungarians lived there. In 1891 agents of the shipping lines had taken the news of South Bend's auto, plow, and sewing machine factories to the community of Hidkő, Sopron County, and quoted the possibilities of such high wages that they created a migration fever in the small town. Among those Hungarians already in America an increasing number likewise started toward the plow factory, swelling the population in the city's Hungarian district. In the census of 1920, there were 5,290 ethnic Magyars. Most were employed in the factories of Oliver plow, Studebaker auto, Singer sewing machine, Bridsell thresher, and Kennedy plow.[25]

Foremen of the Michigan Malleable Iron Works in Detroit, hearing that the best workers in the Toledo foundries were Hungarians, began to lure them to their own factories. From Pennsylvania and West Virginia, at the time of the great strikes when a number of coal mines were closed, workers migrated to Detroit. Later the Detroit factories also transferred workers from Cleveland. In 1920 the census already showed 13,564 people in Detroit claiming Hungarian as their mother tongue, but the decade after that was the main period of development of the city's Hungarian district known as Delray. The migration of Hungarians started rather late to the nearby city of Flint; they began to come around 1910 with the rapid development of the auto industry. The first immigrants settled along St. John Street, in the area of the Buick and Chevrolet factories, and two new streets in the rapidly growing city received Hungarian names: Apponyi and Károlyi.[26]

The occupation of agriculture was insignificant among the Hungarian immigrants, barely 1 percent of them having been attracted by it. In the census of 1920 the number of farm owners and workers was 7,122, which indicates that no more than about 2,000 families worked the soil throughout the forty-eight states.

Those immigrants who established the first Hungarian agricultural settlements in Canada embarked on their journey there from the United States. From the 1880s on, the Canadian government sent agents to the United States to recruit settlers for the cultivation of the territories of western Canada. These settlers were drawn from those new immigrants who wanted to escape a hostile American atmosphere, the persecutions of the native-born American workers, unfamiliar industrial work, and the hot furnaces of the iron and steel industries or the darkness of the mines. The recruiting agents led them to Saskatchewan with the promise of 160 acres of free land, good productive soil, and sunny meadows. There they became the pioneers of the agricultural settlements of Kaposvár (1886) and Békevár (1890s).[27]

The unhospitable natural environment and hard living conditions encountered in the taming of the wilderness forced a number of the Canadian migrants to go back to the United States. Those who did not want to go back to the mines under any circumstances established the only comparatively large Hungarian agricultural settlement in the United States. Named Árpádhon (Árpád's Homeland), it was organized near New Orleans, Louisiana, between Albany and Springfield in Livingston Parish, by two Hungarian settlement agents with the collaboration of officials of the Louisiana Bureau of Colonization and Land Company. They offered the Hungarian migrants employment at the nearby sawmill at $1.15 per day and twenty acres of land for $200, which could be paid in installments over five years.[28] The population grew slowly as others straggled in after the original twenty families, and in 1904 a new settlement action drew sixty families into the circle. Those familiar with Árpádhon state that in the 1910s and 1920s, close to two hundred Hungarian families built houses there. They specialized in raising strawberries, which they sold under the name "Hungarian strawberry."[29]

Other experiments in agricultural settlements are chronicled in contemporary Hungarian-American newspapers. For example, four immigrants from Bodrogköz, who had been involved in grape agriculture in Hungary, in 1894 established Buda, an agricultural settlement in Georgia, for the purpose of cultivating *tokaj* grapes. Twenty-three families were working there by 1896; however, they soon wandered away and established short-lived little colonies of their own named Nyitra, Tokaj, Fordhouse, and, later, Budapest.

Often the establishment of agricultural colonies fell into the hands of swindlers. A typical example of fraud occurred in 1910 and plunged about fifty Hungarian immigrant families into a desperate position. At that time a Hungarian "landowner" whose real name was Gusztáv Weber appeared in New York City, spending money about and talking of his enormous estate, "Balaton Plantation" in Florida. He claimed to be willing to sell part of his land to Hungarian immigrants purely out of patriotism. A clever confidence man, he created a board of better-known Hungarians, whom he entertained on his bogus orange plantation. They, in turn, gave very positive accounts to the Hungarian-American newspapers about the Florida settlement. When some fifty families responded to the tempting offers, the "landowner" transported them to Florida. But after he received an advance payment of $150 per person, he disappeared without a trace. The Hungarians had to turn to the consulate and the Hungarian newspapers for help in obtaining the price of transportation out of Florida. Warrants and complaints lodged against Weber were futile; the land in question was not even his.[30]

There are literally hundreds of industrial and mining settlements outside of the cities where Hungarian migrants turned up and worked, particularly in the states of West Virginia and Pennsylvania. Often they were the first inhabitants of hastily built shantytowns alongside the newly constructed factories and newly opened mines. It was so in West Virginia, where the immigrants from the village of Szamosszeg were recruited for the newly opened mines in the town of Holden.

The name of New Brunswick, a small city in New Jersey, has become rooted in Szamosszegean tradition. Consequently, at the beginning of my research, I believed that I would be able to track down nearly everyone there. Although a series of systematic interviews revealed that New Brunswick always played an important role as a destination for Szamosszegeans, at the beginning of emigration the majority of the men tried to go to Holden, West Virginia. New Brunswick's preeminence only came about in the late 1920s.

"In the beginning almost everybody went to West Virginia—to Holden—to work in the mine," reported the old people in the village.[31] The development of this small mining site began in 1904 with the opening of the coal mine there. It was through the work of labor-recruiting agents that the first Szamosszegeans came to Holden from another mining settlement in Cheswick, Pennsylvania. At that time, Holden consisted only of the makeshift wooden shanties that those who had cleared the forest had left behind them.

Gusztáv, one of the members of the first group that arrived, recalled:

> There was no railway across the mountains to Holden; thus we arrived in a wagon pulled by mules, on which we had packed everything we owned. When we arrived, there was nothing there; it was impossible to buy anything. The men at first had to work in the open, building a road to make us accessible. About six months later the railroad reached us. By then the mine was already opened. My father and my elder brother Kálmán were only two of those from Szamosszeg who worked in the mine; later more came from the village. There was absolutely no mechanization. The generating plant was only barely begun. They situated us in some kind of shack—it consisted of boards held together by tar paper. And it was so cold! This was a wilderness. The women did not like living there. No one liked it, but it was impossible to leave. The wages were very good, but there was nothing to spend them on. Later the farmers came. In the beginning they were afraid to come. They were afraid of us. But then they sold us vegetables, flour, poultry, and eggs. Later when the company houses were built, all of us had cows and pigs.[32]

In the first decade of the century, one or two hundred Slovak and Hungarian migrant workers turned up in every soft coal mining settlement in Pennsylvania. The majority after a longer or shorter period moved on, but there were settlements where the immigrant generation settled down permanently.

Characteristics of Hungarian Settlements

"Hungarian America," little settlements scattered throughout a broad diaspora, developed within the framework of the industrial United States. Not even 1 percent of those living in these small colonies were drawn to agriculture. As a result of industry's dynamic development, changing workforce demands, the migrants' intention of staying only temporarily, and the difficulties of adapting, these settlements took on specific characteristics. They were not as isolated ethnically, nor were they as large as those of the Western European immigrants who arrived earlier. The migrant workers' lifestyle scattered them geographically, and the Hungarians always were a numerically small group within the total population of either a region or city. There was not a single city in which they were in the majority. Even in their largest and ethnically most homogeneous settlement, Cleveland, Ohio, they did not pass the 10 percent mark in the 1910s.[33]

According to American observers, the settlements of the "new immigrants" characteristically formed in those outskirts of large cities that were the "slums." This generalization also applies to the Hungarians, although by no means to such a large extent. At the turn of the century, the U.S. census counted close to 50 percent of them in "rural non-farm" areas, and by the 1910 census, 35 percent of their numbers appeared in the "rural non-farm" category.

The period during which the Hungarians immigrated and their social background influenced the direction of their migrations and the types and forms of their settlements. It was primarily the tradesmen and merchants, as well as the small number of intelligentsia and those who had gone down in the world, who strove for New York, Chicago, and the West Side of Cleveland. By contrast, it was the peasant migrants' socially more homogeneous groups that appeared on the periphery of the industrial cities and in the mining settlements. The immigrants of non-peasant background more easily blended their residences with those of other nationalities, whereas those who came from the peasantry endeavored to remain near one another in settlements which, no matter how small, were ethnically more isolated.

Rigid walls were built not between the habitations of the various nationalities arriving from Hungary, but between the "foreign settlements" and those of the native-born Americans. The former were built in the poorer areas of the cities on the industrial periphery, distant from the dwellings of the native-born Americans.

The seed of the community—particularly in the beginning—was the circle of relatives and acquaintances who originated from the same region in Hungary. "Traditional" colonies developed in the United States where the immigrants from the various villages found one another. These, however, were continually kept in flux by the Hungarians' migrations back and forth across the ocean, as well as by their movements within the United States. When large factories and mining companies expanded, the chain of Hungarian settlements grew in their direction. The younger men in particular continually formed new groups and after receiving a few weeks' wages went from one region to the other. An early commentator writes that

> they came, went, migrated here, there, in the hopes of better work and better pay. Of course, often they were disappointed: they left the certain for the uncertain because every move brought a loss; in the new place they didn't get a job and had to go further. They went sometimes on foot, sometimes by train, scrounging a ride in an empty coal wagon or riding on the top of a wagon filled with coal. When they arrived at their goal after a few hundred miles they were as black as the gypsies, even brother didn't recognize brother, the good friend his friend. They were washed by rain, dried by wind and sun, squeezed by hunger, and the tunnel and railroad bridges cut their bodies down. In the conquering of the new home many lost their lives; those who remained continued until they got stuck, prepared a nest and began a family or brought their loved ones over from home. Those who did not settle down roamed until they received satisfactory pay and after saving money for a few years went back home.[34]

Numerous similar accounts of the immigrants' wanderings can be read in the contemporary Hungarian-American newspapers, and are documented by data on individual lives. For example, information about 143 Hungarian miners from their workplaces shows that all of them worked on many different mine properties until in their old age they either settled in the United States or remigrated to their place of birth.[35]

An important incentive for the immigrants' wanderings was to earn money necessary to realize their dreams and accomplish their plans of returning home to their families within the shortest time possible, whatever hard work was necessary. In addition, contemporaries attributed their mobility to problems acclimating to the new and unfamiliar work conditions and strange environment. Contemporaries often mention the striking migratory fever of the sojourner "new immigrant" Hungarians that made them move about within the United States. We could read about this in the *Szabadság* paper:

> A good part of the Hungarians find their pleasure in the enrichment of the railroads. The Hungarian, who back home prepared for days before going to the market, thinks nothing of going a thousand miles to look for work. Any small excuse, for example the letter of a good friend, persuades them to leave for better work. Today he is in the New York area, the day after tomorrow he will be in Omaha. This is the reason for this epidemic, one can say traveling fever, which in America is in the air itself. However it all goes back to that the large part of our people do not want to become too comfortable with the conditions here, they do not feel at home here; however the immigrant does not want to go back home because he knows very well, that there he will not find in either work or in other circumstances those conditions without which he could no longer remain there permanently.[36]

The fluctuation of the population in the settlements, particularly in the beginnings, is striking. The territory in the United States that the Hungarians wandered through was primarily that of the six industrial states previously discussed, an area several times larger than that of the historical Hungary. The immigrants generally traveled in groups, whose composition was constantly changed by newly woven friendships and contacts. Thus, the Hungarian geographical background of each neighborhood took on a fairly diverse pattern with the passage of time.

It is important to consider whether the Hungarian immigrant settlements signify continuity or an uprooting that tore the inhabitants from their original communities and from the deeply felt intimate relationships that tied them to one another. Although Oscar Handlin writes about such immigrants as the victims of estrangement and alienation, other scholars emphasize how often those who emigrated from a village stayed together in the new environment and thus managed to recreate their original communities and keep their ethnicity constant. Referring to the example of Italian immigrants, historian Rudolph Vecoli first directed attention to this cohesiveness,[37] and he recently summarized the research his work has inspired: "The most remarkable finding of the new immigration studies is that migration customarily involved the transplanting of nuclear families and individuals. By the process of chain migration, particular

Old World sending communities became linked to particular New World receiv-ing communities, held together by shared familial, religious, and social bonds. Cultural maintenance and distinctiveness, not assimilation, were the end result. American society was, and remains, a pluralistic society."[38]

The new studies in immigration strongly emphasize connection and continu-ity with the sending communities in the formation of immigrant communities. However, from the composition of the Hungarian immigrants' settlements, it is not possible to emphasize either "rootlessness" or continuity. There were villagers, relatives, and friends who remained together, and those who scattered in the new environment. From the beginning, the geographical background of the emigrants was varied, and Paula Benkart, for one, emphasizes the conspicu-ous migrations of the Hungarian immigrants within the United States and the influence of this mobility on their communities.[39] To illustrate that even married couples remained mobile for a time after starting families in the United States, she cites the report of a Hungarian Protestant minister, who said that only one-third of the children confirmed by him before World War I lived at the time of their confirmation in the same city where they had been born. Groups of migrants were continually recreated by new places of work, new contacts and, not least, the conflicts among themselves. Their settlement pattern shows that the Hungarian communities that developed in the United States were not simply the results of transferring the original communities to other geographical locations. They were newly organized communities, the supporting pillars of which were the ties of a common fate, language, and homeland rather than the same village or region. Yet the cohesive role of the latter cannot be ignored.

CHAPTER 10

In the Coal Mines
and the Steel Mills

Work and Wages

MAGYAR IMMIGRANTS WERE to be found in every branch of industry where unskilled workers were employed, particularly in the coal mines and steel mills. In fact, the U.S. Immigration Commission estimated that by 1910, 40 percent were employed in the iron and steel industries and another 40 percent in the mines.[1]

Great advances were made in the production of steel after the 1890s as open-hearth furnaces and rolling mills doubled and even tripled the tonnage produced. The steel mills operated continuously, not only to reduce costs but also because the furnaces could not be allowed to cool off for fear of damaging them; they were kept burning even through extended work stoppages. The open-hearth furnaces, with capacities of from fifty to one hundred tons of molten steel, demanded continuous operation of the rolling mills to handle the production of ingots. As a result, after 1890 the twelve-hour shift was universal in pig iron production.[2]

The Carnegie Company introduced the twelve-hour day wherever possible, and after the strike of 1892, all rolling mills went to twelve-hour shifts. The lengthening of the working day also increased Sunday work as mills that used to begin rolling steel at 6 A.M. Monday now started at midnight, forcing the furnace men to go to work several hours earlier to prepare the steel. In 1907–08 most of Pittsburgh's steel mills were actively at work by 5 P.M. on Sunday.

Steel mills were so complex, however, that there was no uniform rule on working hours. In 1907 in the Carnegie steel works, an eight-hour day existed in the Bessemer department where the workers were exposed to the greatest heat; but just 120 of Carnegie's 17,000 employees worked in that department. The prevailing working day was twelve hours for skilled and unskilled workmen engaged in manufacturing and working steel. Although molders and machinists had a ten-hour day in theory, the machinists at times had to finish repair jobs that necessitated working without rest for twenty-four to thirty-six hours, or longer. The work week was six or seven days, with fourteen shifts from Sunday

119

morning to Sunday morning.[3] Steelmaking (as distinct from clerical) employees generally worked split shifts, alternating a week on the night shift with a week on the day shift. In some departments, such as in the blast furnaces, crews worked seven days out of seven.

Clearly documented differences in earnings in the statistical tables compiled by the U.S. Immigration Commission suggest discrimination prevailed in the workplace. The average annual income of foreign-born husbands was $371, compared to $511 for native-born husbands. One-half or more of husbands of all nationalities, except Slovenians and Russian Jews, earned less than $400. All the Hungarians, Slovaks, and Slovenians surveyed did not have one husband earning as much as $1,000, but among Czechs, Moravians, and foreign-born Irish, there were some who had reached this wage level.[4] To be sure, the inability to speak English and the lack of even a modest education or relevant job experience condemned newcomers to the lowest rungs of the economic ladder. Most scholars agree, however, that discrimination added to the burdens of the new immigrants as they were the last hired, the first fired, and the most frequently laid off. They also had little success in advancing within the industries that employed them as they always were considered foreigners even if they learned English and gained job experience.

Unskilled laborers received 16 cents an hour for a ten- or twelve-hour day ($1.60 to $1.93 per day); the semiskilled, including both day and tonnage workers, earned $2.00 or $3.00 a day, and the skilled $2.50 to $5.00 with a small percentage earning more. Sixty hours or more was a common working week, making $10.50 per week the usual pay for an unskilled laborer.[5] This was so low that it barely met the official minimum cost of living in the United States.

Because of the arduous nature of the work, the Carnegie Steel Company directed all its superintendents not to hire anyone over forty in any department and in some departments to hire only men of thirty-five and under. On January 1, 1902, the American Steel and Wire Company decreed: "No inexperienced person over thirty-five years of age and no experienced person over forty-five years of age shall hereafter be taken into the employment of the company."[6] A provision for suspending this rule for special or professional services indicated that the management expected physical workers to deteriorate at an earlier age than professional employees.

While the steel mills paid an hourly wage, mining companies paid each worker on production. Miners—with peasant background—were not given the opportunity to master the more modern techniques of mining but were expected to dig as they had back home—with great physical exertion.[7] Men accustomed to task-oriented farmwork in sunny fields now went underground to monotonous work, under dangerous conditions. "Magyars were considered the most useful employees in mining coal and the North Italians were next in order of preference," stated one representative of the coal mine.[8] Some kept their nerve and strength and refused to compete with one another. Others were able to produce more and did so, happily and boastfully collecting "good money" and planning their departure back to the village where they would carry out their plans.[9] Those not capable of or dissatisfied with such great physical exertion migrated restlessly on, searching for better and easier possibilities.

Numerically and proportionately (84 percent), more miners in West Virginia lived in company towns than in any other state. In West Virginia company towns dominated the entire region. Upon moving into a company town, a miner had to live in a company house and sign a housing contract that the courts of West Virginia subsequently ruled, created a condition not of landlord and tenant, but of master and servant. Consequently the coal company was allowed to unreasonably search and seize a miner's house without any notice. "If we rent a miner a house, it is incidental to his employment, and if a miner would undertake to keep anyone at that home, that was undesirable or against the interest of the company, we would have him leave or have the miner removed."[10]

Through such migrations, they spread over the mining places of Pennsylvania and Ohio. Clusters of Szamosszegeans, for instance, were formed in two other West Virginia mining settlements besides Holden: Granttown, near Fairmont, and Dobra, south of Charleston. First, one Szamosszegean went from Holden to Granttown with a new friend. As one of his countrymen explained, he got tired of the hard coal *diggolás* and went to Granttown, where the mining work seemed easier.[11] Once there, he invited other Szamosszegeans from Holden—and also his brother-in-law and his wife from the village—to join him.[12] Other relatives followed later. Although we do not know who initiated the migration from Holden to Dobra, there already were a number of Szamosszegean families living in Dobra by World War I. During the movements between the three mining sites—Holden, Granttown, and Dobra—families sometimes separated, going their own ways to other mining settlements. With the opening and closing of mines, a few families were almost constantly moving from place to place.[13]

Standardized products were manufactured on a mass scale with wages based on piecework, which was extremely strenuous and very difficult for those unaccustomed to it. The struggling life of the Hungarian migrants inspired their poets and became the theme of short stories and poems.[14] But in the memory of the second generation, there is also a vivid recollection of how difficult, dirty, and hazardous to health their parents' factory jobs were and how ten- to twelve-hour working days wore down the young men physically. "My father always joined the family circle with tired body and soul, and the first thing he did was to put his aching feet into warm water."[15] As had been the case in the coal fields, many were unable to stay at a workplace for any length of time and wandered from one factory to the next, alternating between cities or between the mines and towns. "They tramped long distances from one town to the next looking for jobs on the railroads. Two young men met a horrible end when they walked from Detroit to Cleveland along the railroad. Close to the city a train ran them over."[16]

Unemployment was an additional serious problem faced by the low-paid immigrant workers. Long periods of joblessness shattered their dreams of saving money to return home, as their savings had to be spent on bare necessities. Frequent industrial accidents were another, still greater hazard for the immigrants, especially in the mines and steel mills. Mine accidents often claimed the lives of a large number of workers, many of them immigrants. One such was the accident in 1904 at Cheswick, Pennsylvania, in which fifty-eight Hungarians died. Yet more tragic was an explosion that killed 239 men and boys, many Hungarian immigrants, on December 19, 1907, in Darr coal mine near Van Meter. Some of the victims had come to that mine from the Naomi mine, near Fayette City, after it was closed on December 1 by an explosion that killed thirty-four miners. Over three thousand miners died in 1907, the worst year in United States coal mining history. In Olive Branch Cemetery, seventy-one Darr miners, forty-nine of them unidentified, are buried in a common grave.[17] The Magyar Calvinist minister of Pittsburgh issued a statement on this sad occasion:

> To Our Hungarian Brethren of Jacobs Creek and Vicinity:
>   It was pleasing to God's caring wisdom to put us through these trying times. In the past few days one mine explosion followed the other that caused the number of our widows and orphans to increase steadily. Because of the last explosion at Jakobs Creek, fifty Hungarian women and at least one hundred Hungarian children lost a bread-earner and an earthly caretaker. It is our Christian duty as members of the Hungarian ethnic community, to alleviate their sorrow as much as possible by giving them moral and financial support.
>   We also have duties and responsibilities toward those whose bodies they buried in common graves, unidentified due to the devastating fire, with no one grieving over them and no one praying or singing at their burial. Those missing miners and those buried in the common graves deserve to be buried as Christians. Therefore we summon all our Hungarian brethren and Hungarian organizations of Van Meter, Banning, Whittsett and vicinity to come to Jakobs Creek for a funeral service to be held at the common burialplace Saturday, January 4 at noon.[18]

These disasters illustrate the low esteem in which American society held the immigrant workers. Indeed, fourteen Hungarians who died in another industrial accident had complained about unsafe conditions, only to be told, "Never mind! There are many more Hungarians that will replace you!"[19] In all these accidents, neither the employers nor the states provided any compensation to the injured or to the orphans and widows of the deceased breadwinners. Instead, workers were on their own to arrange for sickness, disability, and death benefits through mutual aid associations.

Some occasional help was given, however, by the Austro-Hungarian Foreign Ministry, which launched a concentrated legal attack on American corporations whose disregard for immigrant safety was overburdening Europe with the migrant workers' widows, orphans, and elderly parents. Paula Benkart writes in her study that in 1910, Consul Ernest Ludwig from Cleveland engaged two lawyers who instituted nine civil suits on behalf of injured Buckeye Steel Casting Company employees in Columbus. They charged that hardly a day passed at the plant without some fatal or disabling accident. According to the consul, the factory posted no safety regulations to prevent these catastrophes, and when accidents did occur Buckeye paid no compensation to the maimed or the widow.[20] It was generally difficult to get valid evidence, as the workers were not willing to speak up in court for fear of losing their jobs. *Szabadság* also wrote about the cases and tried to convince the workers to speak up for themselves: "Those workers who can give information on the causes and details of the catastrophe should present themselves without delay at the consulate in Pittsburgh. They should not be afraid, they should tell the truth; the future lot of many fellow-countrymen depends on their testimony."[21]

The experiences of those who emigrated from the village of Szamosszeg show that the American labor market did not offer similar opportunities to unskilled or semiskilled men and women. In New Brunswick, where the tobacco and cigar factories and Johnson & Johnson's surgical-dressing factory based their production on female labor, the job opportunities attracted the young women from the village. Familiar with wagework at home, where they had worked in the fields as agricultural day laborers, the young women from Szamosszeg did not have an aversion to factory work. In any case, they viewed it as temporary. Most of them married in New Brunswick, sharing life in a single room, and then went on to West Virginia where the men worked in the mines. Those who remained in or returned to New Brunswick generally left work in the cigar factories, however, after their first child was born.

Julianna Szőgyény called up the memory of their migration to and from New Brunswick and a mine in West Virginia:

> I did not work in the cigar factory for long, as I had my daughter and left work for four weeks. Then when my son was born., I did not go back to work at all. When I first arrived to America I lived in New Brunswick for three years. Then we also went to Dobra, West Virginia, where there were a lot of people from Szamosszeg. Dobra was a mining place not far from Charlestown, a large city, down in the valley. My husband went to work in the mine as there was no work available in New Brunswick. There was no work, no earnings, my husband only got thirteen dollars for two weeks and there was the four of us to live on it, as there were two children. We paid fourteen dollars rent. There was no toilet in the house, there was nothing, no gas, only a kerosene lamp. It was no better than it used to be at home. I was sorry I came. It took me a long time to get accustomed to the life here.[22]

Just as men were lured by the piece rates of the mines of West Virginia and Pennsylvania, young girls were attracted by the opportunities of factory work in New Brunswick, prior to World War I. Piroska Puskás, a Szamosszegean in New Brunswick, recalled: "My father came first to New Brunswick; he had two brothers and two sisters-in-law here. Men could not get a job here, only women had an opportunity. By then, in 1914, a number of people from Szamossszeg were already in West Virginia, in Granttown. My father also went there."[23] Factory work was for the young; married women with childen generally stayed at home and supplemented their income by keeping boarders. This was particularily true if the husband went to the coalfields, where women could not find any other jobs.

Living Conditions

When a Hungarian neighborhood began to form in the 1880s on the East Side of Cleveland next to the Eberhardt factory, this part of the city was not yet developed. "Swamp oaks grew and frogs croaked. It was inadvisable to speak Hungarian on the street. At the best the speaker was considered a Tatar, and occasionally even stoned."[24] In Cleveland, Hungarians remember, "on lower Buckeye Road they struck tents, but on upper Buckeye Road they occupied houses."[25] By the turn of the century, however, Hungarians occupied the area from East Seventy-fourth Street to Ninety-second Street and the settlement had changed greatly.

> In those days there were neither lamps nor paving, we only had the all enveloping darkness and the never ending mud. Added to that was the deep contempt of the native born. Today a worker stretches his tired limbs out on a bed covered with quilts, then he was happy if he had somewhere to lay his head. Those first employed at the Eberhardt factory slept six to a bed with five or six under the table! There were few married Hungarians at whose house a Hungarian could lay his head in this strange land; the other nationalities wouldn't have taken them in even for a wagonload of gold.[26]

Information about the networks of religious and secular ethnic institutions and the growing Hungarian neighborhoods was provided at the beginning of the 1910s, by the Austro-Hungarian Consul in Cleveland:

> In terms of population Cleveland is second, but in characteristics it is the first Hungarian city. The East Side with its large territory is completely and purely Magyar. Hardly any other language can be heard and there are hardly any non-Magyar shops with Hungarian institutions, churches, schools, and associations all there together. This is where Hungarian customs are practiced most. The women are not ashamed to wear scarves [one on their head, one on their shoulders], and in the summer can be seen barefoot on the street; the men visibly remain greenhorns for a long time. The houses belong to Hungarians, Hungarian songs can be heard in the streets, and the newsboys announce the Hungarian news in Hungarian.[27]

As regards occupational mobility, in Cleveland they had to be satisfied mostly with blue-collar occupations, while in New York there were quite a few white-collar workers among them. Cleveland Hungarians, on the other hand, moved earlier than the New Yorkers to the outer districts of the city in order to enjoy less congestion and a greater opportunity to buy a house.

Boarding houses played a vital role in the immigrant community and as such are a part of their social history. They were the homes of from twenty to thirty men who usually slept in shifts. The boarding house also was a center of vice and a source of unlawfully naturalized voters for the agents of corrupt political parties as well as a gold mine for the squires and other lower police functionaries who preyed on the ignorant newcomers of the slum sections. At the same time the boarding house had a laudable side. The single man was with members of his own group who could help him in case of distress. He was part of a group in which he could talk over his personal problems as well as those of the group. The lonesomeness of a stranger, in a new environment with totally different cultural patterns, was dispelled. Conditions in the boarding houses have thus far received very scant study, though they often were portrayed by fiction writers in the immigrant press.[28]

According to the report of the Immigration Commission: "The Magyars had the largest proportion of families who add to their income by keeping boarders or lodgers, 53.4 percent of Magyar families having income from this source. Then follow the Poles with 42.7 percent, the South Italians with 40.5 percent, the Slovenians with 36 percent, the Slovaks with 34.6 percent, and the Irish with 10 percent." The comission reported further that "71.3 percent of Magyar wives earned wages, kept boarders, or did both. Of Magyar wives, 22.5 percent earned monetary income; of South Italian wives, 16.8 percent; and of Slovak, 14.6 percent."[29]

Many migrants who were married had left their wives and children in the old country, but not every marriage could withstand a separation that lasted for years. *Szabadság* dealt several times with this subject. For example, in the issue of September 10, 1910, we read, "Among the Hungarians in the United States the number of those who become involved in the crime of bigamy is very large, as they marry in the United States, in spite of the fact that they left a wife and child behind in the old country."[30]

Although this practice caused many problems in the United States, working away from the family in small groups and living in a common household did not represent an unknown way of life for the migrants. In Hungary when they had migrated to do seasonal agricultural work in other parts of the land, they had organized such communal households in order to save more of their meager earnings and create a "pseudo-family" to replace relatives left behind.[31] In those cases, one of the older women went along to run the household and make sure village behavioral norms were maintained. In the United States everyone was young and their village far away; but because they meshed an Old World precedent with the desire of American employers to quicken industrial expansion without investing in communal living facilities, the sometimes troublesome boarding houses flourished. Single people joined together in common households because living became cheaper that way. Similarly families kept boarders (*burdosok*), often combining this venture with selling liquor at home to augument their income. This phase of urbanization was so well covered up by later developments, however, that information about it often is unbelievable even to the immigrants' immediate descendants.

The children were forced into auxiliary work within the family or outside it. Living on the outskirts of town near woods and meadows the immigrants there, like those in the mining settlements, could pursue some of the traditional activities of a peasant household until the expansion of the adjacent city prohibited it. Trying as much as possible to produce what they consumed, they grew their vegetables in a garden next to the house and raised chickens and pigs—just as they did at the mining towns—or kept a cow or two and sold the products. Women and children regularly went by the railroad tracks to gather coal that had fallen off the cars to take home for fuel. "Mrs. Mihály Andrejkovics of Cleveland, as is usual in the Hungarian district, together with her women compatriots gathered coal on the railroad in her spare time and a steam-engine ran over her. She immigrated to America together with her husband and five children half a year ago," a newspaper tersely reported.[32]

For those living in mining settlements, many of the advantages of civilization that even their old villages possessed were nonexistent. Holden, West Virginia, had no doctor or midwife to assist in childbirths; the women had only each other. Nor was there a church or a priest to baptize children. The Kovács children were already several years old before their father was able to have a Hungarian minister brought into the community to baptize them.[33] These early difficulties in particular embittered and exhausted the women who had been in Holden from its beginnings. The Szamosszegeans in Holden packed themselves into boarding houses and tried to remain together as neighbors. Gusztáv Kovács who was taken there as a child in 1904, recalled: "They all lived right next to each other. Sunday morning they had a worship service at our house around the long table, which everyone had in those old houses; there they sang, after which my father said a prayer and read from the Bible. That was the worship service."

When a new arrival came from Szamosszeg they always gathered around to greet the newcomer and hear news from the village. They also gathered if one of them had an accident. The murder of one of the women caused a great panic. "Nobody went to work that day." Because the men frequently tried to escape the bleakness of their life by drinking, the women demanded the closing of the saloon, which had become the community's most popular meeting place. In some respects, the situation in Holden and other similar mining communities actually eased the transition from the Old World way of life to the new. The immigrants, for example, were able to continue farming to supplement their earnings in the mines.[34]

In Dobra we lived in a company house, recalled Julianna Szögyani. Every family got a four-room house and a large garden. It was easier there as rent was not high. For the coal we used in a month, the company deducted two dollars from the pay. We could keep poultry, I had geese, the fowl house was let. At the end, my husband worked in the wire factory. I had chicken. I had a cow, I could milk, there was always milk, curd, sour cream, cream. I grew tomatoes, paprika in the garden, and planted nice flowers. I had everything.[35]

All the West Virginia mines had similar living conditions, and the years there generally are remembered as bitter and difficult. Those born and reared in the mining settlements described them as boring, uncivilized places. "There weren't even any streets in Granttown," Mrs. Szabó recalled. "It looked like a ghost town. The house we lived in didn't even have an address. On the building there was just a post-box with a number 78 on it." In almost every instance, the mines were in isolated localities, and the mining companies owned all the houses in the immediate vicinity."[36] "We didn't know what to do in Granttown, so I kept busy learning how to crochet. It was hard for girls to find work. For a while I did the washing for a family. I could hardly wait to get out of there," Piroska Puskás said.[37] She and her sister went to New Brunswick in the company of a Szamosszegean couple and got work in the cigar factory.

Between 1916 and 1917 the Szamosszegeans began what became a permanent movement away from the West Virginian mining sites. News of job opportunities at the expanding Ford plant attracted the younger generation to Detroit, and by the beginning of the 1920s a small group had already moved there. After a few years hardly any Szamosszegeans remained in Granttown or Holden, while Dobra "was completely abandoned by them."[38] They recalled the migration away from the mining areas as prompted by declining pay, frequent and long-lasting strikes, continual unsuccessful struggles for unionization, and remigration to the village. "I worked in Granttown from 1914 to 1924. The big strike was in 1921. We were on strike for eight months with the mine closed the entire time. The people wanted the union but the company didn't. The Hungarians went on relief and were also helped by the union. During the strike we almost ran out of food. When the eight months were up in November, we went back to work and worked as usual until 1924 when there was another strike. Ah, I said, I'm moving on. And I went too—I went to New Brunswick," Joseph Paragh recalled along with other Szamosszegeans. They had had their first experiences with workers' struggles in West Virginia where they got a taste of the company's cruel attitude toward workers. During the strikes they were driven from the company houses and for months were forced, families and all, to live in tents.[39]

In the early 1920s, conditions in West Virginia were a key factor in the remigration of some to Szamosszeg and the further migration of others to factories. The largest number went to the Johnson & Johnson medical supplies factory in New Brunswick while some went to Detroit, Cleveland, Duquesne, and McKeesport, Pennsylvania. A few, though, "disappeared" somewhere in Pennsylvania. The transformation from emigrant peasants into miners and then into workers in other branches of industry was not unique to Szamosszegeans. Historical sources indicate that masses of immigrant peasants from Hungary and other European countries followed this same path.

In the market economy women's role and worth within the family grew. Especially among the migrants in their new environment. The "boarding mistresses" were the supporting pillars and organizers of the small community; the "good boarding mistress" directed her large "family" of boarders. She was the person whom the peddlers, association organizers, newspaper agents—anyone who wanted to sell something to the migrants—contacted.[40] Although the husband continued as head of the household, the woman took over the decision-making role in family economics. Many new small enterprises were thought up by them.[41]

Despite all their hardships, however, it was possible for most of the Hungarian immigrants to live on their wages and put aside some savings. They were able to survive and save because their lifestyle and their standard of living were much lower than those of American-born workers. At the same time, the obvious evidence of these lower standards was a factor in the negative prejudice towards them. Upon arriving in the United States and finding jobs, the Hungarians began to save with fanatical resolution. As a contemporary critic complained, "We shudder to think of the miserable food they eat; they buy the cheapest, lowest quality of everything. Naturally living this way they are able to save up a tidy sum within a few years."[42] Hungarian-American newspapers and the reports of the Austro-Hungarian ambassadors and consuls and other visiting Hungarians all expressed similar opinions.

To summarize, what looked like attractively high wages to those in Hungary actually were low wages in the United States, where workplaces were dangerous and plagued by a conspicuous number of industrial accidents. The immigrants' intention of staying in America only temporarily and the migratory nature of their existence resulted in a peculiar way of life. Because they wanted to save money at all costs, they reduced their living standards to a subsistence level. Native-born Americans were perplexed and horrified by what they regarded as a lack of ambition, and they explained the differences between their own culture and values and those of the immigrants from Eastern Europe in racial terms.

Strikebreakers?—Strikers?

The east-central European masses who immigrated after the economic depression of 1870 swelled the available labor pool and thus posed a threat to the wages and hard-won gains of the native-born American workers and earlier immigrants. The employers also tried to use the newcomers as strikebreakers against the organized workers, replacing activist workers with new immigrants willing, or, more precisely, obliged to work for lower wages in order to survive. The newcomers, most of whom did not know the language or understand what was going on, failed to realize that they were being used as strikebreakers. A bitter struggle ensued among the various strata of the working class. From this time on, the organized workers in their unions tried to buffer themselves against the immigrants. The American Federation of Labor prescribed conditions of membership—high entrance fees, United States citizenship—that would serve to keep out the newcomers. The unions also aimed at making as many factories as possible closed shops, thus keeping skilled immigrant workers from being employed in jobs suited to their training.

Continuing immigration meant greater stratification and made for a more divided working class in the United States than in Europe.[43] A significant barrier between the native-born and the immigrant workers was their lack of understanding of each other's language and their aversion to each other's customs. The native-born skilled worker, who felt at home in his industrial society, considered the immigrants to be members of a lower species because most of them came from pre-industrial villages and were inexperienced in industrial work. The American workers maintained a most rigid social isolation between themselves and the immigrant workers. The American Federation of Labor, although claiming to represent all workers, in fact represented only the native-born skilled workers. It did not try to organize the "new" immigrants, represent their interests, or get to know them. The core of its efforts and program was to get the biggest share possible for its members from the ever increasing national wealth. It made no political demands; on the contrary, it sharply opposed the workers' parties that advocated socialist ideals. Such attitudes on the part of the unions did not inspire the immigrant workers to feel solidarity with them. Even the skilled workers among the immigrants did not hesitate to work during strikes. Only with the passing of time did some of this hostility begin to subside.

It was in the mining areas that national and racial prejudices first began to let up enough to allow cooperation with the immigrant workers. The first union to open its gates to the new immigrants was the United Mine Workers of America. Work in the mines, because of its peculiarities, provided less of a chance for a worker's aristocracy to develop. The common danger, the greater numbers of immigrants among the miners, and the tendency for them to stay at one job for a longer time all created more favorable grounds for their getting to know and understand each other and thus to learn to cooperate. At any rate, the demands formulated by the mining unions in 1902 took the needs of the immigrants into consideration and tried to draw them into the economic struggle. The United Mine Workers organized most actively in Pennsylvania, Indiana, Ohio, and Illinois, the states where most of the immigrant Magyars worked.

In the successful strikes, the southern and eastern Europeans (Italians, Slovaks, Magyars) generally stood out as steadfast fighters. The Magyar miners were prominent, for example, in the strikes led by the Western Federation of Miners. During the strike of 1912 in Calmeton, Michigan (where a great many Magyars worked): "The Magyar miners stood the fight with admirable tenacity. They gave life to this unforgettable, great struggle. Whenever the strikers held a demonstration, the Magyars always led it with the Verhovay flags."[44] The strikes, along with the mine disasters, became the subjects of their songs, and of Hungarian-American lyric poetry.[45]

The majority of the Magyars, especially those not working in the mines, were not unionized. In the steel industry, for example, as mentioned above, the AFL decidedly closed its gates to them. If one thinks of strikes and wage wars only in connection with organized workers and unions, it is possible to conclude that the unorganized immigrants, isolated from the unions, did not participate in the struggle for improving the living standards of the American workers. In this vein, the earlier literature on the American unions emphasized only the strikebreaking activities of the immigrants. Not until recently, have historians of the American working class begun to take into account the wage wars and strikes from 1905 on that were fought by the "new" immigrants outside the unions and occasionally were fought in spite of the unions' expressed opposition.

Between 1909 and 1912, the period of "great eruptions" the Magyars stood in the ranks of the striking workers in the bitter and bloody strikes at McKeesport, Pennsylvania, South Bethlehem, Ohio, and Bridgeport, Connecticut.[46] Géza Hoffmann, a contemporary observer, has compiled a list of more than seventy great strikes between the years 1905 and 1910 in which Magyars also participated,[47] and his list is by no means complete. Because the marginal status of the immigrants determined the nature of their economic struggle within the American working class, their strikes differed from the classic wage wars of the organized workers. The spontaneity and fierce violence of their actions and their festive demonstrations with flags were more like peasant revolts than class-conscious workers' actions. Wages concerned them the most. They either demanded higher wages or protested against reduced wages and reduced job opportunities; longer working hours and poor working conditions were less of a consideration. According to one historian of the American working class, the forms and characteristics of the new immigrants' strikes seemed a cultural anachronism not only to President Theodore Roosevelt or steel executive Elbert Gary but to union leader Samuel Gompers as well.[48] None of them, of course, bothered to consider that the peculiarities of the immigrants' economic struggles were determined not only by their old-country inheritance and peasant background, but also by the indifference of American society, which paid attention only to conspicuous expressions of their wild despair and, even then, instead of feeling sympathy toward them, disapproved of these "foreign disturbances." Under such circumstances, with no one else to represent their interests, only a few of their lone strikes produced immediate economic results.

CHAPTER 11

The First
Hungarian-American
Businessmen

Saloonkeepers, Shopkeepers

THE FIRST HUNGARIAN shops to open were saloons, grocery stores, butcher shops, and shipping ticket agencies—typically ethnic businesses. At that time, the saloon (*korcsma*) was the most lucrative business. By 1897, on Cleveland's East Side there were seven Hungarian saloons on Holton Street alone. The owners of the saloons and other businesses tried to attract customers by placing short, inviting slogans in local papers: "The Hungarian House's owner is Hungarian, his friendliness is also Hungarian," or "The Buzitai Csárda is on Holton Street, Ferenc Lukács is its good innkeeper."[1] József Pipi, who for a time leased the Hungarian House, advertised his tavern with a three-verse rhyme:

"A Tavern Dedicated to Hungarian Freedom"

The old Hussar is restless because there is no war
For who can stand this peace time, it just becomes a bore
The enemy is nowhere, neither near nor far
The old Hussar gets angry, and opens up a bar.

Hungarian Freedom is the name of the saloon
Open all the time, be it morning, night or noon.
Needless is to say, there is lots and lots to drink,
Food is also plentiful and served in just a wink.

So friend, if you live within, or have to come to town
Come to see the old Hussar, he'll never let you down.
Magyar is the food he serves, and if you taste the wine
You'll feel like a young Hussar, fiery all the time.[2]

131

Another tavernkeeper, János Juhász, also used verse to advertise his business:

> The "Magyar Ház" became Hungarian again,
> Only now did the real life surely begin.
> Boss Juhász is here the owner of land.
> The wine that he offers is fiery brand.
> In the "Magyar Ház" here,
> We shall sing old songs,
> As we did not for years,
> Up till now, not once.

The owner of the "Magyar Ház" in Cleveland is JUHÁSZ JÁNOS, 198 Holton Street.[3]

Especially in New York, on Second Avenue, Hungarian Jews invested in small businesses for which the Hungarian sojourners soon furnished a natural clientele. The best known coffeehouse was the Café Continental on Second Avenue, the meeting place of recently arrived Hungarians. "There is not an intelligent Hungarian who, sooner or later, would not turn up here. Its owner is Hungarian, its kitchen is Hungarian, its music, its air, and every guest or visitor there is Hungarian. Owner: Ignác Rosenfeld."[4]

Stopping at Hungarian stores meant more to the migrants than just buying necessities. The shops also were centers of communication, places where the immigrants could get together with friends and be provided with food, drink, advice, and information. The proprietors themselves served as leaders in establishing community organizations, for it was in the saloons that the Hungarians started almost all of their early community organizations, including the religious societies. One of Cleveland's most popular saloons, the Szabo Hall on Buckeye Road, had grown so popular by the 1910s that it was now far more than a typical saloon. Its advertising boasted: "Szabo Hall has the most modern stage and dance hall with stage sets available for all types of folk theater. It is most suitable for banquets, weddings, and anniversaries. Equipped with electricity, gas lighting, steam heat, it has a separate kitchen, bar, and a dining room with long tables that seat up to 600 persons. The rooms will accommodate 1,000–1,500 people."[5]

The success of the saloon owners and other entrepreneurs depended on how well they accommodated the migrants' wants and customs. There was a market for sausages, bacon, and Hungarian wines and spirits prepared as they were back at home as well as for Hungarian medicines and folk remedies, such as leeches. In its underdeveloped state, the immigrant business community offered a very diverse range of products and services from storefronts crowded together side by side.

"The clientele of the American Hungarian shops developed from the population of the respective settlement. The shops and the goods sold there are of such a nature that they cannot and do not want to draw customers from districts farther away."[6]

The leadership role of the saloon owners was limited to their own locale and was at its height during elections or when social clubs and churches were being founded. Particularly before the turn of the century, the first Magyar saloons and stores belonged to other migrants from the multiethnic peoples of Hungary. Jewish, Slovak, and German tavern owners from Hungary all advertised their Magyar saloons in the Magyar-language press.[7] From many reports, reminiscences, and contemporary advertisements, it is clear that the functions and the atmosphere of the Hungarian shops and saloons were the same in most Hungarian settlements. The atmosphere of the small restaurants and coffeehouses differed only slightly in New York, where they were meeting places of Hungarian immigrants of the most varied type from the 1880s on.

Ticket Agents or "Bankers"

The advertising space of the Hungarian-American newspapers in the first decade of the century was filled mostly with the advertisements of various banks, banking houses, and ship- and train-ticket businesses. Ticket agents, often called "bankers," performed an absolutely essential function within the Hungarian immigrant communities, especially in their formative period. They fulfilled the roles of civil servants and public officials, usually acting as a liaison between the immigrants and both the Hungarian and the American authorities. The inclusive nature of the term "banker" is evident in their advertisements for services that went far beyond the handling, safeguarding, and transmitting to Hungary of the immigrants' money. The banker also sold steamship tickets, acted as an employment agent, interpreted English, handled inheritance and real estate matters, collected debts, and provided a permanent mailing address for the constantly relocating immigrants. In addition, some stocked a large variety of goods to sell to customers who came in to attend to other affairs. The immigrant had to pay for every individual service, and the bankers did very well; by the 1910s the richest of Cleveland's Hungarian immigrants were the immigrant bankers.[8]

The first Hungarian to open a bank, currency exchange, and notary public office in Cleveland, on Buckeye Road, was József L. Szepessy. He started his business in 1891 and by the 1910s had become one of the best known and most respected Hungarian businessmen in the town. Born in 1862 in Abauj County, he completed secondary school in Kassa. At the age of eighteen, with one dollar to his name, he arrived in the United States. His first ten years were a time for wandering from place to place: first he farmed; then he worked in a pencil factory in Brooklyn, hacked coal in Wilkes-Barre, Pennsylvania, became a hardware store salesman there, worked on the railroads in northern Michigan, lived in Cincinnati, and labored on a plantation in the South. From Pittsburgh and McKeesport, Pennsylvania, he moved to nearby Connellsville, where he first worked as a court interpreter, and later, for three years, as a banker, accumulating a small amount of capital. His next stop was Denver, where he entered the tea business but left it to become a cowboy and to wander through Colorado, New Mexico, and Arizona, experiencing what he later recounted as colorful adventures. In the desert he fought Indians, and in Albuquerque, New Mexico, he was a bartender in one of the expensive saloons, where gold miners gambled alongside murders and lynchings. He also went to California to look for gold, but after one week gave it up and moved on to National City, and then to San Diego, where, for the first time in many years, he met up with Hungarians. There he opened a flour business, and shipped into Mexico, clashing with customs. He moved on to Los Angeles and opened a cosmetics store. Having sold the store to a Chinese immigant, Szepessy became a peddler of cosmetics and jewelry in California. In San Francisco, in partnership with another Hungarian, he opened a hotel and lost his money. At his next stop in Oregon, he trafficked in liquor among the miners, and among the Indians, he was a fisherman and hunter. In Alaska, he dug for gold. Eventually he returned to Pennsylvania and became a banker in Punxsutawney and manager of the Chase D. Conner Bank in Uniontown.[9]

When József Szepessy finally settled in Cleveland in 1891, he took a vigorous part in organizing Hungarian institutions. For a short time he was assistant editor of *Szabadság*, which had just begun publication, but soon he went into business for himself as a banker. He initially rented the Hungarian House on Holton Street, where he combined his role as banker, sending the migrants' money back home, with those of grocer and real estate agent. Szepessy was the first to convince Hungarians to purchase houses and lots in Cleveland. He also was the Hungarians' pioneer in city politics, winning election as tax assessor with the support of the Hungarian vote.[10]

The other prominent Hungarian figure in Cleveland's public life in the 1910s was the entrepreneur János Weizer. Like Szepessy, he was from Abauj and was very young when he arrived in America. When the sixteen-year-old János came with his father directly to Cleveland from the village of Csécs, there were only three Hungarian families living on the East Side. The Weizers both went to work for the "old factory" (National Malleable Castings Company) before they moved to the "new factory" (Eberhardt Manufacturing Company). Although the father soon returned to the village, the younger Weizer remained in Cleveland. He became more thoroughly Americanized than the average Hungarian immigrant of those days and in 1888 became a citizen of the United States. Realizing earlier than many others that the majority of his fellow Hungarians would remain in the United States permanently, János urged them to establish Hungarian-American institutions. One of the moving spirits behind the very first Hungarian celebration in Cleveland, which was held in 1887 in Haltnorth's Hall, he was one of the leaders of the Cleveland Hungarians from that time on.[11]

János Weizer began his entrepreneurial career by buyng a grocery store. A few years later, in 1895, he sold it and opened on Buckeye Road the first

Hungarian-owned clothing store, to which he later added a grocery store, a loan business, and a steamship ticket agency. One of his advertisements declared:

> I wish to inform my esteemed fellow countrymen, that in my store you can get tickets for any steamship route. In addition, my fellow countrymen, through me you can inexpensively and securely send ship tickets to Hungary. I also recommend my well-stocked grocery store and the inexpensive and durable work clothes. And my large selection of shirts and underwear.[12]

As the president and one of the co-owners of the Woodland and Rice Avenue Allotment Company, founded in 1907, Weizer owned numerous houses in the Hungarian neighborhood. When, with rare foresight, he established the lively business district on Buckeye Road between 116th and 122nd Streets, his entrepreneurial projects already extended beyond the perimeter of the Hungarian colony. Ultimately, Weizer was responsible for the development of thirty-two streets in Cleveland.[13]

Varied and successful business activities likewise made the name of Ferenc Apáthy well known in Cleveland by the 1910s. From Abauj County as were Szepessy and Weizer, Ferenc Apáthy, born in 1865 in Jászómindszent, was a seventeen-year-old clerk in a store before he emigrated to the United States. He first settled in New York, where with other amateurs he organized the Hungarian Philharmonic Association. Apáthy became chairman of the board of directors of *Amerikai Nemzetör* (American National Guard) the first Hungarian-language newspaper in New York, and took charge of the paper's out-of-town distribution. He arrived in Cleveland in 1888 and began to pursue a business career, soon becoming manager of the Daily Cooperative Company's clothing department. Meanwhile, he organized the out-of-town distribution of *Szabadság* and was involved in founding a new paper, *Magyar Hirmondó* (Hungarian Herald). At the end of the 1890s, Apáthy opened a Hungarian bookstore on St. Clair Street, which he soon relocated to South Woodland and expanded to include a notary public service and a money-transfer and ticket agency. He later moved the business to the corner of Buckeye Road and Bolton Street and then to his home. Along with Weizer, Apáthy was one of the founders of the Woodland and Rice Avenue Allotment Company.[14] An advertisement of his read as follows:

> American Notary Public, 195 S. Woodlawn Ave., Cleveland, O. HUNGARIAN BOOK DEALER, retail, wholesale, STEAMSHIP TICKETS. Buildings and building sites, businesses, bought and sold. MONEY TRANSFERS. Hungarian prayer books and other excellent reading material. FIRE INSURANCE. Musical instruments, watches, chains. Warehouse full of meerschaum pipes, large selection of cigarette holders and tobacco. Preparation and notarization of documents.[15]

Among the wealthiest Hungarians on the East Side in the 1910s was Ferenc (Francis) Boldizsár, who had a money-transfer and ticket agency on

East Seventy-ninth Street. But our knowledge about him is limited. He was born in Hungary, in Gönc, Abauj County, in 1869 and was nineteen years old when he arrived in America, where he worked first for the railroads and later in a factory. He opened a saloon in 1901 and soon was involved in money transfers, selling steamship tickets and everything else that then was a customary part of the immigrant banker's work sphere. In 1911 he described himself in an advertisement in *Szabadság:*

> Money transfer and steamship ticket agency. Also sells books and other imported items. Notary Public, he works for Hungarians, owns five buildings worth over $25,000, all with Hungarian tenants. Annually his trade exceeds well over $10,000 dollars. He supports both associations and churches.[16]

Yet another well-known Hungarian banker in Cleveland was Károly Dobay, a former county magistrate. His business advertisements featured a portrait of himself in Hungarian gala dress:

> Károly Dobay's office. Money transfers, legal matters, steamship tickets, notary public, buildings and lots for sale, all types of insurance: 8820 Buckeye Road. Thanks to my position back home and along with my good connections I can handle legal matters quickly and favorably.[17]

Because money-transfer agents were notorious for taking advantage of the migrants' inexperience, Ernö Kiss, a notary public and steamship ticket agent on Cleveland's West Side during the 1910s, used a photograph of a receipt from the Hungarian Royal Savings Bank in his advertisement:

> HERE IS THE PROOF! the European postal service brought this confirmation receipt along with many others to reassure the Hungarians in America. HERE IS THE PROOF! that not only was my client's money sent, and not only that it arrived in Budapest, but the addressee's own signed receipt is proof that he himself received the money. ANYONE WHO CAN READ can now see that the money which he sends through me is safe, because I transfer it honestly and, using the Hungarian Royal Postal Savings Bank, pay it out in the shortest possible time. YOU NEED NOT BE AFRAID TO SEND MONEY THROUGH ME TO THE OLD COUNTRY, and you may rest at ease, because the money will reach its destination. I SEND YOUR MONEY AT REGULAR RATES to the old country. Tickets available for all the steamship lines. Accurate handling of all legal matters.[18]

> In New York City the oldest and best-known Hungarian banking house is the one owned by Emil Kiss, but other well-known Hungarian bankers are Jenő Kuthy and Gyula Debrovszky, who besides running a bank with bustling trade also engaged in selling imported Hungarian goods.[19]

The bankers' individual paths reflect common patterns in the development of their careers. Most came to the United States before the age of twenty and were much more mobile and independent than the average migrant. They managed to establish social contacts, even outside their own group, relatively quickly. Their geographic mobility apparently helped them to learn English, and their broader, more varied experiences acquainted them with enterprises that were sure to be needed by their compatriots. As a result of their diverse experiences, they also could assume the function of intermediary between their immigrant group and the host society and, in turn, become leaders in their own community's organizations.

However, especially in the beginning, the bankers often defrauded their inexperienced compatriots. "Runaway bankers," those who embezzled the money that they had collected from the immigrants and ran off, reappeared year after year in the Hungarian communities. "It is a sad chapter in the history of the Hungarian Americans that gives an account of the ruffianism of the 'runaway bankers.'"[20] Such are the words introducing a contemporary press report on runaway bankers, giving their names and the amount of money embezzled.

Industrialists

According to Hungarian-American chronicles, the "real American success story" is the career of Tivadar Kundtz (1852–1937) the cabinetmaker's apprentice, who as a millionaire factory owner in Cleveland had around six hundred employees by the 1910s. Tivadar, or in German, Theodor, was born in the village of Untermetzenseifen in Sáros County. He attended the local school and learned his father's trade of cabinetmaking. In May of 1873, twenty-one years old and broke, having spent his last penny on his trip, he arrived in Cleveland.

One of his friends, Jacob Gedeon, from the neighboring town of Metzenseifen, had emigrated to Cleveland years before Theodor. Jacob had been a cooper or barrelmaker in Metzenseifen, but in Cleveland he had a small business in the Flats making wheelbarrows. It is likely that Jacob wrote to relatives and friends back in Hungary telling of the opportunities they would discover in Cleveland. Theodor was among the first to check it out for himself. The largest ethnic group was German, comprising almost one-third of Cleveland's population in 1890. Theodor Kundtz, a German with a multiethnic background, probably adjusted to the New World better than most. Because he was a clever cabinetmaker whose native language was German, he immediately found work.

When he first arrived in Cleveland, Theodor must have been shocked by the contrast between his old and his new home. At that time, Cleveland was a bustling, dirty town. Few streets were paved. Most were a rutted cohesion of dirt and manure that turned into a vile marsh when it rained. There was no electricity. Other than the muted glow of an occasional gas lamp, Cleveland's streets were dark and gloomy after sunset. Teams of overworked horses pulled streetcars along Euclid and Lorain Avenues. Outhouses stood behind many homes. The city's sewage system in 1873 was the Cuyahoga River and its tributaries. Wood and coal smoke from homes and industries hung over the city like a rank fog. Even at its worst, today's air pollution cannot begin to compare with that in 1873.[21]

The clean rushing waters of the Bodva River had been replaced by the Cuyahoga, a sluggish cesspool of industrial and animal waste. The clear mountain air and pristine forests of Hungary had been supplanted by Cleveland's bad air and dirty crowded streets. Within a relatively short time, however, Theodor Kundtz struck out on his own in a one-man shop, which supplied the wooden parts of the sewing machines manufactured by the White Sewing Machine Company. High demand made Kundtz's enterprise a quick success. He expanded his facilities several times, and by the turn of the century he was a well-known manufacturer in Cleveland, drawing a number of his fellow villagers there by the news of his success.[22]

The name of Tivadar Kundtz was often in the Hungarian-American newspapers because of his financial and social activity. He established the Theodore Kundtz Relief Fund, to which all employees had to contribute and from which they received 10 percent of their monthly wages in case of illness. The fund likewise paid a deceased worker's family a death benefit which was augmented by a 25 percent donation from each employee. In the next thirty years, about a thousand of his Metzenseifen neighbors would join him in Cleveland.

Kundtz's contributions and loans are acknowledged in the histories of practically every Hungarian association, newspaper, church, and society in Cleveland. "Tivadar Kundtz is the pride of the entire Hungarian-American community," proclaimed the *Amerikai Magyar Népszava* in its tenth anniversary issue. "Despite his great financial success, he has remained a patriotic, good Hungarian, who is always among the first to act when it comes to a Hungarian cause."[23] Similar praise could be read in other Hungarian-American papers, and because of Kundtz's dual ethnic ties and apparently matching generosity, he was just as highly praised in a publication dealing with the lives of the Germans of Cleveland.[24]

By the 1910s the Hungarian craftsmen and small entrepreneurs operating in Cleveland numbered in the hundreds. They had gone into business following years of working for wages, and quite a few of the artisans had started in Kundtz's factory, moved on to other factories for more pay, saved their money, and became independent in about eight or ten years. The line of business they went into depended not so much on their qualifications as on demand within the Hungarian community. The advertisements placed in the Hungarian papers by eighty enterprises operating in the Hungarian district of Cleveland provide a picture of that demand. There were twenty-one clothiers and shoemakers, nineteen saloonkeepers and general storekeepers, fourteen grocers, seven ticket agents and bankers, six barbers, four hotelkeepers, two hardware store operators, two jewelers and watch repairmen, two bookdealers and bookbinders, one tobacconist, one pharmacist, and one furrier.[25]

As we saw earlier, the customers of each Hungarian-American shop came from the population of that particular settlement, and the shops drew their customers from their neighborhoods. This statement, however, does not apply to Hungarian banks, and that is the reason that the advertising sections of the Hungarian-American papers were mostly filled with advertisements of various banks, banking houses, and shops selling ship and railway tickets.

Biographical data also show that the Hungarian immigrants were more likely to set up a business of their own if they had experience in the same area in the old country. The first Hungarian-American merchants and saloonkeepers had worked in the village store or pub back home; they also were better educated than most of their fellow immigrants and were quicker to recognize the opportunities inherent in providing services that met the group's day-to-day needs. Although most of the Hungarian immigrants would work as unskilled or semiskilled laborers all their lives unless they returned to the old country to resume peasant life, there were exceptions, peasants who became entrepreneurs. First they usually let rooms to boarders as a "boarding boss" (*burdos gazda*); then they used the money earned in that small family business to open a saloon, a butcher shop, or a grocery store.

The ex-peasant petty bourgeoisie that developed in the immigrant community had little in common with today's entrepreneurial class. Friends, relatives, and ethnic contacts formed a virtually captive audience of customers, and the businesses were strictly family enterprises. Like many peasant households, they often were based on a ruthless exploitation of every member of the family. The wife's skills and contributions were the well-kept secret of their success, and the children, too, had to work long hours that left them little time for school or play. One of my sources recalled, with a bitterness that time had not allayed, being made to work in the family saloon "without pay and without rights, with no time off, and having to beg, at the age of twenty, for a few cents to be able, once in a blue moon, to spend an evening out with friends." Two siblings had lost no time getting away from this life of drudgery. Finally my informant fled, running all the way to New Orleans.[26]

Already, during this time of the great labor migration wave, a few Hungarian artists, musicians, lawyers, engineers, scientists, and inventors had sought the possibility of self-realization in America. Their romantic fates developed outside of and separated from the Hungarian communities. One of the famous industrial "firsts" was the work of a Hungarian American, Tivadar Puskás, who was the pioneer of wire-transmitted entertainment, the ancestor of the radio. He became one of the original collaborators of Edison, who praised him highly. Hungarian artists, particularly painters and musicians, began to appear in the United States as career-migrants as early as the labor-migrants' arrival.

Successful intellectuals only occasionally sought contacts with the Hungarian community, or even with its leaders—and their numbers taking part in the formation of the Hungarian-American identity was even smaller. A few intellectuals, lawyers, and physicians did not separate themselves from Hungarian community life. Best known among them were Árpád Gerster,[27] a physician, who was the president, and the driving force of Magyar Társulat (Hungarian Society), a social and cultural organization in New York and Mór Cukor, a lawyer in New York, who played a leading role in the social life of Hungarian immigrants.

CHAPTER 12

Establishing Secular Organizations

THE FIRST PUBLIC forums for socialization were the Hungarian taverns and saloons. Friends and acquaintances met there to talk, drink, sing, play music, and dance, just as though they were back home. The Hungarians frequented the saloons to relax, to ease the loneliness and the spiritual and physical fatigue from their unaccustomed work, and to forget their troubles and homesickness. As the alcohol helped them relax, they ended up drinking more than they had back home and often engaged in loud bravado, senseless arguments, and sometimes knife fights.[1]

In taverns and saloons the immigrants formed Hungarian associations, which preceded even the churches. The establishment of mutual aid associations in most of the Hungarian settlements coincided with some tragedies. In 1886 in Cleveland, for example, a Magyar man with no relatives died. In the middle of the night a hearse took away his body, but it was unclear whether or not he was ever buried. After hearing this disturbing story, a few Hungarian craftsmen, at the urging of a doctor of Polish descent, founded a social and benefit association, named for the martyred prime minister of the 1848 Revolution, Count Lajos Batthyány.[2] At its second anniversary celebration, the mayor of Cleveland was the speaker, and the mother of József Black, who was already a prominent Hungarian citizen of Cleveland, donated a red, white, and green Hungarian flag.

The Batthyány Society had barely begun to function when the Miklós Zrinyi First Cleveland Magyar-Slovak Sick Benefit Society was established. Its main founder was Albert Friedl, a young official who had come to Cleveland from Metzenseifen, Sáros County. There quickly followed the Louis Kossuth Benefit Association and the Ferenc Deák Fraternal Organization, likewise named after persons prominent in the Hungarians' opposition to the Habsburgs.[3]

The earliest Hungarian associations in Cleveland were socialization circles for those who, by the 1890s, had already established their careers and who

141

thought of themselves as "48ers": political, rather than economic, immigrants. Their leaders were the first to promulgate demands for an independent Hungary and the cult of Lajos (Louis) Kossuth. On his name day they organized an elaborate commemorative celebration in the Hungarian Hall, and at the time of his funeral, in 1894, they held wake services.[4] These "body and soul" Hungarians were for the most part not native speakers of Magyar and were not ethnically of Magyar descent. For instance, Tivadar Kundtz was a German-speaking Hungarian, and József Black and Márton Deutsch were Hungarian Jews.[5]

Educated individuals founded the Cleveland Hungarian Young Men's and Ladies' Society in 1891, and it probably was for them that Tihamér Kohányi, the editor of *Szabadság*, wrote "Greenhorns," the first play with a Hungarian-American theme. The Hungarian Drama Society was also established in 1890.

In the beginning, the societies functioned locally, but many soon joined the network of national associations. The idea of federating sick benefit societies originated already in the 1890s. Already in the first decade of the twentieth century many were organized from the start as branches of a national association by migrant workers. who brought their affiliation to their new workplace, especially the coal miners, whose employment opportunities fluctuated from area to area.

In the 1910s there were six national Hungarian fraternal associations in the United States. John Bodnár's statement that "the religious leaders played a major role in shaping early fraternal organizations, especially on a larger territorial basis" does not hold true for the Hungarian migrants.[6] Although these early societies were established primarily for the purpose of providing mutual aid in times of sickness and death, strong nationalistic individualism also influenced their Hungarian founders.

One of the best-known and most popular societies was the Verhovay Segély-egylet (Verhovay Aid Association). It was established by Mihály Pálinkás, a young carpenter, with a few miner friends in 1886 in Hazelton, Pennsylvania.[7] His name is inseparable from the Verhovay Association's history in its first decades; he served as president, vice president, and secretary of the Cleveland branch.

Mihály Pálinkás, a twenty-one-year-old carpenter, migrated to the United States in 1882, and for the next eleven years he worked in a mining community near Hazelton. Then he opened a money-transfer and steamship ticket office in Phillipsburg, but because of the poor economy had to give it up and go back to the mine. Intelligent and extremely popular, Pálinkás is remembered as being so attached to the association, which he always considered his own creation, that he often ended up in direct conflict with its opponents. In 1899 he moved to Cleveland, where he organized one of the largest branches of the Verhovay. Pálinkás worked in one place for seventeen years until, after the end of World War I, he purchased a farm in Mentor, Ohio, and farmed it in cooperation with his three sons.[8]

In the formative period of 1886–1926, unusual mobility and transiency characterized not only the members of the Verhovay Association but also its leaders. During these years it has grown from a small local organization into the largest national Hungarian fraternal association in the United States. By the mid-1920s, the three hundred odd branches of the Verhovay had spread into about twenty states, slightly over one third of them in Pennsylvania.[9]

Two other Hungarian fraternal organizations were started, which had a "national" network in Bridgeport, Connecticut, by the 1910s. Magyar and Slovak immigrants joined to lay the foundation of the Rákóczi Magyar Betegsegélyző Egylet (Rákóczi Hungarian Aid Association) in 1887.[10]

The Magyar Betegsegélyző Egyletek Szövetsége (American Hungarian Aid Society) was also organized in Bridgeport in 1892,[11] uniting several already existing organizations that together gave the society nearly one hundred founding members. At the constituent meeting, the organizers outlined the society's purpose and the direction of the future activities, as follows:

"To bring all Magyars into our camp regardless of religious affiliation, since the main purpose and sacred duty of our organization is to unite all decent Magyars and to win the Americans' respect and honor for the thousand-year-old glorious Magyar name! Furthermore, our goal is to bring into our organization all the existing Magyar societies doing charitable work in America, and to concentrate and strengthen all the forces that provide assistance, so that when misfortune strikes, the future of the workers and orphans may be assured."[12]

Among the founders, an intellectual would appear here and there, but in the main the direction of these societies was undertaken by artisans and craftsmen and the rank and file were mostly peasant-workers.

Six Calvinist ministers and six laymen organized the Hungarian Reformed Federation of America in Trenton, New Jersey, in 1886.[13] Although early proponents of the Hungarian Reformed Federation of America spoke of giving more concrete expression to their faith and creating a medium for the practice of their religion, they decided the Federation needed five hundred members to remain solvent and admitted Protestants, Catholics, and Jews. Immediately they learned the divisive potential of religious differences when some members resigned to protest the admission of Jews and others objected to the Federation's paying suicide benefits. Nevertheless, the Federation survived, stipulating only that all members must "recognize" its Calvinist character and that the president had to be of the Calvinist faith.

The "nationally" functioning Hungarian organizations were much more detached from the churches, as was the case among the Slovak immigrants, for instance. Except for the socialists, they were not anti-church; they assisted the building of churches, but they acted on a "Hungarian," that is to say, on a national basis without any denominational distinction. The socialists were traditionally anticlerical, but the intensity of this sentiment varied according to their branch of socialism. A few other fraternal societies also stepped outside their local boundaries and organized branches in nearby settlements, although on a much more humble scale than the above.

Because of Hungary's late industrialization, its first skilled workers had migrated to Hungary from German-speaking territories. Consequently, as was already mentioned, the language of the skilled workers and artisans was German even if it was not their native tongue: *valcolás* in one of the German-speaking countries continued to be an integral part of training for a craft in Hungary at the end of the nineteenth century. Through the German language, they were able to communicate with other German-speaking immigrants without a problem, so the socialists quickly became familiar with the American workers' movement. Magyar-speaking socialists organized their first small community group as the Sándor Petőfi Workers Society in 1894. Most of them adapted socialist ideas already in their homeland, a sense of class consciousness as members of a trade union. They established the Workers' Publishing Cooperative and published their newspaper, *Amerikai Népszava*, in 1895.[14] The newspaper endeavored to organize the Hungarian-speaking immigrants under the flag of the American labor movement. It popularized the program of the Socialist Labor Party (SLP) and urged the Hungarian workers to support the party. Small in numbers, however, the group could publish the paper for only a few years.

The Hungarian socialists revitalized their small community at the beginning of the century by founding the Munkás Betegsegélyző és Önképző Egyesület (Workingmen's Sick Benevolent and Educational Federation) in New York. Shortly afterward they organized branches from the small groups in the larger Hungarian settlements, and they launched their own paper, *Népakarat* (People's Will) in 1903.

At first the Magyar-speaking workers who had already adopted socialism in their homeland tried to maintain neutrality in debates over the future of the American labor movement. That was possible only for a short time: they soon became divided over the question and in 1904 split up. Those who were with the Socialist Party continued its community involvement, supported by and active in the Workingmen's Sick Benevolent and Educational Federation. Followers of Daniel De Leon broke away from other Magyar socialists and established the Munkás Betegsegélyző Szövetség (Workingmen's Sick-Benevolent Association) in 1906. The falling apart of the small groups of Hungarian socialists influenced by the various trends of the American labor movement was reflected in the propaganda of these two fraternal associations.[15]

Newer associations developed in one of two ways: the increase in the number of immigrants in certain settlements caused further organizing, or some older benefit societies outgrew their local framework and tried to develop a "national" network by creating so-called branches in other parts of the country. In such cases they generally classified the first association as the parent society and designated the societies that joined it or were organized by the same name by the name of the settlement and a serial number indicating its order in the growth of the association (e.g., the Thirteenth New Brunswick Branch of the

Rákóczi Aid Association). The immigrants' wandering throughout the United States facilitated such a form of organization and made it seem natural. Organization members discovered comrades and recruited members at their new places of work, and when the membership grew to eighteen to twenty, they formed a branch. Most of the national network was organized during the first decade of the twentieth century; by 1909, the number and branches of the national organizations had grown considerably. The Magyar Betegsegélyző Egyletek Szövetsége had 245 branches and 10,114 members, the Verhovay Betegsegélyző had 109 branches and 8,883 members. The Rákóczi Betegsegélyző recruited a populous camp on the eastern seaboard, primarily in Connecticut and New Jersey. The Amerikai Magyar Református Egyesület gained ground much more slowly than the above-mentioned organizations, but by 1909 this organization also had 93 branches and 2,500 members.[16]

In the beginning, outward signs of group identification—the organization's pins, flags, uniforms, caps, and seals—were very important in every fraternal society. The officers of the organizations were elected, and initially received no pay. For all that, the number of offices within the organizations continued to grow, indicating the members' desire to hold office and thus to play a public role.

The process of developing the framework of the organizations and their community activities was accompanied by debates, mistakes, and misapprehensions that often shook the very foundations of the organizations. Mistrust of the office holders and accusations against them were common, and so, consequently, was the rapid turnover in these first organizations of men who, in the land of their birth had never heard of organizations, monthly dues, funeral-cost insurance, the way to run a meeting, to keep accounting books, and so forth.

Magyar immigrants were not unique in building nationwide fraternal federations. Other immigrant groups, among them Slovaks and Romanians, also completed federation of their insurance society. In addition to other fraternal societies and federations there were many local societies of various kinds. As the secular organizations consolidated, more varied forms of social life and entertainment developed, naturally at a rate and of a variety depending on the composition of the community. At larger Magyar settlements where the ratio of men and women was somewhat more favorable, Saturday night dances soon became regular. The new goals—"we're organizing a dance to broaden the financial base of our society and to strengthen the organization"—became the catalysts of more constructive activity and more acceptable behavior.[17] The program of dances was augmented by poetry recitals, the performance of comic routines, of plays and choir singing. At this time amateur acting groups and choirs were still organized within the framework of the fraternal societies, or at least with their material support. Besides being good entertainment, these activities also made for group cohesion.[18]

Fourteen young masons formed the Hungarian Educational Workshop on Cleveland's West Side on August 14, 1902. Soon they were joined by some businessmen and intellectuals, including the former lawyer and newspaperman Dr. Henry Baracs, and their programs, which showed the variety of their social activities, quickly turned the group into the most popular and culturally active Hungarian organization in the city. In 1903 it introduced an English course for the migrants, while its theater group regularly put on Hungarian dramas and musical performances. The workshop purchased for itself a home that featured a library and an auditorium with a permanent stage, and other organizations, encouraged by its success, also began to form their own amateur drama groups.

In 1908 eleven other young craftsmen and tradesmen formed the Hungarian Athletic Club, which met in the German Hall. In the same year, the Hungarians' second leading cultural organization, the Cleveland Workingmen's Singing Society, was established by nineteen Hungarian migrants.[19] Major Vendel, a cabinetmaker, took the lead in its political, cultural, and social functions. He was already a master craftsman when he arrived in the United States in 1906, settling first in Painesville, Ohio, and later in Cleveland.[20]

The Hungarian cabinetmakers and carpenters in Cleveland eventually succeeded in organizing the Hungarian branch of the American Federation of Labor, Local 1180. The local was under the influence of the socialists, and its office shared space with the Hungarian Federation of the Socialist Party. Because syndicalist ideas and unions played a central role in Hungary's labor movement, sympathy for the members of the Industrial Workers of the World (IWW), or "Wobblies," came naturally to the radical Hungarian workers, including those who belonged to the Socialist or the Socialist Labor Parties. The IWW's Hungarian "Wobblies" formed into small independent groups in 1912.[21]

Only by considering their European background and the various trends in the American labor movement is it possible to understand the organizations and communities of the immigrant Magyar socialists. From the turn of the century, but especially from 1904 on, the central questions for this group, too, were, first, the possibilities and forms of connecting political action with economic struggle and, second, their relations with the unions. Their "new immigrant" status strongly influenced their views and abilities to judge the situation. After their experience in Europe, they found it incomprehensible that the unions and the worker parties should be traveling on completely different paths, and looked askance at the "practicality" and "ideological poverty" of the American workers' movement.[22] "As for the multitude of socialist papers, they are simply pouring out their ideological stupidities. One does not know whether to be angry or just write off the entire American socialist movement," wrote one of them. The situation in Hungary was so different, the Hungarian labor movement was shaped by such different slogans, that "to create a movement here with the slogans brought from home is impossible."[23]

The majority of the Hungarian socialists, at least until 1910, were drawn to the SLP, which was rapidly declining nationally. They argued that "its ideological stands are closer to the Magyars' and, in general, to the immigrant workers." They felt that "the SP exhausts all its efforts in election campaigns," and, since few of the Magyars were citizens, they could not get involved in this activity. "The SLP, on the contrary, holds that its most important task is to organize on economic lines based on the class war. And in this work even immigrant workers can participate. Through the economic organizations, the foreigners really can become an organic part of the American Workers movement."[24]

Although the socialist sick and death benefit federations were always embroiled in controversy over socialist issues, they adopted a more ambivalent approach toward organized religion. The Workingmen's Sick Benevolent Federation's paper ridiculed religious superstition and denounced the clergy for abetting oppression, but it also invited clergymen to join and promised to work for a world without sin. According to Paula Benkart three Reformed congregations, three Roman Catholic and two Greek Catholic parishes, and one YMCA allowed the Workingmen's Federation to meet in their facilities. In turn, when police appeared to disperse Workingmen's members during a strike, the socialists could claim to be worshipers gathered in the church to sing hymns. In Fairfield, Connecticut, a branch of the rival Munkás Betegsegélyző és Önképző Szervezet (Workingmen's Sick-Benevolent and Self-Educating Organization) carried cultivation of religious groups even further. It convinced two Catholic and one Reformed congregation, as well as the local Red Cross and Community Chest, to help raise funds to build its hall, the "Self-Educating Place." The local Rákóczi branch also donated to the construction fund and later used the hall for its meetings.[25]

No statistical data exist on the number of radical Hungarian laborers. Indications are, however, that even in New York, the center of the Hungarian socialists, only an insignificant minority of the workers identified with radical ideas. At the most, they numbered a few thousand, with great fluctuations due to migration. According to the Austro-Hungarian consul, Hoffmann, in the decade preceding World War I, Cleveland's Magyar-speaking socialists were highly trained, intelligent, and well paid.[26] Most of them started off as skilled workers, or rather as artisans, with city experience after wanderings through Europe. The Social Democratic Party of Hungary also sent educated people to the emigrant socialists' newspaper offices, for example, Dr. Imre Bárd (a social democratic lawyer and newspaperman) and Elek Bolgár (a lawyer and sociologist). However, from the letters and reports they sent to Hungary, it is clear that the American labor movement was unfamiliar to them, and they had a hard time finding their way among its different trends.[27]

Lacking American citizenship, however, few of them could take part in mainstream political movements. Instead, they turned their energies to cultural endeavors and propaganda, in keeping with the social democratic self-educational and self-improvement traditions from back home. After the turn of the century, informative lectures, debates, educational courses, and musical and theatrical performances became a regular part of their community life. As a result, their cultural influence on the Hungarian immigrants was greater than their numbers would suggest.[28]

This period is also important for attaching social programs and cultural activities to their provision of sick benefits. The small community organizations were conducive to the development of an individual's talents; the possibility of playing a role in the group was an incentive for learning and self-education. In meetings, the members became used to performing, giving speeches, debating relatively important issues, and making responsible decisions without out-side pressure.

"Our countrymen of peasant background revel in the association's affairs which give them an opportunity to address one another as 'Dear Mr. President' or 'My Honorable Worthy Speaker,' 'To my dearest friend,' 'Mr. Sárközy,' etc."[29] The great growth of titles in these organizations indicates the immigrants' needs for recognition and social status. In the sick benevolent societies, the usual titles were president, vice president, secretary, treasurer, corresponding secretary, auditor and controller, visitor to the sick, doormen, and flagholders or flagbear-ers, one for the Hungarian and one for the American flag, others for the ceremonial and for the mourning flags.[30]

Especially for the peasant-worker immigrants, the fraternal societies were not only the forum of self-education, but also a school of democracy. It was no wonder that the Magyar clerics complained a great deal about the changes in their parishioners' behavior, and their growing independence, and pointed to the societies as responsible for the change. "At the monthly meetings of the benefit associations, they learned to put forward a proposal, to orate, to vote, to build and to destroy: they would like to see the same forces at work in parish affairs as well," complained a Roman Catholic priest.[31] The outward symbols of solidarity became particularly important to the association members. On patriotic holidays and anniversaries, they paraded bearing the associations' flags, sometimes accompanied by loud brass bands. To generate more respect from the receiving society, whenever possible they marched through American neighborhoods, waving the beautiful, extremely expensive flag that was the most cherished possession of every organization. They also appeared at commu-nity affairs in their uniforms; for example, the Cleveland Greek Catholic society always appeared in military dress. At funerals members wore badges with a black ribbon and accompanied the deceased on his or her last journey, placing a wreath on the grave. With these and countless other rituals, group activities eased the unfamiliar environment's starkness and the absence of the homeland's protective community background.

The associations competed greatly for members, and the members com-peted greatly for office. The means of evaluation of candidates were as varied as the values emphasized by the different types of associations. The "patriotic associations" measured a candidate on how "good a Hungarian man" he was; in the labor movement, on the other hand, his commitment to the class struggle was the most important factor. Amid competition, the network of the centralized associations was formed. The social diversity of the Hungarian-speaking immi-grants was reflected in the diversity of the associations, too. This diversity was expressed in the competition between the organizations, and in those means by which they recruited new members.

The first Hungarian associations were started by educated individuals, lawyers, doctors, merchants, and clergymen, who, either out of idealism or for political motives, tried to gather the Hungarian migrants around themselves. As the organizations grew, leadership slipped unobtrusively into the hands of workers and self-made men, or sometimes was taken over by them amid bitter fighting. The workers' associations tried to keep some distance between their leaders and the intellectuals: the latter were welcome guests only at their festivals and parties.

The peasant worker's distrust of the *kaputos* (the frock coat worn by the middle class) was the product of bitter experience. More than one educated man had taken advantage of the inexperience of the simple villager in the unfamiliar environment. The associations rejected the intelligentsia's direct leadership and opened the way to the rise of a peasant-rooted leadership with a style of its own as the consequences of the associations' transient memberships. The Bridgeport Federation included in its statutes that only such persons might be elected officers in the organization who had been workers in the old country. They further excluded everyone who whether in Hungary or in America was indicted or convicted for an infamous deed.[32]

In the small communities of their local organizations, the peasant workers considered personal friendships, the emotional expression of belonging, as important as re-creating the entertainments and merriments of their village life. The unwritten law of the associations became, "He who doesn't drink with you is not your friend."[33] By contrast, the advocates of self-education were primarily craftsmen and intellectuals.

Within the intimate atmosphere of the small groups, the desire and the opportunity to perform in public put the desirability of culture and education in a new light. There were immigrants who learned to read and write at society evenings, while those who had stopped reading books altogether after grade school were inspired to read regularly and to see learning as a continuous process. Some even tried their hand at writing. The comic routines performed at school functions were usually written by a member; others tried writing plays. The themes of their literary attempts were the experiences gained during their wanderings, the adventures they had had, the homesickness and the conflicts of a "divided heart" expressed comically or satirically with bitter irony, or emotionally with a melancholy romanticism.

The secular organizations were one of the main bases of the Hungarian immigrants' social life, they were congenial soil for the development of individual talent.[34] Their communal importance was great everywhere, especially in the scattered settlements, here they were the only forum of group activity. The local chapters, the so-called branches, rendered it possible to take part directly in social life. As the organizations grew, so did this aspect, until in the 1910s every association annually put on one or more social evenings or theatrical performances.

By examining these programs, it is possible to trace the most important moments in the development of Hungarian-American culture. The literature it gave rise to (of interest here not from the aesthetic but from the historical point of view) and the social events it records are our greatest aid in learning about the strange social world of the Hungarian immigrants, a world the immigrants commonly referred to as "Magyar America," and which they saw as resting on the twin pillars of the fraternal societies and the churches.

The public demonstrations of Hungarian patriotism, the insistence on national independence, the strong anti-Habsburg sentiment, the devotion to the memories of Lajos Kossuth, of the 1848 Revolution and War of Independence, the cult of the war of liberation led by Ferenc Rákóczi to be found among the Magyar immigrants were not entirely original to the immigrant masses with their peasant background. The predominantly middle-class intellectuals, newspapermen, and clerics influenced the communities' ideology.

It should here be mentioned that the Democratic and Republican clubs also grew out of the fraternal societies. Initially the members were mostly intellectuals, small groups of middle-class people or those moving into the middle class. The first Democratic club was organized in New York by a lawyer, Mór Cukor. The members of the Magyar Republican Club participated in the 1900 election campaign of Theodore Roosevelt, and a few of them (e.g., Marcus Brown) received recognition from the President.[35]

By the 1920s, the way in which the centralized Magyar fraternal associations used cultural uniformity and mass communication to achieve both horizontal and vertical integration of the scattered American Magyars is a sharp contrast to the image of primordial solidarity in the ethnic community. However, Magyar leaders worked to prevent the nationally focused loyalties from becoming disruptive at the local level. When members of one religious congregation might belong to any one, or more, of four fraternal associations, and when members of one fraternal association might belong to one of five religious congregations, there were many possibilities for confusion and hard feelings.

CHAPTER 13

Building Religious Institutions

APPROXIMATELY 60 TO 65 percent of the Hungarians of Magyar mother tongue were Roman Catholics; the rest were Calvinists (Reformed Protestants), Lutherans, Jews, and Roman Catholics of the Byzantine rite who were known as Greek Catholics.[1] The first Hungarian religious congregation in Cleveland was B'nai Jeshurun. It began in 1866 with a small Orthodox Jewish *minyan* (prayer group of ten adult males) of working people. These sixteen immigrants began meeting in their homes and then in Gollanter's Hall to pray together. Some could not afford the membership fees in the two established German-Jewish synagogues; others preferred Yiddish or Hungarian to the German they heard there. The congregation soon developed a religious school for the children and by 1875 had hired a preacher-cantor and teacher.[2] The Jewish pioneers easily intermingled with the Christian Hungarians, although the Orthodox Jews from northeastern Hungary kept to themselves. The lifestyle of Hungary's Orthodox Jews did not differ from that of the Galician Jews, who lived only a stone's throw away, but emotionally Hungarians were as negative toward those living in the territories east of Hungary as the Galician Jews were toward them. Hungarian Jews were assimilated to a much greater degree into Hungarian society than those living in other Eastern European countries. The Jewish emancipation in Hungary in the mid-nineteenth century resulted in the integration of the Jews into society as Hungarians.[3] The subculture they then formed later caused their isolation from other Jews in America.

The Slovak and Magyar migrants worked together to build their first Roman Catholic church in Cleveland in 1889, naming it St. László Roman Catholic Church, after a medieval Hungarian king. They agreed that the vernacular parts of the High Mass would be held in Slovak and the Low Mass in Hungarian. A struggle for predominance in status and the use of language, however, erupted when the priest attempted to bless the flag of a Magyar association in Slovak.

Fighting broke out among the spectators, and each group blamed the other for the scandal. After reviewing the problem, Bishop Horstman of the Cleveland diocese dissolved the parish, giving the Slovaks the church building and paying the Magyars one thousand dollars for their investment in it.[4]

Bishop Horstman then requested, in the style of the period, that the archbishop of Hungary send the Magyars a priest: "I request Your Eminence to kindly send me an energetic and worthy priest to the Cleveland diocese to the Hungarians, who have been so long abandoned. Have mercy on these souls who came from your area! . . . Without an offer of help they will all be lost."[5] In response, the archbishop of Esztergom selected Károly Bőhm from the applicants. Bőhm arrived in early December 1892 and after familiarizing himself with the situation, placed the following notice in *Szabadság:* "The next service will be held together with the Slovaks in the St. Ladislaus Church, but after that, the Hungarians will no longer belong there. We must establish our own church through our own strength to be able to call it Magyar, to function as a Magyar community and to allow this community to truly represent the Magyar people."[6] Within six months, on June 4, 1893, the first "purely" Magyar Roman Catholic congregation laid the cornerstone for the Hungarian St. Elizabeth Roman Catholic Church on the corner of lower Buckeye Road and East Ninety-eighth Street.

The Magyar Calvinists began to organize their community in Cleveland under the auspices of the home missions board of the Reformed Church in the United States, originally a German-American denomination. Fifteen to twenty Magyars began singing hymns together in a home and later attended a German church on Seventy-fifth Street on the East Side. After the pastor gave them permission to take communion in their own manner, the Magyar Calvinists' communion hymn "Bread of Life, descend now from heaven, feed our souls for eternal life" rang out to the astonishment of the German congregation, who, not understanding a word, turned and stared at them. The denomination of the Reformed Church subsequently offered them help in organizing a Magyar church, and an English minister in Budapest acted as intermediary between it and the Hungarian Reformed Church. The German Americans asked their Hungarian counterparts to send over an "appropriate young minister" as the "fates of the ever growing number of immigrant Calvinist Magyars and particularly the abandoned state of their spiritual life had come to the attention of the American, English, and German churches."[7] In October 1890 Gusztáv Jurányi, the first Hungarian Calvinist minister, arrived in Cleveland. Paid by the Reformed Church in the United States as a missionary, he held his Magyar-language services in the West Side German church. The establishment of the first Magyar Reformed Church took place on the East Side in 1891, when a community was organized which rented the German Trinity Church on the corner of Rawlings Avenue for two dollars each Sunday.[8]

The first Magyar Greek Catholic church was begun by ten families, who in 1891 founded the Saint Michael Sick Benefit Society to aid the ill and build a church. The Bishop of Munkács in Hungary answered their request to send them a priest, and under the guidance of Father Csurgonics, they built the church and opened it in 1893. The parishioners were of a multiethnic background, individuals who to some degree had been assimilated into the Magyars. In fact, all the Hungarian churches that were established before the great emigration wave of the 1890s were multiethnic. Their elected lay leaders were, as their founders had been, respected members of the evolving communities.

The first fourteen years of the twentieth century witnessed a continuing diversity in Cleveland's Hungarian religious life. West Side Roman Catholics started St. Imre's Church in 1904, and Reformed West Siders organized their own congregation two years later. Meanwhile, with the support of Lutherans in the United States, the Hungarian Lutherans (or Evangelicals) separated from the Reformed congregations in 1905. The Magyar Evangelical congregations remained noticeably multiethnic; most members considered themselves Vends or Magyars.[9] The small groups of Baptists, Seventh Day Adventists, Sabbatarians, and Pentecostals organized churches in the first years of the century with the help of German and English churches. Magyar Baptist congregations were established on the East Side in 1903 and the West Side in 1907. Their best-known "Hungarian" founding preachers were a Slovak, László Zboray, and a Romanian, Béla Szilárd, as separation of the Baptists along ethnic lines only became evident at the beginning of the 1920s.[10] At the first conference of Hungarian Baptist missions in 1908 at Homestead, Pennsylvania, four languages were used in the sermons, addresses, and discussions: Magyar, Croat, Slovak, and German. And in the early days at some of their churches and missions two and three languages were used during worship.[11]

The "Magyar" in the names of first church communities did not so much express their actual derivation, but rather one step in the formation of the Hungarian ethnic community. The social life of the community was markedly advanced by having its own congregations and church buildings when ethnic boundaries became more and more evident. From the beginning the churches functioned as centers of the communities' social life, and so they were symbolic evidence of the existence of the Magyar community.[12]

Pioneer Magyar Priests and Ministers

Serving as priest among the Hungarians who had migrated across the sea was not popular in Hungary in the 1890s. Amusing stories reflect the false images that even the educated gentry had of America. "I am willing to go there," wrote one Calvinist minister applying for a position in Cleveland, "but tell me in complete honesty if there are still Indians there who would make us fear for our lives, as I married only a few years ago and have a wife and two small children whom it is my duty to protect."[13] As a result, the pioneer Magyar ministers were those whose careers in the church, for some reason, were not developing back home. For example, Gusztav Jurányi was an outstanding Orientalist, conversant in as many as seven languages, a philosopher, and a language teacher, who already had served in numerous places in Hungary but was teaching in the secondary school in Pápa, a small city in western Hungary, when the Reformed Church extended its invitation to come to Cleveland.[14]

Jurányi experienced great disappointment among the Magyar migrants: "When the minister appeared at one of the society meetings and addressed those present, without exception Protestants and the majority Calvinists, to join the church, he was received unkindly. There were those who openly asked 'why the minister shoves his way in here' and there were some there who allowed themselves even more disrespectfulness."[15] The main problem was that relatively few migrants wanted to become dues-paying members of a congregation. When asked to join the church many among them replied that they only came to the U.S.A. for a short time, were soon going home, and until then were paying the church tax back home."[16] Jurányi was able to recruit only 50 to 60 members from the 100 to 150 Magyars who attended his first church service. His status as an outsider and the problems involved in organizing and building the church so completely exhausted him that after three years he gave up his career as a Magyar-American minister.

The first Roman Catholic priest, Károly Bőhm (1853–1927), had achieved outstanding success in his studies at the Vienna Pázmáneum. He spoke German, Hungarian, and Slovak fluently and had been the priest at the small Hungarian village of Márianostra, where he had served the inmates of the prison.[17] In Cleveland he soon was able to register 220 families (340 Magyar adults and 507 children) in his parish, although he demanded complete obedience according to the practice of the Roman Catholic churches back home.

In 1894 Bőhm published the *Szent Erzsébet Hirnöke*, which he continued after 1900 as the *Katolikus Magyarok Vasárnapja* (Catholic Hungarians' Sunday). He used his paper as a tool to offer moral and religious instruction to his parishioners and to educate them on how to adjust to American life. Often he wrote about the struggles and sufferings that became the lot of immigrants from Hungary and characterized America as "a country which not only provides bread, but also a gravestone."[18]

The centralized hierarchy of the Catholic Church taught its members to give greater respect to its leaders than did the more self-governing Protestant churches, but Bőhm still had to confront many obstacles. He continually chided the Catholic Magyars for their unwillingness to donate to the church. "Why is it that the Magyar House dance hall is rented months in advance for every payday? Even during Lent it's filled despite the twenty-five cents admission. At the same time, during the week there is hardly anyone who drops a nickel into the church donation basket."[19] Nevertheless, during the fifteen years of Károly Bőhm's leadership, St. Elizabeth Church in Cleveland, the first Magyar Roman Catholic church in America, was built. In addition, the largest Magyar Catholic school was opened, and Bőhm organized churches in other areas, too. In 1907, after a long trip to Hungary, he returned to find his church position filled. A group of church members had begun a revolt against him and managed to get the bishop to name a previous assistant pastor, Gyula Szepessy, to his position. Böhm then became pastor in St. Louis; East Chicago, Indiana; Newark, New Jersey; and Buffalo, New York. From Buffalo he was called back to St. Elizabeth by the Cleveland Magyars after Szepessy's death in 1923, and until his retirement in 1927 Károly Böhm again directed the religious life of Magyar Roman Catholics on Cleveland's East Side.[20]

The second Magyar Calvinist minister, Dr. Sándor Harsányi (1871–1951), arrived in Cleveland on October 26, 1894, after "two weeks' stormy journey across the ocean, memories of which will remain with me until the end of my life."[21] A descendant of a long line of Calvinist ministers, he had graduated from the Theological Institute in Debrecen and applied for the Magyar-American ministerial position on the recommendation of one of his professors, who had been impressed by his noble, enterprising spirit. Because Harsányi often served as a pastor to distant Magyar settlements, his frequent absences caused clashes with members of his Cleveland church presbytery. He also became involved in a dispute with Károly Böhm, the Roman Catholic priest.[22] These conflicts, in turn, led to his departure from Cleveland for the South Side of Chicago after not quite four years. The third minister, who already had fled from the New York Magyars, lasted only a few months in Cleveland before returning to Hungary. One of his colleagues recalled, "He wasn't cut out for the career of an American minister."[23]

Cleveland's fourth Calvinist minister, Elek Csutoros (1865–1950), a son of a carpenter, completed his secondary school and also attended the Theological Institute in Debrecen, but after passing the chaplain's examinations in 1889, did not receive a parish of his own for years. Csutoros embarked for the New World with his wife and a child in October 1898, and on October 20 delivered his first sermon in Cleveland. "The church was packed. I cried! The congregation and I cried together. I cried after my Magyar homeland and the congregation shed tears of joy that after half a year they were again able to hear the preaching of God's word in their mother tongue. This emotional first meeting, however, was followed by far more difficult times.

> If I had known what lay before me in my new work, I wouldn't have dared to begin. Within a half year the small congregation had scattered and I had to go house to house to gather them together. And at least twice a month I had to visit those cities where Magyars lived in larger numbers. I traveled in scorching heat, in rain and cold, at times on railways, by wagon or on foot to visit those Magyars living in the scattered mining settlements. I established approximately fifteen churches.[24]

As immigrant numbers continued to grow in Cleveland, the wooden church became too small, and Csutoros urged the congregation to build a new church. "I began collecting for the church building not only locally, but also in all the Magyar settlements in Ohio. The fall of 1903 we laid the cornerstone and by May of 1904 dedicated the lovely church built of stone."[25]

Elek Csutoros was among the most able of Cleveland's Magyar leaders, in secular as well as religious affairs. During only his second year in Cleveland, the

American Hungarian Reformed Federation, a national fraternal organization, elected him vice president. In 1902 he was a member of the committee that "pressed the placement of Kossuth's statue" in Cleveland, although, as he later wrote to a friend, "because of my stubborn Hungarianism I was on the black list of the government back home."[26] When the American Hungarian Calvinist ministers met to decide whether to join the Hungarian Reformed Church, they elected Csutoros their temporary bishop. He served as the first president and for years as the vice president of the American Hungarian Federation in Cleveland. He was also one of the builders of the American Hungarian Reformed Federation.

When, in 1912, Csutoros was elected pastor to replace his father-in-law pastor in Siter, Bihar County, he remigrated to Hungary with his wife and five children, but his mistake quickly became apparent. "The family was unable to get used to the simple village life."[27] Within a year they were again back in the United States. As another minister had already been installed in Cleveland's East Side Reformed Church, Csutoros was charged with continuing the mission work among the Magyar miners living in southern Ohio. The next year he managed to exchange places with the West Side Calvinist minister in Cleveland and remained there for thirteen years. Under his guidance the church celebrated its tenth anniversary in 1916, and on several occasions Csutoros was asked to mediate between the Kundtz works and its employees on strike.[28]

Between 1907 and 1913, Károly Erdei (1882–1915) led the Calvinist congregation on Cleveland's West Side. He was well known as a student who visited the cities of Europe on a walking tour. After finishing the seminary, Erdei concentrated on getting to America, and on May 5, 1907, he arrived in Cleveland.[29] He was charged with completing organization of the West Side Church, which Elek Csutoros had begun from his post on the East Side. Under Erdei's guidance, the community purchased land and a house on West Twenty-fifth Street and remodeled it into a church and parsonage. He started a Hungarian school on the West Side for the Magyar children and was able to captivate his congregation with his beautiful sermons. With signs of his restlessness ever increasing, however, he exchanged positions with Csutoros in October 1913. On January 28, 1915, facing hospitalization for an illness, he committed suicide.

Unfortunately, little is known about the roles of the Greek Catholic priests, the rabbis, and other Protestant preachers in establishing their congregations. But what is known in no way contradicts the essential picture of the leaders of the Hungarian congregations. As they had difficulties to conform with the different conditions they often changed places, especially in the smaller congregations. The tenth anniversary issue of *Amerikai Magyar Népszava* reveals that often a veritable bartering went on, sometimes owing to the fault of the congregation, sometimes that of the priests. It had become fashionable among the clergymen to exchange places several times a year. Although inner conflicts occurred everywhere, they were more common in larger congregations, in cities where the traditions of the members were more heterogeneous. The Roman Catholic Magyars of Cleveland's West Side, culturally and traditionally more heterogeneous, built a church community amidst more extreme conflicts and disputes than did the East Side's masses of peasant workers. The Greek Catholic church was a special case because the Vatican had allowed its priests in Europe to marry, but the American Catholic bishops were unwilling to recognize its married clergy. As a result, there was a constant turnover of priests in all the Magyar Greek Catholic parishes, including Cleveland's.[30]

Continuity and Change in the Life of the Congregations

From the beginning, changing conditions altered the Hungarian churches' organizational forms, governance, and, finally, their community functions, traditional religious practices. In the United States, where church and state were separate, individuals chose religious denominations according to their own convictions. They also decided the extent to which they wanted to accept the monetary sacrifice of belonging to a church. The church, in turn, relied totally on voluntary donations. It was impossible to coerce payment, and there were no parochial lands and benefice revenue to support the parish priest. Both priests and ministers were without the sources of assured income that existed in Hungary. Financially dependent on their parishioners, the clergy often became victims of the parishioners' whims. Those clergymen arriving from Hungary, who were used to unlimited power and an obedient "flock," had great difficulty accepting the laity's new behavior. Particularly shocked were Catholic priests, who were accustomed to the backing of a rigid hierarchy back home. "A decent and consequently self-respecting priest has to be fed up with the American Misters, who, not having the cane of the *szolgabíró* (district administrator in Hungary before 1945) behind their backs, allow themselves every kind of churlish brutality toward their ordinary priest."[31] In the villages the priests and ministers "counted as gentlemen," but the social distinction gradually diminished in the new environment while tension increased. Without exception, Cleveland's Magyar priests and ministers were educated in Hungary, as they were proud to point out, and they were imbued with the European churches' conservatism.

The church was the earliest Hungarian place where the immigrants were able to act according to the old familiar rituals of conduct. The Magyars, as did other emigrants, tried to follow styles from home in building their churches. Simple naves and high slender towers made the churches look as though they had been transplanted from the Magyar Alföld to the modern factory city. In the cities, however, their pure white color quickly became dark and sooty. When Cleveland's East Side Reformed Church in 1904 replaced its wooden building with a stone edifice, Magyars from far and near were invited for the celebration. The announcement of the dedication boasted:

> On the first Sunday in June of 1904 a great Magyar celebration occurred
> in Cleveland: the new Magyar Reformed church was dedicated. The

celebration was made unforgettable by the mass participation of Cleveland's Magyars, regardless of denomination, along with numerous regional societies participating. There were baptisms, confirmations, marriages, and communions.[32]

In the evening another celebration was held in the Magyar House. Community activities had become an intrinsic function for all denominations. Indeed the Sunday service or Mass was not only a religious occasion but also a functional part of the social relationship. In similar festive fashion was the laying of the foundation stone of the Calvinist church in Johnstown.

> The laying of the foundation stone (which was erected with the powerful help of their English neighbors) was accompanied by a grand ceremony that began at three o'clock in the afternoon. The Hungarians of Johnstown took part in the beautiful and solemn festivities regardless of denomination. Several members of the Reformed Federation attended, five members of the Lajos Kossuth Association clad in hussar dolman acted as guards of honor in the procession accompanying the coach bearing the pastors, whilst two members on horseback rode at the head. The long procession offered a beautiful sight indeed to the inhabitants of the "Cambrian City" and they had reason to be delighted. When they galloped through the streets on horseback all eyes were on them. The Hungarians were all together regardless of denomination and our Slovak kinsmen joined us in the festivities.[33]

Because the religious community was a social organization, societies and cultural organizations, one after another, were established under its auspices. The *Cleveland Magyar Recorder* noted the rivalry that resulted: "The Cleveland Reformed youth hasn't fallen behind either; last Sunday they established the Cleveland Hungarian Reformed Organization."[34] In 1904 the St. Stephen the King Catholic Hungarian Society of St. Stephen Church founded the Szent István Dráma Club (St. Stephen Drama Club), and the Greek Catholics began the Szent János Görög Katolikus Fiatal Férfiak Dráma Club (St. John Greek Catholic Young Men's Drama Club). Amateur theatrical productions and informative lectures presented by the churches' cultural circles clearly reflected the merging of the religious with cultural and social activities. Soon it became a general custom to use the church hall for secular purpose: theatrical practice, school programs, and even dances. Extra areas were sometimes designed for such activities, to thwart the opposition of outraged traditionalists.

Church leaders did cling to the old traditions that protected the national character of the Magyars, but if they did not perceive this character as at risk, they were quick to adopt American customs with a perfunctory protest. Planning and organizing dances, "fairs," games of chance, excursions, and theatrical events that filled the church treasury and protected the members' Magyar identity took up a good part of the pastors' time. The thousand years of Hungarian history offered an inexhaustible wealth of examples for church leaders to use in fostering ethnic consciousness through sermons on patriotism.

The Protestant churches celebrated as important historical events March 15, the beginning of the 1848 Revolution, and October 6, the execution by the Austrians of thirteen Magyar generals who led the War of Independence. For Catholics, the greatest national holiday was August 20, in memory of the Hungarian king St. Stephen, who consolidated and created the Hungarian kingdom. Hungarian Catholics also quickly adopted the cult of Lajos Kossuth, nurturing the ideals of the 1848 Revolution for national independence, which could not be voiced by the Catholic churches in Hungary at that time. The motto of the great Magyar hero in the eighteenth century against the Habsburg rule, Ferenc Rákóczi II, "With God, for Country and Liberty!" was incorporated into the official seal of the Cleveland West Side Reformed Church. The Reformed ministers who described Calvinism as the "Magyar religion" were the leaders in awakening Hungarian consciousness.[35]

Among the migrants were some who were not native speakers of Magyar, but who had started down the road of assimilation in Hungary. In their new environment, the course of ethnicity they had embarked on in Hungary caused them conflict. Some continued their Magyarization, but others found themselves in an identity crisis. "I am a Slovak to the Magyars and a Magyar to the Slovaks," was the anguished cry of one.[36] Finally, there were some who tried to obliterate their Magyar loyalty with outspoken anti-Magyarism. "When he left, he was a loyal Magyar, but later he became an aggressive national organizer. Who can see into his soul?" wrote the Greek Catholic bishop of Munkács to the Hungarian prime minister about the last priest he would send to the United States.[37] This individual belonged to what Glettler has called the "floating nationality element," close to both ethnic groups, but also in conflict with both.[38] Most clerics of this kind eventually moved to an ethnic and national intermediate stage, characterized by a cultural no-man's-land of mixed identities. This small group of switching clergy, insecure and undecided about its own ethnic identity, played an influential part in the development of ethnic consciousness within both the Slovak and the Magyar immigrant communities. Initially, these transitional men of mixed allegiances were mediators, supporting harmony, cooperation, and alliances between the two ethnic groups. The period of mixed identities lasted for at least two decades and in some cases for a good bit longer. However, the conflict generated by the flexible self-identification practiced by some of the clergy was itself an important catalyst in shaping ethnic consciousness.[39]

Although their counterparts and mentors in Hungary did nothing of the kind, the clergymen who were the church builders also assumed responsibility for the immigrant community's social life and worldly problems. They mediated in work conflicts, obtained jobs, and counseled the migrants about marital and personal problems. In the evenings they wrote articles for the Magyar newspapers, and some, such as Sándor Harsányi, wrote for the English papers to dispel prejudices against the "Hunkies."[40] At the same time, the priests and ministers tried to teach the migrants new social norms through their writings, preaching from the pulpit, and personal contacts. In return, the immigrants believed of the clergy, as they did of everyone else, that their deeds were inspired by a financial motive rather than a sense of responsibility. The pastors were respected slightly more than, but distrusted just as much as, other community leaders.[41]

Before World War I, there was as yet no significant difference between parish life in the Magyar-American churches and in the old country. The language of the services was exclusively Hungarian; the Lord's Supper and the hymns sung were determined by Hungarian traditions. The first noticeable innovations, the first American feature, was the Sunday school, the placing of the children's religious education within the framework of parish work.

Church Conflicts

The Magyars brought all of the old-country conflicts between and within the denominations to the United States with them. The differences between Reform and Orthodox Jews that existed in the donor society from the 1880s became the basis for disagreement in Cleveland. "When the immigrants entered the American Jewish world, they could easily feel at home, as the American Jews were also vigorously debating what Judaism should become."[42] The B'nai Jeshurun synagogue in Cleveland, originally founded as an Orthodox congregation in the 1900s, became increasingly more liberal in 1904 when an Orthodox group left and founded Ohev Zedek congregation.[43]

It did not please the Roman Catholic priests that immigrant life brought Hungarians of different denominations closer to each other. In particular, those priests were dissatisfied who tried to isolate their adherents denominationally from others on the basis of the conservative old-country practice. Hoffman quotes from a letter of a worker who relates what happened when members of a Catholic sick relief association brought their flag to a Calvinist church when they attended some festivity. "What happened when we returned to our church? N., the Catholic priest, did not let the flag be carried in until it was consecrated again, as it was contaminated. What effect this had, needless to say, I think."[44] In a central body of fraternals, the Catholics did not send delegates, as reputedly they were not allowed to cooperate with associations that did not make a distinction between denominations. The situation of the Magyar Catholics was made more difficult by the "American bishops' ignorance of the nationality problems within the Monarchy, so that some bishops refused to understand why there was need for a Magyar pastor" especially when there already was a Slovak or other priest from Hungary working in the area.[45] The differences between the would-be organizers of Magyar Roman Catholic parishes and the Irish bishops grew ever more acute, suspicion and mistrust was to be found on both sides, and the propaganda campaign against the Magyar priests conducted by the equally nationalist Slovak priests only added fuel to the fire. "No other nationality gave nearly so much trouble to the bishops all over the country as did the Magyars," recalled the first Magyar parish priest in the memorandum he wrote for the Cardinal of Hungary. "It took years for most Magyar settlements to make the local English-speaking priest or the bishop believe that they were determined to have a priest who spoke their own language."[46]

It is not possible to explain the building of the Roman Catholic churches and community organizations solely with the wish to satisfy the demand of faith. The first priest of Cleveland wrote to the Cardinal of Hungary: "There can be no doubt that our people can be kept loyal to our Holy Mother the Church only if we show and nurture expressly Magyar sentiments. Whatever he has accomplished so far, he has done it as a Magyar."[47] Another Magyar parish priest, commenting in 1901 upon the circumstances surrounding the building of the first Roman Catholic churches, emphasized that "every one of them was created by Magyar national pride wounded to the quick by insult."[48]

Differences between Magyar Calvinism and the American Protestant culture caused conflicts which arose while the churches were being organized. At the turn of the century, immigrant missions of the Reformed and Presbyterian denominations vied with each other as to which could establish more churches and lure the largest flock into theirs. In 1900 the Synod of Philadelphia of the Presbyterian Church emphasized its task concerning the new immigrants in the following: "Here is a work that appeals to both our patriotism and our piety. Good men make good citizens. So we repeat that to be Americanized, they need to be Christianized. If we are to do our duty by 'these strangers within our gates' and their American-born children, we must give them the Gospel."[49]

The General Conventus of the Hungarian Reformed Church began to urge the leaders of the Magyar-American churches to place their congregations under its authority: "Join us in the very real interests of the national and ethnic aspects of religious life, to show a national solidarity and to further the Magyar Calvinist religion."[50] In October 1904, six American congregations formally united with the General Conventus of the Reformed Church in Hungary.

The active interest in the spiritual guidance of the American immigrants by the General Conventus of the Reformed Church was directed by the Prime Minister, who undoubtedly created the "American Action" program because he recognized a steady rise in emigration, generally, and in Magyar emigration, specifically.[51] Magyar-speaking persons accounted for 25 percent of Hungary's emigration in 1899 and 33 per cent in 1902. The trend appeared undiminishing and threatened the delicate population balance in the Hungarian kingdom. As emigration became a mass movement and the anti-Magyar propaganda of Hungary's ethnic minorities in the United States began to be noticed in the old country, the Hungarian government saw the time as ripe in the "highest interests of the Hungarian state" to institutionalize the "nation's care" for the emigrants. For this purpose it worked out a comprehensive program of action, with theoretical and practical directives. The general guidelines for a program were worked out for three main areas (Magyar, Slovak, and Ruthenian), based partly on the recommendations of the Austro-Hungarian ambassador to Washington, and the information he provided, for example, on the communities and organizations of the Monarchy's emigrants to the United States. The various provisions of the "American Action" program outlined the practical means—making contact with churches, supporting clerics and influencing them, if possible, subsidizing schools and newspapers—which it was hoped would promote the theoretical goals of the program.[52]

Although it was very difficult to withdraw from the authority of the Reformed Church in the United States and accept that of the Reformed Church in Hungary, numerous churches did so, especially in the 1910s.[53] Among those transferring their memberships to the Hungarian authority were the Cleveland Calvinists. "It was only after negotiations lasting half a year that the Reformed Church in the U.S.A. released the East Side church from its jurisdiction."[54] The church community on the West Side was supported through substantial loans by the church back home. In the upheaval, the Presbyterian church attempted to divide the large East Side congregation, but on May 24, 1914, only a handful of members left the East Side Reformed church to join the Presbyterians. The minister of the Presbyterian congregation had completed his education in America, and the programs he espoused—English-language classes, kindergarten, and other social activities—reflected his own and his congregation's desire for acculturation.

The creation of the Hungarian-American Reformed Synod further divided the Protestant communities. The hostility among the church communities and primarily among the ministers—formally bilateral—now acquired yet another dimension, for there were the "joiners," the "non-joiners," and the "Presbyterians." The conflict was given expression in press polemics and in floods of pamphlets written in both Hungarian and English. "There were some who pointed a finger at the joiners, and their church delegations as political agents," recalled one source. The "joiners," however, called the "non-joiners" traitors to the Magyars who had sold their Hungarian nationality for the alms of the Americans. The flood of personal abuse even led to some libel suits.[55]

The "American Action" Calvinist branch had sponsored and directed the unification, and its administrative machinery had become the only acceptable channel for Magyar Protestants in America to maintain their ties to the mother country. The only acceptable expression of nationalism was within the Calvinist branch of the "American Action." According to Paula Benkart, those affected by the "American Action," the first generation of Magyar settlers, differed noticeably from other immigrants. They were more certain that their stay in America was temporary and confounded Americanization proponents by taking out citizenship papers far less frequently than other groups.[56] For that reason, they failed to develop the political strength of other Americans to gently cope with the families the Magyars had begun in America.

The nucleus of each community was the small number of activists "who were the doers in both the churches and in the societies." In the words of one of the Calvinist ministers, they were "the saintly minority, who for four centuries have been Magyar Calvinists and who as Magyars, know who they and the members of their household believe in." Organization of the church communities and the building of churches in the midst of the constant fluctuations of the migrants are testimony to the heroic strength of this small group. The migrants were not disposed to the responsibilities of church membership. At the turn of the century, therefore, approximately one-third of the Magyars belonged to a church; in the 1910s the figure was not more than 40 to 50 percent, probably similar to that among the other nationalities from Hungary.

The temporary nature of the migrants' stay away from their homes kept their memories and contacts with the small donor communities alive. Consequently, the authorities of the official Hungarian churches, chiefly the Reformed, but also the Catholic, were able to exercise their control over some of the churches in the United States with the support of reliable priests. Their migratory existence, scattered communities, and variegated ethnic division induced Magyars in even the largest settlements to take advantage of the Hungarian churches' assistance, although lay organizers were the ones who initiated the societies that originally developed the church communities and built the churches.

A mixture of interethnic conflict and cooperation emerged during the churches' early history. The primary cooperation in a multiethnic framework of Hungarians and Slovaks was only shortlived and, instead, was increasingly superseded by animated church building spurred by nationalistic sentiments.

CHAPTER 14

The Function of the Hungarian Ethnic Press

Newspapers and Newspapermen

THE BEGINNING OF real Hungarian-American newspaper publishing is generally dated to 1883, when *Amerikai Nemzetőr* (Hungarian-American National Guard) first appeared in New York. There had been even earlier experiments—*Magyar Számüzöttek Lapja* (Hungarian Exiles' Paper), published in 1853 by the political emigrants of 1848—but *Amerikai Nemzetőr* was the first to recruit its reading public from the "economic" immigrants and the first to accommodate to their needs and demands both in its style and in its content.[1]

A number of newspapers were started in the 1890s but soon folded from lack of an established readership. In Cleveland this was the fate of the *Magyar Recorder, Magyar Hirmondó* (Herald), and the first Magyar-language socialist paper, *Amerikai Népszava* (People's Voice).[2] The only newspaper known to survive into the next century, *Szabadság* (Liberty), found the best tone for expressing the Hungarians' needs. "We have to counteract the Pan-Slavic agitation, which as its goal wants to defame the Hungarians back home and to discredit them in the eyes of the Americans," argued its founder, Tihamér Kohányi.[3]

He was born into an impoverished gentry family of Sáros County. He studied law in Hungary but never took the examinations, working instead as a reporter on various nationalistic newspapers both in Budapest and in the Hungarian countryside. After a number of stormy, thoughtless, and scandal-filled years, he arrived in America a twenty-eight-year-old bachelor with four dollars in his pocket. Later, as an established reporter in the United States, he recollected his early years in Hungary:

> In my youth my life was colorful, if not stormy. I was named in a libel suit, which cost me two weeks; I had three so-called affairs of honor, all of which I must admit I sought. I thoughtlessly threw away my

money on cards and pleasure and had no qualms about making debts. Even my trip to America was paid for from borrowed funds, but since then I have repaid not only that, but all of my debts with monies earned—and I dare say by hard work—in America.[4]

Landing in New York, Kohányi took a fellow countryman's advice to "go, and to go immediately, to the country and take a job as a coal shoveler, live the not particularly pleasant life in the settlements among the simplest people, only don't remain in New York and don't even for one week live the so-called 'Magyar gentleman's' shallow life."[5] He went to a mining area in Pennsylvania but soon migrated further to Chicago and South Bend. After shoveling coal for a while, he began going from house to house peddling books. As a *pedlér* (peddler) Kohányi wandered from one Hungarian settlement to the next. "It was during this time that he saw what a need there was for a Magyar newspaper in this country, which when it became established, would have as its purpose the task, along with the ability, of binding together the great number of Hungarian-Americans."[6]

Kohányi did not have to wait long for his opportunity to publish such a paper. While he was in Cleveland as a *pedlér*, he met businessmen József Black, Tivadar Kundtz, and others who gave him the necessary capital to finance *Szabadság*. It published its first issue in November 1891 in Cleveland, but its history was one of insolvency, bankruptcy, and attachments. The editorial offices were moved to New York and then back to Cleveland, and there were times when the paper folded for all practical purposes. Kohányi was able to keep it going only by undertaking additional ventures. Besides selling books published in Hungary, he sold Hungarian clothes, flags and other insignia, and all sorts of Hungarian memorabilia, and he also took on printing jobs. As a result, *Szabadság* not only survived to observe its tenth anniversary with an impressive, seventy-two-page commemorative edition, but by the 1910s it had become the most widely distributed Hungarian-language daily in the United States.[7]

Newspapers were an essential means of communication in a Magyar community too large and geographically dispersed for face-to-face contact. The fraternal associations about to be formed endeavored to make use of them in their organizational drives. The Bridgeport Association designated *Amerikai Nemzetőr* of New York as their official paper. The Rákóczi Association, after it broke away from the Bridgeport Association, named the East Coast edition of *Szabadság* its official publication. The first officials of the Hungarian Reformed Federation of America started their own newspaper, *Őrálló*, to serve the Federation in 1897. This, however, was shortlived, and from the turn of the century, they chose as their official organ *Reformátusok Lapja* (Journal of the Calvinists). Ethnic newpapers were the most active in urging the establishment of social organizations, and *Szabadság* was no exception. The paper was devoted mainly to social and ecclesiastical problems. One of its aims was, however, to inform Americans of Hungarian events as well as Hungarians of American events. In

1894 Kohányi wondered in an editorial, "Why is it that the larger part of our countrymen remain distant from the organizational movement?"[8] His paper's traveling agents visited scattered Hungarian settlements and developed a network of correspondents to inform the editorial staff about events in the local communities. In this way, the readership was given a role in fashioning the paper's themes and profile. By printing specific employment informations the newspapermen actually made geographic mobility part of the concept of a Magyar community.

Although the Hungarian-language newspapers mushroomed in the first decade of the twentieth century, three Hungarian-language newspapers also reflected the three main ideological trends that characterized the Hungarian migrants in those times: liberal (though slightly nationalist, too), nationalist, and internationalist. All three rose to become national dailies; first among them was *Amerikai Népszava,* in New York (in 1904), then *Szabadság* (Liberty) in Cleveland (in 1906), and the socialist paper, *Előre* (Forward), also in New York (in 1912). In them the immigrants could read about the significance of the benefit associations, of the importance of organizing and the best ways to do it, and what was new in the various organizations. From the 1890s on, the ""Organization Directory" became a permanent feature of the Hungarian-American newspapers. At this time, the space bought by the organizations to publish their news was still an important contribution to the financial resources necessary to the paper's existence. There was keen competition—with irony, contempt, hatred, and disguised rage—among newspaper publishers to become the official newspaper of one or another association. The papers' readers were recruited primarily from among the fraternal societies, and a mutually supportive stance was in the interest of both the organizations and the newspapers.

Szabadság enjoyed its greatest success and underwent its greatest improvement during the first decade of this century. It expanded its format, the quality of its printing improved, and its content attained higher journalistic standards. This newspaper paid the greatest attention to fostering the immigrants' sense of history and national consciousness, although, as a consequence, it also was filled with prejudices. In addition, from 1904 on, it offered *Szabadság Naptár,* an annual review of the activities of the Hungarian immigrant communities, churches, and societies, and sometimes individual memorial profiles. These features reflected the changes that Hungarian culture underwent over time in the United States.

One cannot ascertain how many peasants read the newspaper, but by the 1910s *Szabadság* apparently had a relatively wide readership among them. Those who had already been interested in politics in Hungary were strongly influenced by ideals of the "48-er" and Independence Parties; they were the enthusiasts of the Cult of Kossuth in the Hungarian-American communities. These immigrants especially adopted the romantic, populist, anti-Habsburg stand, which Kohányi urged in the newspaper.

When *Szabadság* elaborately celebrated its twentieth anniversary in 1911, Tihamér Kohányi reported that the paper now had a circulation of forty thousand. He occupied a distinguished position in Cleveland's social and political hierarchy, and among those present at the banquet were other local leaders as well as President William Taft himself.[9] Kohányi's success, however, staved off his total physical exhaustion only for a short time. He was able to go back to Hungary and return to Cleveland with a young bride, but he soon collapsed, and in 1913 he died, leaving a great void in the Cleveland Magyar community and in the Hungarian-American publishing world.

Another outstanding personality in Cleveland's Hungarian intellectual life was Kohányi's competitor Henry Baracs (1860?–1924). After graduating from the law faculty in Budapest in 1890, Baracs emigrated to America to escape some personal conflicts. A short stay in New York preceded his move to Cleveland, where he did translations for *Magyar Hirmondó* (Hungarian Herald) before starting his own newspaper, *Elsö Amerikai Napilap* (First American Daily) in 1902. He was also a notary public and in 1904 advertised his bureau for official English translation. His newspaper career ended when, after six years of fierce competion, Kohányi in 1909 purchased his newspaper and incorporated it into *Szabadság*.[10]

Baracs then went to work as a personal secretary in Tivadar Kundtz's woodworking factory and remained the best-known and most active leader in Hungarian cultural and social affairs. For years he was president of the United Hungarian Societies of Cleveland. When Jenö Pivány, secretary of the American Hungarian Federation, organized the movement to protest the Treaty of Trianon, Baracs as the current president of the Federation spoke in 1919 before the United States Senate's Foreign Relations Committee.[11] Nevertheless, in 1919 Baracs was not reelected president of the American Hungarian Federation. Pivány, in his memoirs, recalls, "The waves of the so-called Christian course which swept through Hungary also reached Cleveland, and this was the reason that at that time the Hungarian Jew, Henry Baracs, was set aside. Understandably, this greatly hurt him, for he had worked hard to revive the American Hungarian Federation from the dead."[12] After Baracs died in 1924, a library was placed in the museum of Case Western Reserve University in his memory.

A Hungarian-language humor periodical, *Dongó* (Wasp), was started in 1903 by György Kemény (1875–1952), who for twenty years was a leading figure in Cleveland's Hungarian public life, serving as president of the American Hungarian Federation and other organizations. He was born in the village of Garatna, Abauj County, and finished secondary school in both Kassa and Eger. He then joined the Cistercian order, under the name of Anyos, and was a novice for two years at Zirc, before leaving the order. After working briefly for Marquis János Pallavinci's family as a tutor, Kemény set out with a half dollar in his pocket to join his parents and brother János in Cleveland: "For weeks he was unemployed before finding a position in a tailor shop, where for a weekly three and a half dollars he pressed clothes for ten hours a day. After a few months he was hired by the *Szabadság* newspaper, where for a weekly five dollars he was the accountant, correspondent, agent, associate and later for five years, editor."[13] *Dongó* became a successful paper, bringing gaiety and humor to the Hungarian immigrants. *Dongó's* regular illustrator was János Kemény. His drawings, which decorated the paper's holiday issues, captured the elements of Hungarian-American life with great expressiveness. Because most of the paper's jokes were sent in by readers, they offer a rare glimpse of the immigrant's frame of reference. Innocent, somewhat clumsy, and naive humor characterizes the majority of jokes. Missing is the intellectual or logical, instead we get an ironic picture of the Hungarian immigrant's sense of awkwardness in a strange environment. "A Magyar can't take part in American dances; therefore they party on their own. At the Hungarian dances the English force them out," went one reflection on the paradox of acculturation. Another joke reveals immigrant perception of American behavior. The "miszter" takes his child to be baptized. The priest asks what the boy's name will be. The miszter thinks a while, then throws out: "Give him some good English name!" "But there are lots of good English names," reckons the priest. "Then let it be 'Godehell' (go to hell)," replies the miszter.[14] In 1908 György Kemény began the literary publication, *Képes Családi Lapok* (Illustrated Family Journal), the only Hungarian-American literary paper, but unlike *Dongó*, it proved unsuccessful. Apparently readers preferred crude humor to high quality. In sketches for *Dongó* and other Hungarian-American newspapers, György Kemény immortalized the lives of the immigrants. An entire series of his tales, *Amerikai magyar életből* (From Hungarian Life in America), appeared in the *Amerikai Magyar Népszava's* Tenth Anniversary Edition in 1910.[15] He published some of the Hungarian-American folksongs he had collected in *Dongó's* Annual Anniversary Edition in 1913.[16] A collection of his own poems, *Száz vers, Magyar énekek az idegenben* (One Hundred Poems, Hungarian Songs in a Foreign Land), was published in Cleveland in 1908, while his epic essays *Huszárék esete* (The Case of the Huszárs) and *Vass András* (András Vass) first appeared in newspaper installments. Such literary activities made Kemény the best-known Hungarian-American poet in Hungary, where the Petőfi Society honored him.

The poet Gyula Rudnyánszky was another writer who worked for a newspaper in Cleveland, where he arrived with his wife in December 1905. Born in 1858 in Özdög, Nyitra County, Rudnyánszky was the son of a hussar first lieutenant of the 1848 Revolution. Young Gyula attended private schools, then studied law. But from 1876 on, he lived for literature alone. A well-known poet in Hungary, by 1904 he was editing the *Szabadság*, a political paper in Debrecen. Following a dispute with the publisher and a brief stay in Budapest, Rudnyánszky emigrated to America, reportedly with the encouragement and financial support of Kohányi. In America Rudnyánszky became one of the apostles of Magyar patriotism.[17]

Yet another unique newspaper writer was Márton Dienes (1866–1917), whose pseudonyms were William Warm and "Old American." In Hungary he was a member of Parliament but emigrated to the United States in 1906, in the wake of a corruption scandal. With the encouragement of Tihamér Kohányi, he wrote the first Hungarian-American novel, *Weinerék Amerikában: Egy magyar kivándorló család küzdelme és sorsa* (The Weiners in America: A Hungarian Immigrant Family's Hardships and Fate). The cheap, trashy novel appeared in installments in *Szabadság* from 1907 through 1911.[18] Dienes also wrote short stories, such as *Találkozás Amerikában: A javító kolónia* (Meeting in America: The Penal Colony). After Kohányi's death in 1913, Dienes wrote a tribute to his employer and friend, *Kohányi Tihamér élete, küzdelmei, sikerei és politikai végrendelete* (The Life Struggles, Successes, and Political Will of Tihamér Kohányi).[19] He also replaced Kohányi as editor until 1915, when *Szabadság* was implicated in a plot to keep American industries from aiding Hungary's enemies in World War I.[20]

Another type of Hungarian newspaperman was represented by Ádám Abet (1867–1949), a tailor and poet. In 1894 in Cleveland, he helped to found the socialist *Amerikai Népszava*, where his verses most often appeared. He had emigrated at the beginning of the 1890s from Nagyvárad, Bihar County. At first he went to New York, then to Cleveland, and sent his verses to newspapers in Hungary. In addition, his *Amerikai levelek* (American Letters) were first published in Hungary's social democratic paper, *Népszava*, before appearing as a separate volume. Abet also wrote musical lyrics and a play, *Csodatükor* (The Magic Mirror). In 1920 he published his philosophical work *Social Conscience or Homocracy versus Monocracy in Story, Verse and Essay*. But by then he had left Cleveland for Bridgeport, and Bridgeport for Phoenix, where he settled permanently.[21]

Formulating National Consciousness

Of all the cultural institutions established by the Eastern European immigrants between 1880 and 1910, the native-language press was most important in forming the migrants' national consciousness and ethnic identity. The press determined the boundaries of the ethnic groups and propagated a sense of belonging and identification with the homeland. Besides continually publishing news from home, the newspapers devoted entire sections to the present undeserved sufferings of their nation only the socialist papers did not extol the glorious thousand years of Hungary's past and its role as the state-creating nation of the Danubian Basin. *Szabadság* demonstrated typical nationalism in 1896 on the occasion of the Hungarian Millennium: "The scorned, misjudged, often snubbed 'Hunky' proudly holds up his head, as though he wants to show every American that he is the son of a nation which can look back on a thousand years of culture convincingly demonstrating the superiority of the Hungarian race with its state-creating abilities and its world-wide historical calling."[22] Contemporaries who objected to *Szabadság*'s Magyar nationalistic tone usually ignored its critical attitude toward Hungary's political and social conservatism. In fact, *Szabadság* enabled the Hungarian democratic opposition to consider the Hungarians in the United States as a base of support for its program of national independence, and the Austro-Hungarian Monarchy briefly withdrew the paper's Hungarian circulation permit in 1907.[23]

It is a cliché of immigration historiography that the peasant masses took no national identity with them to America—only local identification and loyalty. Of course, such a generalization overstates the case, for even a simple emigrant would already have been introduced to nationalism in school, folk games, and stories about historical events, not to mention military service. Nevertheless, the Hungarian immigrants' national identity was shaped primarily by what they encountered in America, above all by the hostility and contempt which they as "Hunkies" met "in the promised land." The definition of Hungarian-American ethnicity emerged from the interplay between the identity Americans tried to assign to the Hungarians and the one that the immigrants brought with them. Hungarian intellectuals believed that it was neither poverty nor religion, but their national origin that prevented the "Hunkies" from being treated as equals in the United States. They were scorned and rejected because they came from a country that was scorned and rejected. *Szabadság*, in an article entitled "'Hunyakia'—The Dishonoring of a Thousand-Year-Old Nation," bitterly criticized the *Indianapolis News* for claiming, "Verbally and in pictures we present our readers with that quarter of the city where 'foreigners' live." In fact, objected *Szabadság*, the article in the *News* was illustrated by a map which "dishonors a thousand-year-old nation: the Hungarian nation. This map, where 'Hunyakia' occupies the place of Hungary, is the dirtying of a bright, internationally admired historical past, the debasement of our ancestors' memories and the humiliating belittlement of that race which for a thousand years was always ready to spill its blood for freedom, and which for a thousand years was the bastion of Christianity."[24]

Ultimately, Hungarians in the United States blamed not American prejudice but rather the Austro-Hungarian Monarchy for their low status, which they attributed to the effects of Austrian rule upon their homeland. The leaders of the Slovak and other immigrant communities reasoned similarly but blamed oppression by Hungarians within the Dual Monarchy as the source of all of their problems. The immigrant newspapers reflect how the leaders of one after another of the non-Hungarian nationalities rejected any trace of Hungarian identity. Immigrants from Hungary distanced themselves from those who were not their own and coalesced with other Hungarian immigrants who were of the same culture and national origin. In time, their spokesmen reinforced the unfavorable view Americans had of Hungary and Hungarians, deviously exploiting American unfamiliarity with European problems and conditions, *Szabadság* charged.[25]

For their part, Hungarian newspaper writers and clergymen attempted to build the "Pan-Slav threat" and the "back-stabbing" by the non-Magyar immigrants into the body of Hungarian-American identity. In defense of the homeland's government, they reasoned that "all the non-Magyars in the kingdom should be compelled to Magyarize themselves, just as aliens coming to America are expected to Americanize themselves."[26] The Hungarian-American press, or at least the "bourgeois" papers, defined love of country and the desire for Hungarian independence as essential attributes of Magyar identity. Magyar identity enabled them to express dissatisfaction with backward social and economic conditions at home and to call for change. Their discussions of the Magyar identity also conveyed the sense that they belonged to a "nationality without kin, caught between the German-speaking Austrians and the awakening Slavs": "A constant threat hangs over the Magyars in Hungary, and over the Magyars in America. There they want to make a Great Austria out of Hungary, they want to annex Hungary. Here the Pan-Slavs slander and defame us, both verbally and in writing. In national assemblies and in books they attack us so that the American people, who once paid homage to Kossuth's greatness, should look at Hungarians in revulsion."[27]

In the early decades, Hungarian-American literature was not considered worthy of publication in Hungary. It appeared almost exclusively in the socialist press and *Szabadság*. The authors were mostly newspaper writers who also had worked in factories and mines for a time and experienced the life of a laborer firsthand. Poetry unfolded as Hungarian-American literature's principal genre, expressing the homesickness, alienation, and unfamiliarity of the work as well as the horror of industrial accidents and the shame of being a "Hunky."[28] Heroes of novels and short stories occasionally included impoverished members of the gentry who became workers and learned to respect physical labor and the peasants whom they would have scorned earlier. Literature thus tried to promote both ethnic and class solidarity.

After World War I, the Hungarian-American newspapers, particularly *Szabadság*, were harshly criticized by Robert E. Park, the famous American sociologist, who made use of a manuscript written by a Hungarian journalist. According to Park, these newspapers did not succeed in becoming progressive tools for educating the people and forming public opinion prior to and during the war. The reasons, he felt, were that newspapermen had not been involved in journalism before immigrating and, indeed, had not had experience in routine work of any kind. They were middle-class men who had fallen on hard times and still remained disdainful of labor. Not proficient enough in English to make a career outside of the Hungarian papers, they took advantage of the immigrant press's monopoly within the foreign-language market.[29]

> The men working on the editorial staffs of the *Szabadság* and *Népszava* are not, for the most part, professional journalists at all—that is, they were not journalists in the old country; they came to the United States, not in the hopeful mood of young men determined to make good, but simply because this seemed to them the only way out of a maze of failures and mistakes. Without any particular training, without in most cases a knowledge of English, but with a strong aversion to strenuous work, they drifted into the offices of Magyar newspapers here, because they were not fitted for anything else; they considered their jobs as a sort of last refuge. In the lack of opportunity afforded by competition, real advancement is blocked to them; they are fully at the mercy of two

employers—those of the *Szabadság* and of the *Népszava*. A few of them are sustained by the hope that they will ultimately be able to get out of the game; the rest, being well up in the thirties, have not even this hope left. They resign themselves to a hand-to-mouth existence, and simply cease to care. It is not merely a matter of being overworked and underpaid; working conditions are notoriously bad in the case of the average American newspaper man, but for him there is always a chance of advancement. In the Hungarian-American press such chance does not exist; there are about a dozen jobs to go around, and no hope to come out on the top. To work on the *Népszava* or *Szabadság* means not only getting into a rut, but being bottled up in a cul-de-sac. From the publishers' point of view, the matter is almost equally hopeless; there is no supply of fresh talent to draw upon, but always the same crowd of twenty to thirty individuals; and in the absence of competition it hardly matters whether you turn out a good sheet or a bad one, except that it is cheaper, all told, to turn out a bad one. In trying to understand the failure of the Hungarian-American press to develop a single genu-inely progressive organ of education and opinion, the psychology of the Hungarian-American editor must be taken into account.[30]

Park's book was written at the beginning of the 1920s, when Americanization was being forced most impatiently on the immigrants. Because he knew no Hungarian, Park relied on an informant, who was a former employee of *Szabad-ság*. If one looks, for example, at the Sunday edition of *Szabadság*, without judging it on the extent to which it has become Americanized, it is possible to see the chronological development of quality in its literature. The migrants, who might at first have read only a prayer book and then only a cheap novel such as the popular *Rinaldo Rinaldini*, the story of an outlaw, in time became newspaper readers and eventually came to know some of the best writers of Hungarian literature, such as Mór Jókai, Kálmán Mikszáth, and Géza Gárdonyi. The weaknesses of the Hungarian-American newspapers are quickly revealed if they are compared with American English newspapers and with those in Hungary. These weaknesses are due as much to the journalists as to the readers. The biographies of the Cleveland journalists prove, however, the aptness of the criticism of Robert Park: "The men working on the editorial staff of the *Szabadság* and the *Népszava* were not for the most part, professional journalists at all—that is, they were not journalists in the old country."[31]

CHAPTER 15

Ties to American and Hungarian Political Parties

SOCIOLOGISTS HAVE REPEATEDLY pointed out that a major function of an ethnic community, in addition to organizing itself and developing an internal structure, is to establish, maintain, and modify relations with its country of origin and its country of settlement. Organized, patterned relations require an ideology explaining the position of the community in both societies, the initiation and maintenance of selected types of relations, and their assimilation into the lifestyle of the society of settlement. As both the formal and the informal relations of an ethnic community with its country of origin and country of settlement are affected by a number of factors, it is important that we study it from the aspect of Hungarian immigrants, too.[1]

As the American press definitely reflects, from the beginning the Hungarian-American elite aspired to play a leading role in establishing relations with American political organizations. Hungarian Jews, who were less likely to plan to return to Hungary, became the primary contacts between Hungarians of all religions and the local political powers.[2] They invited the mayor, judges, and local legislators to the Hungarian community's banquets and celebrations, excellent opportunities for building contacts. As they attempted to convince the American politicians of the importance of the Hungarian vote, however, they surely exaggerated its numbers. And naturally they did not count only those whose mother tongue was Magyar, but all who had emigrated from Hungary. In this way, they could easily speak of a mass of millions.

From the 1890s until the 1930s, politically active Hungarian Americans tended to be members of the middle class, or those who wanted to belong to the middle class. The Hungarian masses did not develop a definite stand toward the American political parties until the 1930s. Before then, their leaders recommended specific candidates not on the basis of party affiliation, but only according to what they had done for the city and for the Hungarians. In

Szabadság's words: "During city elections we must set aside political view-points. What matters isn't whether the person is a good Democrat, or a good Republican, but whether he is a good mayor."[3] "Robert McKisson is running for mayor of Cleveland. Every Hungarian must vote for him, let us reject those who exploit the poor, let us protect the city from the railroad companies' tyranny."[4]

Probably following the Germans' example, prominent Hungarians established an umbrella organization, the United Hungarian Societies of Cleveland, for "coordination of the cultural, charitable, and social activities and the representation of the Hungarian Americans in Cleveland."[5] The activities of the United Societies began in 1902 with the erection and unveiling celebration of a statue of Lajos Kossuth on the one-hundredth anniversary of his birth. A committee of four, three of whom were Hungarian Jews, won the support of C. W. Pollner, an American attorney, who announced that American circles had wanted to set up a Kossuth statue and were only waiting for the Hungarians to begin the action. The leader of the Cleveland Czechs, Istvan Vicar, and the Slovak priest, Stephen Furdek, however, placed an announcement in Cleveland's English-language papers protesting against the statue because they said Lajos Kossuth was "the oppressor of the people."[6] Their committee and one composed of local Hungarian leaders each argued its case before the mayor, and the city council arranged a compromise in which the statue was placed on Euclid Avenue at University Circle, not Public Square.

At the unveiling of the statue, Mayor Johnson gave a very moving speech, and Governor Nash of Ohio and U.S. Senator Mark Hanna attended. The Austro-Hungarian consul estimated that eight to twelve thousand people marched in the parade and sixty to seventy thousand were in the crowds.[7] *Szabadság* reported on the festive procession as follows:

> At noon the Public Square and its vicinity was crowded with Hungarians. Horse riders cantered, coaches rolled, associations in Kossuth hats marched in to music. At exactly one the parade began, and exactly at 1:30 its lead reached the middle of Public Square. It took a good time before the great parade reached Euclid Avenue. But when it all finally was on the wide street it appeared as if there were a real army present.
>
> Six horseback policemen led the parade followed by two flagbearers, then János Weizer in a decorative Magyar hussar uniform with the American flag and Agoston Sztrachovszky in American uniform with the Hungarian flag.
>
> The flagbearers were followed by the main parade with ten horsemen, among whom József Berger of New York presented a worthy display in his decorative costume. After a band, the figure of József Pipi appeared astride a horse leading thirty-six horsemen in their hussars, *csikós,* and decorative civilian dress all looked very handsome.[8]

The parade was a milestone in the Cleveland Hungarians' development of ethnic identity. For years they looked back on it proudly, and it was followed almost immediately by a burgeoning of community organizations.

The inhabitants of "Little Hungary" in Cleveland generally idealized their motherland, as the source of a culture that belonged to all of them. They could identify with a Hungarian village without having to learn English and acquire a new culture. Very often when a church in a Hungarian village or town was built or restored those who came from that place were urged to collect donations. They aimed thereby not only to maintain personal relations with families in Hungary but also to support the community institutions those families were building.[9]

The relative concentration of their settlement and their organized communities made it easier for the political leaders of Cleveland and those of Hungary to reach the Hungarian inhabitants of Cleveland and exert influence on them. The political situation in Hungary, the problem of the country's independence, and the movements of national minorities made life more hectic even in the migrants' communities in the United States. All this became the source of a competition for status. As a result of the communications across the ocean, the traveling to and fro, and the group activities which helped to maintain political contact, everything that happened in Hungary became part of the daily life of the Hungarian communities in Cleveland. The events in Hungary inspired Hungarian-American public leaders repeatedly to develop the idea that the Hungarian migrants had one historical vocation: to help their homeland.

The new migration literature emphasizes that one can hardly speak of any original nationalism among the peasant-workers who migrated to the United States. Their identification with the sending society was entirely personal, as they knew only a very small segment of the country and its people. They were ignorant of the national culture and felt no solidarity with their people as a whole, particularly not with those who were members of other classes.[10] This does not mean that nationalism was utterly missing from those who emigrated from Hungary, only that—when their communities first began to form in the New World—nationalist feeling was confined to the upper classes, the educated members of the migrants.

Moreover, in the years prior to World War I, while they were overseas, nationalist political endeavors became stronger in Hungary. The Hungarian people demanded national independence from Austria; the national minorities demanded cultural autonomy from the Hungarians. The leaders of these movements tried to induce the migrants to support the political struggles pursued at home with donations and the voice of their political presses.

The Hungarian Americans began to build their political connections with the old country after the turn of the century, and Tihamér Kohányi of *Szabadság* played the main role in the process. He first visited Hungary in 1901, when he brought the Hungarian-American donation to set up a statue of the nation's great poet, Mihály Vörösmarthy, in Budapest. Thanks to Kohányi's career in America, this member of the fallen gentry now had prestige among the Hungarian landowners. As a result, he addressed the Hungarian National Agriculture Association, where he dramatically painted the "Pan-Slav threat" to the immigrants from Hungary in the United States.[11] Kohányi suggested that the Hungarian bishops allow only those clergy to migrate whose patriotism was unquestionable.[12] They further proposed that the Magyar Nemzeti Szövetség (Hungarian National Federation) present the emigrants with a flag. Richly embroidered, "To your homeland unfailingly be true, Magyars!" such a flag was taken by a delegation to Bridgeport, Connecticut, in 1902, for the tenth-anniversary celebration of the largest Hungarian association, the Bridgeport Association, where representatives of all the far-flung settlements had gathered.[13]

At the time, Hungary's non-Magyar emigrants considered the Hungarian flag with its inscription a provocation, and they vigorously protested against it. In a memorandum addressed to the President of the United States and to the governors of all the states, they pointed out the flag's anti-American character and complained about the oppression of their nationalities by Hungary.[14] Their various newspapers echoed the same two themes. The Austro-Hungarian ambassador to Washington was also unsympathetic to the symbol of Hungarian nationalism and emphasized to the State Department that the flag was a gift not from the Hungarian government, but from an independent social organization.[15] Every year thereafter the flag was presented to a different Hungarian association until the custom was forgotten. (The American Hungarian Reformed Federation now keeps the flag in its Washington, D.C., headquarters.)

"The Homeland in Danger": The Founding of The American Hungarian Federation

From the turn of the century on, events in Hungary concerned and inspired the elite of the immigrant communities. In 1905 news of chaos back home impelled the leaders of the patriotic Hungarian associations to call a meeting in Cleveland. Leaders of Hungarian organizations from other cities also joined the more than one thousand people from the East Side of Cleveland who responded by assembling at the Magyar House on Holton Street on February 21, 1906. Less than a week later representatives from over two hundred Hungarian settlements created the American Hungarian Federation, which claimed (not without some exaggeration) to represent one million Hungarians.[16]

> Our Compatriots! The freedom of Hungary, its independence, its statutes, the rights of the Hungarian people are in devastating danger. In our new homeland, on the ground of freedom we have learned what we have not learned over there, about which we did not even have time to think, that the strength lies in federation and solidarity!
>
> We, the one million Hungarians in America [sic] do not only demand, but will also achieve that the peoples of Hungary will have the same freedom, the same justice, the same well-being, which freedom, justice and well-being exists in that America, of which we are citizens.

> We want to transplant, we want to implant into the earth of Hungary consecrated with blood all those ideas, which would make our homeland big, strong and powerful.[17]

The opposition Independence and 48er Parties joined Hungary's government coalition, and the crisis was quickly resolved. Almost as quickly, the patriotic fervor for freeing Hungary cooled off in the American Hungarian Federation. In their 1907 program they emphasized the importance of safeguarding the Hungarian immigrants' interest. The idealistic, not realistic, aims of the program, however, were far from the range of thought of the average Hungarian-American worker. One of the officials of the Federation complained to Hoffmann: "It is exceedingly difficult to fire with enthusiasm a great number of my compatriots for goals that only look ideal. They feel averse to the program—they think it is just a machination of the masters. They may be enthusiastic about one or the other part of it, when it appears reasonable and adequate to a certain place, to their town for example. The Hungarians got skeptical owing to failures in the past, in particular on previous settlements. They don't like to overtax their strength, anyhow."[18]

The liberal paper *Bevándorló* (Immigrant) called the program a "dead document" already in the following year, and noted that "there were so few at the meeting that even a motion couldn't be passed."[19] In fact, the American Hungarian Federation existed on paper only until the outbreak of World War I, and even then it could not successfully turn American opinion against the Trianon Peace Treaty.[20] Political movements with ties to the homeland usually interested only the middle class, not the masses, who remained suspicious of the gentry.[21]

When the president of the Independence party, Count Albert Apponyi, went to St. Louis in 1904 to attend the Inter-Parliamentary Union, he used the occasion to visit prominent Hungarian-Americans. In Cleveland he met with several large groups at St. Elizabeth Roman Catholic Church and at the Magyar House. Representing the socialists, Gyula Uchrik and Imre Szemenei gave him a memorandum against conditions in Hungary, and his visit incited a wave of anti-Hungarian propaganda among the non-Magyar nationalities. Even the Slovaks took to the streets.[22] The protests were even more vigorous in 1911 when Apponyi returned after his name had been attached to the Education Act of 1907, which obliged the teachers of the non-Hungarian schools to teach Hungarian well enough so that pupils finishing elementary school should have mastery in both speaking and writing.[23]

For political movements in the interest of the homeland, leaders tried to mobilize the masses through the Hungarian-American press. By the 1910s using such slogans as people's rights, personal freedom, and democracy, both the democratic middle class and the radicals had strengthened the political consciousness of the immigrants. Count Mihály Károlyi, one of the leaders of the united opposition party in Hungary, along with some representatives of the Social Democratic Party, decided to visit the large Hungarian-American communities in 1914 to obtain moral and financial support, much as proponents of Irish independence had done.

Károlyi wrote the following about his American propaganda: "Our policies were clear and well worked out in every detail, and in no country could we have found a better ground for the propagation of our ideals than in the democratic United States with its large Magyar colonies. Our party had to break out of its provincialism and passivity and become a factor to be counted with. The great majority of the half million Magyars living in the United States are people who were forced to emigrate or whose parents had been because of the unbearable social conditions at home. We could be certain that they were no adherents of the existing Hungarian social order."[24]

According to one observer: "Under the influence of the *Szabadság*'s articles for the collection, Cleveland's Hungarians crowded into one unified camp. There was not one dissident voice. All of them, from the wealthiest Hungarian, Tivadar Kundtz, to the most simple Hungarian worker, ten thousands rallied as one at the thought of taking an active part in the continual struggle for an independent Hungary."[25]

The Hungarian opposition parties appeared to be successful in winning the emigrants' support.[26] Certainly, the emigrants' intentions of returning home and continued identification with those left behind inclined them to favor Károlyi's promises of reforms if Hungary again became independent. Formerly impoverished Hungarian peasants in the United States offered tens of thousands of dollars to the political struggle for Hungarian independence.[27] The struggle and their support were both halted by the outbreak of World War I.

CHAPTER 16

The Conflict of Loyalties during World War I

THE WAR CUT off the Hungarian migrant's personal contacts with family members remaining behind; those who were ready to leave were unable to do so for years. The news that loved ones were in danger and that fathers, brothers, and brothers-in-law were fighting at the front strengthened weakening feelings and fading memories. Some Hungarian Americans sought to join the Hungarian army, while the churches prayed for the homeland's victory, the soldiers' lives, and all who remained back home. The associations organized charity events and bazaars to collect money for medical supplies and clothing to send through the Red Cross to the Hungarian soldiers. Soon they were being called upon to buy Hungarian war bonds as well.[1]

Far from responding to Woodrow Wilson's appeal to be neutral in thought as well as in action, millions of American citizen sided with the countries from which they or their ancestors had emigrated. The war destroyed the illusion of the Melting Pot.[2]

Hungarian community leaders hoped that the United States would remain neutral. They constantly reiterated that the United States was not at all an interested party in the war and openly criticized Washington for providing war supplies to the Allies. At the same time, the propaganda within the Hungarian immigrant communities against the Austro-Hungarian Monarchy became stronger as their leaders, particularly the clergy and the journalists, began to demand total national independence.

Two most important national organizations, the Czech National Association and the Slovak League, held a joint conference on October 22–23, 1915, and signed an agreement to work together and make joint public appearances with the goal of securing the Czech and the Slovak nations' political freedom and independence.[3]

Preparation for the war, however, pumped up American nationalism and distrust and animosity toward "aliens." The primary target was the Germans, but the Hungarians also received a share of open hostility; some were attacked or dismissed from their jobs without any reason; Hungarian stores were boycotted. In a booklet published by the Austro-Hungarian Consulate General, such leading members of the Hungarian Parliament as Count Apponyi and such distinguished politicians as Baron Hengelmuller and Consul Nurber tried to explain that Austria-Hungary was free "from guilt in the horrible contest which has been forced upon her, and that she can face it with all the moral power of a pure conscience."[4] As Count Apponyi wrote, "I consider it highly important that the case for Austria-Hungary, in the present international conflict, should be put before the American public with minute precision."[5]

In 1915, the "Dumba Affair" resulted in a tremendous propaganda advantage for the leaders of Hungary's non-Magyar minorities as well as an enormous newspaper scandal in the United States. "Ambassador Dumba has admitted having made proposals to his government for causing strikes in American factories in which ammunition is manufactured." The government of the United States learned this from the copy of a letter from the Ambassador to his government, whereupon the United States directed the following note to the Ministry of Foreign Affairs in Vienna: "The President has charged me with informing Your Excellency that the Ambassador is no longer acceptable to the government of the United States as Ambassador of the Imperial and Royal government at Washington."[6] Because the scheme was to use strikes and sabotage by immigrant workers to keep American companies from fulfilling their contracts with the Allies, it redoubled suspicions against Hungarian immigrants in the workplace.[7]

In Cleveland—as mentioned before—the majority of the Hungarian immigrants worked in iron- and steelworks. The war contracts and later on the war preparations enhanced the key importance of these industries. As the result of war prosperity, job opportunities broadened and wages rose. The state intervened to foster production. Restricting the power of the employers, state authorities supported the struggles of the trade unions for better working conditions, and even in certain places, the demand for the eight-hour day. This was the case, in particular, in the steel industry, which before the war, had long working hours and low wages. Therefore, the trade unions could achieve considerable results during the war.[8] Only during the war years, in 1917 in particular, did large numbers of Hungarian workers join the unions. In the war years strikes multiplied. In the autumn of 1915, a strike broke out in the Kundtz factory in Cleveland. The Hungarian Calvinist clergyman on the West Side, Reverend Csutoros, became the president of the committee which concluded the settlement between the workers and the employers, and under his leadership, a compromise was reached which ended the protracted strike.[9]

In October 1915, the Machinist Union called a strike in the Cleveland Automatic Company. The workers demanded an eight-hour working day, the same wages they had had for the ten-hour day, and reinstatement for the workers, who had been dismissed. In that particular factory, there were some Slovenians and Hungarian-Slovak workers. The strike ended successfully.[10]

The situation became all the more dramatic in 1917 when the United States entered the war on the side of the Allies; from then on hatred flared against immigrants whose homeland was on the side of the Central Powers. At the time most Hungarians, still thinking of themselves as migrants, were not American citizens.

The American socialists reacted to the war differently from their European fellow workers. The American socialists opposed the war. They stated that the war meant an internal conflict between imperialists and had nothing to do with the working class.[11] In a resolution at the congress of the IWW in 1916, they declared their anti-imperialist and anti-war views.[12]

In May of the same year, the federal government sent special agents to Cleveland to investigate the agitation by the IWW among the factory workers there. According to the government, the IWW sent four hundred agents into the Cleveland factories to foster a revolt of the workers. The majority of these agents were said to be Hungarians. These agitators, their accusers claimed, were undermining the basic citizens' rights of the American people and sowing discontent among the workers. As a result of such reports, those who supported the principles of the IWW could not get American citizenship. Every member was threatened with losing his job.[13] When the United States entered the war, unmerciful retributions started to be exercised first against the members of the IWW. They were charged with being "Pro German," and "German agents."[14]

The differences existing within the Socialist Party (SP) first exploded in 1917, when the United States entered the war. At this time, as they were unable to convince the majority of their members to support the Allied war effort, part of the right-wing leadership left the party.[15] Most Hungarian-American socialists took an anti-war position. They rejected the war propaganda of both Hungary and America and did not participate in either side's sudden "patriotic" enthusiasms.[16] The war strengthened the Hungarian socialists' opposition and political activism and widened the gulf between their reformed and radical groups. The Elöre encouraged them to oppose the imperialist war rather than to purchase war bonds.[17]

From the end of 1917 through the first half of 1918, the leaders of the Hungarian-American communities spent their energies trying to convince American public opinion and political officials of their total loyalty. They made various "loyalty declarations" to the states and, on July 4, 1918, publicly celebrated the national holiday of the United States.[18] *Szabadság* and *Amerikai Népszava*, which previously had been "pro-Hungary," had switched to a "pro-America" stance after the United States entered the war. Although the quick about-face confused readers, *Szabadság* and newspapers that were advocating the purchase of Hungarian war bonds in the fall of 1917 now advised the purchase of Liberty Bonds and urged the immigrants to obtain American citizenship.[19] The American Loyalty League was organized in Cleveland with as many as four hundred members. Twenty-three thousand Magyars joined the Loyalty League within a few months.[20]

The Protestant congregations that had joined the church in Hungary were in a precarious position once the United States entered the war. Although in 1917 the Red Cross managed to arrange payment of the ministers' salaries, in 1918 they were cut off, leaving them and their churches in a financial crisis. Church property, being foreign-owned, was confiscated by the Alien Property Custodian. Amid rumors that the ministers would be deported, Mór Cukor, the Jewish attorney in New York who had functioned as mediator for the Hungarian immigrants, arranged for President Wilson to receive a delegation of the clergymen and accept personal statements of their loyalty.[21]

In the history of the American workers—and in that of Cleveland, too—the year 1919 became the year of great hopes and great disappointments. Those who attached great hopes to the year were the radicals, enthusiastic about the news of the European revolutions. But they were not the only ones. The news, for instance, that the working class had taken power in Hungary heartened not only the small groups of socialists, but the masses of the Hungarian immigrants, too. According to *Szabadság*, "One of the almost irreparable results of Bolshevik agitation was that the idea took root in a wide strata of the Hungarians in the U.S., that Hungary changed over into a Paradise without problems for the workers."[22] On the other hand, the Military Intelligence Division sent the following report:

> Recent events in Hungary, notably the rise of Bela Kun, show much radicalism in that country but this does not extend to the Hungarians in the United States. Their only radicalism consists in supporting the movement to break up the great landed estates in Hungary. The American Hungarians are opposed to the return of the Habsburgs and favor a republican form of government in Hungary. The organizations of Hungarians in this country do not participate in radical activities.[23]

The workers' May Day celebration in Cleveland, on May 1, 1919, had tragic consequences. A report entitled "Bloody May Day Demonstration in Cleveland" describes what happened:

> The red flags aroused the anger of the patriotic people. A tank and army truck ran through the long row of demonstrators. The demonstrators who were dispersed were beaten up by the crowd.... "There were many men and women alike among the socialist demonstrators, in particular, because the socialist organizations invited even the members of the IWW, as among them were many Hungarians. But there were one or two participants of Hungarian origin, who also attracted the attention amongst the patriotic people.[24]
>
> In the Hungarian district of East Side, May Day did not pass without excitement either. In front of the branch of the Woodland Bank at the corner of East Eighty-eighth Street, a large crowd gathered and refused to disperse even at the call of the police. Somebody shouted, "Long live the Industrial Republic!" At that the policeman arrested him and wanted to take him to the police station at East Seventy-ninth Street.

The crowd followed the policeman and could have taken the prisoner out of his hands, so the policeman asked for help. Soon a band of mounted policemen arrived and rode into the crowd. The crowd dispersed from the corner of East Eighty-ninth, but met again at other places. The policemen slashed at the crowd everywhere and dispersed them. The clash turned into a fight, and arms were used on both sides.[25]

There were many arrests. From Szabó Hall alone [this Hungarian saloon was the meeting place of the radicals on the East Side] two hundred people at once attacked the police.[26]

Among those arrested by the police, there were few Americans. They wanted to put the blame for the violent events occurring on the first of May on the aliens only because the great majority of the troublemakers were aliens.[27]

Strike activity occurred on an unprecedented scale. Propaganda against the immigrants strengthened in Cleveland after May, and from September 1919, with the outbreak of the steel strikes and mineworkers' strikes, it really gathered momentum.

The increasing power of workers in the United States to mobilize was revealed by the wave of strikes that arose in 1919. "We never knew, never heard of such a number of strikes, as of late." The total number of the participants was estimated to be a million and a half.[28]

With the end of the war the state's control over production stopped. The employers were left to regain their power over the workers. The workers, however, who had acquired more consciousness during the war of their own strength, refused to acknowledge the change in conditions. When the employers rejected the demands of the steelworkers, who were more than 250,000 strong—and were also represented by the American Federation of Labor—they went on strike under the leadership of William Z. Foster.[29] In Cleveland more than 30,000 metalworkers put down their work. Nevertheless attempts to organize the steel industry failed, "and Cleveland witnessed the foundation of the American Plan Association, which aggressively promoted the open shop in Cleveland importing strikebreakers and labor spies as needed."[30]

According to David Brody, an outstanding expert on the American working-class movement, the strikes, at least the big steelworkers' strike, were not the direct outgrowth of radicalism. Rather, they grew out of those economic conflicts which arose between employers and employees following the transfer from war production to peacetime production.[31] At the same time, the employers and those who represented their interests tried to characterize the strikes as revolts of the "foreigners" in order to influence public opinion. "This strike was not initiated by serious and unbiased labor leaders, the people were rushed into it by demagogues intoxicated by the red madness."[32] They deployed police and regular army forces, e.g, in Gary, Indiana, against strikers, where a relatively large group of immigrants from Hungary, Magyars and Slovaks, worked at the time. Confrontations and forceful actions were provoked between the strikers and the armed factory guards and policemen.[33]

In the National Immigration Law Committee, Sidney L. Gulick "showed up the steel strike as proof that the United States should have picked the immigrants and then there would not have been so many superfluous workers amongst the strikers in the steel factories who advocated radical views and Bolshevik principles."[34] In similar vein Senator Kenyon, chair of a Senate subcommittee, stated in his report that "the strike was originated in the first place by incitement and agitation."[35]

Szabadság challenged such remarks and protested that "the defamation of the foreigners was fashionable. The accepted custom to blame the foreigners for our workers' wars was not proven by facts." "For every radical movement, for every strike, the immigrant workers are made responsible."[36] *Szabadság* published many such criticisms on the growth of the American workers' antagonism toward the immigrants in 1919.

At the same time, there were other, more dangerous signs of hostility in the United States. The persecution of the radicals gathered momentum. The "Palmer raids" (ordered by the Secretary of the Interior) began with mass arrests and deportations. At the end of 1919 and in 1920, around New Year's Day, authorities started to arrest the Hungarian adherents of the IWW as well, in Chicago, Detroit, and Cleveland.[37] "Arrested radicals" was the title of the report in the *Szabadság* announcing that in the small restaurant at 3201 Lorain Avenue seven Hungarian men had been arrested. They were accused of having just held a meeting. In December the police raided the club of the Hungarian socialists with the help of the members of the Loyal American League. They arrested its secretary, József Gács, in his home. The detention of the office holders of the Slovenian socialists' club also took place then.[38] *Szabadság* published the frightening news on its front page with a banner headline: "The ruthless persecution of the reds has started,"[39] and added in later issues, "The alien inciters will be chased out"; "The aliens will be deported. Whether they will get convicted or not, they will be sent home to their country."[40]

To try to quell the turmoil of revolutionary fervor transported from Europe, nationwide Americanization programs were begun in 1919. The "Immigrant's Guide to Cleveland" and "Cleveland Citizen's Handbook" were published in nine languages. The city opened an educational center in a school on the East Side on Rawlings Avenue specifically "to educate the Hungarians, to enrich their culture and to entertain them." A similar center in the Woodland Street school offered citizenship classes.

At the same time, the Cleveland Americanization Committee published a small booklet, "The Magyars of Cleveland," to introduce the Hungarians to the Americans. It contained a few highlights of Hungary's history, the immigrants' background, and sketches of the churches and secular organizations they had established in the new environment. In the introduction, Raymond Moley, chairman of the Americanization committee, wrote:

A proper understanding of the Magyars of America cannot be reached without some knowledge of the political conditions existing in modern

Hungary. The Hungarian nation, loosely joined with Austria under the Habsburg dynasty, has been one of the most undemocratic of modern states. A combination of landed aristocrats in alliance with a few financiers of the cities has, under an undemocratic suffrage, ruled the nation. This Junker class has maintained its power chiefly by stimulating hatred between the Magyars and non-Magyar nationalities in Hungary. As a consequence the hatred of the subject races has been directed at all Magyars.

On the other hand a strong liberal movement has been developing in Hungary, which has had as its objective a real democratization of political institutions and a much more tolerant attitude towards the neighboring nationalities. Magyar leaders in America have belonged to both types.[41]

Dr. József Reményi (1891–1952), a Hungarian novelist, poet, and essayist, who was employed by the Cleveland Foundation as a sociological researcher in the 1920s, played a major part in the city's Americanization programs. The young writer had arrived in the United States in 1914 and had become the "Honorary Secretary" of the Austro-Hungarian consul in Philadelphia until the United States entered the war. For a year he was the editor-publisher of the *Philadelphiai Ujság,* before *Szabadság* called him to Cleveland to join its staff. In 1921 the Cleveland Foundation entrusted him with researching the immigration problem. Reményi conceived of the Americanization program as based on harmonic cooperation and advocated an approach that, while urging assimilation, showed a tolerance of ethnicity.[42]

Another Hungarian American, Helén Horváth, led the Cleveland School Board's Americanization program. Since 1901 she had maintained a private English-language school for adult immigrants, and in 1919 the school board asked her to open a new school and broaden the program. Her language schools provided important contacts between the Americans and the immigrants and offered valuable guidance to the more or less confused newly arrived Hungarians.[43] To ensure a supply of students for the schools, city employees, including the Hungarian-American Piroska Hornyák and the American Alice Flint, drove through the immigrants' neighborhoods and at street corners enumerated the advantages of American citizenship. To accelerate Americanization and the Hungarians' assimilation, two new newspapers were established in Cleveland: *Amerika,* which was published in Hungarian by the poet Dr. László Pólya, and *Speak English,* edited by Arthur Winter and Reményi.

The impending truncation of Hungary and the Trianon Peace Treaty threw a shadow over the Hungarian communities and inspired a few prominent individuals to revive the American Hungarian Federation in an attempt to influence American political opinion. The spokesmen for these plans were the president of the Federation, Dr. Henry Baracs, and its secretary, Eugene Pivány. Pivány, a bank official prior to his emigration, lived in the United States from 1899 until the war broke out. How he began his life in America is unknown, but he soon was a bank official in Philadelphia and a Hungarian newspaper editor. The first to chronicle the history of the Hungarian Americans, from 1906 on he regularly published articles on this theme. By the time he took part in the organization of the American Hungarian Federation in 1906, he was an American citizen and had developed good relationships with native-born Americans.

In Budapest, the League for the Protection of Hungarian Integrity entrusted the remigrated Pivány with the mission of returning to the United States and working against the truncation of Hungary among the Americans. In the summer of 1919 Pivány, therefore, arrived back among the Cleveland Hungarians but did not disclose his assignment. He was soon elected secretary of the American Hungarian Federation, which published the English propaganda brochures he wrote on the territorial integrity of Hungary.[44] Pivány succeeded in obtaining a hearing in which he and Baracs spoke before the Senate Foreign Relations Committee, but he was not able to sway American public opinion. In fact, the American Hungarian Federation was unable to move the Hungarian masses to support it. A well-organized radical minority of socialists always managed to disrupt the federation's meetings.[45] Soon Pivány's futile mission made the sharpening of the conflicts between the socialists and the Hungarian patriots obvious during the American Hungarian Federation's short-lived revival. Nevertheless, leaders of the Hungarian-American community later took undeserved credit for the United States' refusal to ratify the Trianon Peace Treaty.[46]

PART THREE

UNDER THE PRESSURE OF ASSIMILATION

CHAPTER 17

The Gates Close

WHEN EUROPEAN EMIGRATION resumed after being halted by World War I, it took on many new patterns. Most noticeably, by 1920, the exodus had substantially slackened, so that from 1921 through 1930, just slightly more than one-half million migrants crossed the ocean annually. The main reasons for the decrease were curtailment of the free international circulation of labor and the worldwide economic crisis.[1]

The United States was the first receiving country to pass laws restricting labor migration. Since the 1880s Americans had watched with growing aversion the gradual shift to the south and east of the European sources of migration. As the trend continued after the turn of the century, approximately 65 percent of all immigrants to the United States came from the Austro-Hungarian Monarchy, Italy, and Russia.[2] "Nativists," as the American opponents of immigration were called, began demanding restriction in the 1890s. Trade unions became a vital part of the movement to limit the largely unorganized new immigrants, who were ready to work for lower wages. Middle-class groups and the intelligentsia objected to the lower cultural level of the peasant and proletarian newcomers.

World War I brought a new upswing of American nationalism, manifestations of the labile loyalty of the new immigrants, and fear of the impact of the European revolutions. The nativists, however, only became successful because their crusade to restrict immigration corresponded with the current interest of American capitalism. The extensive period of economic development and high rate of growth in the United States were over by the 1920s. Indeed, the forces of production had expanded so much during the war that it now became difficult to exploit their capacity, and in 1920–1921 the first signs of a crisis appeared. With the end of the First World War the orientation of capital investment changed substantially: instead of importing capital, in the 1920s the United States began to export it, becoming the creditor of Europe. Consequently, there was a decrease in the American demand for unskilled immigrant labor.[3]

After two decades the campaign for restriction finally achieved results in 1921 when Congress adopted the Quota Act. This act set the number of each immigrant people permitted to enter the United States annually at 3 percent of the group's population in the United States in 1910. The new immigrants' proportion in the "alien" population already was fairly high in 1910. To curtail their influx more severely, the Immigration Restriction Act of 1924 based the immigrant quotas on two percentages from the 1890 census. The obvious but unstated goal of the new American policy was to prevent additional mass immigration of the Italians, Jews, Hungarians, and various Slavic groups, who had made up the majority of migrants in the first decade of the century.[4]

The quota system had almost no influence on emigration from the countries of Western Europe, for overseas migration from that region already had decreased to the extent that their national quotas remained unfilled. But the new restrictions drastically curtailed immigration from East, Central, and Southern Europe, the remainder of the continent. Between 1910 and 1914, 80 percent of all immigrants to the United States came from this region of Europe; in the 1920s this percentage fell to 54 percent and slightly increased to 60 percent only during the Depression, when the actual number of migrants was reduced to a minimum.[5] It closed an era in American history.

The sudden decline in the number of migrants to the United States from countries such as Hungary was not the result of any change in the economic and social conditions of the donor society. Industrialization in Hungary did not develop enough to produce a substantial shift in the social structure. In fact, economic growth was slower there than in the prewar years. In 1910, 57.4 percent of the population of Hungary had subsisted on agriculture; in 1920 it was 56 percent, and by 1930 it had barely dropped to 52 percent. As late as 1941, during the upswing of the war economy, the agrarian proportion remained at 49 percent.[6] Therefore, the movement from agriculture to industry within Hungary still was not great enough to alleviate the internal tensions arising from overpopulation. Only now there was no American safety valve.

The United States Immigration Act of 1921 set the yearly quota for Hungary at 5,747, and the law of 1924 reduced it to 473 before the "National Origins" quota system adopted in 1927 increased the Hungarian quota slightly to 869. As the result of such restrictions, in the early 1920s Central and Eastern Europeans remained on the continent for seasonal work in the agriculture of Germany and France and the mines of Belgium. In the second half of the decade, migration channels began to open in other directions, toward Canada, Argentina, and Brazil, but within a few years they were closed by the Great Depression.[7] Just as the multiethnic composition of the population migrating from historical Hungary makes it difficult to determine the number of Hungarians who migrated between 1880 and 1914, changed borders create a similar difficulty for the interwar period. Generally, Magyar emigrants from the newly created states were registered by American authorities as citizens of those countries.[8]

Between 1920 and 1924, in the largest wave of migration after World War I and before the enforcement of restriction began, more migrants returned to their original communities than emigrated. The United States registered only 25,265 immigrants coming in, but estimated 32,000 emigrants, more than three-fourths of whom were men. In the same period, over one-third of the Magyars who did immigrate to the United States came from Hungary's neighboring countries. In addition, Hungarian Jews from those bordering countries were no longer registered as Hungarians. Though the mother tongue of most of them was Hungarian, the leaders of the new states endeavored to minimize the number of the Magyar national minority in a novel way. Insignificant as their numbers were by prewar standards, the immigrants who arrived between 1920 and 1924 equaled over 80 percent of the total who were recorded between 1921 and 1930. After the restrictions took effect, Hungarians and other would-be immigrants could only try to overcome them in various ways, including crossing the borders illegally from Canada, Mexico, and Cuba to avoid registration.[9]

In the 1920s the regions of emigration were the traditional ones in what had been northeastern Hungary, especially the counties of Abauj, Zemplén, Szabolcs, and Szatmár.[10] Due to the greater emigration to Canada, however, the term *amerikás* villages was replaced by *kanadás* villages, even though the emigrants of the 1920s started their journeys with the financial help of relatives who had emigrated to the United States, or with money borrowed from some returned *amerikás*. After 1924, besides Canada, other important destinations were Brazil and Argentina; but none became as attractive to potential emigrants as the United States had been.

Since late in the nineteenth century, there had been a few small Hungarian colonies in the Canadian prairie provinces of Saskatchewan and Manitoba. Pioneers of the settlements of Eszterháza, Békevár, and Kaposvár had come from the United States, although they and representatives of the Canadian government had recruited a few others to join them directly from Hungary.[11] Mass emigration from Hungary to Canada then developed after 1924, and Canadian immigration authorities registered 29,370 Hungarians between 1924 and 1930. Most of them came from a rural background in the counties of Szabolcs, Szatmár, and Heves in northeastern Hungary.[12]

Canada, Brazil, and Argentina needed labor for agriculture and for the building of the infrastructure, roads and railways. As there was no industrial demand comparable to that of the United States, skilled workers and craftsmen fared better if they declared themselves agrarian workers and contracted to do agrarian work to facilitate their entry into these countries.

Canadian employment agencies took the immigrants they recruited to the vicinity of Winnipeg, Manitoba, where they went into service on farms, hired out for lumbering and bushwhacking, or went to work in the mines and on the roads and railways. Nevertheless, the Depression soon began eliminating those opportunities before the immigrants had had time to adjust to the unfamiliar physical and social environment.[13] They began drifting east where they had a better chance of obtaining agricultural work in the summer and industrial employment in the winter. Entering Ontario, they established their centers in the industrial cities of Hamilton, Windsor, Toronto, and Wellington. In the southern agricultural area of the province, intensive market gardening and tobacco production offered opportunities to the more fortunate among them.[14] Improving economic conditions carried the latter through the stages of journeyman, lessor, and sharecropper, to farm owner. The more unfortunate, who were caught trying to cross illegally from Canada into the United States, were sent back to Hungary as illegal immigrants.

The Changing Social Structure of Migration

From the 1820s to World War I, the characteristic emigrant masses came from the agrarian population who were unable to find agricultural employment. Although proportions varied from period to period and country to country, the peasant character of mass emigration remained unquestionable. Any grouping of the migrants according to occupation, when studied over time, reveals only a few tendencies of change: a gradual increase of nonagrarian workers and a relative increase in white-collar workers, skilled workers, and businesspeople.

The social and political changes that took place in Hungary between the world wars, however, brought significant changes to the half-century-old pattern of emigration. The Austro-Hungarian Monarchy not only suffered military defeat in the war; it ceased to be a state. In Hungary, the first postwar revolution, the bourgeois-democratic revolution of October 1918, associated with the person of Count Mihály Károlyi had been relatively free of violence. This regime was crushed under the weight of external pressure and internal problems by March 1919. It was replaced by the proletarian dictatorship of Béla Kun, the Hungarian Soviet Republic (popularly called the Commune), which lasted from March to August 1919. The new government embarked on a violent class struggle against both the former ruling classes and the basically conservative peasantry. Some six months later this period also was brought to an end. However, after it collapsed, Admiral Miklós Horthy assumed control in the second half of 1919 and remained in power until 1944. It aimed to consolidate the system of large estates and foster large-scale capitalism, rather than the democratic transformation of Hungary.

World War I itself, then revolutions in 1918 and 1919, and the Treaty of Trianon all created new groups of victims and refugees, as well as economic upheavals that drove the poor to emigrate.[15] Popular expectations of social reform had been dashed by 1920, and the Treaty of Trianon deprived Hungary of a large portion of its natural resources, much of the transportation system, and previous trade patterns.[16] The resulting unemployment, inflation, and poverty made emigration a preferred alternative for many, while the Hungarian minorities now in Romania, Czechoslovakia, and Yugoslavia sought to flee discrimination by emigrating either to Hungary or to the New World. Exacerbating all this chaos was the old unanswered question of land tenure. The result was widespread dissatisfaction in the Hungarian countryside, but no substantial change. The regime of Admiral Horthy (1920–44) sponsored only a limited, insufficient land-allotment program.

In the early 1920s, three striking characteristics became apparent in this next period of emigration. In comparison with the 1910s, there is an enormous decline in numbers, and, at the same time, an increase in proportion of urban emigrant most of whom had a Jewish background. Many of the leaders in both revolutions were Jews. In the 1919 Hungarian Soviet Republic, about two-thirds of the "people's commissars" (as the members of the government were then called) and their deputies were Jews. The Jewish presence was particularly noted in the police force and in the Ministry for Culture. Bolshevism was considered "a purely Jewish product," as Oscar Jászi calls it in his reminiscences. Jews as a group were punished for the Commune.[17] Emil Lengyel sees the "New Wave" of immigration as an emphatic mass eruption of the Hungarian intelligentsia. However, Lengyel overstates the proportion of white-collar workers, lawyers, physicians, scientists, engineers, and artists among those who arrived in the United States from Hungary after 1920.[18] Between 1920 and 1924, the proportion of Hungarian immigrants in the categories of white-collar workers and the commercial and financial professions grew to 5.6 percent, possibly even more, as the statistics do not register them all. Nevertheless, the migration of well-known intellectuals stands out more for their talents than their numbers. Until the 1930s, the majority of Hungary's overseas emigrants continued to be from rural areas, even if the proportion of city dwellers increased.[19]

International migration decreased to a minimum throughout the world in the years of the Great Depression. The United States, despite its new restrictions, still admitted the largest number of immigrants after World War I. Between 1929 and 1934, however, more people from the United States returned to Europe than emigrated from Europe to the United States. The same was true for Hungary in the first half of the 1930s, and the number of Hungarians emigrating to Canada and South America at the time numbered only in the hundreds. In 1935 the total number of immigrants from Hungary recorded by the United States was just 130.

Not subject to the restrictive quotas and not counted in the immigration statistics, because they were American citizens, were the children born to migrants in the United States but reared in the old country. Although they did not make up great masses, their uncounted numbers probably were larger than generally thought. For instance, remigrating parents took thirty-four American-born children back to the village of Szamosszeg, and twenty-nine of these children returned to the United States as grown adults before the beginning of World War II.[20]

The migration of intellectuals which began in the early twenties cannot be put unambiguously into a single category of economic, political, or compulsory migration. Economic, political, and scientific considerations all played a role and reinforced one another. In Europe after World War I, economic stagnation had limited the possibilities for scientific creativity and widened the gap between the ambitions of the intellectuals and their opportunities. The American economy was not in very sound shape either, but it was better than Europe's for highly qualified white-collar workers, especially in the natural sciences. As a young country, the United States did not have as many intellectuals and specialists in certain fields as it needed, particularly for its new, well-equipped universities.

After the Anschluss in 1938, the spread of Hitler's fascism gave greater urgency to the emigration of the intelligentsia from Central Europe. Many of the intellectuals with the best qualifications were of Jewish origin. In fact, there were twelve Nobel Prize winners among those who escaped to the United States, and hundreds of additional émigrés held other high scientific or artistic distinctions. Scholars agree that the migration of the intelligentsia would have been much smaller without the Depression and the Nazi expansion but, with those factors in place, it would have been still greater if there had been no economic crisis in the United States.[21]

Although the same general factors that operated throughout Central Europe shaped the emigration of Hungary's intellectuals, some of its special characteristics should be noted. Prior to World War I, the proportion of the intelligentsia among the emigrants from Hungary was smaller than in the groups from northwestern Europe. Within the Austro-Hungarian Monarchy, the possibilities of migration from the less developed to the more developed regions had created a relatively wide and favorable scope for intellectual activity. More important, because of the late development of bourgeois civilization in Hungary, the intelligentsia occupied a very narrow social stratum that was then only in the initial stage of its evolution. Intellectual life was concentrated in Budapest. Secondary schools of good quality were just being established outside the capital after the turn of the century. Although they helped educate the generation of intellectuals that emigrated in the 1930s, these schools had not yet had an impact at the time of the mass migration.

After 1919, political persecutions and racial discrimination were the major factors behind the compulsory or forced migration of Hungarians. Following the Treaty of Trianon the new borders of Hungary contained just 32.7 percent of the country's prewar territory, but from the parts of historical Hungary annexed to the bordering countries, approximately 350,000 persons migrated to the much smaller Hungary established by the Treaty of Trianon. Those who did so between 1920 and 1924 belonged mainly to various middle-class groups or had been white-collar workers in the former state administration. In a period of economic breakdown and stagnation, these immigrations from the formerly Hungarian territories worsened the already unfavorable job opportunities for educated workers in Hungary.[22]

The leaders of the Horthy regime blamed the Trianon Peace Treaty for all its difficulties and proclaimed territorial revision the remedy. Anti-Semitism and irredentism[23] were part of their political arsenal for diverting the inner tensions of society. This counterrevolutionary political system, the Horthy regime, began with the "white terror," which picked its victims from among the radicals and the participants in the two previous revolutions. Fleeing the "terror," the leaders of the revolution of 1918 and the Hungarian Soviet Republic (Magyar Tanácsköztársaság) settled either in Western Europe or in the Soviet Union; only a few migrated to the United States. Soon economic stagnation, lack of perspective in scientific research, and anti-Semitism motivated young Hungarian intellectuals to seek their scientific chances in the research institutes and scientific centers of Berlin, which had come to the fore during the Weimar Republic, and at the universities of Prague, Vienna, and Paris. Study tours, then step-by-step migration through other European countries, led them—after the final blow of the takeover by Hitler—to the United States.[24]

By contrast, the second wave of forced emigrants in the late 1930s went directly overseas to South America or the United States. Almost all the emigrants in this wave were fleeing the advance of fascism or an increase in the persecution of those with Jewish religious or ethnic background that had begun earlier in Hungary. Hungarian statistics show that over a quarter of those who emigrated between 1930 and 1941 were intellectuals, and almost half were tradesmen or businessmen. Peasants and agrarian workers constituted only 8.1 percent of all emigrants in those years, and their ratio was even smaller among those bound for the United States. A breakdown by religion also points out the compulsory nature of this migration: beginning with the 1930s, almost half of all emigrants from Hungary were Jews.[25]

United States immigration authorities registered 1,348 Hungarian immigrants in 1939 and 1,902 in 1940. Then World War II closed the gates so tightly that in 1945 only 55, and between 1941 and 1947 all together only 198 immigrants from Hungary were recorded.[26] The number of actual immigrants was probably somewhat higher, as some escaped to the United States as tourists who were authorized by President Roosevelt to prolong their temporary stay. As those scholars who study this period of international migration frequently note, Hitler's genocidal madness would have had fewer victims if the transatlantic countries had repealed their restrictive immigration laws.[27]

So many of the scientists and artists who emigrated from Hungary between the two world wars became famous in the United States and internationally that Laura Fermi entitled a chapter of her analysis of European intellectual emigration, "The Mystery of Hungarian Genius": "Scholars who tried to solve the mystery gave differing explanations, but they agreed that the achievements of the Hungarian emigrants in almost all intellectual fields were greater than their proportion in the American population would appear to warrant."[28] Although he exaggerated the percentage of intellectuals in the Hungarian immigration after World War I, Emil Lengyel accurately perceived some of the reasons it was as high as it was. The explanation may be Hungary's role as a melting pot which for many years attracted nationalities from all over the Danubian world. Or perhaps the impact in Hungary of the cultures of both East and West is responsible for this amazing fertility. But, in most cases, Hungarian genius came to fruition outside of the country. Hungary's great scientists, artists, and writers became great in foreign countries. The caste policy of the ruling classes may be to blame, or possibly the fact that a peasant country had no need for the products of these great talents. The exodus of those with special abilities from Hungary, therefore, is not only a postwar development. In the postwar period, however, this exodus made history for the United States, as the story of the Hungarian immigrants' contribution to the development of the atomic bomb will show.[29]

Emphasis on the spectacular achievements of Hungarian-born intellectuals has become more popular, both in Hungary and abroad, in the last ten years. But there are no statistical data or methods available to test the claims by international comparisons. What seems plausible is that, on the one hand, favorable research possibilities in the United States attracted the migrants, in contrast to the underdevelopment of such possibilities in Hungary. Yet, on the other hand, Hungary must have been developed enough to have provided the researchers with the educational background indispensable for starting their careers.

To summarize, between the two world wars, Hungary, like most other European countries, showed a significant decrease in the number of its emigrants compared to the previous period. Because restriction of the free movement of labor into the United States stopped the wave of economic mass migration from Hungary before it abated naturally, the safety valve that formerly had existed for the surplus population was now closed. From 1920 onward, various types of migration—economic, political, and compulsory—appeared together and cannot always be distinguished.[30] An important, but sometimes overstated, feature of this new interwar migration was an increased number of intellectuals, particularly among the Hungarians.

CHAPTER 18

"Let's Be American; Let's Remain Hungarian"

Transition to Residence—the 1920s

THROUGHOUT THE HUNGARIAN-AMERICAN communities during the early 1920s, debates continued over permanent settlement and Americanization, as plans to return home were altered by the deterioration of conditions there. In a short period of time, Hungary had been hit by economic destruction from the war, the end of the Austro-Hungarian Monarchy, a bourgeois democratic revolution in the autumn of 1918, and a proletarian dictatorship from March to August 1919. Then, in 1920, the Trianon Treaty ceded two-thirds of the old Hungarian kingdom's territory to the so-called successor states: Czechoslovakia, Romania, and Yugoslavia (the states that arose mainly in the place of the dissolved Habsburg empire). Much of this territory was inhabited by non-Hungarians; however, some of it had a mixed or even a largely Hungarian population. As a consequence of the peace settlement, well over three million Hungarians found themselves under alien rule. Members of all the immigrant groups from Hungary found that new national borders had been drawn around their birthplaces. Meanwhile, the United States of the 1920s was much different from the place to which the new immigrants had come in the 1900s. At the same time, in contrast to Hungary, Czechoslovakia, Romania, or whatever country now was home, America seemed to offer them and their children a far more promising future.

Immediately after World War I, dramatic appeals for help from the old country inundated the Hungarian-American communities. In the words of Cleveland's *Szabadság:* "The Hungarian homeland is completely devastated, torn to pieces, our fathers, mothers, brothers, and sisters are starving, freezing and dressed in rags. Who will help Hungary, if we don't? Who will rise to the protection of the Hungarian homeland, if we are unwilling?"[1] In response, collections were organized for Hungarian war orphans and for repatriation of the prisoners of war who had been held in Siberia and the political refugees who had fled to Austria.[2] With time, however, the never-ending appeals met suspicion and growing indifference as the activists themselves began to tire of

197

the collecting and of the quarrels over appropriating the funds that inevitably followed. At the same time, efforts to represent Hungary's interests politically were tempered by bitter memories of wartime xenophobia and the continuing Americanization campaign as well as by the rivalries between Hungarian groups and individuals in the United States.

During the early 1920s, the Hungarian-American community was itself in a state of upheaval and transformation that modified the geographical pattern of settlement considerably. When an economic slump spawned an outbreak of strikes in the mining regions, waves of migrants left the small mining settlements of West Virginia and Ohio for the larger industrial centers of Cleveland and Detroit.

As it was mentioned, the Szamosszegeans in West Virginia almost emptied their settlements. The majority migrated permanently back to Szamosszeg or went to New Brunswick, New Jersey, but two families moved to Cleveland and a few young men were drawn to Detroit by news of its modern Ford factory.[3]

It was also in the early twenties that Hungarians first began to farm near Cleveland and in New Jersey. They did not want to withdraw from industry into agriculture, but rather to make better use of their family workforce. Husbands generally kept their industrial jobs and dealt with farming only in their spare time; their wives and children worked full-time on the farms.[4]

The transition to permanent residence in the United States required other changes in the Hungarian immigrants' lifestyle, attitudes, and value system. Until the 1920s, they wanted simply to save as much as possible, with little or no investment in homes, furniture, and other amenities. They lived instead as sojourners. At that time, their strategy was a temporary proletarianization to avoid a permanent one. However, after the 1920s, they abandoned their self-imposed custom of strictly saving money, and their interest in the problems of their birthplace diminished as their ties to their small donor communities weakened. They all but gave up the practice of purchasing land in Hungary.

But most striking were the social changes that took place in the United States. At the beginning of the 1920s, Hungarian-American publications enjoyed an explosion in advertising by Hungarian real estate agents, who encouraged their compatriots to purchase houses and plots. From 1922 to 1929, Hungarian Americans built houses with great energy, spending their own savings or taking out bank loans. On the East Side of Cleveland, for example, the modern Buckeye community with its new churches and office buildings sprang up at this time. The upper end of Buckeye Road was completely built-up to 140th Street, and by the next decade Hungarian stores ruled its entire length. János Weizer alone sold over two thousand house plots to the Hungarians. "Never before and never after did the Hungarian accomplish this much."[5] The new houses generally were two-family dwellings built on large lots with fruit trees and vegetable gardens. The more well-to-do moved into the houses on Upper Buckeye; those who found it harder to make ends meet stayed on Lower Buckeye. Place of residence thus became an enduring mark of status within the Hungarian community, and the Depression stalled only temporarily the striving for better neighborhoods. The proximity of wealthy, exclusive Shaker Heights to the Buckeye district of Cleveland helped keep the quest alive, especially among the second generation, for whom the posh suburb symbolized the notion, "We are poor, because we are Hungarians; they are wealthy, because they are real Americans."[6]

From the 1920s on, Hungarian community leaders repeatedly reminded both the immigrants and the dominant society that the Hungarians were no longer migrants but an integral part of the host society, unequivocally tied to their new homeland. The popular new slogan in the Hungarian community was: "Let's be American; let's remain Hungarian."[7] Especially at times of elections, this was a frequent theme in almost all of the Hungarian-language newspapers. By voicing it, either consciously or instinctively, leaders were marking out the place of the Hungarians within a culturally pluralistic American society. Although they did not reject the goal of assimilation, they did place it far into the distant future beyond their most urgent task, the modernization of the Hungarian churches and associations. Modernization is what the leaders meant by Americanization.

In the parents' ambition, the scale of values in the peasant family still asserted itself forcefully in regard to their children. In their childhood they were already treated as exploitable members of the family. In the mining towns, they led the cow to graze and helped to feed the barnyard fowl or care for their younger brothers and sisters. Their parents tried to find a job for them as soon as possible and often stated that they were one or two years older than their age to reach this aim. Boys went to work in the mines at the age of fourteen or fifteen, or at least did auxiliary work next to their fathers. Girls also were drawn into housework as soon as possible; they helped their mothers to cook and clean for the boarders *(burdos)*.[8] They were expected to hand over their pay to the parents. School was regarded by most parents as a waste of time, particularly after the four elementary classes. Even those parents who could afford it were not eager to obtain higher education for their children. They aimed at getting richer, at going ahead. Even for those who had their own businesses, the goal was the broadening of the family venture with the help of their children's labor. Among the Szamosszegean families settled permanently in the United States, only one, formerly a blacksmith in the village, provided for education for all his children. Only two families among those who returned to the village gave one of their sons a higher education (one learned to be a priest, the other studied law).

A favored industry in Detroit was, of course, that of the automobile, at least by the 1930s. A pioneer investigator of occupational mobility among Detroit's Magyars has claimed that engineering had been in vogue with the Hungarian gentry before World War I and that enough aristocratic émigrés worked for the automobile companies after the war to focus the aspirations of Magyar laborers on that profession.[9]

Extensive changes in customs and symbols accompanied the Americanization of the Hungarian immigrants' institutions. The associations replaced their ostentatious badges with smaller, more decorous emblems and no longer engaged in street parades with brass bands. In addition, there were efforts to quell rowdyism in the saloons so that Hungarian Americans could better blend into their environment. As community institutions actively promoted American citizenship and the learning of the English language, the percentage of Hungarian immigrants who had been naturalized virtually doubled, from 28 percent in 1920 to 55.7 percent in 1930.[10] The leaders of fraternal associations, which were organized nationwide, became American citizens, and in the 1920s, there was a general demand to achieve middle-class status. The ethnic elite also encouraged the participation of the community's citizens, old and new, in local politics.[11]

Within the Hungarian neighborhoods of the 1920s, however, human contacts still were reminiscent of those in the former villages. The strongest interpersonal ties had developed along the lines of "in-law" and "godparent-friend," which created roles for selected and fictional relatives. The fictitious kinship derived from friendship that often bound people together more than the blood relationship. Nevertheless, these ties were strong only among the first generation; seldom did entire families, parents, children, and siblings participate in extending them. More often, looking for work separated even blood relatives. The search for work caused even siblings to move very far from one another; there were examples of this among the Szamoszegeans, too.[12]

Customs and Festivals

Some characteristics of the Hungarian homes in the 1920s were described by the Rev. Charles F. Schaeffer, one of the representatives of the Inner Mission of the Reformed Church of the United States:

> Many of them are enclosed by a fence, and we enter through a gate, which seems to indicate the rural spirit that still remains. The houses are usually well kept. When we enter them we find that they are clean and well furnished. The Hungarian people are strong on color. The rugs and tapestries and hangings, the paper on the wall, all are of a rich color. The walls are usually decorated with pictures, many of which are of a historic character. Portraits of great heroes, like Rákóczi, Kossuth, Bocskay, Zrinyi, are found in many homes. Practically every minister's home has a picture of John Calvin. Pictures of the great Hungarian poet, Petőfi, the one hundredth anniversary of whose birth was celebrated for six months in Hungary last year, are frequently displayed. An air of hospitality prevails.[13]
>
> There is also stuffed cabbage, fried chicken, pork, paprika, fish, rétes and many kinds of pastry. Before the days of the Eighteenth Amendment, wine was the favorite beverage in connection with their meals.[14]

Important continuities in Hungarian-American cultural life helped ease in all the organizational, political, and interpersonal changes that accompanied permanent settlement. Throughout the United States in the 1920s, Hungarian culture was embodied in the meetings of associations and clubs, and in dance festivals, picnics, theatrical performances, and sports contests. Good-natured amusement and singing were in full swing in the saloons and at balls and socials. "I remember as a child," related Mr. Stelkovics, a member of the second generation, "when there were balls they took the children; we slept on the benches, while our parents danced and enjoyed themselves."[15] In fact, as the immigrants abandoned the notion of saving money for their return home, their folk customs and festivals, the symbols of their group life, their activities, became more colorful and elaborate than ever before. Because each group "wanted to be the master in his own house" the entertainment was organized within the sphere of the small groups. To celebrate a given occasion there was not just one party, but several. Often their sponsors coordinated their timing to avoid overlapping or conflicting with each other.[16] In most cases, a local *nagybizottság* (generally translated as "central committee") was created from the representatives of the Magyar churches and societies to coordinate major projects. In August, 1928, the Verhovay branches in Cleveland found eleven other Magyar picnics scheduled for the same day as theirs.

Although the grape harvest festival took place at the end of September in Hungary, Hungarian groups in Cleveland sponsored at least a dozen grape festivals throughout the period from Labor Day to October 31 each year. The New Year's Eve gatherings with dances were usually left to the churches and were held in halls next door to the church building, but the radicals had their own versions which they organized in their halls or in the saloons. There likewise was a great deal of less formally organized activity. In the Hungarian settlements on New Year's Day, gypsy bands could be seen going up and down the streets, ready to serenade on request.[17] In the mining places and the industrial villages, the young people supplied amusement for themselves. Mrs. Szakács from Daisytown remembered. "When we were young we sang on the streets. There weren't any cars yet, we just walked. Today if we would go as we did then through the village, well, the police would take us to jail. The girls and boys sang, those were the customs."[18]

A similarly informal practice was Easter sprinkling, which was widespread in Hungary. On Easter Monday the young men visited the young women and sprinkled them with water so that they might blossom like fresh flowers in the spring. Out of gratitude the women gave the men hand-painted eggs. In Cleveland in the 1920s, the Red Cross Drug Store on the corner of East Eighty-ninth Street and Buckeye and the "Saint Elizabeth" drugstore (across from Saint Elizabeth Church) both advertised free rosewater for the sprinkling at Easter time.[19] The Hungarian immigrants in the small mining settlements also sprinkled at Easter, but in the cities of the 1920s the custom became more elaborate. In the old country the eggs had been colored with onion skins; now the Hungarian Americans bought dyes and paints and made them much

fancier.[20] At the age of ninety-one, an immigrant woman in Pennsylvania described the ritual as practiced in her mining community.

> On Easter we baked unleavened bread, as we did in the old country,
> large loaves. The *kolbász* and everything cooked. Even then the men
> enjoyed themselves, that's when they sprinkled. Ah, and the custom
> then was: only a little with the hand, then the whole bucket. Then on
> the third day we went upstairs, and then we sprinkled the men who
> had sprinkled us; we went on the third day. At home it was also the
> custom to sprinkle the men on the third day.[21]

On the first of May the young men would set up a traditionally decorated
"May tree" and serenade their sweethearts as in the old country. It was the
gypsies in Cleveland who went from house to house with their musical instruments to greet the month of May, receiving money in return for playing each
household's favorite song. The gypsies also probably popularized in Cleveland
a custom that was hardly known in Hungary, the funeral of the double bass
from the gypsy band. A more structured and planned event, the burial of the
double bass started the season of Lent, when there was neither music nor
dancing until after Easter. Men, women, and children dressed up as gypsies
and performed with humor how a gypsy caravan buries its double bass in the
midst of heartrending sadness and sobbing. A similar ritual appeared among the
Slovaks on Cleveland's East Side, suggesting the influence of the same gypsies.[22]

Weddings were held throughout the year, but more took place in the
summer. They were community events, for which the preparations were carried
out by friends and relatives. For the most part, even in the 1920s, they retained
the complicated village ceremonies, such as asking for the young woman's hand
in marriage, the role of the best man, the farewell to the bride, and the bride's
dance. A seventy-five-year-old woman in 1977 described her wedding.

> Mine was a Hungarian wedding; we went from house to house. There
> were four bridesmaids, my girlfriends who were all Hungarians, the
> groomsmen all were Hungarians. It was exactly like the weddings back
> home. There was a bride's dance. When I was no longer able to dance
> the bride's dance, a groomsman replaced the bride—not the first, some
> other groomsman, who took his place—there was a brass band and all
> kinds of tunes. "There's a Wedding in Our Street"—we forget, it was
> so long ago—and for the last, "The Wedding Is Over." Our wedding
> lasted for three days.
>
> My aunt cooked and people drank and ate; the table was always
> set, and on Sunday we all went to church again. Our wedding was on
> Thursday and on Friday we were home; [it resumed] again on Saturday,
> and on Sunday it ended.
>
> Every wedding was like that, because that's how the old people
> did it, like back home. And my father wanted a wedding just like in
> the village.[23]

Gyula Kósa, a Szamosszegean migrant, wrote down all the rhymes that the best man customarily said as well as the bride's farewell to her parents, siblings, girlfriends, and neighbors. The best man gave a short speech when the groomsmen started for the bride's house, and again when the wedding party went to the church for their vows. He also spoke when the guests sat down at the table, and he offered toasts with whiskey and wine for each course of the meal: soup, stuffed cabbage, and paprikás chicken. Finally, in America, where money was more readily available, he started a collection of money during supper with a rhyme.[24] Although traditional wedding celebrations in Hungarian villages were held in family homes, in the United States most wedding festivities were held in Hungarian saloons, in facilities such as Cleveland's Hungarian House, or, in the small mining settlements, perhaps in a tent.

Differences based on financial and social circumstances were great. Some did not feast, but had only a plain wedding; others held a feast that lasted three days. The reminiscences show a variegated picture of Hungarian weddings.[25] To the people in the village the wedding pictures sent home showed a completely different world, conveyed the view of a fairyland of white-clad bridesmaids. (The author, as a child, also mused often upon the photo taken on her aunt's wedding, imagining her as something like a duchess. She dreamed about a similar wedding dress for herself; the dress represented richness in her eyes, not a worker's lot.) As big weddings were status symbols within the community, parents tried their best to guarantee them for their children, particularly if the family would not have been able to do so back home, but was better off in the new surroundings. As a result, Hungarian-American wedding pictures display not only ceremonial wealth, but also the immigrant workers' consumer culture.

In the 1920s, those born in Hungary who grew up in the United States, as well as the first wave of the second generation, almost always married Hungarians. A marriage to someone of another ethnic group caused the family great trauma. In Holden when one daughter of a Szamosszegean immigrant family married an Italian, her parents broke off all contact with her. Only fifteen years later, on the occasion of her father's funeral, did she again see her original family.[26]

The solidarity of the former village communities showed up even more clearly at funerals. As in weddings, relatives and personal friends had a central role, but in America they usually participated as members of an organization formed in the earliest days of migration by newcomers afraid of not having a proper burial in a strange, and often deadly, land. At funerals the society escorted the deceased out. If the church was close by, then they went on foot. The deceased was laid out at home. The members of the society kept vigil by the dead body until morning. They did not leave the deceased, stayed around him all night. Some came earlier, some later. Afterwards they took the deceased to the church, where they delivered speeches and then they took him to the cemetery.[27]

The burial ceremonies were influenced not only by the differences in the traditions of the various denominations, but also by ideological differences. Adoption of international ideology, the anticlerical views of the labor movement, required a revolution in the thinking of the proletarian rank and file. They urged the cutting out of church services; instead of the priest, a comrade spoke at the funeral. Secular merry-making accompanied weddings and christenings. It did also occur, that a church leader would refuse to perform the funeral rites, because of the "ungodliness" of the deceased.[28]

Birthday celebrations were not part of the old-country traditions. Instead, name days were observed, especially for the very common "István" and "János," which coincided with holidays. Friends congratulated the celebrant and toasted each member of their circle. Christmas salutations, the Nativity plays, and the chantings became integral parts of Hungarian church life in America, too, in the 1910s when the first photographs of these events are known. Their survival—though in modified form—was assisted by the fact that they served the accumulation of the church income. The community's rationale for main-taining the custom was in part the collection of Christmas donations to the church, for each performance ended in a banquet.[29]

Christmas celebration in the communities combined deep spiritual meaning with a focus on the family. Although we do not know when the custom of setting up a Christmas tree spread within the Hungarian-American community, it apparently had become general by the end of World War I. Decorations, small articles, cookies, honeycakes, and candles were made for the tree. Gifts were prepared at home and usually were simple.[30] In the Hungarian villages, caroling was another widespread custom on Christmas Eve, and it remained common among Hungarian Americans in the small towns and mining communi-ties during the 1920s.

> We went singing on Christmas Eve. Children and adults went separately, with the children going first, followed by the adults. They went from all the churches. They went to every house; there weren't religious considerations here. Most went to Hungarian homes, as the other nation-alities also had singers from their own churches.[31]

Boys and girls would go from house to house with the Bethlehem shepherds' play in the late morning or early afternoon of Christmas Eve and Christmas Day. Wearing appropriate costumes and reciting verses and songs from the Hungarian villages, they performed the scenes where the angel awakens the shepherds and the Magi give gifts to the Baby Jesus.[32] By visiting the homes in their community, the youngsters were recreating the tradition as it had been carried out by groups of relatives and friends in the homeland. In the United States by the 1910s, however, the "shepherds" were organized by the churches, where they were costumed, taught their roles, and photographed. In turn, they gave the churches the coins they received at each house.

The strengthening of "new tradition" played an important role in community organizing. Two types of events became customary which appealed more or

1. Somlószöllő, Veszprém County. The house in which Julianna Papp was born on 20 August 1921.

2. Migrants awaiting departure in Fiume, c.1904.

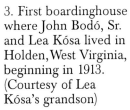

3. First boardinghouse where John Bodó, Sr. and Lea Kósa lived in Holden, West Virginia, beginning in 1913. (Courtesy of Lea Kósa's grandson)

4. Gábor Katkó (*left*), a miner, sent this photo home for his children "to see in what kind of attire your father makes money in America."

5. Eberhardt Manufacturing Company, Cleveland, Ohio. An important workplace of Hungarian immigrants at the turn of the century.

6. At the entrance to a coal mine shaft in the Pittsburgh region, 1907.

7. Children and teachers of the Homestead Church Sunday School in Pennsylvania, 1907.

8. Youth fellowship group, West Seneca, New York, 1907. The greater Buffalo region of the Hungarian Reformed Church organized not only one of the first branches of the Hungarian Reformed Church of America but also a youth fellowship circle and, in 1920, a Sunday school.

9. The synagogue, B'nai Jeshurun, in 1909 in Cleveland, Ohio. (Courtesy of the Western Historical Society)

10. Christmas carolers in Virginia, 1916 – an old custom from home. (From *Képes Világlap*, illustrated newspaper, 29 January 1916. (Courtesy of the collection of Lajos Szathmáry)

11. Gáspár Papp and his wife with their one-year-old daughter, Julianna, en route to the United States, at Port Rotterdam, 4 August 1922.

12. Gáspár Papp, his wife, their two small children, and the Katkó grandparents in 1923.

13. Dedication of the towers and bells of the Hungarian Reformed Church, McKeesport, Pennsylvania, 1925. (Courtesy of the Bethlen Collection, Ligonier, Pennsylvania)

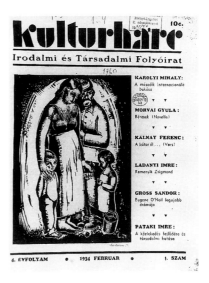

14. Front cover of the newspaper *Kulturharc.* (From *Literary and Societal Journal* 4:1, February 1934)

15. Hungarian burial in Delray during the 1930s.

16. Harvest near Milwaukee, Wisconsin, 1939.

17. American and Hungarian flags at the Zsigmond farm in Logan, West Virginia, in the late 1930s.

18. Company-built modern small family houses in the late 1930s and early 1940s in Holden, West Virginia. (Photo from Victor Bodó, in the author's collection)

19. In memory of Louis Kossuth, the Hungarian Reformed Federation donates an ambulance to the U.S. Army. New York, May 1942.

20. Juliska Dankó's group of young dancers.

21. Three generations of Hungarian tradition in the Dankó family: Juliska Dankó with her daughter and granddaughter.

22. At a harvest festival in 1957, Stephen Dankó Jr. carries the flag of the William Penn Branch 500.

23. The young man was "born in America, brought up in the old country." (J. Kovács and friend, in the village of Bodony)

24. The founders of the Rácz family. In the 1980s, a reunion was attended by more than one hundred relatives.

Elizabeth Ekker

Born: 11-10-1875
Died: 1-20-1964

John Rácz

Born: 4-24-1869
Died: 3-5- 1951

They were married June 5, 1893 in Adony, Fejer County, Hungary. Both are buried in St. Andrew's Cemetery, Elk River, Minnesota

less to the outside world, too: the foundation of their churches (laying of the foundation stone, opening of a new church), and jubilee celebrations of the anniversaries of community organizations. The immigrants tried to outline the borders of their ethnic communities with the symbols of the landed gentry back home, in order to demonstrate to their neighbors that their nation was no worse than any other.

The celebrations of the Hungarian patriotic and national festivals, first promoted by the politically minded immigrants in the early 1900s, became more important in the 1920s and were augmented by observances marking the truncation of Hungary after World War I. Two dates were associated with the War of Independence, which had occurred in the lifetimes of the immigrants' own parents: on March 15, 1848, the revolution against Habsburg rule was declared, and on October 6, 1849, the Austrians executed thirteen Hungarian generals. In Cleveland every year on these anniversaries, the leaders of various community organizations placed a wreath at Lajos Kossuth's statue. The date of June 4, 1920, the signing of the Trianon Treaty, was likewise kept in the public eye with memorial services as well as protests to American lawmakers. The commemoration on August 20 of Saint Stephen, Hungary's first king, remained a largely Catholic occasion for picnics and parades.

The only issue to unite Hungarian Americans in the interwar years was the desire for a revised Treaty of Trianon, which would restore Hungary to its pre-war dimensions. Most of the church organizations resolved to support Hungarian irredentism, that is, the goals of the Revisionist League, an international arm of the Hungarian governments of the 1920s and 1930s, which sought to publicize Hungary's right to the recovery of its lost territories. However, most of the organizations did nothing more than express sympathy, because their members devoted neither time nor money to promoting the cause of revisionism.[33]

The twenties may properly be referred to as the golden age of Hungarian-American ethnic life. The prosperity of the times, the abandonment of plans to return to Hungary, and the tragic plight of the homeland evoked a cultural and organizational reawakening. As an ironic result, many Hungarian Americans of peasant background became more consciously Hungarian and more concerned with Hungarian culture than their counterparts in Hungary.

CHAPTER 19

The Churches
Caught in the Middle

THE IMPACT OF permanent settlement significantly changed the profiles of Hungarian-American religious communities and institutions in the early 1920s. All patriotic Americans and the feverish activities of superpatriots created an unprecedented and speedy demand for planned, aggressive, definitive Americanization.

The boards of the American missionary societies, a large proportion being lay folk, naturally carried these feelings of concern into their programs. It was not possible to determine what other motivations may have played their part—though one might think of several. The fact is that soon practically all of the American Protestant bodies had strong Americanization programs. These included the work of paid volunteer visitors and instructors, who taught English, American history, the ideals and the requirements of citizenship to new Americans in homes, churches and wherever possible, with a view to speedy naturalization. Besides all this, the home missionaries were encouraged, urged, and even compelled (mostly by moral persuasion) to introduce the use of English into all their services and activities.[1]

Because it increased the pressure to adopt the norms of the host society, one of its major effects was to reawaken conflicts between traditionalists and modernists within the Hungarian religious communities. Most of the problems and confrontations arose among the Reformed Protestants after the Hungarian-American ministers took part in the Tiffin Agreement of 1921, in which the Reformed Church of Hungary transferred its two American church districts and all their churches and properties to the Reformed Church of the United States.[2] In a number of places, such as Detroit and McKeesport, the police had to intervene when the people attempted to protect their churches from the "English."[3] Similar turmoil in 1922 in the First Hungarian Reformed Church on the East Side of Cleveland led the pastor, Sándor Tóth, to welcome an appointment for full-time employment on the payroll of the Board of Home Mission of the Reformed Church in the United States to Lancaster Theological Seminary's new Hungarian department.[4] The department's task was to educate second-generation Hungarians as ministers. The Cleveland congregation elected Dr. József Herceg, who had come from Hungary to Lancaster Seminary on a scholarship, to succeed Tóth.

Hungarian Protestant clergymen related how an old German clergyman with a heavy German accent tried to convince them that they should not spoil the growing children's soul with the Hungarian language.[5] The Board of Home Mission of the Reformed Church in the United States in those years acted as a watchdog of Americanization. A remark of Charles E. Schaeffer was often quoted: "We must evangelize the foreigners or they will heathenize us. We must Americanize them or they will foreignize us."[6] The transmission of the two Hungarian church districts took place in the most feverish phase of the Americanization movement. The Reformed ministers, who considered the Tiffin Agreement "the Trianon of the American Hungarians," created the Free Hungarian Reformed Church as a coalition of six congregations independent of both American and Hungarian church authorities.[7] They started their own newspaper, *Magyar Egyház* (Hungarian Church), and by 1930 had added ten more new congregations to their denomination.[8] As the presence of the word "free" and the absence of any mention of America in their organization's name indicated, supporters of the church were determined to rely solely on their own strength to uphold Hungarian traditions and withstand assimilation.[9]

They held on to their own and were averse to everything that characterized American Protestantism. *Magyar Egyház* constantly warned its readers that both of the leading American trends in Protestantism of the times, fundamentalism and modernism, were equally foreign to the Hungarian Reformed faith, as both contradicted the full teachings of the gospel and neither had theological church concept. They recounted with special pleasure the adverse traits of American Protestant church life, which abounded in the 1920s. Although opposing views had existed among the Hungarian ministers joined to the different American denominations, organization of the independent church united them against a common enemy.

By contrast, the ministers who were under the authority of the American Reformed and Presbyterian denominations repeatedly stated that American and Hungarian forms of Protestantism were not significantly different and that use of the Hungarian language within Hungarian congregations was not threatened. American church authorities, the affiliated clergymen said, did not forbid the continuation of ethnic traditions, but simply believed assimilation was natural and inevitable. The Hungarian-American ministers also warned that the congregations of the smaller Hungarian communities could not afford to be independent financially. Finally, they suggested that having the American churchmen as allies could help evoke the attention and sympathy of world Calvinism for the plight of their homeland.[10] As Sándor Tóth wrote in the newsletter of his seminary department, "The American spirit can not be over-come by defiance; rather we must win it to ourselves with love."[11]

The cohesive strength of the Free Magyar Church itself derived from a reaction against too rapid assimilation, from Magyar nationalism, and occasion-ally just from individual efforts: "There is no other goal of our continuance, than the safeguarding and tending to our heritage we received from God, and that is the Hungarian Calvinism."[12] The church reflected the powerful ethnic component of Hungarian Calvinism which had been kept alive and, in some cases, intensified, by the competition to organize American churches before the war. The pastors and members in the sparsely populated communities voluntarily assumed enormous hardships by cutting themselves off from the support of the American denominations at a time when they could no longer depend on material support from the homeland.[13] Individuals in the Reformed Church and in some secular circles in Hungary sympathetically followed and encouraged the activities of the Free Magyar Church, but there is no proof of opponents' claims that it received financial aid from the homeland.[14] The Reformed Church in Hungary officially abided by the letter of the Tiffin Agreement and did not seek even the connection with the Hungarian ministers through the channels of the American church authorities that the agreement permitted. The clergymen were left to feel slighted and ignored.

The bitter struggle between conformists and nonconformists was still con-tinuing during the 1920s. Both sending never-ending memorandums to the Board of Missions here and the Mother Church overseas concerning the relent-less activities of the Free Magyar Reformed Church in America.

In 1929 several Hungarian ministers from the American denominations visited Hungary and unofficially exchanged ideas with leaders of the Hungarian Church. They dismissed the Free Magyar Church's accusations against them, and, while recognizing the enormous sacrifices made by members of the Free Church, questioned whether such a burdensome, futile effort was justified "when we, brothers through His Body and Blood, serve the same purposes, with the same loyal, giving, and Hungarian soul."[15] The delegation's visit only made the conflict worse and the competition rougher. By the next year, Hungarian-American Reformed congregations could be found under the juris-dictions of six different church authorities.

Half a century later, it is easier to see the positive influence of the Free Magyar Church. Its allegations that the ministers within the American denomi-nations had sold out "their faith, their language, Hungarianism, and their church" spurred those ministers to struggle for the relative independence within the American churches that won them, first, a Hungarian diocese and later, their own church districts.[16] In addition, congregations belonging to the Reformed Church in the United States paid strong attention to teaching the Hungarian language in summer schools during the 1920s. So that young people preparing for all phases of church work in the Hungarian community could learn about the Hungarian Reformed Church's history, constitution, and cus-toms, in 1924 the American denomination established a Hungarian department at Franklin and Marshall College in Lancaster, Pennsylvania, and supported it financially for eleven years.[17] Although leaders of the Free Magyar Church often criticized the department's level of instruction and its effectiveness, losing it in the mid-1930s dealt a major blow to Hungarian Reformed religious life in the United States.

Of course, nothing weakened the Hungarian-American Calvinist organizations and communities as badly as the divisions and hostilities did. There were churches that changed denominational masters more than once, according to the direction in which the minister built connections or pursued his own financial and social well-being. Church leadership became notoriously unstable between the two world wars. As soon as a conflict developed between a minister and his congregation or his denominational superiors, the offer of another job often appeared, unsolicited. "The ministers, whenever the ground began to sink beneath their feet in one of the groups, simply turned their backs on their missions and always found new job possibilities in one of the enemy camps, from where they did not miss the opportunity of returning poisoned arrows against their comrades of yesterday."[18] Members of the congregations soon began to follow the example set by their pastors. "The ministers and lay people wandered in and out of congregations, churches and mission groups as though this were the most natural thing in the world. If I become angry at my minister or my fellow worker, I'll go where they will accept me."[19] Eventually some members became so disheartened by the quarrels and bickering that they joined uninvolved denominations or sects turned against all organized religion.[20]

In all the denominations and church communities to which Hungarian Americans belonged, some turmoil was caused by the new phase of accommodation, even if it was not as great as among the Protestants. It was in the 1920s that Hungarian Baptists and other evangelicals built up their churches, and only part of their growth came from the breakup of their existing multiethnic congregations into ethnic ones. In the "national awakening" of the non-Magyar church members, who used to consider themselves Hungarian, and spoke Hungarian, the propaganda against the Hungarians also had a role. As a consequence of this propaganda they discontinued the Hungarian Baptist Seminary and the American Baptists founded the International Baptist Seminary.[21]

Before World War I, Hungarian Jewry maintained several congregations, their Americanization continuing at a quick pace. According to Perlman, in the aftermath of World War I Hungarian Jews were striving to move beyond the parochial concerns of local *Landsmanschaften* and synagogues. They were seeking a national presence and a capability of acting in a concerted manner on the problems left by the war. At the same time, this development on their part marked their growing distance from the national federation of all Hungarians and a recognition that, in a period when conditions were changing for the worse for Jews in Hungary, their interests were diverging sharply from those of Hungarian Gentiles.[22]

The strict discipline and hierarchy of the Roman Catholic Church closed the door much more firmly against attempts to break up the church. In pre-war

Hungarian Catholic communities, the issues of their belonging to a Hungarian diocese or becoming independent from the American Roman Catholic bishop's territiorial authority never would have arisen at all. Undoubtedly, use of the Latin rite made the lack of their own ethnic church more bearable. In fact, prior to 1914 most of the "Hungarian" Catholic churches really were multiethnic. It was only during the 1920s and 1930s that the multiethnic parishes that had survived the earlier conflicts came to be dismantled. The result was the last vigorous period of church building in America's Hungarian Roman Catholic communities. In 1921 alone, eight new Hungarian Roman Catholic parishes were established in the United States.[23] Grievances, a strengthening ethnic consciousness, and a reaction against the intensifying forces of integration all were behind the new regroupings. Because ethnic Catholics received their bishop's permission to form a parish only if the community could guarantee its financial support, the Hungarian parishes usually were larger than the Protestants' congregations, which often were further reduced in size by interdenominational strife.

Although the Hungarian Roman Catholic community always was less fragmented than its Protestant counterpart, the forced assimilation of the 1920s also brought it conflict. Joseph Hartel, pastor of the Cleveland parish, respectfully alerted Cleveland's Archbishop Joseph Schrembs to the problems caused by replacing Hungarian hymns with the Latin chant:

> My people are immigrants from Hungary where from their earliest years, the Mother Church permitted them to sing the praises of God in Hungarian, while the priest at the altar sang his proper part in Latin. They think: "It was good there, why does the church forbid [it] here?" ... Their parents lived in Hungary at a time when nationalism, and especially the love of the national language, had been fanned to the highest pitch, and the national language and the religious service became a thing utterly intertwined; now they think, "Are both to be strangled?"
>
> Incredible as it may seem, many of my people never had the opportunity of even an ordinary grammar school education, and neither read or write. They cannot read a prayer book and if the High Mass is all in Latin, their helplessness is galling to themselves; they cannot understand the Latin, they cannot read, they cannot sing, they are unable to express their sentiments in protracted prayer, and they get the idea that even the church has turned on them and is willing that they lose their nationality, their language; but if they are permitted to sing till it resounds, they remember the hymns they learned in childhood and the sentiments of love and adoration. They awaken and leaving the church, they depart with a sense of having worshiped God as their heart dictated.
>
> Finally, the Baptists, the Protestants, the Socialists play on their love for their mother tongue to alienate them from the church, and [with] this same plea invite them to their ranks where they can use their own language in the worship of God.[24]

On the other hand, in the same year, members of another Cleveland Hungarian parish in conflict revealed how far their own Americanization had proceded when, with no hint of obsequiousness, they firmly insisted that Bishop Schrembs replace their priest.

> The people of the church want no nonsense, and shall not stand for, nor do they want to be ashamed of their priest, therefore it has been decided that, if Rev. E. Rickert is not removed by the 15th of December 1925, the people of the St. Margaret's Church will do as they best see fit to remove Rev. E. Rickert from the parish, if necessary carry the case to public courts.[25]

The Rev. Charles Schaeffer gives us insight to other characteristics of church life, giving a description of some Hungarian American Protestant Churches in the 1920s.:

> The churches themselves are generally of a churchly type of architecture. They are usually well located, with a parsonage in connection or by the side. A church would hardly be considered complete without a steeple and a bell or bells hanging in it. The poet who wrote "The Bells" might have gotten inspiration from the ringing of the Hungarian church bells, for they ring their church bells three times. Three is their national number. It is interesting to note that none of their churches in America is named for a saint. A church named for a saint would be too suggestive of Catholicism. The name of the place is sufficient to designate the church. This is also the New Testament way of naming churches—the Church of Ephesus, the Church of Laodicea, etc.
> In the beginning of the 1920s, the interior arrangement of the Hungarian Calvinist churches was very simple and dignified, as Rev. Schaeffer, Secretary of the Board of Home Mission of the Reformed Church indicates. Great prominence is given to the pulpit. Usually this is located in the center on the side of the church, not at one end. You would not find such a thing as a corner pulpit in our Hungarian churches. A pulpit in a corner would not give it sufficient prominence. The pulpit is central. It is always elevated. The Hungarians believe in a prophetic ministry, although the priestly element is not wanting. The pulpit is usually enclosed, not open like in many of our American churches. There is no altar, but a communion table covered with fine cloths. There is also a baptismal font. Flowers usually are found in profusion, especially on great occasions. Many of the churches have pipe organs, but one seldom sees a piano or another musical instrument in the church. Many, indeed, have no musical instrument whatsoever, and yet the singing is of a very high order. How they do sing! The tunes are the old church tunes, the chorales coming down from the time of Venerable Beza. Very few hymn books, however, are in evidence. The dictator gives out the lines of the hymn and everybody sings. The arrangement of the pews is likewise interesting. When the pulpit is in the center the pews face in that direction, which means that one-half of the audience faces the

other half, the men at one end of the church and the women at the other. Where the pulpit happens to be at one end, with a center aisle, the men sit on one side and the women on the other, and the children are gathered up front near the organ.[26]

The effects of acculturation on both Protestant and Catholic churches were reflected in new social activities and adoption of the American model of financial support. Groups were created for religious-social activities: men's circles, women's circles, sewing circles, young married couples' clubs, Sunday school circles, Sunday school teachers' unions. At the same time, regular community suppers, Sunday dinners and afternoon teas, social evenings and dances, bazaars and parlor games gave the churches a full calendar of social events paralleling those of the secular organizations.

The duties of the priest and minister—or of the minister's wife—expanded to include the teaching of plays, obtaining costumes, and making sure the plays were popular. More noticeably, during these years, the role of lay women expanded as they became the pillars of the church's fund-raising work. Women's groups cooked the community suppers, prepared handicrafts for the church bazaars, and baked nut and poppy seed rolls and made *csiga* (shell) noodles for food sales, creating an important source of financial support for the church. While engaging in this useful work together, they talked, exchanged information, joked, and revived familiar skills from their past lifestyle. In conducting interviews, I spoke with numerous elderly women who every week for over half a century voluntarily went to their church to work in the Ladies Aid Society.[27] Without the many decades of long cooperation on the part of the women, the churches could not have been built or preserved.

It had a religious as well as a secular purpose, for in most Protestant churches the services were held in Hungarian until the end of the 1920s, when the Presbyterians first introduced English. As Father Hartel informed the bishop, Hungarian language remained a vital part of Catholic worship, too.[28]

From the 1890s on, Hungarians in the United States discussed how they could give their American-born children a Hungarian education and teach them the Hungarian language. Their debate was still raging at the turn of the century, when *Szabadság* sharply criticized the Hungarian Catholic schools for neglecting the Hungarian language,[29] and even later in 1908, when Tihamér Kohányi gave the Austro-Hungarian consulary adviser Baron Ambrózy a pessimistic account of the Hungarian schools. The Baron reported to his superiors: "Kohányi belongs among those who do not believe in the immigrant second generation's retention of Hungarian national self-consciousness. He believes that money used for this purpose is thrown out of the window and that the possibility of keeping [it] alive through clergy and newspaper writers is a utopian dream. There is neither a clergyman nor a newspaper writer who will preach against his own interests. But even if this would occur, sermons and articles have no influence."[30]

Intensive Hungarian-language instruction during the regular school year began to ebb in the Protestant communities during the First World War. It was revived on a small scale after the war for several reasons including loss of the subsidies the schools had received from the church in Hungary and the division of many congregations by the organizational conflicts of the twenties. Instead, it was replaced by expansion of the summer schools that some communities had sponsored in the pre-war years. For example, an eight-week morning and afternoon summer school that had been initiated in 1897 was continued in Bridgeport, and some 385 pupils enrolled in its 1926 session. Saturday schools likewise became popular.[31] The students of these schools can be seen in numerous photographs in the annual publications of the Hungarian Reformed Federation of America.[32] If anything, opinions became even more divided in the period of permanent settlement after World War I. At that time, "to help and support the continual cultivation of the Magyar language and culture along with brotherly coexistence" remained a typical goal in the charters of the majority of fraternal organizations,[33] while patriotic leaders continued to proclaim, "The nation lives in its language."

There were only four full-day Roman Catholic Hungarian-American parochial schools before World War I, but some twenty cities witnessed the establishment of such schools in the decade before the Depression called a halt to the activities. The motto of the building campaign was, "Save the second generation." The Catholic church authorities urged the building of schools in the interest of preserving their religious values. From the 1920s on new school laws greatly restricted the possibility of teaching a foreign language in parochial schools. The Roman Catholic and Greek Catholic Hungarian parochial schools concentrated on Americanization and on religious education. Saint Margaret's Hungarian Roman Catholic school, which opened on Upper Buckeye after World War I, never taught in Hungarian. In practice, however, in the early 1920s Cleveland's working-class Hungarians most often sent their children to the public schools, especially to the East Side school located between Rawlings Avenue and Woodlawn Street.[34]

Some Hungarian Roman Catholic churches were seriously burdened by the requirement of building the schools. In St. Ladislaus parish, in New Brunswick, Father Ozseb founded the Magyar Műkedvelő Szinháza (Hungarian Amateur Theater) so that they would be able to pay off their debts, and to cover the cost of maintaining the school. The priest himself taught the "actors, rehearsed with them and was the prompter during the performances. There were also members of the Reformed faith among the actors."[35]

Between the two world wars, churches in fifty-six cities offered Saturday or Sunday Hungarian-language instruction, and sixty-eight churches conducted summer school classes.[36] However the Depression and the introduction of English-language church services in the 1930s suddenly ended the enthusiasm for the Hungarian schools. The expansion of the Catholic parochial schools stopped in its tracks.[37]

The Hungarian-language summer schools, though they were not subject to the new legal restrictions, also lost popularity. According to a teacher at the East Side First Reformed Church, "Within fifteen years there was a drop of 50 percent."[38] Increasingly, the summer schools organized by the Protestant Churches were able to obtain students only by changing into English-language vacation Bible schools.

CHAPTER 20

The Secular Organizations

Divergence of Paths and Goals

The Road to the Insurance Business and the Growth of the Middle Class

THE HUNGARIAN IMMIGRANTS' integration into the American environment after World War I can be seen in the changing characteristics and functions of their secular organizations. As mentioned earlier, since the last decade of the nineteenth century, six "national" Hungarian organizations had developed in the United States: Verhovay, Rákóczi, Bridgeport, the Hungarian Reformed Federation, and two leftist organizations. Each had one or more local branches in the various Hungarian settlements. Before the World War I period, all of the mutual aid societies had customarily charged every member the same dues and gathered the additional amount needed to pay benefits by "assessments" against all the members. When they decided on permanent settlement, however, the old methods were abandoned. The leader of the largest of the organizations explained why:

> The association was put together for migrants, who came and went. The original goal of migration can be seen from the structure of the association. Every migrant started out with the idea that he somehow would get himself together: then home! It was for these types of migrants that the Verhovay was planned. But when it became evident that life developed differently throughout Hungarian America, the Verhovay also recognized that the temporary world had passed and it had to organize for permanency, too, and for an ever more American-Hungarian atmosphere."[1]

The changes needed were to substitute the rate system, which based membership dues on age, for the assessment system and to obtain reinsurance contracts from large Amerian insurance companies. But it was difficult for the members to accept the end of equal rates. A stormy battle ensued between the traditionalists and those who demanded modernization. In the annual membership meeting of the Verhovay held in Cleveland in 1917, the delegates voted down the changes.

After many internal arguments and changes in leadership, in 1920 the general meeting accepted the differential system of dues in a very simple form. From this time on, those 16 to 50 years old were to pay a monthly eighty cents and those 50 years and older, two dollars. The relatively small difference in the rate explains the strength of the opposition which tried to prevent so heavily burdening the older members. However, it did not satisfy those urging Americanization, those better informed about insurance issues, and the ambitious men who were preparing themselves for the top position in the organization. Once again, a complete restructuring of the Verhovay was proposed, only to be voted down by the delegates. When one of the main supporters of reform then resigned his position in disgust, confusion reigned.[2]

All the national organizations went through similar crises until the various state regulatory agencies forced the issue. When New York and Ohio revoked the Verhovay's insurance licenses until it changed over to the differential system, the opposition withdrew and the scales finally were tipped toward the side of modernization. The newspapers took on the crucial role of explaining the new system to the majority of members, who had no knowledge of modern insurance practices. In addition, the Verhovay paper summarized what happened after the 1923 convention which adopted a scale of dues based on the American Mortuary Experience Tables. The total reorganization of the Association laid a new and important burden on the old members although it also permitted them to pay their dues by lowering their insurance level or through encumbrances on their policies. As a result, the old members left the association in large numbers, dropping the Verhovay's membership to under twenty thousand.[3]

The Verhovay Association's modernization and the conflict it generated were typical of what happened in all the other national associations, too. In the same fateful year of 1923, the Rákóczi Segély Egyesület (Rakóczi Aid Association) after a similarly long conflict succeeded in getting the new differentiated rate system adopted by fifty-eight of the eighty delegates at an extraordinary convention.[4] As in the Verhovay, the oldest members repudiated the "capitulation" and left the association; under no conditions were they going to pay the realistic dues.

By the 1920s, the nationwide Magyar associations had hundreds of local branches, which flourished as centers of social life for the members. By 1930, Detroit became one of the most active centers. The largest branch belonged to the Verhovay but all factions of the workers movement were also represented among the organizations. The members had personal contact with one another at the meetings held monthly, and local branches of every fraternal association organized big picnics. To realize how popular these picnics were and how much amusement they gave, one may read, for example, the account given on the "Big Verhovay Picnic in Cleveland" in the Verhovay Association's newspaper.[5]

The decision of the Hungarian Reformed Federation represented their turn toward modernization in the 1920s, too. It is of interest to mention that while leaders of congregations were under different church authorities and stood up against each other, they were kept together by business rationality in the Hungarian Reformed Federation in America. National loyalty could already have been as disruptive for the Federation as religion after some congregations joined the homeland Conventus, but officials worked to keep the association out of religious conflicts. Therefore, when the Free Magyar Reformed Church in America came into being, they got representative positions in the leadership each time they solicited members from both factions.[6] One of their most successful joint efforts in those years was the establishment of their Orphan's home in Ligonier, Pennsylvania: "All Hungarians, irrespective of denominational or religious affiliations, took an active interest in the support of the charitable work so that the Orphan's Home of the Federation was finally dedicated on July 4, 1921, the twenty-fifth anniversary of the Federation."[7]

Nevertheless, despite their rules and perhaps their efforts to avoid religious issues that divided Protestants and Catholics, the fraternal associations—except for the socialists—while vigilantly defending their independence from the churches, maintained strictly Christian organizations.

Every fraternal organization emphasized neutrality in political questions, except for the socialists. The leaders of the Rákóczi Association refused to take part in any such meetings, where the theme could be judged as political. In 1923 the secretary had declined to attend the Connecticut Magyar Citizens' Association convention because the Rákóczi Association shunned all political movements.[8] In the beginnings the statutes generally ordained that members should be born in Hungary. In the 1920s, earlier or later, they opened their doors to others too. In March 1924, as a first step, the Rákóczi's annual convention, for example, decided that non-Magyar members could be enrolled if they lived among and sympathized with Magyars.[9]

As state controls grew from the 1920s on, they created more obstacles to the traditional functioning of the associations. Small associations began to disband, and the larger to merge. Many associations thus gave up their independence and joined others that had greater capital and more—or younger—members. A few clung to the familiarity of their old organizational forms, but the overall effect was to decrease the previously mushrooming number of associations.

With the push from the state regulators, the forces of Americanization and business interests won out over the solidarity of the community. It is unlikely that the advocates of modernization were aware that the rationalization inherent in business methods and the solidarity of the community were incompatible. Instead they seemed to believe that modernization was in the real, best interest of the community.

After announcing the new membership policy the leaders of the federation staunchly proclaimed that their organization was not an insurance company but a brotherhood, while they endeavored to follow the recruitment practices of the American organizations. The need for "experts" made it necessary to give positions to persons whom the association's members earlier would have avoided, intellectuals and "educated men." Still, the presidents and secretaries were mostly "self-made men," who came from simple backgrounds, began as laborers in the United States, and only later worked their way up into the middle class. To give a few examples, there was József Daragó, who from 1917 started to play an important role in the Verhovay Association.

> He was born in 1874 in Szomolya, Borsod County, son of a poor family. He received his teachers' diploma at the Bishops High School in Kassa. As a young man he went to the United States, and first worked on hard labor in factories. He soon started in business in Akron, Ohio. As one of the outstandingly successful Hungarian businessmen he was invited to become the president of the Verhovay Association. As the Association with its nearly four million dollars' wealth was a real economic and social factor in Hungarian public life, Daragó was called upon to take a leading part in it, too.[10]

For years the secretary of the Bridgeport Association, János Walkó was elected to its central leadership on the 1915 convention.

> He was born in 1875 in Szák, Komárom County, son of a small farmer. He finished economic high school and moved to Budapest at the age of 20. There he could not make a living, left for the United States wishing to spend there just a few years. He first tried landscape-gardening, then worked in the Roebling factory in Trenton as wire-strecher for nine and a half years. He became very active in the Trenton branch of the Bridgeport Association.[11]

These leaders, drawn from the immigrant generation, had to be able to manage the business aspects of the association and lead its ethnic social and cultural functions at the same time. Success in this three-in-one position was the result of the individual's own aptitudes and cultural level. As the business duties became more complex and time consuming, most leaders relinquished their social and cultural responsibilities to the newspaper editors, clergy, and other members of the ethnic intelligentsia and limited their own role to insurance business. Consequently, they saw their financial role as being "to provide support for continued education in the Hungarian language and culture and for their advancement."[12] It was the associations that popularized "Let's be American; let's remain Hungarian!" as the slogan of the 1920s. By the latter they meant chiefly maintenance of the mother tongue and its transmittal to the second generation.

Representatives of most Hungarian-American organizations, with the exception of those of the workers' movement, held a "national meeting" in Buffalo, New York in 1929.

The goals were, by expressing everlasting loyalty to America, to establish the long desired Hungarian-American unity in order to prepare for the First Hungarians' World Congress in Budapest and lay down the lines along which a just revision of the Trianon Treaty could be rendered possible. In Buffalo they spoke emotionally about their "vocation as Hungarians," the preservation of their Hungarianism and the Hungarian language, the education of the second generation, the ties that bound them to their homeland, their sorrow over Hungary's truncation, and their other grievances.[13] However, the Hungarian-American newspapers reported critically on the deepening chasm between the promises and pledges the community leaders made at the Hungarian conferences and their behavior in everyday life. The demands of adaptation necessary for their rise to leadership in society quickly wore down the immigrant's nationalism of most but not all leaders of the insurance associations. No other organization, however, appeared to reject Hungarian nationalism in as many ways as the Rákóczi Association did. It was the only one to obtain repayment of the loan it gave to the Hungarian government during the First World War, and Rákóczi leaders did not participate—influenced by the leftists—either in the Hungarian-American meeting in Buffalo or in the Hungarian World Congress in Budapest.[14] There were more radical, socially thinking persons in the leadership of the Association than there were in other "bourgeois" organizations. According to information given by Mr. Stelkovics, they were frequently labeled *cucilists*, communists. Those who upheld a radical view may easily have received those epithets.[15]

The regular work of the leaders required total immersion within the functions of the insurance business. Their management duties increased as the general meetings (conventions) became less frequent. Once held annually, they later met every two years, then every four years. As a result, stability required continuity in leadership. After reorganization, the "new" officers usually were the same persons, or persons repeatedly chosen from the same group of people.[16] Delegates sent to the conventions from local Hungarian-American communities simply could not evaluate the leaders' actual work. Offices in the associations became careers as the officers became managers. Their names became well known throughout "Magyar Amerika," and this gave them social status. Ironically, these managers, in turn, began to resist one of the trends of modernization, mergers that would cost them their positions. The repeatedly renewed attempt to organize one big joint fraternal organization always ended in failure.[17]

The Leftist Organizations

All of the factions of American labor could be found among the Hungarian immigrants: Communists, members of the Socialist Party (SP), the Socialist Labor Party (SLP), and the Industrial Workers of the World (IWW). The beginning of the 1920s was the period of splits and regroupings within the parties, which brought troubled years for the Hungarian-American workers' movement. All radical organizations of the various trends laid great emphasis on publishing political literature in Hungarian.

Groups of leftists who believed in class solidarity but wanted to keep far away from the Communists joined the Worker's Sick Benefit Federation. A split occurred among the members of the IWW Hungarians. Some radicals left and joined the Communists, but others remained in the IWW. After 1924 they published their paper, *Bérmunkás* (Wage Laborer), in Cleveland for more than two decades under the leadership of Joseph Geréb. The Munkásbetegsegé-lyző Szövetség (Worker's Sick Benefit Association) joined the members of the IWW with Hungarians who were drawn to the reformist Socialist Party.

The ideological disputes, factional battles, and personal struggles that continuously raged in the young American Communist Party also beset its Hungarian-language section. As Hungarian political refugees who had participated in the short-lived Hungarian Soviet Republic immigrated to the United States after its fall in 1919, they quickly came into conflict with the "old Hungarian-American" Social Democrats, who had become Communists. Lajos Baksy led the older group and the "1919s" or "Young Communists" were led by János Lékai. When the American Communist Party intervened and in 1925 called a party congress to elect new leaders, the majority of positions went to the Young Communists, who also obtained the key posts in the Worker's Sick Benevolent and Educational Federation. The group's paper, *Uj Előre* (New Forward), then became the main platform for their propaganda efforts. The number of Hungarian-American Communists is hard to estimate. One account in 1925 claimed the Communist Party in the United States altogether had 16,000 members, of whom 600 were Hungarian.[18]

The Communist Party in the U.S.A. in 1925 consisted of seventeen language (immigrant) groups whose work was coordinated by the Workers Party City Committee. Because party connections were loose, the central office gave general directions and stepped in only in case of important problems. In 1925, however, its congress ended the autonomy of the language groups and replaced them with workplace cells and basic organizations in settlements.[19]

Struggling with language difficulties, the smaller number of Hungarian-American Communists continued to focus their activities within the Hungarian immigrant group. Criticism of Horthy's Hungary formed an integral part of its competition with the nationalists for the hearts and minds of Hungarian immigrants. Although the Worker's Sick Benevolent and Educational Federation, which had come under their leadership, reported 136 branches with 5,124 members in 1928, its activities were directed by the largest branch in New York City. The society offered financial and moral support to movements in the political class struggle in which the Communist Party took part. In the early 1920s, for example, it tried to raise financial aid for its imprisoned members and those slated for deportation and organized the protection of their interests. It organized collections for the financial support of the Communists from Hungary scattered throughout Europe after 1919 and supported as well the Communist Party's main propaganda and agitation activities toward the creation of a united industrial party and American recognition of the Soviet Union. In 1922, the Third International sent the Hungarian József Pogány from Moscow to the United States for political work, and there he became one of the leaders of the Central Committee's majority fraction under the name of John Pepper.

The Munkásbetegsegélyző Szövetség had existed since 1906, but its growth exploded in the 1920s. The 177 branches reported in 1925 became 207 with a total membership of 10,849 in 1927.[20] The headquarters of this most rapidly growing of the workingmen's sick benefit associations were in Pittsburgh. It spoke out against the Hungarian "white terror," tried to support the persecuted members of the class struggle such as the Industrial Workers of the World, and, among the Hungarian political refugees, tried to help the Social Democrats who had emigrated to Vienna. The role of political ideology gradually waned within the group as its efforts turned toward the organization of collective life through worker's self-education, choral unions, and so on. The organization backed their papers, *Bérmunkás* and *Munkás*, but with ever less vigor. The organization's paper, *Összetartás* (which began to be published in 1912), was at its beginnings more of a forum for socialist thought and cultural enlightenment than an instrument of corporate communication. However, in the 1920s, it was allowed an ever narrower space for ideological and political debates. Finally, in April, members voted in a referendum to strike the word "socialist" from part of the membership application.[21]

Despite the unification efforts, the leaders of the factions of the labor movement remained engaged in a ruthless struggle with each other deepened by the ideological struggles that in the 1920s ruled the international labor movement. Their ideology made it easier to build connections with different nationalities or with native-born Americans than with each other. Therefore, the leftists started off with a relatively more favorable basis for integrating into American society, but on the other side their foreignness quickly directed attention to their radicalism. In the United States the Communist Party pursued vigorous Americanization in the 1920s, as "development of a united American working class: the destruction of the dividing walls between ethnic groups and the end of the group's isolation."[22]

In the larger Hungarian settlements in the 1910s, "worker's homes" had been the centers of the cultural and social life of the movement, where learning, self-improvement, and entertainment all could find their place.

> It is the duty of every sick benefit society, every IWW class, every revolutionary group to unceasingly recruit amateur groups because the battle must be carried to every front of the capitalist class. The communist ideology can be carried most easily among the masses in plays. Before we can ask the masses to join us, we must first change their way of thinking. This work is done through revolutionary verses, plays, books, and newspapers. For this reason the amateurs must be given better parts, we must produce better productions than those of the stupefying, concerned only with seeking pleasures, bourgeois society.[23]

The audiences, for their part, liked amusing performances better than choral speaking and direct political agitation. Consequently, numerous Magyar settlements were visited by touring amateur groups, and those living in the different localities were able to get to know each other through personal connections.[24]

In the local communities the ideological dividing lines were not as sharp, at least between the different factions of the labor movement. Sometimes it was decreed, "Between the two workingmen's sick benefit associations there was and is an understanding that at one time the selfsame comrade and member could be the president of both."[25] Likewise, the membership of the religious societies and the labor organizations was not always completely distinct; the same person could at the same time be a member of three or four ideologically very different sick benefit organizations. Although political differences placed the leaders in direct conflict with each other, the separate membership walls of the various associations were regularly permeated by day-to-day contact within the Hungarian-American communities. Members of officially feuding organizations not only attended each other's entertainment evenings and plays, but they occasionally shared the same worker's home or Magyar House. They also sometimes found a common cause in the 1920s in the Horthy Ellenes Liga (Anti-Horthy League) formed to protest against the regime in Hungary.[26] The league did not activate masses in the tens of thousands, as one of its chroniclers once claimed, but it did produce several political mass movements.

Organizations of the Hungarian-American Middle Class

Permanent settlement and the maturing of the second generation brought a greater movement of Hungarian Americans into the middle class. That, in turn, in the more numerous Hungarian communities, led to formation of local Magyar Clubs in Cleveland, Detroit, Chicago, and Pittsburgh. The clubs were formed, in the words of the Cleveland group, to enable Hungarians to "be represented on a culturally appropriate level" to the rest of society.[27] That club's organizer and first president was an ambitious college student, the future Judge Louis Petrash, who became the city's outstanding political leader of Hungarian descent in the 1920s.

He was born in Cleveland on the East Side, the son of one of the earliest Hungarian pioneers, Mihály Petrásh and his wife, née Mária Fecso. His parents themselves were community movement leaders, founding members of the St. Elizabeth Church and the original Magyar House, and active participants in the erection of the Kossuth statue. Judge Petrash received his education in the Kinsman Public School and in the St. Elizabeth Parochial School; he received his A.B. and M.A degrees at John Carroll University and his law degree at the Law School of Western Reserve. He finished his legal studies while already a practicing attorney.

Shortly after he began his own law practice, the community drew him into public service and in 1915 he was named Deputy Director of the Cuyahoga County Voting Board. During World War I he was connected to the War Council, and was the Secretary of the Cosmopolitan Liberty Bond Committee as well as a member of the All Nations Activities Committee. In 1921 he was elected to the City Council, the first American of Hungarian parentage to be so honored by the city.[28]

The appearance of the Magyar Clubs and leaders such as Petrash symbolized the way the Hungarian communities and associations from the 1920s on became more socially differentiated and structured and more goal oriented. The new permanent status of the Hungarian migrants who had arrived earlier and an infusion of forced migrants and political immigrants combined with the emergence of the second generation to produce the change. The young artists and classically trained intellectuals who came in the first years of the 1920s and were mostly from Budapest, and even in their new environment they so yearned after the particular form of Budapest's social life that they attempted to reproduce it in various forms. Toward this goal they founded the Fészek (Nest) Club, patterning it after the one in Budapest, and also connected their other social groups and clubs to an established coffeehouse.[29] The main center of the new organizations was almost exclusively New York, along with a few other cities, for example, Chicago and Los Angeles, where the groups were composed of more educated and middle-class Magyar emigrants with an urban background. In New York, the First Hungarian Literary Society had functioned since 1889. It was originally established to promote "debates, recitations, and readings, to improve literary talent and to cultivate the social relations" among its members (particularly merchants, craftsmen, and intellectuals).[30] The main aim of their communal organizations was then to fulfill the cultural demand they were used to (mostly in the German language). The First Hungarian Literary Society, secure in its own building (after 1925), was able to modify its purposes and its programs decade after decade, including the arrival of young Hungarians in the 1920s. In these places, because of their demands a few Magyar concerts and operatic performances were organized.

The post–World War I immigrants' communities and organizations for the most part lasted only for a short period. The possibilities for adapting and the intensity of their attempts at assimilation quickly broke up the not very large groups. Their longings and wishes, however, resulted in attempts at fostering their cultural heritage. Because of this, for example, in 1929 a small group of intellectuals with a radical viewpoint worked at organizing a widely encompassing cultural club. In support of their concept they invited America's Hungarian intellectuals:

> For those with the same language but with different world views and [belonging to different] denominations; individuals with varying social and political views can have as their common connection only culture, the love of beauty and striving after truth. We desire to form a Magyar cultural society, a community in a club where every Magyar can go to refresh their mind and soul as well as rest, where they can meet with friends to talk, exchange ideas, read the best Hungarian magazines and books, be entertained in a fitting manner, and where from time to time learned, artistic and literary presentations and debates will uplift their

intellectual and spiritual level. This Hungarian community will not take part in serving any interest, denomination or any individual's goal or self-interest.[31]

On the basis of this invitation the Ady Endre Society was formed, which emphasized the necessity of building a cultural bridge between the intellectuals of New York and Budapest. For a time the Ady Endre Society, with its high-quality literary and cultural programs, became an attractive meeting place and social cultural center for a part of the New York region's liberal bourgeois Magyar intelligentsia. The Society sponsored guest appearances of a number of famous Hungarian artists from Budapest.[32] But the current of American life broke up this cultural group's momentum, and by the beginning of the 1940s only a few intellectuals remained in it.

The American Magyar Jewish Association, as well as the Freemasons, proved to be stronger and more effective organizations in the 1920s and 1930s.[33] The Federation of Hungarian Jews in America was set up in 1919 for the purpose of rendering support to Hungarian Jews abroad in a social, political, and charitable way. They organized the American Economic Council for American Jews to raise $14 million to aid Jewish refugees expelled during the Communist period under Béla Kun. Several of them had been established in the years preceding World War I, but they became active during the period between the two world wars. Against the anti-Semitism of the government of Hungary the American Magyar Jewish Association protested, too, and issued English-language publications to inform the American public opinion on the white terror and the general situation in Hungary. A new Hungarian law limiting higher education of Jews by quota, and propaganda that questioned the Jews' Hungarian identity, now rallied them against the Hungarian political system.

At the same time, this marked their growing distance from the national federation of all Hungarians and a recognition that, in a period when conditions were changing for the worse for Jews in Hungary, their interests diverged sharply from those of Hungarian Gentiles.[34]

In the 1920s, in the social activities of some communities and in the organizations directing them, the two characteristics of adaptation are more strongly evident: first, the dissociation from one another into various social classes, interest groups, and second, the need for group cohesion and representation. Not only did the newly arrived urban population feel the social organizations as restrictive, but increasingly so did those among them who achieved higher economic and political positions. By the 1920s the numbers of these latter groups which had become detached grew. Particularly in the larger settlements, where the social differentiation was also greater, the Hungarian population divided into communities made up of small groups.

The leaders of local communities could still harmonize various group activities. In the 1920s, in most of the Hungarian settlements they initiated for that purpose an organization, like the Egyesült Magyar Egyletek és Egyházak Nagybizottsaga (United Hungarian Associations' Committee) in Cleveland.[35]

They were also usually the organizers of the Hungarian Days, which were held annually in the larger settlements in picnic grounds with programs, music, and dancing. Not only those local groups which had divided into varying organizations, but Hungarians from other communities attended. Even more, Hungarian Days represented the occasion when Americans not of Hungarian ethnic background were able to partake in their social life.

The first Hungarian Day, according to our information, took place in Pittsburgh in 1916. It was another ten years, at least in the Pittsburgh area, before the next picnic was held. However, after 1926, when it was renewed the example was followed in an increasing number of settlements, becoming the annual meeting place for the local and regional Hungarians, and also providing an arena for the introduction of ethnic traditions. In his dissertation on the characteristics of the Pittsburgh Hungarian Days, J. K. Balogh writes:

> This is Shrove Tuesday and an occasion of pomp in America. On this day countless Hungarians don their colorful Hungarian dress. The day's program is full and varied, the afternoon with many speeches, the main address is usually given by a well-known American. The evening dances are extremely interesting: here the world famous Hungarian *csárdás* can be seen—with the faultless accompaniment of gay Hungarian gypsies. The character of this festival is completely Hungarian, the two main foods are stuffed cabbage and *kolbász* [Hungarian sausage]. It is interesting to note that over 10,000 Hungarians annually participate in this gala event. This is the largest Hungarian Day in America—outdoing even Cleveland's, which has more of a local character. Large Hungarian colonies participate in Pittsburgh's Hungarian Day: McKeesport [estimates are at least 5,000], Duquesne, Hazelwood, Homestead, East Pittsburgh, Braddock, Rankin, McKees Rocks, Corapolis, Springdale, and neighboring cities in Western Pennsylvania. . . . This is perhaps the greatest day for American-Hungarians, since on this day they revive their faded memories of beautiful Hungary in a realistic manner.[36]

Seeing the varied division, the multicolored value system, the experiences in the course of geographical and social distances—a contemporary Hungarian journalist worded his opinion of the Hungarian Americans in the following way:

> The Hungarian American, as an organic body, has never existed. Since immigration began, there have been small and large Hungarian organizations, but they have never had a unified life. One group of immigrants shared no common interests with another group. The Mid-Western miner had no common interest with the New York lawyer . . . the two of them occupying different cultural levels. . . . American Hungarian life has thus grown up around the Hungarian drugstore, the Hungarian butcher shop, the Hungarian sacristy, the Hungarian bank and the Hungarian saloon.[37]

This remark of a contemporary demonstrates well that the Hungarian groups as subdivisions of society were criss-crossed by class and contained their own primary groups of families, cliques, and associations—as Milton M. Gordon relates: Being composed of numerous subcommunities, the class position is the dividing wall in ethnic community.

CHAPTER 21

The Hungarian-American Newspapers

Proposing Different Paths to Integration

As we have seen, the leading Hungarian-American newspapers, *Szabadság* and *Amerikai Magyar Népszava*, changed their position from pro-Hungarian to pro-American in 1917 when the United States entered the war. Although this 180-degree turn originally had been dictated by fear, the newspapers' about-face became even more obvious after the war was over. They agitated against remigration, praised American ways, avidly pushed naturalization, and encouraged modernization of the Hungarian organizations. Meanwhile, they published and acted as patrons of the pleas for help arriving from the old country and advocated preservation of Hungarian values. In the 1920s they were competing to carry out the slogan "Let's be American; let's remain Hungarian."

During the war, an ex-attorney and the manager of a small bank, Dr. Endre Cserna had married Tihamér Kohányi's young widow and had become *Szabadság*'s publisher. Despite his having emigrated to the United States as recently as 1912, Cserna was active in the Hungarian American Loyalty League in 1918 and encouraged *Szabadság*'s readers to buy U.S. war bonds.[1] Nevertheless, his paper's rival, *Amerikai Magyar Népszava* (New York), pulled ahead of it in popularity after the war.

Népszava's publisher, Géza D. Berkó (1871–1927), freed of his great competitor by Kohányi's death, had assumed the leadership of the Hungarian-American press by the 1920s. He moved his editorial office into a palatial building on Times Square and attempted to emulate the career of József Pulitzer, the Hungarian-born American newspaper king.[2]

To meet his readers' demand for news from home, Berkó tried to establish a news service and also attempted to involve his readers in various social or community projects and crusades. The newspaper thus supported the regular shipment of American gift parcels to relatives back home and published much propaganda for the launching of the first "charity boat."[3] In addition, Berkó organized the protest movement against the Trianon Peace Treaty and in 1926 started the campaign for "A Kossuth Statue in New York!" As Berkó explained, "Lajos Kossuth's bronze figure in New York must announce to the American nation, that the Hungarian who loves his homeland will not become reconciled either here, nor across the ocean, to the provisions in the Trianon Peace Treaty. No, no, never!"[4]

Despite the ominous trends appearing in the ethnic press, propaganda for the revision of the Trianon Treaty began in the second half of the 1920s, when the lack of solutions to the European minority problems began to receive greater publicity in the United States. In 1927 the Lajos Kossuth statue in New York City was dedicated before several thousand Hungarian-Americans and a delegation of five hundred distinguished Hungarians, while the Anti-Horthy League organized a large demonstration and from an airplane dropped upon the celebrating crowd leaflets criticizing the Hungarian political situation.[5] The next year, more than eight hundred prominent persons, including about one hundred Hungarian women from Cleveland, made a pilgrimage to Hungary to return the visit of the delegation which had come for the dedication of the Kossuth statue in New York. Their trip was organized by *Szabadság*'s Endre Cserna and Géza Kende and booked through the travel agency of the Szilvássy brothers from Cleveland. In Budapest, Regent Miklós Horthy held a reception for them in the Royal Palace, where the president of the Pro Hungaria Szővetség convinced Mrs. Helén Horváth of the necessity of establishing a parallel association in Cleveland. By December, the Pro Hungaria Society Cultural Association for Hungarian Ladies and American Ladies of Hungarian Origin was already operating with the goal of "promoting the better understanding of Hungarian culture and art in the U.S.A."[6]

The *Amerikai Magyar Népszava* enthusiastically supported the conservative newspaper baron Lord Rothermere, who warned the English public that "all of Europe's ills will be based on the Paris Peace Treaty." It published a long series of articles by Ernő Ludwig, a former Austro-Hungarian diplomat, titled "Lord Rothermere, the Apostle of Revision of Peace." Lord Rothermere himself maintained in his own organization a separate Hungarian section headed by Nándor Fodor.[7] To publicize the revisionists' demands amid the popular fascination with aviation, *Amerikai Magyar Népszava* extensively covered the "Igazságot Magyarországnak!" (Justice for Hungary) transatlantic flight of Hungarian pilots.[8]

Continuity with the past of the Hungarian-American newspapers since 1908 was represented by Géza Kende (1879–1933), whose professional skills and knowledge of Hungarian-American affairs were considered the best even by his rivals. He was assistant editor for five years under Kohányi and rendered great service not only to *Szabadság*, but to Hungarian-American journalism as a whole. Kende and the other newspaper writers often changed jobs. In 1914 as the *Amerikai Magyar Népszava*'s representative, he had organized

Count Mihály Károlyi's American tour, but in the 1920s it was for *Szabadság* that he traveled several times to Hungary. In the 1920s he provided inspiration for most of the Hungarian movements in Cleveland as well as in Hungarian America generally and was the author of "Az amerikai magyarság története" (The History of the Hungarian Americans). Although converted to Greek Catholicism, Kende came from a Jewish background, as did the majority of the Hungarian-American newspaper writers.[9]

Familiar with the readership of *Amerikai Magyar Népszava* and *Szabadság,* the Hungarian government at the beginning of the 1920s sought to reach an agreement and to find common interests with the editors and owners of the two papers, and it succeeded. To persuade the Hungarian Americans that they had a crucial role in the struggle against the Trianon Peace Treaty, in the early 1920s a number of leading Hungarian politicians supplied the papers with interviews reminding Hungarian-American readers of their "sacred duty" and "their historical calling" toward their homeland.[10]

Both *Amerikai Magyar Népszava* and *Szabadság* maintained separate editorial offices in Hungary. At the beginning of the 1920s, these two largest Hungarian-American newspapers seemed to be more than merely exponents of the Hungarian government's propaganda. Citing the overly simplified, one-sided opinions, "pieces from home" the radical newspapers went so far as to call them Horthy's "paid spokesmen." To be sure, the Hungarian government, did not forget that both *Szabadság* and *Amerikai Magyar Népszava* had hailed the Hungarian bourgeois democratic revolution with joy, condemned the "white terror," and criticized conditions in Hungary. The editor of the *Amerikai Magyar Népszava* was even willing to take part in common action with the leftist leaders of labor organizations to protest against the "white terror" in Hungary.[11] The connection on both sides was a matter of necessity. Just as before the war, Hungarian officials, now under much greater pressure, closed their eyes to differences of opinion with the newspaper men they needed to rely on. In turn the readiness of the newspaper editors to work with Hungary's elite was influenced much more by their readers' nationalism, opposition to the Trianon Peace Treaty, and the business potential of sensationalism, than by any subsidy Hungary might give them.[12]

Ties to Hungary, however, did not halt the newspapers' Americanization. From the middle of the 1920s, interest in news from the homeland diminished, stories from around America received central place, and the sensation-seeking tactics of the American newspapers were more and more adopted. Information was briefer, more superficial and less often documented with facts and figures about the Hungarian-American communities.[13] In 1926, for example, *Amerikai Magyar Népszava* organized the first beauty contest, "Who is the most beautiful girl in America?" Publishing the photos of the contestants, it prompted its readers to vote.[14] The immigrants and the struggles of their lives which previously had been the theme of the Hungarian-American literature in the papers' Sunday literary supplements, were replaced by third-rate love stories and stories of success, which the distinguished expert of Hungarian literature, József

Reményi, said were written by "hordes of greedy marauders."[15] However, an entirely different value system was represented by the leftist newspapers, reflecting the problems and activities of the different trends in the labor movement in the 1920s.

The national fraternal associations and the church authorities relied more on their own periodicals, than on "official papers." For example, the Workers Sick Benefit Federation launched its official paper *Szövetség* (Federation) in 1912; *Verhovayak Lapja* (Verhovay Journal) was first published by the Verhovay Fraternal Association in 1917; and *Rákóczi Szemle* (Rákóczi Review) by the Rákóczi Fraternal Association from 1923.[16]

Once again, Clevelanders were the leaders when Hungarian publishers and newspaper writers on January 1, 1929, called upon the communities to send representatives to Buffalo, New York, "where we could form the long desired Hungarian-American Association, could profess our ever-lasting loyalty to America, and could lay the foundation that would make possible the just revision of the Trianon Treaty."[17] In Buffalo, the American Hungarian Federation was revived for a third time to represent "every Hungarian American's activity" and to prepare for the First Hungarian World Congress in Budapest. At that Congress in 1929, the Hungarian-American churches, associations, and newspapers were represented by large delegations, but the events were followed with skepticism by some radicals and liberals among the Hungarian-American elite. On behalf of the latter, Professor József Reményi of Cleveland's Western Reserve University sarcastically commented, "If we think on the League for Revision in Hungary, on the World Federation of Overseas Hungarians, and the whole American-Hungarian complex of similar Hungarian organizations, then it would appear as though the role of savior of the homeland awaits the American-Hungarians."[18]

When the Hungarian-American communists took over *Előre* from the socialists, the financial problems of this newspaper were solved in such a way that *Előre* filed a petition for bankruptcy, and after a few days of stoppage, the *Uj Előre* was launched, with different leadership, late in 1921.[19] Soon it fell into the hands of those young Communists who had emigrated after the fall of the Hungarian Soviet Republic in 1919. The paper, which followed the program of the American section of the Worker's Communist Party, became the official organ of the party's Hungarian-language group. Its policy was determined by the Moscow center of the international Communist movement, but reminiscences of the experiences at home and criticism of the present regime there gave it its individual aspect. From its start, this paper urged the integration of the Hungarian immigrants, meaning their assimilation into the American working class. Repeatedly it published the Communist Party's goal, "To break out as quickly as possible from the ghetto-like seclusion, the ethnic isolation."[20] It was in this direction that the editors of the paper encouraged all social and cultural activities. They did not see their tasks as safeguarding and preserving the consciousness of being Hungarian for the future. Instead, they tried to educate the immigrants to become Americans, and conscious, useful proletarians at the same time, as they could be of value to their old and their new fatherlands only in this way.[21]

The newspaper's rigid and doctrinaire internationalism allowed no room for analysis of why integration might be lagging or how it could be hastened. Yet although the Communist press adopted the language of the working class and the class struggle and made the words "worker," "revolution," and "socialist" central in its vocabulary, in reality the culture of the Hungarian language became a part of its message.[22] That message had to be written in Hungarian for the readers to be able to understand it, but the Communists did not incorporate into their programs the retention of the mother tongue for their children or the protection of the Hungarian legacy and the means of passing it on.

This left *Uj Elöre* with a staff of only three to cope with the task of bringing out a national daily paper. It was very poorly written and edited, and its editor changed often.[23] Nevertheless, the newspaper managed to establish a workers' correspondence network and encourage those who seemed talented. Some of them succeeded in reaching a literary level in depicting social and societal problems, and some by the 1930s were writing in English.[24] Their main form of expression was the report, in which they viewed both their birthplace and the United States through different eyes than had the earlier immigrants. Rather than seeing "the America of limitless opportunities," they tried to show the "other America," the factories and mines where the majority of Hungarian workers were employed to work hard and lead gray lives. From the period of the Great Depression, especially, the reports of these correspondents formed an important legacy for future generations.[25]

According to Gárdos, *Uj Elöre* reported 9,000 subscribers in 1925. Kovács gives the number of all the subscribers as 36,659.[26] When compared with other data, however, Gárdos's estimate seems to be more realistic. Its financial support came mainly from the Worker's Sick Benefit and Educational Society, as part of the organization's central reserve fund was regularly turned over to finance the newspaper. The local branches organized dinners, dances, picnics, and theatrical performances in order to raise funds for the paper. This sort of community support helped the newspaper survive the financial hardships with which most of the radical newspapers continually struggled "to publish a revolutionary workers' paper free of deficit." To enlarge the source of funds, every summer each region or city held an "*Uj Elöre* Day," for cultural and political as well as fund-raising purposes.[27]

Other lines of the Hungarian labor movement were also represented by newspapers in the 1920s, such as the SLP's *Munkás* (Workers) and the IWW's *Bérmunkás* (Wage Laborer). The narrow camp of their readers could have hardly kept them alive if they had not received support from the American centers of these organizations, from the Socialist Labor Party and the IWW.

Finally, there was the "Octobrist" press, published by émigrés who had been part of the bourgeois democratic revolution of October 1918 in Hungary. Best known was *Az Ember* (The Man, 1926), which in Hungary had been the paper of Ferenc Göndör, an employee of the Social Democratic Party. In 1919, Göndör first emigrated with his press to Vienna, then settled in the United States in 1926. His readers were primarily bourgeois radicals, liberal Hungarian Jewish intellectuals who emigrated to the United States after World War I, and some well-informed skilled laborers. The paper tried without success to draw closer to the older immigrants' left-wing masses. "It became the spokesman for a small part of the large camp, the spokesman of the Hungarian radical intellectuals, from whom it received its moral and financial support."[28] Göndör made some early mistakes when he aimed several "unseemly sketches" at members of the clergy and at Count Mihály Károlyi. On the other hand, his involvement in the gathering at Buffalo and his scoffing at the communists did not help him, either.[29]

Instead, as the 1920s were a decade of fierce arguments between the Communists and the Social Democrats, *Az Ember* became locked in a battle with *Uj Előre* that did neither paper credit. *Az Ember* demanded, like the other Octobrist papers, revision of the Trianon Treaty, but in a form different from that sought by the "patriots" or the Hungarian government. The Octobrists generally espoused only peaceful means of revision.[30] As propagandists, they were far less influential, especially among the masses of Hungarian Americans. Göndör and his friends were most successful in organizing cultural programs of high quality for appreciative audiences in New York City. The social evenings of *Az Ember* were attractive in the circle of Hungarian liberals, and social democrats, particularly in the 1930s.

The Hungarian-language working-class papers, like *Magyar Bányászlap* (Hungarian Miners' Journal), proclaimed militant views imbued with the spirit of class struggle. In 1914 such a workers' paper appears, which "shows an equally intense commitment to technical unity among Magyar workers who accepted the capitalist system."[31]

Besides these "nationwide" newspapers, every larger settlement had its own Hungarian language newspaper by the 1920s: Detroit, Chicago, Toledo, Bridgeport, Pittsburgh, New Brunswick, Los Angeles, St. Louis, Trenton, and the list could go on. Their circulation reached the highest levels before the Depression. They were the principal sources of the local communities' social and cultural events.

Hungarian-American newspaper subscribers increased significantly from 72,000 in 1920 to 98,000 by 1930.[32] The problem of dual languages did not yet exist for the newspapers in the 1920s, but with the death of Géza Berkó in 1927, the period of the "pioneer" immigrant newspaper writers came to an end. Symbolically, after he died, the ownership of Berkó's newspaper for a time fell out of Hungarian hands for business reasons alone.[33] In the census of 1930, the number of the Hungarian immigrants was 274,450, and at the same time that of the subscribers to American-Hungarian language papers was 328,400.[34]

The 1920s were the mature period of the Hungarian newspapers. Their various types and the differences in the views, ideologies, and policies represented by them reflect the cultural and social diversity and those stratifications and characteristics, which were then formed by the new environment. In numbers, form, and financial base, they reached the peak of their possibilities, from which their decline, together with the diminishing of the numbers of the immigrant generation, began with the economic depression in the 1930s. By the 1940s, however, virtually all of them could be described according to the following: "The *Amerikai Magyar Népszava* is an independent newspaper in the best of American traditions. It is an American newspaper printed in the Hungarian language. It regards every problem first and last from the American point of view."[35]

CHAPTER 22

The 1930s:
Class and Ethnic Solidarity

THE HUNGARIAN IMMIGRANTS' period of economic prosperity in the United States lasted only from 1922 to the crash of the stock market in 1929. Economic collapse, unemployment, and evictions were to characterize the lives of the masses for almost four years afterward.[1] The crisis brought particularly difficult times for all the "new immigrants." Only African Americans were harder hit by unemployment as the branches of industry with the greatest loss of jobs included the coal mines and the steel mills where the majority of the Hungarian immigrants worked. Some returned to their homelands, and only the fact that the economic situation in the old country was just as hopeless kept mass remigrations from occurring.

Let me quote from a letter of a Hungarian-American Calvinist priest who informed his friend about the impact of the economic depression:

> For the last three years, this country has been suffocating in destitute poverty. Goods are in abundance, but it is impossible to buy anything as there are no jobs available, and so there is no money. Hungarian people here lived on what they could save up to now. Three years of joblessness, together with the failure of the banks, exhausted them. Though I was able to keep the church's finances in some order up to now, we have reached the end of the rope. I loathe the winter, as forty families are already sustained by the city (sustained somehow). But this figure is growing fast. This stupid American system has positioned the various branches of industry in such a way that there are only steel factories in a certain district or only textiles in another. So when a worm gets into one, the workers can go begging. In our district, for example, there are no other but steelworks in a radius of eighty miles. The rust is eating them merrily. Land is bad also, hilly country, the forests are cut out, they dug the coal, so that hardly anything grows on it. If they only could grow their potatoes, at least, but they cannot do even that.
>
> The situation is the same in the whole country as in the Pittsburgh neighborhood, with small differences. Officially they speak of 12 million unemployed in the country, which means that there are about 20 million of them. And that means at least 80 million unprovided for. Up to now

234

except for a few scattered cases, everybody meekly endured hunger and wearing rags. The so-called American is doped with patriotic slogans, the immigrants dare not to murmur, as xenophobia is just large enough by now. The ancient Habsburg principle is working: divide and rule.[2]

At the peak of the Depression, approximately 50 percent of the Hungarian workers in Cleveland were unemployed, and the majority of the jobless remained without any support. If they were not American citizens or if they owned any property, they were ineligible for aid. Instead, their proximity to Shaker Heights made it possible for the women to become the breadwinners, washing laundry and cleaning in the homes of the wealthy for two dollars a day. The impact of the Depression on the evolution of Hungarian ethnic groups is very striking. The crisis was especially hard on some of the older Hungarian community organizations.

The Hungarian American Reformed Federation reported: "Thousands of our members lost their jobs, had hardly a bite to eat, let alone be able to pay their fees. As a result the dropping out of members, the cashing of their bonds, raising, and extending loans, were the order of the day. To these contributed the failing of some banks, where many thousands of our cash deposits got lost, or got depreciated to a considerable extent."[3]

The unemployed were unable to support their associations and their churches financially, but some contributed their labor to repair the churches and put their surroundings, gardens, and paths in order. Having so much free time on their hands enabled the migrants to participate in other community activities, such as dramatic presentations, which reached their peak during the 1930s.[4]

During the crisis, the Hungarian-American communities displayed outstanding examples of ethnic and class solidarity. Because families had only their church communities, sick benefit societies, and one another to rely on for support, new organizations were formed to coordinate efforts. For example, in Cleveland the Hungarian Ladies Charity Committee was established to "help feed the hungry, a great objective, as the majority of the people in this area were unemployed and poverty-stricken during those times."[5] The Small Home Owners Association was organized in 1930 by Cleveland's Hungarians and Slovaks to help each other avoid being evicted once they had been foreclosed, but when their efforts proved unsuccessful, some of their demonstrations resulted in violent clashes with the police.[6] In the same year, Géza Kende started the Old Settler's American-Hungarian Family out of concern for the growing number of Hungarians in Cleveland, who For economic reasons or because they belonged to the workers' movements, no longer were members of the churches and had no one to bury them. For a small fee, it guaranteed members a decent funeral, a casket, and pallbearers and soon became one of the largest organizations in the community.[7] Also in 1930 the city's small businessmen organized the Hungarian Better Business Association "to deal with the ever growing problems of the modern streamlined business life and to help our buyers sell first class merchandise at first class prices. The founding twenty-five merchants further intended to become involved in local political affairs."[8]

On the national level, the crisis years of the Depression brought the New Deal and the Democratic Party's appeal to the ethnic minorities, as well as organization of the industrial unions of the CIO, which held its drive in 1935, the dynamics in the Hungarian-American communities began to change.

The small number of Hungarian communists and some Wobblies worked very actively in the new unions. In the interest of the "united American working class," they helped both the immigrant and the American-born workers to organize strikes, especially in Toledo, Flint, Cleveland, Detroit, and Trenton. Some second-generation Hungarians became well-known union leaders in industrial Ohio; for example Julius Emspak was one of four or five General Electric workers who, during the 1930s, decided to build an industrial union.[9]

The IWW's success began in 1934 when 440 organizers established a liaison with the small nucleus of Cleveland-area Hungarian and Finnish Wobblies.[10] Since most of National Screw's employees were Hungarian, members of one of Cleveland's largest ethnic groups, the IWW approached leaders of the Hungarian community to win public opinion for strikers. In an attempt to rally the Hungarian population against management, a mass meeting was held at 116th Street and Buckeye Road at which the audience was addressed by speakers from the Hungarian Young People's Society, Andrew Weiner of *Bérmunkás*, and ministers from the Hungarian Reformed Church and the Hungarian Presbyterian Church. Members of the Hungarian community who crossed 440's picket line had their names publicly advertised in *Bérmunkás,* which framed the list of strikebreakers with a heavy black border.[11]

In April 1931, the editorial office of *Uj Elöre* moved to Cleveland to be nearer to the workers in this center of heavy industry, according to the reminiscences of one of the correspondents. It led big movements and activities in Cleveland, particularly in favor of the unemployed and small homeowners. "It is a certainty that our paper had not as many readers or subscribers before or thereafter as in Cleveland during the big Depression," recalled one member of the editorial staff.[12]

The hardships of the Depression placed the merger of the Hungarian sick benefit organizations back on the agenda. The movement for a United Sick Benefit Association held unification conferences in the Hungarian settlements. The leaders of the Workers' Sick Benefit and Self-Education Associations, under the control of the communists, urged the members of the other national associations to free themselves of their "bourgeois leaders" and choose representatives who would be truly interested in representing their interests.

Their rationale was that "as long as there are two classes, the capitalist and the working class, there will be two kinds of sick benefit associations, those of the working class and those of the middle-class, supported by capitalism. The workers have no business in the camp of their enemies, the workers' place is in the workers' sick benefit associations."[13]

The extreme Left, however, was in no position to unite the other national associations under their leadership. It is true that the moderate Left, the Általános Munkás Betegsegélyző (General Workers' Sick Benefit Association), lost almost half its members, declining to only 5,100 by the mid-1930s, and reorganization under new leaders in 1935 was unable to stop it from withering away.[14] At the same time, continued futile expenditures in support of the opposition forces within the other sick benefit associations thoroughly burdened the Workers' Sick Benefit and Education Association (WSBEA), which already was struggling with financial problems, and forced it to unite with the other Communist-controlled sick benefit associations. In 1931, two existing leftist groups, the Hungarian Workmen's Sick, Benevolent and Educational Association with 4,736 members and the Slovak Workers Society with 5,815 members, started to discuss a merger. In 1932 the International Workers Order (IWO) was founded and a Hungarian-language group under the name *Testvériség* (Brotherhood) joined it.[15]

After absorption of the WSBEA, the IWO became a Communist-led social organization of 30,000 members, which offered insurance on the age-based rate system. Within it, the Hungarian radicals' connections with persons of similar philosophy in other ethnic groups became more direct.[16] Related to these changes was the emergence of new options for leftists within the mainstream of American political culture, due largely to the birth of the New Deal and the creation of the CIO.

In the CIO the main task of the "Communist factions" was "to conduct a systematic Communist agitation, propaganda and education to bring the foreign language speaking masses closer to the American revolutionary labor movement so that they will take an active part in the class struggle in America under the leadership of the Communist Party."[17] The IWO's cultural activity always reflected political values and ideas. The organization repeatedly emphasized that a unique expression of working-class culture and its variety and profusion represented the high-water mark in the creation of an autonomous, oppositional working-class culture.[18] Aside from cultural activity, the clearest reflection of the IWO's determination to stress class issues over national ones was a decision to organize English-speaking branches.[19]

The IWO claimed 11,000 members for its Hungarian section by the end of the 1930s. It maintained club-rooms and engaged in cultural activities wherever possible. In several eastern communities attempts were made to open club-rooms for groups of mixed ethnicity on a city-wide or community-wide basis but without success. Apparently the older people could not mix. The monthly publication of the IWO *Fraternity* carried language inserts and the copies that went to members of the Hungarian section carried the Hungarian insert.

In their work among the second generation the IWO did not pay attention to the nationality of its members; the Youth Section was "straight American" and only English was used in its activities.[20]

Despite the apparatus at their disposal I did not find that the IWO had been considered a factor in the Hungarian communities. This may be attributable to the fact that even its local leaders were mostly intellectuals, and seemed much more concerned politically with the achievement of a world-wide new deal than with any strictly national grouping—the labor movement was their primary concern.

The leaders of the other Hungarian associations attacked the International Workers Order as an agency of the Communist Party, although *Uj Előre* repeatedly denied it. "The IWO, even with the worst intentions, can't be considered a party organization. . . . There are communists in the IWO, as well as Republicans and Democrats, and other parties."[21]

From the 1930s on the interests of the workers brought the cooperation of wider circles of Hungarian Americans. It is true concerning the Hungarians, too, what Peter Rachleff wrote about the Croatians: "Despite the continuous economic depression, despite widespread unemployment, an air of optimism swept the colonies, not just of Croatians, but of most ethnic groups."[22] Above all, they shared support of Franklin D. Roosevelt's New Deal. The Hungarians of Cleveland's East Side became such mainstays of the Democratic Party that they were rewarded with nominees on the ticket for city positions for the next twenty-five years.[23] Hungarian-American workers also joined in the great political campaign to reelect Roosevelt. The majority of the Hungarian immigrants and their children started to orient themselves toward the Democratic Party.

Caring for the forgotten poor people, laying emphasis on the consideration of the workers' interests, acknowledgement of and support for the right to collective wage agreements, this was the workers' insurance program. The real efforts to create workplaces aligned the majority of the unions behind Roosevelt, moreover part of the socialists, too. These latter realized that the goals of the New Deal coincided with the demands of the socialists' "minimal program."[24]

Then the CIO joined the cause of industrial unionism to the issues of Social Security and unemployment insurance. "More than a majority of the Hungarian immigrant workers function within the framework of the CIO," reported a Hungarian social democratic leader after an American tour. He added, "Long lists can be compiled of Hungarian immigrants, or rather their children, who in leadership positions within the CIO struggled in the vanguard for the interests of the workers."[25] Socialists and Communists were by no means its only enthusiasts. The Rákóczi, the Bridgeport, and later the Verhovay Associations began discussions with the IWO, with the backing of the CIO. The Verhovay convention of 1935 went on record in its support.

In a similar vein, *Uj Előre* wrote:

> The campaign for social insurance went beyond the walls of the churches and called for unity among the Hungarians in America, in the interest of those millions who are thrown out from their workplace through no fault of their own and have to undergo tribulations owing to their being old. The united front work took roots and there is no recess in America

where they would not have heard of its necessity. The worker members and the center of the Rákóczi Relief Association and the membership and the center of the Bridgeport Relief Association work in brotherly cooperation with the membership and the center of the IWO in this work which became necessary a long time ago. The convention of the Verhovay also took up this problem and the members of the Verhovay are there at more than one place in the forging of unity."[26]

On the latter, *Az Ember* observed, "No movement has ever aroused such an interest in such a short time in the Hungarian-American immigrants."[27] In a number of American historical studies it is emphasized, that during the economic crisis among the workers, the communists clearly were the most militant in the economic struggles. They were the harshest critics of the American trade unions and the most unequivocal supporters of the CIO.[28]

The president of the Verhovay, Mr. Daragó wrote several articles even in the *Uj Előre,* on the CIO campaign, calling the members to support this movement, if they agree with its goals. He sent articles in Hungarian weeklies, for which the association itself paid, in order to present the CIO nationally to the Hungarians."[29]

Although the Hungarian socialists replied in the CIO's defense that it at least had planted a seed of class consciousness in the Depression's fallow ground, the majority of the Hungarian immigrants who supported the CIO did not write out any political goals. They wanted collective contracts for protection of all the workers, regulated wages, and the opening of the gates to the unions. According to them, the CIO was just such an organization to fulfill this purpose. It became a milestone in the lives of the immigrants that later was reflected in the periodization of their memories in relationship to it.[30]

> In 1926, my father died; I had to care for my mother. I lived in Maclett, Michigan. I worked for one dollar a day. I worked in a butchery for seven dollars a week. I worked at Sedyside, Tennessee, at the Henry Ford car factory where the workers were addressed in the most degrading manner, and being cursed day and night. One had to take the foreman for a drink at lunchtime, or else one could not keep the job. I lived in Springdale, Pennsylvania. I returned to Detroit, Michigan. I worked in the Brigs car factory, where the foreman beat the worker, if he was not quick enough, and cursed the worker in a way that is beyond description. All these changed after 1935. Thanks to the U. A. W. and the C. I. O.[31]

The Organization of Radical Intellectuals in a Cultural Union

The decade of the 1930s was a time when class and ethnic solidarity did not disturb but sooner complemented each other, when all groups of Hungarian immigrants became more sensitive to leftist values. As masses of workers became open to more radical social concepts, some young Marxists and sympathetic intellectuals, artists, and writers created the Kultur Szövetség (Cultural Union). The Cultural Union aimed to rally all those individuals into one camp, without considering their political divergences, who were receptive to the spirit of progress.[32] Those who inspired it were Communists, but the organization itself operated independently of any political group. On the part of the Communists, it was a great advance compared to their isolation in the 1920s. The organizing committee of the Cultural Union focused on Hungarian settlements. The influence of the Cultural Union was strongest in New York, although it also had branches in the Hungarian communities of Chicago, Los Angeles, New Brunswick, and Perth Amboy. Its president was Dr. Joseph Hollós (1876–1947), a physician, who at the time of the Hungarian Soviet Republic drafted the medical program for the fight against epidemics (tuberculosis). After the fall of the dictatorship he emigrated to Vienna; then, after experimenting with Germany, Czechoslovakia, and Romania, he emigrated to the United States in 1924.

The Cultural Union issued a monthly journal, *Kulturharc*, started in 1931 and edited by Eugen Berkovits, which pursued many activities.[33] Its activists, mostly writers, poets, and visual artists, held lectures and published papers on scientific and art subjects, organized a free science school, and sponsored performances of the amateur theatre group, the Kulturszinpad (Cultural Stage).[34] They organized debates and art exhibitions and ran a school of drawing. Some of their activists worth mentioning were Hugó Gellért, well-known cubist painter, and Imre Ladányi, physician and painter, whose paintings were shown regularly in the yearly exhibitions of the American Artist Congress.[35]

The *New Masses*, which shared the viewpoint of Marxism but did not belong to a party, could serve as a model for the journal *Kulturharc*, the producers of which not only wished to be the Hungarian-language interpreters of progressive and social ideas, with the help of literature and the arts, but also aimed to implant the consciousness of being Hungarian Americans into the immigrants. It tried to gather together and develop the social and cultural life of the Hungarian-American emigration. In such a sense did *Kulturharc* signify a window opening on America and the world. It also represented commitment and a high level of ideas and of art. This endeavor soon made the Hungarian-American *Kulturharc* a recognized journal of the highest rank. It wished to serve general progress, the building of the society of the future, with the threefold slogan: to learn and to teach; to educate and to be educated; to develop and to be developed.[36]

For some years, the association's cultural program of broader perspectives proved successful in the rapprochement of groups advocating left-wing views, and a big step forward on the part of the Communists from their sectarian self-imposed seclusion characteristic of the 1920s.

In a sense, however, the growing political and economic solidarity of Hungarian-American workers during the Depression was misleading. Under the class approach, the Depression was drawing foreign-speaking workers into the general economic struggles of the working class and was weakening national groups' identification and strengthening working-class unity. From a cultural standpoint, the ethnic community was beginning to disintegrate wherever religion was becoming more important than Hungarian identity. In the 1930s, that increasingly was the case among Jews and Roman Catholics, as leaders of these two religious groups especially were starting to leave Hungarian-American concerns largely in the hands of the societies, the Calvinist churches, and a few Hungarian Greek Catholic churches.

If overseas events inevitably shaped the course of American radicalism in the interwar years, this is more emphatically true of the Hungarian immigrants. *Uj Előre* could not become the press organ of the anti-fascist People's Front struggle owing to its sectarian past. Therefore it was discontinued and, as the democratic united front's newspaper, *Amerikai Magyar Világ* (Hungarian World) was issued—leaning on the more liberal, more democratic strata of the lower middle class and the intelligentsia.[37] It existed for barely a year; cooperation with the lower middle class and the intelligentsia did not prove to be enduring. Thus, the outbreak of World War II found the Hungarian immigrants full of inner tension.

To sum up, the Hungarian fraternal associations did not simply survive the Great Depression, but through a lot of new undertakings they transformed themselves and their activities. The community as a whole greatly increased its participation not only in its collective affairs but also in broad-based movements and institutions. The national fraternal insurance associations emerged at the end of the 1930s stronger than they were before the Depression. A dynamic progress welled up within Hungarian communities and helped them to carry through the hard times. In the second half of the 1930s, an upward trend can be seen in the continuation of modernization in their business activities and in the growth of membership. (The Hungarian Reformed Federation in America, for example, increased their membership from 12,720 in 1936, to 20,865 in 1940.) Profiting by the beginning of the ethnic renaissance, they also turned their attention to the old country. The leaders proudly organized the festivities to celebrate the fiftieth anniversary of their national organizations. The problem of the second generation, however, threw a shadow on their future.

CHAPTER 23

The Second Generation

Its Own Identity

MANY CHILDREN OF the Hungarian immigrants had grown up during the pro-Americanization years of the 1920s. The situation in the Hungarian schools reflected how overt coercion by the Americanizers and more subtle pressures to conform combined to influence the second generation's sense of ethnic identity. With the restriction of immigration the community leaders of Hungarians in fraternal organizations and in the churches began to realize that they needed youth to counterbalance the burden of its senior members. The federations began recruiting young members by establishing childrens departments, but there was a demand for youth to be drawn into their governments, too. Their misgivings grew concerning the future of their organizations as they experienced more and more toward the end of the 1920s that the American-born children, upon becoming adults, turned their backs on their parents' ethnic identities. One cannot thus be astonished that from this time on, every one of the organizations was seriously concerned with the question of the second generation.

It was not easy for the Hungarian community leaders to ponder seriously on the phenomenon that immigrants would never completely lose their ethnicity, but, whether the parents liked it or not, their children would become completely American in values and behavior. However, they were more and more concerned about preserving the insurance function of the associations, or the institutional future of the congregation, than their ethnic quality. This could not be achieved without conflicts.

At the start of the 1920s, the Hungarian-American population was almost evenly balanced between 274,400 persons born in Hungary and 271,840 born in the United States. By the next census in 1930, however, the American-born outnumbered the immigrants by 140,000 or, specifically 437,080 to 299,228.[1] Clearly, the deepening of the generational conflict—and the leaders' growing sense of urgency—was related to the demographic changes.

The younger generation was attempting to speed up, while their parents were trying to slow down, the inevitable modernization and Americanization of community institutions. As debates accompanied or delayed the language change in religious services, more and more of the American-born younger generation left the Hungarian churches, just as they had left the secular social organizations.[2] It was not infrequent for young men applying for professional positions to change their names. Some believed an Irish name offered more possibility of advancement in American politics, so when Árpád Szilvássy ran for the office of Ohio state representative in the 1930s, he changed his name to A. S. Harding.[3]

As was mentioned before, the second generation of new immigrants led the strikes of the 1930s and organized the CIO. Emil Mazey (Mezey), son of a Hungarian immigrant was the Chairman of UAW, Detroit, and leader of the most famous sit-down strike in April 1938. Later Emil Mazey described that strike as "among the most exciting in our whole experience in the working movement. It was like seeing men who had been half dead suddenly come to life."[4]

"Can the American Hungarians be saved?" was the question urgently debated in both Hungary and the United States in the second half of the 1930s. In the contemporary Hungarian-American press, the controversy centered on the second generation's flight from their immigrant parents' sentimental, cultural world.[5] The press itself reflected the process of assimilation, even as it attempted to influence and form the identity of the second generation. The church papers and both secular daily papers, New York's *Amerikai Magyar Népszava* and Cleveland's *Szabadság*, devoted numerous articles to the parents' moral obligations to acquaint their children with Hungarian culture. Meanwhile, besides supporting Hungarian-language education within the churches, the press concerned itself with winning over the Hungarian-American youth through other methods, such as contests.

The Hungarian press included numerous articles that expressed its attitude toward the second generation. In August 1930, for the first time, a small single column was published in English for young members, "Junior Order," in the Verhovay Association's journal. In the next year the column was larger, and acquired a new title: "Our Junior Order." This column, intended for the young, gave way gradually to the reports of the English-language branches which had been founded in the meantime. These branches tried to shape the young people's ethnic consciousness by conveying Hungarian historical and cultural information. To this end, in 1930–1931 they published a series entitled "The History of Hungary."

The first English-language branch of the Verhovay Association was established in Cleveland in January 1934, its membership made up exclusively of women. The Verhovay Hall set aside an area for the young people's club to meet, and attempts to involve them during membership campaigns included holding cultural contests with the prize of a trip to Hungary. Most important, not only was business conducted in English, but branches were permitted to offer American sports (bowling, baseball, basketball, football, hockey) and cultural entertainments appropriate for American-born teens and young adults (dances, beach parties, picnics, and the like). Many lodges organized activities through which the second generation not only learned about the traditional culture but actively participated in it.[6] They could not ward off cultural changes reflected in and promoted by these new activities The cultural change was a two-sided process: reinforcement of the traditional went hand in hand with accommodation to the new. Additional young people's organizations were developing independently of the fraternal organization in Cleveland, the Hungarian Junior League, the Four Arts Club, and the Hungarian Civic Club were intended to promote Hungarian culture in the English language.[7]

In the interest of transmitting the Hungarian cultural heritage, the first competition was organized by *Amerikai Magyar Népszava* in 1934 and required entrants to answer four questions: "How did you learn Hungarian?" "What do you know about Hungary, Hungarian history, and culture?" "What does being Hungarian mean for you?" and "In your opinion what can the American second generation do in the interest of Hungary?" Of the 240 essays which the paper received, the ten best papers were sent to Budapest, where a jury of pedagogical specialists and public figures judged them on knowledge of the Hungarian language and overall familiarity with the culture. The authors of the two winning essays won trips to Hungary. The paper published all the submitted works in its Sunday supplement and followed the winners' trips in great detail, trying to make Hungary seem attractive to the second generation

In 1936, a weekly supplementary edition entitled "Second Generation" was established and printed in English for the American youth of Hungarian descent. *Szabadság* also published two handbooks for second-generation high school and college students, containing essays on the cultural connections of Hungary and the United States.[8]

In the second half of the 1930s, there were signs of an ethnic revival, which—according to Oscar Handlin—had been attributed to the humiliation and rejection of the immigration quota. In imitation of the ideals and the actions of the nativist groups that had shut their people out, the newer immigrants rallied around their own distinctive national and racial characteristics. As Oscar Handlin observed of the "new immigrants" generally, an uncritical glorification of the homeland's past and emphasis on the value of their own "racial quality" were reactions to the message of inferiority that they received from their social situation and environment.[9] Through them in this way, all the new migrants groups tried to compensate for the nativist attitude, sanctioned by the immigration laws, that Hungarians were among the "undesirable" immigrants, too, and inferior "Hunkies" to Americans of other backgrounds.[10] The result of the "Hunky" ratings, the brutalized and stereotyped portraits drawn of Hungarian Americans, was the reason that many, especially young people, abandoned their identity or were handicapped with an inferiority complex. However, according to Zoltán Fejős, who analyzed the ethnic culture of two generations of Chicago Hungarians, the short-lived ethnic movement which unfolded in the middle of the 1930s cannot be the immigrants' reaction against their environment which acted contrary to social adjustment. The multicultural festivals, the dance movement promoting ethnic dance in which several ethnic groups were involved, can only be interpreted within the assimiltán process. The movement, the festivals in particular, offered a certain standing and a chance for the members of ethnic society in their sphere of leisure-time activities to be part of an acknowledged section of American life. The ethnic movement, thus, meant one possible road toward American society.[11]

During the ethnic revival, fraternal and cultural organizations were encouraged in their struggles for the "preservation" and "saving" of the generation born in the United States. Community leaders acknowledged, "the future of the Hungarian-American is not very confidence inspiring in respect to the second and third generations. Among the Hungarian immigrants relationships even within the family are often not very close, and are even looser in the churches and associations."[12] They lamented the Americanization of the new generations: "From our children's point of view, too, our being Hungarian is empty, unsubstantial, totally insignificant. We are aliens for them, too. They tolerate us, but are not enthusiastic about us. They live in a different atmosphere in a world of different thoughts. They do not want to be like us."[13] But, they argued, "before we give up on the fight to win back the second and third generations, we must attempt one last experiment."[14]

The "experiment" consisted of two suggestions. First, parents should become more Americanized, particularly in family relationships between parents and children. They should give the young people independence and allow them greater freedom to express American social norms. On the other hand, the parents and other adults should try harder to familiarize the youngsters with Hungarian culture and to interest the second generation in the life of the associations by offering them various new benefits and greater use of English in official publications.[15]

In 1938 *Népszava* started its "Lajos Kossuth and George Washington" competition. Juxtaposition of the two figures was intended to instill the idea that the Hungarian immigrants, too, could be proud of the same kind of historical heroes as the sons of the admired American nation. Eventually, the largest Hungarian-American fraternal association, the Verhovay, joined in, offering its own contest with a free trip to Hungary for the winner.[16] These contests did not attract masses of entrants, but they did demonstrate that institutional attempts to preserve the language and the culture, which until then had mainly occurred within the churches, now had greater possibilities.

Fortunately for the promoters of Hungarian cultural traditions, *Szabadság* at this time was acquired by a new Hungarian owner, Zoltán Gombos (1905–1983). As a young man, after completing his secondary studies in Kolozsvár, he emigrated to Cleveland. In 1925 he began his studies at Western Reserve University, where he received his diploma in 1929. He became the *Szabadság's* news reporter in 1935 and city desk editor the next year. In 1936 he married the daughter of Béla Kolozsy, whose family had arrived in 1921 from Erdély, where Mr. Kolozsy had been a postmaster. Mr. Kolozsy began working at the *Szabadság* in 1928 and quickly became the director of the East Side branch office. Zoltán Gombos was named chief editor in 1938 and became the owner-publisher in 1939.[17] From this time on, until his death, he was one of the main actors in Cleveland's Hungarian public life.

Young Hungarian American, a bilingual newspaper published by *Szabadság*, was to provide the second-generation youth educated in American schools with information about Hungarian history and culture and Hungarian contributions to American civilization. In the process, the publishers of this paper made the 1848 revolution and the cult of Kossuth important elements of the second generation's identity.[18]

The problems of maintaining the ties of the second generation, the methods that could be employed, and the help that was needed from the old country all played an important part in the Hungarian World Congress held in Budapest in 1938. The representative of one of the Hungarian-American organizations, for example, urged that the World Congress of Hungarians from Abroad quickly publish an English-language book to familiarize the second generation with the Hungarian nation and its history, literature, art, and values. Ambitiously, he further suggested that the book be interesting for the young people's American friends to read and that it include a section on the associations, churches, and successful Hungarian-American individuals to win the children over to an integrated American life.[19]

Instead of publishing such a book, the congress translated the English newspaper writer Andor Kun's brochure "What Does the World Owe to the Hungarians?" and the American Hungarian Reformed Federation published Ödön Vasvári's *Lincoln's Hungarian Heroes*, which described the role of Hungarians in the Civil War. *Reformátusok Lapja*, the newspaper of the American Hungarian Reformed Federation, likewise continually reprinted the ecstatic poetical manifestations written in nineteenth-century America about the leaders of the Hungarian fight for independence and the historical meaning of its ideals.[20] The leaders of the churches and of the fraternal associations searched for a way to solve the question: "How can the educated second generation draw close to the Magyar youth?"[21] Joseph Reményi, the man of letters, who as an intellectual was well known among Hungarians, wrote articles about how to solve this generational conflict.

Above all, in the 1930s Hungarian-American ethnic identity became separated from knowledge of the mother tongue. Many community leaders in the United States did not yet realize the fact, and political leaders in Hungary, who were preoccupied with rallying opposition to the Treaty of Trianon, certainly did not. Both, therefore, invested their energy and scarce resources, if not the prestige of the institutions they headed, in the contests and other endeavors that were irrelevant and incomprehensible to most younger Hungarian Americans.[22]

The primary function of the bilingual and the English-language publications was that they supplied the youth of Hungarian descent, educated in American schools, with the knowledge to understand the meaning of the ethnic cultural symbols. The information conveyed can be roughly divided into four groups: (1) the glorious Hungarian past, the thousand years' continuity of Hungarian history, and its historical and cultural facts; (2) popular biographies of those Hungarians who were famous all over the world, particularly scientists and artists; (3) Hungarian folklore, and the cultural traditions and handicrafts derived from and sometimes transforming that folklore: the vintage ball, Hungarian dress, Hungarian embroidery; and (4) those Hungarian achievements which were enriching American civilization, too, condensed in a popular brochure entitled "Do you know what the world can thank the Hungarians for?"

Besides the encyclopedic knowledge, the forming of sentimental factors was also essential. Publications for youth in general—sometimes more openly, sometimes more guardedly—tried to strengthen the sentimental dimension of ethnicity in order to foster ethnic loyalty on three levels: (1) idealizing cultural consciousness by selecting only the positive, the glorious events from the national past; (2) emphasizing solemnity, suggesting that the manifestation of the ethnic link is a ceremonial act of everyday life; (3) awakening the pride of the second generation by overcoming the feeling of inferiority inherited from the first generation and fostering the sentiment of equality, even of a certain cultural superiority.[23]

All the ambitious plans, the contests, and the fraternal associations' outreach to the English-speaking generation had minimal success, however. In 1940, when sociologist Joseph K. Balogh studied the Hungarian-American organizations, more than two-thirds of the members of the fraternal associations were immigrant Hungarians, and the same was true of the other socio-cultural groups.[24] After changing over to English, the churches were more successful in keeping the second generation in their communities.[25]

Children born in the United States to Hungarian-speaking parents were a transitional generation. To compensate for their ambiguous situation, most tried to overemphasize their American characteristics and cover up their ethnic background. Over a lifetime of trying, however, they were unable to free themselves from the feelings of genetic inferiority that were nurtured by the American schools.[26] They rejected their parents' mother tongue and broken English as part of this process and embraced instead a symbolic ethnicity that valued, for example, the performances of Hungarian dance groups at international dance festivals and the youth sports clubs.[27]

The integration of the American-born youth into the value system of the immigrants occurred only to a small degree. Values from the American social milieu had a much greater influence on them. When the publications serving the second generation finally realized this, they tried to secure the acceptance of ethnic ties through a simplified, "cleaned-up" abstract of the old country's culture that functioned as a symbolic language. From the second half of the 1930s, the ideology of the Hungarian-American identity emphasized familiarity and emotional identification with the Hungarian cultural heritage, but not the Hungarian language: "When the children of the foreign born accept from the past certain contributions, it is illogical to say that they destroy the unity of their American life."[28]

The tool for achieving these goals was the English language, the second generation's native tongue. A common motif throughout the English language and bilingual publications was that ethnic cultural individualities can enrich American society. These publications depicted the old country's culture not through intense idealization of cultural consciousness as a value in itself, but as a means of reaching out to the other ethnic groups and to American society as a whole. For them, this was the basis of cultural pluralism. The outbreak of World War II, however, blighted their cultural aspirations before they could unfold.

CHAPTER 24

World War II

A New Identity Crisis

AT THE END of the 1930s, Hungarian Americans could only look on as a tragic future loomed: the approach of another war in which their old and new homelands again would be on opposite sides. Because of its geographical location and the revisionist, anti-Communist policies of its ruling elite, Hungary was bound more and more closely to Germany, while its rulers deluded themselves about the likely outcome of such an alliance. Others wanted to establish contacts abroad in case Germany should lose, and to do so, they sought the support of the largest group of the Hungarian diaspora, the Hungarian Americans.[1]

When the United States entered the war, once again any nonconformity, either cultural or political, became suspicious. As a result, tensions increased within the various Hungarian-American community organizations and between individuals, too. By this time, groups of Hungarian Americans were already formed by the political legacy of the tumultuous period following World War I. in Hungary.[2] The presidency of Count Mihály Károlyi lasted only from October 1918 to April 1, 1919, when the Communists took over under the leadership of Béla Kun. In the autumn of the same year, Kun's Bolshevik government was replaced by a counterrevolutionary regime headed by Admiral Miklós Horthy. Functionaries of the Social Democratic and Communist Parties, as well as the activists of the "red terror," now had to flee the "white terror." Some went to the United States, became American citizens, changed their names in some instances, and remained politically inactive until reawakened by the advance of European fascism.

During World War II, Hungarian Americans drew on identities rooted in their original surroundings to form, roughly, four groups: the conservatives or "revisionists"; the liberal democrats or Octobrists; the Communists; and a few pro-Nazis. The largest group, of conservatives or "revisionists," was supported by their traditional institutions, fraternal associations, churches, and newpapers and was united in the American Hungarian Federation, which was repeatedly reorganized in 1938. Their views were best promulgated by *Amerikai Magyar Népszava,* which at that time became the community's largest daily paper.

The second group consisted of the liberal democrats or Octobrists of 1918 (Õszirózsás). Some had arrived in the United States at the beginning of the 1920s, but others had fled fascism in the second half of the 1930s. Their political weight seems to have been greater than their numbers would indicate, as their leaders were such intellectuals as Rusztem Vámbéry and Oszkár Jászi. Vámbéry, a well-known Hungarian jurist and sociologist, fled fascism and came to the United States in 1938. There he became "the unofficial adviser to the Foreign Ministry and the Strategic Service on questions related to Hungarian affairs" in New York. Oszkár Jászi, one of the outstanding personalities of the bourgeois democratic revolution in Hungary in 1918, emigrated at the beginning of the 1920s and arrived in the United States in 1925. He was the chief representative of bourgeois radicalism in the 1920s, and a brilliant teacher at Oberlin College. Both men had influential contacts on various English-language American newspapers, including *The Nation,* and within the U.S. State Department. The traditional ethnic elite of priests, journalists, and self-made business leaders could not compete with them in this respect.[3]

Communists and their fellow travelers made up the third contingent, most of whom had fled Hungary for the United States in the 1920s. After 1938 the name of their newspaper was changed from *Uj Elõre* to *Amerikai Magyar Világ* (American Hungarian World) and shortly afterward to *Magyar Jövõ* (Hungarian Future), and was published with the financial support of the Hungarian section of the Communist-dominated International Workers' Order.

The small group of Hungarian Communists was brought into a difficult position by the Non-Aggression Pact between the Soviet Union and Germany and by the war against Finland. The varying political tasks could not be followed by some members and they left the party; the majority, however, obediently propagated the directives which were imposed on them by their obligations as internationalists. In 1940, for example, they insisted on the United States' neutrality.[4] During World War II, by concentrating on the anti-fascist struggle, the Communists won the support of a large number of neutrals and successfully penetrated Hungarian relief and insurance associations.

The fourth group consisted of a handful of pro-Nazis. Their views were represented by the Bridgeport newspaper *Egyetértés* (Consensus). When its editor was questioned by the U.S. State Department, he argued that before the outbreak of war, his newspaper had preached the politics of isolation beloved of so many Americans. During the war, he claimed, the newspaper remained strictly loyal to America's war objectives. Because the editor was not able to rid himself of the stigma of Nazism, the paper soon folded.

The principal aim of the conservative nationalist group was to make the firm loyalty of the Hungarian immigrants unambiguous to their American hosts and to portray Hungary in a better light by somehow explaining away its alliance with Germany. On March 4, 1940, the leaders of the Hungarian American Federation wrote a letter to President Roosevelt expressing the unreserved solidarity of American citizens of Hungarian origin with the policy of the United States. On the suggestion of the Hungarian-American Calvinist leaders, the strongest guardians of the spirit of Kossuth, the year 1941 was christened Kossuth Year, in reference to the American round trip of the great Hungarian statesman ninety years earlier. The Hungarian Reformed Federation of America, the Verhovay Sick Benefit Society, the Bridgeport Association, and the 231 local branches of the Rákóczi Association organized Kossuth festivities everywhere. One of the leaders of the Hungarian Americans defined the spirit of the Kossuth Year in the following: "The Kossuth traditions are most suited for discussing the strictly speaking Hungarian inner life on the one hand, and the assimilation to the new life, on the other, as it is characterized by understanding, by patience and a hearty cooperative spirit, just as these characterize the social life of this country."[5]

On January 7, 1941 they addressed a declaration to President Roosevelt and presented it to Assistant Secretary of State A. A. Berle, Jr. The declaration first of all stated that "American citizens of Hungarian origin, united in the American Hungarian Federation, are fully conscious of the duties which citizenship in the world's greatest democracy, the United States, entails and are willing and anxious to fulfill such duties until death."[6]

The declaration further stated that:

> American citizens of Hungarian origin learned with deep regret that the Government of Hungary found it impossible to avoid the signing of the pact with the Axis powers. It is our conviction that by the signing of this pact the Hungarian government lost its power of independent action, that the people of Hungary are no longer free to express their will and that this act is a direct threat to the ancient independence of Hungary.
>
> Therefore, the Executive Committee of the American Hungarian Federation as representative of American citizens of Hungarian origin, through whom also—as we sincerely believe—the silenced people of Hungary convey their thoughts and desires, consider it our gallant duty to lead a movement for the preservation of an independent Hungary and for the freedom of its people within the limitations of the Constitution and laws of the United States."[7]

The anti-fascist movement soon came to be headed by Tibor Eckhardt, former leader of the Hungarian Independent Smallholders Party, who arrived in the United States in 1941. Eckhardt's previous statements opposing the Treaty of Trianon and his good American contacts made him welcome among the majority of Hungarian immigrants' elite, and he seemed to have the approval of the State Department as well.[8] Such favor was no minor consideration for the leaders of the Hungarian-American associations, unions, churches, and newspapers, who had lived through World War I with uncertainty and fear.

Nevertheless, liberals and radicals alike used their newspapers to attack Tibor Eckhardt from the very start, just as they did the American Hungarian Federation. Most Hungarian leaders of traditional organizations were also labeled fascists from time to time by State Department informers. "Supposedly a popular Hungarian American even was reported to be a Communist and a Nazi on the same day by two opposing groups."[9]

On September 21, 1941, in Cleveland, the liberals formed the Association of Democratic American Hungarians under the leadership of Rusztem Vámbéry, who also became the editor of the organization's journal, *Harc* (Fight).[10] Of course, this group too stressed its members' loyalty to the United States. As for Hungary, they felt its future must include dismantling of the outdated anti-democratic and semifeudal structure of the country at the end of the war.[11] The Hungarian radical communists in the International Workers' Order also adopted a manifesto proclaiming, "All our efforts, thoughts and actions are directed towards the elimination of the fascist enemy the day after the attack on Pearl Harbor."[12] At the same time they emphasized: "We solemnly declare that the Hungarian nation is not responsible for the policies and acts of its present government."[13]

Not surprisingly, the leaders of the Association of Democratic American Hungarians rejected all Eckhardt's attempts to unify the opponents of fascism. Oszkár Jászi articulated their claim that Eckhardt's anti-fascists and the American Hungarian Federation both wanted to "preserve for the oligarchy whatever could be salvaged from the collapsing old Hungary."[14]

When Vámbéry showed readiness to cooperate with the movement led by Eckhardt, Oszkár Jászi rendered a sharp criticism of the endeavors to rally together: "You have no right to launch a spontaneous action in defense of political goals which are far from us and are contradictory to us."[15] As a result, Vámbéry also ceased to be an advocate of cooperation. In addition, he told officials of the State Department that Eckhardt had refused to recognize the lawful existence of Czechoslovakia, Yugoslavia, and Romania.[16] When the attacks against Eckhardt and the American Hungarian Federation escalated to calling them "Hitler's fifth column" and charging them with anti-Semitism, they created such a climate of fear in the Hungarian-American communities that Eckhardt had to step aside.[17] "Is there anything wrong with this program?" asked a State Department Official in a report on the controversy. "If there is, the critics and foes of the 'Free Hungary' movement failed not only to prove it, but even to voice it. All they seemed to be concerned with is the personality and political past of Tibor Eckhardt and with that they try to discredit and besmirch the character of each and everyone associated with him or who support the 'Free Hungary' movement."[18]

Though divided, Hungarian Americans of every sort supported the American Red Cross in every conceivable way. War bond drives and civil defense activities were especially popular. Groups also sent packages to members in various branches of the United States armed forces, and women's groups rallied to the support of the mothers and wives of service personnel. Most of the activities, especially assisting the military personnel and their families, were motivated by sincere loyalty to the United States.[19]

> During the war, we made every moral and financial sacrifice not only in order to fulfill our tasks as citizens, but also to prove with deeds our unswerving faithfulness, love and esteem towards the United States.

We could report with understandable satisfaction at our last Convention that among the national groups constituting the people of the United States, we Hungarians gave in proportion most of the soldiers, bought most of the bonds, and made the biggest financial sacrifice. We could also state with special pride that there was no traitor among us.[20]

Early in 1943, under the influence of the increasingly successful Russian offensive against Germany, the American Hungarian Federation convened in Bridgeport, where—with great enthusiasm—they appealed to the people of Hungary to sabotage Nazi war endeavors and to liberate themselves from the Nazi dictatorship. They also condemned persecution based on race, skin color, or religious differences.[21] But a new grouping organized on a wider base than before could now attack the associations from the left. Liberals, social democrats, and Communists united in the Hungarian American Council for Democracy under the unlikely leadership of actor Béla Lugosi. The Council backed the exiled Count Károlyi as an actual political leader.[22] The declaration adopted at its National Conference in June 1943 pledges:

All support for the democratic people's movement of Hungary, our heroic ally the underground National Front for Hungarian Independence, and for the establishment of a democratic Hungary based upon the principles of the Roosevelt-Churchill Atlantic Charter, and guided by cooperation, understanding, good-neighbor policy towards the surrounding countries and their peoples.

We are in uncompromising opposition to any attempted Hungarian-Darlan-deal (with Count Bethlen, Tibor Eckhardt or anyone connected with the Horthy regime, present or past) through which agents of Hungarian fascist feudal reaction attempt to perpetuate themselves and their power in the coming postwar world.[23]

Toward the end of 1943, Hungarian immigrant trade unionists also convened and called upon their counterparts in Hungary to revolt. They then formed an organization and affiliated with the American Hungarian Democratic Council.[24]

The average Hungarian-American worker of the first generation observed the political struggles of the leaders rather passively. Many were no longer interested in political slogans concerning the faraway Hungary they had left several decades before.[25] During the war overfull employment, worker patriotism, and public acknowledgment of labor's crucial role all conjoined to advance the social status of Hungarian organized workers, too. The jump in United States labor union membership from 8.7 million in 1940 to 14.3 million five years later was a hallmark of that advance. Unionists made up over a third of all nonfarm civilian employment by 1945—the historic peak proportion for the twentieth century.[26]

Especially alienated from the homeland that was once more fighting against the United States were those Hungarians whose children of military age were serving in the United States Army after an American high school education that had turned them against Hungary. Many were ashamed of Hungary's alliance with fascist Germany and concealed their Hungarian origin.[27] "In just the three months after Pearl Harbor 1,300 young Hungarians entered army service in Cleveland."[28] The military then helped them erase any lingering traces of their ethnicity as the recruiting and training of a large armed force brought about a remolding of the American population. Members of the more isolated Central and Eastern European ethnic groups were among those whose lifestyles changed most of all. They became familiar with new regions of the United States and saw American social attitudes toward them change in a positive direction. The time spent in the military was a revelation to those who had rarely, if ever, left their ethnic settlements before. Wearing the same uniform, eating the same food, being subject to strict discipline, undergoing heavy training, and facing the challenges of war eliminated the insularity of these young people and placed their identity in a new context of "shared values and traditions."[29] On the home front, migration in search of jobs in the defense industries similarly pushed the ethnic groups out of their linguistic islands and intermingled them with other groups. After the war, as a result, the loyal support the European ethnic groups had given to the war effort was recognized in their "legitimization as patriotic Americans."[30] It also brought about the reformulation of ethnic symbols and rituals. Folk songs, dances, festivals, and other traditional events were often mingled with displays of American patriotism and changed thereby. At the same time, activities such as waste collection, subscription of war bonds, and civil defense exercises frequently became part of ethnic rituals.[31]

Probably the most obvious manifestation of the war's influence was the increase in the number of naturalization cases. The 1940 Naturalization Act (twice modified during the war) simplified the process. Veterans applying for citizenship, for example, were exempt from certain residence, language, and registration requirements. Meanwhile, the Alien Registration Act authorized the fingerprinting and registration of all aliens.[32] "This 'carrot-and-stick approach' led 2.2 million people to become American citizens between 1940 and 1949."[33] To assist them, Hungarian religious congregations began holding English and citizenship classes for adults.

The decrease in the use of foreign languages was dramatic. The number of all foreign-language radio stations fell by 40 percent between 1942 and 1948, while the number of ethnic newspapers declined as well. The use of the English language further accelerated in the churches with the return of veterans who had been ministered to exclusively in English in the military. Some changes were so startling that perceptions of their extent became exaggerated. "Young men returned from the army completely transformed and did not want to take up where they had left off. They did not want to marry only Hungarian girls any more."[34]

Hungarian immigrants' concern for the homeland did not vanish with the war. News that Budapest was in ruins, that there was famine in Hungary, and that Hungarians were trying to build a democratic society pulled together the various Hungarian-American interest groups and their social organizations for the relief effort. In fact, the war had not yet ended when the American Hungarian Relief was established in 1944. The first aid from the brief unified outreach was sent to Hungary in April 1945.[35] Disagreement of the displaced persons became so acrimonious, however, that the Relief Committee was formally dissolved in February 1948.

The considerable progress made in the Hungarian immigrants' integration is shown by the aims of the American Hungarian Federation, declared in its statutes, which were adopted in 1947:

a. To serve with all its might the interest of the United States.

b. To make the Hungarian immigrants acquainted with the American democratic way of life, and point to all those endeavors which aim at the destruction of the laws included in the constitution of the United States, and instruct the immigrants of our flesh and blood in that range of ideas which correspond to the traditional conception of our adopted country and which give everybody the possibility of subsistence and prosperity.

c. To make acquainted the second and further generations of Hungarian origin with the history of the people whose descendants they are and to draw them as natural heirs into every one of the American Hungarian institutions, which were built by the Hungarian immigrants during more than half of a century.

d. To coordinate the joint endeavors of the various Hungarian associations, so that all these bodies may fulfill their function in their civic, social and cultural activities in America and be connecting links in the American Hungarian life.

e. To give attention to the movements contrary to the American spirit and do everything in its power to prevent these endeavors to fulfill their objectives.

f. To help the Americans of Hungarian origin to acquire the means of subsistence and of prosperity and give them assistance against any discrimination.

g. To correct the various attempts to misrepresent and distort the historic justice of the cause of the Hungarian nation.

h. To assist so far as it lies in their power the American and the Hungarian charitable organizations.

i. That within the frame of the constituion and the laws of the United States they promote the movements which aim to achieve Hungary's independence, the liberty and welfare of the Hungarian people.[36]

There is an enormous difference in the identity of the Hungarian immigrants if their attitudes at the time of the two wars are compared. The majority's attitude at the time of World War I was formed by fear; yet, their hearts were entirely turned to the fatherland. By the 1940s, their links were altogether bound to their adopted country, but their ethinc ties were still manifested. These were particularly colored by those emotions instilled in them by the conservative ethnic elite, which stemmed from the peculiar conflicts of the history of their people and from the permanent emphasis of their uniqueness as a nation, being without relatives in the whole universe. These gave them the uncertain feeling of being left alone in the world.

PART FOUR

THE POSTWAR PERIOD

CHAPTER 25

The Arrival of the Displaced Persons: 1948–52

Flight from East Central Europe

FROM THE FORCED migrations for labor to the flight of refugees on a scale never seen before to escape extermination in death camps, World War II and its aftermath produced unprecedented movements of population in Central and Eastern Europe.[1] At the end of the war in Europe, there were over 11 million non-German homeless people, and the Western Allies were caring for nearly 7 million displaced persons, or DPs, by September 1, 1945.

DPs included all types: Nazi collaborators and resistance sympathizers, major criminals and innocent teenagers, whole families, groups of political dissidents, victims of bombings, SS members in flight, Communists, concentration camp guards, agricultural laborers, citizens of ravaged countries and gangs of looters. All European nationalities were represented from both East and West.[2]

Within a month, 5 million of the homeless under the authority of the Western allies had been repatriated. Caravans of people moved along the roads of Central Europe, from north to south, south to north, east to west and west to east, traveling by foot, on bicycles, pulling wagons and carts, driving horses or oxen, or crammed into ox wagons.[3] Their return home from Germany, Austria, or Italy was assisted by the governments of the countries concerned, by the United Nations, and by voluntary organizations.[4]

The 2 million homeless who remained in Western territory after September 1945 represented a more difficult situation. From November 1945 to June 1947 over one million of them were repatriated with the involvement of the UN. "But more than a million homeless people still remained in European camps: 850 thousand in Germany, 148 thousand in Austria and the rest in Italy."[5] These were the people who did not want to return to the place they had come from for political and other reasons.

259

The plight of the remaining displaced persons seemed quite hopeless. Doors everywhere were closed to them as most countries maintained strict immigration restrictions. At the same time, the representatives of the Western powers, having experienced the often tragic consequences of forced repatriation, stated openly that it would be inhumane to force the refugees to leave.[6] The only way out seemed to be resettlement of the refugees in a third country. After intense debates in 1947 the International Refugee Organization (IRO) was formed with the participation of sixteen governments under the auspices of the UN. On July 1, 1947, the IRO began its activities of repatriation, aid, legal and political protection, and the promotion of resettlement overseas and on the continent of Europe.[7] In 1948–1949 the organization obtained sufficient funds from members of the UN to devise a comprehensive immigration policy, and between 1948 and 1950 it carried out the first planned and protected large-scale immigration ever, resettling over a million persons in third countries, most of them overseas. By the end of this operation, just over 100,000 "difficult cases" remained in the refugee camps, those who could not be recommended for emigration due to their age, illness, or physical handicap.[8]

Many displaced persons thought that Europe had become overpopulated with a permanent imbalance between its economic potential and large population masses. Migrating somewhere far away from war-stricken Europe seemed to offer better prospects, especially for those whom both the Germans and Allies classified as former enemies. Most of them, however, had to wait four to five years in German or Austrian army barracks for a chance to start a new life overseas.

Ethnic Hungarians already had begun migrating from territories that no longer were part of Hungary after the conclusion of peace at Trianon in 1920. Their number may be estimated at 350,000.[9] By the end of 1943 many non-Hungarians from neighboring countries had followed in their footsteps.[10] Marrus writes in his book on migration to Hungary:

> Thousands of refugees fled to Hungary from both Poland and Slovakia to escape deportation and death. In 1942 the number of refugees from Slovakia alone was estimated to be over ten thousand. Between March 1942 and March 1944, during the presidency of the aristocratic and peace-oriented Miklós Kállay, Hungary provided refuge to Jews, ex-members of the Polish army, pilots of its allies and deserters. There is no doubt that at this time Hungary was desperate to get out of the clutches of the Germans, and more liberal refugee policies were just one way of indicating a preference for the Allies. These circumstances finally changed in the spring of 1944 when Germany occupied Hungary, putting an end to the Kállay regime and closing the gates to any further refugees.[11]

As the German invasion also opened the door to the Holocaust, Hungary became second only to Poland in the number of Jews dragged off to the concentration camps on Polish and German territory.[12]

On October 15, 1944, Regent Miklós Horthy was captured and forced to resign together with his government. Extreme rightists, members of the Hungarian fascist organization the "Arrow-Cross," got into power. The Hungarian fascists' most important plan of government was to organize the evacuation of all persons and valuables from the country. They had a fanatical belief in the victory of the "German wonder weapons" and that was what they wanted to wait for in Austria and Germany. They started dismantling factories and transporting assets out of the country. The flight to the West before the advancing Russian troops was at its height in Hungary at the beginning of 1945, when the fascist government ordered the evacuation of all important state administrative officers, members of the Arrow-Cross, and the semimilitary formations of young people. Hungarian army units were directed west by their German commanders. In addition, alongside those under military service with the Germans who were retreating from the Russian army, masses of civilians fled west out of Hungary. At Easter 1945 a quarter of a million civilian refugees and at least a quarter of a million Hungarian Royal Army servicemen crossed the borders, amidst huge commotion and tragic accidents.[13]

The Hungarian army, police, and other authorities left in the last days of March 1945 for an orderly resettlement to Austria. The Arrow-Cross government headed by Ferenc Szálasi, several members of Parliament, and many civilians sought refuge after the end of March on German soil. The majority of those who left the country of their own accord immediately after the war "were not so much fleeing communism as they were concerned about how the Hungarian nation and its government would react to their actions under the Horthy regime."[14]

The deportation of German Hungarians under the pressure of the victorious anti-fascist forces created a new wave of forced emigrants in 1946,[15] the same year that the expulsion of Hungarians from Czechoslovakia to Hungary began. Under the civilian exchange treaty between the two countries, Slovaks voluntarily moved from Hungary to Czechoslovakia. Meanwhile, the Hungarian population from Bukovina and Moldova that had been resettled in Bácska had to leave for southwestern Hungary as Bácska had once again become part of Yugoslavia.[16]

After the war, coalition governments of civil and Communist parties came to power in Central and Eastern Europe, including Hungary, which was now in the Russian sphere of interest. In these countries land reform, nationalization, and the Communist yearning for power were accompanied by increasing domestic political struggles. Peace treaties signed in 1947 sanctioned the Communist regimes being formed in Romania, Czechoslovakia, Hungary, and Bulgaria. With the help of the occupying Russian army and the Communist-controlled police force, the Communists created the political monopoly of the Communist Party. Anti-Communist opposition parties were dissolved, and their leaders were threatened, jailed, or deported.[17] From 1947 on the main motive for emigration from Hungary was the confrontation between the Soviet bloc and the Western powers and the growth of Communist totalitarianism. The émigrés were the leaders of the coalition parties, bankers and industrial entrepreneurs who had had their property confiscated, intellectuals, scientists, and artists. The briefly liberal, democratic Hungary lost most of its outstanding public and cultural figures.[18] The 1947–1949 wave of refugees was a great loss, not so much in numerical terms as in quality, that left a lasting void in Hungarian culture. Most of this wave headed for the American zone in Germany, and its illegal border crossings to the West continued until 1952, when the "iron curtain" had become almost impenetrable. After a short stay in Western Europe, most of them found refuge in the United States.

Table 3 shows the number of immigrants to the United States in the years 1948–53.

TABLE 3.

Immigrants Admitted from East-Central Europe to the United States under the DP Act, by Country of Birth, June 25, 1948–June 30, 1953[19]

Country	Immigrants		Displaced Persons		German Ethnics	
	No.	%	No.	%	No.	%
All countries	399,698	100.00	345,952	100.00	53, 766	100.00
Europe	397,177	99.37	343,488	99.29	53,689	99.86
East-Central Europe	238,915	60.15	201,668	58.71	38,347	71.42
East-Central Europe	238,915	100.00	201,668	100.00	38,347	100.00
Hungary	16,032	6.71	12,528	6.24	3,504	9.13
Czechoslovakia	11,663	4.88	8,824	4.40	2,839	7.40
Romania	10,402	4.35	5,049	2.52	5,353	13.97
Yugoslavia	33,026	13.82	17,090	8.52	15,936	41.56
Poland	132,851	55.61	126,459	63.05	6,392	16.67
U.S.S.R.	34,941	14.63	30,618	15.27	4,323	11.27

Nearly 100 percent of the immigrants to the United States came from Europe, and 60 percent of them from East-Central Europe in the years 1948–1953. According to the data regarding the country of their birth, by far the largest number of DP refugees came from Poland, more than 50 percent. A much smaller number of refugees came from the other countries. Though considerably fewer, the Hungarian refugees follow the Polish if comparing their numbers with the population of the sending country. Most of them were torn away from their original surroundings at the end of the war and waited for years at the first station of their asylum in Germany or in Austria for the chance of resettlement.

Demographically and economically the countries of Central and Eastern Europe should have been providers of labor for other countries in the 1950s-

1960s, too, just as they had been during the first decades of the twentieth century. Instead, the new regimes increasingly restricted the freedom of movement between countries. In April 1949 a thirty-mile-wide prohibited zone was established on the western border of Hungary; it was later surrounded by minefields, guard towers, searchlights, and guard dogs. In May 1950 a similar ten-mile-wide zone was created along the Hungarian-Yugoslav border. Shortly afterwards, laws stripped Hungarian citizenship and confiscated property from all those who failed to return from trips to foreign countries within thirty to sixty days of being given notice to do so. When an amnesty was declared in April 1950, virtually no one came back to Hungary by October 4, the deadline for voluntary return.[20] The illegality of all emigration gave political overtones even to that which was economically motivated.

The Hungarian Displaced Person

There are no reliable statistics on Hungarian refugees; the available data almost always are based on estimates. J. Vernant, however, concludes, "Hungarians constituted the largest proportion of displaced persons after the Second World War by population size: this from a country which had already lost two-thirds of its territory and half its population in 1919."[21] The number of Hungarians in Germany and Austria when D-Day arrived was between 800,000 and 1 million. Other estimates concur that approximately 800,000 people, including 100,000 soldiers, 150,000 military youth, 300,000 civilians, (40,000 of them "Arrow-Cross" men), and 250,000 ethnic Germans fled to the West from Hungary.[22] The number of soldiers in the Hungarian units that surrendered to the Americans in southern Germany was put at about 120,000 by László Taubinger in his studies on Hungarian refugees.[23] The total number of Hungarian prisoners of war in the West was calculated by the Comrade Association of Hungarian Prisoners of War to be 280,000 in 1950.[24] "About 100,000 of them were in Germany, including the section of the Hungarian army that was transferred to Germany."[25]

Estimates vary greatly because they refer to different time periods and their calculators did not always have full knowledge of the facts. For instance, Gyula Borbándi states that there were 108,000 Hungarians living in camps and 73,000 outside camps in the American zone of Germany in 1949.[26] Computations based on Hungarian census data, however, show that actual population growth was only 62,000 behind projected natural growth for 1941–1949.[27] That almost precisely equals the 62,001 Hungarian refugees the IRO helped resettle from July 1, 1947, to December 31, 1951.[28] Although Hungarian public opinion considers the true number of DPs to be higher, it is in line with the conclusions of scholars John Kósa of Canada and István Szépfalusi of Austria. Kósa puts the figure for the spring of 1945 at 55,000.[29] Szépfalusi finds 60,971 Hungarian citizens applied for asylum in Austria between 1948 and 1955. But 22,055 of them were ethnic Germans.[30] Szépfalusi further believes Kázmér Nagy's estimate of 200,000 to be exaggerated even for the entire period of 1948–1956.[31] Vernant considers other factors in his study.

Although many of them returned, in June 1945 there were still 400,000 Hungarians in camps in Austria and Germany, and two years later 23,000 of them continued to live in the American zone in Germany. In 1945–1946 approximately 200 war criminals were handed over to the Hungarian government, and only approximately 1,600 Hungarians were repatriated between July 1947 and December 1951.[32]

Countries started opening their borders to the displaced persons and refugees in 1947, and the Displaced Persons Act finally was adopted by the U.S. Congress in the summer of 1948. Thus it was only then that the organization of their settlement in the United States began. The immigration of the Hungarian DPs in large numbers—because of their former enemy status—became possible only at the beginning of the 1950s. Then approximately 16,000 Hungarians were allowed to immigrate to the United States. Let us see their demographic structure.

TABLE 4.

Immigrants Born in Hungary, by Sex and Age, Fiscal Years 1951–1952[33]

Age groups	Male		Female		Total No.	% of males	% of females
	No.	%	No.	%			
Admitted number	5,753	100.00	5,419	100.00	11,172	51.49	48.51
Under 19 years	1,348	23.43	1,193	22.02	2 ,541	53.04	46.95
20 to 39	2,687	46.71	2,444	45.10	5,131	52.37	47.63
40 to 59	1,465	25.46	1,531	28.25	2,996	48.90	51.10
60+	253	4.40	251	4.63	504	50.20	49.80

The statistical data enable us to form a more or less realistic picture of the characteristics of the age structure of the Hungarian DPs. The age of those who made up the group was generally higher at the time of their arrival than the age of those immigrants who came before the First World War for economic reasons. They were far from being as old as the descriptive literature emphasizes it, for 23.43 percent of them—that is, every fifth one—was under nineteen years of age, and 70.14 percent belonged to the age group below forty. It is a fact that every fourth person's age was higher than forty years. We can conclude both from the number of those under nineteen and of the women that it was relatively common for the refugees to flee with members of their family.

Descriptive literature emphasizes that the refugees were recruited from the middle and higher social groups and had higher education almost without exception.[34] The "new Americans" were army officers, businessmen, professionals, landowners, gentry, or even aristocrats, and of course, there were large numbers of petit-bourgeois people. Many of those claiming to be members of the Hungarian nobility, though, were recently assimilated Germans or Slovaks, who had been professional army officers or bureaucrats.[35]

The social structure of the Hungarian DPs was also indicated by the statistics as being essentially more differentiated. The ratio of professionals was relatively high among them (11 percent), but many more claimed to be craftsmen, foremen and kindred workers (17.99 percent), or operatives and kindred workers (14.49 percent). The ratio of those who were formerly physical workers in reality was more likely to have been lower than that given in the statistics. The phenomenon of "devaluation" of occupation in this direction is reported by the preparer of IRO statistics, too.[36] This may be explained by the immigration policies of the receiving countries, with the trend in their demand for the workforce. (This is shown partly by the data of the 1970 Census relating to the occupational distribution of those who arrived after 1945. The number of those in their circle with a diploma was more than 30 percent by then.)

The demographic characteristics, social background, and motivations for immigration set this post–World War II group apart from the older economic immigrants from Hungary. Political views and ideology differentiated the new arrivals both from their predecessors and among themselves even more than their class structure did. Their ranks contained legitimists, national conservative democrats, extreme fascists, and social democrats, but the main dividing line fell between the 1945 "national emigration" and the 1947 "democratic emigration." That line set apart two distinct groups that differed from each other in almost every respect: age, social background, political views, motivations for leaving Hungary, and the year of their departure. Regardless of how much other differences later were smoothed away in the United States as a result of business contacts, friendships, and intermarriage, the date of departure from Hungary always continued to be a reliable indicator of a Hungarian-American refugee's political views.

The Displaced Persons Act of 1948 provided for the issue over the next two years of 200,000 visas to eligible persons located in the American, British, or French zones of Germany, Italy, and Austria. Its order of preference put agricultural laborers first, professionals second, and those with relatives who were American citizens third. The act further stipulated that all resettled families had to be provided with jobs and housing. In a victory for the immigration restrictionists, instead of establishing an extra quota for the newcomers, the act "encumbered" up to 50 percent of each donor nation's annual quota for as many years as were necessary to "repay" the number of places used up by displaced persons who received a residence permit.[37] Yet despite the difficulties, the majority of all Hungarian refugees wanted to settle in the United States.

Displaced persons hoping to go to the United States first had to be screened by the IRO. Only a long and complicated procedure could free a displaced family from the European camps and assembly centers. "It would take a long time to describe how many obstacles hindered the immigration of Hungarians."[38] But perhaps an example can illustrate some of them, although a family immigrating with five children would undoubtedly represent an extreme case.

One Hungarian family, A.L., his wife, and their five children, were among the 140,000 people who underwent the immigration procedure prescribed by the 1948 DP Act. Registration, interview, documentation, medical examination, and countless eligibility and security checks had to be passed until they received the relevant visas and were finally able to pack, say farewell to their friends, and set off to an emigration center. Their story was that of many Hungarians who had been waiting in Austria for a home in a democratic country since 1945. For the L. family, the wait lasted five years. When an American resident finally assured them a job and housing, they still faced four desperate months of administrative details and screening. This was a fearful period of waiting, when any tiny practical detail—the sickness of a child, the sudden filling up of the quotas, etc.—could have put an end to their hopes at any time. The L. family waited in Austria, in a camp in Glasenbach near Salzburg, with nine hundred other people from fourteen or fifteen different ethnic groups. In Glasenbach Mr. L. was a manual worker on an Austrian farm; he also completed a five-month car mechanic's course at an Austrian technical school in Linz and was leader of the local Hungarian DP scout troop.

Because the L. family were Lutherans, Mr. L.'s first interview in 1949 was with the Austrian Director of the Lutheran World Organization, Miss Lund, who then gave detailed information on the family to the New York center of the National Lutheran Council recommending that Mr. L. be offered a suitable job. The New York Council sent Miss Lund an offer from an American farmer who needed a worker on his farm. This offer consisted of a two-room apartment with a garden, thirty-five pounds of meat (excluding bones) per month, three dozen eggs per week, half a gallon of milk a day, and one hundred dollars a month.

Miss Lund then accompanied the L. family to see the head of the IRO's Salzburg immigration center. It was his task to verify that the L. family had been in IRO care up to that time. The next step was to present Mr. L. and his file to the Selector of the DP Committee, whose task it was to check whether Mr. L. was both eligible under the DP Act and qualified for the job offered to him. Then the file had to be sent to U.S. Military Intelligence for security checking. Thereafter the American DP Committee reviewed the papers once again and, if all the papers, including the Military Intelligence report, were in order, they were forwarded to the U.S. Consul; it was the Consul's task to decide whether a visa should be given to the L. family strictly in accordance with existing immigration laws binding on all immigrants without exception.

The most important part of the control procedure was the security check. In addition to a thorough study of the papers, L.'s employers and neighbors were also asked about his conduct. Local police records were checked at his place of residence and German records consulted for any contacts and Nazi collaboration during the war. His political activities and background were put under close scrutiny in order to prevent the entry of subversive elements into the United States. After the check, L. was sent back to the DP Committee and, if found in order, the relevant papers were sent to the U.S. Consul for visa approval.

A thorough medical examination was an important part of the resettlement process. (The first medical examination was carried out by the IRO's medical authority.) The L.'s as persons applying for a visa, were examined in Europe by the U.S. Public Health Service. As a next step, their fingerprints were taken at the U.S. Consulate and their papers checked once again. The L.'s also completed an extensive visa application form at the Consulate. All documents were checked carefully once again, and it was verified that the applicants could be allowed entry to the United States. If everything was in order the Consul gave the applicant an oath and issued the visa.

After Mr. L. received the visa, he was interviewed by an official of the Immigration and Naturalization Service. That official not only examined the relevant papers and documents, but also interviewed each member of the family individually. He checked whether the applicant had been declared a DP in accordance with the Constitution: that is, based on an IRO mandate, that in the course of the various examinations nothing had been found that would prevent immigration to the United States; that the medical papers were in order and that nothing had been revealed in the course of the medical examinations that would cause the authorities to refuse entry to the United States; that the applicants were of good character; that they were not criminals and did not represent a threat to national security; that the submitted documents were authentic, complete and in order; and that the visas had been issued in accordance with the relevant rules and regulations. If everything was in order, the visa was stamped: "Has undergone investigation—Found eligible for immigration," and at last the family could start to pack.

The five children—P. aged 9, A. aged 8, Z. aged 6, K. aged 4, and I. aged 13 months—became very excited when it seemed that something was finally about to happen. One day before departure came the last medical examination. As the family lived in an IRO camp, they had received all the necessary vaccinations. All families with babies came under close observation for three weeks to see that they were in good health and could make the journey.

That Mr. L. spoke several languages, along with his work with the scouts, had made him many friends in the camp, all of whom wished him well when he set off. When he left Europe, Mr. L. left many things behind: a university degree from the law faculty, a career in public life, sixteen years of experience in the wine export-import trade, and four and a half years spent in whatever housing was available and the camp in Austria. After nine days of travel, the family arrived in New York. There they faced more medical examinations and an interview with the Immigration and Naturalization Service.[39]

It is not surprisimg that with the earlier immigrants memories of their "rapid processing" at Ellis Island always remained. Neither is it surprising that the displaced persons were permanently influenced by their prolonged encounter of several years with the suspended animation in the camps and repeated examinations by doctors and bureaucrats who assumed the worst of them.

Political control of immigration and resettlement was tightest in the United States, more liberal in Canada, and most liberal of all in the countries of Latin America. Persons obviously compromised by their fascist or "Arrow-Cross" past were not allowed into the United States, if only to avert the likely public outcry. Hungarians who actually had committed crimes against humanity or who had actively participated in the "Arrow-Cross" regime usually did not even apply for a United States visa but tended to emigrate to Australia, South America, and Canada. Those who did somehow reach the United States and were detected by the immigration authorities at Ellis Island were deported to Europe.[40]

The categorization of Hungarian soldiers was a problem. Under Section 13 of the U.S. Immigration Act, those "who in the Second World War had taken up arms against the United States of America" could not be allowed on the territory of the United States. Although Hungary technically had been at war with the United States, Hungarian soldiers had not actually fought American troops. It therefore was open to legal dispute whether "taking up arms" applied in their case, and representatives of the Hungarian immigrants held extensive negotiations with American authorities over the matter.

A second Displaced Persons Act, adopted in 1950, redefined eligibility for immigration. Among those now excluded were Communist and Nazi (fascist) Party members and supporters of regimes opposed to democratic government and free economic competition. Soldiers barred were those who had fought in the Second World War after December 6, 1941, against the United States or its allies on the Western front (including Africa and Italy), either as a member of a national army or its supporting units. In 1950 as well, the United States raised its immigrant quotas and established a ceiling of 415,000 for the next two years, but maintained the encumbrance of quotas. The latter provision was terminated by the Refugee Relief Act of 1953, permitting U.S. authorities to allow in 205,000 refugees as above-quota immigrants. Besides compulsory migration the mechanism of chain-migration also took place after World War II. While it did not move masses, in the frame of family unification, hundreds of those immigrated to the United States between 1947 and 1949 who were wives or children left behind in Hungary by those who formerly emigrated.

Substantial differences are shown in the direction of the migration of those who move from economic reason and the DPs. While the goal of 80 percent of the former was the United States, only 27 percent of the Hungarians under the IRO's authority went to the United States.[41] The second most common destination was Australia (21.5 percent) although only 1,227 Hungarian-born persons were living there at the time of the 1947 census.[42] Just over 13 percent of the Hungarians chose Brazil, Argentina, or Venezuela, and very few stayed in Europe (Great Britain, Switzerland, and the former West Germany). Some who resettled in European countries were not registered by the IRO, however, because they did not need its assistance. A higher number of Hungarian immigrants were indicated in Swedish immigration statistics, for instance, than in the respective IRO records, and there was legal migration from Hungary to Sweden for agricultural work.[43] Likewise, IRO records show 7,191 Hungarian Jews resettled in Israel, but Israeli immigration statistics put the figure at 15,104.[44]

CHAPTER 26

The Arrival of the Freedom Fighters: 1956–57

ON OCTOBER 23, 1956, an uprising broke out in Budapest against the Communist government of Hungary. When it was soon mercilessly suppressed, 200,000 Hungarians had fled, most to Austria and a few to Yugoslavia. This was the largest spontaneous migration of civilians since the Spanish Civil War, and one still unequaled in modern European history.[1] During 1956, only 1,121 Hungarian refugees were registered in Austria before October 27. After this date the numbers were in the hundreds per day and well into the thousands for some days in November. The emigration wave for all of November involved a total of 113,810 persons; and for December it reached 9,750, before tapering off to 12,862 in January 1957.[2] After further declines in February, only an insignificant number of people left the territory of Hungary in March. Emigration to Yugoslavia started toward the end of December, and the United Nations Refugee Committee reported that a total of 19,857 Hungarians eventually arrived there.[3] However, the great degree of mobility among all the refugees makes it impossible to determine precise totals.

The new wave of flight was made easier by the extraordinary situation which developed at the country's border. As early as the middle of November a radio broadcast by the Kadar government had forbidden people to leave the country, and in the succeeding days the AVH[4] and Russian troops established checkpoints along roads leading to the West. The number of refugees crossing at this time was enormous, and there were insufficient guards and troops to restrain the bulk of them. Many of them crossed into Austria without seeing any sign of guards or troops and without interference. Others met border guards who in general were sympathetic. For example, a group of refugees who crossed the border on December 1 were intercepted by border guards who, at the outset, wanted to prevent their departure. After exchanging some words, however the group was allowed to go and the guards pointed out the way and told them where to look for Russian patrols. Some were ferried across a river on the border by the guards.[5] Even when the refugees were captured, there was no effective means of dealing with them. One refugee who was detained near the border by the secret police was released after two days and put on one of several trucks with about forty others. They were taken to a town about fifty kilometers from the border and crossed at Tothfalu on November 29. Others were taken by the Russians, returned to Győr and told to go back to Budapest. On release they returned to the border and crossed.

Who Left the Country?

The emigrants and refugees of 1956–1957 were characterized by having a large proportion of young people among them: approximately 30 percent of them were minors, a large part of whom left without their parents;[6] 66.4 percent were under 30 years old; only 1 percent was over 60 years old. Two-thirds of them were male, but a relatively high number of women emigrated from Budapest. More than half the refugees of working age had college degrees or were skilled or semiskilled workers, while many of the others were university students.

More than two-thirds of the emigrants were members of the working population, and the remaining one-third were their dependents.[7] Within the latter group, the number of high school and university students was over 3,200, as 11.2 percent of all Hungarian high school and university students left the country. On November 4, approximately 450 university students from Sopron—half of the total number of the students—fled to Austria, from where they finally went to Canada. Of the 450 students, 220 were forest engineers; the rest were mining engineers, surveyors, and geologists. About fifty professors and their families also crossed the Austrian border, twenty-five of them from the Forestry Faculty of Sopron University.[8]

Settled in the new surroundings, some of the 1956 emigrants naturally tended to overstate their qualifications, giving rise to jokes later on. "What's the definition of a shipping engineer? Someone who turned himself into an engineer on the ship taking him to his new homeland."[10] Nevertheless, the high proportion of white-collar workers is supported by statistical data, which put the proportion of skilled and unskilled industrial workers at 52.4 percent. Clearly, the exodus cost Hungary tens of thousands of its most highly educated and highly skilled citizens.[11]

The significant emigration contributed to the demographic problems that became evident in Hungary a few years later, for the number of refugees approximately equaled the number of births in a whole calendar year and corresponded to the natural population increase for three or four years. The greatest blow was inflicted on the demographic policies of the 1950s that had been bent on setting new records for population growth. Despite the tens of thousands of births forced upon women during the so-called Ratko era (named

TABLE 5a.

Hungarian Refugees into the United States by Occupation[9]
(December 31, 1957)

Occupation	Total	Percentage
Professional, technical, and kindred workers	3,513	11.07
Farmers and farm managers	609	1.92
Managers, officials, and proprietors	585	1.84
Clerical	2,189	6.90
Sales	379	1.19
Craftsmen, foremen	5,904	18.60
Operatives	4,746	14.95
Private household workers	197	0.62
Service workers	762	2.40
Farm laborers	246	0.78
Other laborers	1,460	4.60
No occupation	11,148	35.13
GRAND TOTAL	31,738	100.00

TABLE 5b.

Hungarian Refugees into the United States with No Occupation

Category	Total	Percentage
Housewives	2,725	24.46
Retired	9	0.00
Students	2,876	25.82
Children under 14	5,374	48.25
Unlisted	164	1.47
TOTAL	11,148	100.00

TABLE 5c.

Hungarian Refugees into the United States by Sex and Age

Age	Male		Female		Total	
Under 5 years	1,053	5.45	1,002	8.06	2,055	6.47
5–9	1,127	5.84	7,030	8.28	2,157	6.80
10–14	1,028	5.33	833	6.70	1,861	5.86
15–19	2,994	15.51	1,386	11.15	4,380	13.80
20–29	6,888	35.68	3,417	27.48	10,305	32.47
30–39	3,381	17.51	2,622	21.09	6,003	18.92
40–49	2,032	10.54	1,406	11.30	3,438	10.83
50–59	669	3.46	521	4.19	1,190	3.75
Over 59 years	132	0.68	217	1.75	349	1.10

by the people after the Minister of Health made responsible for the anti-abortion laws and their strict enforcement), the masses of young people leaving the country within a few months caused the pace of population growth to plunge.[12]

The Hungarian government tried to persuade the emigrants to return by declaring amnesty for all those who had left the country before November 29, 1956, and by the middle of February 1957, some 14,000 had returned to Hungary. The Hungarian Foreign Ministry had been allowed to send a special commissioner to Austria, and at the end of January a committee of the UN and the International Red Cross, together with Austrian and Hungarian government commissioners, visited refugee camps and disseminated information, travel documents, and free train tickets for Hungarians who wanted to return.[13] Particularly extensive propaganda was put out by the Hungarian government for the extradition and the bringing home of the young people. Even those who went to the Youth World Festival were furnished with English pamphlets on this subject.[14]

Motivations

As those who left Hungary in 1956–1957 were a cross section of society, all possible forms of emigrant attitudes existed among them. Their motivation consisted of intermingled and sometimes just randomly connected factors. Any real analysis of the motivations behind this exodus could not be carried out at the time. The 200,000 refugees were regarded as traitors by the Hungarian government, and as heroes and freedom fighters by the governments of the host countries.[15]

Contemporary interviews already reveal how varied the motivations of leaving the country were. Inquiries about the factors underlying the refugee movement found that there were several reasons motivating these refugees. Quite often immigrants invented political reasons as an ex post facto explanation for having gone abroad.[16] It is true that all witnesses felt strongly against certain features of the regime existing immediately prior to October 23 and were bitterly hostile to the security department, the AVH. Some witnesses drew a distinction between "Communism" and "Communism as it is operated in Hungary."[17] However some refugees were desirous of leaving Hungary well before the events of 1956 took place and were merely waiting for a chance to do so. These people took advantage of the revolution to leave the country at the earliest opportunity. They took no part in the demonstrations or in the fighting which followed.

Nevertheless, the great majority of interviewees showed an intense love of their country. While much of the population would willingly have left Hungary up to 1953, certain events about the time when, in June 1953, Imre Nagy, became prime minister with a liberal program, encouraged the belief that better days were coming. However, this hope had not been realized; Imre

Nagy was pushed out of office and discontent was rife. But while the revolution was succeeding in October 1956, there was no thought of a general exodus. All interviewees heard would have been quite happy to remain in Hungary under the new order, which they hoped the uprising would achieve.

When it appeared that the revolution had failed, many thousands decided it would be necessary or very desirable for them to leave the country. Some had taken an active part on the side of the revolutionaries as elected members of the Workers' Committees, or in organizing the general strike, in actual fighting against the AVH and the Russians. They feared that they would be rounded up by the AVH and would face either execution, a long term of imprisonment, deportation, or confinement in a concentration camp. Indeed, the secret police was already endeavoring to locate offenders. Knowledge of this prompted many to flee immediately.

Others had been in prison at the time of the revolution for political offenses and had been released by the revolutionaries. They felt that as soon as the secret police and the Communist Party had been reorganized, the best they could expect would be a return to prison with additional punishment. Others found that they were no longer able to follow their former professions or occupations, as they were under continual suspicion from the AVH and the party and found it difficult to obtain suitable employment. To them, the prospect of remaining in the country offered no future and no security.

But, above all these other considerations, the overriding reason given for leaving the country was dissatisfaction and discontent with the way of life, with the material hardship of every day in Hungary. People felt that they could no longer live under conditions where the Communist rule was imposed by force on the people; where there was no freedom of expression; where there was a continual fear of the activities of the party and the AVH; where they had no voice in the government of their country; and where the economic situation was such that they were barely able to eke out an existence, even though they worked long hours. They felt that as soon as the Communists were restored to power, they could expect only retaliatory measures, further suppression of their rights, and more stringent conditions in their lives. Rather than face this prospect, they decided to leave without any belongings, in the hope that they could start a new life in a new country. The urgency of their desire to escape was abundantly evidenced by testimony such as that from a husband who left with his eight-months-pregnant wife and of another who carried away a month-old baby in a basket.

Later, Western social psychologists revealed how varied the motivations were. They estimated that participation in the armed uprising and fear of retaliation motivated less than 5 percent of the refugees to leave Hungary. Aspects of the pre-1956 Hungarian political situation, such as social and economic disadvantages and fear of repression or of imprisonment, by contrast, motivated approximately 50–60 percent of the emigrants. In those politically motivated cases, "other reasons" such as psychological factors, individual character traits, and events in an individual's own life history also played a part.[18] For example, some emigrants were trying to escape job-related conflicts or failed marriages, and when the sudden opening of the borders touched off a "now or never" fever, a psychological situation was created in which people—especially young people—who otherwise never would have thought of leaving the country actually did so.[19]

There is a striking difference between the two waves of flight from Hungary. In the immediate postwar period of the 1940s, Hungarian emigration was motivated by various repelling factors inside Hungary. In 1956 the flight was inspired more by the attracting factor of better prospects in the Western world. Isolation from the outside and the prohibition of travel abroad made forbidden Western lifestyles appear more glamorous to the Hungarians than they really were, and the image was reinforced by the rosy picture earlier emigrants conveyed back to those left behind.[20] An inseparable intertwining of the political and economic factors can be seen in the 1956 refugee movement for the first time.

A few hours after the first mass migration into Austria began, the UN Chief Commissioner requested governments to give refuge to as many Hungarians as they could. As Western European countries responded favorably, Hungarians began to leave Austria, although not enough departed to compensate for the additional influx of 6,000 people every day.[21]

Although President Eisenhower said the United States "could not do anything" to assist the rebels because of the threat of war with the Soviet Union, the refugees were another matter. He promised to help "in every possible way" Hungarians trying to escape the "criminal actions of the Soviets."[22] The fighting was still going on in the streets of Budapest when the U.S. Congress committed $20 million to supply the refugees flooding into Austria, as well as those still to come, with food, shelter, and medical services.

At the urging of the State Department, which usually stood for tough immigration policies, President Eisenhower ordered 5,000 Hungarians to be allowed in "as soon as possible."[23] On November 26, he told a group of Hungarian refugees that the United States would offer refuge to 21,500 Hungarians and commissioned the Defense Department to work out a scheme for transporting them. In light of the generous offers of asylum made by other countries, he further promised to ask Congress to adopt legislation allowing highly qualified refugees to obtain permanent residence in the United States.[24]

President Eisenhower appointed a New York lawyer Tracy S. Voorhees, a talented bureaucrat, to head the presidential Hungarian Refugee Relief Committee.[25] Camp Kilmer in New Jersey, vacated by the U.S. Army a short time before, was to become the Joyce Kilmer Reception Center for the refugees, who began arriving on November 21. There, the vice president of the Refugee Relief Committee, Lee C. Beebe, soon established such a high degree of efficiency that official procedures that normally might have taken two years were completed within an hour or so.

The refugees had been classified according to jobs and qualifications before they left Europe. Now government organizations carried out thorough health and security inspections, which resulted in deportation of only 5 of the 32,000 refugees as possible security threats. On May 6, 1957, the last refugee left the center for a new home in the United States, and the largest single immigration to the United States in such a brief period had been completed. Although the jobs found for 38 percent of the refugees did not match their skills, only 9 percent of them subsequently became unemployed in the next five years, and at least half the refugees professed satisfaction with their new careers.[26]

No event in the history of Hungary united Hungarians all over the world as did the tragic Freedom Fight of 1956. Hungarian relief organizations were set up worldwide to accommodate the nearly 200,000 refugees and to assist those remaining in Hungary, and existing associations and institutions made sacrifices that seemed beyond their capabilities. At Camp Kilmer, the Association of American Hungarians (AAH) was represented by the Hungarian-American churches and institutions of New Jersey until it was able to set up an all-encompassing organization, Coordinated Hungarian Relief Incorporated (CHR), in January 1957.[27]

CHR's central office began its operations in Washington, D.C., in the main office of the Hungarian Lutheran Association. Its nationwide organization and fund-raising were carried out hand-in-hand with the American Hungarian Federation. The first important task was to find housing for the refugees, followed by finding sponsors, teaching English-language courses, disbursing cash and material gifts, and dispatching relief to those waiting in the Austrian camps or suffering shortages in Hungary. As the resettlement of refugees was coming to an end, sending secondhand clothing and medication, especially the polio vaccine, to Europe became the focus of the relief work. From the Hungarian-American point of view, however, CHR was not only an overall relief organization, but also an interest group, trying to win public figures and opinion makers to the cause of the refugees. In that respect, it was equally successful.

By far the largest percentage of refugees was brought to the local communities by the national voluntary resettlement agencies of the three major faith groups: Catholic Relief Services, Church World Service—Lutheran Refugees Service, and United HTAS Service. According to information from the Immigration and Naturalization Service as of March 1957, the largest numbers of Hungarians had gone to New York (4,159) and Cleveland (1,487), but hundreds settled in most of the big cities. Percentages with relatives varied from approximately 5 percent in San Francisco and a small percentage in Buffalo, Pittsburgh, and St. Louis to 60 percent in Detroit, Cleveland, and Akron. All of these communities took in sizable numbers of refugees, but some of them contained a high number of relatives and some did not. Cleveland, of course, took a large number. And admittedly Cleveland had a high percentage of relatives. This could be an exception to the general rule, or it could be because of the highly active and successful pattern of local community organization developed there, with all activities concerned with refugees channeled through one agency.[28]

As of December 5, 1957, according to Immigration and Naturalization Commissioner Swing, only 391 of the 38,000 Hungarian refugees admitted to this country had left the United States. Of the 391, twenty-two were deported because of Communist affiliations and fifty-two for fraudulent statements. Some forty-three family members left with these deportees. The 274 other Hungarians left voluntarily. Of the 229 adults in this latter group 145 returned to join close relatives; only 84 returned because they failed to make adjustments in the United States.[29]

In a wave of migration the variety of views and motivations are usually covered since the current political considerations show these much more homogeneous than they really are.

One of the most important morals drawn from examining the wave of migration in 1956 is to see how difficult it is to define "refugee" and to differentiate between political and economic causes in the migration in the second half of the twentieth century. The boundary between political and economic emigration has never been sharp. Special circumstances can give the label of political emigration to any geographical mobility. The relative economic backwardness of the society left behind, and the attraction of the Western countries, political and economic motivations combining, melted to form the waves of migration. What is emphasized when labeling their characteristics, is not independent from the current political interests of the emitting and receiving countries either. For example, in the autumn of 1956 the Western world wanted to see the escape of fighters for liberty against the Russian oppression in the sudden emigration of masses, while the Hungarian government saw the hasty adventure of youngsters deceived by the fake propaganda of the capitalist world, and the escape of criminals and counterrevolutionists from prison. The official political statements degraded them to simple dissidents. As the political points of view are pushed to the background, and the methods of detailed comparative examinations come to the foreground, the facts of social variety and the diversification of motivations can rather be seen in the migration wave of the "56-ers." We can notice, e.g., how much synchronized their structure of professions was with the current profession pattern of the international migration, how high was the number of marketable occupations compared to the "45-ers." There is much evidence to support the fact that it is an important condition of fitting into the new environment, what the receipt is like from its part. It is worth comparing the waves of emigration from this point of view.

Our research has proven that voluntary migration is motivated by attraction, while forced migration is motivated by repulsion. The concrete historic circumstances formed diverse types of both voluntary and forced migrants. Even the category "refugee" can be of several types, depending on whether the refugees look for shelter outside the border of their own country as victims of political, religious, or racial persecution. Many "refugees," in the original sense of the Latin word, are "banished." Many are "exiled" in a modern sense, leaving their homeland persecuted by the future image of the unacceptable fate that would come if they chose staying at home. And others—possibly the biggest group of forced migrants—are "drifting masses" leaving their home in the cross-stream of conflicts.

Since the individuals in every community differ in feeling themselves assimilated to their environment, in the extent to which they share the dominant beliefs of the majority, it is assumed that even in one wave of refugees some feel themselves marginal in relation to the society they leave, some less so. Since in their new environment, in the period of settling, many problems of the refugees and their solutions depend on the emotional ties to their past, we study to what extent the relations of the refugees are marginal to their old homeland, or to what extent they identify with it.

CHAPTER 27

The Newcomers

Integration and Conflict

THE RECEPTION INTO the existing Hungarian-American community organizations of Hungarians who obtained entry under the Displaced Persons Act was very ambiguous. The American Hungarian Federation, for example, did not refuse them a friendly welcome and signed many "assurances" that permitted a sizable proportion of the DPs to enter the country.[1] Many of them were being settled in the midst of the old-timers' community.

The Federation's activities still were viewed skeptically by the leftist Hungarian Americans, who now were concerned that members of the "Arrow-Cross" regime and supporters of the Hungarian extreme right might be among the refugees. "We will make sure that no one is able to take advantage of the good-willed generosity of the United States and that no Nazi, 'Arrow-Cross' member, or Horthy criminal can smuggle himself into this country,"[2] they vowed.

The DP Hungarians, the "45-ers," languished in Austrian and German refugee camps until they could get to their final destinations. Their "ex-enemy" existence followed them, and they were humiliated for it. Even their fellow countrymen settled earlier received them with aversion. One of them describes their situation compared to the "56-ers."

"The 200,000 Hungarians who followed us after October 1956 should know that we—fleeing the same bolshevik regime as they—were not welcomed with burning enthusiasm . . . but instead by the immeasurable misery of an exhausted and bombed-out Europe. . . . We were welcomed not with immigration permits, but with various black stamps reminiscent of the Nüremberg period: Nazi, fascist, war criminal or, at best, former enemy."[3]

The 45-er political emigrants were more likely to sink to the status of unskilled physical workers in their new enviroment. Although many had been trained at the Hungarian military academy or the law faculty of the university, their degrees and doctorates were not marketable in the United States. They had to accept and never found their way out of the lowest jobs. "In the 1950s

279

in Cleveland, for instance, three former Hungarian generals, including the Chief of Staff of the Second Army, who fought against the Soviets in 1942–43, worked as common workers among unskilled workers."[4] Most of the middle-aged remained stuck in this sphere of low-paid unskilled work, the younger ones, however, freed themselves from the burden of manual work after a few years and found employment in some intellectual occupation. Craftsmen and tradesmen fared better in American society than middle-class, even though they were lower in terms of social and cultural standing in the Hungarian community.

Forced to live in a manner entirely out of keeping with their social background, professional qualifications, and past experiences, the postwar Hungarian émigrés adjusted to their new situation by regarding their stay in the United States as a temporary solution until Hungary's inevitable liberation took place.[5]

Most of the 45-er organizations were founded in Germany's many refugee camps. They already had organized themselves in Europe along political, social, and cultural lines. They represented all shades of the deposed elite, from the Monarchy's aristocrats' conservative nationalist gentry groups to specifically military associations and far rightist neo-Nazi groups. In the new surroundings right from the beginning, abstaining from political activity char-acterized many well-known personalities of the emigration.[6] Thus, the circle of political activists was rather narrow in every grouping: there were hundreds rather than thousands, "professional" émigrés. The majority of the members of a group, even if they identified themselves with one or another political line, were occupied rather in laying the foundation of making their living. In the United States these Hungarian immigrants sympathized more with the Republican Party than with the Democratic Party. A role was played in this by the fact that they found unequivocally and deeply reprehensible the Yalta Conference, the joint decision of Roosevelt and Stalin on the future of the small states in Central Europe.

For a long time, the activities of the so-called military emigration were characterized by the competition of two associations: the Magyar Szabadság Mozgalom (Hungarian Movement for Freedom), founded in 1946 by General Ferenc Kisbarnaki Farkas; and the Magyar Harcosok Bajtársi Szövetsége (Fraternal Association of Hungarian Veterans), founded in 1947 led by General András Zákó. They issued papers by the name of *Magyar Szabadság* (Hungarian Freedom) and *Nemzetpolitika* (National Politics).

The Hungarian Movement for Freedom could be joined by former soldiers and civilians, too, in the spirit of the legal continuity of the 1939 anti-Bolshevist Hungarian parliament. Its program was militantly anti-Communist and stood up against all those emigrants, too, who had taken part in the Hungarian government of 1945.[7]

The Fraternal Association of Hungarian Veterans extended its interest only to former soldiers. The character and tasks of the organization were expressed in a 1949 circular as follows: "The spiritual and emotional fellowship for those Hungarians who are willing to take up the fight against bolshevism even with arms collects all forces for the liberation of Hungary and the restoration of its independence, does this work on the basis of Western democratic principles."[8] Though resettlement over the five continents dispersed the members of the organization, their activities were characterized by continuity even in the new surroundings and they built relationships with their fellow sufferers.

The culturally and socially oriented Magyar Társaság (Hungarian Association) represented interwar Hungary's Christian conservative social and intellectual world. It dedicated itself to the preservation and practice of the Hungarian heritage and to helping establish and maintain contact with the Hungarian-American organizations. The organizer, leader, and moving spirit of all activities of the Hungarian Association was John Nádas (1903–1992). He got his degree at the University in Budapest and began his political career as secretary of the Christian Regional Party. Later he became secretary general of another Christian conservative Hungarian political party. The Hungarian Association was already organized in Innsbruck, Austria, when he left Hungary in April 1945. Dr. Nádas immigrated to the United States and settled in Cleveland with other Innsbruck Hungarian Association members. After the difficult period of adjustment to a new life in a new country, he turned his attention to establishing a new Hungarian Association in Cleveland.

On November 24–25, 1961, the Association organized the first Hungarian Conference, soon to be renamed the "Hungarian Congress."[9] The Association's scholarly institution and activities were coordinated by Professor Ferenc Somogyi, a legal expert and constitutional historian formerly of the University of Pécs. The proceedings of the annual meetings of the Congress were published for more than thirty years. From them, the attitudes, political and cultural committments—the conservative nationalist ideology of the members of the Association—as well as its international membership can be traced.[10]

Several studies and monographs already give us information about the many-decades-long political activities of these organizations, but much more information is needed to describe their social and cultural history.[11] A sizable percentage of the postwar immigrants came from Hungary's social and political elite and the relatively well-to-do middle classes. They tried to counter the frustrating influence of their social failure by separating the world of their work completely from the world of their private and social life. The brutal reality of the former was made bearable by the dream world of the latter, in which the hierarchy of their original position in society, the customs and the value systems shaped by it, could guide the ways of their behavior. "They lived in their own Hungarian world; reality was separate from the industrial labor that most of them had to engage in eight to ten hours a day to make ends meet, and in their spare time they isolated themselves from others, although circumstances had thrown them together. They all lived in their own Hungary, as writers, journalists and artists: the old Hungary they had left behind."[12] For them, the old historical Hungary was a spiritual homeland, present wherever Hungarians dwelled, with borders as they were before Trianon and for a short time in the 1940s. Because of their learning and past social status, the majority of them felt superior to the relatively uncultured average Americans they encountered in their new places of employment. So they perpetuated the world they had left behind, which managed to save their sanity and indoctrinate the second generation with their own ideals.[13]

The DP Hungarians' organizations established local chapters in all of the larger centers of Hungarian communities in America. To these were added later a host of local organizations including "self-culture societies"—academic circles, women's guides, and sport clubs in which their social activities could unfold.

The community lived in the informal social gatherings. They organized musical and theatrical events, amateur performances, and film screenings on many occasions. There was hardly a weekend without a memorial festivity, a dinner, or a festive banquet in one of the big cities. The various elegant balls, the recurrent events of their social life, offered themes for discussion for weeks, and the reports appearing in the newspapers reminded them of the Hungarian balls of old. The process of integration and the modifications in the international relationships, however, did not leave the communal life of these organizations untouched either. The influence of the receiving community was reflected in the various forms of social activities, in the regular organizing of balls and parties.

The DPs did not build their connections with other "old-timer" Hungarian organizations (their endeavors in this direction were scarce and very weak) because the DPs felt they had different social, economic, and educational background than the earlier immigrants and were the bearers of urban values, in contrast to the rural values which they ascribed to the old-timers. Many arrived with considerable formal education and with a mastery of several languages. In all, they differed far more from the old-timers (and from the children of old-timers) than either group could accept. They thus constructed their own private world in which they could submerge in order to escape from the trials and tribulations "forced on them" by American society, and they set up political and social organizations separate from those of the earlier Hungarian immigrants.[14]

Their goal was to pass on to their children the culture, learning, and way of life that had virtually been extinguished in the Hungary of the post–World War II years. According to Susan Papp, the postwar Hungarians were successful in instilling a strong sense of cultural identity in their children. This was accomplished mainly through Hungarian-language schools and the Hungarian Scout movement,[15] which was founded in 1945 in Germany. In safeguarding the cultural and moral values of the past, in shaping the minds of young Hungarian-Americans regarding their heritage, the Hungarian Scouts in Exile may have been the most important boy-scout activity aimed first at deepening the knowledge of the Hungarian language, fostering acquaintance with geography, folklore, history, and literature, and mastering Hungarian folk singing and folk dancing, and only thereafter focused on the traditional boy-scout activities. Around 1950, with the onset of immigration, the center of the Hungarian

Scouts in Exile was transferred to Garfield, New Jersey, where its talented leader and organizer Gábor Bodnár lived.[16]

The most striking characteristic of the communal organizations of the postwar immigrants was their strong nationalism, which was also one of the important components of their anti-Communism: Besides the strong emphasis laid on the national goals and the liberation of Hungary from Russian oppression, the final and possibly the most interesting phenomenon was the creation of international émigré committees by the local branches of organizations throughout the world.

The arrival of nearly sixteen thousand Hungarian displaced persons between the years 1948 and 1952 brought a new social stratum into the Hungarian-American population. The world of the "old" economic migrants—whether they were members of the first, second, or third generation—was so fundamentally different from that of the "new" political refugees that the members of the two groups could never find common ground, not even with the passing of years. The social and cultural differences dividing them simply were insurmountable, given the strong class consciousness that characterized the Hungarian political elite both before and immediately after World War II.

The gulf was obvious in the case of the fraternal associations. The new arrivals believed that insurance matters were handled "in an outdated and petty manner," and the social and cultural life of the associations were "neither Hungarian, nor cultural." Instead, careerists among the American-born Hungarians were using them as ethnic tools to build up business. On the other hand, the old immigrants would not tolerate criticism from the newcomers and tried to protect their associations from them.[17] As a result, few post–World War II immigrants joined existing Hungarian-American community organizations but stayed in their own closed circles, which were continuations of the class-conscious societies of Europe.

The right-wing and anti-Communist refugees witnessed and benefited from the decline of left-wing movements among Hungarian-Americans. Bitter enmity began from the start, when the leftists accused the immigrants of being, if not war criminals, at least Nazi collaborators. A shift to the right in U.S. policy, however, led to a ban on immigrating Communists and left-wing socialists alike as threats to national security, while right-wingers were allowed in. During the Cold War, both general and ethnic public opinion turned further against the left. Some leading Jewish figures, for example, were disillusioned by Soviet Communism in the 1950s, and economic prosperity in the 1950s also softened the radicalism many immigrants had developed in the 1930s.[18] In addition, some loyal Communists returned to their homelands to "participate in building socialism" as Communists gained power there.[19] The anti-Communism of the post–World War II Hungarian immigrants was so strong that they rejected any idea of a compromise or cooperation with other groups of immigrants. Their interest focused solely on Hungary, but not the Hungary that could be visited in the period of détente.

The immigrants of the postwar era were themselves divided into two main distinct groups. The characteristics of the first wave were somewhat moderated in those who came after 1947. The latter group of Hungarian émigrés had approved of and supported the 1945 turn in domestic politics that had prompted the former group to leave, although there were some who had held public office before then but were not pro-German or holders of extreme right-wing views.[20] In addition, many outstanding intellectuals, scientists, and artists left Hungary after 1947.[21]

Politicians among the post-1947 immigrants established the Hungarian National Council in 1947, with the financial support of political figures in Washington. It was to unite all democratic forces, to represent the oppressed Hungarian nation in the free world, and to promote the liberation of the Hungarian nation from Communist oppression. It saw it as its task to lead the Hungarian people back into the Western cultural community and into the free political system of a united Europe.[22] Former Hungarian Prime Minister Ferenc Nagy and the former President of the Hungarian Parliament, Béla Varga, were its leaders, and retained their refugee status to the end so they could be bound by loyalty to Hungarian, and not United States, citizenship. The Hungarians of this wave of immigration were not maligned as pro-German or Nazi collaborators. On the contrary, some of them even held important posts with corresponding salaries in United States institutions of the Cold War such as Radio Free Europe. Few 1945 political émigrés could get into those renowned organizations, as recognition and financial support were given to the politicians of 1947 and the few immigrants who had left Hungary in protest against its pro-German policies. The emigrants of 1947 also were better off because more of them had marketable qualifications and skills. In terms of culture and erudition, a whole world divided the Hungarian Americans of 1945 from those of 1947.

By the 1960s the "national" emigrants of 1945 gained control of one of the organization founded by "old" Hungarian Americans, the American Hungarian Federation headquartered in Cleveland, and made it the voice of anti-communism and liberation."[23] Because members of the Hungarian National Council and of the American-Hungarian Federation had so little in common politically, backbiting became a permanent feature of relations between them. Council members strongly criticized the Association because it had "served Hitler, pushed the country into war and, through its policy of fighting to the end, had caused irreparable loss and damage." In reply, the Association pronounced the Council guilty of "serving Stalin, accepting the Soviet occupation of the country, and participating in land redistribution which was nothing more than theft, the sentencing and execution of Hungarian government officials as war criminals, and the communist declassing of the elite strata of society."[24] Finally, the objectives of the American Hungarian Federation became further and further removed from United States foreign policy in the 1960s and 1970s, with the official shift from the Cold War to peaceful coexistence. The American Hungarian Federation's criticism of the American policy change, in turn, caused some dissatisfaction within the Hungarian-American community. While the majority of Hungarian-American spokesmen still seemed to support the politics of liberation, the community itself was becoming more divided on the question.

The "national" immigrants, who left Hungary between 1945 and 1947, concentrated on the restoration of the borders of Hungary as they had been for a thousand years before the Treaty of Trianon.[25] The Hungarian Association has taken every opportunity over the years to protest the Trianon and the Paris Peace Treaties that resulted in the significant reduction of the size and population of Hungary. One of their projects was to put the Trianon and Paris Peace Treaties before the International Court of Justice in The Hague. If the Court then terminated the treaties, these Hungarians hoped, the Western powers would have to reconsider the Hungarian question. The American Hungarian Federation was one of the wholehearted backers of the effort to restore the thousand-year-old Hungary. It believed: "Hungarians in emigration do not have the right to give up a single city or even furrow. The fate of stolen Hungarian territories is not just the concern of the Hungarian ethnic minorities living there but of all Hungarians and what is more it is the primary concern of all Hungarians, and the question must always be considered from this point of view."[26]

The main fields of action of the leaders of the "democratic" emigration of 1947 were the Hungarian National Council and Radio Free Europe. Promising that "upon lifting of the 'iron curtain' the Council will return home and restore order and the continuity of public life until the Hungarian nation decides in free elections what it wants," the members of the Council regarded themselves as a "shadow government formed in emigration."[27] Because the Hungarian National Council, especially the intellectuals, were not so much concerned with the borders or size of Hungary as with liberation, it was willing to work with the representatives of Hungary's neighboring nations,. On February 11, 1951, these Hungarian immigrants, therefore, joined a coalition of similar groups meeting in Philadelphia and adopted the "Declaration of the Aims and Basic Principles for the Liberation of Nations of Central and Eastern Europe."[28]

Some Hungarian Americans supported a third view that fell between the extremes advocated by the two organized factions, that is, the "national" immigrants and the "democratic" immigrants. This middle position would have had Hungary take back only the territories where Hungarians were in the majority. Slovakia, Transylvania, and Croatia, where other groups prevailed, would become independent, although they likely would participate in some kind of union of such states.[29]

Competition and discord became permanent both between and within the individual groups. Advocates of all three political positions claimed to be the sole representatives of the Hungarian nation. Yet the wider Hungarian-American community did not concern itself with the legitimacy of these spokesmen or show much interest in them. At the same time, the more recently arrived Hungarians and their factions did not pay much attention to or seek support from the wider ethnic community. The organizations and positions of the newcomers embodied the divisiveness of political trends, both internally and externally. Setting up a unified representative organization of Hungarians in the United States was on their agenda for four decades, but it was the most futile of all their programs.

In contrast to, and partly because of, deliberate efforts to avoid the difficulties the postwar immigrants had encountered, three important factors contributed to the successful resettlement of the Hungarian immigrants of 1956–1957. Americans in general were positively motivated to take care of the refugees; Hungarian-American religious and other social organizations approached the task of resettlement in a spirit of self-sacrifice; and finally, the majority of the immigrants themselves were very young skilled or semiskilled workers with a lot of students and professionals. Because the positive propaganda carried by the newspapers, radio, and television was almost overwhelming, the Hungarians were received as heroes and Freedom Fighters, and, most important, as ideological allies.[30] Such artificially generated enthusiasm, however, inevitably was followed by a reaction and some degree of disillusionment as reality set in.[31] In the United States and other host countries, public opinion felt somehow cheated when, instead of gallant heroes, the refugees turned out to be ordinary men and women. Critical remarks were also delivered in Congress.[32]

Nevertheless, the unprecedented resettlement effort continued. Government committees were set up to coordinate relief activities in states hosting more than 90 percent of the refugees. With generous support from many philanthropic foundations, these committees helped integrate the Hungarian newcomers into society, organize English and Americanization courses for the young people, and direct the university students toward fields in which the United States had a labor shortage. The Presidential Committee for Hungarian Refugee Relief then continued the process with a program providing scholarships and maintenance costs for Hungarians specializing in needed subjects.[33]

The refugees of 1956, the 56-ers, even at the first station of their asylum in Europe had started to put down foundations of their organizations. As they were neither politically nor ideologically homogeneous, they were from this aspect probably the most heterogeneous refugee wave—their organizations were divided: soon a number of 56-er Freedom Fighter Federations, in competition with one another, announced their programs: the fight for a free independent Hungary. Every one of the various groupings of the Freedom Fighters saw itself the genuine one, and denied the right of the name and representation to the other groups.[34]

The most unique organization was that of the Hungarian refugee students, the Union of Free Hungarian Students (the Szabad Magyar Egyetemisták Szövetsége or "SzMESz").[35] Its leaders—particularly in the beginning—did their utmost to keep themselves apart from external influence and to mark themselves off unequvocally from former Hungarian émigré groups. The Union of Free Hungarian Students described itself as the independent community of Hungarian students of different religions and ideologies, belonging organizationally to no party or political or social associations. It declared that it would

(1) be ready to cooperate with every person or organization which followed similar aims and had the same ideas; (2) support, as part of the Hungarian intelligentsia of the future, the principles of the "56-er" Hungarian Freedom Fight for independence, democracy and neutrality, and act in this spirit in the manner allowed by the constitution of its host state; (3) represent the interests of the Hungarian students, that is to say, help them to foster their scholarly and scientific progress with all the material instruments at its disposal; (4) hold that its important task was to discuss and clarify the problems of "Hungarianhood," both in order to create a forum to develop constructive ideas, and to help acquire adequate information on these questions of "Hungarianhood"; (5) attend to the Hungarian culture and establish exchange relations between the Hungarian and other cultures; and (6) assist Hungarian students to become acquainted with the lives of people in their host nations.[36]

The Freedom Fighters' organization in America was active in order to gain the sympathy of the official circles and arouse the interest of the press. It strove to achieve that the Hungarian question not be removed from the agenda and whenever some event or anniversary warranted it, something should always happen to remind others of the Hungarian October of 1956.[37]

The organizations of the "56-ers" were horizontal; they tried to coordinate internationally those who settled in the various countries. Their member organizations formed themselves in fourteen countries on three continents. In this respect they were similar to the DP organizations, but with the difference, among others, that in their cultural and spiritual centers the Europeans had a much bigger role, than in those of the Hungarian DPs.

At a time when the immigrants of 1956 were being integrated into their new environment, multiculturalism and the respect for other cultures were becoming fashionable in American society. Hungary and its culture, which had never received much coverage in world newspapers, was now presented on the front pages. The gallant Freedom Fight had been defeated, but its spirit appeared to the American public as something glorious:

> "We cannot find words to describe the bravery and sufferings of the Hungarian nation. We cannot find words to describe the uncivilized brutality of their Soviet oppressors. While the light of freedom may still be seen somewhere in the world, the heroic uprising of the Hungarian people against the soul-destroying reign of communism will always make hearts flutter. While the light of freedom may still be seen somewhere in the world, the brutal perfidy of Soviet Russia will always be despised. To such depths of barbarism man, created in the likeness of God, can sink. To such heights of herioism can he rise."[38]

Such assessments of the 1956 Hungarian Freedom Fight in leading American newspapers and similar speeches by public officials greatly influenced Hungarian-born Americans. Many of those who had lost interest in or had decided to keep silent about their Hungarian origins, especially during the

Second World War, now expressed their pride. Some resumed using their Hungarian names.[39]

Hungarians who came to this country before the revolution, and in many instances many years before, were extremely helpful and generous in the early reception of the refugees by providing the indispensable interpreter service needed by them and by the agencies helping them. Many of the refugees found homes and jobs through these older Hungarians, some of whom were relatives and some of whom were not. The churches, of course, have always been tremendously interested and active in helping the Hungarians, opening up their social and religious services to them freely and warmly. Cleveland, like all Hungarian-American communities, welcomed the new refugees. Committees there officially sponsored five thousand immigrants and found them accommodations and jobs suitable to their qualifications.

Difficulties were encountered in the course of integration. Married men and women whose wives or husbands had been left behind in Hungary were frustrated and did not move quickly into the pattern toward integration. Probably the largest and most difficult problem in the resettlement of the Hungarian refugees was the language barrier. Very few Hungarians spoke English or any other language than their native Magyar. Special classes were established by public school systems and by private agencies. Existing adult education classes for newcomers were sometimes specially extended. A wide range of techniques were employed in teaching English. Some of the young men were impatient with the slowness of learning. The remarks of one youth were typical of their reactions: "We don't like to learn words like 'window' and 'door' and 'eat' and 'drink'. We want to learn names of tools and materials." Haste to learn quickly sometimes took the form of resentment toward regular class procedure and Americanization lessons.

One of the major difficulties was that some of the refugee youths in their late teens or early twenties, having no parental guidance or family relationship to sustain them, resented attempts to supply control and supervision by older people with whom they had been placed.[40] The sudden, unplanned flight from Hungary left the refugees no time to accept the idea of emigrating, no time to learn even the rudiments of the English language. Many of them found themselves within a few days or weeks on another continent far away without a period of psychological preparation. Coming from far different cultural backgrounds and from a system of state regulation alien to this country, some of the young people did not understand the necessity of self-imposed restrictions demanded in a free society. They had never had the wholesome recreation Americans have come to regard as their birthright, or had the high wages prevalent in our economy, and as a result they spent their money foolishly. They bought cars, drove them without adequate skill or understanding of our language, and thereby found themselves in trouble. Especially in the beginning of their residence here there was, on the part of some of them, an inordinate amount of drinking. One priest said of the Hungarian youth, "They all were like colts let loose in a pasture when they first got here and tasted freedom."

In fact, the leaders of the Cleveland Hungarian community soon found that the immigrants of 1956 were much more similar to Americans of the same age than any previous wave of immigrants had been. They soon bought cars, took out loans, furnished their homes, and spent what they earned, while demonstrating little or no concern for Hungarian cultural traditions. On the contrary, most of them showed more interest in business; even their personal relationships were essentially career oriented. They certainly did not cultivate the nostalgic memories of Hungary that the economic and political refugees of former generations nurtured.

The behavior of the younger generation, intoxicated by never before felt freedom and much higher incomes, caused a great deal of distress at the beginning.[41] As teenagers and young adults they were particularly receptive to America's contemporary "youth culture." Particularly telling was their espousal of the consumer philosophy, as transmitted to them by radio, television, and movies within a climate of economic prosperity. Many soon entered either the American armed forces or American colleges and universities.

Without an appropriate organization, a true Freedom Fighter cannot be distinguished from those who emigrated from Hungary from pure adventurousness or for fear of being held responsible after the failure of the Freedom Fight. No other group of Hungarian immigrants had received as much paternalistic care from the American people, including Hungarian-Americans, but the newcomers were not at all attracted to the activities of the Hungarian-American communities. Consequently, they left the geographical locations of their Hungarian neighbors as soon as they had the chance. Although a significant number still lived in Buckeye and its surroundings, in 1962 more than 30 percent had already left Cleveland, many for the suburbs.[42]

By 1962, half the newcomers owned their own homes, most of them in Buckeye, and 10 percent owned their own businesses; 20 percent held university degrees. As many as 43 percent of them had already taken American citizenship and another 39 percent had applied for it.[43]

Caring for the Hungarian refugees, the American community has learned through this unusual experience much about human nature and much about refugees. The experience of the problems of Hungarian resettlement therefore may have important relevance for the future.

CHAPTER 28

From Group Identity to Individual Identity

BY THE 1970S, most of the post–World War II immigrants had moved to the suburbs from their Hungarian neighborhoods. Their community feelings and loyalties were now maintained by spiritual ties instead of geographical proximity. They believed that a Hungarian identity could be preserved through shared cultural interests and schools. In contrast, the "old" Hungarian Americans had believed that members of their community should stay together in the literal sense, with their own ethnic institutions, churches, schools, and clubs nearby. The Hungarian refugees who moved to the suburbs were a small part of a mass exodus from the ethnic enclaves that brought about the irreversible decline of the traditional, geographically based Hungarian-American communities. The exodus confirmed their original assessment, as the Hungarian-American community was considerably weakened. Families that might have participated in Hungarian social events, and their children who might have attended Hungarian parish schools, had now left. Meanwhile, death was beginning to take the aging leaders away from the community as well.

The movement out of Cleveland, for example, had begun as early as the end of World War II, but was masked by the influx of postwar émigré newcomers. By the 1960s, however, the suburban migration involved not only the natural desire to leave old and derelict houses in the area of East Seventy-ninth and Holton Streets, but also a flight from middle-class houses and areas built in the 1920s. At the southern and western edges of the Buckeye area, an increasing number of African Americans moved into the houses vacated by the Hungarians.[1]

Beginning in the 1960s, for example, the geographical dissolution of the Cleveland Hungarian-American community and its social repercussions were artificially accelerated. Unscrupulous real estate agents used the arrival of the first African Americans in the Buckeye neighborhood to spur panic selling

290

or "blockbusting." It was mostly solitary elderly people who stayed in their old homes.

The loss of the young Hungarian families was followed by the closure of Hungarian church schools. The Saint Elizabeth Roman Catholic school, for example, had 650 pupils in 1930, but only 40 in 1960; in 1965 it was closed. In addition, some suburbanites began to avoid Hungarian community events for fear of crime.[2] Stores moved out of the former Hungarian districts or were closed down when their owners retired. As a result, by the end of the 1970s not a single store established for Hungarians remained to the west of East 115th and Buckeye Road or to the south of Buckeye.[3] But even without the panic induced in Buckeye, on the West Side of Cleveland, along Lorain Avenue, the number of Hungarian residents fell, too, an indication of how powerfully the suburban lifestyle was attracting urban residents. Therefore, the organization formed in the 1960s to stem the tide in Buckeye probably would not have succeeded in any case. The Buckeye Home Improvement Organization of two thousand member families was to stimulate investment in the Buckeye area. In 1964, its name was modified to the Buckeye Neighborhood Nationalities Civic Association, and it began cooperating with other civic and social organizations to preserve the ethnic profile of the neighborhood: "All of us are interested in a better future for the Buckeye Community. As a civic group, our purpose is to explore various methods of achieving this goal. Your officers have started a study of this matter and have made several contacts. The Buckeye Community was, prior to 1913, the city of Newburg; at that time it voted to join the City of Cleveland. It appears, at this time, that a better future for the community would be assured if our community were to detach from the city and join one of the adjacent suburbs or become independent."[4] The organization operated traditionally on the volunteered talents and efforts of its leaders and members, American-born ethnic Hungarians and Slovaks. It succeeded only in mitigating some of the effects of the sweeping changes that continued to take place.

As the Hungarian-American fraternal organizations were not significantly bolstered by any of the émigrés or refugees, they tried to increase their membership by merging with other associations. At the beginning of 1952, the Verhovay Association persuaded the Rákóczi Association to merge with it. The circumstances at the time were favorable for unification, as the economic boom had widened opportunities for investment and increased the significance of the insurance business through the role of the second generation. Targeting a wider American market and finding the names Verhovay and Rákóczi an obstacle to their business activities, in 1955 they became the William Penn Fraternal Association in honor of the English Quaker who founded Pennsylvania, where the Verhovay Association originally was established.[5] The decisive step in the modification of identity was made visible when the united organization was given an English American name. The second generation wanted to free itself from the Hungarian cultural symbols and Hungarian historical names. These changes shook the sentiments of the older members of the organization, who had never thought of giving up the Hungarian name. The delegates to the

Rákóczi Fraternal Organization's 1930 convention had even put in their by-laws that the name Rákóczi could not ever be changed.

In the 1960s, leaders of all the fraternal associations were working out a new modernization program modeled on the insurance policies and administrative methods of the commercial insurance companies. In order to win the wider American (not only Hungarian-American) market, they now employed professional agents and made the house-to-house collecting of membership fees, and thereby the Hungarian organizers, redundant. They also reduced financial support for fraternal, social, or cultural events. The William Penn Fraternal Association continued to put out the formerly bilingual publication *William Penn,* but from 1963 on it was written entirely in English. All these changes led to the weakening of personal and communal contacts. The lively social activity of the members in the local branches of the organization in many cases diminished, and in other cases discontinued entirely.[6]

The membership and character of the Hungarian-American associations underwent many changes during this period. At the 1971 general meeting, the adjective "fraternal" was removed from the name of the William Penn Association. As a result of its transformation, by the 1980s the William Penn Association had become one of the most significant organizations of its kind in Pennsylvania. Yet the number of new members could not make up for the reduction in its membership due to death. The growth of its assets was dependent on attractive investment conditions.

The Hungarian Reformed Federation of America was best able to keep its Hungarian character by replenishing its membership with postwar immigrants. Their leaders, educated Calvinist clergymen with strong Hungarian consciousness, could make contact easier with those arriving after World War II. Some of those later arrivals even got into the central leading body of the organization.[7]

The American Sick Benefit and Life Insurance Association in Bridgeport, commonly called the Bridgeport Association, was merged with—or more accurately purchased by—a commercial company in the early 1960s. Litigating for many years, the William Penn Association could only acquire this insurance company in 1971, considerably reduced in members and in capital. The fraternal associations of the workers' movements disappeared during the Cold War. The reformist Workingmen's Sick Relief Association merged into the Verhovay Association in 1947. The downward trend in the leftist movements and repression during the Cold War crushed the Communist-controlled International Workers Order in 1950.[8]

Since the 1960s, the use of the Hungarian language had ceased in the majority of Roman Catholic churches. The official position was that the congregations should retain their ethnicity only to the extent that parishioners actively demanded it. The majority of the Catholic leaders emphasized assimilation and losing ethnic identity.[9] Thus in the second half of the 1960s, none of the old Hungarian-language schools still survived in Cleveland. Hungarian education had collapsed completely with the suburban exodus and demographic changes in the Hungarian-American community. Even in the Protestant church communities, which were more persistent in the use of ethnic symbols and the Hungarian language, bilingualism fell quite into the background.

> The bilingual life of four generations in all our congregations created a new situation which was entirely new and most unique. The first and last of the four generations speaking only Hungarian, the second generation speaking English with some broken Hungarian, the third generation speaking exclusively English. What made it yet worse: the opinions and emotions of these four generations, with their differentiated political and historical backgrounds, were as far from each other as east is from west. The members of the clergy as well as the elected lay-representatives coming to our administrative sessions represented all four generations and they themselves came from all the four. We arrived at a time when presiding over legislative, jurisdictional and administrative meetings became the delicate undertaking in our history. Governing the Synod, indeed, needed not only patience and wisdom, but also endurance and art![10]
>
> On the field of our endeavors regarding the total union of all Hungarian Reformed Churches in America, we had arrived at the decisive years of our history. At that time in these United States of America there were already as many as 127 Hungarian (Calvinist) Reformed Churches: 52 in the Evangelical and Reformed Church, 28 in the Presbyterian Church in the United States, 25 in the Free Magyar Reformed Church in America, 3 in the Dutch Reformed Church, others were completely independent.[11]

The 1960s saw the disappearance of such old Hungarian newspapers as *Munkás, Bérmunkás, Magyar Bányászok Lapja,* and others. Even *Szabadság* and *Amerikai Magyar Népszava,* which had had such wide circulation during the war, fell back to a weekly appearance.

After the first easing of the Cold War, however, relations with the old country started to revive. The Hungarian government opened the door in 1963, when it arranged legal relations with the 56-ers. From this time on, the emigrant generation started to visit the old country in ever larger numbers. These visitors were mostly from the group of the 56-ers, but also included the majority of the surviving members of the "old Americans," the *amerikások.* Such was unequivocally true according to my informant for my microanalysis on those who emigrated from Szamosszeg.

On arrival the emigrants were amazed to find that their relatives in Hungary were leading a much better life than was to be expected from the many letters complaining about the circumstances at home. The flow of parcels from overseas, therefore, came to a stop. On the other hand, they invited the relatives from the village to visit them in the United States, to stay with them for about six months, and earn enough money to enable them to make repairs on their homes, erect new fences, and so forth. Dollars were very valuable in those days; one could buy a thousand forints for eighteen dollars.[12]

By 1970, the core of the Szamosszegeans in New Brunswick had changed. It consisted of the earliest members of the second generation, those who had been born in America, grown up in the old country, and returned to the United States in the 1930s, and those who arrived to the United States as part of the movement to unify families after World War II. Competition for prestige is inseparable from community life. Because holding office in the church meant social prestige, since the 1910s there had always been a few Szamosszegeans serving as presbyters in the Hungarian Calvinist Churches in New Brunswick.[13] Those most active in the local ethnic communities accepted office in the churches and fraternal organizations. Having gained a successful foothold financially, they did not as yet have recognition from society.

Microanalyses confirm the marriage pattern of the second and the third generations: the accelerated ethnic and religious mixing. Although the early second generation married Hungarians, only one married a descendant of Szamosszegeans. The grandchildren of the emigrants, without exception, married someone who had no Hungarian background. Those who married non-Hungarians would also not necessarily choose someone of the same religious denomination. If any tendency appears in their marriages it is that they often married children of Central or South European immigrants—Poles, Italians, and Slovaks—although the third generation married into almost every national group.[14] Thus, the grandchildren of pure Magyar Protestant Calvinist immigrants from Szamosszeg married diverse ethnic and religious groups: Polish and Slovak, Catholic and Jewish, as well as, increasingly, Indian and Vietnamese.[15]

Generally members of the third generation chose to belong to American congregations. Those who lived in New Brunswick occasionally attended the Hungarian Church, but only for family-related reasons such as christenings, weddings, or funerals. Most of them did not keep up contact with relatives in the village and only a few visited them.

By the 1970s, attitudes toward education were very different from those of the pioneer generation. Education took on a primary importance, with emphasis placed on it rather than only on the acquisition of wealth, and this is also the trend of behavior of the Szamosszegeans. The grandchildren of Mrs. Bodó, the boarding-house mistress in West Virginia, are college graduates, and this example is not unusual. Most of the grandchildren of Szamosszegean immigrants reached at least high school or university, and left the social strata of the blue-collar workers.[16]

Some among the Szamosszegeans who kept track of the way of life of their companions from the village kept shaping their descendants' fate. An elderly woman in New Brunswick, brought to the United States by her parents as a teenager in the 1920s, is still trying to radiate the norms of community homogeneity. A man from the village put it this way: "I must go to a burial of a Szamosszegean while Aunt Piroska is alive, as she is calling me to account if I don't go. She stated, as long as one of us is alive, he must not stay away from a burial of a Szamosszegean."[17] Thus, one sole event survived for the longest time which brought people from the village together in New Brunswick, and that was the death of someone who came from the village. The ceremony of "a burial, yet in alien grounds" evoked the feeling of togetherness in those who in their everyday life had lost touch with each other. Friends are, however, not chosen from their circle anymore, as their interest in their cultural heritage fades.

With the passing of the first generation, however, the anchor of Hungarian-American culture no longer held. The efforts of subsequent generations to preserve their ethnicity were restricted to going to their own churches and occasionally visiting ethnic institutions, to enjoy Hungarian cuisine and attend attractive ethnic social events, for example, the annual "Magyar Day." At most, some traveled to Hungary in search of the birthplace of their parents or grandparents.

Many Hungarian-American churches were closed by the 1970s, and only some of the children of earlier members, the few who remained in Cleveland, attended. On the East Side, St. Elizabeth Church is protected due to its historical value.[18] The "workers' homes" ceased to exist; in most places the "Magyar Houses" did, too. The surviving immigrants and some of their descendants, likewise the members of the William Penn Association and Hungarian Reformed Federation of America, diminished markedly, too. In some other places, however—for example at New Brunswick and New York—Magyar Clubs still existed whose membership received replacements from the workers' groups of the postwar immigrants.[19]

When immigrants arriving in Cleveland in the years following World War II had observed the disintegration of the Hungarian-American communities and the decline of their cultural heritage, they attributed the estranged behavior of the American-born generation to the uncivilized ways of the peasant immigrants. The associations of the nationalist group of postwar immigrants tried to do everything to encourage the use and preservation of the Hungarian language and the appreciation of Hungarian culture by the younger generation. They developed cultural programs to involve the young people in Hungarian social life, primarily in the 1960s, before their hopes for a return to Hungary finally began to fade. But with time, they too were not exempted from those problems brought about by the second generation's search for its identity. Occasionally, part of forming a value system of their own was the rejection of their parents', or at least stressing their being separate from it. Americanization of the younger generation of the DPs had considerably narrowed the possibilities of passing on the Hungarian cultural heritage.

In the 1970s, though, under the influence of a more general American ethnic renaissance, all the different groups of Hungarian Americans became more interested in their Hungarian heritage. As a part of this movement, the leaders of the William Penn Association began devoting more attention to Hungarian ethnic and fraternal activities. Because of the increasing interest of its members in the old homeland, for instance, the association started to organize regular group tours to Hungary and watched for other opportunities to harmonize business and social activities. As that renaissance developed, it often took the form of multiethnic, multicultural festivals in cities, towns, and surrounding communities with the active support and participation of the leaders of the Hungarian-American fraternal organizations.

The Committee for Hungarian Books and Education and the American Hungarian Foundation had rebuilt a Hungarian-language teaching and school system in Cleveland by the beginning of the 1970s. In addition, they had organized a Hungarian studies program and a cultural history course, taught in Hungarian, at Case Western Reserve University. In Cleveland, the Hungarians were the first ethnic group to launch language courses both within the public school system and at the college level. Their aims were to teach the history of Hungarian culture and to improve the Hungarian-language skills of those who had a good passive vocabulary.[20] The public school programs were followed by Hungarian-language schools on the West Side, within the framework of the Hungarian Scout Association and with the support of the American Hungarian Singing Society. Summer schools also were reestablished in Buckeye with the support of the William Penn Association.

A cult of ethnicity and of bilingualism is an elitist, not a popular, movement and "romantic ethnicity," as a sociologist called it, is also political. The same is true in relation to the Hungarian ethnic community. The end of the Cold War and of the ethnic renaissance moved in particular the small circle of intellectuals from the 56-er and 45-er groups to safeguard the Hungarian cultural heritage: "A heritage that gives into our identity, no matter where we are. Those spiritual values which tend to make us better Hungarians, better Americans and better human beings."[21]

In the 1960s, with signs of the unfolding of ethnic renaissance the narrow intellectual elite judged the possibility of progress of the Hungarian culture and language encouraging, relying not so much on broad empirical facts as rather on the interpretation of M. Hansen's statement regarding the third generation. Beginning in the middle of the 1960s, they started to propagate the teaching of the Hungarian language, arguing that bilingualism would play a personality-enriching role. The future of the Hungarian language and culture was one of the main subjects of the Sixth Hungarian Congress in Cleveland in 1967. In his lecture entitled "Is there a future for the Hungarian language and culture in America?" August Molnár, the director of the American Hungarian Foundation, tried to focus attention on the long history of this theme and on the value of the work of previous generations. He emphasized: "We cannot set the goal for ourselves to raise 'Hungarians' here in America. Our aim can only be to preserve the priceless Hungarian values for mankind and to make the people of the world acquainted with them. The Hungarian-born American citizen—as the bearer of a range of emotions of two mentalities, of bilinguality and of characteristic peculiarities—can be a live bridge, serve as a connecting link, gain esteem for and bear witness to the Hungarian values and to what we are and who we were. The role of being a live bridge is the vocation of the bilingual citizen."[22]

A Hungarian-language weekend school was opened, sponsored by the Alumni Association at Rutgers in New Brunswick. It is this school which launched the idea and the program of the so-called mother-tongue movement, pointing out that it is the teaching of the Hungarian tongue in the diaspora which is the condition of success in establishing direct links with the culture and the intellectuals of the homeland. Their example was followed by other Hungarian organizations, too; an upward trend in the teaching of the Hungarian language was perceivable. The cultural studies programs lasted less than a decade, however. The concentration of the Hungarian population around any institution was so low that it was no longer feasible to organize courses for it.

One of the most enduring and still active community of the 56-er Hungarian students, the Bessenyei György Circle of the Hungarian Alumni Association (Rutgers University), found refuge in the United States.[23] This and the Hungarian-friendly community launched a periodical, *Itt-Ott* (Here and There),[24] and organized yearly meetings in Lake Hope, Ohio, to discuss in a democratic spirit, at an open forum, the historical, political, social, and economic subjects which concerned the Hungarians collectively, both inside or outside Hungary.[25] They invited the better-known figures of the representatives of both the Hungarians who lived in the West, and the intelligentsia at home, in Hungary. Their lectures, free debates, and recitals aimed at fostering Hungarian consciousness. They consciously professed cultural pluralism, they emphasized, for example that knowing two or more languages, being at home in two cultures, would bring a richer self-realization and, at the same time, better understanding among people. For the sake of survival, they included in their program the task of attaining the consciousness of being Hungarian and the decision to throw in their lot with the Hungarian people. This program demanded that they keep in contact with both Hungarians in the old country and those who were dispersed in the whole world, and this communication began an intensive period. The quickening of the information flow from the 1970s, on the other hand, also enlivened those political and ideological influences which had played a part in the change of the system in Hungary .

There was considerable difference in the second generation's knowledge of the Magyar language according to the different immigration waves. In the 1970s, most sons and daughters of the pioneer generation could still speak the mother tongue, even though their reading and writing ability was much more shaky. The following statement on the usage of language made by the person interviewed can be generalized regarding the second generation. "The only time I can honestly say I use the Hungarian language is when I am over here in my mom's house. and talking to my mommy. Now with my brother, he speaks Hungarian but I speak English."[26] The children of the 45-ers managed to retain a Hungarian consciousness, evidently the beneficial effect of Sunday language schools, boy scout activities, Hungarian centers, and dancing ensembles, not to mention the influence of the parental home.

Still, as an observer from Hungary, I could see clearly that beginning in 1972, the conscious acceptance of Hungarian identity was most prevalent among children of the Hungarian wave of immigrants. The American-born generations, and mostly those who immigrated as children with their parents, were the most well read in high Hungarian language and culture, and they were the ones who showed a genuine interest in Hungary.[27]

The situation was different regarding the usage of the Hungarian language among the 56-ers. Though there were some among them who concentrated on preserving and cultivating the Hungarian language, culture, and national and historical identity and on passing it on to subsequent generations, the 56-er refugees' apparent indifference regarding the education of their children about their Hungarian heritage was particularly shocking to the members of the nationalist group of 45-ers.

At the beginning of the 1980s, a symposium held on the questions of the usage of the Hungarian language did not judge the situation optimistically. Only about 10 to 20 percent of émigré Hungarians were really determined to bring about bilingualism, consciously maintaining the use of the mother tongue and successfully teaching their children the Hungarian language. These parents are almost invariably both of Hungarian origin.[28] Parents of mixed marriages find themselves at a great disadvantage, at least from the Hungarian point of view, if the mother, who is the first teacher of the mother tongue, is non-Hungarian. Generally, in mixed marriages the teaching of Hungarian tends to be postponed until the age of ten or twelve or even later; it is certainly not taught from infancy. The roles of parents, grandparents, relatives, and friends is even more critically important in such mixed marriages than in fully Hungarian families. On the other hand, very little can be done if the language of the home is not Hungarian, as unfortunately often is the case when one marriage partner is non-Hungarian, and this is quite common among the 56-ers.

The United States censuses contain little information on the relatively small group of Hungarian immigrants, who were generally registered under the label "others." The 1970 census was the first to collect information and provide a basis for statistics on the Hungarian immigrants, their social classes, employment, professions, and educational and income levels.

By the 1970s, the Hungarian immigrants' remarkable characteristics came to light: the highest ratio of professional, technical, and kindred workers (every fourth working male) was found among them, compared to Czechoslovakia, Yugoslavia, Poland, and the total immigrant population in the United States. On the other hand, it was in their circle that the ratio of blue-collar workers (including farmworkers) was the lowest. The statistics derived from the 1970 census, which support this appraisal of the Hungarian immigrants, show not only individual achievements in science and the arts considered worthy of mention, but also that the Hungarian immigrants as a group were much better educated than the average American. The 1970 census and information given by immigrants at the time of arrival makes it possible to compare their diversity of occupations by immigration period.

Data on the occupational distribution of the immigrant generation according to the period of their arrival in the United States show that the majority of

TABLE 6.

Occupational Distribution of Immigrants to the United States from Hungary, Compared with All Immigrants and Those from Neighboring Countries (percentages)[29]

Male, 16 years old or over	From Hungary	From all countries	From Czechoslo-vakia	From Yugoslavia	From Poland
Total number	49,638	2,536,802	35,589	45,232	133,006
Professional, technical, and kindred workers	22.2	16.9	19.7	13.3	12.3
Managers, administrators, and kindred workers	10.5	10.3	11.2	6.4	12.6
Sales workers	5.2	5.9	6.0	2.1	8.9
Clerical and kindred workers	4.6	6.5	5.1	3.0	5.4
Craftsmen and kindred workers	27.2	21.3	24.2	30.6	23.8
Operatives except transport	15.0	14.7	15.9	22.4	21.6
Transport equipment operators	2.3	3.1	2.8	2.1	2.4
Laborers except farm laborers	3.4	6.0	3.8	6.0	3.5
Farmers and farm managers	0.3	0.9	2.3	0.9	0.6
Farm laborers and farm foremen	0.4	2.3	0.3	0.1	0.3
Service workers, except in private households	8.8	11.9	8.7	13.1	8.2
Private household workers	0.1	0.2	—	—	0.4

those declaring highly qualified occupations arrived in the decade after World War II, for example, 64 percent of the professionals and 56 percent of the managers and administrators. These percentages reflect the most important changes of this last hundred years: in Hungarian immigration the first great masses of unskilled laborers of peasant background were followed by skilled, well-educated, cultured immigrants. Therefore, the Central and East European countries provided the United States not only with masses of unskilled workers but also with masses of highly educated, creative individuals.

By the census of 1970, the majority of first-generation Hungarians were those who had immigrated after World War II, although they were only a minority among Hungarian-Americans if the American-born children and grandchildren of the earlier immigrants were included. The same was true in the 1970s in Cleveland, where the Hungarian-American population was estimated at approximately 80,000, of whom post–World War II immigrants and their children represented approximately 15,000–20,000.[30]

The long historical process and the tremendous changes Hungarian Americans went through, both socially and culturally, were embodied in the changes

TABLE 7.

Social Structure of Immigrants (16 Years Old and Over) Born in Hungary and Migrating to the United States (percentages)[31]

Occupation	Total	Before 1925	1925–1934	1935–1944	1955–1959	1960–1970	Not re-ported
Male employed	100	19.5	5.0	3.7	18.5	39.	—
Professional techni-cal, and kindred workers	100	9.5	3.1	6.4	24.2	40.0	—
Managers, adminis-trators, except farm	100	20.4	7.6	5.4	21.0	35.0	—
Sales workers	100	30.2	8.8	7.8	18.2	20.0	—
Clerical and kindred workers	100	28.8	2.8	2.8	18.0	11.3	—
Craftsmen and kin-dred workers	100	18.5	5.0	2.2	15.6	13.5	0.5
Operatives except transport	100	21.0	5.6	1.6	15.5	13.1	0.9
Transport equipment operatives	100	20.9	7.9	—	22.2	5.0	2.0
Laborers except farm	100	17.6	6.2	2.4	17.2	8.5	2.3
Farmers and farm managers	100	56.2	—	—	27.5	16.3	—
Farm laborers and farm foremen	100	22.1	—	—	12.1	29.3	—
Service workers	100	32.1	3.9	2.5	14.9	11.0	1.0
Private household workers	100	—	42.1	—	57.9	—	—
Female employed	100	23.3	3.7	4.1	19.7	14.0	1.3
Professional, techni-cal, and kindred workers	100	9.1	—	5.2	28.5	19.1	1.7
Managers and administrators	100	27.2	3.4	6.2	28.2	7.1	2.3
Sales workers	100	43.2	7.1	5.0	11.6	9.7	—
Clerical and kindred workers	100	25.3	1.8	4.0	18.3	13.0	1.4
Craftsmen and kindred workers	100	8.5	9.5	2.4	21.0	10.5	—
Operatives except transport	100	17.7	5.3	3.2	16.5	15.0	1.4
Transport equipment operatives	100	100.0	—	—	—	—	—

TABLE 7. *(Continued)*

Social Structure of Immigrants (16 Years Old and Over) Born in Hungary and Migrating to the United States

Occupation	Total	Before 1925	1925–1934	1935–1944	1955–1959	1960–1970	Not re-ported
Female employed							
Laborers except farm	100	14.6	—	—	23.6	24.9	—
Farmers and farm managers	100	31.7	38.3	—	—	30.0	—
Farm laborers and farm foremen	100	100.0	—	—	—	—	—
Service workers	100	25.0	4.3	4.3	20.7	13.2	1.2
Private household workers	100	40.9	3.9	2.9	19.0	13.7	2.1

in their identity and the innovations in their ethnic symbols. By the 1960s, the peasants of the mass migration, those capable of preserving village crafts and folk culture, were greatly reduced in number. For them, Hungary was the subject of sentimental memories and feelings, their mother country, where they were born and had spent their childhood. They remembered the historical Hungary as a world dominated by Hungarians and never could come to terms with the Treaty of Trianon. They remained suspicious and critical of the aristocrats, masters who rallied around that issue. The "old-timer" Magyar Americans, mostly with peasant background, heard with joy the news of the extinction of the Hungarian gentry and the agrarian reform.[31]

Although the post–World War II Hungarians were also sharply divided by ideology, social background, and culture, their common features were a committed anti-Communism and membership in the middle and upper classes. On the other hand, those showing the greatest social diversity were the immigrants of 1956, the welcomed and celebrated "Freedom Fighters." The social support they enjoyed created outstandingly favorable conditions for their integration. At the same time, their memories of wartime and postwar Hungary and their experiences under the Communist regime prevented them from being paralyzed by homesickness or nostalgia.

Churches and fraternal organizations tried to remove the social barriers separating the individual strata of Hungarian immigrants, but with little practical result.[32] Divisions between the groups continue to the present day, passed on from one generation to the next. Nevertheless, the groups did have a common interest in some areas of Hungarian culture, and a wish that Hungary be freed from the Russian yoke, which happened in the 1989. Thereby they were showing a collective self-image as Hungarians, despite its various individual manifestations.

During the years of the general ethnic renaissance in the United States, few Hungarian Americans had completely rejected their Hungarian identity. True, the Hungarian community had become more diffused geographically in comparison with just a few decades before, but local communities had been replaced by cultural, economic, or religious subgroupings. By the 1970s, Hungarian-American ethnicity was very diverse and stratified, and the extent of identity ranged from a complete lack to full awareness. Those conscious of their Hungarian identity, moreover, could belong to any church or income group and could have any degree of culture and education.

The Hungarian-American lifestyle has not vanished completely but has changed fundamentally. As the concept of being Hungarian itself thus underwent fundamental changes during recent decades, the ability to speak Hungarian ceased to be a reliable indicator of the intensity of Hungarian identity. Ethnic meeting places have lost their role, as people now listen to Hungarian radio broadcasts and Hungarian music in their own homes. Individuals do not participate in Hungarian community events; rather, they learn about Hungary at school and university.[33] Nevertheless, these same individuals relate to particular aspects of their Hungarian cultural heritage and take a stand on Hungarian issues much more consciously than the peasant Hungarian Americans of the immigrant generation ever did.

These are promising exceptions, however, which cannot counterbalance the waning of the Hungarian identity in the United States.

SUMMARY AND CONCLUSION

The Migration Pattern

DURING THE FIVE decades preceding World War I, multidirectional labor migration swept through Central and Eastern Europe in the wake of accelerated urbanization and industrialization. The region's progressive incorporation into the Western-centered capitalist system brought to Hungary the demographic, economic, and social changes that from the 1880s on created a mass of potential emigrants. Hungary's transition from feudalism to capitalism was protracted, incomplete, and fraught with contradictions. Without rearrangement of the old sociopolitical order, land reform provided millions of peasants with neither sufficient land nor the means to acquire it. The results included the unrealistic subdivision of land into smaller and smaller parcels, an endless spiral of debt, and creation of a huge agrarian proletariat.

Shortly after serfdom was abolished, the building of railroads eastward across Europe produced a boom time of new jobs and high wages. Soon trains brought in both a whole new array of manufactured goods to be desired and, at the same time, shipments of mass-produced articles that began to capture the market for the pots and pans, baskets, brooms, and textiles which peasant farmer families previously had made to supplement their incomes. Similar in time and impact to the railroads was a series of canal construction and flood control projects that also created a brief demand for wage labor and more lasting changes in land use patterns.

Moreover, these same innovations in transportation not only created a need for migration, but also provided the opportunity for it to occur. Hungary's industrialization was so narrowly based that its own industrial sector could not possibly absorb its surplus agrarian population, especially given the extreme inequalities of Hungary's system of land tenure. Necessarily, the opportunities were located overseas. Merchants, craftsmen, village artisans, and storekeepers were the pioneers. When the agrarian population joined them, the large-scale movement became what is known as peasant migration. The migrants' social composition can be distinguished among the stages of the process, with merchants and artisans coming first, and miners, cottagers, and agricultural workers following them. Although relatively few of the educated upper classes participated in the "Great Migration" overseas, the immigrants' socioeconomic backgrounds were more diversified than contemporary and later historians have suggested. The outbreak of the war, however, cut off Hungarian emigration in full swing. By the time the turbulence of the war, of the postwar revolutions, and of the redrawing of Hungary's boundaries had subsided, domestic factors had led the United States to close its gates to the "undesirable" peoples of Central and Eastern Europe, Hungarians among them.

Overseas emigration cannot be studied without giving due attention to remigration. Although the strong conservatism of Hungarian peasants has to be taken into account, it does not explain adequately why return migration from the United States was a mass phenomenon from the 1880s to the beginning of World War I. To understand this, one has to realize that migration was a temporary emergency solution to a problem at home. Hungarian society resisted permanent emigration for years; it was morally justifiable only in extreme circumstances. Migrants were hoping only for better chances of making money overseas; their ultimate goal was to save and return to the place of their birth with their savings. It was only after several trips back and forth across the Atlantic, and the realization that migration could be an end as well as a means, that a number of Hungarians began to entertain the idea of becoming permanent residents of the United States. Remigration from this view was for many the normal, expected behavior. What has to be explained by scholars studying this phenomenon is not the decision to return, but the decision to remain overseas.

Those who returned to Hungary did so after an average of three to five years in the United States; relatively few migrants returned after a stay of ten or more years. The savings of the returnees bore fruit in new houses built, debts paid off, and land bought, but the peasantry as a whole cannot be said to have advanced socioeconomically through migration because most of the lands the remigrants bought were not parts of big estates but had been peasant holdings in the past, too.

Migration overseas was intensive in some parts of Hungary and almost nonexistent in others. The emigration regions shared some important features, the most salient being that they fell outside the pull of the major industrial center, Budapest. Nevertheless, these features do not entirely explain the increased readiness to migrate. Instead, the objective factors making for emigration in those regions became operative through extra-economic, subjective factors. Most migrants were from non-self-sufficient regions where nature was less benign and the population had been accustomed to using itinerant labor—usually short- and middle-distance harvest migration—simply to survive for generations before railway networks and relatively cheap steamship fares made long-distance, transoceanic movement feasible.

The empiric proof of our microanalysis unequivocally points to the role of the family in "chain-migration." Migrating family members were the models for emigration; newcomers went to relatives or friends, who introduced them to the neighborhood, to the social network, the church, and frequently to jobs. Regional studies demonstrate a poor fit between the international patterns and what appears to be happening at the local level. The results question seriously the relevance of weighted national statistics in accessing migrational motivation.

The concept of chain-migration is better suited to explain the migration process on local levels than the "push-pull" model based only on economic rationality, in which migrants responded mechanically to labor markets. There is evidence that the migration process was not only based on kinship, but on age cohort as well. Chain-migration rather is described in terms of networks based on information, mutual help, and emotional and material resources which provided guidance and sustenance to the voyagers. Such networks mediated by letters of former migrants sent from America, and prepaid tickets, determined timing and destination, assured lodgings and jobs, and ensured social integration into ethnic community. "Migration tradition" is used to suggest that decisions were based on an accretion of knowledge, experience, and social bonds which in effect created bridges between two places thousands of miles apart. The flow of people and information back and forth across the Atlantic Ocean both lured and influenced the adjustment process.

The multinational character of the overseas migrants from the population of Hungary had specific demographic and political consequences. Generally, the geographic mobility initiated by industrialization led to considerable population shifting in all the countries concerned. In multinational Hungary, however, the most mobile groups, with respect to emigration and internal migration alike, were the non-Magyars, particularly the Slovaks, who lived in parts of the country which could not provide a living for them. They were the first to migrate, and the result was a shifting of the ethnic balance in favor of the Magyars. Hungary's minority nationalities lost not only those who sailed overseas and stayed there, but also those who left agriculture to work in industry and settled in cities such as Budapest that were predominantly Magyar with strong forces of assimilation. Therefore, while the Magyars might have lost people through emigration, this loss was compensated by the assimilation of other ethnics that resulted from internal migration. (The impact of this exchange on the population statistics may well be relevant to the research of historians of emigration in other multinational countries, too.)

There was, however, a great deal of contemporary concern about the multinational nature of the Hungarian emigration movement. Magyars spoke of the loss of the "Magyar" population, and the Magyar press was full of jeremiads based on the blatantly unrealistic assumption that the emigrants abroad would have been employed full-time in Hungary. The leaders of national minorities claimed that the problem of emigration was caused by their being oppressed. Another source of alarm, especially for the ruling elite, was the change in the attitude and behavior of those who had had a whiff of New World air.

The effect of remigration on the societies of origin can be seen in their local environment. Changes were visible mostly in their more conscious attitude, the awakening of national feelings, particularly in the Slovaks. Still the old milieu proved to be the stronger influence on the remigrants, who soon adapted to it after resettling permanently.

Although some interest groups claimed the government's anti-national liberalism was allowing the nation to hemorrhage, the Hungarian government initially was not averse to seeing the non-Magyar emigrants go, despite protests from the landowners about the flight of their cheap manpower. Adding to the confusion over migration policy was a lack of statistical data on just how much money was involved. Whatever the sums sent and brought home, they were enough to make a visible improvement in living standards within the emigration regions and thus to add to official ambivalence about curtailing migration.

While emigration from Hungary greatly declined in the 1920s, it did not totally cease. Among the small groups reaching American shores in the early 1920s were comparatively more politically and socially active individuals than had been realized previously. They were the refugees of two unsuccessful revolutions, the "1918-ers" and those from 1919, as well as some of the Hungarians who had become ethnic minorities of other countries owing to the redrawn international borders of the Trianon Peace Treaty, which handed out two-thirds of the old Hungarian kingdom's territory to the so-called successor states, Czechoslovakia, Romania, and Yugoslavia. At this time, the majority of the emigrants were those children who joined the head of the family who had decided on permanent settlement and was awaiting them in America. These immigrants of the 1920s represented a source of new blood primarily for the Hungarian-built churches and the press, which were in the midst of controversies and clashes over ethnic values and inventions.

"Magyar America," especially in its formative period, from the 1880s to the beginning of the 1920s, was comprised of industrial workers' settlements scattered over a large area near steel factories and mines. It was shaped by the dynamic economic development of the United States, by the changing demands of the industrial pool, by the migrants' intentions, and by the difficulties they had in adapting. Centers of settlement developed, but even as mass migration continued, it produced no ethnically homogeneous large colonies such as the earlier immigrants from Western Europe had formed. As sojourners, Hungarian migrants made little effort to put down roots in the United States. Rather, they moved from city to city, especially the single persons, searching for the best-paid jobs for unskilled labor, which is also reflected in the large-scale fluctuation of their settlements.

These communities growing in Hungarian neighborhoods were not simply old communities transplanted into a new geographical setting. They were newly organized communities, whose supporting pillars most often were the shared language and common homeland of the residents, than their ties to a particular village or region.

Although the migrants from Hungary were all regarded in the host society as Hungarians, the pioneers were Hungarian-speaking Jews, Slovaks, or Germans from Hungary. Though some political emigrants from the Revolution of 1848 can still be identified in Cleveland and New York as economic migrants, the network of chain-migration for the overwhelming majority of ethnic Hungarians, the Magyars, who arrived in America came into being during the first fourteen years of the twentieth century.

Bourgeoisie, intelligentsia, aristocrats, and craftsmen were seldom found among the agricultural masses, but were found more often in the circles of the Magyars than among the other nationalities migrating from Hungary. One of the most striking cultural characteristics of the Magyar-speaking Hungarians was their manifold division into religious denominations. Besides the Roman Catholic majority, there were sizable groups of Reformed Protestants, Jews, and Greek Catholics and smaller numbers of Lutherans, Baptists, Unitarians, and Seventh Day Adventists. By the early years of the twentieth century, all these denominations had developed their own community institutions with very dissimilar memberships. This diversity of the Hungarian community in America, which existed from its beginning, made the Hungarian migrants socially and culturally more stratified than any other new immigrant groups that the host society recognized.

Among the Hungarian-American elite—clergymen, journalists, other professionals, small businessmen, and entrepreneurs—can be found members of the gentry who had lost their social positions in Hungary, and also Magyar-speaking Jews, Germans, Slovaks, and others, as well as laborers. As this fairly heterogeneous elite began to take shape, it popularized among the migrants an ideology of Magyar identity that reflected its members' own strong emotional ties to the Hungarian Bourgeois Revolution and the War of Independence of 1848/49. All factions of this elite place the Revolution, the cult of its leaders, and the red, white, and green Hungarian flag at the center of Hungarian identity. As early as the 1880s, the revolutionary leader Lajos Kossuth, who had toured the United States as a hero of democracy in the 1850s, was revered as the most prominent historical personality and symbol by the small Hungarian group in Cleveland, for example—for one hundred years, the Kossuth cult was and remained the symbol of Hungarian ethnic consciousness.

In the founding of Hungarian community institutions in the last two decades of the nineteenth century Hungarian-Jewish tradesmen and artisans played a large role. They had begun their migration to America earlier than the Christian Hungarians and came for the most part for permanent settlement. They generally knew some languages on arrival, having spoken Hungarian, German, Yiddish, and Slovak in Hungary. They soon learned English and assumed the "middleman" role between the Christian Hungarians and the host society.

The intelligentsia, businessmen, village and city tradesmen, and artisans who made up the new Hungarian-American elite began to establish the Hungarians' first associations, churches, and newspapers in the United States. The culture in these institutions was characterized by the continuation of traditions and values brought over from their original environment, but was modified immediately. The culture of the Hungarian migrants, too, was neither entirely extinguished nor entirely unchanged. They quickly recognized the church, for example, as a pivotal component of ethnic existence and American public life, and they made their congregations not only ecclesiastical and religious but also social organizations responsible for all the ethnic, national, and traditional historical commemorations of the community. Preparations for these, in turn, played an important role in the establishment of an internal order in the community and to a large extent strengthened the consciousness of interdependence that supported Magyar-American ethnic identity. As a result, religion and the community system of activity now connected with it formed the nucleus of everyday life, of the ideology of the community. Outwardly, religion became the visual expression of the Hungarian-American community's life, while inwardly, it provided a necessary social forum for its every member, one of the very integral vital stages of social activity.

From first to last, the independent, non-religiously affiliated fraternal organizations had a large role in Magyar circles, larger than in those of the other non-Magyar nationalities such as the Slovaks. The activities of these organizations and their leaders reveal emphatically that the ideas and ritualistic beliefs giving meaning and continuity to the communities' social lives were derived from the culture and traditions of the European artisans, as well as from the European peasantry.

The bearers of the fraternal association concept among the Hungarian immigrants were the tradesmen and the skilled workers. Either directly or indirectly through personal connections, they guided nearly all the fraternal organizations, and it was they whom the agricultural workers imitated in founding their own secular and religious associations. This social group, with its individual artisan culture dating back to the time of the guilds, was a major force in late-nineteenth-century European migration, for its *valcolás* or "waltzers" maintained the tradition of working abroad for further training in skill or craft. Naturally, the agricultural workers attempted to build the traditional values of the agricultural community into their associations, just as it cannot be denied that they took notice and followed other immigrant ethnics' building of fraternal organizations, too.

There were great differences, between the agricultural and nonagricultural migrants in their breadth of vision, experiences, and cultures. Even though the distance between the agricultural workers and the craftsmen in the Old World social hierarchy was blurred in their new environment, it did not disappear. The Hungarian craftsmen living on the West Side of Cleveland, for example, harbored feelings of superiority toward the agricultural workers who settled on the East Side; some looked down on the latter in marked contempt.

In conforming to the host society, the Hungarians encountered advantages and disadvantages as a result of their ethnic, denominational, and sociocultural diversity. Through the mediator or broker role of the socially mobile Hungarian Jews, the Hungarians quickly and more easily became informed about their new surroundings. In addition, most Hungarian Jews with the knowledge of the German language could communicate with groups of other immigrants, learn more about the American workers' movements and the trade unions, and shorten the way to them. Meanwhile Hungarian Protestants established ties between themselves and two older American denominations, the German Americans' Reformed Church and the mainstream Presbyterians.

Nevertheless, the Hungarian migrants' traditions and their cultural variety made formation and integration of their communities particularly complicated. In the early years, the feeling of interdependence was stronger among the multinational groups from Hungary, so they were more favorably disposed to cooperation. Bitter rivalries among the members of the ethnic elite, however, soon led the clergy and journalists to build up the walls between groups. One factor contributing to the discord was the host society's prejudice against all "Hunkies," which the leaders of one group tended to attribute to and blame on another. The resulting desire of each nationality to differentiate itself from the others who came from Hungary was particularly hard on individuals within the minority groups who had begun Magyarization in the homeland. Getting into an identity crisis in their new surroundings, they often bore witness to so-called fluid identity, that is to say that they sometimes owned up to being Hungarian and sometimes to being Slovak under the pressure of the environment.

The Hungarian migrant workers, for the most part, remained in close communication with the families, relatives, and friends they had left behind. Besides the private contacts, from time to time they took part in communal life, too, by organizing collections to renovate their village churches or to alleviate the suffering caused by natural disasters at home. It was primarily the leaders of these migrants who worked to establish institutionalized connections with their original societies. In the period from 1904 to 1914, the Reformed Church of Hungary succeeded in bringing the majority of the Hungarian Calvinist churches in the United States under its direct supervision. At the same time, Tihamér Kohányi, the editor of the newspaper *Szabadság*, using the slogan "For an Independent Hungary!" formed political connections with some leaders of the opposition parties of Hungary, though he and his elite circle were unable to garner much support.

The Hungarian migrant worker's simultaneous ties to his native land and to the host country were brought into question by historical events. Relations between the United States and Hungary were cloudy even before World War I, for Hungary still was considered a "half-feudal country" and an oppressor of its non-Magyar nationalities. Leaders of Hungary's minority nationalities in America exploited this perception and spectacularly increased their efforts during World War I, when the United States and Hungary became actual enemies. In this social environment saturated with prejudices against Hungary and the pressures of Americanization, the community leaders of the Hungarian Americans repeatedly tried to redefine the relationship of the Magyar migrants to their donor and their host societies. The tensions of natural integration and the humiliations of forced assimilation were intensified by their defensive position before their fellow sufferers, the other ethnic groups from Hungary. Under such circumstances, a positive self-definition was virtually impossible, and perhaps the best that could have been hoped for was an ambivalent ethnic identity, a dual loyalty.

The cultural differences between their old and new homes, and the discrimination they encountered in the latter, created a painful situation for the Hungarian elite. The bourgeoisie, whose professions did not tie them to the Hungarian immigrants, endeavored to leave the Hungarian ethnic environment as soon as possible, diminishing the already small number of potential leaders from this social class. In the circle of the new immigrants there was such a unique relationship, which, in particular in the beginnings, brought together Jewish and non-Jewish Hungarians—still, at that time, most of them identified themselves as Hungarian. The connection between Jewish and Christian Hungarians began to loosen after World War I. By this time the Hungarian Jews came into contact with their fellow Jews with mixed background, thus providing for the potential of a cosmopolitan framework for subsequent Jewish life. The negative influence of Hungarian political developments and rising anti-Semitism in Hungary also led them to give higher priority to the Jewish and American aspects of their identity.

Representations of the homeland generally give immigrants the impression of a collective historical continuity that helps them define themselves in a drastically changed sociocultural environment. The essential source of passionate concern for Hungary among them in this period was their driving desire for dignity and status in the United States. The image of the old country was a significant element in the ethnic consciousness of the Hungarian migrants. However, the homeland that served as a foundation for continuity during relocation, and for unity in an unfamiliar setting, soon became a negative symbol that was contrasted with the reality of the new America. In Hungary, the upper social classes, the gentry, and the urban intelligentsia developed a concept of national existence for themselves at the turn of the century. The Hungarian agricultural immigrants considered themselves part of this national "imagined community" only after they left their original society. In America, they took as their own the emblems and metaphors which in Hungary had been those of the cultural ruling class. In Cleveland, the mediators of their transfer or appropriation clearly were members of the declassed gentry, from the lower ranks of the Hungarian intelligentsia. They were the activists for whom passionate nationalism was the most important, if not the only, link with the old-country elite. Although it is a cliché of American ethnic scholarship that the immigrant masses brought only local identities and attachments with them to the United States, in Hungary the evocation of heroic events and the historical past in the schools and in the military had given the immigrants memories that the nationalist elites could evoke and appeal to.

The unfriendly, negative reception the Hungarian immigrants received in the United States influenced both how others defined them and how they defined themselves. Long before it pushed the second generation to reject the Hungarian aspect of their identity, American prejudice against "Hunkies"—and against "Micks," "Wops," and "Polacks," for that matter—combined with a growing indifference to the regional and village loyalties that had originally meant so much to the immigrants, led to focusing ethnic identity on the national level.

Immigrants from diverse backgrounds were thus consolidated under a single grouping, but divided along new lines as conflicts and disagreements broke out over the nature, history, and future of national existence. The role of the congregations, of the fraternal associations, of other informal ethnic organizations, and of the newspapers written in the mother tongue was of great importance historically in the forming of communities, in the preservation of the cultural heritage, in the support of integration, but those immigrating masses cannot be overlooked, either, who did not join them or take part in any of these activities.

The Hungarian-American community was an arena where ideologies, hegemonies, and opposition groups fought for control. Because the ethnic leadership had few possibilities for achieving power, wealth, or status outside the group, they hotly contested the positions within it. As John Higham has observed, all immigrant leaders had to address their own groups in a manner that reflected the position they occupied in American society. In case of Hungarian Americans, leaders had to mobilize a quiet immigrant group slowly and almost indirectly. However, the national tradition, the institutions for transmitting it to the masses, and the elite leadership that the Hungarians enjoyed as advantages in linking their American ethnicity to their national homeland proved in the long run to be grave liabilities.

From Immigrant to Ethnic

With the beginning of the 1920s, the Hungarian immigrants' situation changed considerably, and consequently the character of their communities and the behavior of their members also changed. The decision to remain permanently in the United States placed them in a new context, which itself altered their outlook and attitudes. There emerged a new type of leadership by individuals whose careers directly connected them with the wider American society. They focused the community's attention on the development of a Hungarian-American ethnic consciousness, as they repeatedly reminded the group itself and the broader American society that the Hungarians were already an integral part of American society, unequivocally and exclusively tied to their new home. They did embrace the goal of assimilation and, at the same time, postponed it far into the future.

The local lodges of the Hungarian-American fraternal and cultural societies, congregations, social halls, a profusion of educational efforts, debating clubs, drama circles, and singing societies became prominent in the 1920s. This sort of informal but pervasive education was as important as that provided by the schools through which foreign-born Hungarians successfully attempted "to educate and Americanize themselves." Ethnic culture comes about within a historic process, namely, on the basis of the Americanization of the old country's cultural tradition. Up to the 1940s, ethnic culture characterized the peasant-worker population belonging to the American working class, but the middle strata of the ethnic society was not foreign to it either.

In the communities that showed a homogeneous aspect to the outside world, the competing identities, the changing significance of the definition, and the selective process of ethnic culture were characteristic. At the beginning of the 1920s, however, conflicts continually arose between the traditionalists and the advocates of assimilation. A group of Protestant ministers, for example, openly rebelled against forced assimilation and united in an organization independent of both the American and the Hungarian church authorities. Secular organizations formed in the 1920s specifically served the purpose of political, or rather social separateness, reinforcing the great value members of the immigrant generation already set on their community institutions.

Generational change had a great impact on the course of ethnic identification. The critical period for Hungarian immigrants and their children started in the second half of the 1920s. The conflicts between the first and second generations deepened as it became evident that the majority American-born children of Hungarian immigrants, as soon as they were grown, did not want to belong to but hastened to turn their backs on their parents' ethnic communities.

On the other hand, some were challenging their foreign-born parents for leadership of the ethnic community when they reached adulthood. The younger people wanted to speed up Americanization; their rise touched off disputes over such issues as the use of English in organizational publications and religious worship. They often reacted against the foreignness of their parents with an intensity of identification with American culture painful to the older generation.

In the second half of the 1930s the air became more favorable for ethnic activities, too. For the purpose of binding the second generation to the secular and religious institutions ethnic leaders planned a variety of programs. They moved to establish English-speaking lodges for the second generation within the fraternal organizations. They started to publish English sections for the youth in their magazines, and began to tolerate their children's attraction to much of America. They hoped that the second generation would show more interest in Hungary's history and the culture of their parents' homeland if they could get to know it in their mother tongue, that is, in English. To urge them on, they organized various cultural contests, offering as a prize a trip to Hungary.

It can be noticed that under the Great Depression, the ethnic and class militancy that had begun to coalesce before and during World War I returned in the Hungarian community, too. Owing to the linkage that was created between the labor unions and the Democratic Party, Hungarians felt urged to become more active in the strike-organizing drives and in the political struggle for unemployment insurance. Led by the second generation, born in America, a resurgent ethnic working class built on the experience of the Progressive era. It was the first time that the leaders of their fraternal organizations competing with each other cooperated in backing the CIO. The events of the 1930s show that it is not possible to narrow down class consciousness and that the loyalty of workers can be developed out of the traditional labor movement. In the struggles fought for better conditions of life, for the aims propagated by the Democratic Party, the broad masses of the Hungarian immigrants and their children were there. This was a new beginning of a new era in their history. The cult of Roosevelt and the Democratic Party dates back for them to those times.

Seemingly disproportionately fewer of the second generation accepted their ethnic inheritance than did children of other "new migrant peoples." Those born in America questioned or ignored the protections that had been created with such care by the immigrants to maintain ethnic boundaries, language, holidays, sex roles, marriage, and patterns of respect within the group. All those programs which depended on the English language reflected a new emphasis in the ideology of Hungarian-American ethnic identity, that is, knowledge of and identification with Hungarian culture instead of the labored maintenance of the Hungarian language. Whatever potential for success this new approach possessed was thwarted by the outbreak of World War II, which found Hungary once again an enemy of the United States. The American-born generations of Hungarians did not want to identify themselves with a country that the host society and other ethnic groups alike depicted as undemocratic and intolerant, not to mention being predisposed to wage war on the United States, the land of their birth and citizenship.

The Postwar Period: New Immigrants.

During and after World War II, the domination of ideological chaos, governing the society by violence and making thousands homeless, characterized the whole of East Central Europe. The masses forced to leave their homes reached millions, redrawing the ethnic map of this region. Escaping from the advance of the Russian troops, hundreds of thousands of civilians and soldiers crossed the western border of Hungary in the spring of 1945. "War mobility" drifted nearly one million of the population into Austria and Germany. The majority returned after the "farewell to the arms," but there were an estimated 100,000 at least who found their final home in other countries. The IRO (International Refugee Organization) helped in resettling 61,000 Hungarian refugees from 1948 to 1952, almost 17,000 of them in the United States.

Among the Hungarian DPs, the "45-ers" had been lingering four to five years in Austria and in German refugee camps or other lodgings until they could get to their final places of settling. Their "ex-enemy" existence followed them, and they were humiliated for it. Even their fellow countrymen who had settled earlier received them with aversion.

The main feature of the postwar migration waves was the collapse of the bases of the existing political and social system. By losing World War II, the elite ruling in the decades between the two world wars lost its power position. The advance of the Russian troops drifted hundreds of thousands of civilians to the West, to Austria or Germany, and forced the activists of the collapsed political system to escape from retaliation.

Since these emigrants were motivated by political reasons, most of them have to be looked at as political emigrants in the traditional sense of the concept. Individuals with different views, though, with different social experiences, were present even in this wave of emigration. The survivors of concentration camps choosing to settle in other countries instead of staying home, blighted by the behavior of their original environment, could arrive together with radical nationalists, just as the emigration of anti-fascist representatives of conservative values could also take place at the same time. The variety of views and motivations are usually covered in a wave of migration, since the current political considerations show these much more homogeneous than they really are. In Hungary, for example, the official propaganda wanted to make see the "running of lords and fascists" in the 1945-ers.

From 1949, the political, socioeconomic profile of East Central Europe was changed by the Communist parties' gaining power. Because of their marginal position, most social and spiritual leaders of the short-lived civil democratic Hungary had to emigrate in 1947–1949. With their emigration those small groups tailed off those members who could have played a leading role in building a democratic Hungarian society. In the United States they became the representatives of the so-called democratic emigration, the "47-ers."

Though at the end of the war political motivations combined with the economic ones in mass flights and in the illegal emigration after 1945, it was not so striking as among those in the last big wave of refugees, in November and December 1956. The massive emigration connected to the revolution in 1956 is an independent and individual chapter in the history of Hungarian emigration. One of the most important morals to be drawn from examining the wave of emigration in 1956 is the realization how difficult it is to define "refugee" and to differentiate between political and economic causes of migration in the second half of the twentieth century. Special circumstances can give a political appearance, and the label of political emigration may be attached to geographical mobility. The relative economic backwardness of the society left behind, the attraction of the Western countries—political and economic motivations combined—formed the waves of international migration. When labeling their characteristics, they are not independent from the current political interests of both the emitting and the receiving countries. For example, in the autumn of 1956 the Western world wanted to see the sudden emigration of masses, as the escape of freedom fighters against the Russian oppression while the Hungarian government saw it as the hasty adventure of youngsters deceived by the fake propaganda of the capitalist world, and the escape of criminals and counter-revolutionaries from prison.

The integration of the foreign-born into a new society is always a difficult, complex, and sometimes slow process, affected by many factors that can delay, accelerate, or prevent it. The differences in culture between the old and the new homeland, the adaptability of individuals, the circumstances under which the immigrant or refugee comes to his or her new home, the attitude of the receiving society—these are all important factors in the cultural integration of immigrants. The voluntary immigrant, the displaced person, and the harried refugee all come for different reasons and because of different pressures. The speed with which the entrance is effected is yet another factor, and so is the presence or absence of assistance in adjusting to the new society. Considering that the Hungarians of 1956 came with such speed, without a preparatory period or orientation, and after the traumatic experience of a revolution, their start on the road to integration proceeded extremely well.

The post–World War II immigrants were significantly different from any previous ones from Hungary to the United States. Their communities were not bound together by either geographical or organizational ties as much as by the mass media including radio and publications. These media connections were originally established in the European camps, where the Hungarians started numerous periodicals, as well as schools and scout troops, during their four or five years' wait for entry into their new countries. Later, these periodicals transcended international borders to unite them and similar émigrés in Canada, South America, and Australia in a socially horizontal community.

The support and admiration with which American public opinion regarded the doomed struggle of the Freedom Fighters in 1956 not only encouraged the open declaration of Hungarian-American identity, but reinvigorated the ethnic consciousness of Hungarian Americans. The reevaluation that began in 1956 was strengthened by the ethnic renaissance that provided tolerance as well as social and financial support for cultural preservation. But for the children and grandchildren of the masses of economic migrants, "preservation" per se is not the right term. As ethnic generations come of age, they appear to be especially sensitive to the attitudes and prejudices of their fatherland.

Belonging to one ethnic group is only one form of a person's identity. Religion, social class, and occupation can either support or compete with ethnicity as forms of self-identification, and Hungarians in the United States have been fragmented by one or more of these forms from the very beginning. This trend was continued and intensified by the arrival of each new wave of Hungarian immigrants and refugees. Of course, these multiple forms of identity did not promote ethnic stability. Rates of Hungarian immigrant assimilation were variable and uneven. Hungarian-speaking families always seemed to be more loosely connected to their ethnic heritage and community than immigrants of other groups.

However, large-scale ethnic mobilization regardless of public opinion can be caused by war, persecution, or natural disasters that actually imperil the homeland or family members there. Prime examples are the aid campaigns organized by various Hungarian-American groups for their defeated nation just after each of the two world wars. In 1944, previously opposed groups briefly overcame their own animosities within the ethnic community to heal Hungary's war wounds.

The case of Hungarian immigrants further illustrates how greatly relations between the home and host countries influence ethnicity. Because an unfriendly, hostile attitude discourages immigrants' open declaration of national identity, the strained relations that existed between Hungary and the United States even before World War I made it more difficult for Hungarians than for other Central and Eastern European immigrants to become integrated into American society. Later, prejudices against Hungary and Hungarians only intensified during the two world wars.

Both class and ethnic consciousness sharply declined after World War II. All the local institutions that sustained traditional identities—lodges, taverns, national parishes, political machines, and Hungarian newspapers—were gravely weakened. Keeping an institution running, such as the insurance enterprise of a fraternal organization, or preserving members of a congregation, exhibited the decline of their ethnic nature. Even those members of the second generation who acquired positions in institutions founded by Hungarian immigrants endeavored to cover up their ethnic roots. (See, for example, the change of name of two big Hungarian fraternal organizations, the Rákóczi and the Verhovay to William Penn!)

As the DPs were strikingly different both socially and ideologically from the older group of Hungarian immigrants, they did not revitalize the existing Hungarian organizations and community life. They brought a host of problems the consequences of which are still being felt. They generally preferred to form their own associations. The existing Hungarian organizations, with a few exceptions, appeared to some as lacking in sophistication, breadth, and ability to satisfy their intellectual and political needs and aspirations.

No other group of Hungarian immigrants had received as much paternalistic care from the American people, including all the groups of the Hungarian Americans, as the "56-ers," but the newcomers were not at all attracted to the activities of the Hungarian-American communities, and left the geographical locations of their Hungarian neighbors as soon as they had the chance.

The decades after World War II. immediately preceded the reversal of attitudes toward Hungarian identity. Hungarian culture had been kept alive by the middle-class immigrants of the 1940s, who put strong emphasis upon Hungarian high culture, that is, music, art, and all other aspects of Hungarian culture that formerly had belonged to a small elite. The study of their continued lobbying for the independence of Hungary and their cultural activities in preserving the Hungarian heritage over five decades is largely a task for the future. However, it can be said that they definitely outstripped Hungarians in Hungary in creating a new national tradition of the Kossuth legend and the celebration of March 15, both in memory of the freedom fight of 1848/49, and the celebration of October 23 in memory of the uprising of 1956. Moreover, it was their version of Hungarian culture that was there to be preserved when the ethnic renaissance temporarily gave an impetus to the opening of new Hungarian schools in place of those which had closed down, and to the presentation of Hungarian ethnic symbols in the applied arts and cultural products.

The fact that the Hungarian-American ethnic group has been a part of American society for over a century is the result, not so much of its stubbornness in survival, but of its continuous reinforcement by newer and newer waves of immigrants. During the twentieth century, many culturally and socially diverse groups and individuals emigrated from Hungary to the United States, stratifying the Hungarian Americans socially and using ethnic symbols and expressions of cultural identity in new ways. Before the 1950s, craftsmen, peasants, and workers laid down the foundations of Hungarian-American communities and shaped their image, but afterwards the representatives of the Hungarian ethnic community were professionals and members of the middle class. What gains could be acknowledged by the receiving new home? Steel and coal were furnished, while roads and railways were built by those young able-bodied men of the past. Modern industry and health care were built with the brains and knowledge of the newcomers. Contributions of all the waves proved in one way or another that they did not become a liability but a valuable national asset.

The one hundred years of Hungarian experiences with their congregations, fraternal associations, other informal organizations, and the papers written in the mother tongue reflect the importance of ethnic institutions in the forming of communities. They continually modified the cultural heritage, giving free play to the effects of the environment, preserving what they felt necessary and letting go of what was superfluous in their integration process.

Under the impact of the ethnic renaissance the social scientists, having rescued the migrants from the caricature of uprooted, oppressed, traumatized victims, have exaggerated the degree of autonomy which the immigrants enjoyed. The results of my empirical investigation especially in the frame of microanalysis give a lot of evidence to the accuracy of the portrait of self-determined, free-willed migrants who established cohesive communities, which is troubled, though, by a number of discordant thoughts expressed.

Sufficient evidence proves that the reaction on the impact of the environment is not the same and not all groups respond in the same manner. Each group brings to bear its own background on the forces of the modern city while the homogenizing forces produce countereffects. There is a need to maintain or to find some sources of uniqueness. It is therefore just as important

to study the factors which limit the similarities as it is to study the similarities themselves.

Hungarians had to and still have to surmount extraordinary difficulties in
order to safeguard their ethnic identity. This is due less to their relatively small
numbers than to the particularly manifold division among them. Though it is
true of every one of the postwar immigrant groups that they mostly came from
town dwellers, from a more educated class of their people and represented
various ideologies, the Hungarians were unique with such great variety of
social, ideological, and cultural division among them. Characteristic of Hungarian society was not only that there were big social differences but also the
great gulf between the various strata and cultures. They did not free themselves
even in the United States from the prejudices, the strivings to separate indicated
by them, which were even inherited by the second generation. Only in theory
can we speak of American Hungarianhood, of an American ethnic community—this notion can be used only as an instrument for our research. In reality
one can only find a great number of small, competitive groups, communities
who feel aversion or at least indifference to each other. Uprooted or transplanted, both adjectives are valid for great numbers among them. Only the
first generation had personally experienced the old world heritage which is a
natural source of ethnic identification. The basic fact is, anyway, that generations
differ among themselves not only in degrees but also in the nature of their
identification with ethnicity. For every group, the Hungarian neighborhood
had been rapidly disappearing and with it the heretofore strong emphasis on
communally oriented rather than individually oriented action.

According to the distinguished historian of ethnicity Rudolph Vecoli, the
ethnic revival in general has certainly encountered some difficult moments.
But he is confident that ethnicity is by now "an enduring dimension of American
life." And it is true that the United States has come to conceive of itself as a
pluralistic multiethnic society in the 1970s. Ethnic revival has achieved a
measure of success in salvaging ethnic heritage and instilling pride in ones'
ethnic origin, as well as in promoting community studies.

APPENDIX

BALTIC
SEA

under the
Prussian annexation

POLAND

RUSSIA

Wisła
• Warszawa

under the
Russian annexation

GERMAN
EMPIRE

Odra

SILESIA

BOHEMIA

MORAVIA

GALICIA

BUKOVINA

under the
Austrian annexation

RUTHENIA

Danube

SLOVAKIA

Vienna

AUSTRIA-HUNGARY

• Budapest

CROATIA

KINGDOM
OF
HUNGARY

TRANSYLVANIA

Po

SLAVONIA

BANAT

ROMANIA

DALMATIA

BOSNIA

HERZE-
GOVINA

SERBIA

Danube

ADRIATIC
SEA

BULGARIA

0   100
miles

**The Spread of Overseas Migration in Austria-Hungary and Polish
Territories, 1870–1913**

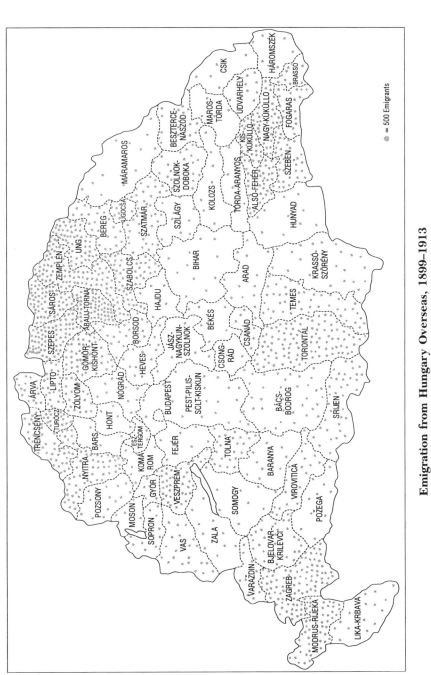

Emigration from Hungary Overseas, 1899–1913

SOURCE: Juliana Puskas, *From Hungary to the United States (1880–1914),* p. 57

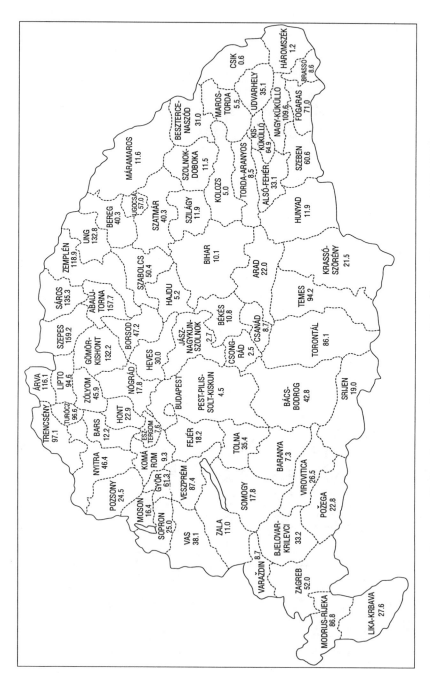

Overseas Emigration as a Percentage of the Natural Increase, 1899–1913

SOURCE: Compiled from MSK 67, Table 44, p. 53.

TABLE 8.

Distribution of the Hungarian Ethnic Group in the United States

STATES	1910	1980	STATES	1910	1980
New York	23.1	13.8	Iowa	0.1	0.3
Ohio	19.3	13.7	Kansas	0.1	0.3
Pennsylvania	20.0	11.4	Kentucky	0.1	0.3
New Jersey	11.1	9.5	Nebraska	0.3	0.3
California	0.8	9.3	Nevada	0.0	0.3
Michigan	2.8	7.1	Oklahoma	0.1	0.3
Florida	0.0	5.0	Tennessee	0.1	0.3
Illinois	6.4	4.8	Delaware	0.1	0.2
Connecticut	4.0	3.0	Montana	0.1	0.2
Indiana	3.4	2.5	New Hampshire	0.0	0.2
Wisconsin	1.5	1.9			
Texas	0.2	1.6	New Mexico	0.0	0.2
Maryland	0.3	1.6	North Dakota	0.2	0.2
Virginia	0.5	1.3	South Carolina	0.0	0.2
Arizona	0.0	1.1	Alaska	—	0.1
Massachusetts	0.4	1.1	Arkansas	0.0	0.1
Missouri	1.2	1.1	District of	0.0	0.1
Colorado	0.3	0.9	Columbia		
Minnesota	0.7	0.9	Hawaii	—	0.1
Washington	0.2	0.9	Idaho	0.0	0.1
West Virginia	1.7	0.7	Maine	0.0	0.1
Georgia	0.1	0.6	Mississippi	0.0	0.1
Oregon	0.2	0.6	Rhode Island	0.0	0.1
North Carolina	0.0	0.5	South Dakota	0.1	0.1
			Utah	0.0	0.1
Louisiana	0.1	0.4	Vermont	0.2	0.1
Alabama	0.1	0.3	Wyoming	0.1	0.0
			TOTAL	100	100

NOTES

Chapter 1: Hungarian Society between Feudalism and Capitalism

1. It resulted in the dual state of Austria-Hungary, which played a significant role in European power-politics until its defeat in World War led to its dissolution in 1918–1919. See *A History of Hungary* edited by Peter F. Sugár, Péter Hanák and Tibor Frank (Bloomington: Indiana University Press, 1990).

2. See László Katus, "Economic Growth in Hungary during the Age of Dualism, 1867–1913," in *Social Economic Researches on the History of East Central Europe,* edited by E. Pamlényi (Budapest: Akadémiai Kiadó, 1970) 35–127. See also Peter Gunst, "Agricultural Development in Hungary, 1860–1939," in *Economic Development in Hungary and Finland, 1860–1939,* edited by Tapani Mauranen (Helsinki: Institute of Economic and Social History, 1985), 63–88.

3. Tibor Kolossa, "The Social Structure of the Peasant Class in Austro-Hungary. Statistical Sources and Methods," *East European Quarterly* (January 1970), 420–37.

4. Scott M. Eddie, "The Changing Patterns of Landownership in Hungary, 1867–1914," *Economic History Review,* (1967), 20:293–310. See also Iván T. Berend and György Ránki, *The European Periphery and Industrialization, 1780–1914* (Budapest: Akadémiai Kiadó, 1982), 40–8.

5. László Katus, "Transport Revolution and Economic Growth in Hungary" in *Economic Development in the Habsburg Monarchy in the Nineteenth Century: Essays*, edited by John Komlós (New York: Columbia University Press, 1983), 204. See also Iván Berend and György Ránki, *Hungary: A Century of Economic Development* (Newton Abbot, Devon: David and Charles, 1974), 20–90.

6. Imre Katona, "Átmeneti bérmunka formák" (Transitional types of wage labor), in *A parasztság Magyarországon a kapitalizmus korában, 1848–1914* (The peasantry in Hungary during the time of capitalism, edited by István Szabó. 2 vol. (Budapest: Akadémia Kiadó, 1965) 2:382–406. See also Scott M. Eddie, "Agriculture and Labor Supply," in Komlós, *Economic Development in the Habsburg Monarchy*, 101–115.

7. Peter Sipos, "Migration, Labor Movement and Workers' Culture in Budapest, 1867–1914," in *Roots of the Transplanted*, edited by Dirk Hoerder and Inge Blank. 2 vol. (New York: Columbia University Press, 1994), 2:155.

8. Ibid., 2:158.

9. On the growth of the tax burden on peasants, the difficulties of getting credit, the incidence of usurious credit, see István Varga, "A közterhek" (General and proportionate tax-sharing), in Szabó, *A parasztság, Magyarországon*, 2:246–287.

10. István Orosz, "A differenciálódás és kisajátítás" (Differentiation and Expropriation), in Ibid., 2:21–22.

11. György Szabad, "A hitelviszonyok" (Conditions of credit), in Ibid., 2:184–214.

12. Ibid., 2:245.

13. Varga, "A közterhek," in Szabó, *A parasztság Magyarországan*, 2:246–287.

14. Károly Keleti, *Magyarország népességének élelmezési statisztikája physiologia alapon* (Statistics on nutriments for Hungary's population on a physiological basis) (Budapest, 1887), 45–46, 53–54.

15. Ibid., 53.

16. Magyar Királyi Földmüvelési Minisztérium: *Mezögazdasági munkabérek Magyarországon*, 1893, 1894, 1895, 1896, 1901, 1908. (Hungarian Royal Ministry of Agriculture, Agricultural wages in Hungary) (Budapest, 1909).

17. *Magyar Statisztikai Évkönyv, 1900* (Hungarian Statistical Yearbook) (Budapest, 1901), 106.

18. On their lifestyle and the characteristics of their working conditions, see Zoltán Sárközi, "A summások" (Seasonal workers), in Szabó, *A parasztság Magyarországon*, 2:321–371.

19. See also Gyula Rubinek, *Parasztszocializmus* (Peasant Socialism) (Budapest: Patria, 1895) and Lajos Zsigmond Szeberényi, *A parasztok helyzete Magyarországon. Szociális tanulmány, különös tekintettel az alföldi munkásmozgalomra és a kivándorlásra* (The position of the peasants in Hungary. A social study with particular attention to the workers' movement of the Great Plain and to emigration). (Békéscsaba: Kókai Lajos, 1907).

20. See Edit Fél and Tamás Hofer, *Proper Peasants: Traditional Life in a Hungarian Village* (Chicago: Aldine Publishing Company, 1969). See also J. W. Cole, "Culture and Economy in Peripheral Europe," *Ethnologia Europea* XV: 3–26.

21. See also Ernö Tárkány Szücs, *Magyar jogi népszokások* (Hungarian popular customs in the law) (Budapest: Gondolat, 1981), 405–460); Fél and Hofer, *Proper Peasants*, 405.

22. See András Bertalan, "Hagyomány és alkalmazkodás baranyai német és magyar falvakban" (Tradition and adjustment in the German and Hungarian villages of Baranya county), in *Paraszti társadalom és müveltség a 18–20. században* (Peasant society and culture from the 18th to the 20th century) (Budapest: Magyar Néprajzi Társaság, 1974), II, 141–148. See also Judit Morvay, "The Joint Family in Hungary," *Europe at Hungarica Congressus Ethnographicus in Hungary* (Budapest: Akadémiai Kiadó, 1965), 231–42.

23. Gyula Illyés, *A puszták népe* (People of the Plains) (Budapest: Nyugat, 1937), 30. In this stifled primordial world which in its entirety fenced off so much from the warmth of the tribes, the women, the mothers ruled in every family.

24. Tárkány Szücs, *Magyar jogi nepzokasok*, 474.

25. Ibid., 422–3.

26. Ibid., 757–74.

27. Folk costumes also expressed social rank in the second half of the 19th century. See Mária Kresz, *Magyar parasztviselet, 1820–1867* (Hungarian folk costume) (Budapest: Akadémiai kiadó, 2 vol. 1956). See also Alice Gáborján, *Hungarian Peasant Costumes* (Magyar Nepviselet) Hungarian Folk Art. 3, edited by Gyula Ortutay (Budapest: Corvina, 1969).

28. Iván Balassa, *Lápok, falvak, emberek. Bodrogköz.* (Marshes, villages, people, Bodrogköz) (Budapest: Gondolat, 1975), 257–87.

29. *History of Hungary from the Earliest Times until the Present Day*, edited by Peter Hanák (Budapest: Corvina, 1991), 143–5.

30. István Balogh, "A paraszti müvelödés" (Peasant education), in Szabó, *A parasztság Magyarországon*, 2:487–550.

31. Linda Dégh, *A szabadságharc népköltészete* (The folk poetry of the War of Independence) (Budapest: Akadémiai Kiadó, 1952).

32. See also Julianna Puskás, Inge Blank, Horst Rössler and Cvetka Knapic-Khren, "Rural and Artisan Protest in Western, East Central and Southeastern Europe from the Early 19th Century to World War I," in Hoerder and Blank, *Roots of the Transplanted*, 2:25–30.

33. Ildikó Kriza, "Ethnic Identity and National Consciousness of the Hungarian Peasantry During the Age of Dualism," in Ibid., 1: 175–97.

34. Ibid., 1:193.

Chapter 2: The Pattern of Migration, 1876–1910s

1. Heinz Fassman, "Emigration, Immigration and Internal Migration in the Austro-Hungarian Monarchy in 1910," in Hoerder and Blank, *Roots of the Transplanted*, 1:253–308.

2. "Annual Reports," Table IX, in *International Migration*, edited by Imre Ferenczi and Walter F. Willcox (New York: National Review of Economic Research, 1969), I, 420–43.

3. Sune Akerman, "Theories and Methods of Migration Research," in *From Sweden to America: A History of Emigration*, edited by Harold Runblom and Hans Norman (Minneapolis: University of Minnesota Press, 1976), 76.

4. Immigration and Naturalization Service, Table 13, *United States Annual Report,* (Washington, D.C., 1976), 62–4. Cited in *Harvard Encyclopedia of American Ethnic Groups,* edited by Stephan Thernstrom (Cambridge: Harvard University Press, 1980), 1047–9.

5. From Hungary alone 181,288 persons emigrated to the United States between 1891 and 1898. See *A magyar szent korona országainak kivándorlása és visszavándorlása 1899–1913* (Emigration and remigration in the countries of the Hungarian Sacred Crown), Magyar Statisztikai Központi Hivatal, *Magyar Statisztikai Közlemények,* Új Sorozat 67. (Hungarian Office of Statistics. Hungarian Statistical Publications. New Series 67). For the first modern processing of the statistical data of overseas migration from Hungary, see Gustav Thirring, "Hungarian Migration of Modern Times," in Ferenczi and Willcox, *International Migration,* II 411–39.

6. Katus, "Economic Growth in Hungary," in *Acta Historica,* 37–127.

7. *Magyar Statisztikai Közlemények* 67:14.

8. See, for example, the estimates of Alajos Kovács, "A kivándorlas statisztikai okai" (The statistical reasons of emigration), *Közgazdasági Szemle* (Economics Review) (July 1909), 445–554; Gustav Thirring, "Hungarian Migration of Modern Times," in Ferenczi and Willcox, *International Migrations,* II, 411–39; István Rácz, *A paraszti migráció és politikai megítélése Magyarországon 1849–1914* (Peasant migration and its political assessment in Hungary) (Budapest: Akadémiai Kiadó, 1980); and Julianna Puskás, *From Hungary to the United States, 1880–1914* (Budapest: Akadémiai Kiadó, 1982) on the scale of the emigration from Hungary.

9. *Magyar Statisztikai Közlemények* 67:38.

10. Ibid., 15.

11. Harry Jerome first proved the cyclical nature of the process in his book, *Migration and Business Cycles* (New York: National Bureau of Economic Research, 1926).

12. *Magyar Statisztikai Közlemények* 67, Table 8, "Emigration from the Hungarian Empire According to Their Routes."

13. *Reports of the Immigration Commission* (1911 reprint, New York: Arno, 1970), 3:359.

14. American industrial wages were five or six times higher than agricultural wages in Hungary. See in Puskás, *From Hungary to the United States,* 53–56.

15. See for example the studies of Keijo Virtanen, *Settlement or Return: Finnish Emigrants 1860–1930* (Turku: The Migration Institute, 1979); Puskás, *From Hungary to the United States;* Monika Glettler, "Slovak Return Migration from the U.S. to Hungary before the First World War," a paper read at the symposium "A Century of European Migration, 1830–1930," University of Minnesota, November, 1986; and Dino Cinel, "Seasonal Emigration of Italians in the Nineteenth Century: From Internal to International Destinations," *The Journal of Ethnic Studies* (Spring, 1980).

16. The most frequent one-sidedness of the evaluations: that only in connection with the diminishing of the remigrants' gross number do they refer to the traveling to and fro of one particular person, and forget about this factor in connection with the migrants. See, for example, Steven Vardy's estimates in his book *The Hungarian Americans* (Boston: Twayne, 1985), 20.

17. Gusztáv Thirring, *A magyarországi kivándorlás és a külföldi magyarság* (Emigration from Hungary and the Hungarians abroad) (Budapest: F. Kilian, 1904).

18. Report to the Prime Minister from Lipót Szmrecsányi, December 4, 1902 in Frantisek Bielik and Elo Rákos, *Slovenske Vystahovalectvo*, (Bratislava: SAV, 1969), 236–8.

19. Report of the subprefect of Szepes County to the Minister of the Interior, in ibid., 354–357.

20. Statement quoted by Lajos Leopold, "A visszavándorlók mérlege" (The balance of the remigrants) *Huszadik Század* (Twentieth Century), I (1908), 143–4.

21. Sándor Tonelli, "Utazás a magyar kivándorlókkal" (Traveling with the Hungarian emigrants), *Közgazdasági Szemle* (1908), 431.

22. See the remigration rates of race and people in Thernstrom, *Harvard Encyclopedia*, 1036–7.

23. The greatest number of remigrants to be found for 1908 is 53,377. "Annual Reports," in Ferenczi and Willcox, *International Migration, 1920–1943*. According to the United States Immigration Statistics the rate of remigrants was 269.0 percent in 1908. In the following years, the rates were 75.4, 76.4, 205.9, 179.7 and 97.7 percent in 1913. Cited in Thernstrom, *Harvard Encyclopedia*, 1036.

24. Ralph Melville, "Permanent Emigration and Temporary Transnational Migration: Jewish, Polish, and Russian Emigration from Tsarist Russia, 1861–1914," in *Overseas Migration from East-central and Southeastern Europe,* edited by Julianna Puskás (Budapest: Akadémiai Kiadó, 1990), 133–142. According to Melville, Jewish mass migration began in conjunction with the 1881 pogroms in Southwestern Russia and with the reactionary transformation of tsarist policies concerning Jews under Alexander II. The massive overseas emigration was restricted almost entirely to the western part of Russia. About 2.4 million of more than 2.8 million emigrants to North America in 1899–1914 came from the Jewish Pale. Recent investigations indicate that over 20 percent of the Jews returned during the period between 1880 and 1900. See Jonathan Sarna, "The Myth of No Return: Jewish Return Migration to Eastern Europe, 1881–1914," in *American Jewish History* LXXI (1981), 256–69.

25. *Magyar Statisztikai Közlemények* 67:38.

26. Ibid.

27. See the data of the United States Bureau of Census 1910, "Population: Country of Origin and Mother Tongue." Total number of immigrants from Hungary: 495,600. Of these: Magyar 227,742, Slovak 107,954, German 73,338. Cited in Thernstrom, *Harvard Encyclopedia*, 1053.

28. Similar observations were made with regard to the Italian remigrants by Cinel, "Seasonal Emigration of Italians," 42–68.

29. See Lars Göran Tedebrant, "Remigration from America to Sweden," in Runblom and Norman, *From Sweden to America*, 201–9 and Virtanen, *Settlement or Return*, 170–5.

30. "Annual Reports 1899–1913," in Ferenczi and Willcox, *International Migrations*, I, 460–70. Data concerning Hungary are based on definite facts only in the 1904/1905, 1907/1908, and 1912/1913 years, otherwise on estimations. The division by mother tongue of emigrants is also registered in the Hungarian emigration

statistics. In the latter, the proportion of Magyars is higher than in the U.S. surveys, though there are no great differences in exact figures. Hungarian statistics are vague mainly in connection with national minorities; for instance, the Slovaks who had had more experience in emigration eluded control easily. The greatest difference in the two sources is in the data on their numbers. See also the ethnic composition of the population in detail in László Katus, "Über die wirtschaftlichen und gesellschaftlichen Grundlagen der Nationalitatenfrage in Ungarn vor dem ersten Weltkrieg" Tables 20, 27, and 28, in *Die nationale Frage in der Österreichischen Monarchie, 1900–1918,* edited by Péter Hanák and Zoltán Szász (Budapest: Akadémiai Kiadó, 1966), 149–214.

31. United States statistics classified all immigrants from Hungary as Hungarians until 1899, after which those of Hungarian mother tongue were classified as Magyars. Although U.S. immigration authorities registered Jews as an ethnic group ("Hebrews"), Hungary registered them as a religious group and did not list them in the census as a national minority. Most of the Jews registered as Magyars.

32. *Magyar Statisztikai Közlemények* 67, "Kivándorlás az egyes törvényhatóságok területéről a kivándorlók anyanyelve szerint" (Emigration from the territory of certain municipalities according to the mother tongue of the emigrants) 18–25. See also József Gellén, "A Systems Approach to Emigration from Hungary before 1914," in Puskás, *Overseas Migration,* 191.

33. Distribution of Immigrant Aliens admitted, by Age and Race of People 1899–1924. "Annual Reports 1899–1913," in Ferenczi and Willcox, *International Migrations,* 1:444–9.

34. United States Annual Reports, in Ferenczi and Willcox, ibid., 433–3, and in *Magyar Statisztikai Közlemények* 67: 19. Hungarian men 16,637, women 13,973. The proportion of women is somewhat smaller than in the American statistics.

35. Ibid., 435–6.

36. Ibid., 439.

37. Ibid., 86.

38. Ibid.

39. Ibid.

40. Ibid., Table 19, 35.

41. Heves Megye (Heves county) 1902, E. 1903, 21–23. Quoted by István Rácz, *A paraszti migráció,* 88.

42. István Rácz, "A parasztok elvándorlása a faluról" (Migration of peasants from the villages), in Szabó, *A parasztság Magyarországon,* 1:433–77.

43. Zoltán Kramar, *From the Danube to the Hudson: U.S. Ministerial and Consular Dispatches on Immigration from the Habsburg Monarchy, 1850–1900* (Atlanta: Hungarian Cultural Foundation, 1978), 69–72.

44. "The decline of the famous Saxon industry of yore made many of our Saxon citizens leave for America from the 80s on." *Magyar Statisztikai Közlemények* 67:26. See also L. Hegedüs, *A magyarok kivándorlása Amerikába* (Emigration of Hungarians to America) (Budapest: n.p., 1899), 61–70, and the 1881 debate on the bill concerning "A kivándorlási ügynökökről" (On emigration agents). The Minister of the Interior, in circular number 62867/1875, had reminded the municipalities that "numerous Hungarian and Austrian subjects, especially craftsmen,

emigrate to North America in the hope of being employed there as artisans and workers, for higher wages."

45. Report of Sáros County's Sub-prefect to the Minister of the Interior, September 23, 1881. OL.BM. Országos Levéltár Belügyminiszterium (National Archives. Ministry of Interior)] 1882.II.17-8078. Report of Zemplén County's Sub-prefect to the Minister of the Interior, April 5, 1881. OL.BM.1882.II.17-6078. See also Gyula Margittay's interpellation in the House of Representatives, "Az emberrel való kereskedés tárgyában, amelyet a nép kivándorlásra való csábitásával követnek el" (On the subject of selling human beings through luring the people to emigrate) April 7, 1886, 22.OKN. [Országgyüles. Kepviselöház, Napló (Parliament, Journal of the House of Representatives.)] XL.141–3.

46. Compiled from the reports of the United States Commissioner General of Immigration, published in *Magyar Statisztikai Közlemények* 67:36. In the occupational distribution there were also decided differences in the ethnic groups emigrated from Hungary. This is particularly remarkable in the "professional" category. In this category they included 1367 persons from among the Hungarians, only 194 Slovaks, and 160 from among the Romanians. "Number of immigrants of specified occupation, fiscal years 1899 to 1910," *Reports of the Immigration Commission* 3:140.

47. Ibid., 3:84.

48. See the maps about the spread of immigration in the studies of John S. MacDonald, "Agricultural Organization, Migration and Labor Militancy in Rural Italy," *Economic History Review.* 2nd Series (1958): 16; Runblom and Norman, *From Sweden to America,* maps: "Migration Overseas from the Nordic Countries 1865–69; 1870–74; 1895–9; 1900–04; 1905–09; 1910–14; Puskás, *From Hungary to the United States,* maps: "Emigration from Hungary Overseas 1899–1913" and "Emigrants from Hungary Overseas and to the Continent, 1899 (according to counties)"; Walter D. Kamphoeffner, maps: on "Index of Relative Intensity of Emigration by Districts"; Robert P. Swierenga, maps. "Dutch International Migration and Occupational Changes: A Structural Analysis of Multinational Linked Files" in *Migration Across Time and Nations: Population Mobility in Historical Context,* edited by Ira A. Glazier and Luigi De Rosa (New York: Holmes & Meier, 1986), respectively 176, 103; 1986, 103–4.

49. See Sárközi, "A summások," in Szabó, *A parasztság Magyarorizágon,* 2:314–71.

50. Report of the Subprefect of Szepes County to the Minister of the Interior, November 6, 1914 in Bielik and Rákos, *Slovenske Vystahovalectvo,* 355.

51. The migration fever spread from the north to the south. Maps show the spread of migration in Puskás, *From Hungary to the United States.* The northern part of Szabolcs County, the districts of Kisvárda and Tisza account for 30 percent of the emigrants. Ferenc Szászi, *Az Amerikába irányuló kivándorlás Szabolcs megyéből az elsö világháborúig* (Emigration to America from Szabolcs County to World War I) (Nyiregyháza: György Bessenyei, 1972), 48.

52. "Those who wanted to emigrate were mostly day-laborers who did not own any land. Most of them did not wish to emigrate with the aim of settling, but to get a job with bigger pay," stated the official report cited by Szászi, *Az Amerikába*

irányuló kivándorlás, 38. One part of this largest emigration region took shape inside of the borders of Hungary within the North-Eastern counties, and the other part in the peripheral crown lands in East Galicia and Bukovina, Ladislav Tajták, "Slovak Emigration and Migration in the Years 1900–14," *Studia Historica Slovacia* 10 (1978), 46–80.

53. Ian Alnas, "Industrialization and Migration of the Transylvanian Peasantry at the End of the Nineteenth Century and the Beginning of the Twentieth Century," *East European Quarterly,* (January, 1970),: 504–505; also Gellén, "A Systems Approach to Emigration," in Puskás, *Overseas Migration,* 89–106. See the studies for example of Mark M. Stolarik, "Slovak Migration from Europe to North America, 1870–1918," *Slovak Studies* 20 (Slovak Institute, 1980), and Ladislas Tajták, "Slovak emigration, its causes and consequences," in Puskás, *Overseas Migration,* 74–88; also Ivan Cizmic, "Emigration from Yugoslavia prior to World War I," in Glazier and de Rosa, *Migration Across Time and Nations,* 255–67.

54. This was already emphasized by J. D. Gould, "European Inter-Continental Emigration, 1815–1914: Patterns and Causes," *Journal of European Economic History,* VIII, 593–679.

55. See the map of the emigration regions in Austria-Hungary in Fassman, "Emigration, immigration and internal migration," in Hoerder and Blank, *Roots of the Transplanted,* 253–308.

Chapter 3: The Pattern of Migration: The Village of Szamosszeg

1. See, for example Robert P. Swierenga. 1991. "Local Patterns of Dutch Migration to the United States in the Mid-Nineteenth Century." In *A Century of European Migration, 1830–1930,* edited by Rudolph J. Vecoli, and Suzanne M. Sinke. Urbana: University of Illinois Press, 134–57.

2. According to the 1910 Hungarian census the population of Szamosszeg was 2800. Of this, earners were 1388, 1207 in agriculture, 2 in other branches of farming, 101 in industry, 24 in commerce, 20 in office or freelance, 12 day-laborers, 15 servants, and 6 were unknown. Szamosszeg is a village in Szatmár County; the nearest train stop is 5 kms away in the neighboring village.

3. The collection "Magyarok az Egyesült Államokban és Kanadában. Szamosszegiek: interjúk, levelek, fényképek" (Hungarians in the United States and Canada. The Szamosszegians: Interviews, Letters, Photos) is in the possession of the author.

4. To conduct interviews with immigrants from Szamosszeg or their descendants, I was able to travel to Holden, WV, Cleveland, OH, Detroit, MI. Pittsburgh, PA, New Brunswick, NJ, Highland Park, NJ, New York, and in Canada to Toronto and Hamilton.

5. Although I reconstructed the lives by relying on collective memory, that is to say, I asked the subjects of the interviews about the others too, I indicate the chief interviewee of every family. Each interview can be found on a separate tape. See Puskás collection of tapes, "Hungarian American interviews, 1977–1994."

6. Robert P. Swierenga, "Ethnic History," *Ethnic Forum* (Spring 1984), 4.

7. See László Horváth, "Az Egyesült Államokba irányult kivándorlás Kál községből az első világháború előtt" (Emigration to the U.S.A. from the village Kál

before World War I) in *Agora,* XXVII (1992), 257–273. and XXVIII (1993), 50–88; Pál Hadházy, "Kivándorlás Turistvándi községből (Emigration from the village Turistvándi), in *Néprajzi dolgozatok Turistvándiból* (Ethnographic dissertations from Turistvándi) (Nyiregyháza: András Jósa Museum, 1986), 3–41. Zoltán Fejős, 'Itt kell az életet leélni.' Adatok a viskiek kivándorlásához egy családtörténet tükrében. Duna-menti népek hagyományos müveltsége ('It is here that one has to live one's life.' Data on the emigration of the Viskis reflected in the history of a family. The traditional education of the people along the Danube), *Tanulmányok Andrásfalvy Bertalan tiszteletére* (Studies as homage for Bertalan Andrásfalvy). (Budapest, 1991), 95–104.

8. Interview with Gusztáv Kovács, Detroit, 1983 and 1985, and with Julia Kovács, New Brunswick, NJ, 1985.

9. Interviews with Lajos Szabó and Lenke Szabó, Szamosszeg, 1983, and with Margit Szabó, New Brunswick, NJ, 1986.

10. Interviews with Ignác Kósa, 1982, with Etelka Balogh, Szamosszeg, 1983, and with Irma Bacskó, New Brunswick, NJ, 1984.

11. "The women, not having enough room elsewhere, kneaded the dough in the attic." Interview with Ignác Kósa, Szamosszeg, 1982.

12. Mária had to leave her fourth daughter in the village at the house of her parents, because her husband did not accept the girl, who was born out of wedlock.

13. Interviews with Piroska Puskás, New Brunswick, NJ, 1984, 1986, 1994. She was one of my main informants.

14. Interview with Ignác Kósa, Szamosszeg, 1982, with Irén Kósa, East Brunswick, and with Béla Puskás, Somerset, NJ, 1984.

15. Interview with Vilma and Zsuzsanna Bodó, New Brunswick, NJ, 1984.

16. Interview with Lea Kósa's daughter-in-law, Julianna Bodó, and her grandson, Győző Bodó, Holden, WV, 1985.

17. Interview with Julianna Szögyény (Mrs. Süldő) and Borbála Gergely (Mrs. Szabó), New Brunswick, NJ, 1984.

18. Interview with István Puskás, New Brunswick, 1984, and with Julianna Bodó on her visit to Szamosszeg, 1991.

19. Interview with Julianna Bodó, when she visited her relatives in the village in 1991.

20. Interview with Gábor Filep and his wife, Emilia Dul, and István Filep's daughters, Lenke and Vilma Filep, New Brunswick and Perth Amboy, NJ, 1984.

21. The memories of those were recollected by Mrs. Joseph Kósa in the course of an interview, Szamosszeg, 1984.

22. Irma Kun spoke frequently at the spinning mill of the fact that the Americans often threw stones at them, as they went to work. Interview with Etelka Balogh, Szamosszeg, 1982.

23. According to the marriage register of the Hungarian Protestant church located on Somerset Street, New Brunswick, NJ, of the 54 marriages, only two involved a bride and groom who were both from Szamosszeg. Research of Paula Benkart and Zoltán Fejős also shows that the territorial background of the marriages is scattered. Their marriage pattern is not similar to that of the Italians.

24. Ignác Kósa recalled this statement, which was a slogan in Szamosszeg, 1982.

25. Gusztáv Kovács mentioned two Szamosszegian boys who were in reality younger (15 years old) than they claimed to be when they went to get work in the mines of Holden, WV, Detroit, 1983 and 1985.

26. Éva V. Huseby-Darvas, "Migration and Gender: Perspectives for Rural Hungary," *East European Quarterly*, XXII, no. 4 (January 1990), 489.

27. Kovács, interview, Detroit, MI, 1983.

28. Szögyény (Mrs. Süldó), interview, New Brunswick, NJ, 1984.

29. Gergely (Mrs. Szabó), interview, New Brunswick, NJ, 1984.

30. Kovács, interview, Detroit, MI, 1983.

31. Interview with Irma Bacskó, New Brunswick, 1984.

32. The childless couple, strictly economizing, bought more than ten acres of land, but never returned. They gave the land to relatives, and the land, unequally distributed, became the source of hatred among those remaining in the village. Interview with Gábor Filep, New Brunswick, NJ, 1984 and 1986, and with quarrelling relatives in Szamosszeg.

33. Gergely (Mrs. Szabó), interview, 1984.

34. Interview with Ida Szabó, New Brunswick, NJ, 1986.

35. See in more detail Danica Simová, Eva Fordinálová, and Anna Stvrtecká, "From Husband's Household to National Activity: The Ambivalent Position of Slovak Women," in Hoerder and Blank, *Roots of the Transplanted,* 1:341–58. See also Mary Eleanor Cygan, "Polish Women and Emigrant Husbands," ibid., 1:359–74.

36. OKN (Országgyülés, Képviselöházi Napló) (Parliamentary Journal of the House of Representatives) 1902.X.,96.; OKN 1907.XI.,71, in Rácz, *A paraszti migráció,* 82.

37. See for example the case of the family of Sándor and Zsuzsanna Kovács from Szamosszeg.

38. The information comes from the correspondence of Mrs. Oláh and her son János in the author's collection of letters.

Chapter 4: "You Ask Me Why I Came"

1. The letters and parts of letters quoted here were chosen from the issues of *Szabadság* (Cleveland) published between 8 January and 9 March 1909.

2. These interviews were taped in villages of Bodrogköz, the main center of emigration from Hungary. Mihály Szentimrei, librarian at the Library of Sárospatak, helped me in this work: I convey my thanks to him here, too. See also the chapter "Történetüket mondják, interjúk anyagából, levelekböl" (They tell their stories, taken from interviews, from letters) in Julianna Puskás, *Kivándorló magyarok az Egyesült Államokban, 1880–1940* (Emigrant Hungarians in the United States) (Budapest: Akadémiai Kiadó, 1982), 551–79. Additional interviews in the author's collection.

3. *Szabadság Naptár* (Szabadság Almanac) published yearly news of family dramas and accidents in industries in its series "Amerikai magyarság krónikája" (Chronicle of Hungarian Americans) from 1904 to 1914.

4. Ferenc Szili, "A somogyi kivándorlók Amerika képe és magyarságtudata a századforduló évtizedeiben (The image of America and their consciousness of being

Hungarian among the migrants of Somogy county at the turn of the century), in *Levéltári Évkönyv* (Yearbook of the Archive) (Kaposvár, 1993), 207–272.

5. Ibid. See also "immigrants' letters" in the author's collection and Linda Dégh, "Two letters from home" in *Journal of American Folklore* 91:361 (1978): 808–822.

6. See Charles Tilly, "Transplanted Networks" in *Immigration Reconsidered: History, Sociology and Politics,* edited by Virginia Yans-McLaughlin (New York: Oxford University Press, 1990), 84–85.

Chapter 5: Repercussions in Hungary of Overseas Migration: 1870–1914.

1. Concerning the former Austro-Hungarian monarchy, researchers concentrated on their own ethnicity's migration losses, mostly exaggerating them onesidedly. See the studies of Cizmic, Prpic, Stolarik, Rácz in the bibliography.

2. *Magyarország történeti demográfiája* (The historical demography of Hungary), edited by József Kovacsics (Budapest: Közgazdasági és Jogi Könyvkiadó, 1963). See also Katus, *Economic Growth in Hungary during the Age of Dualism, 1867–1913.*

3. See the study of Alajos Kovács, "A kivándorlás statisztikai okai" (The statistical reasons of emigration), Közgazdasági Szemle (July 1909), 445–454.

4. Census data: the rate of men and women in the population, 1869–1910. Number of women for 1000 men: 1869, 1014; 1880, 1018; 1890, 1015; 1900, 1009; 1910, 1015.

5. Table 99 in *Magyar Statisztikai Közlemények* 67: 100.

6. See Péter Hanák, "Polgárosodás és asszimiláció Magyarországon a 19. században" (The ascendancy of the bourgeoisie and assimilation in Hungary in the 19th century), *Történelmi Szemle* (Historical Review), IV (1974) 513–536, and also "Magyarország társadalma a századforduló idején (Hungary's society at the turn of the century) in *Magyarország története* (History of Hungary) (Budapest: Akadémiai Kiadó, 1977), 7/2:403–516.

7. See the citation of the manuscript of László Katus in Hanák, "Polgárosodás és asszimiláció Magyarorizágon," 514–5.

8. *Magyarország története* (Statistical data from the Census. The national composition of the Hungarian population.) 7/2:414.

9. Hanák, "Polgárosodás és asszimiláció Magyarországon," 513–36.

10. For example, Gyula Kertész, *A kivándorlás szabályozása* (The regulation of emigration) (Budapest: Várnai és fia, 1910), 107–8. His estimate comes closest to the truth, but it is interesting to note that even this rather high estimate is taken by Rácz, *A paraszti migráció,* 107, as the lower rather than as the higher limit. Stolarik mentioned a surprisingly high figure (1980). In any case the growing number of dollars sent home prompted Baron Kornfeld, submanager of the General Credit Bank of Budapest in July 1911, to go to New York in order to establish there an organization known as the Transatlantic Trust Company. Its purpose was to take over, organize and extend the business of collecting and forwarding to the home country the earnings of Hungarian immigrants. The normal annual export

of Hungarian savings, according to Lajos Steiner, an American Hungarian, amounted to 400,000,000 a year. See Robert Ezra Park, *The Immigrant Press and Its Control* (Montclair, NJ: Patterson Smith, 1970), 418.

11. In other sending countries, too, the loss of manpower was emphasized. See Keijo Virtanen, *Settlement or Return: Finnish Emigrants (1860–1930) in the International Overseas Return Migration Movement* (Turku: The Migration Institute, 1979). At present the differences between the figures relating to the emigration losses of the various ethnicities in the former Austro-Hungarian Monarchy are still striking.

12. See Frigyes Fellner, *Magyarország nemzeti jövedelme* (The national income of Hungary) (Budapest, 1908), 113.

13. *Hungarian Census* 1891, 2:109–110.

14. Bertalan Neményi, *A magyar nép állapota és az amerikai kivándorlás* (The condition of the Hungarian people and emigration to America) (Budapest: Athenaeum, 1911), 46–47.

15. Ibid., 46.

16. Ibid., 47.

17. Fejös refers to the report of the chief constable of Zemplén county, according to whom the houses built by the "amerikások" can be aired and kept clean, in Zoltán Fejös, "Kivándoriás Amerikába a Zemplén középső vidékeiről" (Emigration to America from the central part of Zemplén) (Miskolc, 1980). 316. See also Rácz, *A paraszti migráció,* 176.

18. Returnees from the United States were popularly called "amerikás," "amerikások" in plural.

19. *Hungarian Census* 1891, II, 109–10.

20. See Lars-Goran Tedebrand, "Remigration from America to Sweden," in Runblom and Norman, *From Sweden to America,* 208.; Virtanen, *Settlement or Return,* 66–67 and the chapter "The Individual's Return Decision," 170–221; J. D. Gould, "European Intercontinental Emigration. The Road Home. Return Migration from the U.S.A.," *Journal of European Economic History* VIII (Spring 1980), 41–113. See also Ewa Moravska, "Return Migrations: Theoretical and Research Agenda." In a *Century of European Migrations, 1880–1930,* edited by Rudolph J. Vecoli and Suzanne M. Sinke. 1991. Urbana: University of Illinois Press, 277–92.

21. Report from the subprefect of Trencsén County to the Prime Minister, OL.K-16 (National Archives, The Centrally Registered and Filed Documents of the Prime Minister's Office)

22. *Hungarian Census* 1891, I, 109–10.

23. *Huszadik Század,* January-June 1908, 294.

24. From the speech of Ferenc Kossuth on the 172nd meeting in Parliament 16 December 1902. OKN.X.79.

25. See the 1902 report of the deputy-lieutenant of Heves County, quoted by Gábor Farkas, *Adatok Bodony község történetéhez* (Data concerning the history of Bodony village) (Gyöngyös: Bodony község Tanácsa, 1969), 99.

26. See among the many documents related to this Document No. 129 in *Iratok a nemzetiségi kérdes történetéhez Magyarországon a Dualizmus Korábam,* edited by Gábor G. Kemény (Documents concerning the question of non-Magyar

ethnic groups in the Age of Dualism) (Budapest: Akadémiai Kiadó, 1952–1985) (IV, 1960; V, 1971). See also Bielik and Rákos, *Slovenske Vystahovslectro*, 332–3 and *A Felvidéki Kivándorlási Kongresszus Tárgyalásai, Szervezete, Tagjainak Névsora és Határozatai* (The discussions, organizations, registered members and resolutions of the Emigration Conference on Northern Hungary), edited and published by the Országos Gazdasági Egyesület (National Economic Association) (Budapest: Patria, 1902), a conference held in Miskolc, May 31–June 1, 1902.

27. Report of the Lord Lieutenant of Turócz county to the Prime Minister, November 20, 1902, in Kemény, *Iratok a nemzetiségi kérdés történetéhez*, II (1964), 577–8.

28. Elek Bolgár, "A kivándorlás" (Emigration), *Huszadik Század* (1908), 493–9.

29. In the village of Szamosszeg there were remigrants among the activists during the time of the "Red Republic." Remigrants were forced to dig their own graves, but with the intervention of their priest they were saved. I was able to speak to one of them, János Bacskó. He only recalled his experiences of American democracy and completely forgot his own radical past. He actually took up the attitude of a conservative landed peasant.

30. See more about the consequences of emigration on the Slovaks, Ladislav Tajták, "Slovak Emigration: Its Causes and Consequences" in Puskás, *Overseas Migration*, 74–88.

31. Photographs of remigrants also demonstrate the extent to which peasant work, lifestyle, and the village community drew the remigrants back to their former life even in their outward appearance.

32. Farkas, *Adatok Bodony község történetehez*, 100.

33. See also Iván Balassa, *Lápok, falvak, emberek*, 257–87.

34. Interviews with some old Seven Day Adventists at Telkibánya in my collection. See also László Kardos, *Egyház és vallásos élet egy mai faluban: Bakonycsernye—1965* (Church and religious life in a contemporary village, Bakonycsernye—1965) (Budapest: Kossuth Kiadó, 1969), on sectarianism among the Magyar remigrants.

35. See the reports of the Austro-Hungarian monarchy's ambassadors and consuls from 1895 to 1914, for example, 7 July 1895, "Über panslavistische Agitation unter den Vereinigten Staaten sich aufhaltende Slovaken, October 25, 1895," and "Über die Lage der Slovakischer Arbeiter Bevölkerung in Pennsylvania und die unter ihnen betriebene panslavische Agitation." Ausstellungs Verzeichniss des Politischen Archivs des Ministerium des Äussern, XXII USA-1895, Nr. 14, Nr. 15.

36. Monika Glettler, "The Hungarian Government's Position on Slovak Emigration, 1885–1914." in Puskás, *Overseas Migration*, 107–118.

Chapter 6: Painting Pictures of an El Dorado

1. OL.BM.1928. K.150.

2. In 1880 Prime Minister Kálmán Tisza presents in 1880 the preamble of the bill "On Emigration Agents," OKI (Országgülés. Képviselőhazának Iratai) [Parliament. Documents of the House of Representatives]), vol. XVII, 290.

3. *Pesti Napló*, (Pest Journal) Budapest, 5 August 1880.

4. *Pesti Napló,* 29 November 1895.

5. *Pesti Napló,* 28 March 1901.

6. "Földmüvelök," (Tillers of the Soil), *Népszava* (People's Voice) Budapest, 1 September 1903. The Social Democrats took the following stand: "We're no friends of emigration, though we feel that the miserable economic and social conditions are enough to account for it." See *Népszava,* 4 September 1900.

7. From the speech of Kálmán Török, OKN. XXI-71,73. 13 November 1908.

8. László Vetési, *Boldogország a maga valóságában. Egy magyar munkás anerikai levelei* (The happy land as it really is. A Hungarian worker's letters from America) (Budapest: Lampel, 1902).

9. József Madarász, Jr. OKN.1908. XXI. 73–74. 13 November 1908.

10. From the speech of János Hock, OKN. XXI. 77–79. 13 November 1908.

11. Count József Majláth, *A kivándorlásról* (On emigration) (Budapest: II. Gazdaszövetség kiadványa, 1907), 42.

12. See Table 7, "Distribution of the migrants by sex, in percent, 1899–1913," in Puskás, *From Hungary to the United States,* 40.

13. See map "Emigrants from Hungary Overseas and to the Continent, 1899," in ibid., 59.

14. Report from Szepes County's subprefect to the Minister of the Interior, 8 September 1882. OL. BM. II-17-8361/1883.

15. See also reports from Abauj-Torna, Borsod, Bereg, Gömör, Szepes, Szatmár, Zemplén and other counties' subprefects to the Prime Minister. OL-K 16 (National Archives. The Centrally Registered and Filed Documents of the Prime Minister's Office) 1905-XVI-1450.

16. See Decree Nr. 205578/1913 of the Minister of the Interior, in Bielik and Rákos, *Slovenske Vystahovalectuo,* 349.

17. Of the 585,344 emigrants who went to the United States between 1908 and 1913, 221,596 returned. See Puskás, *From Hungary to America,* 27

18. Report from the prefect of Borsod County to the Prime Minister. OL.ME (Országos Levéltár Osztrák-Magyar monarchia Követségének iratai [Documents of the Austro-Hungarian Monarchy's Embassy in Washington, D.C.]) K26, 29, February 1904.

19. Fejős, "Kivándorlás Amerikába." See also Lajos Beck's speech on the 367th Session of the Parliament, 18 November 1908. OKN. XX. Vol. I, 62–6.

20. Neményi, *A magyar nép állapota,* 46–49.

21. Béla Gunda, "America in Hungarian Folk Tradition," *Journal of American Folklore,* 88: 406–416, 415.

22. Minutes of the Szabolcs County Assembly, 7 November 1901.

23. Interview with Piroska Puskás, New Brunswick, NJ 1983.

24. Interview with Gusztáv Kovács, Detroit, MI, 1983.

25. "Amerikás" dalok (Songs of "amerikások") in Dezsö Nagy, "Az amerikai magyarok folklórja" (The folklore of Hungarian-Americans), in Folklor Archivum (Folklore archive), edited by Mihály Hoppál, manuscript, II, 635–47.

26. From the letter of András Molitorisz, Allegheny, PA, in *Szabadság* (Liberty), 29 January 1909.

27. In January 1909, *Szabadság,* published in Cleveland as the Hungarian-language paper in America with the largest circulation, asked its readers for letters

telling why they came to America. Nineteen hundred letters were received in response. Most of these were published by the paper in its Sunday issues.

28. From the letter of Mrs. Farkas, in *Szabadság*, 22 January 1909.

29. From the letter of A. Margit, in *Szabadság*, 15 January 1909.

30. From the letter of Mrs. L. Joós, Wilkes-Barre, PA, in *Szabadság*, 5 February 1909.

31. Cited by Fejős, "Kivándorlás Amerikába," 322.

32. From the letter of J. Neuman, Passaic, NJ cited in *Szabadság*, 5 February 1909.

33. A summary of my research in the village of Szamosszeg.

34. From the letter of Mrs. L. Joós, Wilkes-Barre, PA, in *Szabadság*, 5 February 1909.

35. The richest source in this respect is the comic paper, *Dongó* (Wasp), edited by György Kemény, which appeared from 1903 to 1933, first in Cleveland and later in Detroit.

36. Quoted from István Jovicza's poem "Amerika" in Hoffmann, *Csonka munkásosztály* (Truncated working class) (Budapest: Pesti Könyvnyomda, 1911), 229–231.

37. From the letter of Mrs. Ferenc Tóth, New Philadelphia, PA, in *Szabadság*, 22 January 1909.

38. Letter from Mrs. Joós, Szabadság, 5 February 1909.

39. Cited by Fejös, "Kivándorlás Amerikába," 304.

40. *Eperjesi Lapok* (Eperjes Papers) 1882.l.nr., cited by István Rácz in his "A paraiztok kivándorlása a falúról (Migration of the peasants from the villages), in Szabó, *A parasztság magyarenszágon*, 463.

41. *Report of the Immigration Commission,* 4:388.

42. "We may say with good reason that every returnee, when he goes back the second time, takes 2 or 3 other persons along."

43. *Szabadság 10. jubileumi száma* (1901), 38.

Chapter 7: Emigration and Public Opinion in Hungary

1. See the introduction of the bill on regulating emigration in Parliament, 3 December 1902. OKN. Vol.IX, 271–4.

2. See the Memorandum of Sáros County, 29 May 1880 for an end to illegal emigration and for aid to those who want to return. No. 3898,OK.I. (Országgyülés. Képviselőházi jegyzökönyvek [Parliament. Minutes of the House of Representatives].) II., 11. Interpellation on the question of the Magyars emigrating from Sáros County, at the 266th session of Parliament 22 May 1880. IKN Vol.XII., 93. Petition submitted on 18 March 1882 by the communities of the royal free borough of Szatmár-Németi and Zemplén County concerning the implementation of measures to restrict emigration and to do away with its causes. OKN. Vol.IV, 224.

3. See Mary Boros Kazay, "The Emigration Problem and Hungary's Lawmakers, 1880–1910," *Hungarian Studies Review* 8:1 (Spring 1981): 25–44. See also István Rácz, "Attempts to Curb Hungarian Emigration to the United States before 1914," *Hungarian Studies in English*, VII (Debrecen, 1973), 5–33, and Puskás

From Hungary to the United States, Chapter: "Free Emigration—with restrictions: The Hungarian Government's Emigration Policy," 92–98.

4. The bill "A kivándorlási ügynökségekről" (On the emigration agencies), XXVII: tc. Országos Törvénytár (National Legal Code) (1881), 165–7.

5. Preamble to the bill "On the emigration agencies." OKI. Országgyülés Képviselöházi iratai (Documents of the House of Representatives of Parliament) 1878–1881 Cycle of Parliament Sessions. XXIV, 242–5.

6. The introduction of the bill "On regulating emigration" in Parliament 3 December 1902. OKN. Vol.IX., 271–2 and 1903. IV. tc. Országos Tövénytár (National Legal Code).

7. *Népszava,* Budapest, 8 November 1902.

8. *Népszava,* Budapest, 8 November 1902.

9. OL Miniszterelnökség (National Archives-Prime Minister's Office) K 26. 29 July 1902.

10. Prime Minister Kálmán Széll's answer to Ferenc Buzáth's interpellation. See OKN. XV. 274–275, and the supplement to document No. 195, Preamble to the bill "On the Regulation of emigration" OKI. VII., 265–284. The Text of the Bill—1903. IV.tc. Magyar Törvénytár (Hungarian Legal Code) (1904), 45–69.

11. Extract from the public order issued by the Minister of the Interior: According to the authorization contained in the 1903 IV. §b. "I hereby point out that the sole course for overseas emigration must be via Fiume, and I declare that for the time being I shall only grant permission for transporting emigrants on this course."

12. For more details on the Alliance of the Atlantic Shipping Companies for the years 1902–04, see OL.BM.1928.K 150., 25–37.

13. For details see OL Prime Minister K 150, 42–44. MP Károly Hencz's interpellation, and the Minister of the Interior, Count Gyula Andrássy's reply, 21 November 1908. OKN, XI, 202–206.

14. This was expressed, for example, by the fact that the Dillingham Bill (Senator Dillingham had submitted a bill to restrict emigration) was given an appendix which proposed 1) to fine immigrants arriving in a ship subsidized by foreign countries thirty dollars each, and 2) to prohibit the landing of emigrants whose trip was supported by foreign countries through contracts with shipping companies. OL.BM.1928.K150, 37–38.

15. See the detailed statistical reports on "The role of Fiume and the shipping companies in transatlantic emigration" based on data collected by the Royal Hungarian Commissary Office of Emigration. *Magyar Statisztikai Közlemények* 67, II, 71–81.

16. See "A kivándorlásról" (On Emigration) Article 1909 II. 2–3, in Magyar törvénytár (Hungarian Legal Code) (Budapest, 1920), 4–29.

17. "Indoklás a kivándorlásról szóló törvényjavaslathoz" (Preamble to the Bill on Emigration) OKI.XXII, 415.

18. György Szmrecsányi MP's interpellation on the subject of one of the most important social and economic questions of the last two decades: on the question of emigration 21 December 1910. OKN. II, 233–7. Repeated interpellation of Szmrecsányi, 17 January 1911. OKN, III, 327–34. See also Barna Budai "The Cunard, the Hungarian Emigrants and the Pool," *Pesti Napló,* 18 January 1911.

19. Barna Budai, "A Pool szerződés" (The Pool contract), Köztelek, 19 November 1913.

20. In 1895 Géza Polányi, opposition deputy from Hajduszoboszló, called attention to the eradication of the entailed estates. He saw them as "an anachronism in the present era of equality before the law," and he also supported the revision of the inheritance laws as an ameliorating measure. 6 November 1895. OKN. XXVI, 195–9. See also Mary Boros-Kazay, "The Emigration Problem," 29. See the minutes of the Emigration Congresses (1902). See, for example, *A Felvidéki Kivándorlási Kongresszus Tárgyalásai, Szervezete, Tagjainak Névsora és Határozatai.*

21. OKN. 1901–1906. X. 16 December 1902, 81–2.

22. The newest literature also criticized the activities of the agents of shipowner societies, but it did not ascribe to the agents as great a role in the incitement of emigration as many contemporaries did. The leaders of some countries were apt to see the reasons for emigration explicitly in agents' activities.

23. The bill was introduced by the Minister of the Interior, Count Gyula Andrássy, on 9 May 1908. For its text and appendix, "Preamble to the Bill on Emigration," see OKI. XXII, 415–49.

24. See, for example, the minutes of the Emigration Congresses in 1902 in Miskolc, (note 21 above)

25. OKN. 1884–1887. XVI. 2 April 1887, 279.

26. From Endre Ady's poem, "Ülj törvényt Verbőczy!" (Sit in Judgement, Verbőczy!).

27. "Stahovanie" *Národné noviny,* 15 March 1892. Cited by Tajták, "Slovak Emigration," 83.

28. Quoted by Cizmic "Emigration from Yugoslavia prior to World War I," in Glasier and de Rosa, *Migration Across Time and Nations,* 257.

29. Ibid.

30. See more details in the chapter "Kivándorlási politika—propaganda és gyakorlat" (Emigration politics—propaganda and practice), in Puskás, *From Hungary to the United States,* 92–115.

31. See, for example, the debate of the Social Science Association on emigration and remigration. *Magyar Társadalomtudományi Szemle* (Hungarian Sociological Review) I (1908), 281.

Chapter 8: American Immigration Policy: The Era of Regulations, 1882–1914

1. See William S. Bernard, "Immigration: History of the United States Policy," in Thernstrom, *Harvard Encyclopedia,* 486–95.

2. Ibid., 490.

3. Ibid., 491.

4. Quoted by Maldwyn Allen Jones, *American Immigration* (Chicago: University of Chicago Press, 1960), 252.

5. John Higham, *Send These to Me: Jews and the Immigrants in Urban America* (New York: Atheneum, 1975), 29–66.

6. Ibid., 102–16. See also Thomas J. Archdeacon, who emphasized that "the identification of immigration with left-wing radicalism added a fresh dimension to American xenophobia. Nativists had usually stereotyped aliens as the agents of reactionary regimes." In *Becoming American: An Ethnic Heritage* (New York: Collier Macmillan, 1983), 57–111.

7. Tibor Frank, "Amerikai 'uj bevándorlók' antropometriai vizsgálata. 1908–1911" (Anthropometric study of "new immigrants" in America), *Antropometriai Közlemények* (Antropometric Publications) 36 (1994), 69–77. Social Darwinism enjoyed immediate success in American universities. The most important person in the transfer of the ideology from Europe to the United States was an Englishman named Herbert Spencer, who coined the phrase "survival of the fittest." The attraction of Social Darwinism also reflected a need by many citizens to find an explanation for the growing disparity of wealth evident in the new industrial order. See also Archdeacon, *Becoming American,* 159–60.

8. Ibid., 162–3.

9. In 1887 President Grover Cleveland vetoed a bill that would have established a literacy requirement for immigrants. Cleveland argued that the test was contrary to American tradition and measured prior opportunity rather than innate ability. Presidents William H. Taft and Woodrow Wilson repeated the argument of Grover Cleveland and vetoed bills incorporating literacy tests. Ibid., 163.

10. According to Philip Taylor the lobbying of powerful Irish, German, and Jewish groups against further restrictions is part of the explanation. Even more important probably is the fact that once prosperity had returned, there were powerful business forces favorable to free entry. See Philip Taylor, *Distant Magnet: European Emigration to the U.S.A.* (New York: Harper Row, 1971), 247.

11. Higham, *Send These to Me,* 48–9.

12. Archdeacon, *Becoming American,* 166–9.

13. John R. Commons, *Immigration and Its Economic Effect* (New York: Henry Holt, 1906). See also Richard Hofstadter, *Social Darwinism in American Thought* (Boston: Beacon Press, 1955), 49.

14. Edward A. Ross, *The Old World in the New* (New York: The Century Co., 1914), 146.

15. As the head of AFL, Gompers also supported the restriction of immigration. He visited sending countries, too, and in his reports showed no sympathy towards immigration.

16. Tibor Frank, "Ellis Island követei. Az osztrák-magyar kivándorlás titkos amerikai megfigyelése, 1906–1907" (Ellis Island's envoys. The secret American supervision of the Austro-Hungarian emigration, 1906–1907), *Valóság* 35 (1992) no. 7, 77–90.

17. Tibor Frank, "From Immigrant Laborers to Emigré Professionals: Studies in the Social History of Hungarian American Migrations, 1880–1945." Manuscript (Budapest: Lóránt Eötvös University, 1995).

18. Marcus Braun summarized his experiences in his book *Immigration Abuses: Glimpses of Hungary and Hungarians* (New York: Pearlon Advertising Co., 1972). First published as *Certain Reports of Immigrant Inspector Marcus Braun* (Washington, D.C.: Government Printing Office, 1906).

19. *Reports of the Immigration Commission,* Immigrants in Industries, vols. 19–20.

20. Ibid., "The Emigration Situation in Austria-Hungary," vol. 4, 349–88.

21. Ibid., Statements and recommendations. Submitted by societies and organizations interested in the subject of immigration.

22. When Boas gave an account of his research and its results in March of 1909, he noted that the descendants of immigrants are more advanced than the immigrants themselves, and start developing earlier. The effect of American conditions increases as more time elapses between the parents' immigration and the birth of their children in the United States. The changes observed in the second generation are not confined to the rate of development, but we can observe a change in cultural characteristics, too, which seem to approach those of Americans. Franz Boas, *Changes in Bodily Form of Descendants of Immigrants,* Senate Documents, 61st Congress, 2nd Session, 1909–1910, vol. 8.

23. Franz Boas, *Kultur und Rasse* (Culture and Race) (Leipzig: Welt und Comp, 1914), 61–7. Boas' influential *The Mind of Primitive Man* (New York: Macmillan, 1911), a series of lectures presented at the Lowell Institute in Boston and the National University of Mexico, 1910–1911, and considerably enlarged in a 1937 edition, is quoted by Frank, "Immigrant laborers," 485, a manuscript.

24. Richard A. Easterlin, "Immigration: Economic and Social Characteristics," in Thernstrom, *Harvard Encyclopedia,* 485.

Chapter 9: Settlement Patterns

1. Károly Rácz-Rónai, "An American Hungarian poet," from his poem "Immigrants" in Hoffman, *Csonka munkásosztály,* 229.

2. *Magyar Statisztikai Közlemények* 67: 45, textual commentary.

3. Since 1881 migrants were also using a new generation of fast steamers, which shortened the ocean crossing to 9 days. Missler's firm had a main agency in Budapest too. His name became so well known that people said they "traveled with Missler." See Dirk Hoerder, "The Traffic of Emigration via Bremen/Bremenhaven—Merchants' Interest, Protective Legislation, and Migrants' Experience," in *Journal of American Ethnic History,* XIII, no. 1 (1993), 68–101.

4. Publications of contemporaries on their traveling experiences with emigrants. See also Tivadar Kompolthy, *Tengeren és szárazföldön* (On sea and on land) (Nagyvárad: Wügel Nyomda, 1890); Kramar, *From the Danube to the Hudson; Magyar Statisztikai Közlemények* 67; Sándor Tonelli, *Ultonia. Egy kivándorló hajó története* (Ultonia. Story of a migration ship) (Budapest: Egyetemi Nyomda, 1929). Edward A. Steiner, *On the Trail of the Immigrants* (1906: reprint New York: Arno Press, 1969); Albert Tezla, *Valahol túl, Meseországban. Az amerikai magyarok 1895–1920.* 2 vol. (Somewhere in a distant fabled land: The American Hungarians) (Budapest: Európa Könyvkiadó, 1987). Under the titles "Megy a hajó" (The ship departs), and "Elisz Ájlend" (Ellis Island), he cites information received from contemporaries, I, 125–26.

5. From the proceedings of debates in Parliament. See in more detail OL K 150, 42–44; and the interpellation of Károly Hencz and the answer of the Minister of the Interior, Count Gyula Andrássy, on 21 November 1908. OKN.XI. 202–206.

6. According to the *Előre* (Forward), 17 January 1914. "On Ellis Island they no longer look for a reason to deport an emigrant. They do it and that's all there is to it." Another article of 6 February 1914 describes how a Hungarian immigrant on Ellis Island burst out against the crudeness of the examining physician, upon which the latter declared him insane. According to the statistics of the Immigration and Naturalization Office, the number of deportees tended to increase. See also Edward A. Steiner, "The Hungarian Immigrant," in *Outlook,* LXXIV (1903), 1040–44.

7. See also the detailed report based on the data in Table 25 in the "Annual Report of the Commissioner General of Immigration," in *Magyar Statisztikai Közlemények* 67, Tables 47, 56.

8. It is difficult to follow the establishment of Hungarian emigrants' settlements and even more difficult to determine the actual numbers in the various locations. The United States Census numbers are only rough estimates, not only because the counting of the emigrants was faulty, but because, as was previously pointed out, the registration of immigrant national groups ran into problems as a result of the complex nationality relationships. Fortunately the contemporary Hungarian-American sources contain much information about the settlements. These sources are very useful for tracing where the scattered Hungarian settlements developed and for reconstructing the characteristics and types, even if their numerical data are rough estimates and their exaggeration require critical examination.

9. "Hungarians," in *The Encyclopedia of Cleveland History,* edited by David D. Van Tassel and John J. Grabowski (Bloomington: Indiana University Press, 1987), 533.

10. Susan Papp, *Hungarian Americans and Their Communities of Cleveland"* (Cleveland: Cleveland State University, 1981), 155. See also *Szabadság 10. jubileumi száma* (Szabadság's 10th Anniversary issue) (1901), 19.

11. "Immigration to Cleveland by country of origin, 1874–1907," in Van Tassel and Grabowski, *The Cleveland Encyclopedia* (1987), 542–543.

12. Hoffmann, *Csonka munkás osztály,* 37. and *Szabadság Naptár* (1908), 205.

13. Ira Rosenwaike, *Population History of New York City* (Syracuse: Syracuse State University Press, 1972), 123.

14. Hoffmann, *Csonka munkásosztály,* 36.; Edward A. Steiner paints a vivid picture with his personal recollections of New York's Hungarians, including the "Little Hungary" restaurant. Steiner, *On the Trail of the Immigrants* (New York: Revell. 1960, Reprint, Arno Press, 1968.

15. This Hungarian enclave is also described in Rosenwaike, *Population History* of New York City. See also Robert Perlman, *Bridging Three Worlds: Hungarian Jewish Americans, 1848–1914. Settlement Pattern of Hungarian Jews* (Amherst: University of Massachusetts Press, 1991), 135–148.

16. *Szabadság 50. jubileumi száma* (Szabadság's 50th Anniversary issue) (1941), Cleveland, OH. 92–93.

17. Kálmán Káldor, *Magyar Amerika irásban és képben* (Hungarian America in writing and pictures) 2 vols. (St. Louis: Hungarian Publishing Co., 1937), 53–73.

18. For more about the Hungarians settling in Toledo, see John M. Hirnyák, *Birmingham. Toledo's Hungarian Communities* (Toledo: OH., 1975).

19. Kádor, *Magyar-Amerika írásbam és képben*, 1:102–103. *Szabadság 50. Jubileumi száma*, 106.

20. See *Szabadság Naptár*, 1905–1908. Most migrants arrived from the counties of Abauj-Torna, Zemplén, Bereg, and Szablcs.

21. "Trentoni magyarság története" (The history of the Hungarians of Trenton), in "Magyar telephelyek Amerikában" (Hungarian settlements in America), *Szabadság Naptár* (1905), 225–229. See also David Burden Smith, "The Hungarians in New Brunswick, New Jersey to 1920: A Social Biography" (M.A.thesis, Rutgers State University, 1965).

22. August J. Molnár, "Hungarian Pioneers and Immigrants in New Jersey Since Colonial Days," in *The New Jersey Ethnic Experience,* edited by Barbara Cunningham (Union City, NJ: W. H. Wise, 1977), 249–266.

23. *The Hungarians in Bridgeport. A Social Survey,* edited by Hillel Bardin (Bridgeport, CT: University of Bridgeport, Department of Sociology, 1959).

24. See the detailed description of the Hungarians' settlement in Chicago in Fejős, *Chicagoi magyarok,* 39–83. A good overview of the changes in the census methods is contained in "The People of Chicago" (1975), "Census Data of Foreign Born" (1976), and in "The Historic City" (1976), a historical, statistical compilation. See also *Szabadság 50. jubileumi szama* (1941), 186–7; *Szabadság 10. jubileumi száma* (1901), 31; Káldor, *Magyar Amerika írásban és képben,* 1:153–5; Károly Rácz-Rónay, "Az amerikai magyar telepek története" (The History of American Hungarian settlements), *Külföldi Magyarság* (Hungarians Abroad), 13.

25. *Szabadság 10. jubileumi száma* (1901); Káldor, *Magyar Amerika írasban és képben (1937); Szabadság 50. jubileumi száma* (1941), 1:307.

26. Káldor, *Magyar Amerika írásban és Kepben,* 178; Interviews with Mr. and Mrs. Danko, Detroit, MI, 1983; *Magyar Hírlap* (Hungarian News, Detroit), 28 September 1916; Malvina Hauk-Abonyi and James A. Anderson, *Hungarians in Detroit* (Detroit: Wayne State University Center for Urban Studies, 1977). See also *Szabadság 50. jubileumi száma* (1941), 253.

27. M. L. Kovács, "The Saskatchewan Era, 1885–1914," in *Struggle and Hope: The Canadian Hungarian Experience,* edited by N. T. Dreisziger (Toronto: McClelland and Stewart, 1982), 61–3.

28. Elek Csutoros, "Az Árpádhoni településről" (The settlement in Árpádhon), *Árvaházi Naptár* (Orphanage Almanac) (1917), 120–131. See also I. H. Janda, *Hungarian Place Names in the United States* (El Paso, TX, 1976), 219–227. Contemporary documents were reproduced by Tezla, *Valahol túl,* 2:153–173, on the settlement in Árpádhon published in the *Árpádhoni Kertészlap* (The Árpádhon Gardeners Journal). 1913–1914. Hammond, IN.

29. Robert Hosh, "Árpádhon, Louisiana: An Example of Hungarian Immigration Acculturation," (M.A. thesis, Columbia University, 1969).

30. Géza Kende, *Magyarok Amerikában: Az amerikai magyarság története* (Hungarians in the United States: The history of Hungarian Americans), 2 vol. (Cleveland: Szabadság kiadó 1927). unpublished. (One copy in the author's collection.) In the chapter, "A telepítések története" (The history of the colonies) the

author wrote that in the second half of the 1920s, Hungarian settlements (Buda, Nyitra, Tokaj) consisting mostly of a few families did not exist anymore owing to the fact that the settlers were obliged to find work in industry.

31. Interview with Ignác Kósa, Szamosszeg, 1982.

32. Interview with Gyula Kovács, Detroit, 1983.

33. US Census 1910, "Population," vol. 2.

34. *Szabadság 10. jubileumi száma* (1901), 17.

35. See *Magyar Bányásznaptár* (Hungarian Miners' Almanac) (1940), 271–91.

36. *Szabadság 10. jubileumi száma* (1901), 17. See also Edward A. Steiner, *On the Trail of the Immigrants* (1906) (reprint, New York: Arno Press, 1969), 213–24. The date published in the *Szabadság 50. jubileumi száma* (1941) from the over 2,000 biographies in 354 settlements attest to their migrations within the United States.

37. See Rudolph J. Vecoli, "Contadini in Chicago: A Critique of 'The Uprooted,'" *Journal of American History,* 51:401–17.

38. Swierenga, "Ethnic History," Ethnic Forum. 4.

39. Paula K. Benkart, "Hungarians" in Thernstrom, *Harvard Encyclopedia,* 465. For more detail see her study "The Hungarian Government, the American Magyar Churches, and Immigrant Nationalism" (paper presented to the Hopkins-Harwichport Seminar in American Religious History, August 1973), 1–20. This paper can be found in the Balch Institute library, Philadelphia, PA.

Chapter 10: In the Coal Mines and Steel Mills

1. *Reports of the Immigration Commission,* vols. 19–20, 23. In the iron and steel industry the years between 1890 and 1910 brought a similar change in the composition of the work force. By 1907, some 73.2 percent of its foreign workers were Slovaks, Magyars, Germans, and Croatians. See Bureau of Labor, "Report on Conditions of Employment in the Iron and Steel Industry," III (Washington, D.C., 1910), 85.

2. John A. Finch, *The Steel Workers.* 2d ed. (Pittsburgh: University of Pittsburgh Press, 1989), 183.

3. Raymond A. Mohl and Neil Betten, *Steel City: Urban and Ethnic Patterns in Gary, Indiana, 1906–1950.* (New York. Holmes & Meier, 1986), 5. Margaret F. Byington writes, "The nature of the work, with the heat and its inherent hazard makes much of it exhausting. Yet these men for the most part keep it up twelve hours a day." In *Homestead: The Households of a Mill Town* (Pittsburgh: Russell Sage Foundation, 1974), 36.

4. On the wages see *Reports of the Immigration Commission,* vol. 26, I–II, 577.

5. Ibid. See also L. Ferenczi, *Amerika. Az Egyesült Államokban élö magyarok megélhetési viszonyai, helyzete, munkája, keresete és a Carnegie vasmüvek ismertetése* (America. The conditions of subsistence, position, work, and earnings of the Hungarians living in the United States and the presentation of the Carnegie ironworks) (Zombor: Kollán József, 1909), and A. S. Glenn, *Amerikai levelek* (Letters from America) (Budapest: Lampel, 1913). Contemporary reports on the working conditions of the iron and steel factories are published by Tezla, *Valahol túl,* 2:7–95.

6. Finch, *The Steelworkers,* 192.

7. The greatest expansion of coal mining in West Virginia occurred after 1893. More than one half of the miners in 1910 are of foreign birth, and belong principally to races of Southern and Eastern Europe. See more details in *Reports of the Immigration Commission,* Vols. 19–20. Immigrants in Industries.: Pt. 23. Summary report on immigrants in manufacturing and mining. Senate Document No. 633. 61ˢᵗ Congr. 2ⁿᵈ Session.

8. Ibid., 6, 2:228.

9. Ibid., 6, 1:50.

10. David Alan Corbin, *Life, Work and Rebellion in the Coal Fields: The Southern West Virginia Miners, 1880–1922.* (Chicago: University of Illinois Press, 1981) 9. See the chapter "Solidarity For Ever," 87–105. See also *Reports of the Immigration Commission,* (1911, 1970) 6:511.

11. Gusztáv Kovács, interview, Detroit, 1983.

12. Gusztáv Kovács, interview, 1983.

13. Second interview with Gusztáv Kovács, Detroit, 1985.

14. The mine, the hard and dangerous work, the frequency of accidents—the main subjects of Hungarian-American literature. See, for example, the following verse:

> "In the Bluefield cemetery
> a lot of graves men dig.
> Many poor dead miners,
> a lot of graves they need.
> In a fit of temper
> the mine did smother them!
> They were Magyar peasants,
> So who cares about them!"

> (Rough translation from Hungarian by György Kemény. Hungarian text in Hoffmann, *Csonka munkásosztály.* 234.)

15. Interview with Mrs. Seres, Cleveland, 1988. See also István Eszterhás, *Amerikai magyar regény* (American Hungarian novel) (Cleveland, 1989) on the lot of the Hungarian worker in Cleveland.

16. From the First Hungarian Reformed Church's Death-Register, Cleveland, 1892–1914, 57. It can be ascertained that this was the cause of their death. *Szabadság Naptár* reported on many fatal accidents in the column "On the Field of Work" and in the 20th anniversary issue, 21 December 1911.

17. A marker was placed in 1909 in memory of the 239 miners killed in an explosion in the Darr Mine on 19 December 1907. For accounts of the accidents in the factories and explosions in the mines see the collection of American Hungarian Newspapers, see Tezla, *Valahol túl,* 2:7–130, and in the *Szabadság Naptár,* 1904–1912.

18. Sándor Kalassay and Sándor Harsányi, "Temetik a magyarokat" (They are burying the Hungarians), *Amerikai Magyar Reformátusok Lapja* (Journal of the American-Hungarian Reformed), 4 January 1908, 9–10.

19. This was repeatedly the theme of Hungarian-American poems: "Any trouble, any hatred there exists, the Hungarians are charged with it. Be it a Pole, a Slovak, a Czech, anyone coming from the eastern part of Europe will all be called collectively coming from 'Hungaria.' The xenophobe English newspapers take every opportunity to deal a blow at a foreigner, and the American working people, reading these articles deriding the aliens, feel an even bigger hatred for them." *Szabadság*, 13 May 1897.

20. On the Austro-Hungarian Foreign Ministers Actions against American employers, OL. ME. K. 126/1910/386, in "The Hungarian Government, the American Magyar Churches and immigrant nationalities." A paper presented by Paula Benkart to the Hopkins-Harwichport Seminar in American Religious History. 23–25 August 1973.

21. *Szabadság*, 3 December 1907.

22. Interview with Julianna Szögyény, New Brunswick, NJ, 1984.

23. Interview with Piroska Puskás, New Brunswick, NJ, 1984 and 1986.

24. *Szabadság 10. jubileumi száma*, "A clevelandi magyar kolónia" (The Hungarian colony of Cleveland) (1901), 18–19.

25. Ibid., 19.

26. Ibid., 18.

27. Hoffmann, *Csonka munkásosztály*, 36. Essentially the same was written on the Hungarian settlement of Cleveland by Károly Rácz-Rónai in his series of articles quoted above, "IX. Cleveland," *Külföldi Magyarság* (1923), 2.

28. For example, György Kemény, "Az amerikai magyar életből. Karcolatok (From Hungarian Life in America) Sketches, in *Amerikai Magyar Népszava Jubileumi Díszalbuma 1899–1909* (Amerikai Magyar Népszava Deluxe Anniversary album) (New York, 1910) 210–35.

29. *Reports of the Immigration Commission*, 26:579. See also Frank J. Sheridan, "Italian, Slavic and Hungarian unskilled immigrant laborers in the United States," *Bulletin of the Bureau of Labor*, no. 72 (Washington, D.C., September 1906).

30. *Szabadság Naptár* (1905). Records of some bigamies can be found in the Marriage Register of the First Reformed Church of Cleveland.

31. Sárközi, "A summások," in Szabó, *A parasztság Magyarországon*, 2:321–381.

32. *Szabadság*, 13 January 1892. An article entitled "Rossz szokás" (Bad habit) relates that some of the Cleveland parents have the bad habit to send their children to collect coal dispersed on the rails.

33. Interview with Gusztáv Kovács, Detroit, 1983.

34. Interviews with J. Szögyény, P. Puskás, Mrs. Szabó, G. Kovács, and others. All mentioned that they continued some peasant household activities in their new environment.

35. Interview with Julianna Szögyényi, New Brunswick, NJ, 1984.

36. Interview with Margit Szabó, New Brunswick, NJ, 1986.

37. Interview with Piroska Puskás, New Brunswick, NJ, 1983.

38. Interview with Joseph Paragh, Highland Park, NJ, 1986.

39. Interview with Joseph Paragh, Highland Park, NJ, 1986.

40. *Amerikai Magyar Népszava Jubileumi Díszalbuma* (1910), 216.

41. All persons who were interviewed emphasized this and it could be seen unambiguously in the case of the Szamosszegians.

42. *Amerikai Magyar Népszava Jubileumi Díszalbuma* (1910), 41.

43. More detailed in Ewa Morawska, "The Sociology and Historiography of Immigration," in Yans-McLaughlin, *Immigration Reconsidered,* 199–200.

44. L. Tarcai, "A Verhovayak a munkásharcokban" (Members of the Verhovay in the workers' struggles) (Verhovay Journal, Verhovay Relief Association's 50th Anniversary Publication) (Pittsburgh, 1936), 58–64. (*Verhovayak Lapja, Verhovay Segélyegylet 50. éves jubileumi kiadványa* 1936).

45. Such for example is the following:

> Mister pitboss we won't work
> We are striking to a man
> We are striking to show you
> That we won't load the coal."

Quoted by the famous Hungarian writer Zsigmond Móricz
in his collected works (1921, vol. 1. no. 1., 250) from the book
Amerikai Magyar Költök (American Hungarian poets)
Budapest, 1920. Compiled by Jenö Rickert.

See further on the strikes the immigrants took part in, for example: Lajos Tarcai, "A Verhovayak a munkásharcokban." (Members of the Verhovay in the workers' struggles) *Verhovayak Lapja, Verhovay Segély egylet 50 éves jubileumi kiadványa* (1936), 58–64. For more on the strikes the immigrants took part in, see the Report on the Miners' Strike in the Bituminous Coal Fields in the Westmoreland County, Pennsylvania in 1910–1911 (Washington, DC, 1912).

46. See the description of various strikes by Fred Thomson, *The I.W.W.: Its First Fifty Years 1905–1955.* (Chicago: Industrial Workers of the World, 1955), 43. During the McKees Rocks strike (August 1909), members of the so-called "Unknown Committee" decided after a striker, Istvan Horváth, was killed, that for every striker killed they would take the life of one of those fighting against them. On the 29th of August, the state troopers, who the workers called "the Cossacks of Pennsylvania," attacked the living quarters of the Hungarian strikers, sneeringly called 'Hunky-ville,' and started shooting. "The strikers, as good as their word, used weapons in self-defense," according to József Geréb, *Forradalmárok könyve* (Book of revolutionaries) (Chicago: I.W.W., 1921), 85. For the steel strikes of 1909–10 and the new immigrants' determined participation, see also David Brody, *Steelworkers in America: The Nonunion Era,* (Cambridge, MA: Russell and Russell, 1960), 123–46. See also Melvyn Dubofsky, *We Shall Be All. A History of the Industrial Workers of the World* (Chicago: Quadrangle Books, 1969), 204–9. John N. Ingham, "A Strike in the Progressed Era, McKees Rocks, 1909," in *The Pennsylvania Magazine of History and Bibliography,* X, 6 (July 1966), 2:353–77; and also Graham, Adams, Jr., *Age of Industrial Violence, 1905–1910,* (New York: Columbia University Press, 1966).

47. Hoffman, *Csonka munkásosztály.* In the chapter "Strikes" interesting information can be found on the strikes in which Hungarians took part. The numerous spontaneous strikes of the Hungarians reflect that the work stoppages were not

the work of agitators (116). The Americans attribute the disturbances to the violent, half-savage nature of the immigrants and call those workers, once despised for being modest but fighting now for better working conditions, a host of rabble (117). "Nagy sztrájkok és szerencsétlenségek" (Huge strikes and disasters) *Szabadság 20 jub. szám* (Szabadság 20th Anniversary Nr.) 11 December 1911.

48. Herbert G. Gutman, *Work, Culture and Society in Industrializing America: Essays in American Working-class and Social History* (New York: Knopf, 1976), 80–91.

Chapter 11: The First Hungarian-American Businessmen

1. *Dongó,* 6 October 1904. In a notice entitled "Clevelandi kocsmárosok" (Innkeepers in Cleveland) the advertisements of seven Hungarian pubs in the East Side on Holton Street can be found, *Clevelandi Magyar Recorder* (Cleveland Hungarian Recorder), May 1897.

2. Ibid.

3. Ibid.

4. *Amerikai Magyar Népszava Jubileumi Díszalbuma* (1910), 335.

5. *Napsugár* (Sunbeam) Cleveland-New York-Chicago, 9 January 1910. "János Szabó, the oldest saloonkeeper of the earliest days on the Cleveland Buckeye Road" *Szabadság Naptár* (1915), 194.

6. *Amerikai Magyar Népszava Jubileumi Díszalbuma* (1910), 330.

7. Their advertisements lead one to this conclusion. See them in *Clevelandi Magyar Recorder,* Cleveland, 5 May 1897; *Szabadság Naptár* (since 1904) and *Napsugár* (1910).

8. Hoffmann, *Csonka munkásosztály,* devotes a special chapter to "the banker" (A bankár). See further in G. Kemény, "Az amerikai életből," in *Amerikai Magyar Népszaua Jubileumi Díszalbuma (1910),* 220–222. József Szepessy had already advertised in *Szabadság* on 13 March 1893: "I notify the Hungarians of having opened a ship-ticket selling and money-sending business." In one of his advertisements in 1910, the expansion of his business activities is well reflected: "József Z. Szepessy, notary public, is the chief banker of the Hungarians. He is therefore not a runaway banker. The only Hungarian man in Ohio state who is director of an American bank. He is the legally appointed agent of all the shipping companies, there is none other in the Hungarian district. He sends money home three times a week. The money is always sent in a sealed envelope or hand-delivered, and the postal receipt from Hungary can always be seen at Szepessy's office. All kinds of selling, inheritance or transfer of land, agreements, promissory notes, etc., are practicable in this office. He arranges naturalization papers. He lends money on real estate. Fire insurance. Selling of houses." *Napsugár,* 10 April 1910.

9. *Szabadság,* 17 September 1918.

10. *Napsugár,* 22 May 1910, and *Szabadság,* 21 December 1911.

11. *Szabadság 50. jubileumi száma* (1941), 79.

12. *Magyar Hírlap Naptár* (Almanac of the Hungarian Journal) (1915), 52.

13. *Szabadság Naptár* (1920), 192, *Szabadság 50. jubileumi száma* (1941), 79.

14. *Napsugár,* 10 April 1910.

15. *Amerikai Magyar Népszaua Jubileumi Díszalbuma* (1910), 385.

16. Ibid., 338, 402, and *Szabadság 20. jubileumi száma* (1911) (Szabadság's 20th Anniversary issue).

17. *Magyar Hírlap Naptár* (Almanac of the Hungarian Journal) (1915), 190. Another advertisement of the same kind: "I get legal matters transacted whether here or in the old country by the best advocates. The largest and most Hungarian bookseller in Cleveland. I store all kinds of merchandise imported from home." *Amerikai Magyar Népszava Jubileumi Díszalbuma* (1910), 402.

18. *Magyar Hírlap Naptár* (1915), 189.

19. *Amerikai Magyar Népszava Jubileumi Díszalbuma* (1910), 335.

20. See the chapters "Futó bankárok" (Runaway bankers) in the *Szabadság Calendars,* 1904–1913.

21. Cristopher J. Eiken, *Tori in Amerika—The Story of Theodor Kuntz* (Cleveland: Orange Blossom Press, 1994), 7–9.

22. Ibid., 15–16.

23. *Amerikai Magyar Népszava Jubileumi Díszalbuma* (1910), 336.

24. "Theodor Kundtz" in *Cleveland und sein Deutschtum,* (German American Biographical Publication, Cleveland 1897–98), 335–337. See also Tihamér Kundtz's advertisement in ibid., 339.

25. On 27 February 1910, *Napsugár* published a list of Hungarian shops in Cleveland under the title "Reliable Hungarian shops and firms." The article "Magyar üzleti élet Amerikában" (Hungarian business life in America) contains short information on notable businessmen and their social significance. Ibid., 330–346.

36. Interview with Mr. Szabó, Cleveland 1988.

27. Árpád G. Gerster, *Recollections of a New York Surgeon* (New York: P. B. Hoeber, 1917). This memoir of a well-known and respected Hungarian surgeon, who spent most of his life in New York, sheds light on the problems faced by those who engaged in or supported Hungarian activities in the United States.

Chapter 12: Founding Secular Organizations

1. See Kende, *Magyarok Amerikában,* II, 27–28.

2. The Society's first aim was to provide sick benefits and funeral expenses; secondary aims included protecting the rights of Hungarian immigrants and informing Clevelanders about the Hungarian people, customs, and traditions. Papp, *Hungarian Americans and their Communities of Cleveland,* 172.

3. *Amerikai Magyar Népszava Jubileumi Díszalbuma* (1910), 324. See ibid., 172–173.

4. *Szabadság,* 4 April 1894.

5. According to Perlman there is little doubt that before 1900, Jews constituted the majority of Hungarians in Cleveland, as is clear from the list of members of the Hungarian Society and the fact that the first Hungarian Church was not established until 1891. Perlman, *Bridging Three Worlds,* 142. This is an overstatement in my opinion. There is no doubt about it that the Hungarian Jews generally had German family names in those days, but there were also Germans from Hungary in the fraternal organizations at that time. Most important, however, is

that membership in an organization was not yet acceptable to the majority of the Magyar migrants.

6. Bodnár's statement that the religious leaders played a major role in shaping early fraternals, especially on a larger territorial basis, is not valid for the Hungarian migrants. John Bodnár, *The Transplanted: A History of Immigrants in Urban America.* (Bloomington: Indiana University Press, 1985), 125.

7. For details of the process by which a small, local ethnic mutual association developed into a large national insurance organization, see also Béla Vassady, Jr. "The Early Decades of the Hazleton-based Hungarian Verhovay Sick Benefit Association," in *Hard Coal, Hard Times: Ethnicity and Labor in the Anthracite Region,* edited by David L. Salay (Scranton, Anthracite Museum Press, 1984), 17–33. See also Steven Béla Vardy, *The Centennial History of the William Penn Association. One Hundred Years of a Hungarian Fraternal Association in America* (Pittsburgh,: The William Penn Association, 1989), 5–7.

8. For the biographic data on Mihály Pálinkás, see Káldor, *Magyar Amerika írásban és képben,* 58. Béla Vassady, Jr., discusses some themes, such as the circumstances of the founding of the Verhovay Sick Benefit Association and the mixture of interethnic conflicts and cooperation which emerged during the association's early history. Salay, *Hard Coal, Hard Times,* 17–33.

9. Between 1896 and 1926 the Verhovay Association was known variously as "Verhovay Aid Society," "Verhovay Association," "Verhovay Sick-Benefit Society," "Verhovay Sick-Benefit and Death-Benefit Society," "Verhovay Fraternal Association," and "Verhovay Fraternal Insurance Association." Vardy, *The Centennial History of the William Penn Association,* 8.

10. Ferenc Rákóczi was a prince of Hungary in the eighteenth century who fought for Hungarian independence from Habsburg rule. The Hungarians in Bridgeport—many of whom immigrated from northeastern Hungary, where Rákóczi held huge estates, named their association after him. They regarded themselves as "Rákóczi's people," and enthusiasm for Rákóczi would always be a significant force within the association.

11. The Rákóczi Association issued an ornate album to celebrate its twenty-fifth anniversary, edited by Vince Troll, secretary of the association (Bridgeport, 1913). On the occasion of its fiftieth anniversary, the association published *Rákóczi Segélyezõ Egyesület Arany Jubileumi Könyve* (Rákóczi Aid Association's Golden Jubilee Book), edited by László Lakatos, (Bridgeport CT: Rákóczi Segélyezõ Egyesület, 1938). This fifty-year history included an abridged version in English for the second generation. See also János Valkó, *Az Amerikai Betegsegélyzö és Életmentö Szövetség ötven éves története, 1892–1942* (Fifty years' history of the American Sick Relief and Life Insurance Federation (Pittsburgh: Expert Printing Company, 1942).

12. Quoted in *Szabadság 10. jubileumi száma* (1901), 21.

13. By 1 January 1898, there were already 936 members in the Federation, of whom 816 were Calvinists, 31 Lutherans, 86 Roman Catholics, and 3 Jews. For more details see Sándor Kalassay, *Az Amerikai Magyar Református Egyesület müködésének 25 éves története, 1886–1921* (The 25 year history of the functioning of the American Hungarian Reformed Federation) (Pittsburgh: Fodor, 1923).

14. Ádám Abet, the editor-in-chief, with his colleagues Jakab Schön and Armin Weltner, and attorney Vilmos Löw. See *Amerikai Népszava,* 1 October 1895.

15. From their newspapers, *Népakarat* (People's Will), started in 1903, follow-ing of Daniel De Leon, and *Elöre* from 1905, adhering to the Socialist Party, their diversity can be emphasized.

16. See "Egyletek" (Associations), in *Amerikai Magyar Népszava Jubileumi Díszalbuma* (1910), 33–45.

17. Puskás, *From Hungary to the United States,* 170.

18. After having visited the McAdoo mining place Lajos Ambrózy reported the following from Hazelton, PA, 20 December 1908: "Our compatriots brought the love of singing here with them. The night before leaving we went to see the rehearsal of 'The yellow shoe,' the well-known popular play. People enjoy playing peasant parts, which remind them of the old country. They perform the songs and dances with vigour and temperament." OL.ME.K26.1909.XXII.1695.

19. "Hungarian Workingmen's Singing Club" was organized on 5 August 1908 and after a short time it had become one of the leading cultural institutions of the large Hungarian-American colony of Cleveland. *Szabadság 50. jubileumi száma* (1941), 48.

20. Short biography of Vendel Major in ibid., 58. The first Hungarian singing circle was organized in Cleveland on 22 March 1886. *Clevelandi Magyar Recorder,* 21 March 1897. This was followed by a number of other attempts until 1908.

21. The number of the adherents of the I.W.W. grew particularly after 1911 because of the zest of the strike struggles and the debates of the Hungarian socialists. The I.W.W.'s central organ and the board of the newspaper were headquartered in Chicago, but the group was relatively strongest in Cleveland. *Felszabadulás* (Liberation), 18 January 1919. The newspaper changed its name to *Bérmunkás* (Wageworker) in 1923. See more details in *Testvériség* (Fraternity), New York, 5 April 1911 and Julianna Puskás, "Hungarian Immigrants and Socialism, 1890–1914," in *In the Shadow of the Statue of Liberty,* edited by Marianne Debouzy (Saint Denis: Presses Universitaires de Vincennes, 1988), 139–151.

22. Imre Bárd's letter to Ervin Szabó, Budapest, 26 February 1909, *Szabó Ervin levelezése, 1905–1918* (The correspondence of Ervin Szabó), edited by György Litván and László Szücs (Budapest: Kossuth Kiadó, 1978), 2:671.

23. Ibid.

24. F. Paál, "Magyar szocialisták Amerikában" (Hungarian socialists in America) *Szocializmus* (1911) (Socialism), 122.

25. Paula Benkart, "Religion, Family, and Community Among Hungarians Mi-grating to American Cities, 1880–1930" (Ph.D. diss., Johns Hopkins University, 1975).

26. Hoffmann, *Csonka munkásoszfly,* 212.

27. See Imre Bárd, "Magyarok az amerikai munkásmozgalomban." (Hungarians in the American labor movement) *Szocializmus,* 1911, 298–309; Ferenc Paál, "Magyar Szocialisták Amerikában" (American socialists in America). 117–126; and János Jemnitz, "The Relations of the Hungarian Americans' Labor Movement as Revealed in the Correspondence of Ervin Szabó," *Acta Historica* IX, no. 1–2 (1965), 179–214.

28. Lecture series were introduced and made regular by the socialists. During the winter of 1910/1911, they opened a "Modern School" in New York with a

curriculum of world history and economics. They started a workers' school in Chicago with 32 lectures. They held open lectures fortnightly in Cleveland, and regular classes were formed in Pittsburgh, and Milwaukee. Only a small fraction of the Hungarian immigrants were drawn into their circle.

The Pittsburgh classes covered the following subjects: What is the aim of social democracy; the duties of socialist workers; a sermon against the stories of Genesis; morality in socialist society; technical progress; the Erfurt Program, anti-alcoholism; questions of principle and tactics; women and socialism, and problems in technology. Hoffmann, *Csonka munkásosztály,* 212.

29. Report of Lajos Ambrózy, New York, 19 November 1908. OL.ME.K26. 1909. XXII. 1946.

30. Hoffmann, *Csonka munkásosztály,* 174.

31. Sándor Várlaky, "Javaslataim a nagygyűlésen" (My suggestions at the general meeting), *Családi Lapok* (Family Papers), 13 January 1913. Várlaky, a Catholic priest, enclosed the 1913 Memorandum in the Hungarian Archbishop's Archive, Esztergom.

32. They repeatedly emphasized the labor character of their associations. The Federation of the Bridgeport and other associations prohibited any member who had not been a manual laborer in the old country from holding a leadership position. Report of Lajos Ambrozy, New York, 19 November 1908. OL.ME.K26. 1909.XXII,.-1946.

33. *Verhovayak Lapja, Verhovay Segélyegylet 50 éves jubileumi kiadványa* (1936), 65.

34. Interview with Albert Stelkovics, Pittsburgh, PA, 1982. Stelkovics recalled his father's cultural activities in the fraternal organization, and he still had in his possession the text of a popular play copied by hand by his father. Others also recalled names of prominent activists, and long lists of names could be made up from the Almanacs, too.

35. Biographical data of Marcus Braun and Mór Cukor in Vasvári Collection, Szeged. C2: 6–14; H5-24; B 5/c: 16; Sz2/b:57.

Chapter 13: Building Religious Institutions.

1. See the statistical data about the distribution of Hungary's emigrants by religious affiliation. Puskás, *From Hungary to the United States,* 182–3.

2. These were beginnings of what emerged as B'nai Jeshurun, and after changes, as today's Temple on the Heights. Perlman, *Bridging Three Worlds,* 187. See also Lloyd P. Gartner, *History of the Jews of Cleveland* (Cleveland: Western Reserve Historical Society and the Jewish Theological Seminary, 1978), 120–1. The First Hungarian Congregation Ohab Zadek on Norfolk Street was the first (and for many years the only) Hungarian synagogue in New York. It opened its doors in 1872 or 1873 and soon had three hundred members. Perlman, *Bridging Three Worlds,* 137.

3. Yeshayahu Jelinek, "Self-Identification of First Generation Hungarian Jewish Immigrants" *American Jewish Historical Quarterly,* LXI (1972): 213. Also George Bárány, "Magyar Jew or Jewish Magyar? Reflection on the Question of

Assimilation Part II," in *Jews and Non-Jews in Eastern Europe, 1918–1945,* edited by Béla Vágó and George I. Mosse (New York: Wiley, 1974), 51–98.

4. The documents of the quarrel can be found at the Cleveland Bishop's Archive under "Hungarian St. Elisabeth Church 2" (1891).

5. Bishop Hartman's letter to the Archbishop of Hungary, 1890, Hungarian Archbishop's Archive, Esztergom. CD, 181.

6. *Szabadság,* 25 December 1892.

7. The prejudices of American (native) Protestant church authorities described in detail in Aladár Komjáthy, "The Hungarian Reformed Church of America: The Effort to Preserve Denominational Heritage" (Ph.D. diss., Theological Seminary, Princeton, NJ, 1962).

8. On the organization of the church communities of Protestant Hungarians see Sándor Kalassay, *Az Amerikai Magyar Református Egyesület,* 211.

9. Mrs. István Ruzsa, "Ruzsa István, első magyar ág.h.e. amerikai magyar lelkész életrajza és müködése" (Biography and work of István Ruzsa, first Hungarian minister of Augustan Confession) (Cleveland, 1967). Manuscript in the Szathmáry Collection, Chicago. One copy in author's collection.

10. On the history of the Baptist Church communities, see Edvin L. Kautz, "The Hungarian Baptist Movement in the United States: A Socio-Historical Study" (M.A. thesis, University of Pittsburgh, 1946), which presented the basis of the book *Amerikai Magyar Baptisták Története* (The history of the American Hungarian Baptists), edited by Gábor Petre, György Balla, and Ferenc Dér, 1958 (Cleveland, OH.: Amerikai Magyar Baptista Szövetség); and Mihály Almási, *A clevelandi magyar baptista misszió 85 éves története* (The 85 year history of the Hungarian Baptist Mission in Cleveland) (Cleveland, 1984).

11. E. L. Kautz, "The History of the Hungarian Baptist Work in America," 1957.

12. Churches as main ethnic institutions are described by Benkart "Religion, Family, and Community" (1975), 80–140, and Peter Niedermüller, "Egyházi élet, vallás és kulturális hagyomány egy amerikai magyar közösségben" (Church life, religion and cultural tradition in a Hungarian community in America), in *Vallási néprajz* (Ethnography of religion), edited by Imre Dankó and Imola Küllös (Budapest: Eötvös Loránd Tudományegyetem, 1985), 274–306. See also Louis A. Kalassay, "Educational and Religious History of the Hungarian Reformed Church in the United States." (Ph.D. diss., University of Pittsburgh, 1939), 24–27. "Our fellow countrymen kept up the habit of improvising Xmas pastorales on the larger Hungarian settlements. At least in Cleveland, Xmas would not be Xmas without a pastoral play." *Szabadság,* 21 January, 1897.

13. Elek Csutoros's letters to his friend Józsi, 1925. A copy is in the collection of the author.

14. Biographical data on Gusztáv Jurányi in the Somogyi Library, the Vasvári Collection, Szeged, 40–3.

15. *Jubileumi Emlékkönyv 1940* (Memorial Anniversary Album) (Pittsburgh: Expert Printing, 1940), 52.

16. Ibid., 54.

17. Ferenc Kapri, *Böhm Károly pápai prelátus élete és korrajza, 1885–1907* (The life history of Károly Böhm, papal prelate and a portrait of the period) (Cleveland: Classic Printing, 1994), 11–21.

18. *Szent Erzsébet Hírnöke,* (St. Elizabeth's Herald) (1899), described in Papp, *Hungarian Americans and Their Communities of Cleveland,* 164.

19. Károly Böhm, "I revoke," *Szent Erzsebét Hírnöke* 14 April 1899, Papp, 170.

20. See more details on the way of his life in Kapri, *Böhm Károly pápai prelatus élete és korrajza,* 19–119.

21. Sándor Harsányi, "Visszaemlékezések—ötven esztendövel ezelötti idökre" (Reminiscences—on times fifty years ago), in *Jubileumi Emlékkönyv* 1940, 166.

22. The subject of the discussion was published by Sándor Harsányi under the title *In defence of the Protestant faith* (Cleveland, 1895).

23. This is how a contemporary chronicler, Kalassay, asserted him. *Jubileumi Emlékkönyv* 1940, 334–335.

24. Elek Csutoros's letter to his friend, 1927. A copy is in the collection of the author.

25. Ibid.

26. Ibid.

27. Interview with the son of Elek Csutoros, Rev. Stephen Csutoros, 1988, in his home in Cleveland.

28. *A Clevelandi West Side Egyház történetének 10 éve* (The ten-year history of the Cleveland West Side Church), edited by Elek Csutoros (Cleveland, 1916), n.p.

29. *Jubileumi Emlékkönyv* 1940, 1981

30. The Hungarian government made repeated efforts through diplomatic channels at the Vatican, to prevent the Galician Greek Catholics and Hungarian Catholics from merging into church communities. The Austro-Hungarian ambassadors and consuls gave information regularly on the peculiar difficulties and problems in the integration of the Greek-Catholic churches and of the linkage and the separation between religion and ethnicity. Greek Catholic documents. OL.ME.12.26.-1904.XXI., 605.1907. XXIII.b., 748. Documents in connection with support to the Hungarian Greek Catholic Bishop and priests working in the United States. XXIII/b.-871. See also *Amerikai Magyar Népszava Jubileumi Díszalbuma* (1910), 225, and Glettler, *Pittsburgh, Wien, Budapest,* 102–6.

31. PL.E. Memorandum 1913. Priest Sándor Várlaki's article is attached.

32. Sándor Kalassay, *Az Amerikai Magyar Reformátusok története* (The history of the American Hungarian Calvinists) (Pittsburgh: Magyarság, n.d.), 151.

33. Ibid., 200.

34. *Clevelandi Magyar Recorder,* 24 March 1897.

35. Csutoros, *A Clevelandi West Side Egyház történetének 10 éve,* n.p.

36. Quoted from a letter of a magyarized Slovak, OL ME K 26-1903.

37. The Greek Bishop of Munkács to the Archbishop, "The care of the soul of the Catholics in the United States," Office of the Archbishop, Esztergom, CD 1910. See also Béla Vassady, "Mixed Ethnic Identities among Immigrant Clergy from Multiethnic Hungary: The Slovak Magyar Case, 1880–1903," in *The Ethnic Enigma,* edited by Peter Kivisto (Philadelphia: Balch Institutes, 1989), 47–66.

38. Glettler, *Pittsburgh, Wien, Budapest,* 398.

39. The small group of wavering clergy, insecure and undecided about its own ethnic identity, played an influential role in the development of ethnic consciousness within both the Slovak and the Magyar immigrant communities. Initially these transitional figures of mixed allegiances were mediators, supporting harmony, cooperation and alliances between the two ethnic groups; Béla Vassady Jr., 1990. "Mixed

Ethnic Identities among Immigrant Clergy from Multiethnic Hungary: The Slovak-Magyar Case, 1885–1903," in *The Ethnic Enigma*, edited by Peter Kivisto. (Philadelphia: The Balch Institute Press, 1989), 47–66.

40. For example, the letter of Rev. Harsányi to the *Pittsburgh Leader*, "A minister's arrangement," in *Szabadság*, 1 July 1909.

41. Hoffmann, *Csonka munkásosztály*, 275.

42. Perlman, *Bridging Three Worlds*, 187.

43. In 1917 Rabbi H. A. Libowitz, one of the organizers and leaders of that new congregation, wrote the first history of the Cleveland Hungarians. H. A. Libowitz and Mihály Paragh, *A clevelandi magyarok története* (History of Cleveland's Hungarians) (Cleveland: H. A. Libowitz, 1917).

44. Quoted by Hoffmann, *Csonka munkasosztály*, 268.

45. "Memorandum to the Prince Primate" from Károly Böhm, Roman Catholic pastor of Cleveland, The Hungarian Archbishop's Archives, Esztergom, CD 1913.

46. Ibid.

47. Ibid.

48. *Szabadság 10. jubileumi száma* (1901), 35.

49. "Our work," minutes of the Pennsylvania Synod, 1900, Archive of the Presbyterian Church, Philadelphia. See also Glettler, *Pittsburgh, Wien, Budapest*, 109–39.

50. Zoltán Kuthy, *Almanac of the American Hungarian Reformed Church* (New York, 1911). 33–40. See also *Emlékkönyv 1929, Emlékkönyv az Amerikai Magyar Egyházak évesfordulójára* (Memorial Album for the 25th anniversary of the Hungarian-American Reformed Diocese) (Bridgeport, 1929), 29.

51. "The guidelines for the 'American Action,' March 17, 1903," OL.ME.K126. See also Kemény, (1964), III, 90–92, 222–240.

52. Regarding this subject, lengthy documents can be found in the OL.MFK126 and in the Archives of the Calvinist Synod in Budapest, "Documents of the Convent's Committee for External Affairs."

53. The number of the "affiliated" church communities rose to 18 by 1911 and to 22 by 1914. See list in Kuthy, *Almanac of the American Hungarian Reformed Church*, 41.

54. Csutoros, *A Clevelandi West Side Egyház történetének 10 éve* (Cleveland: n.p., 1916) and OL.ME.K26.XX., 859.

55. For the ecclesiastical work the Presbyterian Church among the Hungarians see John Dikovics, *Our Magyar Presbyterians, New York*. (New York: Board of the National Mission of the Presbyterian Church in the United States, 1945). See also *Amerikai Magyar Reformátusok Lapja*, the newspaper of the Hungarian Calvinists (from 1900). Kuthy, *Almanac of the American Hungarian Reformed Church*, 33–40; *Emlékkönyv 1929*, 19.

56. Paula Benkart, "The Hungarian Government, the American Magyar Churches, and Immigrant Nationalism" (unpublished paper; Philadelphia: Balch Institute, 1973), 1–27.

Chapter 14: The Function of the Hungarian Ethnic Press

1. In his newspaper the publisher-editor Gusztáv Erdélyi Szász ran a regular, characteristically American-Hungarian column, often ridiculed in Hungary, called "Guide to Fraternal Organizations."

2. *Amerikai Népszava* since 1895, editor Ádám Abet; *Amerikai Magyar Népszava* since 1899, owner and editor Géza D. Berkó; *Népakarat,* the paper of the social democrats, since 1903, editor József K. Szabó.

3. Márton Dienes, *Kohányi Tihamér élete és küzdelmei* (The life and struggles of Tihamér Kohányi) (Cleveland: "Szabadság" Nyomda, 1913), 48. Part dealt with the personal characteristics of Kohányi. He believed that by judging the foreign language press, Americans were too apt not to consider the personal factor. Park, *The Immigrant Press and its Control,* 347–50.

4. Ibid., 47.

5. Ibid., 53.

6. Ibid., 54.

7. *Szabadság 20. jubileumi száma* (1911).

8. *Szabadság,* 14 November 1894.

9. Dienes, *Kohányi Tihamér élete,* 96. He published the photo that shows Taft at the banquet.

10. Ottó Táborszky, "The Hungarian Press in America" (M.A. thesis, Catholic University of America, Washington, D.C., 1955), 22–3.

11. Jenõ Pivány, *Egy amerikai kiküldetés története* (The history of an American mission) (Budapest: Magyar Nemzet Szövetség, 1943).

12. Ibid., 41–2.

13. György Kemény's biography (1929) in MTA Kézirattár (Hungarian Academy of Science's Manuscript Archive). See also his biography in Pál Gulyás *Magyar írók élete és munkái* (The life and work of Hungarian writers) (Budapest: Magyar könyvtárosok és Levéltárosok Egyesülete, 1939-).

14. *Dongó,* 18 June and 18 January 1910, in Hoffmann, *Csonka munkájsosztály,* 244–5.

15. *Amerikai Magyar Népszava Jubileumi Díszalbuma* (1910), 210–35.

16. *Dongó 10. jubileumi száma* (Dongo's 10th Anniversary issue), "Magyar nóta Amerikában" (Hungarian songs in America), July 1915, 5–12.

17. Published under the name of *Napsugár,* this weekly professed the ideas of Hungarian national thought and independence. When Rudnyánszky did not succeed in establishing his paper in Cleveland, he moved to Chicago. He did not enjoy success there either. Disappointed, sick, almost completely blind, he returned to Hungary in 1914 before the outbreak of war. His book aimed at transplanting traditions and using them in the new surroundings. See Gyula Rudnyánszky, *Amerikai Felköszöntő. Ünnepi beszédek, alkalmi és hazafias szónoklatok, egyleti zászlószentelési, lakodalmi, keresztelő üdvözlések, pohárköszöntők, bordalok, rigmusok és vöfélykönyv* (American toasts. Festive speeches, occasional and patriotic addresses, consecration of the flag of an association, wedding, christening greetings, toasts, drinking songs, rhymed sayings, and bridesman-book) (Cleveland: Caxton Nyomda, 1907).

18. More details about these in József Kovács, "A társadalom és a nemzeti haladás gondolata az amerikai magyar irodalomban" (Society and the idea of national progress in the Hungarian-American literature) (Ph.D., Budapest, MTA Kézirattár 1–137, 1973).

19. *Szabadság,* 1913.

20. Benkart, "Hungarians," *Harvard Encyclopedia,* 159–60. For more about Dienes see "Vasvári Gyüjtemény," Szeged, Somogyi Könyvtár.

21. "A. első amerikai költő" (The first American Hungarian poet), in Kováes, "A tarsadalom és a nemzeti haladás gondolata," 68–88.

22. *Szabadság* 1896.

23. Puskás, *From Hungary to the United States*, 301.

24. *Szabadság*, 2 May 1908. "Egy ezer estendős ország meggyalázása" (The desecration of a thousand-year-old nation).

25. *Szabadság 10. jubileumi száma* (1901), *Amerikai Magyar Népszava Jubileumi Díszalbuma* (1910).

26. "The Americans will esteem the Hungarians much more and will wipe out the disgrace which was cast on them by the Pan-Slavs." *Szabadság*, 28 January, 1897. The paper repeatedly reverts to the danger of Pan-Slavism, see in detail in *Szabadság, 10. jubileumi száma* (Szabadság 10th anniversary issue). Cleveland 1901 and in *Szabadság 20. jubileumi száma* (Szabadság 20th anniversary issue). Cleveland, 21 December 1911.

27. *Bevándorló* (Immigrant), 6 April 1911. "The Hungarian is slandered, belittled at every step," *Napsugár*, 16 January 1910. "Every one of the English papers in Cleveland made use of the smallest occasion to strike a blow at the foreign element, at the Hungarians in particular," *Szabadság*, 15 August 1894.

28. Hungarian-American writers and poets frequently mentioned the rejection of the Hungarian immigrants, for example, the poem by György Kemény entitled "Hunki," as well as his other poem "And they kicked you." See "Poetry" in Hoffmann, *Csonka munkásosztaly*, 223–243.

29. Robert E. Park, *The Immigration Press and Its Control*. New York: Harper, 1922. Reprint St. Clair Shores, MI: Scholarly Press, 1970), 173.

30. For his analysis Park used "The Hungarian press in America," an unpublished manuscript written by Hungarian newspaperman named Eugene S. Bagger. Bagger worked for some time in the editorial office of *Szabadság*, and his prejudice was likely caused by the termination of his employment. His personal interest must have guided him in criticizing the "low standard" of *Szabadság*, while praising *Elöre*'s. Such a difference in the level of their work can hardly be judged in a fair comparison. Ibid., 352.

31. Park strongly criticized the *Szabadság* for its attitude during World War I. At first the paper was pro-Hungary, but it changed its tone after the United States entered the war. Park quoted an editor of a Hungarian weekly in Chicago who described the amazement of readers of the Hungarian dailies at the sudden turn-about in the attitude of their papers. "This sudden change was incomprehensible to their readers, the American Hungarians. The wise men of our societies put their hands together and waited, waited patiently for sincere explanations. These explanations never came, and so all joined in the not very complimentary explanation: 'Poor papers, what shall they do, how can they write differently? They are forbidden to.'" Ibid. 347–349. Park illustrates the trends of the *Amerikai Magyar Népszara* with examples, 207–9.

Chapter 15: Ties to American and Hungarian Political Parties

1. Helena Znaniecki Lopata, *Polish Americans* (Englewood Cliffs, NJ: Prentice-Hall, 1967), 21.

2. According to Perlman, "it was the Hungarian professionals and business men—by definition predominantly Jewish—who made the first attempts to enter the mainstream of American politics." Perlman, *Bridging Three Worlds*, 204. See for example the role of the Black family in Cleveland, of Marcus Braun, of Mór Cukor in New York, and also that of the Hungarian Reformed Club and the Democratic Club in New York and Cleveland at the turn of the century. The Hungarian Republican Club of the City of New York published *Proceedings of the banquet tendered to His Excellency Theodore Roosevelt, February 14, 1905* (New York, 1905). See also "A kivándorolt magyarság politikája" (The politics of emigrant Hungarians), *Amerikai Magyar Népszava Jubileumi Díszalbuma* (1910), 205–209, and "Mihály Károlyi in America," and "Hungarians of the United States for New Hungary," in *Szabadság Naptár* (1915), 82–94.

3. *Szabadság*, 23 February 1897.

4. *Szabadság*, 19 March 1897.

5. The leadership of the United Societies of Cleveland came from the representatives of Hungarian associations: leaders of churches and secular organizations, for example, and newspaper men. They sponsored the annual commemoration of the 1848 War of Independence held on March 15, in addition to the Magyar Day Festival held every summer in July. Papp, *Hungarian Americans and Their Communities in Cleveland*, 182.

6. Slovaks, along with other Slavic groups and Romanians, opposed the erection of a statue of Louis Kossuth on a public square. Kossuth was considered an enemy of the non-Magyar nationalities of the Austro-Hungarian Monarchy. See Glettler, *Pittsburg, Wien, Budapest*, 193.

7. From the report HHSTA.P.A.XXIII. Kasse I. Kart. 55. Nr. 529 (5.10.1902). Cited by Glettler, *Pittsburg, Wien, Budapest*, 193.

8. *Szabadság*, 30 September 1902. See also Kende, *Magyarok Amerikában*, 2:208–227.

9. Acknowledgments of donations or of collections for one or the other church in Hungary often appeared in *Szabadság*.

10. Researchers have different opinions to this day about the development of the migrants' ethnic consciousness. Some of them (like Victor Greene and followers) maintain that this consciousness only developed after the migrants arrived in America; others (like Kuzniewski) reckon that old-world animosities fueled the development of a sense of collective ethnicity in the migrants before their arrival in the New World. It cannot be questioned that one should not generalize and that there were important differences between the various ethnic groups. By now scholars mostly agree that the national and ethnic identity of emigrants in America evolved considerably faster than it did in the rural areas of their country of origin.

11. Tihamér Kohányi, "The position of Hungarians in the US," a lecture given in OMGE (1901), *Szabadság 10. jubileuma száma* (1901), 39–48.

12. *Ibid.*, 40.

13. József Zseni, *Nemzeti zászlónk Amerikában* (Our national flag in America) (Budapest: Eggenberger, 1903).

14. Non-Magyar emigrants from Hungary not only protested in the newspapers but also turned directly to the President of the United States and to other high

authorities. See Glettler, *Pittsburgh, Wien, Budapest,* 192. They demanded in a memorandum that the position of the Slovaks in Hungary should be improved. OL.ME.K26.1904.-XV.5089.

15. See the report of Ambassador Hengelmüller, SA PA W-XXXIII-USA. 481. Nr. 201. 10 September 1902.

16. The first officials in the American Hungarian Federation were as follows: Tihamér Kohányi, owner of *Szabadság* newspaper, chairman; Imre Fonó, journalist, vice-chairman; Rev. Elek Csutoros, and Rev. János Bíró treasurer; János Németh, banker, chief treasurer; V. Gusztáv Hámory, banker, treasurer; György Kemény, journalist, secretary; Henrik Baracs, journalist, assistant-secretary.

17. *Szabadság,* 28 February 1906.

18. Quoted from a letter written by one of the officials of the Federation. Hoffmann, *Csonka munkásosztály,* 190.

19. *Bevándorló* (Immigrant), 10 May 1907.

20. Pivány, *Egy amerikai kiküldetés története,* 42.

21. Hoffmann, *Csonka munkásosztály,* 190. Tihamér Kohányi was also a leader in that social movement, which worked to bring the donor and host countries closer together. In the name of Hungarian-Americans, adherents erected a statue of George Washington in Budapest, but neither the Hungarian nor the American government officially acknowledged the action. Kohányi found it necessary to allay the misgivings of the leaders in Budapest in advance by emphasizing that "the Washington statue does not want to express support for the ideals of the Republic; the statue's erection has no seditious purpose." It was officially unveiled in July 1906, aand it was the first George Washington statue erected in Europe. Kende, *Magyarok Amerikában,* 2:228–250.

22. It is interesting to note that in his memoirs Count Apponyi never mentions his meeting with Hungarian immigrants in 1904. He relates in detail his visit to Theodore Roosevelt, but he only mentions the demonstration of the nationalities against him in 1911 as an unsuccessful movement. Count Albert Apponyi, *Memoirs of Count Apponyi* (New York: Macmillan, 1935). Studies of I. Cizmic, F. Bielik, and M. Stolarik deal with the demonstration of Slovaks and Croats against Apponyi's visit.

23. More details on this in Vassady, Béla. 1984. "The 'Homeland Cause' as Stimulant to Ethnic Unity. The Hungarian-American Response to Károlyi's 1914 American Tour." *Journal of American Ethnic History.,* 1984. Vol. 2. No. 1. 39–64.

24. Mihály Károlyi, *Hit illuzió nélkül* (Belief without Illusion) (Budapest: Magvető, 1977), 77–78.

25. *Szabadság Naptár* (1915), 92–4.

26. In 1914 at the Passaic Convention of the Verhovay Fraternal Association, Count Mihály Károlyi was elected "Honorary President" of the Association and was offered 18,000 dollars, which was to be paid from a one-dollar per person levy on the 18,000 members of the association.

Chapter 16: The Conflict of Loyalties during World War I

1. See more about these in the 1915 issue of *Szabadság Naptár.* The "national" sick relief organizations—except for the socialists—invested a part of their funds

in Hungarian war loans. But even the general meeting of the Kossuth Association of Detroit decided that it should put six thousand dollars, two-thirds of its total assets, into war loans for the Hungarian homeland. See *Kossuth Lajos Magyar Férfi és Nöi Betegsegélyzö és Temetkezö Egylet 20 éves jubileumára* (Kossuth Album for the 20th anniversary of the Lajos Kossuth Hungarian Men's and Women's Sick Relief and Burial Society) (Detroit, MI 1911), 65. Ottó Táborszky notes in his dissertation that for a while after the outbreak of the war the Hungarian press gave more attention to the events of the war than did the American press. Táborszky, "The Hungarian Press in America." According to the *Amerikai Magyar Reformátusok Lapja,* Hungarian Americans subscribed 15 million crowns worth of war loans at the Transatlantic Trust Company.

2. Maldwyn A. Jones, *The Old World Ties of American Ethnic Groups* (London: Published for the University College by H. K. Lewis, 1974), 4.

3. In 1917 the First Catholic Slovak Union headquartered in Cleveland partially changed its constitution to make it possible for its members to fight for the destruction of the monarchy. In February of 1918 the Slovak League's Congress in New York recognized that the Czech-Slovak Executive Committee, consisting of eight Slovak and eight Czech members, had to be the "head and heart" of the actions for liberation. Nevertheless the Austro-Hungarian monarchy became stronger even as Hungarian-American leaders of the nationalities, particularly the clergy and newspaper writers, demanded total national independence. See more details in Mark M. Stolarik, *Slovak Migration from Europe to North America, 1870–1918* (Cleveland: Slovak Institute, 1980), 116–22.

4. Austro-Hungarian Consulate General, *Austria-Hungary and the War* (New York: Austro-Hungarian Consulate General, 1915), 3.

5. Ibid., 4.

6. Concerning the "Dumba affair," the American Embassy in Vienna reported that according to a letter from Dr. Konstantin Dumba of the Austro-Hungarian Embassy in Washington, "this incident has been distorted and greatly exaggerated by the enemies of the Monarchy and the German Empire." National Archives, State Department, Dumba affair, Washington. 1915. "One of the editors of *Szabadság* was suspected of being involved in the plan and therefore was dismissed by Mrs. Kohányi, who was at the head of the corporation owning the paper at that time." Táborszky "The Hungarian Press in America," 32. According to Park, Dr. Martin Dienes as editor of the *Szabadság* in 1915 made an attempt, in conjunction with Dr. Konstantin Dumba, then Austro-Hungarian Ambassador, to disorganize American munition industries. As soon as his activities were disclosed by the United States Secret Service, he was dismissed. Park, *The Immigrant Press and Its Control,* 351. See also Benkart, "Hungarians," in Thernstrom, *Harvard Encyclopedia,* 141.

7. At several places the native-born workers drove the immigrants from their workplaces. For example, in 1917 the miners, anxious about their livelihood, armed themselves and chased away several thousand immigrant miners, Hungarians among them, from the lead mines in Flat River, Derlage, Bonne Terre and other mining places in Missouri. *Szabadság Naptár* (1919), 101–2.

8. David Montgomery, *Workers' Control in America* (Cambridge: Cambridge University Press, 1979), 95.

9. *Szabadság,* October 1915, and Csutoros, *A Clevelandi West Side 10 éve* (1916 n.p.).

10. *Szabadság,* October 1915. The "munitions strike" swept across the whole northeastern part of the country in the hot summer of 1915. Montgomery, *Workers' Control,* 95.

11. The SP platform declared that the competitive nature of capitalism is the cause of modern wars, and that war is "one of the natural results of the capitalist system." Milton Cantor, *The Divided Left: American Radicalism, 1900–1975* (New York: Hill and Wang, 1978), 56.

12. See Thomson, *The I.W.W.: Its First Fifty Years,* 109–110 and Melvyn Dubofsky, *We Shall Be All: A History of the Industrial Workers of the World* (Chicago: Quadrangle Books, 1969), 376–93.

13. Richard O. Boyer and Herbert M. Morais, *Labor's Untold Story* (New York: United Electrical, Radio and Machine Workers of America, 1975), 197–8.

14. Thomson, *The I.W.W.: Its First Fifty Years,* 109–110.

15. The Socialist Party's (SP) declaration of principles in the annual report at the 1916 party congress. See also the annual pocket calendar of 1917 of *Előre.*

16. *Uj Előre Huszonöt éves Jubileumi Albuma* (1927), 42. For further details see H. E. Neuman's article, "Visszaemlékezés" (Reminiscence): "Every lead article, every article in which the war is mentioned must also be translated into English." *Emlékkönyv 1902–1967* (Memorial album) (New York: Amerikai Magyar Szó, 1967), 85–89.

17. Táborszky, "The Hungarian Press in America," 31–34.

18. "Magyarok a Díszfelvonuláson" (Hungarians on Parade) *Szabadság,* 5 July 1918. Twenty-three associations took part in the festive procession. See also the article of László Harsányi, a Calvinist clergyman, "Magyarok, Testvérek, Vigyáz-zunk" (Hungarians, Brothers, Let us take care), in which he stated what kind of attitude Hungarians must take in such an extraordinary situation. For example, he counsels them to "forgo any declaration of opinion, as this can be possibly misunderstood and you may get into trouble. . . . Don't discuss political issues, as you are not competent to do so, and don't criticize any official measures, just obey!" *Amerikai Magyar Reformátusok Lapja,* 17 February 1917.

19. See also Aladár Konta, "Naturalized Hungarians, their rights and duties," delivered under the auspices of the Hungarian Relief Society, Yorkville Public Library, 7 December 1915.

Mór Cukor urged the Hungarians to obtain citizenship papers "so that our loyalty towards our adopted country should not be doubted. Our patriotic spirit and sentiment will not be damaged by anything, if we adapt ourselves to the country on the land of which we found prosperity." "Polgárosodjunk" (Take up American citizenship), *Amerikai Népszava* (1917).

20. According to George Barany, 23,000 members joined the American Loyalty League in a very short time. "The Magyars," in *The Immigrant's Influence on Wilson's Peace Policy,* edited by Joseph O. Grady (Lexington: University of Kentucky Press, 1967), 148.

21. War lent the Americanization crusade an urgency, because it was discovered in the midst of war that diversity smacked of disloyalty. The resulting demands

for a 100 percent Americanism epitomized the political culture of a period that stretched from 1914 through the mid 1970s. (97). A great many foreign-born people, whether because of a genuine desire to become more "American" or because of external pressures (or because of some combination of the two) did start the classes. Less than half, so far as we can tell, stayed around to finish. (103). John F. McClymer, 1982. "The American Labor Movement and the Education of the Foreign-Born Adult, 1914–25," in *Education and the European Immigrant 1840–1940,* edited by Bernard J. Weiss. (Urbana: University of Illinois Press, 1982), 117–41. See also Ödön Vasvári, "Amikor húsz esztendeje Washingtonban jártunk" (When we went to Washington twenty years ago) *Amerikai Magyar Református Ujság* (Newspaper of the Hungarian American Reformed Church), 1938, 2–4.

22. National Archives, State Department, report of the I.W.W. in Cleveland, 1916.

23. National Archives, Military Intelligence Department, Washington, 1921, 269–64.

24. *Szabadság,* 2 May 1919.

25. *Szabadság,* 2 May 1919.

26. *Szabadság,* 2 May 1919.

27. *Szabadság,* 3 May 1919.

28. *Szabadság,* 1 November 1919.

29. See in detail David Brody, *Labor in Crisis: The Steel Strikes of 1919* (Philadelphia: Lippincott, 1965), 179.

30. Van Tassel and Grabowski, *The Encyclopedia of Cleveland History,* 606.

31. See details in Brody, *Labor in Crisis,* 123–146.

32. *Szabadság,* 1 November 1919.

33. Boyer and Morais, *Labor's Untold Story,* 34, Chapter "Big Steel," 205.

34. *Szabadság,* 17 October 1918.

35. *Szabadság,* 14 November 1919.

36. *Szabadság,* 1 November 1919.

37. See details in Robert K. Murray, *Red Scare: A Study in National History, 1919–1920* (Minneapolis: University of Minnesota Press, 1955).

38. *Szabadság,* 2 December 1919.

39. *Szabadság,* 3 November 1919.

40. *Szabadság,* 18 and 23 December 1919.

41. Raymond Moley, Foreword, *The Magyars in Cleveland,* by Huldah F. Cook (Cleveland: Cleveland Americanization Committee, Mayor's Advisory War Committee, 1919), 2–3.

42. József Reményi's biography in the Vasvári Collection, Somogyi Library, Szeged.

43. "Helen Horváth," Van Tassel and Grabowski, *The Encyclopedia of Cleveland History,* 519–520. See also *Szabadság* 50th Anniversary (1941), 49–50.

44. Eugene Pivány, *Some Facts about the Proposed Dismemberment of Hungary* (Cleveland: American Hungarian Federation, 1919) and *The Case of Hungary,* a brief submitted to the Committee on Foreign Relations of the Senate of the United States on 1 September 1919. (Cleveland: Hungarian American Federation).

45. Pivány, *Egy Amerikai kiküldetés története,* 41–63.

46. The leaders of the reorganized American Hungarian Federation repeatedly referred to this claim at the time of World War II.

Chapter 17: The Gates Close

1. Internationales Arbeitamt, *Die Wanderungsbewegungen 1925–1927* (Genf, 1929), 42.

2. See the statistical data based on United States Annual Reports in Thernstrom, *Harvard Encyclopedia*, 1048.

3. Thomas Brinley, *International Migration and Economic Development: A study of Great Britain and the Atlantic Economy.* 2d ed. (Cambridge: Cambridge University Press, 1973), 15–7.

4. The aftermath of World War I further contributed to racist propaganda. Books, articles, and speeches demanded that immigrants become thoroughly Americanized and argued for restrictionist legislation. See *Americanization Studies: The Acculturation of Immigrant Groups into American Society,* edited by William S. Bernard. 10 vol. (Montclair, NJ: Patterson Smith, 1971).

In 1921 the first quota law set the level of annual immigration at 3% of the 1910 Census with respect to every foreign country. Nativists, eugenecists and restrictionists were quick to push Congress even further. The second quota law increased the severity and regarded the 1890 Census as the basis for the calculation of the quota.

5. United States, "Annual Report of Immigration and Naturalization Service" (Washington, DC, 1976), 62–64.

6. Iván T. Berend and György Ránki, *Hungarian Economy in the Twentieth Century* (New York: St. Martin's Press, 1985); Gunst, "Agricultural Development in Hungary," in Mavrenen, *Economic Development in Hungary and England,* 63–88.

7. On Hungarian emigration to Canada see Paul Bödy, "Emigration from Hungary, 1880–1956," in *Struggle and Hope: The Hungarian Canadian Experience,* edited by N. F. Dreisziger, M. L. Kovács, Paul Bödy, and B. Koevrig (Toronto: McClelland and Stewart, 1982), 27–60.

8. Fortunately the immigration authorities at this time were still asking about the mother tongue; so some information on the mother tongue of those who emigrated from the successor states is available.

9. The crossing place was near Niagara Falls. From among the Szamosszegian emigrants it was here that the Olah couple entered the United States the second time. We could enumerate at length further cases we got to know in the course of our field-work. According to Andor Kun, "no matter how strong the sealing of the frontiers—the Canadian and the Mexican borders are long—many people slipped through them into the United States against the law. Andor Kun "Hogyan megy veszendőbe Európa magyarsága?" (How are Europe's Hungarians wasted?) *Magyar Szemle* (Hungarian Review) (December 1934), 440.

10. See the data in the *Magyar Statisztikai Évkönyv* (Hungarian Statistical Yearbook), 1920–30.

11. See Martin L. Kovács, "Searching for Land: The First Hungarian Influx into Canada," *Canadian-American Review of Hungarian Studies,* VII (1980), 37–43.

12. Dreisziger et al, *Struggle and Hope*, 41–46.

13. Carmela Patrias, *Patriots and Proletarians: Politicizing Hungarian Immigrants in Interwar Canada, 1924–1946.* (Montreal: McGill-Queen's University Press, 1994), 70–4.

14. Linda Dégh, *People in the Tobacco Belt: Four Lives in Ottawa* (Ottowa: National Museums of Canada, 1975).

15. George Borsányi, "Az emigráció elsö éve" (The first year of emigration), *Valóság, no. 12 1977, 36–49.* See also Frank, *"From Immigrant Laborers to Emigré Professionals, 203–39.*

16. Tibor Hajdú and Zsuzsa L. Nagy, "Revolution, Counterrevolution, Consolidation," in Svgár and Hanák, *A History of Hungary,* 295–318.

17. Oscar Jászi, *Revolution and Counterrevolution in Hungary,* 1st ed. London 1929, (2nd ed. New York: Howard Fertig, 1969), 723.

18. Emil Lengyel, *Americans From Hungary,* 2nd ed. (Philadelphia: J. B. Lippincott, 1948), 224. A new approach to this vast territory of post-WWI Hungarian intellectual emigration is provided by Lee Congdon's magisterial *Exile and Social Thought: Hungarian Intellectuals in Germany and Austria, 1919–1933* (Princeton: Princeton University Press, 1991). For a recent general introduction to the period in English see Hajdú and Nagy, *Revolution, Counterrevolution, Consolidation,* 285–318, and Frank, *From Immigrant Laborers to Émigré Professionals,* 203–230.

19. Ferenczi and Willcox, *International Migration,* I, 273.

20. Interviews with most of them in New Brunswick, NJ. Remigration of those born in the United States helps to explain the relatively high number of U.S. citizens from Hungary recorded in the United States Annual Reports of Immigration in the 1930s.

21. Laura Fermi, *Illustrious Immigrants: The Intellectual Migration from Europe, 1930–1941.* 2d ed. (Chicago: University of Chicago Press, 1971), 407–430.

22. István Mócsi, *The Effects of World War I: The Uprooted Hungarian Refugees and their Impact on Hungary's Domestic Politics, 1910–1921,* War and Society in East Central Europe. Vol. 12. (New York, Social Science Monographs, Brooklyn College Press, XIII, 1983), 252.

23. Irredentism was a movement built on the belief that the decrees of the Treaty of Trianon were unjust and could be altered by peaceful means, and that the historical territory of Hungary could be retrieved. A popular slogan of the movement was: "Justice for Hungary!"

24. Tibor Frank, "Pioneers Welcome: The escape of Hungarian Modernism to the U.S., 1919–1945," *Hungarian Studies* 8/C (1993), 237–60.

25. *Magyar Statisztikai Évkönyv,* 1936–1941. See also Alajos Kovács, *Magyarország népe és népességének kérdése* (The people of Hungary and the question of its population) (Budapest: Stephaneum Nyomda, 1941).

26. United States Annual Report of Immigration and Naturalization Service (1948).

27. Michael R. Marrus, *The Unwanted: European Refugees in the Twentieth Century* (London: Oxford University Press, 1985), Chapters: "Flight from Fascism" and "Under the Heel of Nazism."

28. Fermi *Illustrious Immigrants,* 53.

29. The magnificent works of American scientists of Hungarian origin Leo Szilárd (1898–1964), John von Neuman (1903–1957), and Edward Teller (1908-) have been of universal significance. See "Genius Welcome: The Hungarian Contribution to an 'American Race,'" in Frank, *From Immigrant Laborers to Émigré Professionals,* 313–352. See also the strikingly long "List of Prominent Americans of Hungarian Origin," in *Hungary, Past and Present,* edited by Joseph Szentkirályi (New York: Hungarian Reference Library, 1941).

30. Defining the various groups of emigrants from Hungary became very problematic as early as the 1920s, owing to the intertwining of the political émigré, the refugee, and the career-emigrant.

Chapter 18: "Let's Be American, Let's Remain Hungarian"

1. *Szabadság,* 23 December 1920.

2. See the information on these in *Amerikai Magyar Népszaua 25 éves jubileumi száma* (Amerikai Magyar Népszava 25th anniversary issue), 20 April 1924.

3. Two brothers of Gustav Kovács migrated from the mining place to Detroit before he also settled there. Interview with Gusztáv Kovács, Detroit, 1983.

4. Interview with Mr. Szabó, son of a Hungarian immigrant family who bought land after World War I. The interview was conducted on his farm near Cleveland, 1988.

5. *Szabadság 50. jubileumi száma* (1941), 79.

6. Interview with John Palasics, the son of a Hungarian immigrant. Cleveland, 1988.

7. *Amerikai Magyar Népszava 25 éves jubileumi száma* 20 April 1924.

8. Interview with Mrs. Takács, Cleveland, 1977, and Mrs. Bodó, Holden, WV, 1986.

9. Endman D. Beynon, "Occupational Succession of Hungarians in Detroit," *American Journal of Sociology,* 1934, 39:600–10.

10. Percent of Hungarian-born Persons Naturalized to Date, in Paula K. Benkart "Religion, Family and Community Amongst Hungarians Migrating to American Cities, 1880–1930" (Ph.D. diss., Johns Hopkins University, 1975), 136.

11. *Naptár's* (Calendars) Published annually by newspapers, repeatedly described in detail the conditions of naturalization. Some branches of the national fraternal associations even organized naturalization classes.

12. The Hunyady siblings moved to Pennsylvania and Detroit, the Kovács brothers to New Jersey and Detroit.

13. All of these Hungarians were heroes in the fight against the rule of the Habsburgs in the 17th, 18th and 19th centuries.

14. The Rev. Charles E. Schaeffer, *Glimpses Into Hungarian Life* (Philadelphia: The Board of Hungarian Mission of the Reformed Church in the United States, 1923), 6.

15. Interview with Mr. A. Stelkovics, Pittsburgh, 1983.

16. In every populous Hungarian settlement in the 1920s, representatives of church and secular organizations formed so-called United Big Committees. One of their tasks was to coordinate local social events.

17. Papp, *Hungarian Americans and Their Communities of Cleveland*, 235.

18. Interview with Mrs. Takács, Cleveland, 1977.

19. Papp, *Hungarian Americans and Their Communities of Cleveland*, 237.

20. The wedding of John Bodó in Holden lasted three days. The wedding party pitched a tent for the occasion and invited other ethnicities (Italians) from this small mining village. Interview with Mrs. Bodó, Holden, WV, 1984. For more on the Hungarian wedding, see Malvina Hauk Abonyi and James A. Anderson, *Hungarians of Detroit*. (Detroit: Wayne State University, 1977).

21. Interview with Mrs. Szakács, Daisytown, PA, 1982.

22. Interview with J. Palasics, Cleveland, 1988.

23. Interview with Mrs. Takács, Cleveland, 1977.

24. The copybook of Gyula Kósa containing the chants was given to the author for her collection by Gusztáv Kovács, Detroit, 1983.

25. The photos sent to the village were displayed conspicuously in homes, so that visitors would notice them.

26. Interview with Victor Bodó in Holden, WV, 1984.

27. The associations sent a wreath, and their members, wearing black ribbons, participated in the funeral.

28. Written complaints addressed to the bishop can be found in the dossiers of St. Emerick Church in the Cleveland Roman Catholic Archbishop's archives.

29. Zoltán Fejős, *A chicagói magyarok két nemzedéke, 1890–1940* (Budapest: Közép-Európa Intézet, 1993), 113.

30. Reminiscences of Mr. Árvay, New Brunswick, NJ, 1994.

31. Fejös, *A chicagói magyarok két nemzedéke*, 114.

32. Ibid., 132. A colorful picture was given of the customs of Hungarian immigrants and the family experiences of their second generation childhood by the siblings based on their own recollections, in Yolan and Emil Varga's book *Children of Ellis Island: This Side of the Rainbow* (New Brunswick, NJ: I. H. Printing Co., 1988).

33. Paul Kirchner and Anne R. Kaplan, "Hungarians in Minnesota," in *They Chose Minnesota*, edited by June Denning Holmquist (St. Paul: Minnesota Historical Society Press, 1981), 423–439.

Chapter 19: The Churches Caught in the Middle

1. In this respect, the most active were the Presbyterians. However, in new Roman Catholic schools, all classes were taught in English. Edvin L. Kautz, "History of the Hungarian Baptist Work in the United States" (MA. thesis, University of Pittsburgh, 1946.), 19.

2. The official English text of the "Tiffin agreement" can be found in the United States in the report of the Board of Home Mission, Reformed Church, 1922 and in Hungary in the Archives of the Synod Foreign Affairs Papers: Amerika, 1922. See also Dr. Géza Takaró, "Az egyetlen út. A Tiffini Egyezmény története" (The sole way. The history of the Tiffin agreement), *Jubileumi Emlékkönyv* 1940, 57–61.

3. Minutes of the Reformed Church in Detroit for the years 1920–22 contain information about these conflicts.

4. Tóth Sándor, "Lancasteri levelek" (Lancaster letters), *Jubileumi Emlék-könyv* 1940, 125–135.

5. The clergyman speaking with a bad accent to Lajos Nánássay, who studied in Oxford and Edinburgh, said the attitude formed a turning point in his life. He determined that neither he nor his church could be forced into a church community where he could not teach the "little Hungarians" in Hungarian. "Egyháztárgyalások története" (History of Church Negotiations), *Magyar Egyház* (Hungarian Church), 18 August 1923. Cited in Aladár Komjáthy, *A kitántorgott egyház* (The Church that straggled out) (Budapest: Református Zsinati Irod a Sajtóosztála, 1984), 178.

6. Quoted in Zoltán Király, *50th Anniversary Album of the Calvin Synod of the United Church of Christ* (n.p., 1988), 18.

7. "Tiffin is our Trianon," wrote György Borsy-Kerekes in his book *Az egyetlen út. Az amerikai reformátusok problémája* (The sole way. The problem of the Reformed in America) (Duquesne, PA: Magyar Egyház Társaság, 1930), 24. Borsy-Kerekes sharply condemned the agreement and the leaders of the Hungarian church functioning under the rule of the American Church authorities. See also A. Komjáthy, *The Hungarian Reformed Church in America. An effort to preserve a denomination heritage.* NJ: Princeton Theological Seminary, diss. 1974. Microfilm: Ann Arbor, MI, 1974.

8. *Magyar Egyház* was first published in March 1922 and edited by Endre Sebestyén, leader of the "Independents" in the 1920s.

9. This is reflected in *Magyar Egyház, 1922–1938.*

10. These arguments were often repeated in the discussions between the opposing camps as published in *Reformátusok Lapja* (Reformed Church Newspaper) and *Magyar Egyház* in the 1920s and 1930s.

11. *Tájékoztató az Amerikai Magyar Református Egyházak küzdelmeiről és jövendő feladatairól* (Bulletin on the struggles and future tasks of the American Hungarian Reformed Church) (1929), 24.

12. Ferenc Ujlaki (1890–1984), a Protestant clergyman arrived in Cleveland, OH in 1913, and began his service at the First Hungarian Reformed Church. From 1935 to 1957 he was the president of the Hungarian Reformed Federation in America. He wrote several articles on the cultural tasks of the official review of the Federation. For example: "A magyar kultúra fáklya. Jegyzetek a Református Egykáz közgyűléséhez." (The torch of Hungarian culture. Notes to be read at the General Assembly of the Federation.) *Református Újság* 1939 1:1–2 Komjáthy, "The Hungarian Reformed Church in America," 265.

13. Borsy-Kerekes, *Az egyetlen út,* 33.

14. Bishop Dezső Baltazár visited the United States for the first time in 1922 and on that occasion he collected one hundred thousand dollars for the College of Debrecen, the orphanage and the diocese. When he visited again in 1924, the editor of *Reformátusok Lapja* started a hostile campaign against him. "It was our firm resolve to wreck the bishop, not only here in America, but also over there in Hungary. Twenty-five Hungarian Calvinist congregations shut their doors before the Bishop." *Jubileumi Emlékkönyv, 1940,* 168.

15. *Tájékoztató az Amerikai Magyar Református Egyházak küzdelmeiről,* 23.

16. Komjáthy, *A kitántorgott egyház,* 207–230.

17. Sándor Tóth, *Jubileumi Emlékkönyv,* 1940, 125–135. He also issued a monthly news bulletin entitled *Lancaster Letters* to awaken interest in the work of the institute.

18. Borsy-Kerekes, *Az egyetlen út,* 33. See also the letters written by Sándor Daróczi, dean in the second half of the 1930s of the "Independents". Bethlen Collection Ligonier.

19. Ibid., 32.

20. Ibid., 33.

21. Almási, *A clevelandi magyar baptista 85 éves története,* 21.

22. Perlman, *Bridging Three Worlds,* 218.

23. See the list of the Hungarian Roman Catholic churches and congregations in *Amerikai Magyar Népszava 25 éves jubileumi száma* (20 April 1924). For the history of every church see István Török, "Katolikus magyarok Észak-Amerikában" (Hungarian Catholics in North America), *Katholikus Magyarok Vasárnapja* (The Sunday of Catholic Hungarians) (Youngstown, OH, 1970).

24. Joseph Hartel, the priest of St. Emerick Church, to Cleveland's Archbishop, 5 March 1925, Archive of the Roman Catholic Archbishop in Cleveland.

25. Letters of the St. Margaret Church members to the Bishop in Cleveland, 15 December 1925, Archive of the Roman Catholic Archbishop in Cleveland.

26. Schaeffer, *Glimpses into Hungarian Life,* 6–9. See also Komjáthy, *A kitántorgott egyház,* 240.

27. On the activities of women in support of the Hungarian churches, see Eva V. Huseby, "A bevádorló nők mint a kontinuitás fenntartói Delray amerikai magyar közösségében" (The immigrant women as the preservers of continuity in the Hungarian community in Delray), *Ethnographia,* no. 3–4 (1991), 294. Group interviews with old ladies in Hungarian churches in New Brunswick, NJ (1984), Cleveland's East Side (1980), and East Chicago (1982). As knowledge of English spread, contact between Magyars and Jews diminished. See also Benkart in Thernstrom, *Harvard Encyclopedia,* 466.

28. Father Hartel to Cleveland's Archbishop, Joseph Schrembs, 5 March 1925. The accusatory letter of some members of St. Margaret Church against their priest, 15 December 1925, Archive of the Roman Catholic Archbishop in Cleveland.

29. "Kohányi's critics, the leaders of these schools, the two clergymen, justify the obligation of a Hungarian to study English, so that he should be able to stand firmly on the field of action in life. The hard facts prove, on the other hand, that the child, as soon as he has shaken the dust of these schools off his shoes, goes straight into the factory, where he starts the struggle of life at the early age of 19. Yet at school he did not learn enough about either Hungary or America, to withstand competition with an average American." "Magyar templomok és iskolák" (Hungarian churches and schools), *Szabadság 10. jubileumi száma* (1901), 25–31.

30. Baron Lajos Ambrozy was a Councillor of the Embassy who was sent by the Austro-Hungarian Ambassador, Hegelmüller, to the Hungarian immigrant settlements on a study tour in 1908–9. Many of the reports on his experiences can be found at the Hungarian National Archives and at the Haus-Hof-und Staats

Archivum in Vienna, in the documents of the "Ministerium des kaiserlichen und königlichen Hauses und des Äussern," and in the Archives of the Synod of the Reformed Church in Budapest. See OL.K26-1909-XXV. 1953 for the quoted document.

31. *Letter of Father Hartel*, March 5, 1925. See additional data on the Hungarian weekend schools in *Jubileumi Emlékkönyv* 1940; see also Komjáthy, *A kitántorgott egyház*.

32. Several *Árvaházi Naptár's* (Calendar of the orphanage) of the 1920s in particular contained photos and reports about Hungarian summer schools of the Protestant churches.

33. This goal was written into the by-laws of the Rákóczi and the Verhovay Fraternal Association from the 1920s on.

34. Five hundred thirty-seven of the 724 pupils in the Rowling Street school, and 504 of the 1019 pupils in the Woodland Street school were Hungarian children. *Church and School Reports* for the year ending December 31, 1922.

35. Father Julian Füzér writes about the work of St. Ladislaus parish in *Katholikus Magyarok Naptára* (Calendar of the Catholic Hungarians), 1987.

36. Joshua A. Fishman, *Language Loyalty in the United States* (The Hague: Mouton, 1966), 26.

37. See L. Monoki: "Nyári magyar iskolák" (Hungarian summer schools) *Jubileumi Emlékkönyv*, 1940, 75–76.

38. Ibid.

Chapter 20: The Secular Organizations: Divergence of Paths and Goals

1. *Verhovayak Lapja, Verhovay Ségélyegylet 50 éves jubileumi kizdványa* (1936), 66.

2. "Fifty years history of the Verhovay Relief Association," Ibid., 24–55.

3. Ibid., 67.

4. *Rákóczi Szemle* (Rákóczi Review) 1 August 1923. See also József Vadas, "A Rákóczi Segélyegylet története" (The history of the Rákóczi Relief Association) in *Rákóczi Segélyező Egyesület, 1888–1938* (Rákóczi Relief Association), edited by László Lakatos. Bridgeport, 1938, 38–39.

5. "Nagy Verhovay Picnic Clevelandben" (The big Verhovay picnic in Cleveland) *Verhovayak Lapja* (The periodical of the Verhovays), 1 September 1928.

6. In the 1930s György Borsy-Kerekes, one of the outstanding leaders of the "Independents" became a highranking official of the Association.

7. "Hungarians from around the country were present in great numbers for this ceremony." Sándor Kalassay, "Az Árvaház története" (The history of the orphanage) *Bethlen Naptár* (Bethlen Calendar) (1941), 72–78.

8. "Jegyzőkönyv" (Minutes), *Rákóczi Szemle*, 1 August 1923.

9. According to Benkart, "Perhaps as the result of similar changes, names such as Angela Baptista and Clement Marchetta appear in the columns of the *Verhovay* paper during the 1920s." Benkart, "Religion, Family, and Community."

10. "Daragó József" in Káldor, (1937) 1:244.

11. Ibid., 1:76. Other self-made businessmen were János Dezső, president of the Bridgeport Association and István Varga, in the bottling industry and president of the Rákóczi Association.

12. The Verhovay Association laid down in its statutes, too, that the transfer of Hungarian culture and the Hungarian language is to be emphasized by the Hungarian Reformed Federation.

13. Hungarian journalists announced the planned "National Assembly" for January, 1928. István Molnár, the secretary of the Hungarian Reformed Federation was elected chairman of the meeting.

14. *Rákóczi Segélyezö Egyesület, 1888–1938* (1938), 36–37.

15. Interview with A. Stelkovics, who was chief secretary of the William Penn Association for about 30 years, Pittsburgh, 1983.

16. József Vasas was a skilled worker before becoming secretary of the Rákóczi Association. He held this position from 1917 until 1955. He was a professional association man and a nationally respected leader among the American Hungarians, "known for his liberal, Hungarian oppositional views, and has been an unrelenting opponent of the Horthy regime." United States National Archives. State Department. Office of Strategic Services. Foreign National Branch Files," 1942–45. HU-304

József Daragó remained president of the Verhovay for more than two decades, until 1943 when he was removed from his position. Reverend Ferenc Ujlaki was the president of the Hungarian Reformed Federation in America from 1931 until 1956.

17. Various plans were drafted for the merging of the Verhovay, the Bridgeport and the Rákóczi Association. The leaders blamed each other for the failure; instead of cooperating, they were in a very fierce competition. See *Verhovayak Lapja, Verhovay Segélyegylet 50 éves jubileumi kiadványa* (1936), 81.

18. Emil Gárdos, "Az amerikai magyar munkásmozgalom történetéhez, 1919–1929" (On the history of the Hungarian labor movement in America, *Párttörténeti Közlemények* (Party historical Publications) (Budapest, 1963), 4–25.

19. According to Cantor, "Defections reduced the total communist membership to about 25,000, with some disconsolately estimating it at 10,000, a four-fifths decline." Cantor, *The Divided Left*, 82.

20. The main source of growth was the joining of a number of small associations in the first half of the 1920s. News about these is available in *Összetartás* (Solidarity), 1928 and *Bérmunkás Naptár* (Wageworker's Calendar) 1929. The Workers' Sick Relief Association, on the advice of the Insurance Department adopted the system of payment based on the American Experience table in the 1920s. "Reorganization of our Federation and the problem of Hungarian associations" *Bérmunkás Naptár* (1931), 51–2.

21. "Referendum," *Összetartás*, 30 April and 30 June 1929.

22. János (Lassen) Lékai was a political emigrant of 1919, sent from the Soviet Union to the United States to do Party work. As soon as he arrived he advocated "Americanization" in *Uj Előre* (New Forward).

23. Communists assigned historical importance to amateur drama groups. Lajos Egri, *Néhány szó a proletár színjátszásról* (A few words about proletarian theatricals) (New York: *Előre*, 1934), 47. See also József Kovács, *A szocialista magyar*

irodalom dokumentumai az amerikai magyar sajtóban, 1920–1945 (Documents of Hungarian socialist literature in the Hungarian Americn press (Budapest: Akadémiai Kiadó, 48–56.

24. György Cincár, in "A munkás színpad" (The worker's stage) He recalled that his group toured New York with an anti-war play, "Don't be afraid, Mother, I shall return!" and other plays, and took part in an amateur competition of Newark, Bridgeport, New Brunswick and other cities. *Magyar Naptár* (Hungarian calendar) (1977), 55–8.

25. *Uj Elŏre Naptár,* (New Forward Calendar), 1929, 79.

26. "The Anti-Horthy League" from the autobiography of Hugo Gellért in *The Noble Flame: An Anthology of a Hungarian Newspaper in America,* edited by Zoltán Deák (New York: Heritage Plan, 1982), 83–6.

27. The Magyar Club established a position for Hungarian professionals in the civic and political arena of Cleveland. Founded by lawyers and city politicians in 1924, the Magyar Club has become one of the most prestigious organizations in the community. Hungarian professionals organized "Magyar Clubs" in a similar way in more populous Hungarian settlements, for example in Pittsburgh and Chicago. Papp, *Hungarian Americans and Their Communities in Cleveland,* 145.

28. *Hungarians in America. Az amerikai magyarság aranykönyve* (Golden Book of American Hungarian), edited by John Körösfŏy (Cleveland: "Szabadság," 1941) 62–63.

29. Lengyel, *Americans from Hungary,* 172.

30. *Amerikai Képeslapok* (American illustrated magazine) 19 November 1895.

31. Appeal to America's Hungarian intellectuals" in *Az Ember* (The Man) 4 December 1929.

32. Ödön Vasvári compiled a long list of the famous Hungarian artists from Budapest in the *Amerikai Magyar Népszava Arany Jubileumi Albuma* (1949), 60–69.

33. Most of the lodges functioned in New York. Best known among them was the József Kiss Lodge. See the list of the associations and lodges of New York and reports on their meetings in the newspaper *Egyleti Élet* (Life in the associations) 1935, which was a weekly newspaper of a Hungarian Jewish fraternal order, founded in 1922.

34. Perlman, *Bridging Three Worlds,* 218.

35. Egyesült Magyar Egyletek és Egyházak Nagybizottsága: *Petőfi Emlékkönyv,* 1930, (United Hungarian Associations' and Churches' Grand Committee: *Petőfi Memorial Book* [Cleveland,] 1930). It contains information on thsoe groups of the Hungarians, whose cultural activities were coordinated by the Grand Committee with other settlements (e.g., Bridgeport, Detroit, Chicago).

36. J. K. Balogh, "An Analysis of Cultural Organizations of Hungarian Americans in Pittsburgh and Allegheny County" Ph.D.diss., University of Pittsburgh, 1945), 28.

37. Imre Déri, *Az Ember,* 19 September 1927. Cited by Lengyel, *Americans from Hungary,* 177.

Chapter 21: The American-Hungarian Newspapers: Proposing Different Paths to Integration

1. *Szabadság Naptár* (1918). The results that issued from the "Proclamation" published in *Szabadság,* when the United States entered the war and also declared

it on Austria-Hungary have already been mentioned. The bilateral loyalty was suddenly replaced by an ardent enthusiasm for the American cause. See page 62, footnote 316. See also Puskás, *From Hungary to the United States,* 308 and Táborszky, "The Hungarian Press in America," 31–4.

2. G. Gáspár, "Az *Amerikai Magyar Népszava* története" (The history of the American Hungarian People's Voice), in *Amerikai Magyar Népszaua Arany Jubileumi Albuma* (1950), 146–51.

3. Ibid., 152.

4. Ibid., 153.

5. Hugó Gellért, "Reminiscences," in Deák, *This Noble Flame,* 83–86.

6. See "Pro Hungaria—Ladies Society." *Szabadság 50. jubileumi száma* (1941). 63.

7. Ibid., 15.

8. The protest against the Treaty of Trianon which the Congress held in 1929 in Buffalo, NY, brought forth an idea typically Hungarian in its daring and romantic nature. Two brave pilots, George Endressz and Alexander Major, set out to fly across the ocean from America to Hungary on a plane built on American Hungarian contributions and named "Justice for Hungary."

9. "Géza Kende," biographical data in the "Vasvári Collection" in Somogyi Könyvtár, Szeged.

10. See Géza Kende's interviews. in *Amerikai Magyar Népszava* vol. 1921–1922.

11. Jenő H. Neuwald, a socialist, the editor-in-chief of *Előre* (Forward) at the time of World War I until 1921, later joined the IWW. His articles appeared in the *Bérmunkás* (Wage laborer). When it ceased publication, he continued to write for the *Értesítő* (Gazette), a paper issued in mimeographed form for the remaining IWW members. See for example *Értesítő,* 8 October 1969. See also Gárdos, "Az amerikai magyar munkásmozgalom, történetéhez, 11 and *Amerikai Magyar Népszava,* 14 April 1920.

12. On the subsidizing of the American Hungarian newspapers see "The documents of the branch in charge of the Hungarian aliens, 1919–1945" OL.K.71. 1919/I/C item.

13. There was striking evidence for this in the changes of the contents of the *Calendars,* "Chronicles of American-Hungarians," which was a regular column before World War I. The column stops appearing in them. The course followed by the *Szabadság* in Cleveland and the *Amerikai Magyar Népszava* in New York became typical of commercial papers: they were primarily business enterprises.

14. Juliska Lovas (Flint, MI) was the one to win first the title of "Miss Magyar Amerika," *Amerikai Magyar Népszava Arany Jubileumi Albuma* (1950), 155.

15. József Reményi, "Miért nincs amerikai magyar irodalom?" (Why is there no American Hungarian literature?) *Korunk* (Our Era), Kolozsvár, 1929, I, 425–430.

16. "Beköszöntő" (Inaugural), *Rákóczi Szemle,* 1 July 1923. The official newspapers of fraternal organizations gave information mainly on internal matters, organizational developments, and on the financial situation, but also on labor questions and the social activities of the local branches, such as "Rákóczi Day," an annual festivity.

17. *Szabadság 50. jubileumi száma* (1941), 15.

18. Reményi, "Miért nincs amerikai magyar irodalom?" *Korunk,* I, 425–430.

19. *Új Előre Huszouöt éues Jubileumi Album* (Új Előre's 25th anniversary album) (1927), 112.

20. *Új Előre,* 26 May 1922, "A proletár kultúra" (The proletarian culture).

21. See János Lékai, writings in *Új Előre,* vol. 1923–1924.

22. Patrias, *Patriots and Proletarians,* 208.

23. Sándor Vörös, *American Commissar.* Philadelphia: Chilton Company, 1961), 183.

24. Kovács, *A szocialista magyar irodalom dokumentumai Amerikában.*

25. See in more detail in the chapter "Az amerikai magyarság és a munkáskultúra" (The American Hungarians and the workers' culture) in ibid., 42–56.

26. Gárdos, "Az amerikai magyar munkasmozgalom történetéhez," 25. Separate reprint, 64–74.

27. Ibid., 28, also *Új Előre Huszonöt éves Jubileumi Albuma* (1927), 124

28. Göndör celebrated the tenth anniversary of his paper in 1936 by publishing a special issue for the occasion. *Az Ember,* 17 October 1936.

29. Mihály Károlyi in his letters to Ferenc Göndör and Oszkár Jászi criticized the steps Göndör took. *Károlyi Mihály levelei* (Mihály Károlyi's correspondence), edited by Tibor Hajdú (Budapest: Akadémiai Kiadó, 1991), 354, 371–373.

30. See for example the following in *Az Ember,* 2 July 1927: "we turn away from us any Hungarian sabre-rattling irredentist and whilst we protest against any kind of warlike adventure with all our might, we shall never cease to demand the revision of the Trianon decision with peaceful means."

31. Martin Himmler's *Magyar Bányászok Lapja* (Hungarian Miners' Journal) also claimed to be the largest American Hungarian weekly. Its circulation ran in excess of 10,000. Published in Detroit, "it concerns itself primarily with the news directly affecting the large groups of Hungarian miners working in the coal fields of West Virginia and Pennsylvania. In second place, it was a personal mouthpiece of Martin Himmler on politics at home and in Hungary. Martin Himmler is one of the chief leaders among the American Hungarians. He wields influence not only among the miners whom he knows so intimately, but also among other leaders who to a certain extent are dependent on the press Himmler controls." Benkart "Religion, Family, and Community Among Hungarians," 195. Martin Himmler, publisher of the *Magyar Bányászok Lapja* and *Detroiti Magyarság,* managed seven weeklies in Ohio, in 1934. Táborszky, "The Hungarian Press in America," 35.

32. Fishman, *Language Loyalty in the United States,* 14

33. In the 1930s, *Szabadság* weathered two financial crises. Bankrupt early in this decade it passed into the hands of a group of Cleveland Hungarians who, however, could not maintain it. It was then owned by a drug concern. The next owner and editor, Zoltán Gombos, who had been on its staff, acquired the paper in 1939 with money he made on the exhibition of foreign films in Cleveland. Office of Strategic Services, Hungary: HU-August 21, 1942.

34. Fishman, *Language Loyalty in the United States,* 14.

35. Ladányí (1943).

Chapter 22: The 1930s: Class and Ethnic Solidarity

1. Lester V. Charles, *America's Greatest Depression, 1929–1941* (New York: Harper and Row, 1970) The chapter "Unemployment and Labor incomes" records

the great increase in the totally unemployed: in 1929, only 3.2 per cent of the labor force was totally unemployed. This rose to 8.7 per cent in 1930, 15.9 per cent in 1931, 23.6 per cent in 1932 and 24.9 per cent in 1933.

2. Letter from Rev. Sándor Daróczy to a friend in Hungary, September 2, 1932. McKeesport, PA. One copy is in the author's collection.

3. Minutes of the Hungarian-American Reformed Federation 1933, 1934. (Ligonier Collection.) Reports on similar difficulties in other "national" organizations appear, for example, in *Rákóczi Segélyező Egyesület, 1888–1938* (1938), 43–45 and in *Új Előre Naptár* (1935), 93.

4. Imre Király (Cleveland) "How does our churchlife flow?" *Emlékkönyv* 91–99.

5. *Szabadság 50. jubileumi száma* (1941), 36.

6. Interview with John Palasics, Cleveland, 1988.

7. Papp, *Hungarian Americans and Their Communities of Cleveland*, 252.

8. *Szabadság 50. jubileumi száma* (1941), 31.

9. See in detail Art Preis, *Labor's Giant Step. Twenty years of the CIO* (New York: Pathfinder Press, 1972), 3–72.

10. With a few hundred members backing them, this group contacted similar organizations at fifteen other GE plants who came together in 1936 to set up what became the United Electrical, Radio and Machine Workers of America, commonly known as U.E. See Deák, *This Noble Flame*, 133–134. Pál Petrás states in his report "Pictures from Chicago": "I can tell without exaggeration, that the Hungarian workers stood their ground in every fight; moreover, I can also state that they took the first place in the steel strike, while the Hungarian women took part in relief work for the strikers. We saw members of the second generation standing in the picket lines." *10 Jubileumi IWO Naptár* (10th anniversary *IWO* calendar) (1940), 101.

11. Roy Wortam, *From Syndicalism to Trade Unionism: The IWW in Ohio, 1905–1950* (New York: Garland, 1985), 139–140.

12. Flórián Paczier, "Kilenc Évig a Lapnál (With the paper for nine years), in *Magyar Naptár* (Hungarian Calendar), *1902–1977,* 44–45.

13. József Fehér, "Előre a betegsegélyzők egyesítése felé" (Forward to the merger of the sick relief organizations), in *Új Előre Naptár* (1931), 7.

14. See the almanacs of *Bérmunkás*, 1935–1937 and *Új Előre Naptár* (1936), 7–18.

15. See more in detail in *IWO Emlékkönyv* (IWO Memorial Album), 1900–1935.

16. Roger Keeran, "National Groups and the Popular Front: The Case of the International Workers," *Journal of Ethnic History*, XIV, no. 3 (Spring 1995) 23–51.

That the Hungarians were becoming more radical is also reflected in the letter written by B. T. Tárkány, the editor of the *Jó Pásztor* (Good Shepherd), a Hungarian Catholic weekly, August 3, 1936. He writes about the Hungarians in West Virginia: "The sad fact is that our people are turning, slowly but surely, from our Church. Bolsheviki agents appear now and then on the mining places, inciting the poor miners against God and owners of the mines. The result is that many of our people read the so-called *Új Előre* (The New Forward), which makes attacks almost daily against our religion, priest and churches. There is no wonder why no room is left in the soul of the people for a religious newspaper." Archives of the Roman Catholic Archbishop in Cleveland.

17. *Thesis and Resolutions for the Seventh National Convention of the Communist party of the U.S.A.* (A pamphlet published by the Central Committee plenum, March 31–April 4, 1930), 78–84.

18. Keeran, "National Groups and the Popular Front," 33.

19. By 1935, the IWO had 175 English-speaking branches consisting of 5500 members, the English-speaking branches being the fourth largest adult branch with 8.7 percent of the membership, after the Jewish 33.4 percent, Hungarian 9.4 percent, and Slovak 8 per cent.

20. Office of Strategic Services, Hungary: HU 304 August 21, 1942.

21. *Új Előre Naptár* (1935), 91–93.

22. Peter Rachleff, "Class, ethnicity and the New Deal. The Croatian Fraternal Union in the 1930s." in Kivisto, *The Ethnic Enigma,* 95.

23. Papp, *Hungarian Americans and Their Communities in Cleveland.* See also the volumes of the Chicago Hungarian paper *Interest.* Similarly, *Az Ember,* Ferenc Göndör's journal in New York, raised its banner for Roosevelt's New Deal ideas. Hungarians were very active in 1936 in the campaign to reelect President Roosevelt.

Members and leaders of the Rákóczi Association were "anti-Horthy" and also "in American politics militantly New Deal." "Liberalism is in the character of the association which early lent its support to general oppositional movements abroad." This can be read about in a report. Office of Strategic Services, Hungary: USS3-HU-August 21, 1942. Even the Free Hungarian Church supported the reelection of Roosevelt. *Magyar Egyház,* XV (November 1936) -quoted by Komjáthy, "The Hungarian Reformed Church of America," 279.

24. See in more detail Cantor, *The Divided Left,* 97–127.

25. Sándor Garbai, "Az amerikai magyarság szociális elhelyezkedése" (The social settling down of the Hungarians in America) *Korunk,* (1937), 500–506.

26. Minutes of the Convention in 1936. (The documents are deposited at the Archive of the Hungarian Foundation in New Brunswick, N.J.) The mobilization of the members was aimed at by an informative pamphlet of the Verhovay Association: *Amerikai magyar útmutató a polgárosodás és munkásnyugdíj általánosságokban való megismertetésére* (American Hungarian guide to general information on naturalization and workers' pensions) (Pittsburgh: Verhovay Segély Egylet, n.d. [After 1937]).

27. *Az Ember, 10. Jubileumi Száma* (As Ember's 10th Anniversary issue) (1936).

28. Montgomery, *Workers' Control in America* 161–8; Cantor, *The Divided Left,* 122–3. Preis, *Labor's Giant Step,* 34–49.

29. *Uj Előre,* 31 December 1936, 8.

30. Interview with second generation Lajos Antal, who was an activist in the union, Pittsburgh, 1986. In his company, I visited some small mining places in Pennsylvania, where old women, widows of miners, emphasized the same experiences.

31. Interview with N. N., Detroit, 1986.

32. See more details on the Cultural Federation: József Hollós, "A Kulturszövetség feladata" (The task of the Cultural Federation) in his *Két világháború között.*

(Between two world wars) (New York: Kultúrszövetség, 1936) and Sándor Szent-miklóssy, "Mit akarunk?" (What do we want?), *Kulturharc* (Struggle for Culture) (1932), 3, 52–53.

33. *Kulturharc*, a social and literary periodical, was published from 1931 to 1938 in New York by the Kulturszövetség.

34. Its theatrical committee founded a theatrical group. The "Kulturharc Műkedvelő Gárda" (The Struggle for Culture Amateur Set) organized evening debates, free schools, exhibitions of paintings, and schools of design. *Kulturharc* (1933), 113.

35. Featuring excerpts from the autobiography of Hugó Gellért in Deák, *The Noble Flame,* 81–91; Personal data and history of Imre Ladányi in "Memory Ladá-nyi," *Woodcuts* (New York: Kövesdy Gallery, 1986), 11–12. Emory (Imre) Ladányi was born in 1902, in the town of Kecskemét, Hungary. Although he became a doctor, he was since childhood drawn to woodcarving and painting. He emigrated to New York in 1929, and became licensed to practice medicine. In his spare time, he continued to create pieces of art. In the 1930s, during the Depression, he joined the Hungarian Cultural Federation (Magyar Kulturszovetseg) where he gave lectures on hygiene and taught courses in fine arts. Some of his linocuts served as cover illustrations for *Kulturharc,* the journal of the Federation. The Federation organized an exhibit of his works and he also became a permanent member of the Contemporary Art Gallery exhibitions. See Walter I Straus, *Emory Ladányi, Visual Artist* (New York: Albaris Books, 1977). By the 1940s "The List of Prominent Americans of Hungarian Origin" was remarkably long, though far from complete. *Hungary, Past and Present,* edited by Joseph Szentkirályi (New York: Hungarian Reference Library, 1941), 98–123.

36. According to Emil Lengyel, the life of these societies was ephemeral. Sometimes an ambitious program chairman arranged good lectures, debates and musical performances but interest languished. The struggle for life dulled receptiv-ity for cultural matters. The intellectually curious newcomers drifted away from Hungarian settlements. Card playing in many cases replaced cultural activities. Lengyel, *Americans from Hungary,* 172.

37. The new publication was "a paper for Hungarians of progressive mentality." It wished to be a more effective tool for the unification of the Hungarian immigrants' various groups. From the title *Amerikai Magyar Világ* (Hungarian World in America) the words "of America" were soon left out and it appeared with the name *Magyar Világ* (Hungarian World) from November 3, 1938

Chapter 23: The Second Generation: Its Own Identity

1. The foreign born Magyar population of 1930 was just about half of the total Magyar immigration to the United States for the period 1899–1930. United States Census 1930. Commissioner General's Report 1930. 214.

According to Hutchinson, the distribution of the second generation Hungarians (foreign parentage, males) by major occupational group was rather close to that of the white male labor force, except for a low proportion among farmers (20) and farm laborers (23). Comparison with all foreign parentage showed slightly more employment as operatives, less as farmers, service workers, and farm laborers. Occupational specializations continued the concentration of the immigrant generation among workers in heavy industry and were relatively high among toolmakers, accountants and auditors, and welders and flame cutters. Edward P. Hutchinson, *Immigrants and Their Children, 1850–1950* (New York: Chapman G. Hall, (1956), 251–2.

2. For example, by the end of the 1930s, of the 198 members of the East Chicago Hungarian Reformed community 150 still belonged to the immigrant generation. *Egyházi és gyülekezeti Krónika az East-Chicagói Elsö Magyar Evangéliumi és Református Egyház és Templom harmincöt éves Jubileumára.* (Church and congregational chronicle commemorating the 35th Anniversary of the East Chicago First Hungarian Evangelical and Reformed Church and Congregation) (East Chicago, 1942). A similar picture is shown in *A chicagoi South Side-i Magyar Református Egyház Albuma* (The Album of the Chicago Southside Hungarian Reformed Church) (Chicago, 1942) and in *Az Indiana Harbori Elsö Magyar Evangéliumi és Református Egyház családi albuma* (The Family Album of the Indiana Harbor First Hungarian Evangelical and Reformed Church) (Indiana Harbor, 1993).

3. "A Szilvássy testvérek története" (The History of the Szilvássy siblings) in *Szabadság 50. jubileumi száma,* 72–73.

4. Irving Berstein, *Turbulent Years: A History of the American Workers, 1933–1941.* (Boston: Houghton Mifflin, 1971), 744 (United Automobile Workers of America, 734–51).

5. A few articles on the subject: Andor Kun, "Megmenthetö-e az amerikai magyarság?" (Is it possible to save Hungarianhood in America?), *Magyar Szemle,* VII (1929), 15–24; Andor Kun, "Hogyan megy veszendöbe az amerikai magyarság?" (How does Hungarianhood in America get lost?), *Magyar Szemle,* XXII (1934), 440–445; and Sándor Gondos, "Elpusztult-e az amerikai magyarság?" (Did Hungarianhood in America go to waste?), *Magyar Szemle,* XXVII (1936), 137–145.

6. Juliska Dankó, described her ties to Hungarian ethnicity very colorfully. She was actually of the second generation, because she was only an eight-month-old baby when her parents took her to America. She was brought up in the Hungarian community of Delray-Detroit. In her recollections she emphasized that in their home the children had to speak Hungarian only. Her father especially demanded that. She learned to write and read Hungarian. For decades Julia Dankó taught Hungarian dances and took part in amateur theatricals as a member of the Verhovay's Detroit branch, as well as participating regularly in its other cultural activities. The interview was conducted in Detroit, 1986.

7. Papp, *Hungarian Americans and Their Communities of Cleveland,* 244.

8. *Szabadság 50. Jubileumi száma* (1941), 74.

9. Handlin, *The Uprooted,* 85.

10. Higham, *Send These to Me,* 222 and Archdeacon, *Becoming American.*

11. Fejős, *A chicagói magyarok két nemzedéke,* 224. See also Nicolas V. Montalto's study, "The Intercultural Education Movement, 1924–41. The Growth of Tolerance as a Form of Intolerance," in which he emphasized that cultural education as defined by powerful professional educators and government leaders was not as much the antithesis of Americanization as one might surmise from the rhetoric of

the movement, since it was a more "scientific" Americanization, a modified expression of the same impulse. The goal remained the same, only the methodology had changed. The demands for the "100 percent Americanism" epitomized the political culture of a period that stretched from 1914 through the mid-1920s. See more details in Bernard J. Weiss, *American Education and the European Immigrants, 1840–1940*, edited by Bernard J. Weiss (Urbana: University of Illinois Press, 1982).

12. Mihály Varga, "Az amerikai magyar élet jövője" (The Future of Hungarian Life in America) *Verhovayak Lapja, Verhovay Segély Egylet 50 éves jubileumi kiadványa* (1936), 47.

13. Ibid.

14. For the second generation, part of the anniversary publication was written in English, 1–45.

16. Some of the winners wrote about their journey and their experiences in Hungary in *Verhovayak Lapja,* 1938. Trips to Hungary were also organized by the American Hungarian Federation in the years from 1935 to 1939.

17. *Szabadság 50. jubileumi száma* (1941), 41.

18. The *Young Hungarian America,* Vol. I, (1936) and *Second Generation Almanac for the American Youth of Hungarian Origin,* edited by Andor Sziklai (Cleveland: *Szabadság,* 1937). For more detailed analysis of these papers see Fejős, *A chicagoi magyarok két nemzedéke,* 176–88.

19. See the suggestions of the American Hungarian Federation in "A magyarok II. világkongresszusának tárgyalásai" (The Deliberations of the 2nd World Congress of Hungarians), 16–18 August 1938, 45.

20. A popular column was started for the Second Generation in the *Református Újság.* It contained articles on the history of Hungarians, 1937–1939. The preservation of the values of Magyar-America was aimed at by Edmund Vasvári's book: *Lincoln's Hungarian Heroes: The Participation of Hungarians in the Civil War, 1861–1865* (Washington, D.C.: Hungarian Reformed Church of America, 1939).

21. *Református Újság,* XVI (January–April 1938). The story of Colonel Michael Kovács (1724–1779), who became the Master of Exercises of the famous Pulaski Legion, America's first hussar regiment, was also written at that time. Református Újsag, February 1940, 8–9. Julius Melegh, "For the Second Generation in the 1930s," *Testvériség (Fraternity),* 13–14 May 1940. Clarence A. Manning, "Kossuth's place in American History," ibid., 11–12 October 1940. American poets' verses about Louis Kossuth which were written at the time of his trip to America were republished in *Testvériség.*

22. Balogh, *An Analysis of Cultural Organizations,* 50.

23. See for more details Fejős, *A chicagoi magyarok két nemzedéke,* Chapter, "The second generation" 161–213

24. Bologh, *An Analysis of Cultural Organizations.* The leftist organizations did not pay any attention to passing ethnic heritage on to the second generation: they emphasized assimilation and a united working class.

25. A somewhat more favorable picture is shown of the second and the third generations in church life by John Butosi in his "Church Membership Performance of Three Generations in the Hungarian Reformed Churches of Allegheny County" (Ph.D.diss., University of Pittsburgh, 1961).

26. In the interviews, most people spoke openly of the bad feelings caused by the prejudices against the Hungarians. Similar problems are raised in connection with Polish-Americans by James S. Pula, "Image, Status, Mobility and Integration in American Society: The Polish Experience," *Journal of American Ethnic History* VI, no. 1 (Fall 1996), 78–95.

27. Astonishingly similar attitudes of the second generation of other ethnic groups are described in *Studies in Ethnicity: The East-European Experience in America,* edited by Charles A. Ward, Philip Shashko, and Donald E. Pienkos (New York: Columbia University Press, 1980).

Chapter 24: The Second World War: A New Identity Crisis.

1. Nándor F. Dreisziger, "Bridges to the West: The Horthy Regime's Reinsurance Policies in 1941." *War and Society,* VII, no. 1 (May 1989), 1–23.

2. There is a series of documents in the National Archives, Washington, DC entitled "Office of Strategic Services, Foreign National Branch Files," 1942–1945: Hungarians on political activities of the conservative and of the leftist factions. INT-15HU-1 to INT-15 HU-823.

3. On Oszkár Jászi's wide circle of intellectual relationships see his correspondence in *Oszkár Jászi's Selected Letters,* edited by György Litván and János F. Varga (Budapest: Magvető, 1991) 441.

4. "Communists thus once again cynically subordinated consistent policy to Soviet needs and manoeuvres." Cantor, *The Divided Left* 144–145.

5. György Borsy-Kerekes, *Testvériség,* 1941. Quoted by István Gál, *Magyarország, Anglia és Amerika.* (Hungary, England, America), Chapter: "Az amerikai Kossuth kultusz" (The Kossuth cult in America) (Budapest: Officina, 1944), 193.

6. Declaration of the American Hungarian Federation to President Roosevelt January 7, 1941, in Paul Nadányi, *The "Free Hungary" Movement* (New York: Amerikai Magyar Népszava Press, 1942), 13.

7. Quoted by Nadányi in ibid.

8. David Montgomery was the United States ambassador to Hungary in the 1930s. He had close relations with Tibor Eckhardt. Paul Nadányi quotes at length the letter of the former ambassador, in which he defends Eckhardt against the slanders. See ibid., 22–25.

9. Interview with Louis Tóth, Chairman of Victory Council, Office of Strategic Services, Hungary: HU.95. July 21, 1943.

10. *Harc* (Fight), official weekly of the American Federation of Democratic Hungarians (Demokratikus Magyarok Amerikai Szövetsége), edited by Rusztem Vámbéry, New York, 1941–45. In the first issue (December 25, 1941), the editor stated, "The interests of the United States and the Hungarian people are united in all essential points for those who know the following: The present feudal fascist political structure was a very important factor in pushing Europe toward catastrophe."

11. *The Proclamation of the Association of Democratic American Hungarians,* 21 September 1941 (Cleveland) One copy is in the author's collection.

12. *The Proclamation of the International Workers Order* (New York, 1941), quoted by Imre Komlós, "Az International Workers' Order és a háború" (The International Workers Order and the war), *Magyar Jövő Naptára* (Magyar Jövő's Calendar) (1943), 48–49.

13. See the newspaper, *Magyar Jövő* (Hungarian Future) and its Almanacs, 1941–1945. The Hungarian American Federation was called a "fifth column" organization. "Organizing fascist propaganda was their task here, too." János Nagy, "Magyarország és az amerikai magyarság a háborúban" (Hungary and the American Hungarians in the war), *Magyar Jövő Naptára* (1944), 22–23.

14. "In the case of Hungary the test of every other movement against Nazi Germany is whether they reject without condition the Hitlerite revision of the Hungarian frontiers and want peace with the neighboring countries." Oszkár Jászi, "A magyar egységfront kérdéséhez" (On the issue of the Hungarian United Front) *Magyar Fórum* (Hungarian Forum) I, no. 3 (1942), 55–56.

15. Oszkár Jászi's letter to Rusztem Vámbéry in Litván and Varga, eds. *Oszkár Jászi's Selected Letters, 441.*

16. "The Professor's main objection to Eckhardt's programs was that Eckhardt never came out with a statement against the Horthy regime, refused to recognize the legal existence of Chechoslovakia, Yugoslavia, Romania, and often referred to them in offensive terms. Office of Strategic Services, Hungary: HU 60. April 7, 1942.

17. The continuous attacks against Eckhardt were published not only in the *Magyar Fórum* and *Harc* but in the English language newspapers (for example, *Nation*).

18. The resignation of Tibor Eckhardt as President of the Independent Hungary Movement. Office of Strategic Services, Hungary: HU 113. July 14, July 20, 1942 (1943) 53.

19. See the pictorial documents about their donations (ships, Mobile Disaster Units, war bonds) in the *10th Anniversary Almanac of the American Hungarian Federation. (AHF).* Compiled by Stephen Balogh. (Washington, D.C. 30 September 1948).

20. Ibid., the President's report at the 10th Anniversary meeting of the American Hungarian Federation, 1948.

21. "The Stratification of Hungarian Politics in the United States. Office of Strategic Services, Hungary: HU 285. March 3, 1943.

22. Free Hungarians organized similarly in England, Canada, Mexico, Uruguay, Argentina, Brazil, and Bolivia around the banner of Mihály Károlyi, former president of the Hungarian People's Republic, who was exiled from his home and lived in England. He believed in the ideals of Kossuth and Lincoln, and fought for them. His friends worked for a visa to the United States for him, but they did not succeed.

23. "Declaration and Guide to Policy and Action of the Hungarian-American Council for Democracy," adopted by the National Conference held in Chicago, June 27, 1943. A copy of the document is in the author's collection.

24. "Conference of Hungarian-American trade unionists." Office of Strategic Services, Hungary: HU-464 December 5, 1943.

25. József Hollós, "Miért a *Magyar Fórum?*" (Why the *Magyar Fórum?*) *Magyar Fórum,* I (1 April 1941).

26. Harold G. Vatter, *The United States Economy in World War II* (New York: Columbia University Press, 1985), 119–120.

27. Interview with Steven Dankó, Detroit, 1986.

28. *Szabadság,* January–July, 1942, quoted by Papp, *Hungarian Americans and Their Communities of Cleveland,* 258. In World War II, 1145 members of the New Brunswick Hungarian community served in the army. List of their names appeared in *Hungarian Defense Council Souvenir Album* "In honor of our boys who were in the service" (New Brunswick, 23 June 1946). See also Philip Gleason, "Americans All: World War II and the Shaping of American Ideals," *The Review of Politics,* XLIII (October 1981), 515.

29. George E. Pozetta, "From Rustbelt to Sunbelt: Patterns of Ethnic Migration and Integration in America, 1940–1989," in *From 'Melting Pot' to Multiculturalism: The Evolution of Ethnic Relations in the United States,* edited by Valeria Gennaro (Roma: Bulzoni Editore, 1990) 263–280.

30. Ibid., 268.

31. Ibid., 269

32. 111,464 Hungarian immigrants were registered as aliens in 1940: 44,773 males, 66,691 females. "Alien Registration" Immigration and Naturalization Service, United States Department of Justice 1940. Table VI.

33. Pozetta, "From Rust Belt to Sunbelt," in Lerda, *From 'Melting Pot' to Multiculturalism,* 270. Another scholar put it somewhat differently "The war gave young men a shared experience, different from and more intense than of previous generations." William McNeil *America High: The Years of Confidence, 1945–1960* (New York: The Free Press, 1986), 27. Quoted by Pozetta, "From Rustbelt to Sunbelt," in Lerda, *From 'Melting Pot' to Multiculturalism, 267*

34. Interview with Albert Stelkovics, Pittsburgh, 1984.

35. For more about the postwar relief work, see Ferenc Ujlaki, "Egymás terhét hordozzátok" (Carry each others' burden!), *Bethlen Naptár* (1949), 127–8. "The appeal for such collaboration issued by the Aid to Hungary Committee, which is now in the process of organization, has met with a great deal of favorable reaction—all local Hungarian-American spokemen whom I have interviewed have declared themselves as ready to support such organization." Office of Strategic Services, Hungary: HU 627. September 22, 1944.

36. *Declaration of the Hungarian Reformed Federation of America, 1944.* Proceedings of the convention in Bethlen Collection, Ligonier.

Chapter 25: The Arrival of the Displaced Persons, 1948–1952

1. Eugene M. Kulisher, *Europe on the Move. War and Population Changes, 1917–47* (New York: Columbia University Press, 1948), 805.

2. Marrus, *The Unwanted,* 299. See also Jacques Vernant, *The Refugee in the Postwar World* (London: Allen and Unwin, 1953), 32. "During the second world war, sixty million European civilians had been forced to move—more than ten times the number of refugees generated by World War I and its aftermath." Malcolm J. Proudfoot, *European Refugees, 1939–52. A Study of Forced Population Movement* (Evanston, IL: Northwestern University Press, 1956), 21. See also Kum Salomon,

Refugees in the Cold War. Toward a New International Refugee Regime in the Early Postwar Era (Lund: Lund University Press, 1991).

Important documents about the problems of the displaced persons in the United States: (1) *Displaced Persons Operations:* Report of Central Headquarters for Germany, (Washington: UNRRA, 1946): Legislation Advocated for the Entrance of Displaced Persons in the United States; (2) "Message of the President to the Congress" Read in the Senate and House of Representatives on July 7, 1947, and released to the press by the White House on the same date, II. Doc. 332. Department of State Bulletin, July 20, 1947; (3) Howard Alexander Smith, *Displaced Persons Problem,* (Washington, D.C.: Government Printing Office, 1948): Report on displaced persons problem submitted to Senate Foreign Relations Committee by Senator H. Alexander Smith, advisory member of the Senate Foreign Relations Committee to special subcommittee of the Judiciary Committee of the Senate, dated March 15, 1948; (4) Rabbi Philip S. Bernstein, "Status of Jewish Misplaced Persons," *Department of State Bulletin* (1947), 22–25: Rabbi Bernstein was Adviser on Jewish Affairs to General Lucius D. Clay, Military Governor of the European Theater. His statement was made before the House of Representatives Subcommittee on Immigration and Naturalization on June 20, 1947, and released to the press on the same date. Kurt R. Grossmann, *The Jewish DP Problem. Its Origin, Scope and Liquidation* (New York: Institute of Jewish Affairs, World Jewish Congress, 1951).

3. Gyula Borbándi, *A magyar emigráció életrajza: 1945–1985* (The biography of Hungarian emigration) 2nd ed. 2 vols. (Budapest: Európa), 1:15.

4. Marrus, *The Unwanted,* 320. See also Mark Elliot, *Pawns of Yalta: Soviet Refugees and America's Role in Their Repatriation* (Urbana: University of Illinois Press, 1982).

5. See the chapter "Problem of Repatriation," in Mark Wyman, *DP: Europe's Displaced Persons, 1945–51* (Philadelphia: Balch Institute, 1989), 61–85. See also Julius Epstein "American Forced Repatriation," *Ukrainian Quarterly* X, no. 4 (Autumn 1954), 254–265.

6. The US Army training packet on the 1945–46 occupation revealed the interpretation of the Yalta document: "Individuals identified by the Soviet repatriation representatives as Soviet citizens were subject to repatriation without regard to their personal wishes. The realization that many DPs did not want to return home and would refuse to be repatriated, even to the point of committing suicide, was to prove a continuing, nagging problem to the Western allies." Wyman, *DP: Europe's Displaced Persons,* 65.

7. Louise Holborn, *The International Refugee Organization: A Specialized Agency of the United Nations. Its History and Work, 1846–1952* (London: Oxford University Press, 1956). See also Kim Solomon, *Refugees in the Cold War: Towards a New International Refugee Regime in the Early Postwar Era* (Lund, Sweden: Lund University Press, 1991).

8. On the International Refugee Organization's activities and functioning, see IRO Reports (1956), Table IV, 12–13.

9. István Mócsi, "Partition of Hungary and the Origin of the Refugee Problems," in *Essays on World War I: Total War and Peacemaking, a Case Study on Trianon,* edited by Béla Király, Péter Pastor and Iván Sanders (New York: Brooklyn College Press, 1982), 494–5.

10. Kulisher, *Europe on the Move*, "Hungary," 105.

11. Marrus, *The Unwanted*, 251. See also Livia Rothkirchen, "Hungary—an Asylum for the Refugee of Europe," *Yad Vashem Studies*, VII (1968), 127–42.

12. See the statistical report on the victims of the Holocaust. Rudolph I. Braham, *The Politics of Genocide. The Holocaust in Hungary*. 2 vol. (New York: Columbia University Press, 1981), I, 200. See also *Third Semi-annual Report to the President and the Congress*. February 1, 1950. (Washington, D.C.: Government Printing Office, 1950), and the *Displaced Persons Commission and Memo to America. The final report of the Commission* Washington, D.C.: Government Printing Office, 1952.

13. Béla Tarcai, *Magyarok a nyugati hadifogoly táborokban* (Hungarians in the prisoner of war camps in the West) (Budapest: Kötes Kereskedelmi és Szervezö Társaság, 1992), 9.

I gathered information by listening to reminiscences about the bitter experiences of the civilians in flight, the congestion of the masses on some parts of the road, and the bombings they suffered. Interviews with O. Zoltai, St. Paul, MN. 1983 and G. Gracza, Budapest, 1994. Besides some oral testimonies, there are written reminiscences, novels, and official accounts, for example those from Barna Dienes, American Reformed clergyman, who visited the European refugee camps on behalf of the Protestant World Federation. His accounts of his experiences contain information on the every day life of the refugees. (A collection of Barna Dienes' documents are filed at the Bethlen Archive, New Brunswick, NJ. Hungarian-American Foundation.

József Nyirő, Hungarian writer, one of the refugees himself, described the difficulties of the physical and mental trials of homelessness and homesickness in his novels *Ime! Az emberek* (Behold! the humans) and *Zöld Csillag* (Green Star) (First published in Youngstown, *Katolikus Magyarok Vasárnapja*, 1979. Second edition Debrecen, 1991.) We know of a few more recollections, happening mostly in refugee camps, where the older people recollected their experiences with bitterness, the younger ones in a more optimistic tone.

In 1949, *Új Magyar Út* (New Hungarian Way), the paper of the *Magyar Szellemi Munkaközösség* (Hungarian Cultural Fellowship) still appeared in Münich, Germany. Its founder was Géza Soós. Professing at the time the ideology of "a particular Hungarian way" seemed to be left-wing in the eyes of the "national emigration." The journal was published in the United States from the beginning of the 1950s, edited by Elemér Bakó. See Miklós Béládi-Béla Pomogáts *Nyugati irodalom 1945 után* (Western literature after 1945) Budapest: Gondolat. 34-5. The 45-er emigrants did not only raise the number of papers published and their level, but boosted their circulation, tried to get them to their companions in distress into several countries on various continents.

A big role in stopping the dispersion of the teenagers was played by the schools and the boy-scout movement organized in the refugee camps. Tibor Zoltai gives an attractive description of a boy's character taking shape in the boy-scout community in his novel *Pali fel a fejjel* (Pali, cheer up!). Garfield, NJ.: Magyar Cserkészszövetség. 1978. See also László Könnyü, *Egy költő visszanéz*.

14. Whether to return home or to settle, "the decision was mostly influenced not by political considerations, but by individual points of view and personal interests." Borbándi, *A magyar emigráció életrajza*, I, 22.

15. Stephen Kertész, "The Expulsion of Germans from Hungary. A Study in Postwar Diplomacy," *Review of Politics*, 1953, 179–208; *Documents on the Expulsion of the Germans from Eastern-Central Europe*, edited by Theodore Schieder. 4 vol. (Bonn: Federal Ministry for Expellees, Refugees and War Victims, 1960), I.

16. A detailed and dramatic report is given in Miklós Füzes, *Forgó szél. Be- és kitelepitések Dél-Kelet Dunántúlon, 1944–1948 között.* Tanulmány és interjú kötet (Whirlwind. Settlements and deportations in South-East-Transdanubia, between 1944 and 1948. Studies and interviews) Pécs: Baranya megyei Levéltár, 1990.

17. See, for example, the dissolution of bourgeois parties under the leadership of Stephan Barankovics, Demokratikus Néppárt (Democratic People's Party), and Dezső Sulyok, Szabadság Párt (Liberty Party) in 1947. Both parties took refuge from the country in 1949.

18. In the summer of 1947, Ferenc Nagy, the prime minister of the country, did not return from his trip to Western Europe and the deputies of parliament and leaders of the bourgeois parties who were being pushed into the background followed him. After a short stay in Western Europe, most of them found refuge in the United States: Zoltán Pfeiffer, of the Függetlenségi Párt (Independence Party), Károly Peyer, former leader of the Social Democratic Party and the Council of Trade Unions, Imre Kovács, former General-secretary of the Nemzeti Parasztpárt (National Peasant Party), Vince Nagy, Minister of the Interior in 1918, former joint-secretary of the Szabadság Párt (Liberty Party). A well-known scholar, Zoltán Bay, described his escape very colorfully in his book *Az élet erősebb* (Life is stronger) (Debrecen and Budapest: Püski, 1990).

19. Compiled from the "Annual Reports of the Immigration and Naturalization Service, For the Fiscal Years 1948–1953" (Washington, D.C.: Government Printing Press, 1954).

20. *Hungarian Statute-Books*, 1945–1963, Budapest.

21. Vernant, *The Refugee in the Postwar World*, 181.

22. Ferenc Kisbarnaki Farkas' estimate in *Az altöttingi országgyülés története* (The history of the session of parliament in Altötting) (Munich: Mikes, 1969), 12. Most of the members of the formations which surrendered to the Americans were set free at the beginning of 1946. A large part of them went home immediately. Most of those remaining abroad went to the area of Passau, Regensburg and Bad Aibling. László Taubinger's data are quoted by Borbándi, *A magyar emigráció életrajza*, I, 21

23. Ibid., I, 20–21.

24. *Fehérkönyv a Szovjetunióba elhurcolt hadifoglyokról és polgári deportáltakról* (White Book on the position of the prisoners of war and civilian deportees who were dragged to the USSR). Issued by the Fraternal Association of Hungarian Veterans (1950), 181. Pál Kéri, "A földönfutó DP-ik letelepítése" (The settling of the homeless DPs [in the state of New York]) in *Az Ember*, 22 May 1948. See also Zsigmond Gyallay Papp, "Magyar földmunkások Svédországban" (Hungarian agricultural workers in Sweden), *Szociáldemokrata Népszava* (Social Democratic People's Voice), January 1950; Egon F. Kunz, *Blood and Gold. Hungarians in Australia* (Melbourne: Cheshire, 1969).

25. Borbándi, *A magyar emigráció életrajza*, 1:22. Interview with T. Tóth, Ligonier, Pa., 1996.

26. Ibid., I, 115.

27. Kovacsics, *Magyarország történeti demográfiája,* 230.

28. IRO. Office of Statistics in Holborn (1956), 486.

29. John Kósa, "A Century of the Hungarian Emigration," *The American Slavic and East-European Review,* XVI (1957), 513

30. István Szépfalusi, *Lássátok, halljátok egymást mai magyarok. Mai magyarok Ausztriában* (See each other, hear each other, Hungarians of today. Hungarians of today in Austria) (Bern, 1980), 50–70.

31. István Szépfalusi. "Százezerrel kisebb veszteség" (A loss a hundred thousand smaller). *Élet és Irodalom,* 17 July 1983; Kázmér Nagy, *Az elveszett Alkotmány* (The lost Constitution) (Budapest: Gondolat Kiadó, 1984), 210. See also Paul Bödy's estimates in "Emigration from Hungary, 1880–1956," in Dreisziger, *The Hungarian Canadian Experience,* 47.

32. Vernant, *The Refugee in the Postwar World,* 701–721.

33. The figures are from the "Annual Reports" United States Department of Justice. Immigration and Naturalization Service. Washington, D.C., 1951, 1952, 1953. Under the Displaced Persons Act of 1948, altogether 16,032 persons born in Hungary arrived in the United States. Annual Report 1953, Table 68.

34. In all, the refugees included a wide spectrum of Hungary's middle and upper elite from government, military and police society and conservative and right wing political parties. James Patrick McGuire. *The Hungarian Texans* (Texas: The University of Texas, Institute of Texan Cultures at San Antonio, 1993).

35. Vardy, *The Hungarian Americans,* 121.

36. IRO Reports 1956. Table IV, 12–13.

37. See in more detail M. T. Benneth, *American Immigration Policies* (Washington, D.C.: Public Affairs Press, 1963), Chapter VII, "Public Laws, Immigration Restrictions, 1941–1951," 70–93.

38. In the chapter "Tevékenységem az emigrációban" (My activities in emigration) of his book *Magyarország sorsa Kelet és Nyugat között* (The fate of Hungary between East and West), Gustav Hennyei, the leader of the Hungarian Refugee Bureau, wrote about the difficulties experienced in the course of the Hungarian refugees' admission into the IRO: "It would lead us far if we should want to describe here how many obstacles impeded and hindered the migration of Hungarians to America." The political control was more strict in the United States. Persons obviously politically compromised, with fascist or "iron-cross" past were not permitted to enter in consideration to the public opinion of the Americans, 158. It often happened that the IRO refused the registration of Hungarians, 159. In his reminiscences, Hennyei relates that in the first years after the war, Archduke Dr. Ottó Habsburg often paid visits to the camps of Hungarian refugees. "He was the first to assist our admission to the IRO," 180. See also Gyula Borbándi. *A magyar emigráció életrajza.* 2:111.

39. IRO: *The Ludwig Family,* 1951 (booklet). One copy is in the collection of the author.

40. Cases of deportation are reported in the 1950–1952 issues of *Az Ember.*

41. Report of IRO Office of Statistics in Holborn (1956), 486. See also Borbándi, *A magyar emigrácio életrajza,* I, 121

42. *Australian Immigration Consolidated Statistics.* No. 11. Canberra. Department of Immigration and Ethnic Affairs. 11–13, and see also Kunz, *Blood and Gold,*

43. Under the agreement between the Swedes and the Government in Budapest close to 500 families, more than 1000 people, went to work in Sweden. After the communists came into power, most of them did not return to Hungary. Borbándi, *A magyar emigráció életrajza,* I, 114.

44. The Israeli data in *United Nations (UN) Demographic Year Book, 1949–1959,* 1960

Chapter 26: The Arrival of the Freedom Fighters, 1956–1957

1. Marrus, *The Unwanted,* 359.

2. "The Exodus from Hungary," *United Nations Review,* January 1957.

3. Report of the Governmental Committee for European Migration (ICEM) on the Hungarian Refugee Situation. Austria. December 31, 1957.

4. AVH—acronym for Államvédelmi Hatóság—State Security Authority, Department of the Ministry of the Interior, Budapest. (Formerly AVO—Államvédelmi Osztály).

5. James A. Michener, *The Bridge at Andau* (New York: Random House, 1957). In this book the author tells the story of how thousands of Hungarians, satiated with terror, fled their homeland and sought refuge elsewhere. It is from their mass flight into Austria that this book takes its title, for it was at the key bridge at Andau that many of them escaped to freedom.

6. *Az illegálisan külföldre távozott személyek főbb adatai.* (Principle data on persons illegally departed abroad). October 23, 1956 to April 30, 1957. Központi Statisztikai Hiuatal (Central Office of Statistics) (Budapest, 1974). The report and the statistics were published in *Regio,* 1991/4, 174–211.

7. Ibid., 190.

8. Kálmán J. Roller, *The Sopron Chronicle.* (Toronto, Canada: Rákóczi Foundation, 1980), I, 51–70.

9. The United States Department of Justice. Immigration and Naturalization Service. 85th Congress 2nd Session, Senate Report No. 1817. Calendar No. 1851. 6 and "I and N Reporter-45." April 1958.

10. In the course of interviews in the United States, I was often asked by Hungarian immigrants to solve this riddle, and they were amused to see that I could not solve it. According to Henry Gleitman and Joseph Greenbaum, "Over half of them described themselves as belonging to the intelligentsia." *Preliminary Results of Depth Interviews and Attitude Scales. Inquiry into Political and Social Attitudes in Hungary* (New York: Free Europe Press, 1957), 20.

11. "Report to the President by the President's Committee for Hungarian Refugee Relief." May 14, 1957, Government Printing Office 5–7 and "Report to President Eisenhower by Vice-President Nixon," January 1957. Department of State Bulletin, 36 (Washington, D.C., 1957), 94–95

12. Ferenc Szabó, "Egy millióval kevesebben. Embervesztességek, népesedési tendenciák és népesedési politika Magyarországon, 1941–1968." (With a million

less. Loss of people, tendencies in the changes in the population, demographic policy in Hungary) (Dissertation, Budapest, 1990).

13. Ibid., 220.

14. *Help Hungarian Youth to Return Home,* a leaflet distributed by the Hungarian Delegation at the 6th World Festival of Youth and Students and *Return my Children* (Budapest: Hungarian Red Cross, 1957). Beginning from 1957, publications appeared to promote a return home. See, for instance, Peter Rényi, *"Szabad földről" üzenik: disszidáltakról, hazatértekről* (A message from the "free land": regarding dissidents and those who returned home.) (Budapest: Kossuth Könyvkiadó, 1957) *Kommentár nélkül. Disszidensek levelei* (Without comment. Letters of dissidents), edited by Rudolf Szamos (Budapest: Kossuth Könyv Kiadó, 1958, and Congressional Records, 1956–1957).

15. This is well demonstrated in articles in American and Hungarian newspapers of those days.

16. The American Hungarian Foundation in New Brunswick, N.J. received a large document collection from the UN about the Hungarian revolution, among them were "Reports" about the interviews with refugees. A collection of interviews by *Szabad Európa* (Free Europe) broadcasting station can be found at the Central European University, Budapest.

17. Ibid. Various motivations influenced the departure of those individuals I interviewed: the unfavorable turn in the political situation on the 4th of November 1956, with the entering of the Russian troops, was mentioned by all of them. György Dózsa (Gy.D.), a university student took part in student activities and his fear of reprisals gradually increased: he left in December. The dispersion of his colleagues played a part in his decision; hardly any of them stayed on. He intended to go to American relatives, but had to wait for three years in Vienna for a visa. (Interview Gy.D., Washington, D.C., 1992) The departure of László Lipóczky, a technician, was motivated by his having served on one of the local revolutionary committees, but his professional and career-building plans also affected his decision to leave. (Interview L.L., New Brunswick, NJ, 1992). Maria Bales (M.B.) a twenty-year-old girl, followed enthusiastically the course of the events of the revolution in Budapest. While returning to her father in a small trans-Danubian town on the 4th of November, the news of the Russian invasion and family conflicts compelled her to leave suddenly, and she stopped a passing truck and left the country in it. (Interview M.B., Minnesota, 1994.) Maria Gindele (M.G.) was only a high school student in western Hungary when the open frontiers lured her into the free world. Difficulties with the Viennese refugee quarters and resettlement forced her quick return to the family home. (Interview with M.G., Budapest, 1994.

18. Emil Pintér, *Wohlstandflüchtlinge. Eine Socialpsychiatrische Studie an Ungarische Flüchtlinge in der Schweiz* (Basel: Karger, 1969), 43–62. Henry Gleitman and Joseph Greenbaum, "Attitudes and Personality Patterns of Hungarian Refugees. *Public Opinion Quarterly,* XXV, no. 3 (Fall 1961), 352–365.

19. Vardy also relates that a very small percentage participated in the actual fighting; most of them were really apolitical and left Hungary simply because the borders were suddenly thrown open. Vardy, *The Hungarian Americans* 118.

20. On the pre-eminence of the Western life-style Radio Free-Europe broadcast lectures regularly, which molded the image of the Western world in Hungary, too.

21. League of Red Cross: Societies Hungarian Refugee Relief. *Report on the relief measures for Hungarian refugees undertaken by the League and member national societies in Austria, Yugoslavia and countries of transit and settlement.* October 1957. (Geneva, 1957).

22. Dwight D. Eisenhower, *The White House Years.* 2 vol. (Garden City, NY: Doubleday, 1965), II, 84.

23. United Nations. Department of Public Information. "The Exodus from Hungary." Reprinted from the *United States Review,* January 1957. Washington, D.C., Government Printing Office.

24. Arthur Markowitz, "Humanitarianism Versus Restrictionalism: The United States and the Hungarian Refugees," *International Migration Review,* VII (1973), 48.

25. Ibid., 49.

26. Ibid., 53.

27. Béla Máday. "Az 1956 utáni Magyar Segély szervezése és abban az Amerikai Tudományos Akadémia szerepe" (The organization of Hungarian Relief after 1956 and the role of the American Academy of Sciences) in Bakó, (1990), 59–64.

28. Local Hungarians were active in all stages of the State's relief programs. For example, in the month of December 1956, the Minneapolis Symphony Orchestra-conducted alternately by Antal Doráti and by Zoltán Rozsnyai (a recent refugee from Hungary) played a concert for the benefit of Hungarian refugees in Austria. The program, featuring works of Bartók, Kodály, and Liszt, was intended to commemorate "the heroism and artistic genius of the Hungarian people." Paul Kirschner and Anne R. Kaplan, "Hungarians" in Holmquist, *They Chose Minnesota,* 433.

29. Annual Report of J. M. Swing, Commissioner of Immigration and Naturalization, Washington, D.C., 1958.

Chapter 27: The Newcomers: Integration and Conflict

1. Balogh, *The 10ᵗʰ Anniversary Almanac of the American Hungarian Federation* (1948); Arthur Dobozy. "Az American Hungarian Relief, Inc. eddigi munkája" (The work up to date of the American Hungarian Federation Inc.). First published in *Az Amerikai Magyar Népszava Aranyjubileumi Albuma* (Golden Jubilee Album of the American Hungarian People's Voice) 1949, 96–97, reprinted in *Emlékkönyv az Amerikai Magyar Szövetség 80. Évfordulójára* (Memorial Book of the 80ᵗʰ Anniversary of the American Hungarian Federation) edited by Elemér Bakó. (Washington, D.C.: Amerikai Magyar Szövetség, 1988), 56–68.

2. Kéri, "Földönfutó DP-k letelepítése (The Settling of the homeless DPs). *Az Ember,* 22 May 1948. Similarly, in *Az Ember,* Ferenc Göndör sharply attacked the 1945 emigrants even before they arrived.

3. Böszörményi (1960), 155–6.

4. Vardy, *The Centennial History of the William Penn Association,* 268.

5. Ibid., 267.

6. Steering clear of political activity were, for example, Count Géza Teleki, former minister of religion and public education and Sándor Szent-Iványi, Unitarian

vicar, two leading members of the Bourgeois Democratic Party of 1945. Borbándi (1989). I. 508.

7. See in more detail ibid., I, 72.

8. Magyar Harcosok Bajtársi Szövetsége (Fraternal Association of Hungarian Veterans), Tájékoztató körlevél (Information circular), November 1949. Quoted in ibid., I, 77.

9. *MagyarTalálkozó Krónikája* (Chronicle of the Hungarian Congress). Proceedings of the First Hungarian Congress, edited by Béla Beldy. Vol. I, Cleveland: Árpád Könyvkiadó Vállalat, 1962.

The resolutions of the Hungarian Congress are filled with strong statements concerning Hungary, the Hungarian-American community, and the changing relationship between the two. Among the many recurring themes, the most popular and the most emphatically expressed appear to be the following: the need to preserve the traditional and political values of old Hungary, to pass these values on to future generations along with thorough knowledge of the Hungarian language and culture, to preserve the Hungarian-American community by encouraging marriage among Hungarians, and to work constantly for the liberation of the homeland, the withdrawal of Soviet forces and the creation of a new democratic Hungary. About these see more in Steven Béla Vardy and Agnes Huszár Vardy, *The Austro-Hungarian Mind: At Home and Abroad* (New York: Columbia University Press, 1989), 312–3.

10. Ferencz Somogyi, *A Magyar Társaság. Három évtizedének vázlatos története* (The Hungarian Association. A brief history of its first thirty years) (Cleveland: Magyar Társaság, 1983).

11. See the publications of Gyula Borbándi, and Steven Várdy in the Bibliography. According to two Hungarian-American historians, Susanne Papp and Steven Várdy, the DP Hungarians published both in quality and in quantity more in one decade than the *old amerikások* in the previous half-century. There were many writers and journalists among them; several newspapers were founded in Cleveland during the 1950s and 1960s. These groups published more books than any other wave of Hungarian immigrants. Papp in *Encyclopedia of Cleveland*, 534. A considerable part of their work was political literature, criticism and repudiation of the political regime that took shape in Hungary after 1945. They also laid stress on the Hungarian classic literature, and in particular on those writings that were rejected by the official cultural policy in Hungary. They had no reasons to experience feelings of inferiority when confronted by American society—as did their more humble predecessors. In fact, because of their learning and past social status, the majority of them felt superior to the relatively uncultured average American they encountered in their new places of employment. Várdy, 1985, *The Hungarian American,* 133.

12. Reminiscences of Joe Esterhas, in Papp, *Hungarian Americans and Their Communities of Cleveland,* 2–3. To assess the development of culture among the DP emigrés, one of the most important sources could be found in *Hirünk a világban* (Our reputation in the world), edited by András Csicsery Rónai in the 1950s. This was a guide published periodically beginning in January 1951. In its supplement, *Bibliográfia* (Bibliography), it gave information about well-known Hungarian scien-

tists' achievements, books published by Hungarian writers, and the activities of Hungarian emigrant publishers. It would be beyond the limits of this book to list all the data to be found in this bibliography.

István Csicsery-Rónai, a politician and editor in Hungary in 1919, emigrated to the US in 1949. From 1949 to 1959 he was the political commentator of the Free Europe Committee. He was the owner of the Occidental Press in Washington from 1949 to 1956, and became the editor and publisher of *Hirünk a Világban* (Our Reputation in the World) from 1951 to 1964, and also the editor of *Bibliográfia* (Bibliography) from 1954 to 1964. He published a number of books such as the *Russian Penetration in Hungary* (Washington, DC., 1950. *Száműzöttek Naptára*).

13. István Csicsery-Rónai, *Száműzöttek Naptára* (Calendar of the exiles) (Washington, D.C.: Occidental Press, 1954), 10.

14. These are well reflected in the "Proceedings of the Hungarian Congresses" published since 1962, approximately 30 volumes. Cleveland. To observe and report the cultural achievements of Hungarians the Hungarian bimonthly *Hírünk a világban* (Our Reputation in the World), edited by István Csicsery-Rónai was launched in 1950.

15. Papp, *Hungarian Americans and Their Communities of Cleveland*, 267–268.

16. Vardy, *The Hungarian Americans*, 122–8. See also Gábor Bodnár, *Külföldi magyar oktatás 1974-ben* (Hungarian teaching abroad in 1974) (Garfield, NJ, 1981); *70 Jahre des Ungarischen Phadfinderbunds* (Garfield, NJ: Magyar Cserkészszövetség Kiadványa, 1981).

17. Interview with A. Stelkovics, who secured a position at the Rákóczi Association and for decades was one of the leaders of the William Penn Fraternal Association Pittsburgh, 1984, and Steven Dankó and Gyula Mecker, director for decades of the Verhovay Association (later William Penn Association), Detroit. 1986.

18. See for example the autobiography of Sándor Vörös. In the "Epilogue" he wrote: "Communism creates its own antibodies. There is but one group of people in the entire world who are totally immune to all threats and blandishments from Moscow or Peking—the former communists. The Communist party which I quit over twenty years ago has by now all but disintegrated. Yet, I and my fellow former rebels have been degraded to second-class citizens, denied the right of serving our country in the capacities we were best fitted for because of a punchy law that demands a negative answer to the question "Are you now, or have you ever been a member of. . . ." Vörös, *American Commissar*, 475–76.

19. The best known were Emil Gárdos and János Gyetvai Nagy, the editors of *Új Előre* and *Magyar Jövő*.

20. Before their emigration Ferenc Nagy was, the Prime Minister and Béla Varga, the Chairman of the House of Representatives. Others were leaders of bourgeois parties or held high positions in postwar Hungarian diplomacy.

21. For example the Nobel prize winner Albert Szentgyörgyi. See more about the emigration of famous Hungarian scientists and artists in Stephen Sisa, *America's Amazing Hungarians* (Huddleston, VA: The Author, 1987). *Amerikai Magyar Népszava Arany Jubileumi Albuma* (1950), 60–68. See also Gyula Borbándi, *Nyugati Magyar Irodalom. A magyar emigráns irodalom lexikona.* (Hungarian literature in the West. Encyclopedia of the literature of Hungarian emigrants) edited by Csaba

Nagy (Budapest 1990). Published by the Institute of Literature-Science of the Hungarian Academy of Sciences and the Petőfi Literary Museum. *Nyugati magyar esszéírók antológiája* (Anthology of Hungarian essay writers in the West). Compiled and edited by Gyula Borbándi. (Bern 1986). *Nyugati magyar tanulmányok antológiája* (Anthology of studies by Hungarians in the West). Compiled and edited by Gyula Borbándi. (Bern 1967). Tibor Frank, *From Immigrant Laborers to Emigré Professionals.* Studies in the Social History of Hungarian-American migrations. Inaugural Papers. Budapest. Eötvös Lóránd University. Manuscript.

22. On the activities of the Nemzeti Bizottmány (National Committee) see the official journals, *Bizottmányi Közlöny* (Gazette of the Committee), the monthly—bimonthly journal, which was started by the presidium of the Executive Committee of the Hungarian National Committee on January 19, 1949. See also Borbándi, *A magyar emigráció életrajza,* I, 514.

23. See János Nádas's article on the organizing and uniting America's one and a half million Hungarians. *Magyar Találkozó Krónikája* (1966), IV–V, 206–210.

24. Borbándi, *A magyar emigráció életrajza,* I, 139–130.

25. In 1960, on the fortieth anniversary of the Trianon Peace Treaty, the Association again took the political steps necessary to voice the protest of Hungarian Americans to this treaty. Ferenc Somogyi, *Küldetés: a magyarság története* (Mission: the history of the Hungarians) (Cleveland: Árpád Publishing Co., 1973), 93.

26. János Nádas, "Egységes magyar külpolitika kialakítása, ki képviselje a magyarságot az emigrációban" (The formation of a uniform Hungarian foreign policy: who should represent the Hungarians in emigration?) *Magyar Talákozó Krónikája* (1962), 35–57.

27. *Bizottmányi Közlöny* (Gazette of the Committee), the Gazette of the Hungarian National Committee (December 1949); *Amerikai Magyar Népszava Arany Jubileumi Albuma* (1950), 86–97. See also Ernő Ács, *A Magyar Nemzeti Bizottmány, mint politikai szervezet* (The Hungarian National Committee as a political organization) (New York, 1952) "Barankovics István előterjesztése az emigráció kulturpolitikai programja tárgyában a Magyar Nemzeti Bizottmány Végrehajtó Bizottsága ülésén" (István Barankovics's presentation on the subject of the emigration's program on cultural policy to the Executive Committee of the Hungarian National Committee) (New York, 1952). The work of the Committee was sharply criticized by Dezső Sulyok, *A magyar emigráció tragédiája* (The tragedy of the Hungarian emigration) (New York: Magyar Október 23, Mozgalom, 1962).

28. *Bizottmányi Közlöny,* 1951.

29. Nádas, *Magyar Tálkozó Krónikája* (1962), 37–57.

30. See the appraisal of the Hungarian revolution in the United States of America. Congressional Records November 1956 to May 1957 (Washington, D.C.: Government Printing Office, 1956, 1957). In American newspapers a flood of articles informed Americans about the Hungarian revolution. Little Hungary, which hardly appeared on the front pages of newspapers with world-wide circulation, on the occasion of the 1956 events became immediately well known.

31. Interview with J. Palasics, Cleveland, 1988. See also his manuscript on Cleveland Hungarians (note 42 below). The loss of the illusions entertained for the "56-er" Freedom Fighters was also expressed by others in interviews. To quote

only one of many, Michael A. Feigham of Ohio: "Any scholar of revolutionary events knows that actual conditions of life best prepare the way for any revolution. But I repeat, the youth, the ones that many have given up as lost to freedom's cause, were the ones who sparked it. That's a lesson we must never forget. It may very well be that the youth will save the world of tomorrow, because we, in this generation of leadership may fail to understand our opportunities or may lack the courage to take advantage of them. February 14, 1957.

32. Arthur A. Markowitz (1972), "Humanitarianism versus Restrictionism: The United States and the Hungarian Refugees." *International Migration Review,* 7, No. 1:46–59.

33. Report of the Presidential Committee for Hungarian Refugee Relief. Washington, D.C. 1957 The committee was founded at Bard College in New York on February 2, 1957.

34. "Hungarian Refugee Students and United States Colleges and Universities one year later (February 1957–January 1958)" (New York: Committee on Educational Interchange Policy, 1958).

35. See more details in László Papp, *Az EMEFESZ az amerikai magyar egyetemisták mozgalma az 1956–os forradalom után* (The AHSUS, the movement of the American Hungarian Students after the 1956 revolution) (New Brunswick, NJ: Magyar Öregdiák Szövetség, 1988). The Union of Free Hungarian Students held its first national congress in Chicago June 12–14, 1957. In 1958, it changed its name to "Association of Hungarian Students in the United States, (AHUS)." The organization launched two papers: in English *The Hungarian Student* and in Hungarian *Magyar Diák* (Hungarian student).

36. Gyula Várallyay, *Tanulmányúton. Az emigráns magyar diákmozgalom 1956* után (On a study tour. The Hungarian émigré student movement after 1956) (Budapest: "Századvég," 1992), 55. See also the special number of the *Magyar Diák* (Hungarian student) published on the occasion of the organization's congress.

37. It was made possible by the effective intervention of the Freedom Fighters: The governors of some states declared June 17 "the Day of the Hungarian Freedom Fighters" to commemorate the day when the execution of Imre Nagy and his associates was made public. Borbándi, *A magyar emigráció életrajza,* I, 45.

38. Washington: Library of Congress. Congressional Record, November 1956.

39. Interview with Steven Dankó, Detroit, 1986. Others also emphasized the positive effect of the Hungarian revolution on the Hungarian ethnic consciousness in the United States.

40. "Hungarian refugee resettlement in the United States. An inquiry into selected problems, trends and solutions at the community level, prepared by the Joint Committee on Integration of the American Immigration Conference and the National Council of Naturalization and Citizenship" (New York: American Immigration Conference, National Council of Naturalization and Citizenship, January, 1958).

About the conflicts of integration concerning the "56-ers" see also Violet Head, *The 1956 Hungarians: Their Integration into an Urban Community* (Chicago: University of Chicago, 1963).

41. Papp, *Hungarian Americans and Their Communities of Cleveland,* 276. According to John Kósa the social differentiation also shows in the settlement

pattern. See in "A Century of Hungarian Emigration," *The American Slavic and East European Review,* XVI (December 1957), 513.

42. *History of the Cleveland Hungarians,* edited by John Palasics (Manuscript). Cleveland, 1976. Interview with J. Palasics, Cleveland, 1988. We may quote many interviews with the 1956 escapees on their opinion that joining an ethnic community would have meant a decline in status for them. The new immigrants were, after all, more highly skilled and better educated than their predecessors. They regarded the Hungarian American newspapers, radio programs, theater groups, and other cultural institutions as inferior to those they had left behind in Hungary. Even the religious groups, usually the mainstay of ethnic cohesion, did not interest the newcomers. Moreover, their political views were so radically different from those of their predecessors, that communication between the two groups was difficult. Alexander S. Weinstock, *Acculturation and Occupation: A Study of the 1956 Refugees in the United States* (The Hague: Nijhoff, 1969), 43.

Chapter 28: From Group Identity to Individual Identity

1. The changes in the ethnic composition of the population on the East Side in Cleveland are illustrated by maps, in Karl Bonutti and George Prpic, *Selected Ethnic Communities of Cleveland. A Socio-Economic Study for the Cleveland. Urban Observatory: City of Cleveland* (Cleveland: Cleveland State University, 1977).

2. *Magyarorszagi Szent Erzsebet Templom 1892–1992* (The Church of St. Elisabeth of Hungary) (Cleveland, 1992).

3. Interview with J. Palasics, Cleveland, 1988.

4. Buckeye Neighborhood Nationalities Civic Association, BNNCA *Newsletter* June 1967. Cleveland, vol. 4, no. 7. 5

5. See the minutes of the merging convention. The documents of the William Penn Association can be found at the Hungarian Foundation, New Brunswick, NJ. Gyula Mecker, one of the organizers of the merger, who in his recollections, gives a most interesting account of the preparations for it, the fights for the leading positions and the encouraging of the "old leaders'" withdrawal by founding an old-age pension fund. Interview with Gyula Mecker, Detroit 1986. See also *Verhovayak Lapja* and *Rákóczi Szemle* for the years 1954 and 1955.

6. In and around Pittsburgh I interviewed a number of old members of the Verhovay Association in 1984. All of them complained and criticized the attitude of the leaders of William Penn at that time who—according to them—turned their back on the Hungarians, and were interested only in business.

7. László Eszenyi, a former officer of the Royal Hungarian General Staff, arrived in the United States in 1949 and was already working at the headquarters of the Hungarian Reformed Federation in 1950. He became treasurer and for years until his retirement served as vice president. Imre Bertalan, a Protestant minister who arrived in the United States in 1946 and filled major posts in the Federation for decades, was a member of the board, and president for more than a decade. Some DPs and "56-er" Hungarians secured positions at the Board as field organizers.

8. See more details about the last period of the IWO in Artur J. Sabin, *Red Scare in Court: New York Versus the International Workers Order* (Philadelphia: University of Pennsylvania Press, 1993).

9. Fishman emphasized that "the majority of Catholic leaders has constantly moved in the direction of de-ethnization," in "Hungarian Language Maintenance," 19. See also James S. Olson, *Catholic Immigrants in America*. (Chicago: Nelson-Hall, 1987), 200–217. In sketching the history of Magyar Roman Catholic parishes, István Török mentions their "slow depopulation" in *Katolikus Magyarok Észak-Amerikában* (Hungarians of the Catholic faith in North America). (Youngstown, OH: Katolikus Magyarok Vasárnapja. 1978), 52.

10. Király, *The 50th Anniversary Album of the Calvin Synod* (1988), 34. The assimilation process is well reflected in the work of John Butosi, *Church Membership Performance of Three Generations*, 270–80.

11. Király, *The 50th Anniversary Album of the Calvin Synod* (1988), 82.

12. At that time those in the village who got dollars from relatives working in the United States were viewed with envy. See interviews with Ignác Kósa and with other Szamosszegians, 1982–86.

13. Two "56-er" persons from Szamosszeg became also curators at the church in New Brunswick on Somerset Street. Interview with György Dózsa, Washington, 1992.

14. Julianna Puskás, "Hungarian Overseas Migration: A Microanalysis," in *A Century of European Migrations, 1830–1930*, edited by Rudolph J. Vecoli and Suzanne M. Sinke (Urbana: University of Illinois Press, 1991), 335.

15. I obtained this picture from the interviews with Piroska Puskás, Mrs. Szabó, Irma Bacskó, and some descendants of Szamosszegians in New Brunswick, NJ. Of the two granddaughters of Mozes Bacskó, one married a Pole, the other a Jew. The granddaughter of Béla Kovács married an Indian; the grandson of Szabó married a Korean, just to mention a few. In relation to the Hungarians we cannot ascertain the validity of the three melting pots in the process of assimilation.

16. Interviews with Victor Bodó, Holden, WV, 1984 and 1986. He informed me about the education of the descendants of Lea Bodó. Concerning other families, I was informed mainly by the women mentioned in Note 15.

17. Interview with Steven Puskás, New Brunswick, NJ, 1986

18. In 1988, even on the festive occasion of Easter, when I visited the church, the few congregants were almost lost in the huge church. A small group of second generation, all about 70 years old, was still attached to the church. "The accumulative impact of the integration and assimilation of many members of an ethnic group would cause the gradual fading of its earlier cultural distinctiveness and the weakening of its cultural institutions, customs and practices." Elliott R. Barkan, "Race, Religion and Nationality in American Society. A Model of Ethnicity—From Contact to Assimilation," *Journal of Ethnic History*, XVI, no. 2 (Winter 1995), 38–75.

19. For example, in the "Magyar Club" in New Brunswick, NJ, which was built in 1916 and ever since has been one of the centers for Hungarian social activities, the intellectuals, many of them "56-ers," are avoiding the simple people, who are the main visitors of the club.

20. Gábor Papp, *Magyar iskola Clevelandban* (Hungarian school in Cleveland) 1967.

21. Albert Wass, *Our Hungarian Heritage* (Astor, Florida: Danubian Press, 1979). See also Károly Nagy, *Magyar szigetvilágban ma és holnap* (In the world of the Hungarian archipelago today and tomorrow) (New York: Püski, 1984), 141. and Somogyi, *Küldetést.*

22. August Molnár "Is there a future of the Hungarian language and culture in America?" *Proceedings of the VI. Hungarian Congress,* edited by János Nádas (Cleveland, 1967), 113–127.

The "American Hungarian Foundation started as a separate Department of Hungarian Studies at Elmhurst College (Illinois) in 1941 under the direction of Barabás Dienes "for the promotion of the Hungarian cultural and historical heritage." After his death, the American Hungarian Studies Foundation was taken over by Rev. August Molnár and moved to New Brunswick, NJ. The Foundation owns an archive, gives financial assistance to research and studies concerning the history of American Hungarians, and organizes exhibitions. In the late 1970s the word "Studies" was dropped from the name of the Foundation and its publications. Its sponsors are mostly successful descendants of immigrants

23. Károly Nagy is one of the founders of the "Mother Tongue Movement" which was started in 1970. See Károly Nagy, *Külföldi magyar iskoláink gondjairól* (On the problems of our Hungarian schools abroad) (New Brunswick, NJ, 1972) and *Tanítsunk magyarul!* (Let us teach Hungarian) (New York: Püski, 1977). See also András Sándor, *Hungarian Saturday lessons. Hétvégi magyar iskola, 1960–1970.* At Rutgers University. (New Brunswick, 1970).

24. Two founders of the periodical, András Ludányi and Lajos Éltető, were former ÉMEFESZ members.

25. The ITT-OTT Movement was renamed later as "Magyar Baráti Közösség" (Hungarian Society of Friends). Its aim was and still is "the cultivation of Hungarian traditions and Hungarian culture, the improvement of the Hungarian language and Hungarian consciousness, the safeguarding of the youth as Hungarian Americans." The leaders have organized an annual conference since 1973.

26. Miklós Kontra and Gregory Nehler, "Language use: an interview with a Hungarisan American," *Hungarian Studies Review,* VII, no. 1, 105.

27. Particularly memorable in this respect was my meeting the Zoltai couple in St. Paul, MN in 1972. They were teenagers at the end of the Second World War when they escaped from Hungary with their parents. Their strong ties to Hungarian culture are reflected by the many Hungarian books and journals in their library and by their cultural social activities in various Hungarian programs.

28. *Lármafa:* "Magyarságtudat Szimpózium", (Symposium on Hungarian consciousness) Toronto: Rákóczi Press, 1984) 159–162 Similar thoughts can be read in the study: "The Attenuated Ethnicity of Contemporary Finnish-Americans," in Kivisto, *The Ethnic Enigma,* 67–88

29. *United States Census* 1970. Vol. II, Population. "National Origin and Language" 466–478.

30. Ibid., Table 18, 478.

31. Ibid. The 1960 Census contains data about the educational level of immigrants. According to these, the level of Hungarian immigrants was superior to that of other immigrant groups by this time. The percentage of persons at the college

level by country of origin was: Hungary 22.2, Czechoslovakia 19.7, Yugoslavia 13.3, Poland 12.3, total from the rest 16.9. Information is furnished on professionals separately by László Papp, *Who is who among professionals of Hungarian origin in the Americas* (New York: Hungarian Alumni Association, 1961); Tibor Szy, *Hungarians in America. A Biographical Directory of Professionals of Hungarian Origin in the Americas* (New York: Hungarian University Association, 1963); *Hungarians in America. A Biographical Directory of Professionals of Hungarian Origin in America,* edited by K. Dési and Dezsö Bognár (Mt. Vernon: Alpha Publications, 1971). See also Tibor Frank, 1995. "From Immigrant Laborers to Emigré Professionals." Studies in the Social History of Hungarian-American migrations. Inaugural Papers. Budapest. Eörvös Lóránd University. Manuscript.

32. See Paul Bödy, "First Generation Values in Different Waves of Hungarian Immigration to the United States" in *Search for American Values: Contributions of Hungarian Americans to American Values,* edited by Ilona Kovács (Budapest: Széchényi Könyutár, 1990), 63–69.

33. According to a Hungarian Protestant minister, "Az egyház beszorult az öreg amerikások és a DP-k közé." (The church got squeezed in between the old "amerikások" and the DPs).

34. In the 1970s, many studies were published on bilingualism, on the Hungarian language, and its teaching in the preceding half-century. See Ágnes Huszár Vardy, "Alsó és középfokú magyarságtudományi oktatás Észak-Amerikában" (Instruction in Hungarian Studies on the Elementary and Secondary Levels in North America) in *Magyar Találkozó Krónikája,* XIII (1974), 39–56; and Stephen Béla Vardy and Agnes Huszár Vardy, "Historical, Literary, Linguistic and Ethnographic Research on Hungarian Americans. A Historiographical Assessment in Hungarian Studies," *Journal of the International Association of Hungarian Studies,* I, no. 1 (Budapest, 1985), 71–122.

35. *A magyar nyelvért és kultúráért.* Tájékoztató az 1970 augusztus 1–15 között Debrecenben és Budapesten megrendezett anyanyelvi konferencia anyagából (For the Hungarian Language and Culture). Selections from the material of the mother tongue conference organized in Debrecen and Budapest between August 1 and 15, 1970), edited by Imre Samu (Budapest, 1971). See also Solomon Kun, *Refugees in the Cold War. Toward a New International Refugee Regime in the Early Postwar Era* (Lund: Lund University Press, 1991.

BIBLIOGRAPHY

SOURCES
Archives and libraries consulted in Europe
      in the United States

PRIMARY SOURCES
Statistics
Publications of the Hungarian ethnic organizations
    a.) Anniversary Publications of newspapers and associations
    b.) Anniversary Publications published by congregations
    c.) Newpapers, Journals
    d.) Books, Studies

SECONDARY SOURCES
Bibliographies
Books, pamphlets, articles
    International section
    Hungarian section

398

ARCHIVES AND LIBRARIES CONSULTED

Europe

Budapest, Hungary. Országos Levéltár (National Archives).

A Miniszterelnökség központilag iktatott és irattározott irata (The centrally registered and filed documents of the Prime Minister's office): OL.ME.K26.

A külföldön élő magyar állampolgárok gondozását ellátó osztály iratai (Documents of the department administering affairs of Hungarian citizens living abroad): OL.ME.K27.

Az Osztrák-Magyar monarchia washingtoni követségének iratai (Documents of the Austro-Hungarian Embassy in Washington): OL.ME.K106.

A Belügyminiszterium általános iratai (Ministry of Interior, General Documents): OL.BM.1928.K 150.

Budapest, Hungary. Parlamenti Könyvtár (Parliamentary Library).

OFI: Országgyülés. Förendiházának irományai (Documents of the Upper House of Parliament).

OKI: Országgyülés. Képviselőházának iratai (Parliament, Documents of the House of Representatives).

OKJ: Országgyülés. Képviselőházi jegyzőkönyvek (Parliament, Minutes of the House of Representatives).

OKN: Országgyülés. Képviselőházi Napló (Parliament, Report of the House of Representatives).

A Magyarországi Református Egyház Zsinati Levéltára (Archives of the Synod of the Hungarian Reformed Church).

2.1. Konventi Külügyi Bizottság iratai 2.1. (Documents of the Convent's Committee for Foreign Affairs) e./ Amerikai ügyek. Az amerikai egyházi ügyek iratai (e./ American affairs. Documents of the American church's affairs.)

Politikatörténeti Intézet Archivuma (Archives of the Institute of History of Politics).

MTA Történettudományi Intézet Archivuma (Archives of the Institute of History of the Hungarian Academy of Sciences).

Esztergom, Hungary. Hungarian Archbishop's Archive, CD.

Pl. E.-USA-Püspöki értekezletek jegyzökönyve, 1890–1914 (Minutes of the Bishops' meetings, 1890–1914).

Memorandum to the Prince Primate from Károly Böhm, R.C. pastor of Cleveland, CD, 1913.

Miskolc, Hungary. Archives.

Nyiregyháza,Hungary. Szabolcs-Szatmár Megyei Levéltár (Archives of Szabolcs-Szatmár County).

Administrative Committee, Reports of the lord-lieutenants and subprefects on emigration.

Sárospatak, Hungary. A Tiszáninneni Református Egyházkerület könyvtára (Library of the Reformed Church District West of the River Tisza).

Amerikai Magyar Gyüjtemény (Hungarian American Collection). Books, calendars, congregational anniversary publications.

Sátoraljaujhely, Hungary. Zemplén megyei Levéltár (Archives of Zemplén County).

Szamosszeg-Szabolcs-Szatmár County, Hungary. Parish Register of the Calvinist Church in Szamosszeg, 1860–1914.

Szeged,Hungary. Somogyi Könyvtár (Library of Somogy County).

Vasvári gyüjtemény (Vasvári collection).

Vienna, Austria. Haus-, Hof-und Staatsarchiv (State Archives).

SA PA W: Ausstellungs Verzeichnis des Politischen Archivs des Ministerium des Aussern. 1890–1914 XXXIII. Washington, USA.

United States

Washington, DC. National Archives.

Department of Justice, Hungarian Files, RG. 65 FBI documents-OSS.

Library of Immigration and Naturalization Service, Annual Reports on Immigration.

Congressional Records: Justice for Hungary. Petition submitted by the Executive Committee of Arrangement, National Convention of American Citizens of Hungarian descent to the Congress of the United States relative to a Plea for Justice for Hungary and Peace for Europe. Written by Louis K. Birinyi, presented by La Follette, 67th Cong., 4th sess., 3 March 1923.

Congressional Records, 1956–1957. Hungarian Question, Refugees.

American Hungarian Reformed Federation. List of members, 1897–1904; by-laws and minutes of conferences, 1896.

Cleveland, OH. Episcopal Archives.

Documents of St. Elizabeth, St. Emeric, and St. Margaret Hungarian Catholic Churches.

Detroit, MI. Archives of Labor History and Urban Affairs, University Archive.

Wayne State University, Mazey Collection, Hungarian leftists.

Philadelphia, PA.

Archives of the Presbyterian Church.

Balch Institute, Hungarian collection.

Minneapolis, MN.

Immigration History Research Center, University of Minnesota.

Madison, WI.

Archives of the Socialist Labor Party, Documents of the Hungarian SLP.

Pittsburgh, PA.

Industrial Archives, accidents in industries.

Ligonier, PA.

"Bethlen Collection," documents of the Hungarian protestant churches and the American Hungarian Reformed Federation, Árvaházi Naptárak, Bethlen Naptárak (Almanacs of the Orphanage, of the Bethlen Home).

New Brunswick, NJ.

Hungarian Foundation. Documents, manuscripts, books, pamphlets concerning the history of Hungarian-Americans.

PARISH REGISTERS

Cleveland, OH. The First Hungarian Reformed Church (1891–1909); West Side Hungarian Reformed Church(1907–8); Roman Catholic Churches: St. Elizabeth (1894–1914), and "St. Emerich" (1905–23).

Additional Protestant Churches: Allen Park, MI (1918–23); Bridgeport,CT (1894–1902); Carteret, NJ (1895–1904); Homestead, PA (1904–8); New Brunswick, NJ (1906–35); Pittsburgh, PA (1891–94).

PRIMARY SOURCES

Statistics

A Magyar szent korona országainak kivándorlása és visszavándorlása 1899–1913 (Emigration and remigration in the countries of the Hungarian Sacred Crown, 1899–1913). Hungarian Statistical Publications, New Series, vol. 67. Budapest: Magyar Statisztikai Központi Hivatal.

Magyar Statisztikai Évkönyv, 1900–1901 (Hungarian Statistical Yearbook). Budapest: Magyar Statisztikai Központi Hivatal.

Magyar Statisztikai Közlemények. (Hungarian Statistical Publications).

Dillingham Commission. *Report of the United States Immigration Commission,* 41 vols., 1907–1911. Second edition, 1970.

Ferenczi, Imre, and Walter F. Willcox, eds. *International Migrations.* 2 vols. New York: National Bureau of Economic Research. Second edition, 1969.

Keleti, Károly. 1887. *Magyarország népességének élelmezési statisztikája physiológiai Alapon* (The nourishment statistics of Hungary's population on physiological basis), 45–46. Budapest.

United Nations (UN) Demographic Yearbook, 1949–59. 1960.

United States Bureau of the Census. Population, general report and analytical tables, taken in the years 1910, 1930, 1940, 1950, 1960, 1970.

United States Departments of Commerce and Labor, and the Immigration and Naturalization Service. Annual report of the Commissioner General of Immigration, 1899–1970. Washington, DC.

Publications of the Hungarian ethnic organizations

a.) ANNIVERSARY PUBLICATIONS OF NEWSPAPERS AND ASSOCIATIONS

Szabadság 10. jubileumi száma (Szabadság 10th Anniversary). Cleveland, 1901.

Szabadság 20. jubileumi száma (Szabadság 20th Anniversary). Cleveland, December 1911.

Szabadság 50. jubileumi száma (Szabadság 50th Anniversary). Cleveland, 1941.

Amerikai Magyar Népszava Jubileumi Diszalbuma, 1899–1909 (Deluxe Anniversary Album of the American Hungarian People's Voice). Edited by Géza Berkó. New York, 1910. (Hereinafter AMN 10th Anniversary, 1910)

Hungarians in America, Az amerikai Magyarság Aranykönyve. Edited by John Kõrösfõy. (Szabadság Golden Book) Cleveland, 1941.

Amerikai Magyar Népszava 25 éves jubileumi száma (25th Jubilee of the American Hungarian People's Voice). Edited by Géza Berkó. New York, 1924.

Amerikai Magyar Népszava Arany Jubileumi Albuma (Golden Jubilee Album of the American Hungarian People's Voice). Edited by I. Székely. New York, 1950.

Az Uj Elõre Huszonöt éves Jubileumi Albuma (Uj Elõre 25th Anniversary 1927) Edited by János Kiss. New York, 1927.

Az Ember Jubileumi Szám (Az Ember 25th Anniversary 1936). Edited by Ferenc Göndör. 17 October 1936.

A Katolikus Magyarok Vasárnapja 1945 évre szóló jubileumi népnaptára (Catholic Hungarians' Sunday: Jubilee People's Calendar for 1945). Edited by Tarzicius Kukla. Cleveland, 1944.

Arvaházi Naptár (Orphanage Calendar). 1922–40, Bethlen Naptár from 1941 issued by the Hungarian American Reformed Association in Ligionier, PA.

Californiai Magyarság 25. Jubileumi szám (Californian Hungarians' 25th Anniversary 1948). Edited by Z. Szabados. Los Angeles, CA.

Chicago és környéke I. Magyar Társalgó és Betegsegélyzõ Egylet 25. éves jubileumi kiadványa (Chicago and its environs. The 25th Anniversary Publication of the Social and Benefit Association). Chicago, 1916.

Verhovayak Lapja, Verhovay Segélyegylet 50 éves jubileumi kiadványa (Verhovay Relief Association's Verhovay Journal 50th Anniversary). Edited by József Daragó. Pittsburgh, PA, 1936.

Rákóczi Segélyző Egyesület, 1888–1938 (Rákóczi Relief Association, 1888–1938). Edited by László Lakatos. Bridgeport, CT, 1938.

Amerikai Betegsegélyző és Életbiztositó Szövetség (Bridgeporti szövetség) ötven éves története, 1892–1942 (Fifty-year history of the American Sick Relief and Life Insurance Federation [Bridgeport Federation] 1892–1942). Edited by János Valkó. Pittsburgh, PA, 1942.

10 Esztendős Jubileumi IWO Naptár (IWO 10th Anniversary Calendar). New York: The Hungarian Section of International Workers Order, 1940.

Emlékkönyv és program az "Előre Mükedvelő Kör" húsz éves jubileumára. (Memorial album and program for the 20th Anniversary of the "Előre Amateur Circle") New York, 1934.

Emlékkönyv 1902–1967 (Memorial album) Publ. by New York: Amerikai Magyar Szó, (Hungarian Word in America) 1967.

Bulletin of the Hungarian American Federation. Cleveland, OH, 1908–1924.

Emlékkönyv az Amerikai Magyar Szövetség 80. Évfordulójára. (80th Anniversary Memorial Album of the American Hungarian Federation); edited by Bakó Elemér Washington DC: Amerikai Magyar Szövetség, 1980.

Magyar Hirlap Naptár. (Calendar of the *Magyar Hirlap*). Cleveland, OH, 1915, 1916.

Magyar Naptár 1902–1977. (Hungarian calendar). New York: Amerikai Magyar Szó, 1977.

Magyar Találkozó Krónikája (Chronicle of Hungarian Reunion). Edited by János Nádas and Ferenc Somogyi. Cleveland, OH, 1961–annually.

Petőfi Emlékkönyv. A Clevelandi egyletek szövetségének kiadványa (Petőfi memorial book. Publication of the Federation of Cleveland's Societies). Cleveland, 1930.

Kossuth Album, Delray-Michigan (Detroit). Kossuth Lajos Magyar Férfi és Női Betegsegélyző és Temetkezési Egylet 20 éves jubileumára. (Kossuth Album for the 20th Anniversary of Lajos Kossuth Hungarian Men and Women Sick Relief and Burial Society). Edited by: Ferenc Ujgyulai-Prattinger. Detroit, MI, 1922.

Emlékkönyv—Anniversary Book "in honor of our boys who were in the services." Hungarian Defense Council, New Brunswick, NJ. 23 June 1946.

Remember Hungary, October 23, 1956–1971. Hungarian Freedom Fighters Federation of the United States. Union City, NJ, 1971.

B.) ANNIVERSARY PUBLICATIONS PUBLISHED BY CONGREGATIONS.°

Árvaházi Naptár (Almanac of the Orphanage of the Western American Hungarian Reformed Church). Edited by Gyula Melegh. McKeesport, PA, 1917.

A Magyarországi Református Egyház Amerikai Egyházmegyéjének Naptára az 1911 évre. A New York-i Első Magyar Református Egyház tizenötéves jubileumára (The 1911 Calendar of the American Diocese of the Reformed Church of Hungary for the 15th Anniversary of the First Hungarian Reformed Church). Edited by Zoltán Kuthy New York, 1910.

Az Amerikai Nyugati Magyar Református Egyházmegye Árvaházi Naptára, 1917 (The Almanac of the Orphanage of the Western American-Hungarian Reformed Church, 1917). Edited by Gyula Melegh. McKeesport, PA, 1917.

Emlékkönyv az Amerikai Magyar Református Egyházmegye 25. éves évfordulójára. Az Egyesült Államokbeli Református Egyház Keleti Magyar Egyházmegyéje 1904–1929

° This compilation contains only a fraction of the many hundreds of published church memorial albums or "anniversary books." Owing to the volume we could not aim at completeness.

(Memorial Album for the 25ᵗʰ Anniversary of the Hungarian-American Reformed Diocese. The Hungarian Diocese of the Reformed Church of the United States in the East, 1904–1929.) Compiled by Géza Takaró, Ernő Komjáthy, and István M. Böszörményi. Bridgeport, CT, 1929.

Jubileumi Emlékkönyv (protestáns egyházi közösségekről) (Jubilee Memorial Book on Protestant congregations). Edited by Sándor Tóth. Pittsburgh, PA, 1940.

Emlékalbum a clevelandi első magyar református egyház 45 éves jubileumára (Memorial Album for the 45th anniversary of Cleveland's first Hungarian Reformed Church) Cleveland, OH. 30 May 1936.

St. Elizabeth's Hungarian Catholic Church, Golden Jubilee, Cleveland, 1892–1942.

St. John's Hungarian Greek Catholic Church, 75ᵗʰ Anniversary Album. Cleveland, 1967.

First Hungarian Lutheran Church, Golden Anniversary. Cleveland, 1906–1956.

Négy évtized a Clevelandi Első Magyar Ágostai Hitvallású Evangélikus Egyházban (Four decades of the Cleveland First Hungarian Lutheran Church of the Augustan Confession) Cleveland, OH, 1946.

Jubileumi Emlékkönyv, 1904–1929. (Jubilee Memorial Book, 1904–1929). Compiled by Lajos Varga. Pittsburgh, PA, 1929.

A South Norwalki Magyar Református Egyház Aranyjubileuma, 1893–1945. (The Golden Jubilee of the Hungarian Reformed Church of South Norwalk). 1944.

Az Evangélikus Református Egyház Husz éves jubileumi Emlékkönyve (20ᵗʰ Anniversary Memorial Book of the Lutheran Reformed Church). Compiled by László Bernáth.

Evangéliumi Hirnök (Gospel Messenger). Official Organ of the Hungarian Baptist Union of America since 1908. Cleveland, OH.

Emlékkönyv a Magyar Református Egyház Harmincöt Éves Jubileumára (Memorial Book for the 35th Anniversary of the Hungarian Reformed Church). New Brunswick, NJ, 1950.

60 éves Jubileumi Évkönyv (60ᵗʰ Anniversary Album of the Magyar Reformed Church). Edited by Imre Bertalan. New Brunswick, NJ.

Jubileumi Emlékkönyv a passaici Magyar Református Egyház 60 éves fennállása alkalmából. (Jubilee Memorial Book for the 60th Anniversary of the Hungarian Reformed Church of Passaic). Passaic, NJ 1895–1955.

Az Indiana harbori (Ind.) Első Magyar Evangéliumi és Református Egyház Családi Albuma (Family Album of the First Hungarian Evangelical and Reformed Church of Indiana Harbor, Indiana). Compiled by Zsigmond Balla, 1943.

Magyar református egyház 35 éves jubileumára (The 35th Anniversary of the Hungarian Reformed Church). Compiled by János Dezső. Wharton, NY, 1940.

A Chicagoi South Side-i Magyar Református Egyház Családi Albuma, (Family Album of the Hungarian Reformed Church of Chicago South Side). Compiled by Barna Dienes. Chicago, 1942.

25 éves Emlékalbum (25ᵗʰ Anniversary Memorial Album). Edited by Károly Bogár. McKeesport, PA, 1935.

Ezüst Jubileumi Emlékkönyv. A Gary, Ind. Első Magyar Evangélikus és Református Egyház Huszionöt éves jubileuma alkalmából (Silver Jubilee Memorial Book. On the occasion of the 25th Anniversary of the First Hungarian Lutheran and Reformed Church in Gary, Indiana). Compiled by Béla Bacsó, 1941.

50ᵗʰ Anniversary of The First Hungarian United Church of Christ, 1914–1964. Edited by Csaba Baksa. Akron, OH, 1964.

Négy évtized. a los-angelesi elsõ magyar református egyház életébõl, 1926–1966. (Four decades from the life of the First Hungarian Reformed Church). Compiled by Antal Szabó. Los Angeles, 1966.

A Philadelphiai Elsõ Magyar Református Egyház (tiz éves) története (The ten-year history of the First Hungarian Reformed Church in Philadelphia.) Compiled by Jenõ Pivány, 1914.

A Detroiti Egyházközség húsz éves története, 1904–1924. (The twenty-year history of the Congregation of Detroit). Edited by Mihály Tóth, 1925.

A Toledoi Szent István hitközég Jubileuma. (Jubilate-Church of St. Stephan, King of Hungary). Toledo, OH, 1924.

Emlékkönyv 1903–1953. A Toledoi Magyar Református Egyház ötvenéves fennállásának alkalmából (Memorial Book 1903–1953. On the occasion of the 50th Anniversary of the Hungarian Reformed Church of Toledo) Compiled by Ferenc Ujlaki, n.d.

Szent István hitközség ezüst jubileuma, 1902–1927 (St. Stephen Congregation's Silver Jubilee, 1902–1927) New York, n.d.

"The History of the Trenton and Roebling Hungarians." Trenton: *The Fifteenth Anniversary Album of the Independence Hungarian News*. Edited by Orosz J. Antal, 1929.

c.) Newpapers, Journals

AMN: *Amerikai Magyar Népszava* (Hungarian American People's Voice). New York, NY, 1899. First editor-publisher: Géza D. Berkó (before 1914).

Amerikai Magyar Reformátusok Lapja (The Newspaper of the Hungarian American Reformed Church). Bridgeport, CT; Pittsburgh, PA; New York, 1901. Editor-publisher: Sándor Kalassay, later László Harsányi.

Amerikai Magyarok Vasárnapja (Hungarian Americans' Sunday). Cleveland, 1928. Previously: *Katholikus Magyarok Vasárnapja* (Catholic Hungarians' Sunday); *Magyarok Vasárnapja* (Hungarians' Sunday). Later, *Katholikus Magyarok Vasárnapja, 1935, No. 36; Magyarok Vasárnapja*.

Amerikai Népszava (American People's Voice). New York, NY, 1895–98.

Arpádhoni Kertészlap (Arpádland Gardeners' Journal). Hammond, IN, 1913–14.

Bérmunkás (Wageworker). New York and Chicago, 1912. Editor: József Geréb.

Bevándorló (Immigrant). New York, NY, 1901. New York, NY, and Passaic, NJ, 1906–11.

Bulletin of the Hungarian American Federation. Cleveland, 1908–24. Source: AMN 1924.

Californiai Magyarság (Californian Hungarians). Los Angeles, 1923–41.

Clevelandi Magyar Recorder (Hungarian Recorder in Cleveland). Cleveland, 1896.

The Commentator. Cleveland: Hungarian American Federation. 1924. Source: AMN 1924.

Dongó (Wasp). Cleveland; later Detroit. 1903–1933. Editor: György Kemény.

Egyleti Élet (Club-life). New York, NY, 1923–1924. Editor Simon Szerényi.

Elõre (Forward). New York, NY 1905-November 1921. Later: *Uj Elõre* (New Forward) beginning 5 November 1921.

Az Ember (The Man). New York, N.Y. 1918–44. Editor-publisher: Ferenc Göndör.

Felszabadulás (Liberation). Chicago, 1919.

Interest. Chicago, 1932. Editor: Sándor Kálmán.

Az Irás (The Writing). Chicago, 1925–53. Editor: Gyõzõ Drózdy, later Ignác Izsák.

Kulturharc (Struggle for Culture). New York, NY, 1931. Editors: Jenõ Berkovits, Ferenc Kálnay, Péter Moór, Viktor Candell.

Magyar Bányászlap (Hungarian Miners' Periodical). New York, NY 1914; later Himler-ville, KY. Publisher-editor: Márton Himler.

Magyar Egyház (Hungarian Church). Editor: Endre Sebestey, Duquesne-McKeesport, PA, 1921–41.

Magyar Fórum (Hungarian Forum). New York, NY, 1942–43. Gen. Editor: Rusztem Vámbéry. Editor: János Terebessy.

Magyar Hirlap (Hungarian Journal). New Brunswick, NJ, 1933. Editors: József Szebényi, László Dienes.

Magyar Szenterzsébet Amerikai Hirnöke (Hungarian St. Elizabeth's American Herald) Cleveland, 1893–1901; merged with *Magyarok Vasárnapja.* Editor: Károly Bōhm.

Magyar Ujság (Hungarian Newspaper). Detroit, MI, 1910–17. Later *Detroiti Ujság* (Detroit Newspaper). Owner-editor: Antal Féder, later Gyula Fodor.

Munkás (Worker). Cleveland, 1909.

Napsugár (Sunbeam). New York, NY; later Cleveland. Source: AMN 1924.

Népakarat (People's Will). New York, NY, 1903–11. First editor: József K. Szabó.

Otthon (Home). Cleveland and Chicago, 1910–44. Founder: Dr. Artur Winter, handed it over to editor: Sándor Desseffy.

Ōrálló (Guard). Bridgeport, CT. Editor: Sándor Kalassay. Source: Amerikai Magyar Református Naptár, 1909.

Összetartás (Solidarity). Pittsburgh, PA, 1913–31.

Rákóczi Szemle (Rákóczi Review). Bridgeport, CT, 1924.

Second Generation Almanac for the Youth of Hungarian Origin. Journal 1936, n.p.

Szabad Magyar Tájékoztato (Free Hungarian Guide). Magyar Bizottsag (Hungarian Committee) New York, Vol. 1, 1958.

Szabadság, Cleveland, OH, 1891.

Testvériség (Brotherhood). New York, NY, 1911.

Testvériség (Fraternity). Washington, DC, 1923.

Új Magyar Út (New Hungarian Way), Sept.–Oct., 1954, edited by Elemér Bakó. Vol. 5, Nr9. Washington, DC, 110.

Uj Elōre (New Forward). New York, 1921. Previously: *Elōre.*

Verhovayak Lapja (The Periodical of the Verhovays). Detroit, MI, 1918.

D.) BOOKS, STUDIES.

American Hungarian Federation. 1946. *A Just Peace for Hungary:The American Hungarian Federation's Position on the Hungarian Peace Problem.* Washington DC: American Hungarian Federation.

Bagger, Eugene S. 1921. "Importing the White Terror—Articles Reprinted from *The Nation.*" In *The Jewish Chronicle* (New York).

Bárd Imre levele Szabó Ervinhez Budapestre (Imre Bárd's Letter to Ervin Szabó in Budapest) 26 February 1909. In *Szabó Ervin Levelezése, 1905–1918* (The Correspondence of Ervin Szabó, 1905–1918). Budapest: Akadémiai Kiadó, 1978.

Birinyi, Louis K. 1928. *A Plea for Justice for Hungary.* Memorandum submitted by American citizens of Hungarian descent, all the Hungarian Christian Churches and Hungarian United Societies of Cleveland, Ohio, to the World Conference on International Justice, Cleveland, 7–11 May 1928.

Birinyi, Louis K. 1929. *The Tragedy of Hungary.* Cleveland: published by the author.

Boas, Franz. 1911. "Changes in bodily form of descendants of immigrants." *Senate Documents,* 61st Cong., 2nd sess., 1909: 38; 1910. I. Vol.38. Washington, DC: Government Printing Office.

Bobula, Ida Miriam. 1953. *The Hungarian Material in the Library of Congress*. Washington, DC: Library of Congress.

Bodnár, John. 1985. *The Transplanted*. A History of Immigrants in Urban America. Bloomington, IN: Indiana University Press.

Bogár, Károly. 1941. *Verhovay's Spelling-Book: Magyar Betü, Magyar Szó* (Hungarian Script, Hungarian Word). Pittsburgh, PA: Verhovay Fraternal Association.

Borsy-Kerekes, György. 1930. *Az egyetlen ut. Az amerikai magyar reformátusok problémája* (The only way. The problem of the Hungarian Calvinists in America). Duquesne, PA: Magyar Egyház Társaság.

Braun, Marcus. 1972. *Immigration Abuses: Glimpses of Hungary and Hungarians. Experiences of an American Immigrant Inspector while in Hungary*. New York: Pearlon Advertising. First published as *Certain Reports of Immigrant Inspector Marcus Braun*. Washington, DC: Government Printing Office, 1906.

Byington, Margaret F. 1910. *Homestead: The Households of a Mill Town*. The Pittsburgh Russel Sage Foundation. Reprint 1974, Pittsburgh, PA: University Center for International Studies, University of Pittsburgh.

Cook, Huldah F. 1919. *The Magyars of Cleveland*. Cleveland: Cleveland Americanization Committee Citizen's Bureau.

Csutoros, Elek. 1917. *Az árpádhoni településről* (The Árpád Home Colony) *Tiz év a clevelandi West sidei magyar Református Egyház történetéből. (*Ten Years of the History of the Hungarian Reformed Church Life, 1906–1916). Cleveland, OH.

Daniel, Ferenc, and István Orosz. 1988. *Ah, Amerika! Dokumentumok a kivándorlásról, 1896–1914* (Documents on the emigration, 1896–1914). Budapest: Gondolat.

Deák, Zoltán, ed. 1982. *This Noble Flame: An Anthology of a Hungarian Newspaper in America*. NewYork: Heritage Press.

Dienes, Márton. 1913. "Kohányi Tihamér élete, küzdelmei, sikere és politikai végrendelete" (The life, struggles, successes and political testament of Tihamér Kohányi). In *Szabadság* (Cleveland).

DiKovics, J. 1945. *Our Magyar Presbytarians*. New York: Board of National Missions of the Presbytarian Church in the United States.

Dreisziger, N. F. "Oszkár Jászi and the 'Hungarian Problem'. Activities and Writings during World War II." *Hungarian Studies Review*, Vol. XVIII, Nos. 1–2 (Spring 1991), 59–79.

Dreisziger, Nandor. "The 1956 Hungarian Student Movement in Exile." *Hungarian Studies Review*, Vol. XX, Nos. 1–2 (Spring-Fall 1993), 103–116.

Erdély, Stephen. 1964. "Folksinging of the American-Hungarians in Cleveland." *Ethnomusicology* 8:14–26.

Füzes, Miklós. 1990. *Forgószél. Beés kitelepülések Dél-Kelet-Dunántúlon 1944–1948 között. Tanulmány és interjúkötet.* (Whirlwind, emigration, and immigration in southern and eastern Transdanubia 1944–48. A study and volume of interviews). Pécs: Pécs-Baranya Megyei Levéltár.

Gáspár, G. 1910. "Az Amerikai Magyar Népszava Története." (The History of the AMSz). In *Amerikai Magyar Népszava 10 jubileumi Album*.

Gellért, Hugó. 1982. "Reminiscences." In *This Noble Flame: An Anthology of a Hungarian newspaper in America*, edited by Zoltán Deák, 83–86.

Gonda, Fredric. N.d. *The History of Cleveland Hungarians*. Cleveland: H. A. Liebowitz.

Hoffmann, Géza. 1911. *Csonka munkásosztály*(Truncated working class). Budapest.

Incze, Sándor, ed. 1921. "Magyarok Amerikában"(Hungarians in America). *A Szinházi Élet Albuma.*Budapest.

Kalassay, Sándor. 1937. *Az Amerikai Magyar Református Egyház története* (The history of the Hungarian-American Reformed Church). Pittsburgh, PA: Magyarzag.

Kalassay, Sándor. 1922. *Az Amerikai Magyar Református Egyesület müködésének huszonötéves története, 1896–1921* (The history of twenty-five years' of activities of the Hungarian American Reformed Federation). Detroit: Fodor.

Káldor, Kálmán. 1937, 1939. *Magyar Amerika irásban és képben* (Hungarian America in words and pictures). 2 vols. St. Louis: Hungarian Publishing Co.

Kampis, György. 1957. *Az 1956. Október hó 23 napját követöen jogellenesen külföldre távozott személyek vagyonjogi helyzetének rendezése* (Settling the position in regards to the rights of property for people who left the country illegally after 23 October 1956). Budapest.

Kemény, G. Gábor. 1952, 1956, 1964, 1966, 1971. *Iratok A Nemzetiségi Kérdés Történetéhez Magyarországon a Dualizmus Korában* (Documents concerning the question of non-Magyar ethnic groups in the age of dualism). Budapest. Vol. 1, 1952; Vol. 2, 1956; Vol. 3, 1964; Vol. 4, 1966; Vol. 5, 1971. Budapest: Akadémiai Kiadó.

Kende, Géza. 1927. *Magyarok Amerikában* (Hungarians in America). 2 vols. Cleveland: Szabadság Publisher.

Kertész, Gyula. 1910. *A kivándorlás szabályozása* (The Regulation of Emigration). Budapest.

Király, Zoltán. 1988. The 50th Anniversary Album of the Calvin Synod of the United Church of Christ. N.p.

Kohányi, Tihamér. 1901. "Az Amerikai Magyarság multja, jelene és jövöje. A *Szabadság* Tizéves Jubileumára" (The past, present and future of the Hungarian Americans. 10th Anniversary of *Szabadság*). In *Szabadság* (Cleveland).

Könnyü, László. 1977. Egy Költő visszanéz/önéletrajz (A poet looks back/curriculum vitae). St. Louis, MO: Amerikai Magyar Szemle.

Kovács, Ernő. 1926. *I Accuse! Reply to the Lies of Uj Előre.* Cleveland.

Kovács, József. 1977. *A szocialista magyar irodalom dokumentumai az amerikai magyar Sajtóban, 1920–1945* (Documents of Socialist Hungarian Literature in the Hungarian-American Press, 1920–1945). Budapest: Akademiai Kaido.

Kramar, Zoltán. 1978. *From the Danube to the Hudson: U.S. Ministerial and Consular Dispatches on Immigration from the Habsburg Monarchy, 1850–1900.* Atlanta, GA: Hungarian Cultural Foundation.

Kretzoi, Charlotte. 1985. "United States History in Hungary: Research and Teachings." in *Guide to the Study of United States History Outside The US, 1945–1980,* edited by Lewis Hanke, 2:538-44.

Kuthy, Zoltán. 1915. *Amerikai magyarok imádságos könyve háborus idöben* (Hungarian-American prayerbook in wartime). 2d.ed.

Litván, György, and Varga F. János, eds. 1991. *Oszkár Jászi's Selected Letters.* Budapest: Magvetö.

Loew, William Noah. 1883. "Alexander Petőfi." A lecture delivered before the Hungarian Relief Committee of Cleveland, 1 February 1883. Cleveland: Nevins Printing House.

Máday, Béla. 1988. "Az 1956. utáni Magyar Segély szervezése és abban az Amerikai Tudományos Akadémia szerepe" (The organization of Hungarian Relief after 1956 and the role of the Hungarian Academy of Sciences). In *Emlékkönyv az Amerikai Magyar Szövetség 80. Évfordulójára* (Memorial Alum for the 80th Anniversary of the Hungarian American Federation), edited by Elemér Bakó. Washington DC: Amerikai Magyar Szövetség.

Magyar, József. 1982. *Szemelvények a chicagói Szent István templom életéböl (1930–1974)* (Excerpts of the life of the St. Stephen Church in Chicago, 1930–1974). Sïo Paulo, Brazil: Editora Grafica Nagy LTDA.

Marchbin, A. A. 1934. "The Origin of Migration from South-Eastern Europe to Canada." *Canadian Historical Association Report,* 110–20.

McGuire, James Patrick. 1993. *The Hungarian Texans.* San Antonio, TX: University of Texas, Institute of Texan Cultures.

Mészöly, Gedeon. 1932. *Amerikai magyar fiu Magyarországon.: Olvasókönyv magyar tanulók számára* (Hungarian American boy in Hungary. Reading-book for Hungarian students). Budapest: Koltann.

Nadányi, Paul. 1942. "The Free Hungary Movement." *Amerikai Magyar Népszava* (New York).

Nagy, Károly. 1977. *Tanitsunk magyarul! Tanulmányok, cikkek, beszélgetések, A szórvá-nymagyarság nyelvoktatásáról, kultúra-müveléséröl* (Let us teach Hungarian. Studies, articles, discussions. On the teaching of language and the cultivation of culture of the scattered Hungarians). New York: Püski Kiadó.

Novak, M. 1972. *The Rise of the Unmeltable Ethnics: A New Political Force of the Seventies.* New York: Macmillan.

Nyirő, József. 1991. *Ime, az emberek!* (Behold, the humans!). Debrecen. n.p.

Nyisztor, Zoltán. 1973. *Idegen az idegenben. Visszaemlékezések* (Foreigner in a foreign land. Recollections). Munich.

Ölvendi, Tamás. 1948. *Levelek a számüzetésböl* (Letters from exile). Munich.

Papp, László. 1988. AÉMEFESZ: Az amerikai magyar egyetemisták mozgalma (The movement of the American-Hungarian university students). New Brunswick, NJ: Öreg Diákok Szövetsége.

Petre, Gabor, György Balla, Ferenc Dér. 1958. Amerikai Magyar Baptisták Története (The history of the American Hungarian Baptists). Cleveland, OH: Amerikai Baptista Szövetség.

Pintér, E. 1969. *Wohlstandsflüchtlinge. Eine Socialpsychiatrische Studie an Ungarischen Flüchtlinge in der Schweiz.* Basel.

Pivány, Eugene. 1919. *The Case of Hungary in the Light of Statements of British and American Statesmen and Authors.* Budapest: Hungarian Territorial Integrity League.

Pivány, Eugene. 1919. *Some Facts about the Proposed Dismemberment of Hungary.* Cleveland: Hungarian American Federation.

Rácz, Rónai Károly. 1911. "Immigrants." In *Csonka munkásosztály,* edited by Géza Hoffmann, 229.

Rácz, Rónai Károly. 1922–1923. "Az amerikai magyar telepek története. Cikksorozat. a *Külföldi Magyarság.* ujság 1922–1923 számaiban" (A series of articles entitled "The History of American-Hungarian settlements," in the 1922–1923 issues of the newspaper *Külföldi Magyarság).*

Radnóti, Agoston, ed. 1966. *Vienna Dossier.* Budapest: National Committee of the Hungarian Student Organization.

Reményi, József. 1937. "A magyarnyelvü alkotószellem lélektana Amerikában" (The psychology of the Hungarian-language creativity in America). In *Magyar Szemle,* May.

Reményi, József. 1936. "American children of foreign born parents." *Verhovayak Lapja* 50th Jub. Nos. 10–12. Rt.

Rickert, Ernő, ed. 1920. "Amerikai magyar költők" (American Hungarian poets). Budapest: *"Magyar Jövő"* Ifjusági Irodalmi Lap.

Roller, Kálmán J. 1985. *The Sopron Chronicle.* Sopron 1956. Vancouver.

Rudnyánszky, Gyula. 1907. *Amerikai felköszöntő ünnepi beszédek, alkalmi,és hazafias szónoklatok egyleti zászlószentelési, lakodalmi, keresztelői üdvözlése, pohárköszöntők* (American festive toasts, speeches on special occasions, patriotic orations, consecration of the flag of an association, speeches at weddings, christenings). Cleveland.

Schaeffer, The Rev. Charles E. 1923. *Glimpses into Hungarian Life.* Philadelphia: The Board of Hungarian Mission of the Reformed Church in the United States.

Schultz, Ignac. 1941. "Budapest's Fake Mission." *The Nation,* 27 September.

Somogyi, Ferenc. 1978. *A Clevelandi magyar nyelvoktatás* (Teaching the Hungarian language in Cleveland) *Emlékkönyv* 1958–78 (Memorial book) (Cleveland), 321–71.

Souders, D. A. 1922. *The Magyars in America.* Reprinted 1969, San Francisco: R. and E. Research Associate.

Stibran, T. D. 1961. *The Streets Are Not Paved with Gold.* Cleveland: Printing Co.

Sulyok, Dezsö. 1962. *A Magyar Emigráció Szerencsétlensége* (The distress of the Hungarian emigration). New York Magyar Október 23 Mozgalom (The Hungarian 23rd October Movement).

Szamos, Rudolf. 1958. *Kommentár nélkül. Disszidensek Levelei* (Without comment. Letters of dissidents). Budapest.

Szili, Ferenc. 1993. "A somogyi kivándorlók Amerika képe és magyarságtudata a századfordulò évtizedeiben" (The image of America and the consciousness of being Hungarian of the emigrants of Somogy in the decades at the end of the century). Levéltári Évkönyv). Yearbook of the Archive, Kaposvár: 24, 207–272.

Szy, Tibor. 1963. *Hungarians in America.* New York: Hungarian University Association.

Taggart, Spencer. 1943. *Memorandum on the Activities of Hungarian Nationalists in the United States, 8 December 1943.* 47, 69f. Department of Justice Records, 864 01 B 11/73. Washington DC: National Archives of the United States.

Tezla, Albert. 1987. *Valahol túl, Meseországban: Az amerika's magyarok, 1895–1920.* (Somewhere in a distant fabled land: American-Hungarians in America). 2 vols. Budapest: Európa Könyvkiadó.

Tonelli, Sándor. 1929. *Ultonia. Egy kivándorló hajó története* (Ultonia. Story of an emigration). Szeged.

Vámbéry, Rusztem. 1942. "The Hungarian problem." New York: *The Nation.*

Vetési, László. 1902. *Boldogország A Maga Valóságában. Egy Magyar Munkás Amerikai Levelei* (The happy land as it really is. A Hungarian worker's letter from America). Budapest: Lampel.

II. SECONDARY SOURCES

Bibliographies

Bakó, Elemér. 1973. *Guide to Hungarian Studies.* 2 vols. Stanford, CA: Hoover Institution.

Bognár, Dési K. 1972. *Hungarians in America,* 3rd ed., Mt. Vernon, NY: AH Publication.

Kovács, Ilona. 1975. "The Hungarians in the United States: An Annotated Bibliography." Master's thesis, Kent State University.

Nagy, Csaba, ed. 1990. *A magyar Emigráns Irodalom Texikoma* (Enclyclopedia of the literature of Hungarian emigrants). Vols. 1–3. Budapest: Institute of Literature. Hungarian Academy of the Sciences and the Petőfi Literary Museum.

Széplaki, Joseph. 1977. *Hungarians in the United States and Canada: A Bibliography.*
Minneapolis, MN: Immigration History Research Center, University of Minnesota.

Szilassy, Sándor. 1973. "Amerikai magyar könyvtári és levéltári gyüjtemények" (Collections of Hungarian-American library and archival materials). In *Magyar találkozók krónikája,* 1964–1965. Cleveland, 139–46.

Vitéz, Francis. N.d. "A Bibliographical Survey of the Hungarian Reformed Literature in the United States." Master's thesis, Columbia University.

Wynar, Lubomyr R. 1975. *Ethnic Groups in Ohio with Special Emphasis on Cleveland: An Annotated Bibliographical Guide.* Cleveland: Cleveland Ethnic Heritage Studies Development Program, Cleveland State University.

BOOKS, PAMPHLETS, ARTICLES

INTERNATIONAL SECTION

Books, pamphlets

Ahern, John, ed. 1987. *The Preservation of Ethnic Heritage: An Examination of the Birmingham Experience.* Toledo: The University of Toledo.

Album, Gerald. 1973. *Immigrant Workers: Their Impact on American Labor Radicalism.* New York: Basic Books.

Alexander, June Sylvia. 1987. *The Immigrants' Church and Community: Pittsburgh's Slovak Catholics and Lutherans, 1880–1915.* Pittsburgh, PA: University of Pittsburgh Press.

Anderson, Benedict. 1983. *Imagined Communities: Reflections on the Origin and Spread of Nationalism.* London: Verso.

Archdeacon, Thomas J. 1983. *Becoming American.* New York: The Free Press.

Barkan, Elliott R., 1995. "Race, Religion and Nationality in American Society: A Model of Ethnicity—From Contact to Assimilation." *Journal of American Ethnic Studies,* Vol. 14, No. 2, 38–75. Comment by Rudolph J. Vecoli, 76–81. Comment by Richard D. Alba, 82–90. Comment by Oliver Zunz, 91–94. Comment by Elliott R. Barkan, 95–101.

Beckhofer, F., ed. 1969. *Population Growth and the Brain Drain.* Edinburgh: Edinburgh University Press.

Benneth, Marion T. 1960. *American Immigration Policies.* Washington, DC.

Bonutti, Karl, and George Prpic. 1977. *Selected Ethnic Communities of Cleveland: A Socioeconomic Study for Cleveland.* Cleveland: Urban Observatory, Cleveland State University.

Böszörményi, Endre. 1960. A menekülő orzág (The fleeing country). In Trianoni Almanach, 1920–1960. München: Hidtő Kiadó, 158–159.

Brinley, Thomas. 1961. *The Decline in International Migration.*

Brody, David. 1965. *Labor in Crises: The Steel STrikes of 1919.* Philadelphia: Lippincott.

Cantor, Milton, ed. 1979. *American Working-Class Culture: Explorations in American Labor and Social History.* Westport, CT: Greenwood Press.

Cantor, Milton. 1978. *The Divided Left: American Radicalism, 1900–1975.* New York: Hill and Wang.

Caroli, Boyed Betty. 1977. *Italian Repatriation from the United States, 1900–1914.* Staten Island, NY: Center for Migration Study.

Charles, Lester V. 1970. *America's Greatest Depression, 1929–1941.* New York: Harper & Row.

Chmelar, Hans. 1974. *Höhepunkte der österreichischen Auswanderung* (Highlights of the emigration from Austria). Vienna: Verlag der österreichischen Akademie der Wissenschaften.

Corbin, David Alan. 1981. *Life, Work, and Rebellion in the Coal Fields: The Southern West Virginia Miners, 1880–1922.* Urbana: University of Illinois Press.

Cumbler, John. 1977. *Working-Class Community in Industrial America: Work, Leisure and Struggle in Two Industrial Cities, 1880–1930.* Westport, CT: Greenwood Press.

Debouzy, Marianne, ed. 1988. *In the Shadow of the Statue of Liberty: Immigrants, Workers and Citizens in the American Republic, 1880–1920.* Saint Denis: Presses universitaire des Vincennes, 139–51.

Dinnerstein, Leonard, and David M. Reimers. 1977. *Ethnic Americans: A History of Immigration and Assimilation.* New York: New York University Press.

Divine, Robert A. 1954. *American Immigration Policy, 1924–1952.* New Haven, CT: Yale University Press.

Dubofsky, Melvyn. 1969. *We Shall Be All: A History of the Industrial Workers of the World.* Chicago: Quadrangle Book.

Feingold, Henry L. 1970. *The Policies of Rescue: The Roosevelt Administration and the Holocaust, 1933–1944.* New Brunswick, NJ: Rutgers University Press.

Fermi, Laura. 1971. *Illustrious Immigrants: The Intellectual Migration from Europe.* Chicago: University of Chicago Press.

Finch, John A. 1910. *The Steel Workers.* Pittsburgh, PA: University of Pittsburgh Press. Second edition, 1989.

Fishman, Joshua A. 1978. *Language Loyalty in the United States.* New York: Arno Press.

Fleming, Donald. 1969. *The Intellectual Migration: Europe and America, 1930–1960.* Cambridge, MA: Belknap Press of Harvard University.

Friedman, Saul S. 1972. *No Haven for the Oppressed: United States Policy towards Jewish Refugees, 1938–1945.* Detroit, MI: Wayne State University Press.

Gabaccia, Donna. 1988. *Militants and Migrants: Rural Sicilians Become American Workers.* New Brunswick, NJ: Rutgers University Press.

Garis, Roy L. 1927. *Immigration Restriction: A Study of the Opposition to and Regulation of Immigration into the United States.* New York: Macmillan.

Gartner, Lloyd P. 1978. *History of the Jews of Cleveland.* Cleveland: Cleveland Western Reserve Historical Society and the Jewish Theological Seminary of America.

Glaitman, Henry. 1957. *Youth in Revolt: The Failure of Communist Indoctrination in Hungary.* New York: Free Europe Press.

Glazier, Ira A. and Luigi De Rosa, eds. 1986. *Migration Across Time and Nations: Population Mobility in Historical Context.* New York: Holmes & Meier.

Goldwin-Gill, Guy S. 1990. "Different Types of Forced Migration Movements as an International and National Problem." In *The Uprooted. Forced Migration as an International Problem in the Post War Era.* Edited by Göran Rystad. Lund: Lund University Press.

Gordon, David, Richard Edwards, and Michael Reich. 1982. *Segmented Work, Divided Workers: The Historical Transformation of Labor in the United States.* New York: Cambridge University Press.

Gordon, Milton M. 1964. *Assimilation in the American Life: The Role of Race, Religion and National Origins.* New York: Oxford University Press.

Gordon, Milton M. 1978. *Human Nature, Class and Ethnicity.* New York: Oxford University Press.

Green, Nancy L. 1994. The Comparative Method of Poststructural Structuralism. New Perspectives for Migration Studies. *Journal of American Ethnic Studies,* 13: 3–22.

Guerin-Gonzales, Camille, and Carl Strikwerda, eds. 1993. *The Politics of Immigrant Workers: Labor Activism and Migration in the World Economy since 1830.* New York: Holmes & Meier.

Gutman, Herbert. 1976. *Work, Culture and Society in Industrializing America.* New York: Knopf.

Handlin, Oscar. 1951. *The Uprooted.* Boston: Little, Brown. Second edition, 1973.

Hansen, Marcus Lee. 1940. *The Immigrant in American History.* Cambridge, MA: Harvard University Press.

Hansen, Marcus Lee. 1938. *The Problem of the Third Generation Immigrant.* Rock Island, IL. Reprinted in *Commentary,* November 1952.

Hartmann, Edward G. 1948. *The Movement to Americanize the Immigrant.* New York: Columbia University Press.

Harzig, Christiane, and Dirk Hoerder. 1985. *The Press of Labor Migrants in Europe and North America, 1880s to 1930s.* Bremen: The Labor Newspaper Preservation Project, 385–402.

Herberg, Will. 1960. *Protestant, Catholic, Jew: An Essay in American Religious Sociology.* Garden City, NY: Anchor Books.

Higham, John. 1975. *Send These To Me. Strangers In The Land. Patterns of American Nativism, 1860–1925.* New Brunswick, NJ: Rutgers University Press.

Higham, John. 1990. "From Process to Structure Formulations of American Immigration History" in Peter Kisvisto and Dag Blanck, eds. *American Immigrants and their Generations. Studies and Commentaries on the Hansen Thesis after Fifty Years.* Urbana: University of Illinois Press.

Higham, John. 1994. The Ethnic Historical Society in Changing Times. *Journal of American Ethnic Studies.* 13: 30–44.

Hoerder, Dirk, and Horst Rössler, eds. 1993. *Distant Magnets: Expectations and Realities in the Immigrant Experience, 1840–1930.* New York: Holmes & Meier.

Hoerder, Dirk, and Inge Blank, eds. 1994. *Roots of the Transplanted.* 2 vols. New York: Columbia University Press.

Hoerder, Dirk, ed. 1996. *Struggle a Hard Battle: Essay on Working Class Immigrants.* DeKalb: Northern Illinois University Press.

Hoerder, Dirk. 1986. *Why Did You Come? The Proletarian Mass Labor Migration.* Bremen: University of Bremen.

Hoerder, Dirk, ed. 1985. *Labor Migration in the Atlantic Economies.* Westport, CT: Greenwood Press.

Hofstadter, Richard. 1955. *Social Darwinism in American Thought.* Boston: Beacon Press.

Holborn, Louise W. 1956. *The International Refugee Organization. A Special Agency of the United Nations. Its History and Work, 1946–1952.* London: Oxford University Press.

Holborn, Louise W. 1975. *Refugees: A Problem of our Time. The Work of the United Nations High Commissioner for Refugees, 1951–1972.* Vol. 1. Metuchen, NJ: Scarecrow Press.

Hutchinson, E. P. 1956. *Immigrants and their Children, 1850–1950.* New York: Russel and Russel. Second edition, 1976.

Jaffe, Julian F. 1972. "The Anti-Radical Crusade." In *Crusade against Radicalism during the Red Scare, 1919–1924.* New York: Prot. Work.

Jerome, H. 1926. *Migration and Business Cycles.* New York: National Bureau of Economic Research.

Kivisto, Peter. 1990. "The Transplanted Then and Now: The Reorientation of Immigration Studies from the Chicago School to the New Social History." *Ethnic and Racial Studies* (October): 455–81.

Kivisto, Peter, and Dag Blench. 1990. *American Immigrants and their Two Generations: Studies and Commentaries on the Hansen Thesis after Fifty Years.* Urbana: University of Illinois Press.

Kivisto, Peter, ed. 1989. *The Ethnic Enigma: The Salience of Ethnicity for European-Origin Groups.* Philadelphia: The Balch Institute Press.

Lockwood, W. G., ed. 1984. Beyond Ethnic Boundaries: New Approaches in the Anthropology of Ethnicity. Michigan Discussions in *Anthropology.* Ann Arbor, 51–84.

Lucassen, Leo. "The Gulf between Long-Term and Short-Term Approaches in Immigration Studies. A Reassessment of the Chicago School's Assimilation Concept." Universitat Osnabrück. In *IMIS-BEITRAGE,* Heft 5. 1997. Apr. 5.

Marrus, Michael R. 1985. *The Unwanted: European Refugees in the Twentieth Century.* Oxford: Oxford University Press.

Miller, R. M., and Thomas D. Marzik. 1977. *Immigrants and Religion in Urban America.* Philadelphia: Temple University Press.

Mohl, Raymond A. and Neil Betten. 1986. *Steel City, Urban and Ethnic Patterns in Gary, Indiana, 1906–1950.* New York: Holmes and Meier.

O'Grady, Joseph P., ed. 1967. *The Immigrants' Influence on Wilson's Peace Policies.* Lexington: University of Kentucky Press.

Ostergen, C. Robert. 1988. *A Community Transplanted: The Transatlantic Experience of a Swedish Immigrant Settlement in the Upper Middle West, 1835–1915.* Madison: University of Wisconsin Press.

Park, Robert Ezra. 1921. *Immigrants and their Press.* New York. Second edition, Monclair, NJ: Petterson Smith, 1970.

Park, Robert Ezra, and Herbert A. Miller. 1921. *Old World Traits Transplanted.* New York.

Park, Robert Ezra. 1950. *Race and Culture: Collected Studies.* Glencoe, IL.

Pozetta, E. George. 1990. "From Rustbelt to Sunbelt: Patterns of Ethnic Migration and Integration in America, 1940–1988." In *From 'Melting Pot' to Multiculturalism,* edited by Valeria Gennaro Lerda. Rome: Bulzoni, 263–80.

Pozetta, E. George. 1981. *American Immigration and Ethnicity: Themes in Immigration History.* New York: Garland Publishing.

Preis, Art. 1972. *Labor's Giant Step: Twenty Years of the CIO.* New York: Pathfinder Press.

Prpic, George J. 1980. *The Croatian Immigrants in America.* New York: Philosophical Library.

Roberts, Peter. 1970. *The New Immigration: A Study of Industrial and Social Life of Southeastern Europeans in America.* 2d ed. New York: Arno Press.

Ross, Edward A. 1914. *The Old World in the New.* New York: Century Co.

Runblom, Harold, and Hans Norman. 1976. *From Sweden to America: A History of Emigration.* Minneapolis-Uppsala.

Salomon, Kum. 1991. *Refugees in the Cold War. Toward a New International Refugee Regime in the Early Postwar Era.* Lund: Lund University Press.

Sanders, Ronald. 1988. *Shores of Refuge: A Hundred Years of Jewish Emigration.* New York: Henry Holt.

Schechtnan, B. Joseph. 1962. *Postwar Population Transfer in Europe, 1945–1955*. Philadelphia.

Serene, H. Frank. 1979. *Immigrant Steelworkers in the Monangahela Valley, their Communities and the Development of a Labor Class Consciousness*. Pittsburgh, PA.

Skardal, Dorothy Burton. 1974. *The Divided Heart. Scandinavian Immigrant Experience through Literary Sources*. Oslo-Bergen-Tromsö: Universitetsforlaget.

Smith, Anthony. 1981. *The Ethnic Revival in the Modern World*. Cambridge: Cambridge University Press.

Sollors, Werner. 1986. *Beyond Ethnicity. Consent and Descent in American Culture*. New York: Oxford University Press.

Sollors, Werner, ed. 1989. *The Invention of Ethnicity*. New York: Oxford University Press.

Steinberg, Stephen. 1981. *The Ethnic Myth: Race, Ethnicity and Class in America*. New York: Atheneum.

Steiner, E. A. 1906. *On the Trail of the Immigrants*. New York: Revell. Reprint, New York: Arno, 1969.

Stolarik, Mark, and Murray Friedman, eds. 1986. *Making it in America: The Role of Ethnicity in Education, Business Enterprise and Work Choices*. London: Associated University Press.

Stolarik, Mark. 1980. *Slovak Migration From Europe to North America, 1870–1918*. Slovak Studies, vol. 20. Cleveland, OH: Slovak Institute.

van Tassel, David D., and J. John Grabowski. 1987. *The Encyclopedia of Cleveland History*. Bloomington: Indiana University Press.

Thernstrom, Stephan. 1964. *Poverty and Progress: Social Mobility in a Nineteenth Century City*. Cambridge, MA: Harvard University Press.

Thernstrom, Stephan. 1973. *The Other Bostonians: Poverty and Progress in the American Metropolis, 1880–1970*. Cambridge, MA: Belknap Press of Harvard University.

Thernstrom, Stephan. ed. *Harvard Encyclopedia of American Ethnic Groups*. Cambridge, MA: Harvard University Press.

Thomas, W. I., and Florian Znaniecki. 1918. *The Polish Peasant in Europe and America*. New York.

Thomson, F. 1955. The IWW. Its First Fifty Years. 1905–1955. Chicago, IL.

Vecoli, Rudolph, and Suzanne M. Sinke, ed. 1991. *A Century of European Migration, 1830–1930*. Statue of Liberty/Ellis Island Centennial Series. Urbana: University of Illinois Press.

Virtanen, Keijo. 1979. *Settlement or Return: Finnish Emigrants (1860–1930) in the International Overseas Return Migration Movement*. Turku, Finland: Migration Institute.

Weiss, B., ed. 1982. *American Education and the European Immigrants, 1840–1940*. Urbana, IL.

Wimmer, Irene Portis, ed. 1983. *The Dynamics of East European Ethnicity Outside of Eastern Europe*. Cambridge, MA.

Wyman, David S. 1968. *Paper Walls: America and the Refugee Crisis, 1938–1941*. Amherst: University of Massachussetts Press.

Wyman, Mark. 1989. *D.P. Europe's Displaced Persons, 1945–51*. Philadelphia: The Balch Institute Press.

Yans-McLaughlin, Virginia. 1990. *Immigration Reconsidered: History, Sociology and Ethnic Differences*. Boston: Little, Brown.

Znanieczki, Helena. 1976. *Polish Americans: Status Competition in an Ethnic Community*. Englewood Cliffs, NJ: Prentice-Hall.

Studies, Articles

Alnas, Ion. 1970. "Industrialization and Migration of the Transylvanian Peasantry at the End of the Nineteenth Century and the Beginning of the Twentieth Century." *East European Quarterly* (January): 504–5.

Abramson, Harold. 1980. "Assimilation and Pluralism Theories." In *Harvard Encyclopedia of American Ethnic Groups,* edited by Stephan Thernstrom, 150–60.

Archdeacon, Thomas J. 1985. "Problems and Possibilities in the Study of American Immigration and Ethnic History." *International Migration Review* 19.

Asher, Robert. 1982. "Union Nativism and the Immigrant Response." *Labor History* 23 (Summer): 325–48.

Barrett, James R. and David Roediger, 1997. "In Between Peoples: Race, Nationality and the 'New Immigrant' Working Class." *Journal of AEH* (Spring) 16: 3–7.

Bernard, Williams S. 1980. "Immigration: History of the United States Policy." In *Harvard Encyclopedia of American Ethnic Groups*, 486–95.

Beynon, Endman D. 1934. "Occupational Succession of Hungarians in Detroit." *The American Journal of Sociology* 39 (March): 600–10.

Beynon, Endman D. 1936. "Occupational Mobility and Social Distance among Hungarian Immigrants in Detroit." *Journal of Sociology* 41 (January): 423–34.

Bodnár, John. 1995. "Remembering the Immigrant Experience in American Culture." *Journal of American Ethnic History,* (Fall) 1: 3–27.

Bonacich, Edna. 1973. "A Theory of Middleman Minorities." *American Sociological Review* 38.

Breton, Raymond. 1964. "Institutional Completeness of Ethnic Communities and Personal Relations of Immigrants." *American Journal of Sociology* 70: 193–205.

Cantor, Milton. 1986. "Ethnicity in the World of Work." In *Making it in America: The Role of Ethnicity in Education, Business Enterprise,* edited by Mark Stolarik and Murray Friedman, 98–115.

Cinel, Dino. 1980. "Seasonal Emigration of Italians in the Nineteenth Century: From Internal to International Destination." *The Journal of Ethnic Studies* 19 (Spring): 43–68.

Cohen, Abner. 1974. "Introduction: The Lesson of Ethnicity." In *Urban Ethnicity,* edited by Abner Cohen. London: Tavistock Publications.

Commons, John R. 1900–1902. "Immigration and its Economic Effect." *Reports of the United States Commission.* 19 vols. Washington, DC: Government Printing Office, 1911. Reprint Arno Press and New York Times, 1970.

Elliott, Robin B. 1985. "The Eastern European Immigrants in American Literature: The View of the Host Culture, 1900–1930." *Polish American Studies* 24, no. 2: 25–45.

Gands, Herbert. 1979. "Symbolic Ethnicity: The Future of Ethnic Groups and Cultures." *American Ethnic and Racial Studies* 2.

Gleason, Philip. 1980. "American Identity and Americanization." In *Harvard Encyclopedia of American Ethnic Groups,* Stephen Thernstrom, ed. 31–57.

Gould, J. D. 1979. "European Intercontinental Emigration, 1815–1914: Patterns and Causes." *Journal of European Economic History* 8:593–679.

Gould, J. D. 1980. "European Intercontinental Emigration, The Road Home: Return Migration from the U.S.A." *Journal of European Economic History* 8, no. 1(Spring): 41–113

Harrington, Mona. "Loyalties: Dual and Divided." In *Harvard Encyclopedia,* 676–686.

Hechter, Michael, et al. 1976. "Ethnicity and Industrialization: On the Proliferation of the Cultural Division of Labor." *Ethnicity* 3: 214–24.

Hoerder, Dirk. 1993. "The Traffic of Emigration via Bremen: Bremenhaven-Merchants' Interest, Protective Legislation, and Migrants' Experience." *Journal of American Ethnic History* 13, no. 1: 68–101.

James, A. Henrietta. 1977. "The Study of Social Mobility: Ideological Assumptions and Conceptual Bias." *Labor History* 18 (Spring):165–78.

James, A. Henrietta, 1979. "Social History as Lived and Written." *American Historical Review* 84 (December): 1293–1323.

Keeran, Roger. 1995. "National Groups and the Popular Front." *The Case of the International Workers* 14, no. 3 (Spring): 23–51.

Macdonald, John S. 1958. "Agricultural Organization, Migration and Labor Militancy in Rural Italy." *Economic History Review,* 2d ser., vol. 16.

Macdonald, John S., and Beatrice D. Macdonald. "Chain Migration, Ethnic Neighborhood Formation and Social Networks." *Milbank Memorial Fund Quarterly* 42:82–97.

Morawska, Ewa. 1991. "Return Migrations: Theoretical and Research Agenda" in *A Century of European Migrations, 1880–1930.* Edited by Rudolph Vecoli and Susanne M. Sinke. Chicago: University of Illinois Press. 277–282.

Rosenblum, Gerald. 1973. *Immigrant Workers: Their Impact on American Labor Radicalism.* New York: Basic Books.

Salt, John, 1989. A Comparative Overview of International Trends and Types, 1950–80. In *International Migration Review,* Fall 1989. 23: 431–456.

Sarna, Jonathan. 1981. "The Myth of the Return: Jewish Return Migration to Eastern Europe, 1881–1914." *American Jewish History.*

Smith, Timothy. 1983. "Religion and Ethnicity in America." *American Historical Review* 83:1171.

Swierenga, Robert P. 1991. "Local Pattern of Dutch Migration to the United States in the Mid-Nineteenth Century" in *A Century of European Migration, 1830–1930.* edited by Rudolph Vecoli and Susanne M. Sinke. Chicago: University of Illinois Press.

Swierenga, Robert P. 1994. "Ethnic History." *Ethnic Forum* 4 (Spring).

Tedebrand, Lars-Göran. 1976. "Remigration from America to Sweden." In *From Sweden to America: A History of Emigration,* edited by Harold Runblom and Hans Norman, 201–27.

Thistlethwaite, Frank. 1991. "Migration from Europe Overseas in the Nineteenth and Twentieth Centuries." In *A Century of European Migration, 1830–1930,* edited by Rudolph Vecoli and Suzanne M. Sinke, 17–57.

Vecoli, Rudolph. 1964." Contadini in Chicago: A Critique of *The Uprooted.*" *Journal of American History* (December).

Vecoli, Rudolph J. 1985. "Return to the Melting Pot: Ethnicity in the United States in the Eighties." *Journal of American Ethnic History.* Vol. 5. 7–20.

Vincent, Joan. 1974. "The Structuring of Ethnicity." *Human Organization* 33:375–79.

Wallerstein, Emanuel. 1973. "The Two Modes of Ethnic Consciousness: Soviet Central Asia in Transition?" In *The Nationality Question in Soviet Central Asia,* edited by Edward Allworth. New York: Praeger.

Ward, David. 1980. "Immigration: Settlement Patterns and Spatial Distribution." In *Harvard Encyclopedia of American Ethnic Groups,* edited by Stephan Thernstrom, 496–598.

Weinberg, Daniel E. 1977. "Ethnic Identity in Industrial Cleveland: The Hungarians 1900–1920." *Ohio History* 86 (3), 171–186.

Williams, Emilio. 1970. "Peasantry in the City: Cultural Persistence and Change in Historical Perspective. A European Case Study." *American Anthropologist* 72:528–43.

HUNGARIAN SECTION

Books, pamphlets

Almási, Mihály. 1984. *A Clevelandi Magyar Baptista Misszió 85 Éves Története* (The eighty-five year history of the Cleveland Hungarian Baptist Mission). Cleveland.

Balassa, Iván. 1975. *Lápok, Falvak, Emberek. Bodrogköz* (Marshes, Villages, People. Bodrogköz). Budapest.

Balch, Emily Greene. 1910. *Our Slavic Fellow Citizens.* New York: Charities Publications Committee.

Baráth, Tibor. 1974. *A külföldi magyarság ideológiája* (The ideology of Hungarians abroad) Montreal: Történetpolitikai Tanulmányok.

Bardin, H. 1959. *The Hungarians in Bridgeport.* Bridgeport, CT: University of Bridgeport.

Barth, Fredrik. 1969. *Ethnic Groups and Boundaries: The Social Organization of Cultural Difference.* Results of a symposium held at the University of Bergen, February 1967. London: Allen & Unwin.

Barton, Josef J. 1975. *Peasants and Strangers: Italians, Rumanians and Slovaks in an American City, 1890–1950.* Cambridge, MA: Harvard University Press.

Béládi, Miklós, Pomogáts Béla, and Rónay László, eds. 1986. *A Nyugati Magyar Irodalom 1945 után* (Hungarian literature in the Western countries after 1945). Budapest: Gondolat Kiadó.

Berend, T. Iván, and György Ránki. 1974. *Hungary: A Century of Economic Development.* Newton Abbot, Devon: David & Charles.

Berend, T. Iván, and György Ránki. 1982. *The European Periphery and Industrialization.* Cambridge: Cambridge University Press.

Bielik, Frantisek, and Elo Rákos. 1969. *Slovenske vystahovalectvo.* Dokumentary I. Bratislava.

Borbándi, Gyula, ed. 1967 *Nyugati magyar tanulmányok antológiája* (Anthology of studies by Hungarians in the West). Bern: European Protestant Hungarian Free University.

Borbándi, Gyula. 1985. *A Magyar Emigráció Életrajza—1945–1983* (The biography of the emigration from Hungary, 1945–1983). Bern: Az Europai Protestáns Magyar Szabadegyetem. Second edition, 2 vols. Budapest: Europa, 1989.

Borbándi, Gyula, ed. 1986. *Nyugati magyar esszéírók antológiája.* (Anthology of Hungarian essay-writers in the West). Bern: European Protestant Hungarian Free University.

Brody, David. 1960. *Steelworkers in America: The Nonunion Era.* Cambridge, MA: Russell and Russell.

Dégh, Linda. 1952. *A szabadságharc népköltészete* (The folk poetry of the war of independence). Budapest: Akadémiai Kiadó.

Dreisziger, N. F., et al. 1982. *Struggle and Hope: The Hungarian Canadian Experience.* Toronto: McClelland and Stewart.

Eröss, Ferenc. 1961. *Magyar "munkásvezérek" Nyugaton* (Hungarian "labor leaders" in the Western countries). Budapest.

Farkas, Gábor. 1969. *Adatok Bodony község történetéhez* (Data concerning the history of Bodony village). Gyöngyös: Bodony Közég Tanacsa.

Fejős, Zoltán. 1993. *A chicagoi magyarok két nemzedéke 1890–1940* (Two generations of Hungarians in Chicago, 1890–1940). Budapest: Közép-Európa Intézet, 299.

Fél, Edit, and Tamás Hofer. 1969. *Proper Peasants: Traditional Life in a Hungarian Village.* Chicago: Aldine Publishing Company.

Fellner Frigyes. 1908. *A nemzetközi fizetési mérleg és alakulása Magyarországon.* (The international balance of payment and its develoent in Hungary) Budapest: Politzer.

Ferenczi, Imre, and F. Walter Willcox, eds. 1929, 1931. *International Migrations.* 2 vols. New York: National Bureau of Economic Research. Second edition, New York, 1969.

Fishman, Joshua A. 1966. *Hungarian Language Maintenance in the United States.* Uralic and Altaic Series, vol. 62. Bloomington: Indiana University Press.

Gergely, Ernő Joseph. 1947. *Hungarian Drama in New York: American Adaptation, 1908–1940.* Philadelphia: University of Pennsylvania Press.

Glatz, Ferenc, ed. 1990. *Ethnicity and Society in Hungary.* Budapest: Történettudományi Intézet.

Glettler, Monika. 1980. *Pittsburg-Wien-Budapest. Programm und Praxis der Nationalitätenpolitik bei der Auswanderung der ungarischen Slowaken nach Amerika um 1900.* Vienna: Verlag der österreichischen Akademie.

Gracza, Rezső, and Margaret Gracza. 1969. *The Hungarians in America.* Minneapolis, MN: Lerner.

Gunst, Peter, and Tamás Hoffmann, eds. 1976. *A magyar mezőgazdaság a 19.- 20.században 1849–1949* (Hungarian agriculture in the nineteenth and twentieth centuries). Budapest.

Győrffy, István. 1939. *Néphagyomány és nemzeti művelődés* (Folk tradition and national education). Budapest.

Hadházy, Pál. 1986. *Kivándorlás Turistvándi községböl* (Emigration from Turistvándi village). In *Néprajzi Dolgozatok Turistvándiból.* Nyiregyháza, 3–41.

Hanák, Péter, and Zoltán Szász. 1969. *Die Nationale Frage in der Österreichischen Monarchie, 1900–1918.* Budapest: Akadémiai Kiadó.

Hauk-Abonyi, Malvina, and James A. Anderson. 1977. *Hungarians of Detroit.* Peopling of Michigan Series, Ethnic Studies Division. Detroit, MI: Wayne State University.

Hennyei, Gusztáv. 1992. *Magyarország sorsa Kelet és Nyugat Között* (The lot of Hungary between East and West). Budapest: Europa-Historia.

Hirnyák, John M. 1975. *Birmingham: Toledo's Hungarian Communities.* Toledo, OH.

Hofer, Tamás, and Edit Fél. 1979. *Hungarian Folk Art.* Oxford: Oxford University Press.

Illyés, Gyula. 1937. *A puszták népe* (People of the plains). Budapest: Nyugat.

Janos, Andrew. 1982. *The Politics of Backwardness in Hungary, 1825–1945.* Princeton, NJ: Princeton University Press.

Kardos, László. 1969. *Egyház és vallásos élet egy mai faluban: Bakonycsernye* (The church and religious life in a contemporary village, Bakonycsernye). Budapest: Kossuth Kiado.

Károlyi, Mihály. 1977. *Hit illúziók nélkül* (Faith without illusions). Budapest.

Katus, László. 1970. *Economic Growth in Hungary during the Age of Dualism, 1867–1913.* Studa Historica Budapest: Akadémiai Kiadó..

Kecskeméti, Paul. 1961. *Unexpected Revolution.* Stanford, CA: Stanford University Press.

Kemenes, Gálfi László, ed. 1980. *Nyugati Magyar Költök Antológiája* (Anthology of Hungarian poets in the West). Bern: Európai Protestáns Magyar Szabadegyetem.

Komjáthy, Aladár. 1984. *A kitántorgott egyház* (The staggered-out church). Budapest: A Református Zsinat Sajtóosztálya (The press department of the Synod Reformed Church).

Kósa, János. 1957. *Land of Choice: The Hungarians in Canada.* Toronto: University of Toronto Press.

Kosáry, Dominic G. 1971. *A History of Hungary.* New York: Arno Press.

Kovács, Ilona, ed. 1990. *Search for American Values: Contribution of Hungarian-Americans to American Values.* Budapest: Országos Széchényi Könyvtár.

Kovacsics, József, ed. 1963. *Magyarország Történeti Demográfiája* (The historical demography of Hungary). Budapest: Közgazdasági Könyvkiadó.

Könnyü, Leslie. 1962. *A History of American Hungarian Literature.* St. Louis: Cooperative of American Hungarian Writers.

Kraljuk, Frances. 1978. *Croatian Migration to and from the United States, 1900–1914.* Palo Alto, CA: Ragusan Press.

Kulisher, Eugene M. 1948. Europe on the Move. War and Population Changes, 1917–1947. New York: Columbia University Press.

Lackó, Miklós. 1968. *A magyar munkásosztály fejlödésének fő vonásai a tőkés korszakban* (Main characteristics of the development of the Hungarian working class in the capitalist period). Budapest: Kossuth.

Lengyel, Emil. 1948. *Americans from Hungary.* Philadelphia: J. B. Lippincott Co.

Lukacs, John. 1986. *Immigration and Migration: A Historical Perspective.* Monterey, VA: American Immigration Control Foundation.

Makár, János. 1969. *The Story of an Immigrant Group in Franklin, New Jersey. Including a Collection of Hungarian Folk Songs Sung in America.* Franklin, NJ.

Mayer, Maria. 1977. *Kárpátukrán (ruszin) politikai és társadalmi törekvések, 1860–1910* (Transkarpathian-Ukrainian [Ruthenian] political and social endeavors). Budapest: Akadémiai Kiadó.

Montgomery, David. 1979. *Worker Control in America: Studies in the History of Work, Technology and Labor Struggles.* Cambridge: Cambridge University Press.

Montgomery, J. F. 1947. *Hungary, the Unwilling Satellite.* New York: Devin Adair, reprinted by Vista Books, Morristown, NJ, 1993.

Morawska, Ewa. 1985. *For Bread and Butter: The Life-World of East Central Europeans in Johnstown, Pennsylvania, 1880–1940.* Cambridge: Cambridge University Press.

Morvay, Judit. 1965. *Asszonyok a nagy családban* (Women in the big family). Budapest.

Nagy, Kázmér. 1974. *Elveszett Alkotmány* (Lost constitution). Munich. Second edition, Budapest: Gondolat, 1984.

Pap, Michael E. 1973. *Hungarian Communities in Cleveland.* In *Ethnic Communities of Cleveland: A Reference Work.* Cleveland: Institute for Soviet and East European Studies, John Carroll University.

Papp, Susan. 1981. *Hungarian Americans and their Communities of Cleveland.* Cleveland: Cleveland Ethnic Heritage Studies, Cleveland State University, 155.

Patrias, Carmela. 1994. *Patriots and Proletarians: Politicizing Hungarian Immigrants in Interwar Canada.* Montreal: McGill-Queen's University Press.

Perlman, Róbert. 1991. *Bridging Three Worlds, Hungarian-Jewish Americans, 1848–1914. Settlement Pattern of Hungarian Jews.* Amherst: University of Massachusetts Press.

Polányi, Imre. 1987. *A szlovák társadalom és polgári nemzeti mozgalom a századfordulón, 1895–1905* (The Slovak society and the bourgeois national movement at the turn of the century, 1895–1905). Budapest: Akadémiai Kiadó.

Postrineau, Abel. 1978. *Hegyvidék és sikvidék a XVIII. században* (Mountain regions and plains in the eighteenth century). In *Egyetemes Történeti Tanulmányok 12,* Debrecen, 125–38.

Puskás, Julianna. 1982. *Kivándorló magyarok az Egyesült Allamokban, 1880–1940* (Emigrant Hungarians in the United States). Budapest: Akadémiai Kiadó.

Puskás, Julianna. 1982. *From Hungary to the United States, 1880–1914.* Studia Historica 184. Budapest: Akadémiai Kiadó.

Puskás, Julianna, ed. 1990. *Overseas Migration from East-Central and Southeastern Europe, 1880–1940.* Studia Historica. Budapest: Akadémiai Kiadó.

Rácz, István. 1980. *A paraszti migráció és politikai megítélése Magyarországon, 1849–1914* (Peasant migration and its political assessment in Hungary, 1849–1914). Budapest: Akadémiai Kiadó.

Salay, David L., ed. 1984. *Hard Coal, Hard Times: Ethnicity and Labor in the Anthracite Region.* Scranton, PA: Anthracite Museum Press.

Sári Gál Imre. 1966. *Az Amerikai Debrecen* (The American Debrecen). Toronto: Patria Publishing Co.

Sisa, Stephen. 1987. *America's Amazing Hungarians.* Huddleston, VA: published by the author.

Stark, Tamás. 1989. *Magyarország második világháborús embervesztesége* (Hungary's population loss in World War II). Budapest: MTA Történettudományi Intézet.

Szabó, István, ed. 1965. *A parasztság Magyarországon a kapitalizmus korában 1848–1914* (The peasantry in Hungary during the time of capitalism, 1848–1914). 2 vols. Budapest: Akadémiai Kiadó.

Szántó, Miklós. 1984. *Magyarok Amerikában* (Hungarans in America). Budapest: Kossuth Kiadó.

Szászi, Ferenc. 1972. *Az Amerikába irányuló kivándorlás Szabolcs megyéböl az elsö világháborúig* (Emigration to America from Szabolcs County to World War I). Nyiregyháza. Bessenyei György Kiado.

Szászi, Ferenc. 1982. *Adatok a magyarországi zsidóság kivándorlásához, különös tekintettel Szabolcs megyére, 1919–1941* (Data relating to the emigration of Jews from Hungary, with particular regard to Szabolcs County). Magyar Történeti Tanulmányok 15:69–89.

Szászi, Ferenc. 1982. *Kivándorlás Szabolcsmegyéböl a két világháború között, 1920–1941* (Emigration from Szabolcs County). Nyiregyháza.

Tárkány Szücs, Ernö. 1981. *Magyar jogi népszokások* (Hungarian popular customs in the law). Budapest: Gondolat Kiadó.

Török, István. 1970. *Katolikus Magyarok Észak-Amerikában (Catholic Hungarians in North America),* Youngstown, OH: Katolikus Magyarok Vasárnapja.

Vardy, Steven Béla. 1985. *The Hungarian-Americans.* Boston: Twayne Publishers.

Vardy, Steven Béla. 1989. *The Centennial History of the William Penn Association: One Hundred Years of a Hungarian Fraternal Association in America.* Pittsburgh, PA: The William Penn Association.

Vasváry, Ödön. 1988. *Magyar-Amerika* (Magyar America). Szeged: Somogyi Könyvtár.

Voigt, Vilmos. 1987. "Az amerikai magyar folklór kutatása" (Research in the Hungarian-American folklore). In *Modern Magyar Folklorisztikai Tanulmányok,* Debrecen, 113–23.

Völgyes, I., ed. 1980. *The Peasantry of Eastern Europe.* 2 vols. New York: Pergamon.

Weinstock, S. Alexander. 1969. *Acculturation and occupation: A Study of the 1956 Hungarian Refugees in the U.S.* The Hague: Martinus Nijhoff.

Studies, Articles

Alnas, Ion. 1970. "Industrialization and Migration of the Transylvanian Peasantry at the End of the Nineteenth Century and the Beginning of the Twentieth Century." *East European Quarterly* (January 1970): 504–5.

Bakó, Elemér. 1961. "Hungarian Dialectology in the USA." *The Hungarian Quarterly* 4:48.

Ball, John. 1958. "The American Government and the Hungarian Refugees. Contemporary Issues," *AA Magazine for Democracy*, 8:549–557.

Balla, Bálint. 1971. "Az 1956-os kivándorlások elözményei a magyar kivándorlás-történelemben. Egy szociológiai kutatómunkáról." (The precedents of the 1956 emigrations in Hungarian emigration history. A sociologist research work.) in *Együtt Európában* (Together in Europe), edited by Szépfalusi István. Conference 1965. Vienna: Utitárs. 11.26.

Balogh, István. 1965. "A paraszti müvelödés" (Peasant Culture). In *A parasztság Magyarországon a kapitalizmus korában 1848–1914,* edited by István Szabó, 2: 487–550.

Balogh, István. 1965. "A paraszti gazdálkodás és termelési technika" (Peasant economy and production technique). Ibid., 1: 349–93.

Bárány, George. 1967. "The Magyars." In *The Immigrants' Influence on Wilson's Peace Policies,* edited by Joseph P. O'Grady, 140–72.

Barton, Josef J. 1978. "Eastern and Southern Europeans." In *Ethnic Leadership in America,* edited by John Higham, 150–75. Baltimore: Johns Hopkins University Press.

Benkart, Paula K. 1980. "Hungarians." In *Harvard Encyclopedia of American Ethnic Groups,* edited by Stephan Thernstrom, 462–71.

Benkart, Paula K. 1983. "The Hungarian Government, the American Hungarian Churches and Immigrant Ties to the Homeland." *Church History* 52 (September): 312–21.

Benke, Zsófia. 1985. "Documents in the Hungarian National Archives relating to United States History." In *Guide to the Study of United States History outside the U.S., 1945–1980,* vol. 2, 5 ed., 546–62. White Plains: Lewis Hanke.

Bidia, Karel D. 1982. "Hunkies: Stereotyping the Slavic Immigrant, 1890–1920." *Journal of American Ethnic History* 2: 18–19.

Bodnár, John. 1980. "Immigration, Kinship and the Rise of Working Class Realism in Industrial America." *Journal of Social History.*

Böty, Paul, ed. 1981. *Hungarian Ethnic Heritage Study of Pittsburgh.* Pittsburgh, PA: Hungarian Ethnic Heritage Study Group.

Böty, Paul. 1990. "First Generation Values in Different Waves of Hungarian Immigration to the United States." In *Search for American Values,* edited by Ilona Kovács, 63–9.

Böröcz, József. 1987. "Name Language Shift in Árpádhon, Louisiana: A Content Analysis of Tombstone Inscriptions." *Hungarian Studies* 1–2:227–41.

Boros-Kazai, Mary. 1981. "The Emigration Problem and Hungary's Lawmakers, 1880–1910." *Hungarian Studies Review* 8(1): 25–44.

Csicsery-Rónai, György. 1954. Russian Cultural Penetration in Hungary, Washington, DC, 1950; *Számüzöttek Naptára* (Calendar of the Exiles), Washington, D.C.

Dégh, Linda. 1972. "Two Hungarian-American Stereotypes." *New York Folklore Quarterly* 28:3–14.

Dégh, Linda. 1980. "The Ethnicity of Hungarian Americans." In *Congressus Quantus Internationalis* Tenno Ugristorum. Turku, 20–27. VIII. Pass. N. Red. Osma Ikola, 225–290.

Dégh, Linda, and Andrew Vázsonyi. 1969. "Field Report on Hungarian Ethnic and Language Research in the Calumet Region," section 1. In *The Ethnic Research Survey of Northwest Indiana,* edited by Richard M. Dorson, 66–67.

Dreisziger, N. F. 1989. "Bridges to the West: The Horthy Regime's Reinsurance Policies in 1941." *War and Society* 7, no. 1 (May 1989): 1–23.

Farkas, Zoltán J. 1971. *Hungarian City and County Names in the United States.* Vol. 9, 141–3.

Fassman, Heinz. 1994. "Emigration, immigration and internal migration in the Austro-Hungarian Monarchy in 1910." In *Roots of the Transplanted,* edited by Dirk Hoerder and Inge Blank, 253–308.

Fejös, Zoltán. 1980. *Kivándorlás Amerikába a Zemplén középső vidékéröl. Vázlat a századeleji emigráció tanulmányozásának néprajzi kérdéseihez* (Emigration to America from the Central Part of Zemplén. Outline for the ethnographic study of emigration for economic reasons during the early part of the century). Miskolc.

Fejös, Zoltán. 1987. "Magyar Ruha," "Szüreti Bál" és az amerikai-magyar etnikus kultúra néhány kérdése ("Hungarian Dress," "Vintage Ball," and some questions concerning Hungarian ethnic culture). Magyarságkutatás (Research on Hungarianhood). Budapest: A Magyarságkutató Csoport Évkönyve, 267–82.

Frank, Tibor. 1992." Ellis Island követei. Az osztrák-magyar kivándorlás titkos amerikai megfigyelése, 1906–1907" (Emissaries of Ellis Island. Secret U.S. Government Surveillance of Ausztro-Hungarian Immigration, 1906–1907). *Valóság,* 35: 7.

Frank, Tibor. 1994. "Amerikai 'Uj Bevándorlók' antropometriai vizsgálata, 1908–1911" (Anthropometric study of the "new immigrants" in America, 1908–1911). *Antropometriai Közlemények* 36 (1994): 69–77.

Gellén, J. 1982. "The Geographical Origins of Two Hungarian Immigrant Parishes in Toledo, Ohio." *Angol Filológiai Tanulmányok* 15:35–49.

Gunda, Béla. 1970. "America in Hungarian Folk Tradition." *Journal of American Folklore* 88:406–16.

Gunda, Béla. 1982. "The Ethno-Sociological Structure of the Hungarian Extended Family." *Journal of Family History* 7 (Spring): 40–51.

Hajdu, Tibor. 1973. "A két világháború közötti magyar történelem Amerikai forrásaiból" (From the American sources of inter-war Hungarian history). *Valóság* 16 (10): 84–87.

Hammerton, Elizabeth, and David Cannadine. 1981. "Conflict and Consensus on a Ceremonial Occasion: The Diamond Jubilee in Cambridge in 1897." *Historical Journal* 24:111–46.

Hanák, Péter. 1974. "Polgárosodás és assziniláció Magyarországon a 19. században" (Assimilation and the ascendancy of the bourgeoisie in Hungary in the nineteenth century). *Történelmi Szemle* 4:513–36.

Hegedüs, István. 1979–80. "Maintaining Hungarian in Canada." *Polyphony: The Bulletin of the Multicultural History Society of Ontario* 2: 2–3, 76–80.

Hofer, Tamás. 1968. "Anthropologists and Native Ethnographers in Central-European Villages: Comparative Notes on the Professional Personality of Two Disciplines." *Current Anthropology* 9:311–15.

Hofer, Tamás. 1980. "The Creation of Ethnic Symbols from the Elements of Peasant Culture." In *Ethnic Diversity and Conflict in Eastern Europe,* edited by Peter F. Sugar. Santa Barbara, CA: ABC Clio.

Hofer, Tamás. 1988. "A népi kultura jelentésváltozásai a századfordulón" (Variations of the concept of folk culture around the turn of the century). *Valóság* 31 (December): 42–48.

Horváth, László. 1992. "Az Egyesült bllamokba Irányuló Kivándorlás Kál Községböl az elsö Világháború Elött" (Emigration to the United States from Kál village before World War I). Hevesmegyei Kivándorlás I (Emigration from Heves County I). In *Agora* 27–28:257–73.

Horváth, László. 1993. "Kivándorlás az Egyesült bllamokba Bodonyból 1914–ig" (Emigration from Bodony to the United States until 1914). Hevesmegyei Kivándorlás II (Emigration from Heves County II). In *Mátrai Tanulmányok*, 56–88. Gyöngyös: A Múzeum.

Huseby, Éva Veronika. 1991. "A bevándorló nõk mint a kontinuitás fenntartói Delray amerikai magyar közösségében" (The immigrant women as the preservers of continuity in the Hungarian community in Delray). *Ethnographia*, nos. 3–4: 279–309.

Janda, Izabella Horváth. 1977. "English Hungarian and Hungarian English Language Interference Phenomena in Chicago." In *The Second Lacus Form*, edited by Peter Reich, 590–5. Columbia, SC: Hornbeam Press.

Jelinek, Yeshayahu. 1972. "Self-Identification of First Generation Hungarian Jewish Immigrants." *American Jewish Historical Quarterly* 61 (March): 214–21.

Jemnitz, Janos. 1963. "The Relations of Hungarian Americans Labor Movement as revealed in the Correspondence of Ervin Szabó." *Acta Historica* 9, no. 1–2:179–214.

Katona, Imre. 1965. "Atmeneti bérmunka formák" (Transitional types of wage labor). In *A parasztság Magyarországon a kapitalizmus korában 1848–1914*, edited by István Szabó, 2:382–406.

Katus, László. 1966. "Über die wirtschaftlichen und gesellschaftlichen Grundlagen der Nationalitätenfrage in Ungarn vor dem ersten Weltkrieg." In *Die Nationale Frage in der Österreichischen Monarchie, 1900–1918*, edited by Peter Hanák and Zoltán Szász. Budapest: Akadémiai Kiadó.

Kerek, Andrew. 1978. "Hungarian Language Research in North America: Themes and Directions." *Canadian-American Review of Hungarian Studies* 5 (2):63–72.

Kertész, Stephen D. 1978. "Peace Making in the Dark Side of the Moon: Hungary 1943–1947." *The Review of Politics* 40.

Kirshner, Paul, and Anne R. Kaplan. 1981. "The Hungarians." In *They Chose Minnesota*, edited by June Holmquist, 423–39. St. Paul: Minnesota Historical Society Press.

Kolossa, Tibor. 1970. "The Social Structure of the Peasant Class in Austro-Hungary: Statistical Sources and Methods." *East European Quarterly* (January): 420–37.

Könnyű, Leslie. 1963. "Eagles of Two Continents." *The American Hungarian Review*, St. Louis, MO.

Könnyű, Leslie. 1967. "Hungarians in the U.S.A.: An Immigration Study." *The American Hungarian Review*, St. Louis, MO.

Kontra, Miklós. 1981. "Language Usage: An Interview with a Hungarian." *American Hungarian Studies Review* 8:99–118.

Kontra, Miklós. 1985. "Hungarian-American Bilingualism: A Bibliographic Essay." *Hungarian Studies* 1:257–82.

Kontra, Miklós, and Gregory L. Lehler. 1981. "Ethnic Designations used by Hungarian-Americans in South Bend, Indiana." *Ural-Altaische Jahrbücher* 53:105–11.

Korányi, E. K., A. Kerenyi, and G. J. Sarwer-Foner. 1958. "On Adaptive Difficulties of Some Hungarian Immigrants." *Medical Services Journal* (Canada) 14 (June): 383–405.

Kósa, John. 1956. "Hungarian Society in the Time of the Regency" *Journal of Central European Affairs*, 16.

Kósa, János. 1957. "A Century of Hungarian Emigration, 1850–1950." *American Slavic and East European Review* 16:501–14.

Kovács, Alajos. 1909. "A kivándorlás statisztikai okai" (The statistical reasons of emigration). *Közgazdasági Szemle* (July): 445–54.

Kovács, Martin L. 1979. "Aspects of Hungarian Peasant Emigration from pre-1914 Hungary." In *The Peasantry of Eastern Europe*, edited by Ivan Völgyes. 2 vols. 1: 119–32. New York: Pergamon Press.

Kriza, Ildikó. 1994. "Ethnic Identity and National Consciousness of the Hungarian Peasantry during the Age of Dualism." In *Roots of the Transplanted*, edited by Dirk Hoerder and Inge Blank, vol. 1.

Kunz, Egon. F. 1971. "Political Events: 'At Home' and the Concept of Catharsis. Naturalization among Refugees". *International Migration* IX, no. 1–12. 55–67.

Leopold, Lajos. 1908. A visszavándorlók mérlege (The balance of the remigrants). *Huszadik Század* I: 143–44.

Marácz, László. 1995. "Western Images and Stereotypes of Hungarians" in *Vampires Unstaked: National Images, Stereotypes and Myths in East Central Europe*, edited by Gerrits and Adler. Amsterdam: Koninklije Nederlandse Akademie van Wetenschappen, 25–40.

Markovitz, Arthur A. 1973. "Humanitarianism Versus Restrictionism: The United States and the Hungarian Refugees." *International Migration Review* 7: 46–59.

Molnár, August J. 1977. "Hungarian Pioneers and Immigrants in New Jersey." In *The New Jersey Ethnic Experience*, edited by Barbara Cunningham, 249–66. Union City, NJ: W. H. Wise.

Morawska, Ewa. 1991. "Return Migrations: Theoretical and Research Agenda." In *A Century of European Migration, 1830–1930*, edited by Rudolph Vecoli and Suzanne M. Sinke, 277–92.

Morawska, Ewa. 1992. "In Defense of the Assimilation Model." *Journal of American Ethnic History*, 76–87.

Nagy, B. 1993. "The Hungarian Refugee Law." In *Refugees in Hungary*, edited by H. Adelman, E. Sik, and G. Tessényi. Toronto: York Lane Publishers.

Niedermüller, Péter. 1989. "National culture symbols and reality." *Ethnologia Europaea* 19 (1): 47–56.

Niedermüller, Péter. 1990. "An anthropological approach in the study of immigrants. Overseas migration from East-Central and Southeastern Europe, 1880–1940." In *Overseas migration*, edited by Julianna Puskás. Budapest: Studia Historica, 191.

Orosz, István. 1972. "A differenciálódás és kisajátítás" (Differentiation and expropriation), in *A parasztság Magyarországon a kapitalizmus korában 1848–1914*, edited by István Szabó, 2:9–107.

Papp, Susan. 1987. "Hungarians." In *The Encyclopedia of Cleveland History*, by David D. van Tassel and John J. Grabowski.

Pelényi, John. 1964. "The Secret Plan for Hungarian Government in the West at the Outbreak of World War II." *Journal of Modern History* 36:170–77.

Pentzell, Raymond J. 1977. "A Hungarian Christmas Mummers' Play in Toledo, Ohio." *Education Theater Journal* 29: 179–98.

Puskás, Julianna. 1975. *Emigration from Hungary to the United States before 1914.* Budapest: Studia Historica Academiae Scientiarum, 65–105.

Puskás, Julianna. 1985. "The Process of Overseas Migration from East Central Europe- Its Periods, Cycles and Characteristics. A Comparative Study." In *Emigration from Northern, Central and Southern Europe: Theoretical and Methodological Principles of Research.* International symposium, Uniwersytet Jagellonski, Krakow, November 1981.

Puskás, Julianna. 1986. "Hungarian Migration Patterns, 1880–1930: From Macroanalysis to Microanalysis." In *Migration Across Time and Nations,* edited by Ira Glazier and Luigi De Rosa, 231–354

Puskás, Julianna. 1988. "Hungarian Immigrants and Socialism, 1890–1914." In *In the Shadow of the Statue of Liberty,* edited by M. Debouzy, 139–51.

Puskás, Julianna. 1991. "Hungarian Overseas Migration: A Microanalysis." In *A Century of European Migration, 1830–1930,* edited by Rudolph Vecoli and Suzanne M. Sinke, 221–42.

Puskás, Julianna. 1993. "Hungarian Images of America: The Sirens' Song of Tinkling Dollars." In *Distant Magnets: Expectations and Realities in the Immigrant Experience, 1840–1930,* edited by Dirk Hoerder and Horst Rössler, 180–98.

Puskás, Julianna, Inge Blank, Horst Rössler, and Cvetka Knapic-Khren. 1994. "Rural and Artisan Protest in Western, East Central and Southeastern Europe from the Early 19th Century to World War I." In *Roots of the Transplanted,* edited by Dirk Hoerder and Inge Blank.

Rácz, István. 1965. "Parasztok elvándorlása a faluról" (Migration of peasants from the villages). In *A parasztság Magyarországon a kapitalizmus korában 1848–1914,* edited by István Szabó, 433–77.

Roucek, J. S. 1945. "Hungarians in America." In *One America,* edited by F. J. Brown and J. S. Roucek. New York: Prentice Hall.

Sárközi, Zoltán. 1965. "A summások" (The seasonal workers). In *A parasztság Magyarországon a kapitalizmus korában 1848–1914,* edited by István Szabó, 2:321–71.

Scott, Eddie. 1967. "The Changing Patterns of Landownership in Hungary, 1867–1914." *Economic History Review,* 2d ser., 20:293–310

Simova, Danica, Eva Fordinalova, and Anna Stvrtecka. 1994. "From Husband's Household to Natinal Activity: The Ambivalent Position of Slovak Women." *Roots of the Transplanted,* edited by Dirk Hoerder and Inge Blank, 1:341–58.

Sipos, Péter. 1994. "Migration, Labor Movement and Workers' Culture in Budapest, 1867–1914." In Hoerder (1994), 155.

Soskin, Philip. 1967. "The Adjustment of Hungarian Refugees in New York." *The International Migration Review* 2:40–46.

Szabad, György. 1965. "A hitelviszonyok" (The conditions of credit). In *A parasztság Magyarországon a kapitalizmus korában 1848–1914,* edited by István Szabó, 2:184–217.

Szász, Zoltán. 1983. "Az Amerikai Magyar Szövetség nemzetközi tevé kenysége" (The international activities of the American-Hungarian Federation) in *Emlékkönyv az Amerikai Magyar Szövetség 80. Évfordulójára.* (Memorial Book for the 80th Anniversary of the American Hungarian Federation), edited by Elemér Bakó. Washington, DC.: Amerikai Magyar Szövetség. (1988) Washington, DC: 66–78.

Szuch, Yolanda Danyi. 1987. "A Church's Response to the Preservation of Ethnic Heritage: Religious Traditions at St. Stephen's Church." In *The Preservation of Ethnic Heritage: An Examination of the Birmingham Experience,* edited by John Ahern, 60–77.

Tajták, Ladislav. 1978. "Slovak emigration and migration in the years 1900–1914." *Studia Historica Slovacia* 10:46–80.

Tajták, Ladislav. 1990. "Slovak Emigration, Its Causes And Consequences." In *Overseas Migration From East-Central And South-Eastern Europe, 1880–1940,* edited by Julianna Puskás, Studia Historica. Budapest: Akadémiai Kiadó.

Thirring, Gusztáv. 1931. "Hungarian Migration of Modern Times." In *International Migrations,* edited by Imre Ferenczi and F. Walter Willcox, 2:411–39.

Thirring, Lajos. 1963. "Magyarország népessége, 1869–1949" (The population of Hungary, 1869–1949). In *Magyarország Történeti Demográfiája* (The historical demography of Hungary), edited by József Kovacsics. Budapest: Közgazdasagi Könyvkiadó.

Vardy, Steven Béla. 1982. "Hungarians in America's Ethnic Politics." In *America's Ethnic Politics,* edited by Roucek and Eisenberg. Westport, CT.

Vardy, Steven Béla and Agnes Huszár Vardy. 1985. "Historical, Literary, Linguistic and Ethnographic Research on Hungarian Americans." *Hungarian Studies* 1:77–122.

Várdy, Steven Béla and Ágnes Huszár Várdy. 1989. *The Austro-Hungarian Mind at Home and Abroad.* New York: East European Monograph, Boulder.

Varga, István. 1965. "A Közterhek" (General and proportionate tax-sharing). In *A parasztság Magyarországon a kapitalizmus korában 1848–1914,* edited by István Szabó, 2:164.

Vassady, Béla, Jr. 1984. "Themes from Immigrant Fraternal Life: The Early Decades of the Hazleton-based Hungarian Verhovay Sick Benefit Association." In *Hard Coal, Hard Times: Ethnicity and Labor in the Anthracite Region,* edited by David L. Salay, Scranton, PA, 17–33.

Vassady, Béla, Jr. 1989. "The 'Homeland Cause' as Stimulant in Ethnic Unity: The Hungarian-American Response to Károlyi's 1914 American Tour." *Journal of American Ethnic History* 2:39–61.

Vassady, Béla, Jr. 1990. "Mixed Ethnic Identities among Immigrant Clergy from Multiethnic Hungary: The Slovak-Magyar Case, 1885–1903." In *The Ethnic Enigma: The Salience of Ethnicity for European-Origin Groups,* edited by Peter Kivisto, Philadelphia: Balch Institute Press, 47–66.

Vázsonyi, Endre. 1978. "The Cicisbeo and the Magnificent Cuckold: Boarding House Life and Lore in Immigrant Communities." *Journal of American Folklore* 91:641–56.

Voigt, Vilmos. 1981. "Etnikus szimbolumok létrehozása a folklórban" (Creating ethnic symbols in folklore). In *A Folklórizmus Fogalma és Jelenségei. Előadások* (The concept and phenomena of folklorism. Lectures), edited by Kincsö Verebélyi, 2:91–116.

Unpublished Dissertations, Theses, and Essays.

Balogh, J. H. 1945. "An Analysis of Cultural Organizations of Hungarian-Americans in Pittsburgh and Allegheny County." Ph.D. diss., University of Pittsburgh.

Benkart, Paula. 1973. "E Pluribus Unum: Ethnic Identity in a Religiously and Geographically Diverse Magyar Community." Unpublished manuscript at the Balch Institute.

Benkart, Paula. 1973. "The Hungarian Government, the American Magyar Churches and Immigrant Nationalities." A paper presented to the Hopkins-Harwichport Seminar in American Religious History. August 23–25.

Benkart, Paula K. 1975. "Religion, Family and Community amongst Hungarians Migrating to American Cities, 1880–1930." Ph.D. diss., Johns Hopkins University.

Beynon, Endman D. 1935. "Occupational Adjustment of Hungarian Immigrants in American Urban Communities." Ph.D. diss., University of Michigan.

Bodó Ibolya. "Magyar nyelvű szinjátszás az Egyesült Államokban 1870–1970." (Hungarian language dramatic art in the U.S.) Unpublished paper. Budapest: The National Széchenyi Library. Manuscripts.

Boros, Alexander. 1959. "Their New World: A Comprehensive Study of the Assimilation of Four Waves of Hungarian Immigration" (Honors dissertation) Kent State University.

Butosi, John. 1961. "Church Membership Performance of Three Generations in the Hungarian Reformed Churches of Allegheny County." Ph.D. diss., University of Pittsburgh.

Frank, Tibor. 1995. "From Immigrant Laborers to Émigré Professionals." Studies in the Social History of Hungarian-American Migrations, Inaugural Papers. Budapest: Loránd Eötvös University. Manuscripts.

Győry, György. 1979. "Nyelvi interferencia az Egyesült bllamokbeli magyar sjtóban" (Language interference in the Hungarian press in the United States). Dissertation, Loránd Eötvös Univeristy.

Hrivnyák, J. M. 1975. Birmingham-Toledo's Hungarian Community. M. A. thesis, University of Toledo, OH.

Hosh, Robert. 1969. "Árpádhon, Louisiana: An Example of Hungarian Immigration Acculturation." Master's thesis, Columbia University.

Kalassay, Louis A. 1939. "The Educational and Religious History of the Hungarian Reformed Church in the United States." Ph.D. diss., University of Pittsburgh.

Kautz, Edwin L. 1946. "The Hungarian Baptist Movement in the United States: A Socio-Historical Study." Master's thesis, University of Pittsburgh.

Komjáthy, Aladár. 1962. "The Hungarian Reformed Church of America: The Effort to Preserve Denominational Heritage." Ph.D. diss., Princeton, NJ Theological Seminary. Microfilm: Ann Arbor, MI, 1974.

Kovács, Ilona. 1993. "Az amerikai könyvtárak magyar gyüjteményeinek szerepe az asz-szimiláció és identitás megőrzése kettős folyamatában" (The American libraries' Hungarian collections' role in the double process of assimilation and the safeguarding of identity). Ph.D. diss.

Kovács, József. 1973. "A társadalmi és nemzeti haladás gondolata az amerikai magyar irodalomban" (The idea of social and national progress in Hungarian-American literature). Candidate's Degree diss., Budapest: MTA archive of manuscripts.

Kresz, Mária. 1981. "Possibilities of Researching Material Folk Art among Hungarians of North America." Paper presented at the First Conference on Hungarian American Folklore, Budapest.

Mócsi, István Imre. 1976. Radicalization and Counterrevolution: Magyar Refugees from the Successor States and their Role in Hungary, 1918–1921. Diss. University of California. Ann Arbor, MI, University Microfilms.

Neiger, Stephen. 1957. "Report on the mental health situation of Hungarian immigrants." Unpublished paper.

Nelson, Agnes Denman. 1956. "A Study of the English Speech of the Hungarians of Albany, Livingstone Parish, Louisiana." Ph.D. diss., Louisiana State University.

Palasics, John. 1976. "History of Cleveland's Hungarian Community." Unpublished paper. One copy is in the author's manuscript collection.

Primes, Agnes. 1940. "The Hungarians in New York: A Study in Immigrant Cultural Influences." Master's thesis, Columbia University, Political Science, faculty.

Ruzsa, Mrs. István. 1967. "Ruzsa István elsö magyar ág.h.e. amerikai magyar lelkész életrajza és működése" (Biography and work of István Ruzsa, first Hungarian minister of the Augustan Confession). Unpublished. Szathmáry Collection, Chicago.

Smith, David Burden. 1965. "The Hungarians in New Brunswick, New Jersey to 1920: A Social Biography." Master's thesis, Rutgers State University.

Szabó, Ferenc. 1990. "Egy millióval kevesebben. Emberveszteségek, népesedési tendenciák és népesedési politika Magyarországon, 1941–1968" (With a million less. Loss of people, tendencies in the population changes and demographic policy in Hungary,) Dissertation, Budapest.

Szamek, Pierre Ervin. n.d. "The Eastern American Dialect of Hungarian: An Analytical Study," Ph.D. diss., Princeton University.

Táborszky, M. A. 1955. "The Hungarian Press in America." Master's thesis, Catholic University of America.

INDEX

AAH (Association of American Hungarians), 276
Abauj County, Hungary, 32, 71, 109, 111, 133–35
Abet, Ádám, 169
Acculturation. *See* Americanization; Assimilation
Activism: social and political, 78
Advertisements, Hungarian establishments, 131–32, 135–36
Ady, Endre (poet), 94; society, 224
Age of Dual Monarchy, 16
Agents, emigration, 89, 93, 107, 131–37, 198
Agriculture, 5–7, 114, 191, 265
Aid, to Hungary, 179, 197
Alien Property Custodian, 182
Alien Registration Act, 254
All Nations Activities Committee, 223
Allegheny, PA, 59
Ambrózy, Baron, 212
"American Action," 161
American Artist Congress, 240
American Communist Party, 220
American Economic Council for American Jews, 224
American Federation of Labor, 98, 101, 129, 146, 183
"American Houses," 83
American Hungarian Aid Society, 143
American Hungarian Federation, 167,176–78, 185–86, 249, 253, 255, 276, 284, 296
American Hungarian Foundation, 296
American Hungarian Reformed Federation, 156, 246
American Hungarian Relief, 255
American Hungarian Singing Society, 296
"American Hungarian Settlements," 111
American Hungarian World (newspaper). See *Amerikai Magyar Világ* (newspaper)
American Letters, 169
American Magyar Jewish Association, 224

American Mortuary Experience Tables, 216
American Plan Association, 183
American Red Cross, 252–53
American Sick Benefit and Life Insurance Association, 292
American Steel and Wire Company, hiring practices, 120
American Workers movement, 147
Americanization, 232, 245; differential dues system, 216; education, 312; language, 207; newspapers, 229; organizations, 312; religion, 161, 209
Amerikai Nemzetör (newspaper), 164
Amerika, 185
Amerikai levelek, 169
Amerikai Magyar Népszava (newspaper), 168, 227, 228, 233; clergymen, 156; contests, 244; disappearance of, 293; Hungarian propaganda and, 229; revisionists and, 249; second generation and, 243; Tivadaor Kundtz, 138
Amerikai Magyar Református Egyesület, 145
Amerikai Magyar Világ (newspaper), 241, 250
Amerikai Nemzetör (newspaper), 135
Amerikai Népszava (newspaper), 144, 164–66, 169, 181
Amerikások, 74–75, 77, 83
Amerkai Magyar Életből (series), 168
Ancient Order of Hibernians, 99
András Vass, 168
Andrejkovics, Mrs. Mihály, 126
Anschluss, 1938, 194
Anti-communism, 270
Anti-Horthy League, 222, 228
Anti-Semitism, 93, 167, 195, 224, 252
Apáthy, Ferenc, 135
Apponyi, Count, 177, 180
Áprádhon, LA, 113
"Arrow-Cross," 261, 263, 268

429

438

22, 25, 32; mining, 120; nationalism, 170; New Jersey, 111; New York, NY, 110; newspapers, 171–72; occupations, 31; Philadelphia, PA, 109; population, 1880, Hungary, 71; priests and ministers, 153–57; racism, 101; rate of emigration, 93; Reformed Church (Calvinist), 152; religion and, 161, 307; Republican Club, 150; socialism division in, 144; social interaction, 216; South Bend, IN, 112; unions, 129–30; Youngstown, OH, 111

"Magyar America," 150, 306–7

Magyar Bányászok Lapja, 293

Magyar Bányászlap (newspaper), 232

Magyar Betegsegélyző Egyletek Szövetsége, 143, 145

Magyar Day, 295

Magyar Egyház (newspaper), 207

Magyar Harcosok Bajtársi Szövetsége, 280–81

Magyar House, 176–78, 177, 222

Magyar Hirmondó (newspaper), 135, 164, 167

Magyar Jövő (newspaper), 250

Magyar Műkedvelő Szinháza, 213

Magyar Nemzeti Szövetség, 176

Magyar Recorder, 164

Magyar Szabadság Mosgalom, 280

Magyar Szabadság (paper), 280

Magyar Számüzöttek Lapja (newspaper), 164

Magyar Társág, 281

"Magyars of Cleveland," 184

Majláth, Count, 63, 82–3

Man, The, (newspaper), 231, 232

Manitoba, Canada, 191

Marriage: ethnicity and, 203, 254; language and, 298; non-Hungarian ancestry and, 44; patterns, change in, 294

Mass migration, 95

Matol, Antun C. (poet), 94–95

May Day celebration, 182–83

May Tree, 202

Mechanism of migration, 48–54

Medical exams, 267

Meeting in America: The Penal Colony, 169

Megyaszó, O. F., 62–63

Megyaszó, Hungary, 65

Melting pot, 179, 196

Mentor, OH, 142

Mészáros, Lajos, 61

Metzenseifen, Hungary, 137

Mexico, 191

Mezokövesd, Hungary, 83

Michigan Malleable Iron Works, 113

Middle class, 110, 173,215–19, 222–26

Migrants, 25, 31, 142, 223

Migration, 20, 29, 116, 133–34, 303–4; changing social structure, 192–96; children, 49, 52, 53; destinations, 268–69; division of labor, 53; economics, 33–34; effects, 69–72, 87; Europe, 18–19, 21, 263; family affiliation, 49; farm management, 53; forced, 33, 194, 277–78; goals, 53; growth, 18; Jewish, 23; land ownership, 51; mobility, 49; nature of, 23; patterns, 18–35, 33–34, 36–49, 121, 303–11; populations, 21, 25; theories of, 118, 277–78; voluntary, 277–78; women, 49–50; to work sites, 16. *See also* Chain migration; Emigration; Immigration; Remigration

Miklós Zrinyi First Cleveland Magyar-Slovak Sick Benefit Society, 141

Mikszáth, Kálmán, 172

Military service, 92, 254

Mining, 38–40, 46, 47, 53, 127; accidents, 122; settlements, 109, 198

Missler Agency, 108

Mobility: migration and, 49

Moley, Raymond, 184–85

Molitorisz, András, 59

Molnár, August, 296

Monaville, WV, 39

Monyha ranch, 63

Morgantown, WV, 39

Moskowitz, J. D., 111

Mother tongue movement, 297

Motivation, 33, 314–15

Munkács, Bishop, 152–53

Munkás Betegsegélyző és Önképző Egyesület, 144, 147

Munkás Betegsegélyző Szövetség, 144

Munkás (newspaper), 221, 231, 293

Munkásbetegsegélyző Szövetség, 220

Mutual aid associations, 122, 141, 215

"Mystery of Hungarian Genius," 195

Nádas, John, 281

Nagy bandák (large work teams), 50

Nagybizottság (central committee), 201

Nagy, Ferenc (Prime Minister), 284

Nagy, Imre, 273–74

Nagy, Kázmér, 263–64

Nagycsalád, 12

Names: Americanization, 232; use of Hungarian, 288

Narodne Noviny (National Newspaper), 94

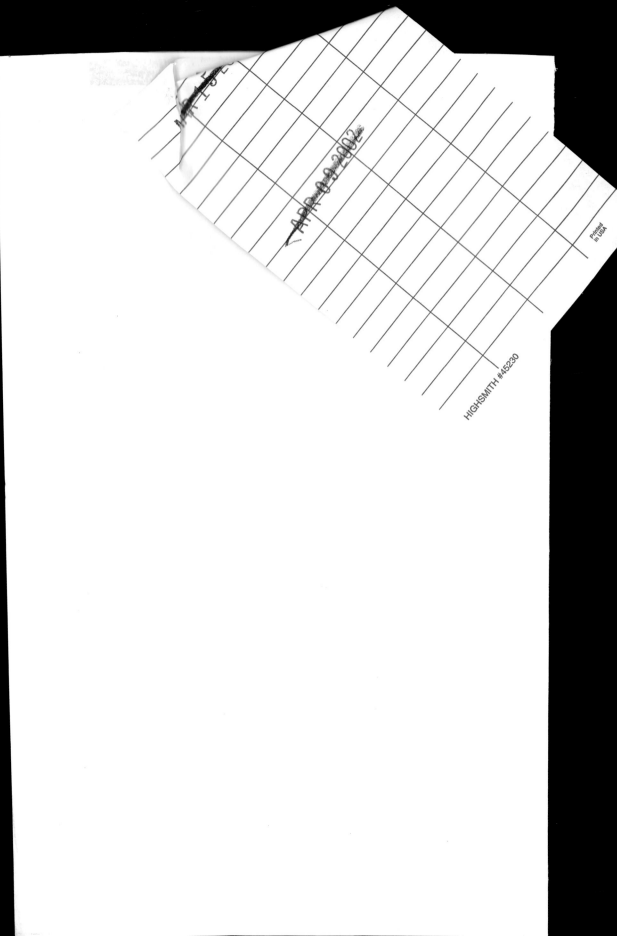

APR 09 2002